ADOLESCENCE

Development, Diversity, **Context, and** Application

Richard M. Lerner
Tufts University

Jason D. Brown
University of Manitoba

Cheryl Kier
Athabasca University

PEARSON
Prentice
Hall

Toronto

National Library of Canada Cataloguing in Publication

Lerner, Richard M.
     Adolescence : development, diversity, context, and application /
Richard M. Lerner, Jason D. Brown, Cheryl Kier. — Canadian ed.
Includes bibliographical references and indexes.
ISBN 0-13-102370-5

1. Adolescence—Textbooks. I. Brown, Jason, 1968– II. Kier, Cheryl A.
(Cheryl Ann), 1959– III. Title.

HQ796.L38 200   305.235   C2004-900564-2

ISBN 0-13-102370-5

Vice-President, Editorial Director: Michael J. Young
Acquisitions Editor: Ky Pruesse
Executive Marketing Manager: Judith Allen
Signing Representative: Ryan St. Peters
Senior Developmental Editor: Martina van de Velde
Production Editor: Charlotte Morrison-Reed
Copy Editor: Debbie Viets
Proofreader: Karen Alliston
Production Manager: Wendy Moran
Photo Research: Sandy Cooke
Page Layout: Susan Thomas
Art Director: Mary Opper
Cover and Interior Design: Lisa Lapointe
Cover Image: Mel Yates/Getty Images

1 2 3 4 5   09 08 07 06 05

Printed and bound in the United States of America.

BRIEF CONTENTS

CONTENTS

MEET THE RESEARCHERS

PREFACE

The word *adolescence* can be traced to the Latin word "adolescere," which means to grow into maturity. Growing into maturity involves change, and today, adolescence is regarded, perhaps with the exception of infancy, as the most change-filled period of life. It is a period of transition in which the biological, psychological, and social characteristics typical of children become the biological, psychological, and social characteristics typical of adults.

Most researchers define the second 10 years of life (from ages 10 to 20) as the adolescent period. All people who study adolescence—or who experience it, as either parents or as young people themselves—agree the period is characterized by numerous major changes and also dramatic ones that often are remembered for all the years of life thereafter.

The hopes, challenges, fears, and successes of adolescence have been romanticized or dramatized in novels, short stories, and news articles. It is commonplace to survey a newsstand and find a magazine article describing the "stormy years" of adolescence, the new crazes or fads of youth, or the "explosion" of problems with teenagers (e.g., involving crime or sexuality).

To what extent are these characterizations of adolescence correct? Just what do we know about adolescents and if some adolescents do experience problems, what can be done about it? In turn, aren't there strengths of adolescents? How may knowledge about adolescent development be applied in ways to promote positive, healthy development among all the diverse young people experiencing this period of life? How, in the span of 10 years, does the individual bridge the gap between coping with the several challenges of early adolescence and the launching of a young adult life?

The Goal of This Book

Answering these questions fascinates and engages the energies of scientists, practitioners, parents, teachers, and young people themselves. Providing the key information to answer these questions is the goal of *Adolescence: Development, Diversity, Context, and Application*.

This book will help you to understand the bases of the *developmental changes* young people experience during the adolescent period; to appreciate the important instances of *diversity* of individuals, families, communities, and cultures that give texture and richness to adolescent development; to recognize the important role played in adolescent development of the different instances of the *context*, or ecology, of human development—for example, the family, the peer group, schools, communities, the media, and culture; and to understand the ways in which knowledge about adolescent development, diversity, and context may be *applied* to promote positive development among young people. In short, the aim of *Adolescence: Development, Diversity, Context, and Application* is to present the best information currently available about the adolescent period and the ways in which scientists and practitioners both understand the period and take actions to promote positive development among youth.

Why Is There a Need for This Canadian Edition?

In the process of writing this edition, numerous people asked us, "How do Canadian adolescents differ from American adolescents? Doesn't it all just boil down to hormones?" As will become clear in this book, adolescence involves more than just hormones. A major theme of this text is that differences in context can affect adolescent development. While Canada and the United States are similar in many ways, there are also important differences between them. These include differences in ethnocultural diversity, social values, economic conditions, crime, education, and health policies. Thus, the social environment of Canadian youth differs in some very important ways from that of youth in the United States. Data from the U.S. may not always transfer well to the Canadian situation.

This Canadian edition aims to examine adolescence within the context of the Canadian social environment. Each chapter focuses on studies conducted with Canadian adolescents and those conducted by Canadian researchers. Many Canadian researchers have made significant contributions to our knowledge about adolescence, and we aim to highlight their work here. We also include issues relevant to the Canadian population, such as experiences of

Aboriginal youth, youth from different ethnocultural backgrounds, and francophone youth. These additions aim to make the textbook more relevant to the experiences of Canadian readers.

How Is Adolescence Discussed in This Book?

Throughout this book we illustrate that, by understanding the relations of diverse adolescents and their contexts, we may formulate *applications* that may help improve these relations. These applications may involve community-based programs, professional practices, education curricula, and public policies. But all applications aim to resolve or ameliorate challenges to healthy adolescent development, to prevent problems of adolescent behaviour from developing, or to promote positive development among youth.

Accordingly, this book emphasizes that adolescence is a dynamic developmental period marked by diverse changes for different youth, changes brought about because development involves changing *relations* among biological, psychological, and social/ecological processes. Together, these diverse developmental changes involve the relations adolescents have with their biological, social, and cultural contexts, and provide the basis for innovations, in the types of applications just noted, aimed at increasing societal ability to improve the lives of adolescents. If the basis of the development of young people lies in their particular relationships with their social world—with their specific family, peer group, schools, and neighbourhoods—then by taking actions to improve these relations we may be enacting the key steps needed to promote positive development.

You will find that the four themes in the title of the book—development, diversity, context, and application—are interwoven. Together these themes will help you understand how scholars and practitioners contribute to identifying knowledge that matters in respect to enhancing the lives of the diverse young people in Canada, the United States, and around the world.

Foci and Features of the Book

The themes of developmental diversity, adolescent-context relations, and the links among theory, research, and applications to programs aimed at enhancing the life chances of young people are key foci in contemporary scholarship and practice pertinent to adolescence. As such, these themes frame the discussion in all chapters of this book. Across chapters, we emphasize several types of information:

- The stress on adolescent *development* involves both the antecedents in earlier life periods of changes in adolescence and the consequences of these changes for later adult development and aging. The treatment of development in this text includes a discussion of the intertwining of the development of youth with the development of their parents and other relatives, with peers, and with other individuals important in their lives (for instance, teachers, mentors, and coaches).
- The focus on *diversity* provides understanding of the variation among adolescents associated with race, ethnicity, gender, sexual orientation, and physical characteristics.
- The emphasis on the *context* of adolescence involves discussing (1) the role of culture and history in shaping the processes and products of adolescent development; (2) the role of the social, interpersonal, familial, and physical context in influencing youth development; (3) institutional contributions to adolescent development, including educational, political, economic, and social policy influences; and (4) community needs and assets, including programs promoting positive youth and family development. In addition, several disciplines and several professions involved in understanding the contexts that influence human development are discussed.
- The fact that the changes of adolescence derive from the relations between youth and their contexts constitutes an optimistic and powerful approach to *applications* (for instance, community-based programs, school curricula innovations, professional practices, and public policies) aimed at promoting positive adolescent development. By changing the character of the relations youth have with their social world, we may be able to enhance their chances for healthy development. Accordingly, the stress on application involves indicating current foci of policies and programs pertinent to youth intervention programs, education, retraining, and services.

The several foci of the book are not only interwoven throughout the discussions in each chapter but they appear as well in the feature boxes. The book includes "Implications for Parenting" boxes about **parenting adolescents** and "Applications" boxes about **policies** and **programs** pertinent to promoting positive adolescent development. In addition, "Meet the Researcher" boxes present **personal reflections** by leading scholars of adolescence about their current research or applied efforts.

The information in these boxes and in the text itself is enhanced by several learning tools: **vignettes** about adolescent development that begin the text of each chapter, **chapter overviews, learning objectives, issues to consider, chapter summaries, discussion topics,** and **glossaries.**

Aspirations for This Book

Certainly, it is a daunting task to understand the bases of the healthy and successful development of diverse adolescents and to apply such knowledge to ensure that young people are eventually capable of leading themselves, their families, their communities, and their nations productively, responsibly, and morally across the 21st century. We believe all citizens, worldwide, must rise to this challenge if we all are not only to survive but to prosper.

The young people of today represent 100% of the human capital upon which the future health and success of all nations rest. To enhance the lives of adolescents requires that we continually educate all citizens—young and old—about the best means available to promote enhanced healthy lives among *all* youth and the families, schools, and communities involved in their lives. It is our hope that *Adolescence: Development, Diversity, Context, and Application* will motivate you to contribute to this effort. In so doing, this book may play a role in an educational and community collaborative effort to help ensure, for the new millennium, a socially just and civil society populated by healthy and productive children and adolescents.

Changes to the Canadian Edition

With the aim of increasing the appeal to Canadian students and emphasizing the important contributions made by Canadians to the study of adolescence, we have increased the number of Canadians represented in "Meet the Researcher" boxes. Almost half of the more than 30 boxes highlight Canadian

researchers. As well, examples of Canadian research are interspersed throughout this textbook and we have included settings, examples, and political issues that relate to Canadian students' experiences.

Overview of Changes

CHAPTER 1
- Expanded discussion of "storm and stress" debate, which includes viewpoint of Canadian researcher Jim Côté.
- Added material about cultural differences between Canada and the United States.

CHAPTER 2
- Expanded discussion of nature-nurture debate.

CHAPTER 3
- New research regarding age of menarche in various countries, including Canada.
- New material on evolutionary theory.
- New section about body image, with Canadian statistics on body image and eating disorders.
- New research about eating disorders among males.

CHAPTER 4
- Addition of Canadian material about IQ tests, including effects of language on performance.

CHAPTER 5
- Updated material on gender differences in morality.
- Addition of Canadian material about programs for adolescents and the Developmental Assets approach.
- A new section on the values of Canadian adolescents.

CHAPTER 6
- New research about collective identities and identity development among ethnic minorities.
- New research about the effects of context on identity development.

CHAPTER 7
- Updated information about nontraditional occupations.
- Addition of Canadian material about youth employment and regional variations in employment, including employment among Aboriginal youth.
- New research on volunteering among adolescents, particularly among Canadian adolescents.

- Additional material about the development of gender stereotypes.
- Updated discussion of students' views of the two sexes and their abilities, as well as inequality, in the workplace.
- New material about androgyny, including Canadian research.

CHAPTER 8

- Addition of Canadian statistics on the demographics of families.
- A new section about Canadian residential schools and their effects on parenting.
- Updated and Canadian material about the effects of divorce on adolescents, and the effects on adolescents of having two working parents.

CHAPTER 9

- Updated and Canadian material on the relationship between parents and peers.
- A new section on bullying.

CHAPTER 10

- Addition of Canadian statistics about homosexuality.
- Addition of Canadian material about age at which youth first have intercourse, use of contraception, teen pregnancy and birthrates, STDs, programs for AIDS prevention, sexual harassment and sexual assault, and "rape drugs."
- A new section on prostitution, particularly in the Canadian context.

CHAPTER 11

- Expanded section about the different roles of schools.
- Addition of material on French Immersion schools, Aboriginal students, refugee youth and the school system, Canadian statistics on early school leavers, and discussion of school violence in Canada.

CHAPTER 12

- Addition of Canadian material about Internet use.
- New Canadian material on community-based learning.

CHAPTER 13

- Addition of domestic statistics on poverty, youth crime, and suicide.
- Added discussion about homeless youth in Canada, and substance abuse among youth in Canada.

CHAPTER 14

- Additional discussion of programs for youth in Canada and about national social programs.
- A new section about community development.

CHAPTER 15

- Addition of Canadian statistics about the influence of family on the transition to young adulthood.

APPENDIX

- New information about constructs, quasi-independent variables, and internal and external validity.
- A new section about qualitative research.
- Additional examples for research designs.

Acknowledgements

We are indebted to numerous colleagues for helping us develop this book. We are grateful to all whose basic and applied scholarship about adolescence has provided the information and expertise reflected in the following pages. We are especially appreciative of all the colleagues who contributed to the "Meet the Researcher" boxes, features that enable readers to understand the scholarship and passion that researchers bring to their work, efforts aimed at both furthering understanding of young people and improving their lives. We would like to acknowledge our gratitude to the reviewers of this Canadian edition. Their thoughtful comments and suggestions were invaluable:

Gerald Adams, University of Guelph; Jody L. Bain, University of Victoria; Sandy Bozak, Mohawk College; Denise Buote, University of British Columbia; Jennifer Connolly, York University; Maureen Drysdale, University of Waterloo; Verian Farnsworth, Kwantlen University College; Laurain Mills, University of Victoria; Alexa Okrainec, Brandon University; Verna Raab, Mount Royal College; Sandra Rollings-Magnusson, Grant MacEwan College; Joseph Snyder, Concordia University; Kimberely Vaughan, University of Calgary; Theresa Zolner, University of Saskatchewan.

We would also like to thank the people at Pearson Education Canada, particularly our acquisitions editor, Jessica Mosher, and developmental editor, Martina van de Velde. Jessica's contributions to the project were never-ending. Martina's efforts on the part of this publication were astounding. We are extremely grateful for her thoroughness and dedication. We would also like to thank Deborah Viets, who skillfully copy edited the manuscript.

Richard Lerner wishes to express his love and gratitude to his family. His wife, Professor Jacqueline V. Lerner, has been his most important colleague in his research and scholarship about adolescent development. She has also been his partner in the development of their three children—Justin, Blair, and Jarrett. He knows Jackie would agree that their children have taught them more than perhaps they want to recognize about adolescence.

Jason Brown would like to thank his partner, Shelley Reiser, for her encouragement and support during the many evenings and weekends spent on this project. He is also grateful to the coauthor of this Canadian edition, Cheryl Kier, who, because of her keen interest, knowledge, and careful attention to detail, made his contributions comprehensible. He is most indebted to traditional people, who have taught him to listen, and the young people and families who have shared their experiences with him.

Cheryl Kier would like to express appreciation to her husband, Mike Procter, for all his support and patience while she devoted her attention to this project. She also wishes to thank Mount Royal College's librarians Margot Millard and Margot Calvert, who went out of their way to locate relevant material for this book. Cheryl couldn't have asked for a better coauthor than Jason Brown. His insight, devotion, and encouragement made it a pleasure to collaborate on this edition.

R. M. L.
Medford, Massachusetts
October 2000

J. D. B.
Winnipeg, Manitoba
September 2003

C.A.K.
Calgary, Alberta
September 2003

ABOUT THE AUTHORS

Richard M. Lerner is the Bergstrom Chair in Applied Developmental Science at Tufts University. A developmental psychologist, Lerner received a Ph.D. in 1971 from the City University of New York. He has been a fellow at the Center for Advanced Study in the Behavioral Sciences and is a fellow of the American Association for the Advancement of Science, the American Psychological Association, and the American Psychological Society. Prior to joining Tufts University, he was on the faculty and held administrative posts at Michigan State University, Pennsylvania State University, and Boston College, where he was the Anita L. Brennan Professor of Education and the director of the Center for Child, Family, and Community Partnerships. During the 1994–95 academic year, Lerner held the Tyner Eminent Scholar Chair in the Human Sciences at Florida State University. Lerner is the author or editor of 40 books and more than 275 scholarly articles and chapters, including his 1995 book, *America's Youth in Crisis: Challenges and Options for Programs and Policies*. He edited Volume 1, *Theoretical Models of Human Development*, for the fifth edition of the *Handbook of Child Psychology*. He is known for his theory of, and research about, relations between life-span human development and contextual or ecological change. He is the founding editor of the *Journal of Research on Adolescence* and of the new journal, *Applied Developmental Science*.

Jason Brown is a licensed clinical psychologist, registered social worker, and assistant professor of Family Studies at the University of Manitoba, where he teaches courses on youth and community issues. He is interested in participatory approaches to research with youth, their families, and communities. He is the proud father of two daughters, Kaylee and Jenna, and in his spare time enjoys listening to and playing drums.

Cheryl Kier was brought up in the United States but received her B.A. and M.S. degrees (in psychology) in Canada and her Ph.D. (also in psychology) from the University of Reading in England. Having worked in England at the University of East London, she is now teaching at both Mount Royal College in Calgary and Athabasca University (Canada's Open University). Her research interests began with the effects of divorce on children and their mothers, as well as sibling relationships, infant-mother attachment, and infant-sibling attachment in married and divorced families. They have expanded to include identity development among adolescents and human rights issues.

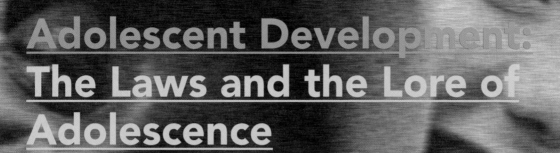

1

Adolescent Development: The Laws and the Lore of Adolescence

Lise Cardinal sat alone in her room. If it were not for the steady sound of her CDs drifting down the stairs, her parents would not have even known she was home. Such relatively unobtrusive behaviour was not typical of Lise, but her mother thought she understood why this was occurring.

It had been just two days ago that Lise and Daniel had broken up and, it seemed, only a few days before then that Mrs. Cardinal had heard her daughter explain how fulfilled she was by her new relationship with Daniel. No other 15-year-old, Lise assured her mother, had ever loved as deeply, as totally. No one had ever felt such intense compassion, devotion, and overwhelming sense of completion.

But now, less than two weeks after it began, it was over. Lise was certain that her pain—her depression and feelings of physical agony—had not been experienced as deeply by anyone else. At least, she pointed out to her mother, she was sure that no one who had been so true had been treated so callously, so rudely and publicly humiliated: told by Daniel, in front of everyone, that he just wanted to be friends!

And so Lise sat in her room hardly evidencing enough energy to place a new disc in her CD player. Friday afternoon turned into Friday evening, and then Saturday morning and afternoon. Another evening was now at hand.

Mrs. Cardinal could not take it any longer. Dinner was on the table and, by Monday morning, there would be chores to do and homework to complete. She had indulged Lise long enough.

She strode up the stairs to her daughter's room. "Lise! Enough is enough now. Come down, eat your dinner, and then start your homework."

"Mom! Leave me alone!" Lise shrilled back. "You don't understand. What do *you* know about love?!"

Learning Objectives

1. To appreciate that adolescent development is influenced by biological, psychological, and social contexts.
2. To recognize the inherent diversity of the possible developmental pathways through adolescence, and to recognize that this diversity involves changes within the person across time and between the individual adolescent and parents and peers.
3. To appreciate the life-span approach to human development and its emphasis on multiple levels of the ecology of human development.
4. To recognize that the changing relations between the developing individual and his or her complex and changing ecology constitute the critical process of human development.
5. To appreciate the relevance of applying intervention studies to better understand how healthy and successful development across the life span can be promoted.
6. To understand how the Canadian context may differ from the American one.
7. To know the major developmental tasks of adolescent development.
8. To recognize that adolescent development is influenced by multiple factors, including hormonal development, family, and culture.
9. To appreciate why policies and programs must be tailored to a specific target population and must address that group's particular developmental and environmental circumstances.
10. To understand the stereotypes about young people that have historically defined adolescence and how these stereotypes have created the lore of adolescence.
11. To appreciate the research that supports the existence of different developmental trajectories and thereby challenges the lore of adolescence.

The hopes, challenges, fears, failures, and successes of **adolescence** have been romanticized or dramatized in novels, short stories, and news articles. It is commonplace to survey a newsstand and find a magazine article describing the "stormy years" of adolescence, the new crazes or fads of youth, or the "explosion" of problems with teenagers involving crime or sexuality. Until the past 35 years, when medical, biological, and social scientists began to study intensively the adolescent period, relatively little sound scientific information was available to verify or refute the literary characterizations of adolescence. Today, however, such information does exist, and it is clear that although adolescence presents many challenges, the evidence is not consistent with the frequently reported belief that adolescence is a protracted period of **storm and stress** for most individuals (Feldman & Elliott, 1990; Lerner, 1993a, 1993b, 1995; Lerner & Galambos, 1998; Offer, 1969; Petersen, 1988). As this chapter discusses, although adolescence has its share of challenges and problems, as do all periods of life, for most young people it is a period when health and positive growth predominate.

Adolescence spans the second decade of life (Lerner, 1991a; Petersen, 1988). Young adolescents elicit both curiosity and frustration in many observers, especially—it seems—parents. By the end of the second decade, however, the person seems to be in a time of constant commitment—to partners, family, and work. The middle portion of this period may be a time of mystery, self-examination, and emerging identity. It is a time to bridge the gap between the awkwardness (for both youth and their caregivers) of early adolescence and the launching of a now young adult life at the end of this period.

Each period of adolescence holds its own promise and fascination. For this reason alone it is useful to study adolescent development. But there are other reasons for interest in this period. Only through such a focus can we understand the diversity of life paths that characterize different people. Only through a focus on the scope of development across this period can we evaluate whether paths on which we embark in early adolescence are the ones on which we continue to walk. This book discusses the diversity and scope of adolescence while attempting to answer the following questions:

- Is there a necessary connection between development at age 10 or 12 and the behaviours of the late adolescent period, as the individual enters college or university, career, or marriage?

- Are there ways in which adolescents may change—for better or worse—as they move from one point of life to the next?

- Are there particular aspects of adolescents' biology (for instance, genes or hormones) and/or their contexts (for example, families, schools, workplaces, or cultures) that either promote connections across life (continuity) or lead to change (discontinuity)?

- *If* adolescents can change, and *if* the bases of these changes can be identified, can means be found to improve their development?

- Can the study of adolescent development help people live lives of greater health, opportunity, and achievement?

A Definition of Adolescence

ISSUES TO CONSIDER
- How do the biological, psychological, and social contexts of adolescence impact development?
- What accounts for the diversity of the developmental trajectories of adolescents?

Adolescence may be described as a phase of life beginning in biology and ending in society (Petersen, 1988). This characterization of adolescence underscores the idea that, whereas pubertal changes may be the most visible and universal features of this period, the social and cultural context within which youth develop textures this phase of life. Adolescence is a period of transition, one when the biological, psychological, and social characteristics typical of children change in an integrated manner to become the biological, psychological, and social characteristics typical of adults (Lerner & Spanier, 1980). When most of an individual's characteristics are in this state of change, that person is an adolescent.

Adolescence is a period of dramatic challenge, one requiring adjustment to changes in the self, family, and peer group. In contemporary society, adolescents typically experience institutional changes as well. As Chapter 11 discusses, among young North American

---

Adolescence Period of transition spanning the second decade of life during which a person's biological, psychological, and social characteristics undergo change in an interrelated manner and the person goes from being childlike to adultlike.

Storm and stress Phrase often used to stereotype general and universal turmoil throughout the adolescent years.

Young people test different roles during adolescence, often in the context of part-time jobs.

adolescents, there is a change in school setting, typically involving a transition from elementary school to either junior high school or middle school. In late adolescence there is a transition from high school to either the world of work or postsecondary education.

Understandably, for both adolescents and their parents, adolescence is a time of excitement and anxiety, happiness and troubles, discovery and bewilderment. Although some childhood behaviour continues, the adolescent also begins to break with the past. Adolescence is a confusing time for the adolescent experiencing this phase of life, for the parents who are nurturing the adolescent during his or her progression through this period, and for the other adults charged with enhancing the development of youth during this period, such as teachers, coaches, and so on.

The feelings and events that bring about parents' reactions to their adolescent children are well known to parents, teachers, and many writers who have romanticized or dramatized the adolescent experience in novels, short stories, or news articles. Even when "storm and stress" is not attributed to adolescence, the period is often characterized by conflicting behaviours, for example, both trying to "fit in" and attempting to define oneself as a unique person. The famous writer George Bernard Shaw once said, "Youth is a wonderful thing. Too bad it is wasted on the young." This view epitomizes the idea that adolescence is characterized by a unique combination of assets and deficits. Adolescents possess many positive and valued characteristics—health, fitness, and energy, for example—and yet also possess characteristics that place them at risk for problems of development—poor judgment, a tendency to make dangerous choices, a propensity to take risks (binge drinking, driving drunk, engaging in unprotected sex; Lerner & Galambos, 1998), and a "live for today, don't worry about tomorrow" attitude. Many of these issues will be discussed in Chapter 4. Writers, poets, and members of the mass media focus on the assets and deficits of people experiencing this stage of life. Such a focus often helps sell books and magazines, and it creates high ratings for television shows. This media depiction of adolescence is popular because it builds on this stereotypical view of young people.

Given the multiple transitions and adolescent experiences, this period is clearly a dramatic challenge. Not all young people undergo these transitions in the same way, with the same speed, or with comparable outcomes. There is diversity in their paths through life, which are known as **developmental trajectories**. A major source of this diversity is the **context** within which youth live and develop—the family, peer group, school, workplace, neighbourhood, community, society, culture, and niche in history.

The Goal of This Book

The aim of *Adolescence: Development, Diversity, Context, and Application* is to present the best information currently available about the adolescent period and the ways scientists and practitioners successfully promote positive development among youth. The book emphasizes that adolescence is a dynamic, developmental period marked by diverse changes for different youth, changes brought about

Developmental trajectories Individual's path through life as influenced by combinations of biology, psychology, and context unique to each person.

Context Environments in which an individual exists, such as family, school, work, and culture.

because development involves changing *relations* among biological, psychological, and social/ecological processes.

Diversity in adolescent development occurs as a consequence of systematic relations between youth and their contexts (Lerner & Castellino, 1999). The importance of understanding this system is underscored by the life-span developmental framework—a perspective particularly useful for discussing adolescence in relation to the periods of life preceding and following it and in respect to the important contexts of one's life.

Conflict with parents is a normal part of adolescence.

Features of the Life-Span Perspective

ISSUES TO CONSIDER

• How might an adolescent's ecology influence her or his behaviour and development?
• What are the two types of diversity stressed in the life-span perspective?
• According to the life-span perspective, what is the goal of intervention studies?

When the life-span perspective was introduced in the 1970s, its features included certain ideas, specifically:

 ■ Development occurs across the life course. It does not end with physical maturity (puberty).

 ■ Individual development occurs in relation to social, cultural, and historical changes. It does not occur because of internal (biological, genetic) influences acting alone or by the isolated action of environmental stimuli.

 ■ Across life, there are important differences between people and within individuals. Not only do people change across life, but also different people change in ways specific to them.

■ Attempts to describe, explain, and optimize development across life involve understanding the connections between individuals and their contexts. If we understand development we should be able to improve it. To facilitate optimal development we need to alter the connections between people and their social and cultural worlds.

A life-span approach to adolescence employs concepts pertaining to the nature of human development—for instance, diversity, context, and application. It uses a specific set of scientific methods, which address issues about these concepts. For example, do youth from different ethnic and/or socioeconomic backgrounds experience comparable changes in their personality development? What family, school, or community resources are most effective in attempts to promote the development of positive self-esteem among these different groups of youth?

The life-span perspective emphasizes that human behaviour and development arise as a consequence of individuals' relationships with the several aspects, or *levels,* of their social context. These levels constitute the **ecology** of human development (Bronfenbrenner, 1979; Bronfenbrenner & Morris, 1998) and include the family, community, society, and culture. In addition, research has demonstrated that the period in history within which people live influences their development as they experience unique combinations of economic, political, and technological conditions (e.g., Glen H. Elder, Jr., 1974; 1998).

Ecology Levels of a person's social context that influences individual development.

As a result, the life-span perspective emphasizes that variability, or diversity, arises in people as a consequence of their relationships with particular combinations of family, community, society, culture, and historical conditions. Two types of diversity are stressed in the life-span perspective. First, there are important differences *among people*, for example, in their ethnic, religious, gender, physical, age-related, community, and cultural characteristics. These may be associated with differing patterns of life-span development. Second, there are often underappreciated differences *within a person* over the course of his or her life. Here life-span scholars emphasize two principles: (1) Development occurs throughout life; children differ from adolescents and adolescents differ from adults; the way you are in childhood or adolescence does not completely determine the rest of your life. (2) Development always involves a combination of gains and losses.

For example, in infancy, gains in visual acuity are accompanied by a loss of neurons that could have been used in other potential visual pathways. In childhood, growth in fluency in one language decreases the probability of gaining similar proficiency in another language. In adolescence, commitment to one **social role** and to its associated beliefs or ideology is associated with a loss of other life paths as potential routes to self-definition. For example, if an individual is committed to becoming a computer engineer and subscribes to the accompanying belief in the importance of technology for society, that choice influences the individual's self-definition and eliminates other choices. In the adulthood and aging years, physical or cognitive losses may be compensated by gains associated with accumulating experience, expertise, or "wisdom" in a particular domain (Baltes, Lindenberger, & Staudinger, 1998; Baltes, Staudinger, & Lindenberger, 1999).

The life-span perspective emphasizes that variations in the changing links, or relationships, between individuals and contexts create diversity in the course of human development. To life-span scholars, *basic* processes of human development are relational in character. Changing *relations* between the developing individual and his or her complex and changing ecology constitute the critical process of human development. To understand human development across life, scholars and students must appreciate the diversity of life paths, or "trajectories." These variations arise as a consequence of differences across life in the familial, community, cultural, and historical niches of people. This influence of multiple levels implies another important idea of the life-span perspective: To understand the influences of contextual levels requires knowledge that goes beyond psychology or any other single discipline. Knowledge about multiple disciplines and from multiple professions must be combined to understand the complex ecology of human development.

Another important goal of the life-span perspective is to understand how healthy and successful development across life can be promoted. If we understand the forces that shape development we should be able to influence those forces, especially when they relate to relatively changeable characteristics, such as behaviour, family relations, or social conditions, including housing, street safety, and human services. And if we can test our knowledge about development by trying to change it, we have an obligation to change it for the better. Scholars have an ethical responsibility to study human life and to use the knowledge they gain to improve life (see Appendix 1). They must go beyond understanding how both positive and negative trajectories occur in adolescence. They must test this understanding in an effort to promote positive trajectories among youth.

In order to accomplish this goal, life-span scholars conduct **intervention studies** in laboratories and in the actual ecologies of human development. Gaining theoretical understanding of how and why development occurs may lead to research designed to explore how people's lives may be improved through change. For example, an individual's social world could be changed through public **policies,** and an individual's functioning might be changed by modifying problem-solving strategies. The importance of public policies and community programs are highlighted in Chapter 14, and problem-solving strategies

Social role Socially prescribed set of behaviours that society believes is important for its maintenance and perpetuation.

Intervention studies Research designed to understand how changing aspects of the social world or an individual's behaviour can lead to improvements in a person's life.

Policies Actions (e.g., the enactment of laws) taken by social institutions, such as governments, to ensure or increase desired behaviours (e.g., better school performance) or to decrease unwanted behaviours (e.g., drunk driving).

are addressed in Chapter 13. Life-span scholars view application as a way to evaluate their assumptions, descriptions, and explanations of human development, so application of topics is featured prominently throughout this text.

In short, *diversity, context,* and *application* constitute key components of a **life-span perspective** on human development. Individual differences between and within persons, the role of the context of human development, and the emphasis on applications and interventions are hallmarks of this view. We integrate these theoretical themes throughout this book and apply them specifically to the adolescent period.

Why Is There a Need for a Canadian Edition of *Adolescence: Development, Diversity, Context, and Application?*

In many ways Canada and the United States are similar. Ouimet (2002) mentions that 90% of Canadians live within 100 miles (167 km) of the U.S. border. Immigration is common to both countries, as is a history of British colonization. With the possible exception of Quebec, movies, television, music, and other media are shared by the two countries.

However, there are many differences as well. As a major theme of this book suggests, differences in context can affect adolescent development. One key difference between the two countries is ethnic and cultural diversity. Canada has a greater Asian population than its southern neighbour. Also, fewer Canadians have English as their main language and more have French as their main language than is true for Americans (Doyle, 2000). Quebec society has influenced Canadian culture with its distinct language, history, symbols, ideas, and perceptions (Ravelli, 2000). Canadian diversity is increasing. Twice as many refugees come to Canada as to the United States and a greater proportion of Canadians are foreign-born. The greatest proportion of Canadian immigrants comes from Asian countries, whereas the greatest proportion of immigrants to the U.S. comes from Central and South America. Visible minorities constitute 13% of Canada's 15- to 24-year-olds and Aboriginals constitute 3.7%. (HRDC, 2000a). Youths represent one-fifth of the Aboriginal population, yet just 13% of the general population are youths. Human Resources Development Canada (2000a) predicts that the population of Aboriginal youths will continue to grow by another 20% before the end of the decade. This

Canadian edition focuses on issues relevant to the Canadian population.

A second commonly stated difference between these two North American countries is the higher crime rate in the United States. However, there are many similarities in crime between Canada and the U.S. For example, an equal number of Canadians and Americans report being victims of crime (Sauve, 1994), and rates of illicit alcohol, cigarette, and cannabis use are similar in surveys of adolescents in the U.S. and in Ontario (Idvis & Adlaf, 1999). However, the homicide rate is higher in the United States than in this country (Ouimet, 2002). There is also greater gun use there (Tonry, 1999), and more people are in prison (Jackson, 2002). These differences can influence the trajectory of problem development in adolescents, and therefore, data from the U.S. may not always transfer well to the Canadian situation.

A third difference between Canada and its southern neighbour may lie in citizens' values. While not all scholars agree with this (e.g., Baer, Grabb, and Johnston [1993] argue that value differences between regional/geographic districts *within* each country are greater than value differences *between* the two countries), Lipset (1968) claimed there is a greater emphasis on individual self-interest and a lesser emphasis on the collective interest in the United States than in Canada. He postulated that despite their origins as British colonies, the two countries evolved differently and thus developed different values. According to this theory, Americans value individualism, equalitarianism, and universalism. In contrast, Canadians value authority, collectivism, elitism, and particularist tendencies. Evidence of particularism can be found in the acceptance of a "mosaic" of cultures in Canada. This is in contrast to the "melting pot" valued by the United States, which encourages all individuals, whatever their ethnic or cultural roots, to be treated the same, to assimilate, and to accept that their interests will not be given special attention. Although there is some disagreement about whether the "mosaic"/"melting pot" distinction is accurate (Reitz & Breton, 1994; as cited in Levitt, 1996), Ravelli (2000) argues that Canada's tendency to welcome and encourage multiculturalism distinguished this country from the U.S., and is perhaps

Life-span perspective Approach that characterizes individual development as occurring across a lifetime through the combination of internal and external influences; the approach stresses differences within and between people and attempts to optimize lifetime development.

Understanding Canadian and American Cultural Differences

Bruce D. Ravelli is a sociologist who teaches at Mount Royal College, Calgary, Alberta. He continues his research into understanding cultural diversity. Bruce is also the co-founder of the *FAST©* assessment initiative, which employs data obtained from students anonymously to improve teaching effectiveness. See www.ravelli.ca and www.getfast.ca

One defining feature about Canadians is our preoccupation with trying to understand ourselves by reflecting on what we are not—Americans. In fact, as Canadians we share a long tradition of distinguishing ourselves from the social, economic, and military dominance of our southern neighbours. Most Canadians would agree that our two cultures are very similar. (For example, we speak the same language, share an integrated economic and financial system, watch and read similar news and entertainment items, eat comparable foods, and celebrate many of the same holidays.) But as Canadians we are also aware of, and promote, things that distinguish us from Americans and make us unique. From the national passion for hockey, the preference for stronger beer, the "I AM Canadian" rant, to our preoccupation with peacekeeping abroad, Canadians revel in anything that appears to separate us from Americans.

My own interest in Canadian/American differences began during my teens and early twenties when I travelled to the United States for reasons having to do with both pleasure and work. During these trips I was always aware that I was in a different country but struggled to identify the subtle differences between our countries and our peoples. The opportunity to systematically explore these differences came when I began my Ph.D. and selected Canadian and American values differences as my primary focus of study.

To examine whether the two countries' cultures varied, and if so how, I began reading the works of the American sociologist Seymour Lipset, who has spent a career documenting how Canadians and Americans differ. Lipset's assertion is that the American Revolution was the primordial event that set both countries' future development on different paths. For Lipset, the revolution established each country's founding ideology—America as revolutionary, Canada as counter-revolutionary.

Lipset argues that evidence of Canadian and American founding ideologies is found in each country's literature. For example, he suggests that American literature is based on themes that stress winning, opportunism, and confidence, while Canadian writing focuses on defeat, difficult physical circumstances, and abandonment by Britain. Lipset cites the well-known Canadian novelist Margaret Atwood, who believes national symbols reveal a great deal about the cultural values a nation embraces. For Atwood, the defining symbol for America was "the frontier," which inspired images of vitality and unrealized potential while "survival" summed up Canada's national character: "Canadians are forever taking the national pulse like doctors at a sickbed; the aim is not to see whether the patient will live well but simply whether he will live at all" (Atwood, 1972:33 cited in Lipset, 1986:124). Lipset suggests that the symbols, attitudes, and values of a people do not exist in a vacuum, rather that social and political institutions embody and reinforce them. For Lipset, then, values are the basis upon which society builds its social and political structures, and different value systems manifest themselves in all social realms, not just literature.

My own research investigated Lipset's assumptions through a comparison of Canadian and American media portrayals of Aboriginal issues. My study included an analysis of 50 years of national media content (as presented by *Maclean's* and *Newsweek* newsmagazines) and their coverage of Aboriginal issues to see if there was any evidence to support or refute Lipset. My findings indicated that the coverage of the issues in each magazine was in fact different, but that the differences were not consistent with what Lipset would have predicted. In fact, Lipset's predictions were supported in only 4 of 14 separate tests I devised to compare value differences in media content.

While my research found little support for Lipset's founding principles argument, I did detect underlying thematic differences between how the Canadian and American media present one topic in particular (i.e., Aboriginal issues) and the world in general. For example, Canadians adhere to a more global and collectivist world view than do Americans, while Americans believe in and promote a society that supports the social values of personal achievement and equality more than Canadians.

Clearly, there is a great deal of social scientific literature demonstrating how Canadians and Americans differ. By using this Canadian edition of *Adolescence: Development, Diversity, Context, and Application* you will find that it presents a thorough review of the world's leading-edge research about adolescence while at the same time providing examples and analyses from a Canadian perspective.

"one of the defining elements of who we are as a people" (p. 54). Bruce Ravelli describes his research in the Meet the Researcher Box 1.1.

Lipset's beliefs are strengthened by the findings that more Canadians turn out to vote than do Americans (Jackson, 2002), and by Feather's findings (1998) that U.S. university students have a higher level of self-esteem than Canadian (and Australian) students, and rate values concerned with competence and accomplishment as being more important than do Canadians and Australians. Feather concludes (p. 756), "These results reinforce the view that the American culture is somewhat distinctive in having a stronger emphasis on individual achievement and the importance of recognizing and rewarding success." Thus the question arises as to whether U.S. research on adolescent values and involvement in civil society applies to Canadians (see Chapter 5).

A fourth difference between Canada and the United States concerns the countries' economics. There is a greater proportion of people living in poverty in the U.S. and the gap between rich and poor is greater there (Doyle, 2000). Child poverty is also a bigger problem in the United States. One in six Canadian children lives in a family with less than half the income of the average family, in comparison to almost one in four American children (Jackson, 2002). Canada does have a higher unemployment rate (6.8% versus 4.0% in the U.S.), but fewer workers fit the definition of being low paid (i.e., earning less than one-third of the national average). Also, fewer men in Canada work more than 45 hours per week. Although Canadian families tend to earn 21% less income than American families (when income is adjusted for purchasing power), the Canadian government subsidizes health care and higher education costs to a greater extent (Jackson, 2002).

A fifth difference between Canada and the United States involves health and education. Both men and women tend to live two to three years longer in Canada than in the U.S., and infant mortality rates are lower in Canada (Jackson, 2002). This may be due to the presence of a universal health care system in Canada, and the absence of one in the U.S. A slightly higher proportion of adults in Canada has received postsecondary education (38.8% versus 34.9% in the U.S.). Based on an international survey of math and science, Grade 12 math scores were higher in Canada than in the U.S. (Jackson, 2002), and the illiteracy rate among youth aged 15 to 25 is lower in Canada than in the U.S. (Willms, 1999).

These differences in ethno-cultural diversity, social values, economic conditions, crime, education and health issues underlie our position that the social environment of Canadian youth is different in some very important ways from that of youth in the U.S.

Key Features of Adolescent Development

ISSUES TO CONSIDER
- What are the major developmental tasks of adolescence?
- How do developmental tasks converge to influence an adolescent's self-definition?

Over the past 35 years, the results of research on adolescence have demonstrated for biomedical, behavioural, and social scientists the importance of individual differences and contextual influence for understanding the nature of human life and development (Lerner & Galambos, 1998; Petersen, 1988). Research on adolescence is an example of the importance of collaborations among multiple disciplines. We have learned that to understand adolescents we need to combine knowledge from biology, medicine, and nursing, the social and behavioural sciences, social work, law, education, and the humanities. The study of adolescence today is not dominated by a purely biological, psychological, or sociological viewpoint. Instead, there is a **multidisciplinary** literature that allows several generalizations to be made about the life of young people and provides information about how best to intervene when adolescents are experiencing difficulties.

Multiple Developmental Challenges of Adolescence: Biology, Psychology, and Society

By the beginning of the second decade of life, numerous types of changes begin to occur. Internal and external bodily changes, cognitive and emotional changes, and social relationship changes all take place. Adolescence involves more than just the internal physiological and external bodily changes associated with puberty; it is a period involving changes in the biological, psychological, and social characteristics of the person. To move adaptively across the

Multidisciplinary Research and knowledge from diverse fields.

MEET THE RESEARCHER   Box 1.2   Nancy L. Galambos

Understanding Images of Maturity Among Adolescents

Nancy L. Galambos did this work as a professor in the Department of Psychology at the University of Victoria in British Columbia, when she was director of the Life-Span Developmental Psychology program at that university. She is currently working in the area of Applied Developmental Science in the Department of Psychology at the University of Alberta. She is assistant editor for the *Journal of Adolescence* and has served on numerous editorial boards in the area of adolescence.

When you think back to junior high or high school, can you remember teens who seemed more "mature" than the other kids in your class? Were you one of these teens, or did you feel young and inexperienced? Did you ever have the sense that some kids who appeared to be older on the outside were *not* mature on the inside? Over the past several years, I have been fascinated by the issue of what it means to be mature in adolescence. I have been interested in both the outer sort of maturity, which includes physical or behavioural maturity, and an inner sort of maturity, which includes characteristics such as a strong work ethic and knowing and being comfortable with who you are.

Through this research, which has been funded by the Social Sciences and Humanities Research Council of Canada, I have found three groups of adolescents who differ reliably on a number of important characteristics. The first group comprises adolescents who engage in "adultlike" problem behaviours such as drinking and smoking. These adolescents feel older or more mature than their same-age peers, but paradoxically, they score low in terms of inner maturity (e.g., they do not believe in the value of hard work). These adolescents may be labelled as pseudomature (or adultoid), for they demonstrate adultlike behaviours in the face of an inner or psychological immaturity. A second group of adolescents—the immatures—have dabbled in problem behaviours, feel younger than do their same-age peers, and are psychologically immature. The third group of adolescents appears to be genuinely mature; they have experimented with adultlike problem

behaviours, they feel slightly older than their chronological ages, and they report a strong sense of themselves and a strong work ethic.

Along with Lauree C. Tilton-Weaver and Erin T. Vitunski, I have looked further into what it means to be pseudomature, immature, or mature. We have found that these groups differ in many ways. For example, pseudomature adolescents are likely to be early maturers. They have a very strong desire to be older and although they are peer oriented, they do not feel that they matter a lot to their friends. Immature adolescents also (perhaps appropriately) feel the desire to be older, but they are less peer-oriented, and have some strengths such as being involved in school. Mature adolescents seem to be pretty happy with where they are in the world: They are not heavily involved with peers but they have close friends and are engaged in school.

Although our initial research has demonstrated the existence of these groups of adolescents, important questions remain. For example, what are the antecedents of becoming pseudomature, immature, or mature? We do not know, but we have found that pseudomature adolescents are more likely than immatures and matures to have older brothers and to hang out with older friends. Are parents aware of their adolescents' levels of maturity? In some respects, yes. Mothers of pseudomature adolescents know that their adolescents have a strong desired age. And mothers of mature adolescents rate their children as highest on socioemotional maturity, whereas mothers of immature adolescents rate

their children as lowest. Whereas fathers of pseudomature adolescents are least satisfied with their adolescents' maturity, fathers of mature adolescents are most satisfied. What are the longer-term consequences of belonging to one of these groups in adolescence? We think that pseudomature adolescents may be at higher risk of developing difficulties in the future and that mature adolescents are likely to continue to be well adjusted. The direction that will be taken by immature adolescents is unknown. To answer all of these questions requires a longitudinal design following these groups of adolescents and their parents over time.

By learning more about adolescents' maturity, we are gaining an understanding of sets of behavioural and psychological characteristics that together tell us about the relative emotional health of the adolescents. Such knowledge can potentially help us to identify adolescents who may be at risk, to design interventions to increase maturity, and to provide support and guidance to parents who are concerned about their adolescents' levels of maturity.

period of adolescence, the adolescent needs to deal with these three sets of changes, which constitute the major **developmental tasks** of this period of life (Demos, 1986). Meet the Researcher Box 1.2 describes how one investigator, Nancy Galambos,

approaches the study of these several facets of adolescent development. She describes her work investigating the experience of feeling or acting older than one's same-aged peers.

Biological Challenges

Adolescence is a matter of biology. As discussed in Chapter 3, the adolescent must cope with changing physical characteristics, such as bodily appearance, and with physiological functions, such as the beginning of the menstrual cycle or the first ejaculation. Adolescents see themselves differently: Hair is growing in places where it has not grown before; their complexion is changing; and their body is taking on a different shape. Moreover, new feelings, new "stirrings," are emanating from the body, and adolescents begin to wonder what this all means and what they will become.

Adolescents spend a great deal of time contemplating themselves—their thoughts, feelings, and appearance.

Understanding and accepting these biological changes as part of the self protects the adolescent from fear, confusion, or alienation about what is happening. For an adaptive sense of self to emerge, adolescents must understand and cope with these biological changes. This constitutes a developmental task of this period.

Psychological Challenges

Interrelated with the biological changes are psychological changes—as shown by the way adolescents react to biological changes. Psychological changes—of cognition and emotion—arise because adolescence is also a matter of psychology (Demos, 1986). New characteristics of thought and emotions emerge. Cognition becomes abstract and hypothetical, and emotions involve feelings about sexuality and changing relationships. The adolescent's developmental task is to cope with these new psychological characteristics. To interact adaptively in the world, the adolescent needs to recognize abstractions and hypotheses as different from reality. And to avoid problems of health and adjustment, adolescents need to find ways to deal in socially acceptable ways with their sexuality. Thus psychological tasks clearly involve adolescents in their social world and illustrate the interwoven nature of the tasks of this period.

New cognitive abilities (discussed in Chapter 4) allow adolescents to understand their current physical and physiological characteristics and to project what these characteristics are likely to mean to them as individuals. Given their changing characteristics of individuality, it is adolescents' thought capabilities that allow them to know who they are, guess who they might become, and plan what they may do with their new feelings.

The psychological changes of adolescence require the individual to deal with his or her changed biology by forming a revised sense of self—a new **self-definition.** Individuals' self-definition fosters the selection of the niche they pick to occupy in life, that is, the role or roles they plan to play in society. Chapter 6 discusses the process of developing an identity.

The Challenges of Society and Culture

The psychological nature of adolescence blends inextricably into the third type of challenge of the period. Because adolescents are a part of society and culture, they must learn the range of activities and roles available in the social world and come to understand their

Developmental tasks Behaviour that must be achieved at a particular age or stage in order for adaptive development to occur.

Self-definition Understanding of who you are as a person based on how you view yourself physically, psychologically, and socially.

value. The developmental task is to find the appropriate role in society by combining who one is physically with who one is psychologically. To fit optimally into a social role, one's sense of self must be well formed.

Self-definition allows the individual to meet the role tasks of the social world. Finding a social role is a crucial developmental task for **adaptive functioning,** that is, functioning that is healthy, positive, and successful. Roles give meaning to life. Responsible and successful performance of roles elicit from society protections, rights, and privileges, which safeguard individuals and allow for continued healthy functioning.

Finding a social role that contributes to society in ways that best suit the individual and is helpful to society will be adaptive for both the individual and the social world. Thus ideally there is a convergence among the three tasks of adolescence, one which allows the person to best integrate his or her changing self with his or her particular social world. Finding one's place in a civil society is discussed in Chapter 5.

The Influence of Multiple Levels of Context During Adolescence

ISSUE TO CONSIDER

• What other factors, besides hormonal changes, influence adolescent development?

Individual differences are an important part of adolescent development. They involve connections among biological, psychological, and societal factors. No single influence acts alone or as the "prime mover" of change (Brooks-Gunn & Petersen, 1983; Lerner, 1987, 1993b, 1995; Lerner & Foch, 1987; Lerner & Villarruel, 1994; Petersen, 1988). Thus it is possible to characterize the study of adolescence as a field that focuses on the *relations* between the developing individual and the several levels of his or her changing context (e.g., Lerner & Galambos, 1998; Petersen, 1988).

For example, hormonal changes are part of the development of early adolescence (Susman, 1997), but they are not primarily responsible for the psychological or social developments during this period (Finkelstein, 1993; Petersen & Taylor, 1980; Susman, 1997). The quality and timing of hormonal or other biological changes influence and are influenced by psychological, social, cultural, and historical factors (Elder, 1980; Gottlieb, 1992; Magnusson, 1988; Stattin & Magnusson, 1990; Surbey, 1990; Tanner, 1991).

Other examples of the integrated, multilevel changes in adolescence arise in regard to cognitive development during this period (Graber & Petersen, 1991). Global and pervasive effects of puberty on cognitive development do not seem to exist. When biological effects are found, they interact with contextual and experiential factors, such as the transition to junior high school, to influence academic achievement (Simmons & Blyth, 1987). Perspectives about adolescence that claim behavioural disruptions or disturbances are a universal part of this period of life (e.g., A. Freud, 1969; Hall, 1904) might lead to the assumption that there are general cognitive disruptions over adolescence. However, evidence does not support this assumption. Rather, cognitive abilities are enhanced in early adolescence as individuals become faster and more efficient at processing information—at least in settings where they feel comfortable in performing cognitive tasks (Ceci & Bronfenbrenner, 1985). Moreover, pubertal timing is not predictive of gender differences on such tasks as spatial cognition (mental rotation, spatial visualization, spatial perception), in which boys tend to perform better than girls. Girls' earlier maturation does not result in general sex differences in cognition (Graber & Petersen, 1991).

The relations among biology, problem behaviours associated with personality, and the social context of youth illustrate the multiple levels of human life that are integrated throughout adolescent development. For example, the biological changes of early pubertal maturation have been found to be linked to delinquency in adolescent girls, but only among girls who attended mixed-sex schools (Caspi et al., 1993) or among early maturing girls who socialized with older friends instead of same-age ones (Magnusson & Stattin, 1998; Stattin & Magnusson, 1990). Early maturation among girls in single-sex schools or in same-age peer groups is not linked with higher delinquency.

Adaptive functioning
Development that responds to biological, psychological, and social influences in ways that are healthy, positive, and successful.

Changing Relations Among Adolescents and Their Contexts

The period of adolescence is one of continual change and transition between individuals and their contexts (Lerner, 1995). These changing relations constitute the basic process of development in adolescence and underlie both positive and negative outcomes (Lerner, 1995).

Most developmental trajectories across this period involve positive adjustment on the part of the adolescent. For most youth there is a continuation of warm and accepting relations with parents (Grotevant, 1998; Guerney & Arthur, 1984). The most optimal adjustment occurs among adolescents who are encouraged by their parents to engage in age-appropriate autonomy while maintaining strong ties to their family (Galambos & Ehrenberg, 1997). (See Chapter 8.)

The risk of problems occurring in a youth's development is greater when the multiple biological, psychological, cognitive, and social changes of adolescence occur simultaneously, for example when menarche (a girl's first menstrual period) occurs at the same time as a school transition (Simmons & Blyth, 1987). In these circumstances, the adolescent is more often involved than younger individuals in making the behavioural and contextual choices associated with problem behaviours, such as engaging in drug use with a particular peer group (see J. S. Lerner, 1995). In adolescence, poor decisions, for example, those involving school, sex, or drugs, have more negative consequences than in childhood (Dryfoos, 1990), and the adolescent is more responsible for those decisions and their consequences

Most adolescents maintain close and warm relationships with their parents.

than in childhood (Petersen, 1988). Adolescent problem behaviour is discussed in Chapter 13.

When necessary, adolescence is an opportune time to intervene into family processes. As discussed in more detail later in this chapter, minor parent-child conflicts are normative in adolescence, for example, regarding chores and privileges. Major conflicts are less frequent, however, and when they occur often in a family, parents should be concerned (Galambos & Almeida, 1992). The continued importance of the family in the adolescent period makes such conflicts an appropriate intervention target. We discuss the influence of family on adolescents in Chapter 8.

Individual Differences Among Adolescents

ISSUES TO CONSIDER
- What characterizes the developmental trajectories of adolescence? Why do problems often occur?
- What is a key feature of policy making in the study of adolescent development?

Normal adolescent development involves both **inter-individual differences** and **intra-individual changes,** that is, both differences between individuals and differences within individuals. Good examples of differences among adolescents are temperamental characteristics involving mood and activity level (Lerner & Lerner, 1983, 1987). Inter-individual and intra-individual differences in mood and activity level may influence adolescent behaviours such as substance use and delinquency (Henry et al., 1996). Diversity also exists between and within all ethnic, racial, or cultural groups. Therefore, generalizations that confound class, race, and/or ethnicity are not useful (Lerner, 1995).

Unfortunately, there is a major limitation in the contemporary scientific literature about adolescent development. Despite the value of the existing knowledge base about development in adolescence, the majority of studies in the literature have involved the study of European American, middle-class samples (e.g., Fisher & Brennan, 1992; Graham, 1992; Hagen et al., 1990; Lerner, 1995). There are, of course, some prominent, high-quality investigations that have studied samples other than European

Inter-individual differences
Variability between people that leads to different developmental outcomes.

Intra-individual changes
Alterations within a person that occur with development.

American middle-class ones (e.g., Brookins, 1991; Reid, 1991; Spencer 1990, 1991; Spencer & Dornbusch, 1990; Spencer & Markstrom-Adams, 1990) or that have studied adolescents from national or cultural settings other than the United States (e.g., Magnusson, 1988; Mead, 1928, 1930, 1935; Silbereisen, 1995; Stattin & Magnusson, 1990; Whiting & Whiting, 1991). Many of these studies are discussed throughout this book, especially research that involves Canadian adolescents.

In regard to policies and **programs,** any intervention must be tailored to the specific target population and, in particular, to a group's developmental and environmental circumstances (Lerner, 1995; Lerner & Miller, 1993; Lerner & Villarruel, 1994). Because of inter-individual and intra-individual diversity among adolescents, any single policy or intervention cannot reach *all* of a given target population or influence every adolescent in the same way (see Chapter 14).

The breadth and depth of the high-quality scientific information available about development in adolescence underscores the diversity and dynamics of this period of life. The theoretically interesting and socially important changes of this period constitute one reason why the field of adolescence has attracted an increasing degree of scientific attention. To enhance further both basic knowledge and the quality of the research base used for applications aimed at enhancing youth development, scholarship in adolescence should be directed increasingly to elucidating the course of development of diverse adolescents.

As a result of the diversity of adolescence, any generalized statement about what is true for "all adolescents" is apt to be inaccurate. Therefore, a stereotyped belief that there is only one type of pathway across the adolescent years—for instance, one characterized by inevitable "storm and stress"—would not be expected to stand up in the face of current knowledge about diversity in adolescence. The life-span perspective provides concepts with which to evaluate this **stereotype,** or cultural lore, that frequently defines the adolescent period.

Programs Standardized procedures followed to enable a person or group to increase desired behaviours (e.g., the enhancement of literacy through instruction in reading) or to decrease unwanted ones (e.g., school dropout).

Stereotype Exceptionless generalization or commonly held belief about a group (e.g., adolescents) or social institution (e.g., fraternities or sororities).

Adolescence: The Myth of Universal Storm and Stress

- What is the lore of adolescence?
- How does context frame the lore of adolescence?

We have defined adolescence as a period of both change and transition. Certainly, other developmental periods also involve changes in both individual and social characteristics, involving biology and psychology as well as relationships with parents and peers. The uniqueness of adolescence is that it is also a period of transition, of development from being childlike to being adult. As already noted, this transition spans almost a decade of life. In fact, with the exception of infancy, adolescence is the major transitional period in the life span (Brooks-Gunn, Petersen, & Eichorn, 1985; Lerner & Foch, 1987).

Because of the dramatic and major ways in which change occurs in this period of life, the developmental tasks of adolescence can be especially problematic. Because it is a period of such pronounced transition in comparison to other life transitions and the person undergoing the changes of this period is physically bigger and stronger than a child, adolescent changes can often appear more disruptive and disturbing in their effects on the individual and his or her social world than is the case with changes occurring in other periods of life. It may be that the nature of adolescent change is so great that it can be experienced as especially stressful and the net effect of the transition may be felt as a time of "storm," or conflict, for the developing person and his or her social world.

Does this possibility of adolescence as an especially stormy and stressful period strike you as fitting or as far-fetched? It may be that your answer is shaped by the events of adolescence that you, your friends, and/or your siblings experienced. It may also be that your answer is shaped by the influences on you of stereotypes that exist in our culture about what is believed to be the inherent nature of adolescence. These stereotypes, if not held by you, may pervade your own or your parents' generation.

A stereotype is an overgeneralized belief or, in other words, an exceptionless generalization (Allport, 1954). The overgeneralized belief about adolescence is that it is a universal period of storm and stress, of emotional turmoil, and of problem behaviours (e.g., see Anthony, 1969; Lerner, 1986; Lerner & Spanier, 1980; Petersen, 1985). This exceptionless generalization is predicated on the idea that the universal biological changes of puberty inevitably create a developmental disturbance in emotions, thoughts, and social relationships (A. Freud, 1969; Anna Freud's theory is discussed in more detail in Chapter 2). According to the stereotype, stormy and stressful inner and outer conflicts inevitably complicate developmental change in adolescence.

The stereotype about adolescence arises from an interpretation about the meaning for the person of an invariant set of individual changes he or she undergoes, those associated with pubertal maturation. For this reason, it is important to discuss the stereotype, or cultural lore, of adolescence.

Bases of the Lore of Adolescence

All individuals and families have conflicts and negative experiences. Such experiences are a normal part of life. Yet many people believe that the adolescent period is a particularly stormy and stressful one—for youth and their families. Is such conflict actually prototypic of adolescent development? Is there a single nature to, or trajectory for, this period? Is there one universal, inevitable type of adolescent development that exists regardless of historical period or culture?

The word *adolescence* itself is not a new invention. It can be traced to the Latin word "adolescere," which means to grow into maturity. However, the word is especially relevant for people today (Demos, 1986). One reason for this importance is that in this century there has been both popular and scientific debate over the nature of the developments that occur in this period.

Psychologist G. Stanley Hall (1904), discussed in more detail in Chapter 2, believed that "human development everywhere included a period of *Sturm und Drang* [German for "storm and stress"] between childhood and adulthood" (i.e., during adolescence) (Demos, 1986, p. 94). As a more or less direct refutation of Hall's theory of universal and inevitable storm and stress in adolescence (Demos, 1986), anthropologist Margaret Mead designed her classic study, *Coming of Age in Samoa* (1928). Mead's view was that storm and stress are **culturally conditioned** and are quite specific to developmental experiences in modern Europe and North America (Demos, 1986). However, more recent researchers have challenged Mead's conclusions, stating that she had been fooled by some of the people she interviewed in Samoa and had not conducted sufficient fieldwork to fully understand

Samoan culture (Freeman, 1983; 1999; as cited in Côté, 2000a). This gave rise to "'the biggest debate in the social sciences for years'" (Crocombe, 1989, p. 38) and is listed among the ten 10 "'liveliest disputes ever'" in Hellman's *Great Feuds in Science* (Hellman, 1998). (Côté, 2000a, p. 526). University of Western Ontario sociologist James Côté entered the fray, thoroughly reviewed the raw data, and firmly supported Mead's work, concluding that "Freeman's theory does not have much to offer when his rhetoric, hyperbole, and outright misrepresentations are discounted" (Côté, 2000b, pp. 584-585). Researchers from England (Rutter, Graham, Chadwick, & Yule, 1976), Canada (Schonert-Reichl & Muller, 1996), as well as the United States (Bandura, 1964) have suggested that while adolescents' lives are not completely smooth and harmonious, the notion of constant storm and stress has been exaggerated.

In his review of the history of the adolescent period, Demos (1986) indicates that the presence and degree of storm and stress in adolescence is related to historical, cultural, and subcultural variations. For instance, teenage pregnancy—one possible instance of a stressful event for the adolescent—is neither a universal nor an inevitable phenomenon of adolescence (Modell, 1985). Instead, the occurrence and rate of teenage pregnancy, and the public's reaction to it, seem to be related to historical and societal trends (Modell, 1985). For example, a comparison of pregnancy rates from 33 countries found only one (the Russian Federation) that exceeded the U.S.'s rate of 83.6 per 1000 women aged 15 to 19 (Singh & Darroch, 2000). Despite any geographical or cultural similarities between Canada and its southern neighbour, Canada's pregnancy rate was almost half that of the United States (45.4 per 1000 women aged 15 to 19). Also, despite popular belief, the rate of teen births in the United States was actually higher in 1957 than in the 1990s, but more adolescents were married during the earlier time period (Coontz, 1992). In addition, as will be discussed in Chapter 10, although the pregnancy rate among Aboriginal adolescents is higher than the Canadian national average, the great value placed on children by many Aboriginal peoples means that, often, adolescent sexual activity and pregnancy are

Culturally conditioned Ideas, views, beliefs, attitudes, or values engendered by the social, cultural, and historical environment in which we live.

not looked down upon or considered disgraceful. Thus, the perception of teenage pregnancy depends on its context. This is also true of other possible sources of stress for adolescents.

The characteristics attributed to the adolescent period vary historically and culturally (e.g., Demos, 1986; Keniston, 1970; Modell, 1985). Given its social character, it should not be surprising that in modern Western societies there is a social stereotype (Anthony, 1969), a lore of adolescence (Lerner, 1986; Lerner & Spanier, 1980; Petersen, 1985; Siegel & Shaughnessy, 1995). As noted, its most general feature is the view that adolescence, universally and inevitably, is a period of storm and stress. There are specific components of this stereotype that are important to note.

Features of the Lore of Adolescence

ISSUE TO CONSIDER

• How does society's view of the developmental tasks of adolescence (e.g., forming a self-definition) contribute to the lore of this period?

At least since the time of G. Stanley Hall (1904), the idea of "storm and stress" captures what many people in Western culture believe is the essence of the adolescent period. Romanticized and envied in fiction, caricatured and condemned in the media, and idealized in song, the stereotype, or lore, about adolescence is that it is a period wherein raging hormones and complicated and contradictory social messages confuse the adolescent about who he or she is and lead erratically from one personally unsatisfying and socially unproductive activity to another (Anthony, 1969; Bandura, 1964; Petersen, 1985). Lacking an enduring sense of self—anchored with accurate understandings of one's emotions, values, and ideology— the adolescent is portrayed as unpredictable and often uncontrollable. Such an individual is simultaneously a victim of his or her own inner turbulence and a victimizer of the social institutions and agents charged with guiding the individual successfully into the stability, success, and serenity of the adult years (Anthony, 1969; Lerner & Spanier, 1980; Petersen, 1985).

The emergence of our culture's lore of adolescence has been aided and abetted by the speculations and theorizations of social scientists and psychoanalysts. Undeterred either by contradictory historical and cultural data (Demos, 1986) or by an invariably incomplete and often nonexistent database (Lipsitz,

1977), these pronouncements have painted adolescence as an inevitable and indeed necessary period of developmental disturbance, as a period of negative and difficult disruptions caused by universally tumultuous and trying transitions in the young person's biological, emotional, cognitive, and social processes (e.g., Erikson, 1968; A. Freud, 1969; Hall, 1904). Here too the adolescent's false or unstable sense of self, derived from the simultaneity and stress of these several transitions, has been said to lead, in a manner seemingly unpredictable to either the adolescent or his or her caregivers, from one adult-like guise to another (e.g., Erikson, 1959, 1968). As each facade is adopted, the adolescent believes, albeit temporarily, that he or she has coped with the storm and is now mature, directed, and committed. Chapter 6 presents alternative ideas about adolescent development of a sense of self.

Not surprisingly, it is little comfort to parents to know that within the mere passage of no more than 10 years the adolescent will look back to these days, understand the individual and interpersonal turmoil produced by this behaviour, and, as did the folksinger Bob Dylan (1964), recognize that:

> Yes my guard stood hard
> When abstract threats
> Too noble to neglect
> Deceived me into thinking
> I had something to protect
> My existence led by confusion boats
> Mutinied from stern to bow
> Ah but I was so much older then
> I'm younger than that now . . .

This lore of adolescence is a story fulfilling the purposes of many sectors of society: educators, social and health care providers, novelists, journalists, and poets included (Meyer, 1988). However, the historical and cross-cultural data we have noted (Côté, 2000a; Demos, 1986; Mead, 1928; Modell, 1985) indicate that storm and stress and/or developmental disturbance is neither universal nor inevitable. But does storm, stress, and disturbance characterize today's adolescent in modern Western societies? Did it characterize your own adolescence and those of your friends? Did it characterize the adolescence of your *parents*?

Certainly, many facets of the lore may have the ring of truth to them, especially to those people trying currently to cope with an adolescent son or daughter. Nevertheless, we may question whether the changes stereotyped to follow from pubertal change— conflict and turmoil, **cognitive reorganization**, and emotional upheaval and personal redefinition—in fact occur prototypically among today's adolescents. For today's youth—at least those in modern Western societies—do the biological transitions of adolescence directly produce a special quality of developmental tasks marked by a psychological disturbance in the young adolescent's cognitive and emotional developments (A. Freud, 1969), and by storm and stress for both the individual and the caregivers? The information available to answer this question consistently and convincingly points to "no."

Research Evidence Regarding Adolescent Storm and Stress

ISSUE TO CONSIDER

• How did research contribute to the debunking of the stereotypes related to the period of adolescence?

Every period of life has stresses. There are always challenges imposed by newly emerged or diminishing psychological and behavioural capacities and by changes in our social world, changes to which we must react to be adaptive. Thus across life we must develop the ability to cope with the stressors imposed by our inner and outer changes.

For some youth, the need to cope with the stress of these changes does produce an adolescent period that is stormy. However, research spanning about 35 years—a period that includes the adolescent years of many of the students reading this book and some of their parents—indicates that for most youth this is simply not the case (Laursen, 1995; Lerner & Spanier, 1980; Petersen, 1985; Rutter et al., 1976).

It is important to evaluate the validity of the lore of adolescence over the course of history. As emphasized by the life-span perspective, development during one period of history may differ from development at other times. Wars, economic depressions, changes in laws, epidemics, and natural disasters may create quite different developmental contexts for youth (Elder, 1974, 1980, 1998). It is possible, therefore, that during a time of considerable social unrest, or of particular quiescence, a pattern of adolescent development may arise that differs from those of other historical eras.

However, we can confidently reject the idea of universal storm and stress for youth if there is no evidence for it over a historical period when wars have begun and ended (for example, in Vietnam and Iraq), major political systems have eroded (communism),

countries have disappeared or emerged (for example, in Africa and in Europe), diseases have reached epidemic proportions (for example, AIDS), and human life has changed fundamentally due to advances in technology (the computer, the Internet). It is important, then, to critically evaluate research pertinent to any feature of adolescent development that has been conducted across such a broad historical period. Given the prominence of the lore of adolescence, such evaluation is critical.

A study by Albert Bandura (1964) provides a useful point of departure for this historical analysis. Investigating male adolescents in California, Bandura not only found that most youth did not experience a stormy adolescence, but he also found virtually no evidence for the general conflicts thought to exist between adolescents and their parents. Most of the boys Bandura studied adopted parental values and standards and formed friendships with peers who shared these same values and standards. Thus there was no struggle by the adolescents to break unwanted ties with parents and turn instead to peers. Bandura found that parents actually encouraged greater autonomy in their adolescents and began training them for such behaviour during their childhood. More about the relation between adolescents and their peers can be found in Chapter 9.

In a portion of his study, Bandura (1964) observed a sample of antisocial boys, whose excessive

Across adolescence, young people spend more time with peers than with parents.

Cognitive reorganization
Changes in the way a person thinks or reasons.

aggression did lead to an adolescence associated with storm and stress. However, their problem behaviours were present throughout their childhood. Other data are consistent with Bandura's (1964) findings that youth who show problem behaviours during adolescence showed similar problematic behaviours in childhood (Spivack, Marcus, & Swift, 1986). A child who is overly and disruptively involved socially and who fails to modulate his or her behaviour to accommodate others is likely to show misconduct and to have conflict with authority figures in adolescence. Similarly, drug use in adolescence was predicted by childhood personality as well as by contemporaneous adolescent personality (Brook et al., 1986). These findings suggest that some, but not necessarily all, paths through adolescence begin in the childhood years.

Offer (1969) also found evidence for multiple paths through early adolescence. Most boys experienced either "**continuous growth**" or "**surgent growth.**" Offer described "continuous growth" as involving smooth, nonabrupt change; he described "surgent growth" as involving abrupt spurts or changes in behaviour but with no necessarily accompanying crisis, problems, or storm. Only a minority of boys experienced what Offer termed "**tumultuous growth,**" which was the only path deemed "stormy" (Offer, 1969).

In Offer's study (1969), the adolescents in the "**continuous-growth**" type of development, the category into which most fall, were not in any major conflict with their parents and did not feel that parental rearing practices were inappropriate or that parental values were ones they did not share. In the "**surgent growth**" trajectory, there was abrupt change but it did not necessarily involve the turmoil associated with storm and stress. Finally, with the "**tumultuous growth**" type, crisis, stress, and problems are present. The nature of this change is aptly characterized by major emotional and interpersonal distress.

Additional research finds evidence of several different types of developmental trajectories in adolescence. Block (1971) identified at least five different paths through adolescence for males and at least six different paths for females. However, for both males and females only a few of these pathways could be characterized as crisis-ridden or stormy.

In a study of both male and female adolescents, Douvan and Adelson (1966) found very little evidence of either conflict with or rebellion from parents. Adolescents were satisfied with their families and with how they were treated by their parents. Douvan and Adelson (1966) found that both boys and girls shared their parents' basic values and standards. In fact, adolescents were again seen to choose peers who had these same values and standards. Although adolescents spend increasingly more time with peers than with parents (Petersen, 1988; and see Chapter 9), and the influence of peers may actually increase across adolescence (Petersen, 1988), parents remain central in the adolescent's world.

These studies lead to two key conclusions: (1) Even when storm and stress is seen in adolescence, it is not necessarily the result of events in adolescence, but instead may be associated with prior developments. (2) Storm and stress is not necessarily characteristic of the adolescent period; many possible types of adolescent development, many trajectories, can occur.

Across the adolescent period youth maintain a high level of discussion with their parents in regard to academic/vocational, social/ethical, family, and peer issues (Petersen, 1998). At the same time, discussions with peers about these issues increase across this age range. Friends may be more influential than parents in some areas such as peer relationships. In other areas parents and peers may have equivalent influences (Chassin et al., 1986). On most major issues, for example, life plans, parents have the most influence on adolescents (Kandel, 1974; Kandel & Lesser, 1969, 1972; Petersen, 1987).

The means by which this influence occurs can vary in relation to the structure and/or function of the family. In regard to family functioning, families with good parent-adolescent communication show high cohesion as a unit, high adaptability to change, and high satisfaction with the characteristics of the family (Barnes & Olson, 1985). However, there may be **cross-cultural variation** in the influence of particular types of family functioning. Among Korean

---

Continuous growth
Developmental path through adolescence characterized by smooth, nonabrupt change.

Surgent growth Developmental path through adolescence characterized by abrupt spurts or changes in behaviour, but not necessarily with turmoil, storm, or stress.

Tumultuous growth
Developmental path through adolescence experienced by a minority of adolescents, characterized by turmoil, storm, and stress.

Cross-cultural variation
Differences in values, beliefs, attitudes, and actions that occur between societies.

adolescents, high parental control is associated with high warmth and low neglect in the parent-adolescent relationship. However, among youths and their parents in Western societies' majority cultures, the relationship between control and warmth and neglect is reversed (Rohmer & Pettengill, 1985).

Family interaction, including among the subsystems in the family, also affects the influence of parents on adolescents. For example, in a study of adolescent-father, adolescent-mother, and adolescent-mother-father interactions in married two-parent families, the presence of the father enhanced the quality of mother-son relations; but the presence of the mother reduced the quality of father-son interactions (Gjerde, 1986). In addition, mothers treated sons and daughters more differently when the father was present in the group; but fathers treated sons and daughters more differently when the mother was absent from the group. In families with male adolescents, parental role differences increased in the presence of the spouse. In contrast to adolescents in households with two parents, youth in mother-only households are more likely to make decisions without direct parental input and are more likely to show problem behaviours (Dornbusch et al., 1985). However, when another adult joins the household, there is an increase in parental control and influence and a decrease in problem behaviours. This change is especially true for male adolescents, and may depend on the reason the one-parent family was formed.

Although there are structural and functional variations in how influence is expressed, parents do continue to influence their adolescents and share with them key orientations to life. Lerner and Knapp (1975) found substantial attitude and value similarity among male and female adolescents and their mothers and fathers. In the great majority of cases, members of both generations had similar attitudes about such issues as sexuality, drug use, war and peace, and civil and human rights.

The adolescents studied by Lerner and Knapp (1975) believed their attitudes were quite different from those of their parents. Despite the actual high level of similarity that existed, adolescents exaggerated the differences between them and their parents and overestimated the extent to which they differed from their parents. Parents, however, underestimated even the small extent to which they differed from their children. The parents saw fewer differences than actually existed. Although the different generational groups present in a family do not actually differ very

much in their attitudes, members of one generation (adolescents) overestimate this difference and members of the other (parents) underestimate it.

Recent information indicates that among contemporary adolescents, parents are not the exclusive or even necessarily the major source of social disagreements (Laursen, 1995). Adolescents report that disagreements occur most often with their mothers, but the next most frequent sources of conflict are friends, romantic partners, and siblings (Laursen, 1995). Fathers trail behind these groups as a source of disagreement. In other words, adolescents' disagreements are more likely to involve people of their own generation than their parents. Disagreements with parents are likely to involve responsibilities, school, and autonomy, whereas disagreements with peers tend to arise in respect to friendships and sexuality (Laursen, 1995).

Even in regard to disagreements with peers, there are perhaps more agreements than conflicts. In a study of about 3500 youth from five countries (the United States, Israel, Costa Rica, the Philippines, and Scotland), there was significant agreement among adolescents and their peers in regard to ideas about major life events involving the nature of and the transition to adulthood (Seltzer & Waterman, 1996). Consistent with past research (Lerner & Knapp, 1975), adolescents also *perceived* that their attitudes were in agreement with those of their peers (Seltzer & Waterman, 1996). Even though adolescents are more likely to have disagreements with age-mates than with both their parents, they believe they have— and in fact do have—marked agreements with their peers. Chapter 9 discusses further aspects of adolescent-peer relationships.

When the precise nature of conflicts between youth and their parents is examined, there is little evidence for the lore of adolescence (Laursen, Coy, & Collins, 1998). Across the adolescent period there is a decrease in the *rate* of conflict between adolescents and their parents and also a decrease in the *number* of conflictual exchanges youths have with them. Although there is an overall decrease in the frequency of conflict between youths and their parents across adolescence, when they do have conflicts the intensity of emotions increases across adolescence, as well as in relation to pubertal maturation (Laursen et al., 1998).

The findings of recent research, consistent with research from several decades ago, indicate that the patterns of inter- and intra-generational conflict and compatibility are hardly the base on which to build the notion of universal adolescent storm and stress. There may always be stress, conflict, or interpersonal disagreements in the adolescent period, but there are several paths through adolescence, and storm occurs only sometimes. For most youth there is a continuation of generally good and satisfying parent-child relations, relations predicated on the adoption by the adolescent of parental values and standards (Lerner & Spanier, 1980; Petersen, 1985).

As the findings of Laursen (1995) and Laursen et al. (1998) suggest, parents do not always experience their children as perfect and amenable to all their rules and requests. Conflicts can and do occur. As illustrated by Lise Cardinal and her mother at the beginning of the chapter, these disagreements may even take the form of heated verbal exchanges. However, disagreements, arguments, and even "backtalk" from teenagers are normal parts of parents' experiences with their teenage children. As explained in Implications for Parenting Box 1.1, parents should keep such interactions with their adolescents in perspective.

The lore of adolescence is not fully accurate in depicting the nature of the changes involving the physiological, cognitive, emotional, self-definitional, and role characteristics associated among contemporary youth with the challenges of this period of life. Nevertheless, the way the adolescent meets the developmental challenges of the period will influence the quality of development during this portion of life.

Contemporary scientific literature does not support the belief that adolescence is a period of general disruption of parent-child ties or the belief in the emergence of problematic social behaviours among virtually all youth. The facts of adolescent

development allow the study of the social problems that *do* occur during this period to be put in appropriate perspective.

It is also important to highlight the nature of the individual and social problems that do exist within this period of life. Although only a minority of youth exhibits these problems, on a population basis this frequency translates into millions of people. This book presents information about these problems of adolescent development in Chapter 13. However, in order to identify what is problematic or atypical it is crucial to know what is typical and normative (Fisher et al., 1993). This book also describes the prototypic characteristics of adolescent development.

Conclusions

Contemporary scholarship about adolescence focuses on the themes of developmental diversity; adolescent-context relations; and the links among theory, research, and application (to youth policies and programs). As such, these themes frame this book in the following manner:

- The emphasis on adolescent development involves both the antecedents of development in earlier life periods and the consequences of changes in adolescence for later, adult development and aging. The treatment of development in this text includes a discussion of the intertwining of the development of a youth with the life-span development of parents and other relatives, with peers, and with other individuals important in the life of an adolescent, such as teachers, mentors, and coaches.
- The emphasis on individual *diversity* includes a focus on developmental variation between adolescents associated with race, ethnicity, gender, sexual orientation, and physical characteristics. In addition, this emphasis on diversity involves an appraisal of within-person variability, such as that associated with the gains and losses that characterize human development across life.
- The emphasis on *context* involves a discussion of (1) the role of culture and history in shaping the processes and products of adolescent development; (2) the role of the social, interpersonal, familial, and physical context in influencing youth development; (3) institutional contributions to adolescent development, including educational, political, economic, and

Parents remain sources of support and guidance for adolescents.

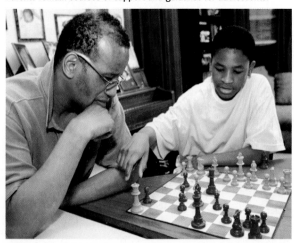

Does Your Preteen Have to Argue About Everything? Yes, But You Can Keep It All in Perspective

Mark Twain once wryly noted, "When I was a boy of 14, my father was so ignorant that I could hardly stand to have the old man around. But when I got to be 21, I was astonished at how much he had learned in seven years."

If you're the parent of a preteen, you know all too well what it's like to be on the receiving end of that attitude. The youngster who once saw you as the source of all wisdom now cuts you off in midconversation with utterances such as "You can't tell me what to do" and "Why do I bother explaining things to you? You can't possibly understand." In addition, he suddenly seems to question every statement that comes out of your mouth. He may even use the occasional obscenity.

It's easy for a parent to lose patience when a child starts mouthing off this way; none of us enjoys being treated disrespectfully or having to justify everything we say. Back talk is also disturbing because it signifies your loss of control over your child's behaviour.

But as inappropriate and disrespectful as a preteen's language might be, it's actually a step toward mature behaviour. Learning to assert individual opinions is a developmental milestone every bit as significant, and universal, as cutting teeth or walking. As annoying as this stage in your child's life can be at times, there is no way you can absolutely abolish back talk. There are, however, a number of ways for you to recognize and provide outlets for your child's opinions, emotions, and growing skills at debate.

Begin by understanding why your child needs to talk back.

Her "smart mouth" is, in some ways, exactly that—a sign that she's smarter. Her logic is growing more sophisticated, although it's not quite up to adult level yet. She now sees her parents' opinions, once regarded as the absolute truth, as one possible truth—and a version of it that she sometimes finds hard to swallow.

Chalk that up to another aspect of adolescence: your child's need to establish herself as a person separate from you. Just as it is your job to watch over and protect your child, it is your child's job to stake out her own emotional turf, to discover who she is and what she stands for.

An increase in back talk often coincides with a developmental transition, such as starting middle or junior high school. Hanging out with a new group of kids may lead your child to think that a certain level of repartee is expected of her. You may need to tell your adolescent, "I know you talk this way with your friends, but I find it unpleasant to hear that kind of language at home."

Don't belittle your child.

In the heat of the moment, this rule can be tough to follow, but it's crucial. No matter how adult your teen wants to be, he is still a child, with easily hurt feelings and little experience in the art of persuasion.

For example, if you take your child to task for doing his homework in front of the television, he may answer you dismissively with, "This isn't homework. It's just answering questions." You could easily reply by saying something like, "That's ridiculous! Do you think I don't know what homework is?"

Although understandable, this response will only serve to embroil you further in an unproductive argument. What you might do instead is say something such as, "Whatever you call it, I want you to try your best at your schoolwork, and I don't think you can do that if you're working in front of the television."

Similarly, if your child is using unpleasant language toward a sibling and you tell him to stop it, he might say, "I'm not being mean; I'm just defending myself!" Your impulse might well be to say, "That's baloney! I heard the way you talked to her." But it's probably more helpful if you respond by saying something like, "Standing up for yourself is a good thing, but you have to try to do it without using words that hurt others' feelings."

Fight fair, even when your child doesn't.

Resist the temptation to fight fire with fire, especially if your teen gets so angry during an argument that she curses at you, shoves you, or even spits on you. If something like this happens, as calmly as you can, say, "I want you to let me know how you feel about things, but I can't tolerate this behaviour. The conversation is over." Follow up with appropriate discipline.

Stick to your values.

Debates with your child will be more fruitful for both of you if you know what is negotiable and what is not. If you have a habit of arguing and then giving in, you'll get more of an argument from your child because he knows that it pays off. Put forward your deeply held values, and don't retreat from them—but be prepared to justify your position to your child.

Set limits on profanity.

Preadolescents often use foul language to signal their grown-up status. It's hard to deny that cursing is an activity associated with adults. It is as reasonable to set limits on profanity, however, as it is on other adult behaviours, such as staying up late. What those limits are depends on how much foul language upsets you.

If your child says, "How come you get to use any words you want, and I don't?" tell her that using profanity is a habit of yours that you don't especially like and are trying to control, but that it sometimes happens when you're very angry or upset. You can also say to her, "By using those words, you're going to offend someone or create an impression you'll regret later on."

Make sure you give your child credit for what he does right.

Because one of your child's primary motives for talking back is to show that he is capable of holding his own in a grownup conversation, acknowledge him when he succeeds. You won't lose ground by saying, "That's a good point you've made."

Suppose your 12-year-old son wants to sleep over at a friend's house and you say, "No, I don't want you to spend the night there. Blair's parents are lax about supervision."

>

Your child might respond with "How do you know? *You've* never spent the night there."

Instead of treating this response as insolence, you might reply, "That's absolutely true. I've heard from other parents, however, that Blair's mom and dad sometimes go out and leave the kids alone. Maybe that isn't so, but the possibility worries me because I'm concerned about your safety."

After some discussion, your child might suggest a solution: "I'll call and make sure his parents will be there all night." After you agree to this—with the understanding that you can telephone the parents to confirm the arrangement—praise your child for respecting your concerns and solving the problem creatively.

Don't expect conflicts—or back talk—to be solved overnight.

Arguments often do not have clear-cut resolutions. If you've both had your say and the conversation has become unpro- ductive, you may have to tell your child, "We've been over this too many times. Let's wrap it up. Maybe if we think about it and talk tomorrow, it'll be easier for us to agree on something."

And remember that arguing with a child you love can be a highly emotional and exasperating experience. Don't expect perfection from yourself. Stay as calm and evenhanded as you can, and keep reminding yourself how smart you're going to be in just a few years.

Source: Lerner, R. M., & Olson, C. K. (1994, December). "Don't talk back," *Parents* pp. 97–98.

social policy influences; and (4) community needs and assets, including programs promoting positive youth and family development. In addition, the text discusses several disciplines and professions involved in understanding the contexts that influence human development.

- Finally, the emphasis on *application* focuses on how the life-span perspective embraces both theoretical and applied research in adolescents' lives. The text also discusses **applied developmental science** (ADS), and how this approach to research about adolescence frames policies and programs pertinent to youth intervention programs, education, retraining, and services.

Many chapters of the book feature an Implications for Parenting box, a key dimension of application. Traditionally, there has been keen interest in understanding how developmental science may be applied to enhance adults' ability to parent their preadolescent offspring. A life-span perspective extends this domain to include issues of parenting youth, such as helping a young person make a successful transition to work. It also includes issues of adolescents' parenting their own children, that is, the issue of teenage parenting.

Summary

- Adolescence spans the second decade of life and is a period of transition wherein a person's biological, psychological, and social characteristics go from childlike to adultlike.

- Not all young people undergo the period of transition in the same way. There is variation in the timing, speed, and outcome of the transition.
- Developmental trajectories are the diverse paths through life that an individual experiences, based on biology, psychology, and social characteristics.
- The life-span perspective seeks to understand development across the entire course of life, in relation to combinations of biological, psychological, and contextual influences. It stresses differences within and among people and

Applied developmental science Approach that uses research about human development to promote positive changes in individuals, families, and communities.

attempts to optimize development by understanding these different bases of development.

- The life-span perspective emphasizes two types of diversity: differences among people (inter-individual differences) and changes within a person (intra-individual changes).

- It is important to use knowledge from multiple disciplines and professions to understand human development.

- Life-span scholars use intervention studies to optimize people's development through changes in the social world and changes in individual functioning.

- The major developmental tasks of adolescence are to deal with changes in biology, psychology, and the social world.

- Adolescents must cope with changing physical characteristics and physiological functions.

- Adolescents must deal with new thoughts and emotions and their changed biology to form a revised sense of self.

- The social developmental task of adolescence involves finding an appropriate role in society by combining who one is physically with who one is psychologically.

- Ideally, the three developmental tasks of adolescence converge to allow the adolescent to integrate his or her changing biology and psychology with the social world.

- Adolescents' changing relations with their contexts influence positive and negative outcomes of adolescence.

- When the biological, psychological, and social changes of adolescence occur simultaneously, there is a greater risk of developmental problems.

- The study of adolescence is limited in that the majority of the studies conducted are focused on European American, middle-class adolescents. However, we aim to address this limitation by highlighting research conducted on Canadian adolescents from diverse backgrounds.

- Because of differences among adolescents, policies and programs must be tailored to specific target populations, and any policy or program should not be expected to reach all members of a given target population.

- The lore or stereotype of adolescence is that it is a period of universal storm and stress involving emotional turmoil and problem behaviours.

- Research indicates that the lore of adolescence is not accurate and that storm and stress is neither universal nor inevitable.

- Adolescence is generally a time of continued positive relations with parents, and most adolescents adopt their parents' values and standards as their own.

- How adolescents meet the developmental tasks of coping with changing biology, psychology, and context will influence the quality of their development during adolescence.

Discussion Topics

1. How do *you* define adolescence?
2. How does the life-span approach to adolescence employ concepts pertaining to the nature of human development such as diversity, context, and application?
3. Why is it important to take a multidisciplinary approach to adolescent development?
4. In what way did the onset of puberty affect your development? What other biological, psychological, and/or social/cultural factors influenced your developmental trajectory?
5. What is missing in studies that make broad generalizations about adolescent development?
6. What is your opinion about the lore of adolescence? How do your experiences and/or the experiences of those you know contribute to your opinion on this matter?
7. How do the media contribute to the stereotypes you might hold about the period of adolescence? Is the media portrayal of adolescence harmful? Is the media more or less harmful in their portrayal of males or females?
8. What should parents know about adolescent development to support healthy relationships with their children?

Key Terms

adaptive functioning, p. 12
adolescence, p. 3
applied developmental science, p. 22
cognitive reorganization, p. 17
context, p. 4
continuous growth, p. 18
cross-cultural variation, p. 18
culturally conditioned, p. 15
developmental tasks, p. 11
developmental trajectories, p. 4
ecology, p. 5
inter-individual differences, p. 13
intervention studies, p. 6

intra-individual changes, p. 13
life-span perspective, p. 7
multidisciplinary, p. 9
policies, p. 6
programs, p. 14
self-definition, p. 11
social role, p. 6
stereotype, p. 14
storm and stress, p. 3
surgent growth, p. 18
tumultuous growth, p. 18

2

Theories of Adolescence

Robbie's biggest concern about leaving his small central Saskatchewan school for Edmonton was about how he would make new friends in the city. His father, a respected man in their small community, had lost his seat in the last council election. During his tenure as a council member, he had been invited to speak in different communities throughout the prairies. These engagements had given his father many contacts, and it wasn't long after he started looking for work that he received a job offer. After taking some time to consider it, his parents made their decision. The family would move to Alberta.

Robbie's sister and brother felt happy about the move. It seemed that they had already carved out their niches. His sister, an outgoing 14-year-old, was probably the smartest of the three. She consistently got top grades in her class, and, according to her teachers, had great academic potential. She wanted to go to university to train to become a doctor or a lawyer. His brother, an athletic 18-year-old, was a very good hockey player. A forward who was fast and smart on the ice, according to his coach, and a star on the local team, he would've been even better had he faced more competition. He often travelled to Saskatoon for tournaments and talked about moving to the city.

In contrast to his sister and brother, Robbie was very ambivalent about moving. On the one hand, being in Edmonton would give him a better chance as a musician. A music teacher at his school told Robbie that he had a talent for playing guitar but needed more advanced teaching than could be provided there. In Edmonton he could find a guitar teacher and maybe some people to jam with. Maybe they could start a band, write some songs, and even play some gigs. He hoped eventually to tour with an alternative band and make big money. That was his dream, though, and not the one his parents had for him. They were aware of the difficulties new musicians had making ends meet, and wanted to see him get a university education that would give him a stronger chance for a well-paid start in a career.

On the other hand, Robbie realized he would have to make new friends and keep up his grades in a new school. It certainly would be difficult to meet new people that he liked as much as the friends he'd grown up with at home. And while he took the high school courses necessary for university entrance, they had always been challenging for him. With a lot of effort and some extra help he'd gotten average grades in Grade 10. He was putting in even more effort this year, and reaping the benefits; he had achieved better than average grades in each of his Grade 11 courses by the end of the year.

The family moved that summer. At school in the fall, Robbie went from feeling like a small fish in a pond to a minnow in the ocean. Fortunately, there were other new students starting Grade 12 that year, and with some help from the school guidance counsellor, he managed to find some interesting options in addition to the required courses he would need to graduate.

While his brother went on to play junior hockey and his sister maintained the honours average, Robbie, to his parents' chagrin, became even more focused on being a musician. In a high school music class, he met another student who played drums in a band that needed a rhythm guitar player. Robbie started jamming and writing songs with the other band members, who also became his friends. By the time his first report card came, his heavy time commitment to the band had seriously hurt his grades. It was apparent that he was spending much more time with the band than on his schoolwork. His parents wanted Robbie to be tutored in order to improve his grades to the level necessary to get into university. That would mean less time for practising with the band.

He needed to make a decision. Mid-term was over, and to get the English and Social Studies grades he required for admission to university he'd have to cut out week-night band practices. The band members wanted him to practise, and told Robbie that if he couldn't commit to the band, they'd have to replace him. He was caught between the wishes of his parents and his new friends. As he realized that he couldn't do both, Robbie became angry. He was angry with his parents for not seeing his point of view and angry with his friends who were ready to toss him out of the band if he couldn't practise enough. He was also angry with himself for not being able to make this decision on his own. It really did matter to him what his parents and friends wanted him to do.

After some reflection, Robbie decided that being a professional musician was a good goal, but not the only goal he would work toward. He decided to combine his interests in music with the better job prospects that a post-secondary education offered. Although it meant giving up the band with his friends, he decided that he would find another one to jam with that didn't require such a heavy commitment for practising. So, he gave up the band and spent more time studying.

That winter Robbie applied to a university music program. When the letter from the university arrived the following summer, he opened it quickly to learn that he had been accepted. It appeared that his decision to study more and leave the band was a good one. He felt confident that the program he would enroll in would give him more options for a career in music, if not as a performer, as a writer, copyist, teacher, or recorder.

Learning Objectives

1. To understand what is meant by the statement "Development occurs as a consequence of relations among multiple levels of organization."
2. To recognize the importance of the diversity of development when designing intervention programs.
3. To understand the theoretical debate of nature versus nurture.
4. To know how developmental contextualism differs from other theories of human development.
5. To recognize that genes can be influenced by characteristics of the context and that, inversely, the context can be influenced by the biological characteristics of those who live within it.
6. To understand the contributions of G. Stanley Hall to the study of developmental psychology and to recognize the problems inherent in Hall's belief that "phylogeny recapitulates ontogeny."
7. To recognize what McCandless meant by *drive states* and how drive states come to influence and determine behaviour.
8. To recognize and be able to describe the three different types of interaction theory.
9. To define and describe the five stages of psychosexual development.
10. To recognize Erikson's view on the role of the ego in contributing to development.
11. To understand the special alterations in personality that Anna Freud associates with adolescence.
12. To recognize that Piaget believes that cognitive development occurs in stages and involves the individual's attempt to maintain an equilibration between the processes of assimilation and accommodation.
13. To recognize that Kohlberg's work, like Piaget's, describes a stagewise progression in moral reasoning and to be able to identify the stages of moral reasoning as described by Kohlberg.
14. To define and describe the four levels of human ecology according to Bronfenbrenner. Specifically, to recognize the reciprocal relationship between the individual and his or her contexts within and across levels.
15. To identify and be able to differentiate the components of the SOC model and to recognize that successful development includes the coordinated integration of selection, optimization, and compensation processes.

What Robbie experienced during his transition from one school to another illustrates what may be the key challenge for people during adolescence: discovering what they can do—given their particular biological, psychological, and social characteristics—to develop successfully in their context. To attain the goal of peer acceptance and peer popularity, Robbie had to understand his physical abilities (a talent for playing guitar), his psychological attributes (his ability to achieve academically), and his social context (what his friends and parents expected of him). He had to attain a self-definition, an identity that fit his specific individual attributes and situational circumstances.

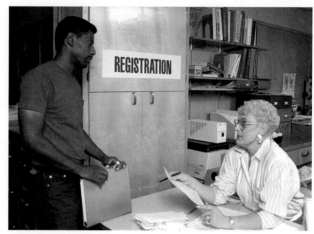

Adjusting to the requirements of life at college or university may be a challenging experience.

The actions adolescents take to meet the biological, psychological, and social challenges they confront determine whether or not they develop in a healthy, positive, or successful (that is, an "adaptive") manner (see Chapter 1). Explaining how adolescents select goals for their behaviours, how they find the means or resources to achieve these goals (that is, to "optimize" their ability to attain their objectives), and what adolescents do to compensate for failures, that is, for the loss of opportunities, arguably are the essential tasks for theories of adolescence (Baltes, 1997; Baltes & Baltes, 1990; Freund & Baltes, 1998). Theories of adolescence must explain three different actions of young people, actions that may be summarized by the terms **selection**, **optimization**, and **compensation** (Lerner et al., 2001).

First, theories must explain how goals are *selected* and developed. For example, why did Robbie, when confronted with the loss of his connections with the peers from his former high school, elect to try to gain acceptance and popularity with the students in his new high school rather than spend his free time with his parents? Why do adolescents in general elect to spend more and more time with peers and increasingly less time with their parents?

Second, theories of adolescent development must explain how youth develop the skills and/or find means to attain the goals they select. How do they learn to act in ways that *optimize* their opportunities to reach their goals? For example, why did Robbie initially elect to reach his goal of peer status through high achievement in music and academics?

Third, to maintain a high level of functioning, losses must be compensated. The means we use to reach the goals we select do not always result in success. Failure is a normative experience for all people. However, healthy development rests on finding ways to *compensate* for failures or losses, to find other means (new resources) to reach goals, or to adopt new goals when original ones prove to be beyond one's biological, psychological, and social resources or capacities. Faced with the realization that he would not immediately be a star musician, and to try to achieve that goal would detract from his time (his resources) to attain academic success, Robbie increased his efforts in academics. Thus Robbie has learned how important it is to make choices and focus personal resources on a domain of functioning matching one's skills and potential when all options cannot be pursued.

Explaining the actions of adolescents and their implications for adaptive outcomes is complicated because the life of adolescents is full of transitions. What makes sense to select as a goal changes across development. For example, the goal of peer relations in middle school might be sufficient popularity to be invited to desired parties, whereas the goal at the end of high school might be to establish a meaningful romantic relationship. The means to reach goals differs across adolescence. For instance, parents must be relied on for transportation to peer events in early adolescence, but by the end of the adolescent period, reliance on parents for transportation to and from dates might be seen as humiliating. How a person compensates for failure or loss varies across adolescence. For instance, more sophisticated cognitive rationalizations for failure are available to older adolescents.

The selections youth make across the adolescent period involve changes in their relations with their contexts (e.g., "Should I spend more time practising with the band or studying?"). Adolescents also consider anticipated future contexts when making selections. Given what young people know of their physical and psychological strengths and weaknesses and the social world they wish to inhabit as an adult, they may ask, "What choices now will lead me to where I want to be when I am an adult?" (Oettingen, 1999). The selections made by adolescents can vary in their significance for life outcomes. Some selections can affect their entire life, such as decisions about substance use, unsafe sex, and postsecondary aspirations (J. S. Lerner, 1995).

When the adolescent understands his or her characteristics of biological, psychological, and social individuality and acts accordingly, successful development is promoted. Adaptive outcomes occur when actions involving selection, optimization, and compensation can foster diversity in the adolescent's behavioural repertoire. Robbie can elect to spend more time in enhancing his academic abilities rather than devoting time to improving his guitar-playing skills.

Theories of adolescence must explain how the individually distinct adolescent acts in relation to the particular context within which he or she is embedded. Theories must account for how the particular "context" of the adolescent provides feedback. Finally, theories must explain how the reciprocal nature of the adolescent and his or her context results in differences in adaptive development.

How successful are theories of adolescence in meeting these explanatory goals? Although earlier theories were perhaps less successful because context was held more constant, *contemporary* theories of adolescence are in fact meeting these goals quite well due to increased focus on the influence of the communities that adolescents live in. The next section of the chapter reviews past and current theories. The usefulness of contemporary theory lies in its stance in regard to a core, perhaps the core, conceptual issue in the study of human development: the **nature-nurture controversy**. The positions of current and past theories in regard to this controversy are discussed.

Understanding Adolescence: Contemporary Theory

ISSUES TO CONSIDER
- What are some concrete examples which illustrate that development has multiple levels of organization?
- How is the individual adolescent an "active agent" in his or her own development?

The study of adolescence has provided a model for scholarship dedicated to the study of the life span. Today, theory and research in adolescence stresses that *development occurs as a consequence of relations among **multiple levels of organization*** (e.g., see Muuss, 1996). The levels considered in contemporary theory are typically the subject matter of different disciplines. For example, genes are one level and are the subject matter of biology. The adolescent and his or her behaviour is another level and involves the discipline of psychology. Groups or institutions such as the family, peers, and schools are part of a level that is most often studied by sociology. Culture is a level studied most often by anthropologists.

Developmental system theories stress that development occurs as a consequence of organized and

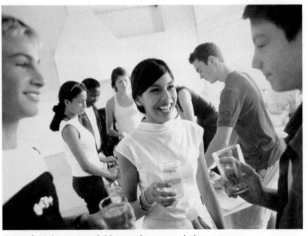

A lot of adolescent social interactions occur in large groups.

Nature-nurture controversy
Debate about whether or how biology and/or environment provide the basis of human behaviour and development.

Multiple levels of organization
Idea that development occurs as a consequence of relations among biology, person, social groups, culture, history, and other levels in the ecology of human development.

Developmental systems theories
Theories which stress that development occurs as a consequence of organized and mutually influential relations among different levels of organization (e.g., biology, society, culture, history).

mutually influential (or "systematic") relations among the levels. These theories emphasize that development occurs because of interconnections among biological, psychological, sociological, as well as other influences (for example, economics, historical events, and the occurrence of wars or disease epidemics). Changes at one level within the developmental system affect other levels. For example, parents' marital problems can affect a young person's psychological health (e.g., depression may arise as a consequence of witnessing parents arguing a lot). In turn, changes in the adolescent's psychological or behavioural characteristics (for instance, becoming involved in alcohol use) can place stress on parents and influence the quality of their marriage.

There are many versions of developmental systems models of human development (Baltes, 1987; Baltes, Reese, & Nesselroade, 1988; Brandtstädter, 1998; Bronfenbrenner & Morris, 1998; Elder, 1998; Featherman & Lerner, 1985, Ford & Lerner, 1992; Gottlieb, 1997; Gottlieb, Wahlstein, & Lickiter, 1998; Lerner, 1986, 1991b, 1995, 1998; Magnusson & Stattin, 1998; Overton, 1998; Sameroff, 1983; Thelen & Smith, 1998). One of these models—*developmental contextualism* (Lerner, 1982, 1986, 1998; Lerner & Kauffman, 1985)—is regarded by many scholars around the world as a general frame for studying adolescent development (e.g., Muuss, 1996) and, more broadly, for understanding the life-span perspective of human development.

The developmental contextual approach to life-span development suggests that to understand adolescence we must consider influences from multiple disciplines in an integrated manner. The theory emphasizes *the need to consider development as systematic change*. We must view the young person as a dynamic entity, the centre of a network of influences involving his or her inner (biological, psychological) and outer (peer group, family, society) worlds. Developmental contextualism stresses that the individual is an active agent in his or her own development. The individual acts on the context just as the context acts on him or her, often in direct response to the actions (the selection, optimization, and compensation behaviours) of the individual (Brandtstädter, 1998, 1999; Lerner, 1982).

Theory, Method, and Application

ISSUES TO CONSIDER
- Why is multilevel, multivariate, longitudinal research effective in studying adolescence?
- What are some variables that might be relevant to intervention programs designed to support adolescents?

The developmental contextual approach to adolescence has specific implications for scientific methods used to study the multiple and changing connections between young people and their worlds (see Appendix 1). A life-span and developmental systems view of adolescence requires that several variables from different levels (e.g., biological ones relating to puberty, psychological ones relating to self-image or identity, and social ones relating to parent-child relations) be studied repeatedly (over time), in order to provide observations of the changes involved in development. Technically, this means that **multivariate** (many variables), **longitudinal** (repeated observations), and **multilevel** (e.g., biological, psychological, and social), and thus multidisciplinary, research should be used to study adolescence.

When we understand something about how adolescents' relationships with their peers, parents, schools, communities, and societies propel their development, we know how development might be improved in real-world settings. We may learn why some adolescents, despite growing up in poverty and in neighbourhoods where there is a lot of crime, few social services, and poor schools, succeed academically, develop a strong commitment to a productive career, and end up having a healthy and positive life. We may also understand why other adolescents in these same circumstances succumb to the risks around them and do poorly in school, in their career or work life, and in their personal development (McAdoo, 1995; Spencer, 1990; Werner & Smith, 1992). Knowledge about the **diversity** (systematic differences) involving adolescents and their contexts provides information about how development occurs and suggests what *might* happen if relationships between young people and their settings were changed.

Multivariate research/studies Research involving several variables.

Longitudinal research/studies Research composed of repeated observations.

Multilevel research/studies Research focusing on biological, psychological, and social facets of a phenomenon.

Diversity In development, systematic differences among individuals, groups, or institutions of society.

Characteristics of Applied Developmental Science

Applied developmental science (ADS) has been conceptualized by the United States' National Task Force on ADS as scholarship that represents

the programmatic synthesis of research and applications to describe, explain, intervene, and provide preventive and enhancing uses of knowledge about human development . . . . [It is] *applied* [because it has] direct implications for what individuals, practitioners, and policy makers do . . . . [It is] *developmental* [because it] focuses on systematic and successive changes within human systems that occur across the life span. [It is] *science* [because it is] grounded in a range of research methods designed to collect reliable and objective information that can be used to test the validity of theory and applications. (Fisher et al., 1993, p. 4)

As discussed by Fisher and her colleagues (e.g., Fisher & Lerner, 1994a, 1994b; Lerner & Fisher, 1994; Lerner, Fisher, & Weinberg, 1997, 2000a, 2000b), ADS, defined in terms of the convergence of application, development, and science, stresses the reciprocal relationship between theory and application, a relationship wherein:

- Empirically based theory not only guides intervention strategies, but also is influenced by the outcome of these interventions.

Of equal import are the assumptions that valid applications of developmental science depend on:

- Recognition of the reciprocal nature of person-environment interactions;
- The influence of individual and cultural diversity on development;
- The importance of both within-person change and differences between people in their respective within-person changes;
- The temporality (historical embeddedness) of change;
- An understanding of both normative and atypical developmental processes;
- Science-based knowledge and intervention strategies;
- Use of methodologically rigorous research designs, measures, and analyses that are developmentally and contextually sensitive; and
- A multidisciplinary perspective aimed at integrating information and skills drawn from relevant biological, social, and behavioural science disciplines.

Throughout this text, examples of applied development science are included in applications boxes such as this one. The ADS work described in these boxes illustrate how ADS scholars engage in one or more of the following activities:

- Conducting contextually sensitive research;
- Identifying developmental correlates of phenomena of social importance;
- Constructing and using developmental assessment instruments;
- Designing and evaluating developmental interventions; and
- Disseminating knowledge.

As do all scholars involved in the study of youth, applied developmental scientists follow strictly the canons of ethics involved with research with children and youth. These ethical principles are presented in the Appendix. In addition to these principles, ethics in ADS involve a commitment to:

- Beneficence and non-malfeasance;
- Respect for the dignity of individuals;
- Social justice; and
- Civil society.

Source: Based on Fisher et al., 1993; Fisher & Lerner, 1994b; Lerner & Fisher, 1994; Lerner, Fisher, & Weinberg, 1997, 2000a, 2000b.

Basic knowledge about adolescent development may be used for purposes of designing or testing **interventions** (actions planned to reduce or prevent problems or to promote positive development). By focusing on development, diversity, and context we may interrelate basic and applied knowledge of adolescence and apply developmental science to promote policies and programs enhancing the life chances of youth (e.g., Fisher & Lerner, 1994). Applications Box 2.1 presents some of the key features of **applied developmental science** (ADS). In turn, Meet the Researcher Box 2.1 illustrates how the ideas associated with ADS are used in the scholarship of a prominent contributor to this field.

Interventions Actions planned to reduce or to prevent problems or to promote positive development.

Applied developmental science Field of science that focuses on development, diversity, and context to interrelate basic and applied knowledge. Knowledge is applied to promote policies and programs to enhance the life chances of youth.

MEET THE RESEARCHER
Box 2.1
Celia B. Fisher

Understanding How Racial Discrimination Affects the Lives of Teenagers Living in Our Multicultural Society

Celia B. Fisher is director of the Center for Ethics Education and professor of applied developmental psychology at Fordham University in New York. She is a founding editor of the journal *Applied Developmental Science* and is chair of the American Psychological Association's (APA) Task Force to Revise the (APA) Ethics Code.

Young people growing up in North America today have many more opportunities than their parents had to meet and get to know teenagers and adults from different ethnic groups. Although many of the old prejudices that were a part of North American history are fading away, racism and ethnic discrimination still exist and can be confusing and stressful for adolescents.

I am studying groups of African American, Hispanic, East and South Asian, and non-Hispanic white teenagers who live, shop, and go to school in the ethnically diverse city of New York. My collaborators in this research—Scyatta Wallace and Rose Fenton—and I have created two new scales to help us understand what types of discrimination are experienced by adolescents from different ethnic groups, how racial discrimination affects how they feel about themselves, and how their parents prepare them for the challenges of living in a multiethnic society.

One scale we created is called the Adolescent Discrimination Distress Index. It asks teenagers whether they have experienced different types of racial discrimination from teachers in school, from adults in stores or restaurants, or from other adolescents their age. Another scale we developed is called the Racial

Bias Preparation Scale. This scale measures how often parents talk to their teenagers about race and what they say. For example, some parents feel they can best help their children deal with discrimination by making them aware that racism exists. Other parents feel they can be most helpful to their children by encouraging them to be proud of their race. In creating these scales we relied on the work of other psychologists such as Harold Stevenson, Diane Hughes, Jean Phinney, and Claude Steele.

The results of our research suggest that teenagers from all ethnic backgrounds have experienced discrimination in stores and restaurants. As might be expected from some news reports on racial profiling, some African American and Hispanic teenagers said they had been hassled by police just because of their race. In all racial groups, some high school students felt that teachers sometimes expected too much of them or too little from them based on racial prejudice and that they were excluded from peer activities because of their race. East Asian American (Korean, Chinese, Japanese) teenagers most often reported racial name-calling by other students. Many teenagers found being the target of discrimination very stressful. We also

found that the more a teenager felt distressed about discrimination, the lower his or her feelings of self-worth.

Although more frequent in ethnic minority families, teenagers from all ethnic groups reported that their parents spoke about racial discrimination and ethnic pride. An interesting finding was that adolescents whose parents tried to help their children by warning them that they would face racial discrimination were more distressed when they had such an experience than teenagers whose parents talked about ethnic pride.

Researchers have just begun to study the effect of racial discrimination on teenagers' well-being, their ability to achieve in school, and their relationships with their peers. As we learn more about how adolescents and their parents prepare for and react to racial discrimination, we can begin to recommend programs aimed at reducing discrimination at school and in the community and at helping teenagers develop ways of confronting discrimination that strengthen their sense of self-worth.

Conceptual Implications of Contemporary Theories of Adolescence

ISSUES TO CONSIDER

- Why might it be important to recognize the vast diversity within life pathways when designing intervention programs?
- Why might the developmental systems approach to supporting youth development be seen as an optimistic one?

Contemporary theories of adolescence have forwarded ideas that are also found in the life-span view of human development. The conceptual themes of development, diversity, context, and application highlight the individual differences and contextual variation that characterizes adolescent development, and they underscore the idea that development during this period is open-ended, malleable, or "plastic" (Lerner, 1984).

Because persons and contexts may change in unexpected ways, individuals' developmental pathways take unexpected courses. This potential for diversity does not mean an unlimited number of possible developmental pathways exist for each person. Viewing development as open-ended and a product of current conditions means an adolescent's future is not prisoner to his or her past circumstances or conditions. Because of the relative plasticity of person-context interactions, future developmental pathways can deviate from previous pathways, be discontinuous as well as continuous (no changes from one period of life to the next).

Scholars disagree about what causes either continuity or discontinuity across life and whether the specifics of development are associated with our genetic inheritance or our experience. This disagreement is termed the nature-nurture controversy. Views about this controversy influence the theories of adolescent development. The features of this controversy organize our discussion of theories of adolescent development that differ from developmental systems theory in regard to the roles of nature and nurture in development, the bases and characteristics of plasticity in human development (and the extent to which adolescent behaviour can be enhanced), and how adolescents act to promote their own adaptive development (Brandtstädter, 1998).

The Nature-Nurture Issue

ISSUES TO CONSIDER

- What characterizes the theoretical debate of nature versus nurture?
- How does developmental contextualism differ from other theories of human development?
- How do developmental and contextual variables "dynamically" interact?

The philosophical roots of the nature-nurture issue are apparent in the writings of Rousseau and Locke. The French philosopher Jean-Jacques Rousseau (1712–1778) believed that humanity was inherently good, and that society corrupts human beings. His thoughts are reflected in the nature perspective. The English philosopher John Locke (1632–1704) believed that the mind was a blank slate or "tabula rasa" at birth, and that ideas were learned or acquired through experience, both outer (through the senses) and inner (processing sense data) experience.

The nature-nurture issue pertains to whether behaviour and development derive from *nature* (heredity, maturation, and genes) or *nurture* (environment, experience, and learning). The issue raises questions about how inborn characteristics (e.g., genes) may contribute to development and/or how acquired characteristics (e.g., stimulus-response

Table 2-1 **Terms Associated with Nature or Nurture Conceptions of Development**

Nature Terms	Nurture Terms
Genetic	Acquired
Heredity	Education
Inborn	Empiricism
Innate	Environment
Instinct	Experience
Intrinsic	Learning
Maturation	Socialization
Nativism	Preformed

connections) may play a role in development. Table 2.1 lists some of the terms that pertain to nature and nurture contributions.

Theories of human development have stressed either nature as the primary basis for development, nurture as the major impetus for change across life, or some combination or interaction of nature and nurture. However, when interaction was stressed, maturation and experience were regarded as separate sources of human development, ones that came together to cause development but that did not really affect each other.

Developmental contextualism stresses that nature *and* nurture are involved in development, but stresses that variables associated with a person's biological characteristics **dynamically interact** with variables from contextual levels. Dynamic interaction means that biological variables *both* influence and are influenced by contextual ones. In developmental contextualism, nature and nurture are not separate; they are completely integrated or fused, mutually shaping each other over the course of life.

Fused Influences on Development of Biology and Context

ISSUES TO CONSIDER

- In what ways, by what factors, are possible developmental outcomes constrained?
- How might genes be influenced by context and vice versa?

In developmental contextualism, influences of biology on human behaviour and development are

Dynamic interaction Interaction characterized by two different variables simultaneously influencing one another. For example, biological variables influence and are influenced by contextual variables.

Ethnic and Racial Identity of Internationally Adopted Adolescents and Young Adults

Anne Westhues is a professor in the Faculty of Social Work at Wilfrid Laurier University.

Children who are adopted in Canada are now as likely to be born outside the country as to be born domestically. This is a major change in the makeup of adoptive families, as intercountry adoption was largely unknown 30 years ago. Not only are children who are adopted from out of the country generally of a different cultural background than their adoptive parents, they are also often visibly different. This means that in addition to the usual developmental challenges of adolescence, these young people have to negotiate identity issues in relation to being adopted and to being of a different cultural background and skin colour than their parents', and they must learn the survival skills needed by people from their culture without having the benefit of parents who are also from a visible minority.

Many research questions can be formulated to guide inquiry in this area of research. My colleague Joyce Cohen and I began with the broad question "How do children adopted internationally fare developmentally at adolescence?" This raised the further question of which aspects of development would be measured to assess how these youth had fared. Possibilities included self-esteem, peer relations, school performance, sexual identity, and occupational identity. We were especially interested in the adopted youth's sense of belonging in the family because of their adoptive status, and in their comfort level with their ethnic and racial background because of the transracial nature of their family life.

Our interest in issues of racial and ethnic identity stemmed from the growing adoption literature that suggested children who are adopted transracially, whether born within country or out of country, experience difficulties with this aspect of identity formation. Specifically, we wanted to know how these young people thought of themselves ethnically

and racially, how important ethnicity and race were to them, how comfortable they felt with their ethnic and racial background, whether they had experienced discrimination, and what their parents had done to promote a sense of ethnic or racial identity. We also wondered whether how people thought about themselves ethnically and racially, how important these aspects of identity were to them, and how comfortable they were with these aspects of their identity were related to the kinds of education their adoptive parents had engaged in about these issues and the experience of these young people with discrimination.

Another question we considered was, What was the appropriate comparison group when assessing how these youth had done? Comparisons might be made to norms for all adolescents in Canada, to other children who immigrated to Canada, to immigrants within the same cultural background as the adoptee, or to birth siblings of the children who were adopted internationally. We decided to make two comparisons—to norms for Canadian adolescents generally, and to birth siblings.

Our sample was drawn with the assistance of social service ministries in three Canadian provinces: British Columbia, Ontario, and Quebec. A record search was conducted to identify families with an internationally adopted child who was at least 12 years old, as we considered this the beginning of adolescence. A letter of invitation was mailed to families whose addresses could be confirmed as current. Fifty families took part in the study from British Columbia, 36 from Quebec, and 40 from Ontario, a total of 126 families. Interviews were conducted with 155 adolescents or young adults who were adopted internationally, 121 of their birth siblings, 123 adoptive mothers, and 113 adoptive fathers. Youth were interviewed

separately from each other and from their parents.

With respect to gender, 74% of the intercountry adoptees were female and 26% male. They came from South Korea (40%), Bangladesh (29%), Vietnam (8%), Haiti (7%), India (4%), and other countries (12%) such as Brazil, Columbia, Guatemala, Bolivia, Chile, Mexico, Jamaica, the Philippines, Hong Kong, Cambodia, China, and Zambia. About half (54%) were two years of age or younger when they arrived in Canada. Most came from orphanages, and most were in good health, or with correctable health problems such as malnutrition at time of arrival. The mean age of intercountry adoptees when interviewed was 17.3 years, with a range from 9 (one family requested that we include a child under the age of 12) to 37.

Our findings showed that 51% of males and 40% of females thought of themselves as Canadian or Québécois, that is, they identified with the majority culture. An additional 10% of males and 5% of females thought of themselves as "hyphenated Canadians," for example, Korean-Canadian. One quarter of males and one third of females identified only with their country of origin and about 10% of each gender said that they did not think of themselves ethnically. A further 5% (male and female) said that they didn't know how to think about themselves ethnically. With regard to racial identification, 11% of males and 17% of females said that they didn't think of themselves racially; 11% of males and 10% of females said that they thought of themselves as white; and the remainder chose descriptions such as Asian, brown, or black to describe themselves.

A large majority of both males (82.5%) and females (70.5%) indicated that they

>

were comfortable or very comfortable with their ethnic and racial background. Fifteen percent of both groups said that they were neither comfortable nor uncomfortable with this aspect of their identity, and 2.5% of males and 12.5% of females said they were uncomfortable with their ethnic background. Ten percent of both males and females said that they were uncomfortable with their racial background. A large majority of the youth—85% of males and 82% of females—said that they had experienced "incidents when people were nasty or unpleasant about their racial or ethnic background." For most, these incidents consisted of racial or ethnic slurs made by elementary school age peers, though some were the target of such behaviour by adults.

While some gender differences can be seen in the data reported above, these were not found to be significant. Parents of intercountry adopted children are encouraged to educate their children about their culture of origin and to help them learn survival skills in relation to being visible minorities in Canada. No significant differences were found in comfort with ethnic or racial background based on whether adoptive parents had engaged in a series of educational activities such as reading about the child's cultural or racial background, attending cultural events, joining cultural groups, or travelling to the child's country of origin. Nor were there any significant differences in comfort with racial and ethnic background in relation to experiences of discrimination or racism.

Racial and ethnic identity is an important aspect of identity. These data suggest that most adolescents who have been adopted transracially and transculturally manage to come to terms with their difference from their adoptive parents in a way that we would consider healthy, but some do not. We were not able to identify factors that differentiated those who successfully manage this developmental task from those who do not.

Further research in this area might be undertaken using both quantitative and qualitative approaches. In-depth interviews with young adults who are comfortable with their ethnic and racial background, as well as with those who are not comfortable with these aspects of their identity, would allow us to generate a theory about factors that predict whether a person will or will not manage this developmental task well. A quantitative study with a large sample of young adults from culturally and racially diverse backgrounds would allow us to test this theory. An increasingly diverse Canada would benefit from this knowledge, which would help us understand the developmental challenges of internationally adopted youth, as well as young people who immigrate here with their birth parents.

---

acknowledged, but are not seen to act independently of environment. Genes function neither as the primary nor as the ultimate causal influence on behaviour. Instead, genes (heredity) and environment are seen as equal forces in the determination of development and as completely fused in life.

Genes are influenced by the specific characteristics of their context. Humans have genes, which, under normal human environmental conditions, are involved in the development of two arms and two legs. Under different conditions a different result might occur. Even a slight change in the chemicals in a baby's prenatal environment may result in an infant born without limbs, as illustrated by some unfortunate cases in the 1950s and 60s when many pregnant women took the drug thalidomide to treat morning sickness.

However, some children prenatally exposed to thalidomide were not adversely affected, suggesting that they may have had genetic material that protected them from the negative effects of the drug. Thus, the extent to which the environment influences behaviour depends on the specific characteristics or hereditary makeups of the people who live within it.

Relative Plasticity and Variability in Development

The thalidomide example in the previous section illustrates the relative **plasticity** of human development. Although different kinds of outcomes are possible depending on the specifics of gene-environment fusions, the diversity of possible outcomes is constrained by both the character of a person's genes and context. *No two people in the world have the same fusion of genes and environments across their lives.*

There are multiple levels of the environment or context of life and differences exist within each level. For example, within the physical environment are differences in noise, pollution, climate, and terrain. Even identical (**monozygotic**) twins, that is, twins who are born from one fertilized egg that has split into two separate fertilized eggs, or **zygotes**, after conception, do not share the same environments across life. Each twin meets different people, may eat different foods or suffer different accidents or illnesses, may have different teachers, and will fall in love with a

---

Plasticity Potential for systematic change across life.

Monozygotic (MZ) twins Twins developed from one fertilized egg that splits after conception. In contrast, dizygotic (DZ) twins develop from separate fertilized eggs.
Zygote Fertilized egg.

different person. As such, even for identical twins, behaviour and development are different.

Genotypes are also equally variable among people. The fusion of different genotypes and environments means that each person is distinct. The potential magnitude of individual differences among people underscores the gross errors we make when characterizing entire groups of people—racial, religious, or gender groups—as homogeneous and undifferentiated in significant ways.

Genetic Variability

Our genetic endowment provides a basis for the uniqueness of each human life. Estimates of the number of gene pairs in humans typically range between 10 000 and 100 000. If we consider how many different combinations can be produced by the reshuffling process of meiosis (the division that forms sex cells—sperm and ova) occurring with this number of gene pairs, then the potential for genotypic variability is enormous. Based on a conservative estimate, there are more than 70 trillion potential human genotypes. In turn, geneticists have estimated that each human has the capacity to generate any one of 10^{3000} different eggs or sperm. By comparison, their estimate of the number of genotypes of all people who have ever lived is only 10^{24}. Thus with the "10^{3000} possible eggs being generated by an individual woman and 10^{3000} possible sperm being generated by an individual man, the likelihood of anyone ever—in the past, present, or future—having the same genotype as anyone else (excepting multiple identical births, of course) becomes dismissibly small" (McClearn, 1981, p. 19).

Environmental Variability

What makes this enormous genetic variability among humans all the more striking is that genes are fused with environments that have at least equal variation. As comparative psychologist Gilbert Gottlieb explained in 1991, the most significant feature of this fusion "is the explicit recognition that the genes are an integral part of a larger system, and genetic expression is affected by events at other levels of the

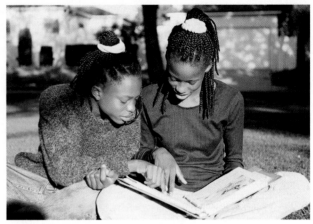

Identical (monozygotic) twins are born from one fertilized egg that splits after conception.

system, including the environment of the organism" (Gottlieb, 1991, p. 5).

As emphasized by comparative psychologist Ethel Tobach (1971, 1972, 1981; Tobach & Schneirla, 1968), genes *must* be fused with the environment if they are to be involved in the development of *any* physical or behavioural characteristic of a person. Gottlieb explains,

> [G]enetic activity does not by itself produce finished traits such as blue eyes, arms, legs, or neurons. The problem of anatomical and physiological differentiation remains unsolved, but it is unanimously recognized as requiring influences above the strictly cellular level (i.e., cell-to-cell interactions, positional influences, and so forth). . . . Thus, the concept of the genetic determination of traits is truly outmoded. (Gottlieb, 1991, p. 5)

Examples of Gene-Environment Fusions

How might gene-environment fusions influence human development? Consider the case of a child born with Down syndrome. Genetic material (DNA) is arranged on stringlike structures present in the nucleus of each cell called chromosomes. The typical cells of the human body have 46 chromosomes, divided into 23 pairs. The only cells in the body that do not have 46 chromosomes are the gametes—the sex cells (sperm

---

Genotype Complement of genes transmitted to people at conception by the union of the sperm and ovum.

Meiosis Process of division resulting in formation of sex cells, sperm, and ova.

Down syndrome Genetic anomaly characterized by extra chromosome in the 21st pair of chromosomes.

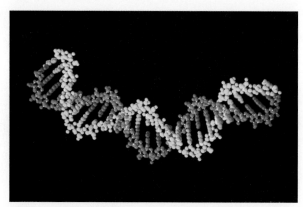

DNA is arranged in stringlike structures in the nucleus of each cell.

in males, ova in females). These cells carry only 23 chromosomes, one of each pair. This arrangement ensures that when a sperm fertilizes an ovum to form a zygote, the new human will have the 46 chromosome pairs appropriate for the species. However, in a child born with Down syndrome, a genetic anomaly exists in that there is an extra chromosome in the 21st pair—three chromosomes are present instead of two.

Children with Down syndrome have a specific inheritance. Yet, even though the genotype has the same chromosomal anomaly, for all children with Down syndrome the developmental outcomes differ.

As recently as 40 to 50 years ago, children with Down syndrome were expected to have maximum life spans of about 12 years and to have low IQ scores. They were typically classified into a group of people who required custodial (usually institutional) care. Today, however, children with Down syndrome often live well beyond adolescence and tend to lead more self-reliant lives. Their average IQ is now higher, often falling in the range allowing for education, training, and employment. Indeed, there is at least one quite striking instance of substantial intellectual accomplishment on the part of a person with Down syndrome. Nigel Hunt, a child born with Down syndrome, grew up to author his own autobiography (Hunt, 1967).

How did these vast differences come about? The chromosomal anomaly itself did not change. What changed was the environment of the children. Instead of being put into institutions that severely constrained the children's developmental possibilities, different and more advanced special education and training techniques were provided, often on an outpatient basis. These contrasts in environment led to patterns of individual development quite different from patterns displayed by children in previous years.

Heredity exerts its effects indirectly through environment in the development of physical characteristics as well as behavioural characteristics. To illustrate, the disorder **phenylketonuria** (PKU) involves an inability to metabolize fatty substances because of the absence of a particular digestive enzyme, and it leads to the development of distorted physical features and severe mental retardation in children. The lack of the necessary enzyme results from the absence of a particular gene. PKU is therefore another instance of a disease associated with a specific genotypic anomaly.

Today, however, many people have PKU without having either the physical or the behavioural deficits formerly associated with the disease. If the missing enzyme is put into the diets of newborns identified as having the disease, *all* negative effects can be avoided. Rather than the gene providing the enzyme, the environment does. A change in the environment changes the outcome, illustrating once again that when genes and environment interact dynamically, alternative outcomes, both physical and behavioural, can occur.

There would be no one *in* an environment without heredity, and there would be no place to see the effects of heredity without environment (Anastasi, 1958). Genes exert their influence on behaviour in an environment having specific characteristics at each of several levels: physical, social, cultural, and so on. At the same time, if there were no genes (and consequently no heredity), the environment would not have an organism in it to influence. Nature and nurture are inextricably tied together, and they never exist independent of the other. Youth themselves stress the importance of both nature and nurture influences on their abilities. Participants in a study of 14- to 19-year-old Quebec youths gifted in dance, music, or academics believed there were strong causal roles in both nature and nurture that led to giftedness in these areas (Tremblay & Gagne, 2001).

Very often in community services, personal and environmental changes are targeted. For example, a study of the intervention strategies used by over 300

Phenylketonuria (PKU) Illness characterized by body's inability to metabolize fatty substances due to lack of a particular digestive enzyme.

prevention and promotion projects targeting children, youth, and families in Quebec (Chamberland, Dallaire, Hebert, Frechette, Lindsay, & Cameron, 2000) provides evidence that change in clients, their living environments, and policy are complementary goals; many of the projects in the study simultaneously addressed all three levels.

Thus, for *any* theory of human development to be logical and to reflect accurately life situations (that is, to have **ecological validity**), it must stress that nature and nurture are always interdependently involved in all behaviour. It is simply not appropriate to ask which one is involved in a behaviour because they are *both* necessary for any person's existence or for the existence of any behaviour. The proper question to ask is, "How do nature and nurture interrelate to provide a basis for behaviour?"

Nature, Nurture, and Theories of Adolescent Development

Across the history of the study of adolescence most theories have not taken the nature-nurture, fusion-type approach to development. Rather, they tend to take one of the three approaches described previously, emphasizing nature, nurture, or some "weak" interaction between the two. To provide an overview of the range of theories of human development it is useful to discuss how different theories are "located" in regard to their approach to the nature-nurture issue. Table 2.2 summarizes the theories reviewed in this chapter.

An Example of a Nature Theory: G. Stanley Hall and the Theory of Recapitulation

ISSUES TO CONSIDER
- What might Hall have meant by the statement "early adolescence is thus the infancy of man's higher nature"?
- How did Hall misinterpret Darwin's theory of human evolution?

Table 2-2 Theories of Adolescence Differ in Regard to Their Approach to the Nature-Nurture Issue

Nature theorists	G. Stanley Hall
Nurture theorists	Boyd R. McCandless
Weak nature-nurture interaction theories	Sigmund Freud Erik H. Erikson Anna Freud
Moderate nature-nurture interaction theories	Jean Piaget Lawrence Kohlberg
Strong nature-nurture interaction theories	Urie Bronfenbrenner Paul B. Baltes and Margret M. Baltes

G. Stanley Hall (1844–1924) was one of the most influential and prominent psychologists at the turn of the 20th century (Misiak & Sexton, 1966). He helped shape the nature and direction of the relatively new science of psychology. (The birthday of modern psychology is dated as 1879, with the opening of the first psychological laboratory in Leipzig, Germany, by Wilhelm Wundt.)

Hall organized the American Psychological Association and became its first president. He also started the first American journal of psychology (aptly titled *The American Journal of Psychology*) and the first scientific journal devoted to human development (originally titled *Pedagogical Seminary*, and then given its present name, *The Journal of Genetic Psychology*). Hall also authored the first psychological texts on adolescence (a two-volume work titled *Adolescence*, 1904) and old age (*Senescence*, 1922).

Hall had his most specific influence in shaping developmental psychology. As implied by the title of one of the journals he founded—*The Journal of Genetic Psychology*—Hall saw development from a nature point of view. Although not many people (including his influential former students, such as Arnold Gesell and Lewis Terman) adopted his specific nature-based theory of development, many did adhere to his general nature, or organismic, orientation. In devising his nature viewpoint, Hall saw himself as the "Darwin of the mind" (Dixon & Lerner, 1999; White, 1968), and he attempted to translate Darwin's phylogenetic evolutionary principles into conceptions relevant to **ontogeny.**

Ecological validity A theory or an observation that reflects accurately real-life situations.

Ontogeny Development, or life course, of an individual organism.

Features of Hall's Recapitulation Theory

Hall believed that the changes characterizing the human life cycle are a repetition of the sequence of changes the species followed during its evolution. That is, Hall's theory specified a parallel between the evolution of humans and life-span changes, starting from conception and moving across prenatal (prebirth) and postnatal life. However, Hall believed that, during the years from birth through sexual maturity, the **recapitulation** was more limited than was the case for prenatal life (Gallatin, 1975). According to Gallatin (1975, pp. 26–27), Hall's recapitulation theory stated that:

> Rather than reflecting the entire sweep of evolution, childhood was supposed to proceed in stages, each of which mirrored a primitive stage of the human species. Very early childhood might correspond, Hall speculated, to a monkey-like ancestor of the human race that had reached sexual maturity around the age of six. The years between eight and twelve allegedly represented a reenactment of a more advanced, but still prehistoric form of mankind, possibly a species that had managed to survive by hunting and fishing.

Hall believed that adolescence represents a specific period in ontogeny after childhood. Not only was Hall the first person to present a scientific theory of development that conceived of adolescence as a distinct portion of the life span (the term *adolescence* first appeared in the first half of the 15th century; Muuss, 1975), but he also did so in a manner consistent with a life-span view of development. Hall saw the capacities and changes of childhood continuing into adolescence *but* at a more rapid and heightened pace. He also saw adolescence as a period of transition between childhood and adulthood. The stages of life previous to adolescence stressed the innate characteristics of humans held "in common with animals," whereas the stage of life following adolescence was said to raise a human "above them and make him most distinctively human" (Hall, 1904, Vol. 1, p. 39). Adolescence is a period of transition from being beastlike to being humanlike (i.e., civilized and mature). This ontogenetic transition mirrored the evolutionary change involved when humans moved from being essentially like the apes to becoming civilized.

According to Hall, human evolution moved the person through this ontogenetic period and put the person in the position of being able to contribute to humans' highest level of evolutionary attainment: civilization. To quote Hall, "early adolescence is thus the infancy of man's higher nature, when he receives from the great all-mother his last capital of energy and evolutionary momentum" (1904, Vol. 2, p. 71).

Because of the acceleration and heightening of capacities in adolescence, and the difficulty in casting off the characteristics of animal-like behaviour while attaining the characteristics of civilization, Hall perceived the adolescent period as stressful and difficult. Because adolescence was an ontogenetically and evolutionarily "betwixt and between" (Gallatin, 1975) phase of human development, it was, to Hall, a period of storm and stress.

Criticisms of Recapitulation

Hall's recapitulationist ideas met criticism that severely diminished their usefulness. The application of Darwinian evolutionary ideas to ontogeny was based on a totally incorrect understanding of the meaning of evolution. Darwin's theory of evolution states that humans did not always exist as they presently do. Previous forms of being existed, and through natural selection some forms were adaptive and continued to evolve until eventually the human species as it is presently known came to exist. This evolutionary process occurs for all animals, not just humans, so all animals that exist today have an evolutionary history. They are as currently adaptive as is the human, albeit to their own environmental settings, or **ecological milieus.**

Thus a rat, monkey, or ape cannot be an ancestor of a human because all exist today. All are equal in evolutionary status—equally as evolved and as adaptive. When we look at a monkey embryo or at monkey behaviour, we are not looking at humans as they existed in a former, lower evolutionary status (Hodos & Campbell, 1969). Although humans and monkeys may have had a common ancestor millions of years ago, that ancestor is long extinct because it was not fit to survive. Whatever exists today is, by definition, fit to survive and thus adaptive at this point in time (Hodos & Campbell, 1969). Hall did not

Recapitulation Developmental changes within the human life cycle that are the hypothetical repetition of the sequence of changes the species followed during evolution.

Ecological milieu Particular environmental settings of a species/individual.

appropriately understand the evolutionary process. Human ontogeny cannot repeat a phase of its evolutionary history if that phase never occurred.

Even as an analogy, a recapitulationist description of human ontogeny is inappropriate. As initially pointed out by Thorndike (1904), and reemphasized by Gallatin (1975), by two or three years of age a human child has already exceeded the capacities of monkeys, apes, or prehistoric humanlike organisms (e.g., the Neanderthals). Sensorimotor, verbal, and social behaviour, for example, are all more advanced in the three-year-old than in the "adults" of any of these other organisms. Additionally, no evidence whatsoever indicates that the events in adolescence are but a mirror of the history of evolution.

In short, Hall's theory that ontogeny recapitulates **phylogeny** is not correct. Although his work is historically quite important in that his is the first scientific theory of human development, and of adolescence in particular, his specific nature theory was not widely adopted. However, because of his influence and position in American psychology, his general nature orientation was often followed.

Nurture Theories of Human Development

Nurture theories of development stress the influence of experiential and environmental variables on behavioural change and view behaviour as a response to stimulation. The explanation of why adolescent behaviour develops in a particular manner (or direction) lies in the environment and not in the person. There are many different versions of nurture theories (White, 1970). McCandless's (1967, 1970) drive reduction theory was directed explicitly to understanding adolescent development.

The Drive Reduction Theory of McCandless

Boyd R. McCandless (1970) proposed a "drive theory" of human behaviour. He viewed a drive as an energizer of behaviour and specified that several drives exist in the person (e.g., a hunger drive, a drive

to avoid pain, and a sex drive). The nurture component of McCandless's theory involves the direction behaviour takes as a consequence of being energized by a particular drive.

We learn in society that certain behaviours *reduce* **drive states** such as hunger, pain, or sexual arousal. McCandless asserts that drive-reducing behaviours are rewarded as a consequence of having the drive diminished and are thus repeated in comparable social situations. Behaviours that do not diminish a drive state are punished behaviours and are less likely to be repeated.

As a consequence of repeating behaviours, people form habits. When a particular drive state is aroused, it is probable an individual will execute the corresponding habit to reduce the internal state. To McCandless, although drive states need not be learned, and may be biologically based, what people do in response to the arousal of a drive is socially learned.

According to McCandless, a new drive emerges in adolescence: the sex drive. To reduce this drive in a way that will be rewarded, new social learning and habits must be formed. McCandless specifies that society does not reward males and females for the same sex drive–reducing habits. Males and females are channeled into developing habits that are socially prescribed as sex appropriate. Thus adolescence becomes a time of defining oneself in terms of new sex-specific habits, which are socially defined as rewarding for one or the other sex. McCandless argues that until new habits are formed, and new self-definitions attained, adolescence could be a period of undiminished drives, thus providing a nurture explanation of adolescent "storm and stress" (see Chapter 1).

Nature-Nurture Interaction Theories

ISSUE TO CONSIDER

• What are the differences among the three types of nature-nurture interaction theories?

A theory can be classified according to the type of stress it places on nature and nurture relations (Lerner & Spanier, 1978a). Although all interaction theories stress that both nature and nurture are involved in human development, not all such theories stress the fusion of nature and nurture. A **weak interaction theory** places primary stress on one source (usually nature) as the determiner of the sequence and character of development. A

Phylogeny Evolutionary history of a species.
Drive state Energizer of behavior that exists within the individual.

Weak interaction theory Places primary stress on one source (usually nature) as the determinant of the sequence and character of development.

moderate interaction theory places equal stress on nature and nurture but sees the two sources as independent of each other. Although they interact to provide a basis for any and all development, one source does not change the quality of the other over the course of the interaction (Sameroff, 1975). A strong interaction theory is one that not only sees both nature and nurture as reciprocally related, but also sees the two as inextricably fused in all development. Examples of weak, moderate, and strong interaction theories are presented here. I discuss first the theories of Sigmund Freud, Erik Erikson, and Anna Freud.

Sigmund Freud and Psychoanalysis

ISSUES TO CONSIDER

- By focusing so extensively on the influence of the libido, what is Freud's theory of development missing?
- In what ways is Freud's work considered "biased"?
- What role does the libido play in adult emotional problems?

Sigmund Freud was born in Freiberg, Moravia, in 1856 and died in London, England, in 1939. He lived most of his life in Vienna, where in 1881 he obtained his medical degree. Freud's theory represents an example of weak interaction because he sees experiences of people as acting only to support or hamper fixed and universal biologically based changes; experience cannot in any way influence the presence or sequence of these changes. Freud hypothesized that human mental life is governed by an energy, termed libido. Humans are born with a finite amount of libido. Its area of localization within the body changes over the course of development. Where the libido is concentrated determines what stimulation is appropriate, or gratifying, and what sort of stimulation is not appropriate.

Nature determines where and when libido moves. Experiences of the person may determine if appropriate stimulation is forthcoming, but does not alter the order of bodily concentration or, in Freud's terms, the stage of psychosexual development. Experience can only facilitate or hinder the development of certain feeling states. Freud specified five stages of psychosexual development: oral, anal, phallic, latent, and genital.

Stages of Psychosexual Development

The first psychosexual stage is the **oral stage**. During the first year of life, gratifying stimulation occurs in the region of the mouth, and pleasure is obtained by sucking and biting. If the baby's attempts at oral gratification are frustrated often enough, some of the libido may become **fixated** (arrested) at this stage of development, and not free to progress to the next stage. Freud believed adult emotional problems result from fixation and involve attempts to obtain missed gratification of the oral stage. An example of a fixation in the oral stage might be overeating as an adult. However, fixation is a potential problem at any stage.

The next stage is the **anal stage**, which lasts from about ages one to three years and occurs when libido centres in the anal area. Children get pleasure through exercising their anal muscles, expelling or holding bowel movements. The anal stage corresponds to the period when children in many societies are toilet trained. Frustration resulting from severe toilet training can cause fixation in the anal stage. This fixation can lead to adult problems such as messiness and wastefulness or the holding back of everything, including emotions.

For both sexes, the **phallic stage** is the third stage, which to Freud spans the period from about the third

---

Moderate interaction theory Places equal stress on the influence of both nature and nurture but sees the two sources as independent of each other.

Strong interaction theory Sees nature and nurture as reciprocally related and inextricably fused in all development.

Libido Freudian term that defines the finite amount of energy that each human is born with which governs human mental life. Localization of the

libido within the body changes over the course of development. Placement of the libido within the body determines what stimulation is appropriate and what stimulation is inappropriate to the developing individual.

Oral stage First psychosexual stage defined by Freud. Occurs during the first year of life when the libido is said to be located in the region of the mouth. Gratification is obtained through stimulation

of this region through sucking and biting.

Fixation Freudian term to describe an arrest of the development of the libido; the person attempts to obtain missed gratification of a previous stage.

Anal stage Second psychosexual stage as defined by Freud. Occurs during second and third years of life, when the libido centres in the anal area. Gratification is obtained through exercising anal muscles,

expelling or holding bowel movements.

Phallic stage Third psychosexual stage as defined by Freud. Spans the period from about the third through fifth years when the libido moves to the genital area. Males and females experience this stage differently because their genitalia differ. See *Oedipal complex* and *Electra complex*.

through the fifth years. This stage involves the libido moving to the genital area. Because of structural differences in genitalia, this stage is different for males and females.

As the libido moves to a boy's genital area, gratification is obtained through stimulation of the genitals that may occur during bathing or dressing. Freud believed that the boy's mother is most likely to provide this stimulation, and he labelled the boy's emotional reaction to the mother the **Oedipus complex**, after a character in Greek mythology who unknowingly killed his father and then married his mother. Freud saw a parallel between this myth and events in the lives of boys.

Freud believed that when the boy realizes his father is the rival for his mother's affection, the boy comes to fear his father will punish him by castrating him, and he experiences **castration anxiety**. The power of this anxiety leads the boy to give up his desires for his mother and to identify with and model himself after his father. The boy forms a structure of his personality termed the **superego** by Freud, which has two components. The first component, the **ego ideal**, is the representation of the perfect, or ideal, man (the "father figure"). In modelling himself after his father, the boy becomes a "man" in his society. The second part of the superego is the **conscience**, the internalization of society's standards, ethics, and morals (Bronfenbrenner, 1960).

In regard to the female phallic stage, the libido moves to the genital area as with males. And, as also the case with males, gratification is obtained through stimulation of the genitals. The mother provides the major source of this stimulation for the girl, but the girl falls in love with her father (for reasons not perfectly clear even to Freud, and as a result, Freud himself was never satisfied with his formulation of

this stage). Nevertheless, Freud said that, analogous to what occurs with boys, the girl has an incestuous desire to possess her father, but realizes that her mother stands in her way.

At this point, Freud's theory of female development becomes different from that of male development. In his theory, the female becomes afraid that the mother will punish her for her incestuous desires toward her father. Although it is possible that the girl first fears this punishment will take the form of castration, her awareness of her own genital structure causes her to realize that, in a sense, she already has been punished. The girl perceives that she does not have a penis, but only an inferior (to Freud) organ, a clitoris. Hence the girl experiences **penis envy** and this impels her to resolve her Oedipal conflict. She relinquishes her incestuous love for her father and identifies with her mother. The girl then forms a superego, as the boy does. Freud termed the reaction of girls to the events of this stage the **Electra complex** (Bronfenbrenner, 1960).

After the phallic stage, at about five years of age, the **latency stage** occurs. Freud said that the libido is not localized in any bodily zone and no erogenous zones emerge or exist. This stage continues until puberty occurs, at about 12 years of age. Here, the **genital stage** occurs. During this final stage, the libido reemerges in the genital area, but now in a mature or adult form. If the person has not been too severely restricted in psychosexual development in the first five years of life, adult sexuality can occur.

A Critique of Freud's Ideas

Freud worked in Victorian Europe, a period of history noted for its repressive views about sexuality. As a practising psychiatrist, Freud attempted to

---

Oedipus complex Boy's emotional reaction to his mother at the time when the libido has moved to the boy's genital area and when he obtains gratification through stimulation of the genitals. When the boy realizes his father is his rival for his mother's affection, the boy comes to fear his father will punish him by performing castration. The boy is so moved by his anxiety that he gives up desires for his mother and identifies with his father.

Castration anxiety Boy's fear that father will punish him for his affections for his mother by performing castration. Fear leads boy to alter affection and turn to identify with father.

Superego Freudian personality structure made up of two components: the ego ideal and the conscience. Formed as a result of the resolution of the Oedipal complex.

Ego ideal Component of the superego that represents the perfect, or ideal, person.

Conscience Component of the superego that represents the internalization of society's standards, ethics, and morals.

Penis envy Girl realizes she does not have a penis but, rather, an inferior (to Freud) organ, the clitoris. The girl experiences envy of the penis and this envy impels her to relinquish her incestuous love for her father and identify with her mother.

Electra complex For girls, the purported emotional crisis that

occurs within the phallic stage of development in Freud's theory.

Latency stage Fourth psychosexual stage as defined by Freud. Occurs around the fifth year of life until puberty. The libido is said to be latent in this stage.

Genital stage Fifth psychosexual stage as defined by Freud. Occurs during puberty as the libido reemerges in the genital area, in an adult form.

Across history, relationships with parents have remained a key part of adolescence.

construct a theory of *early development* from the memories of adult neurotic patients from one particular historical period. Freud constructed a theory about early development without actually observing children.

Freud's adult patients reconstructed their long-gone past through **retrospection**. With Freud's help, they tried to remember what happened to them when they were one, two, or three years of age. Because it is quite possible that adults forget, distort, or misremember early memories and because his data were unchecked for failures of early memories, Freud likely obtained biased information.

We might question whether Freud's ideas represented all the possible developmental phenomena that could occur in each stage of life. Is latency actually a period of relative quiescence, a time when few significant events occur for the child? Is adolescence just a time when events in preceding life make themselves evident or are there characteristics of adolescence special to that period?

Although they accepted most of Freud's ideas as correct, other psychoanalytically oriented thinkers

led the way in showing that Freud was incomplete in his depiction of developmental phenomena within and across stages. Freud's theory emphasized the movement of the libido and focused on a structure of the personality, the **id**, which he believed innately contained this mental energy. Freud stressed also the idea that there was a primary process through which the id energized the person to gratify libidinal impulses. Erikson (1959, 1963), however, focused on societal demands placed on the individual—or, more precisely, the ego (which along with the super-ego and the id comprises the third of the structures of personality that Freud specified). Erikson emphasized that as the person developed, important phenomena related to the ego could be identified in latency, adolescence, and across the rest of the life span as well.

As compared to the id's primary process, which involves urges to gratify the libido in any way possible, even through fantasy, Freud believed that the **ego** develops only to deal with reality, to allow the person to adjust to the demands of the real world and hence survive. Accordingly, Freud said the ego functions in accordance with the **reality principle**. The ego has characteristics that enable it to adjust to and deal with reality. This **secondary process** involves such things as cognition and perception. Through the functioning of these processes, the ego is capable of perceiving and knowing the real world and hence adapting to it. Although Freud did not spend enough time discussing the implications of the ego, this focus was provided by Erikson (1963).

Erik Erikson and Psychosocial Development

ISSUES TO CONSIDER

- By focusing so extensively on the ego, what is Erikson's psycho-sexual theory of development missing?
- What might happen, according to Erikson, if and when an ego capability is not developed in a balanced manner?

Erikson, once a student of Freud's, also proposes a stage theory of development; however, unlike Freud's theory of psychosexual development, Erikson's theory

---

Retrospection Constructing the past through memories. A technique used by Freud.
Id One of the three structures of the mind in psychoanalytic theory. The initial source of the libido.

Ego One of three structures of the mind in psychoanalytic theory. Enables person to adapt to reality.

Reality principle Ego develops only to deal with reality, to allow the person to adjust to demands of real world and hence survive.

Secondary process Functions (e.g., perception, reasoning) that enable ego to adjust to and deal with reality.

speaks of **psychosocial development**. Whereas Freud focused primarily on the contributions of the id to development, Erikson focused on the role of the ego. Erikson emphasized the role of society in determining what the ego must do to fulfill its function of adapting to the demands of a reality textured and shaped by society.

Society does not expect the same things of all people at all times of their lives. We may expect a one-year-old to do no more than eat and sleep, but we expect a 21-year-old to prepare for a career, and we expect a 31-year-old to be engaging in his or her career. To meet each of these successively different demands, the ego must develop different capabilities. The development of ego capabilities passes through eight stages of psychosocial development. Erikson believed that the time we have to spend at each stage is fixed by a maturational "ground plan" for development.

Within each stage a particular capability of the ego must be developed if the ego is to meet the adjustment demands placed on it by society. Each stage is thought of as a **critical period** in the life span (that is, it is a time in life when particular developments must occur if development is to proceed normally). Stage development proceeds whether the capability is developed or not. Even if a person does not develop a capability within the time limits imposed by the person's maturational ground plan, development proceeds. However, that part of the ego (that capability) does not have another chance for adequate development.

Within each stage of psychosocial development there is a crisis of development. For the person to feel he or she is progressing through the stages in an adaptive manner, the person must sense he or she has moved closer to rather than further away from developing the needed ego capability. Erikson delineated eight psychosocial stages and accompanying crises.

Within the first stage of psychosocial development, termed by Erikson **oral sensory** (what lasts from birth through about one year of age), a crisis exists between developing a sense of basic trust versus mistrust toward one's world. If favourable sensory experiences are encountered, the child develops toward the former feeling state. If unfavourable experiences occur, a feeling closer to the latter state develops. In this stage, as well as in the seven others, a person typically develops somewhere in between the two extreme ends of the crisis state. In this first stage, where the crisis is between trust and mistrust, healthy ego development proceeds if the ratio of the trust to mistrust is greater than one. Unhealthy ego development proceeds if this ratio is less than one.

Stage 2 is termed **anal musculature** (which usually lasts for the second and third years of life), and here the crisis is between developing a sense of autonomy (e.g., being able to use one's muscles, to feed oneself) versus a sense of shame and doubt (e.g., not being able to feed oneself). Stage 3 is termed **genital locomotor** (and involves ordinarily the fourth and fifth years of life), and the crisis involved here is between developing initiative (e.g., being able to walk around and find your way, without having parents completely directing you) versus guilt (e.g., feeling you are inappropriately tied to your parents). In Stage 4, **latency** (which spans from about the end of the fifth year through puberty), the crisis is between developing toward a sense of industry (e.g., learning how to read and write, in our society) versus a sense of inferiority (e.g., not being able to do what you feel others can do). In Stage 5, **puberty and adolescence**, the crisis is between developing a sense of identity (e.g., knowing one's role in society, knowing what one believes in) versus role confusion or identity diffusion (e.g., not knowing what one believes in or what one can do with oneself in society).

Psychosocial development Emphasizes the role of the ego and, specifically, the role of society in determining what the ego must do to fulfill its function of adapting to the demands of reality.
Critical period Time in life when particular developments must occur if development is to proceed normally.

Oral sensory stage Stage 1 of Erikson's psychosocial theory. Involves a crisis between developing a sense of basic trust versus mistrust toward one's world.
Anal musculature stage Stage 2 of Erikson's psychosocial theory. Involves a crisis between developing toward a sense of autonomy versus a sense of shame and doubt.

Genital locomotor stage Stage 3 of Erikson's psychosocial theory. Involves a crisis between developing toward a sense of initiative versus guilt.
Latency Stage 4 of Erikson's psychosocial theory. Involves a crisis between developing toward a sense of industry versus inferiority.

Puberty and adolescence Stage 5 of Erikson's psychosocial theory. Involves a crisis between developing toward a sense of identity versus role confusion.

The remaining three psychosocial stages occur during adulthood, and Erikson offers no precise ages for their onset or termination. In Stage 6, **young adulthood**, there is a crisis between developing toward a sense of intimacy (e.g., establishing a strong love relationship) versus a sense of isolation (e.g., feeling alone and unable to be close to anyone). In Stage 7, **adulthood**, the crisis is between generativity (e.g., being able to produce those goods or services associated with one's role) versus stagnation (e.g., being unable to continue to produce what is associated with one's role). Stage 8, the final stage of psychosocial development, is **maturity**. Here the crisis is between ego integrity (e.g., feeling that one has led a full, rich life) and despair (e.g., feeling that one's life is ending before one has had a good life).

Erik Erikson's stage theory of psychosocial development offers descriptions of personality development consistent with a life-span perspective. Although Erikson's explanations of psychosocial development are limited for many of the same reasons that other psychoanalytic conceptions, such as Freud's, are, the descriptions of development Erikson provides have served as a major basis for research about human personality. Later chapters focus on Erikson's ideas.

Anna Freud: Adolescence as a Developmental Disturbance

ISSUES TO CONSIDER

- Why does Anna Freud see adolescence as a unique period of time?
- What are the three specific roles of the structures of the personality in adolescent development?
- Based on what you have learned in Chapters 1 and 2, how might you critique the work of Anna Freud?

As emphasized by both her father and by Erikson, Anna Freud believed the ego's only function is survival. As a consequence, she emphasized that the ego must defend itself from dangers, whether those dangers come from within or without. The conflict between the id and the superego represents a danger to survival. If a person spent all of his or her time in conflict about action, no energy would be left to deal with the demands placed on the person from outside the self (for example, from society). Accordingly, the ego develops defence mechanisms, or ways to avoid dealing with at least one set of the conflicting demands imposed from within. Such avoidance rids the person of the internal conflict and frees up energy for external adaptive demands.

The **defence mechanisms** developed by the ego (mechanisms like **repression, rationalization, substitution**, and **projection**) involve taking the pressures imposed by the id and placing them in a particular area of the mind—the *unconscious*. This area contains material most difficult to bring into awareness—the *conscious*. Id pressures are defended against, but those of the superego are not. The superego's pressures represent the demands and rules of society. If we got rid of those demands and rules, we would have no morality. It would not be adaptive for the ego to put the superego in the unconscious because society would severely punish amoral behaviour. As such, it is the id material that is placed in this area of the mind.

To both Freuds, the typical person establishes a balance among the id, ego, and superego by five years of age. By the time latency has been reached, ego defences appropriate for dealing with all pressures or drives from the id have been established. The person is thus in equilibrium. However, although people may differ in regard to the character of this balance, depending on events in the first three stages of life, Anna Freud (1969) claimed that all people have their balance *destroyed* in adolescence.

Unlike her father, Anna Freud saw adolescence as a period in life presenting demands for the person that are not *just* those relating to earlier life. These demands involve new pressures on the ego that require adaptive solutions for the person. The new demands on the ego

Young adulthood Stage 6 of Erikson's psychosocial theory. Involves a crisis between developing toward a sense of intimacy versus isolation.
Adulthood Stage 7 of Erikson's psychosocial theory. Involves a crisis between developing a sense of generativity versus stagnation.

Maturity Stage 8 of Erikson's psychosocial theory. Involves a crisis between developing toward a sense of ego integrity versus despair.
Defence mechanisms Developed by the ego to take the pressures imposed by the id and place them into the unconscious part of the mind.

Repression Ego defence mechanism by which unwanted desires and/or pressures are placed in the unconscious.
Rationalization Ego defence mechanism of applying plausible but untrue reasoning for behaviour.
Substitution Process of replacing one goal for another.

Projection Process of attributing one's own feelings to other objects or people.

are universal, she contended, because the pressures that create them are universal. To understand this, it is necessary to consider the special alterations that Anna Freud (1969) associated with adolescence, alterations in drives, ego organization, object relations, and ideals and social relations.

With puberty comes an adult genital drive. Thus the balance among the id, ego, and superego is upset as this new feeling state comes to dominate the person's being. Because this alteration is an inevitable, universal one, Anna Freud argues that an inescapable imbalance in development occurs. As such, and as explained in Chapter 1, she believes that adolescence is necessarily a period of developmental disturbance.

Anna Freud claims that the new drive throws the person into upheaval. The adolescent tries out all the formerly useful defences to deal with the new drive. This testing of the use of best defences puts strain on the person because what would be adequate for one state may not be adequate for another, quantitatively greater and qualitatively different state. As such, not only does the adolescent try more of the same defences, but also he or she eventually forms new types of mechanisms causing alterations in ego organization. For example, in relation to the new cognitive abilities that emerge in adolescence, the adolescent uses for the first time highly abstract, intellectual reasons to justify his or her behaviour. This new ego defence mechanism is termed **intellectualization.**

Despite the new ego defences, the danger of inappropriately acting out the genital drive is so great that "nothing helps here except a complete discarding of the people who were the important love objects of the child, that is, the parents" (A. Freud, 1969, p. 8). Indeed, the new defences are useful in helping the adolescent to alter the relations he or she has had with these "love objects." Defences like intellectualization often involve elaborate rationales for why the parents are "stupid," "ineffective," or possess "useless . . . beliefs and conventions" (A. Freud, 1969, p. 8).

When the adolescent has broken the ties with the parents, he or she has also rejected the attitudes, values, and beliefs formerly shared with them. Anna Freud argues that the adolescent is thus left without

Intellectualization Ego defence mechanism of highly abstract, intellectual reasoning used to justify behaviour.

social ties or ideals. Alterations in ideals and social relations are made with substitutes for both of these found in the peer group. Attachment to the peer group provides a mechanism wherein the new genital drive—which started all alterations initially—may be dealt with in a setting less dangerous to the adolescent's adaptation than the family setting.

A Critique of Anna Freud's Ideas

By stressing the primary influence of biologically determined stages of development on psychological and social development, both Sigmund and Anna Freud are taking a weak interactionist stance in regard to the nature-nurture issue. Both Freuds describe human development in a manner inconsistent with what we know about the character of the transition that occurs from childhood to adolescence. Anna Freud described adolescence in terms that acknowledge little plasticity within people and few differences between people. She depicted adolescence as stormy and stressful.

Contrary to what she indicates, the research reviewed in Chapter 1 clearly indicates that most young people do not have stormy, stressful adolescent periods, do not break ties with parents, continue to share the ideals of their parents, and choose friends who have ideals consistent with those of their parents. Chapters 8 and 9 present additional research supporting these findings.

Jean Piaget and Cognitive Developmental (Structural) Theory

ISSUE TO CONSIDER
• How does the equilibration process, as defined and described by Piaget, account for his belief that environment and heredity are independent sources of developmental influence?

Swiss scientist Jean Piaget (1896–1980) presented a theory reflecting moderate nature-nurture interaction. Piaget considered both heredity and environment to be independent sources of cognitive (or knowledge) development. Piaget began writing in the 1920s, but because of his unique methods of observing and of describing his ideas, his work was not well regarded until the 1950s. Like Freud, Piaget believed that stages of development are universal and their sequence is invariant. Unlike Freud, Piaget believed that the stages unfold in response to both environmental and biological forces.

Cognitive development is said to arise from the action of the organism on the environment and from the action of the environment on the organism. Through this bidirectional process, Piaget proposed that cognition develops through four stages: sensorimotor, preoperational, concrete operational, and formal operational. Our progression through these stages involves our attempt to maintain a balance, an **equilibration**, between **assimilating** (changing external stimulation to fit already existing knowledge) and **accommodating** (changing already existing knowledge to fit external stimulation).

In the **sensorimotor stage**, the child develops the knowledge that objects continue to exist even when not sensed by the person. When the person can represent mentally (through images) absent objects and can use symbols (e.g., words) to represent objects, the major characteristics of the **preoperational stage** are evident. Thought about objects in the world is internalized mentally by children at this stage. However, the operations are not yet **reversible**. The child knows that a ball of clay can be rolled into a sausage, but he or she does not yet know that by reversing one's actions with the clay one can return the sausage to the original ball of clay.

Knowledge about the reversibility of actions occurs in the **concrete operational stage**. **Operations**—internalized actions that are reversible—now exist. The child can visualize or mentally represent that the ball of clay can be made into a sausage and vice versa. But thought is limited in that the person can think only about objects that have a concrete, real existence. Clay is real and can be thought about, but a substance that does not exist cannot be dealt with mentally. The child does not

have the ability to deal adequately with counterfactual, hypothetical phenomena and does not recognize the subjective and arbitrary nature of thought. Such recognition characterizes the next stage, the stage most representative of adolescents and adults in modern Western society.

In the **formal operational stage** the person can think of all possible combinations of elements of a problem to find a solution, both real and imaginary. Because the person centres so much on this newly emerged thinking ability, some scientists believe the adolescent is characterized by a particular type of **egocentrism** (Elkind, 1967). An adolescent may believe others are as preoccupied with the object of his or her own thoughts—himself or herself—as he or she is (this is termed **imaginary audience**). Because of the attention, the adolescent comes to believe that he or she is a special, unique person (this is termed **personal fable**) (Elkind, 1967).

A Critique of Piaget's Ideas

Piaget's (1950, 1970) theory accepts a fuller role for experience in providing an interactive basis of stage progression and may be seen as a more moderate stance in regard to the interaction between nature and nurture. However, there is not as full a consideration of environmental or experiential changes as there is of organism changes.

Although Piaget continually emphasized that developmental structural change arises from an interaction between organismic and environmental processes, it is only the organism that is seen as going through changes. Although the organism's *conception* of the environment changes, constant flux of the

---

Equilibration Individual's attempt to maintain cognitive balance between existing cognitive structures and what is encountered in the environment. Maintained through continuous process of assimilation and accommodation.
Assimilation Piagetian term to define process of changing external stimulation to fit already existing knowledge. With accommodation, part of the equilibration process.
Accommodation Piagetian term used to define process of changing already existing knowledge to fit external

stimulation. With assimilation, part of the equilibration process.
Sensorimotor stage First stage of cognitive development as defined by Piaget. The child develops the knowledge that external stimulation continues to exist even when not sensed by the person.
Preoperational stage Second stage of cognitive development as defined by Piaget. The child can represent mentally absent objects and can use symbols to represent objects.
Reversibility Ability to know that by reversing one's actions on

an object one can return the object to its original state.
Concrete operational stage Third stage of cognitive development as defined by Piaget. The child is capable of internalized, reversible actions.
Operation Piagetian term referring to the internalized actions that are mentally reversible.
Formal operational stage Fourth stage of cognitive development as defined by Piaget. Most representative of adolescents and adults in modern Western society. The person is capable of thinking counterfactually and hypothetically. Can think of all

possible combinations of elements of a problem to find a solution.
Egocentrism Cognitive focus on the self. Egocentrism changes as the child moves throughout Piagetian stages.
Imaginary audience Adolescents' belief that others are as preoccupied with the object of their own thoughts as they are.
Personal fable Due to attention of the imaginary audience, adolescents come to believe that they are special and/or unique.

physical and social world was never systematically considered. In addition, the impact of these physical and social environmental changes on the character of the child's progression is viewed in a narrow way. That is, such environmentally based differences between people can only pertain to the rate of change and to the final stage of development reached; but any changes in the environment are irrelevant to the sequence and characteristics of the stages themselves. For Piaget, the organism changes but the environment does not (Riegel, 1976).

Lawrence Kohlberg and Cognitive Development in Moral Reasoning

ISSUE TO CONSIDER

- Why is Kohlberg's theory viewed as a moderate interaction theory?

Lawrence Kohlberg's (1927–1988) theory of the development of moral reasoning is derived from a cognitive developmental viewpoint, as represented in Piaget's theory. As such, it adopts the same moderate nature-nurture interaction view found in Piaget's theory. Kohlberg (1963a, 1963b, 1970) proposed a theory of moral development that has served as the impetus for much research and discussion. To study moral reasoning, Kohlberg presented children with a moral dilemma—a situation where there is no right or wrong answer—and asked them to give reasons for their particular responses to the situation.

Kohlberg described a progression in moral reasoning that involves **preconventional morality**, involving the stage of punishment and obedience reasoning and the stage of naive egoistic reasoning; **conventional morality**, involving the good-person orientation to morality and the stage of social order and institutional maintenance morality; and **postconventional morality**, involving the stage of contractual legalistic moral reasoning and the stage of conscience and principle orientation.

The work of Kohlberg and Piaget is discussed in later chapters (see Chapters 4 and 5). Note here, however, that by minimizing the impact on development of continual social and physical environmental changes, Piaget and Kohlberg did not sufficiently attend to the source of developmental progression: person-environment interactions. If only the person's changes are considered, and the environment's are not, then no variation in stages may be attributed to variation in the environment, and nothing can be related to environmental change. The only source of variation can be the person, the "organism," and only organism changes can predict organism changes.

Accordingly, Piaget's and Kohlberg's supposed interaction is reduced to an account of development that stresses primarily, if not exclusively, organism processes to the omission of environmental ones. Piaget and Kohlberg are left with only being able to account for organism changes on the basis of organism changes. A problem of circular logic is raised because of Piaget's and Kohlberg's failure to consider environmental changes as contributing to development as actively as do organism changes.

However, the last category of interaction theory, labelled strong interaction theory, regards nature and nurture processes as completely fused in life. Genes and contexts are interdependent, part of a unified, coherent system, wherein each influences the structure and function of the other (Ford & Lerner, 1992). Developmental contextualism illustrates well the strong interaction approach. Because it has been presented in some detail already, we discuss other key instances of such theoretical models.

Bronfenbrenner's Model of the Ecology of Human Development

ISSUE TO CONSIDER

- How does the social ecology of life play a role in a person's development?

Urie Bronfenbrenner (1977, 1979; Bronfenbrenner & Morris, 1998) argues that human development needs to be understood as it occurs in its real-world setting,

---

Preconventional morality First level of moral development as defined by Kohlberg. The individual is bound by issues of punishment and obedience and naive and egoistic reasoning.

Conventional morality Second level of moral development as defined by Kohlberg. The individual is bound by issues of the good-person orientation and is concerned with upholding social order and the institutional maintenance of morality.

Postconventional morality Third level of moral development as defined by Kohlberg. The individual is concerned with legalistic reasoning oriented around principles and conscience.

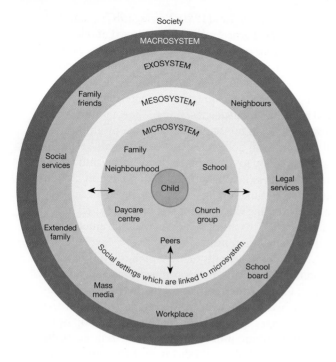

Figure 2.1
Bronfenbrenner's concentric circles representing human ecology.

fields, malls, or other neighbourhood gathering places that most often involve just adolescent-peer interactions.

An adolescent's microsystems may be interrelated. What occurs in school may affect what happens in the family, and vice versa. Bronfenbrenner notes that such microsystem interrelations constitute a second ecological stratum, termed the **mesosystem**. He defines it as "the interrelations among major settings containing the developing person at a particular point in his or her life" (Bronfenbrenner, 1977, p. 515).

What happens in a microsystem (e.g., in an interaction between an adolescent and a parent within the family context) may be influenced by events that occur in systems in which the adolescent takes no part. For example, an adult who is a parent also has other social roles, such as worker. The adolescent is probably not part of his or her parents' workplace interactions, but events that affect the parents at work can influence how they treat the youth. If a parent has a particularly good day at work, he or she may respond to adolescents more positively than otherwise by choosing to spend additional time with them in the evening.

The adolescent lives with people who interact in and are affected by contexts other than those containing the young person. The adolescent may be affected by settings in which he or she plays no direct role. Bronfenbrenner sees such influences as constituting a third system within the ecology of human development. He labels it the **exosystem** and defines it as "an extension of the mesosystem embracing . . . specific social structures, both formal and informal, that do not themselves contain the developing person but impinge upon or encompass the immediate setting in which the person is found, and thereby delimit, influence, or even determine what goes on there" (Bronfenbrenner, 1977, p. 515).

Within the ecology of human development exists a fourth system, the **macrosystem**. This system is

or **ecology**. He believes the ecology of human development is composed of four distinct although interrelated systems or types of settings: the microsystem, mesosystem, exosystem, and macrosystem.

The **microsystem** is composed of "the complex of relations between the developing person and environment in an immediate setting containing the person" (Bronfenbrenner, 1977, p. 515). For example, the family is the major microsystem for youth development in our society (Belsky, Lerner, & Spanier, 1984). It involves interactions between the child, his or her parents, and any siblings present in the home. Other microsystems of youth include the school setting, involving both adolescent-teacher and adolescent-peer interactions, and athletic courts or

Ecology Real-world setting(s) of the individual and/or species.
Microsystem As defined by Bronfenbrenner, the first of several interrelated systems whose composition defines the ecology of human development. Composed of relations between the developing person and the environment in the immediate setting within which the person exists.

Mesosystem As defined by Bronfenbrenner, the second of several interrelated systems whose composition defines the ecology of human development. Composed of interrelations among the major settings containing the individual, the developing person at a particular point in his or her life.

Exosystem As defined by Bronfenbrenner, the third of several interrelated systems whose composition defines the ecology of human development. The formal and informal social structures that do not themselves contain the developing person but impinge on the setting within which the person exists.

Macrosystem As defined by Bronfenbrenner, the fourth of several interrelated systems whose composition defines the ecology of human development. Composed of cultural values and beliefs and historical events that affect the other ecological systems.

composed of cultural values and beliefs and historical events (e.g., wars, floods, famines), both of which may affect the other ecological systems. For instance, natural disasters may destroy the homes, schools, or other microsystems of a person or a group of people, and/or they may make certain necessities of life (e.g., food, fresh water) less available. Cultural values influence the developing person in many ways. In infancy, cultural beliefs about the appropriateness of breastfeeding and about when weaning from the breast should occur can affect not only the nutritional status of the infant but, because mother's milk may make some children less likely to develop allergies later in life, it can also affect their health status. In adolescence, values about child rearing, and indeed the value or role of youth in society, not only affect the behaviours developed by a young person (e.g., Baumrind, 1971, 1991) but can even have implications for whether the person survives adolescence (e.g., see Taylor, 1990, 1993).

Bronfenbrenner's model of the ecology of human development allows us to devise a means to represent the idea that the bidirectional socialization which occurs between adolescents and parents is embedded in a still more complex system of social networks and of societal, cultural, and historical influences.

The Baltes and Baltes Selection, Optimization, and Compensation (SOC) Model

ISSUE TO CONSIDER

- What are the different components of the SOC model, and how do they relate to adolescent development?

We have noted that theories of adolescent development need to explain three aspects of the actions of youth—those involved with selection, optimization, and compensation. These are precisely the three processes discussed by Paul B. Baltes and Margret M. Baltes (1990) in their selection, optimization, and compensation (SOC) model.

Baltes and Baltes (1990; Baltes, 1997; Freund & Baltes, 1998; Lerner et al., 2001) argue that selection, optimization, and compensation need to be considered simultaneously to adequately describe and understand development. The SOC model assumes there are constraints and limitations of internal and external resources in life (e.g., stamina, time, money, social support). As a consequence, a range of alternative developmental goals needs to be selected. **Selection** gives direction to development by directing and focusing resources (i.e., means to reach goals) on certain domains of functioning (e.g., academic achievement) and preventing diffusion of resources (e.g., trying to devote time to both academic achievement and athletic achievement).

In order to actually achieve higher levels of functioning in a selected area, optimization needs to take place. **Optimization** is the process of acquiring, refining, coordinating, and applying resources in the selected area or goal. Typical instances of optimization are acquiring specific goal-related skills (e.g., study skills workshops and tutoring to get higher grades) and persistence in the pursuit of a goal (e.g., keeping up with homework, writing several drafts of a term paper until the best one is produced).

Optimization describes a process geared toward achieving higher levels of (or growth in) functioning. Throughout the life span, however, development can be characterized as multidirectional, that is, as encompassing both growth and decline, or loss and failure (P. Baltes, 1997; P. Baltes, Lindenberger, & Staudinger, 1998; Brandtstädter & Wentura, 1995; Labouvie-Vief, 1981). The SOC model addresses the decline and the management of loss by stressing the importance of **compensation**. When loss or decline in resources threatens our level of functioning, it is necessary to invest additional resources or substitute or apply additional means geared toward the maintenance of functioning (Carstensen, Hanson, & Freund, 1995; Marsiske et al., 1995; Staudinger, Marsiske, & P. Baltes, 1995; see also Bäckman & Dixon, 1992). Typical instances

Selection How youth develop, structure, and commit to their goals. Gives direction to development by directing and focusing resources on certain domains of functioning and preventing diffusion of resources.

Optimization How youth acquire and refine the means to reach their goals. Describes process geared toward achieving higher levels of functioning.

Compensation Investing additional resources, or substituting or applying additional means, geared toward the maintenance of functioning when the pathways youth follow to reach their goals fail.

The Plasticity of Adolescent Development

Adolescence is one of the critical periods in which the foundation of a successful life is laid down: intellectually, socially, motivationally, spiritually, and physically. If we grow successfully during the adolescent phase of life, the doors to a good life are open wide. At the same time, in my research on lifelong (life-span) development, I have been continuously impressed with the fact that the doors to a good life are never completely shut. We humans have the ability to come back and redirect our lives toward more desirable states and outcomes at later periods of life as well. This is called lifelong human plasticity. Three topics and research findings of my work are of special interest to young people.

First, there is the topic of the meaning of life. What makes life worthwhile? The key to a meaningful life is to have goals, to aspire to develop the means (cognitive, motivational, social, and economic) necessary to reach these goals, and in the face of obstacles to find ways for alternative ways to reach goals. When these three activities form a coalition we make progress in life. In technical terms, the theory behind those three modes of successful life management is called the "orchestration of selection, optimization, and compensation."

Second, and this insight owes much to my work in the Jacobs Foundation on Youth Research and Youth Policy, I have learned there are three general domains of "literacy" that adolescents—in addition to a concern with academic school knowledge and the ability to think critically—may want to focus on in order to achieve a good pool of resources and forward-looking perspective on life: (1) life skills literacy, (2) environmental or nature literacy, and (3) computer literacy. If adolescents move

forward in knowing, for instance, how to take care of their bodies and how they can promote their own lives in cooperation with others (life skills literacy), in understanding and nurturing the conditions of their physical environment (environmental or nature literacy), and in using the information technology that the modern world offers (computer literacy), they possess the essential building blocks for becoming mature and future-oriented adults. These three types of literacy are the best insurance policy for moving forward in life and creating the potential to be a good citizen.

The third topic of my research that is relevant to understanding how adolescents live their lives but at the same time prepare themselves for a good future deals with the more specific behavioural and cognitive elements that make us develop and use the best of our potential. With more specific elements, I mean the cognition and behaviours that pervade everything we do, for instance, as we select, optimize, and compensate or as we engage ourselves in the acquisition of the three literacies I described earlier.

Many of these insights about the specific elements involved I have gained from research on another stage of life, that is, aging. Adolescents often worry about their well-being and face what is called critical life events and challenging obstacles. The same is even more true for older people. Their everyday lives are full of challenges and losses. Thus studying the extreme conditions in the lives of older people helps scientists to better understand what happens in other stages of life, such as adolescence.

In this research with older adults we have identified some of the specific elements relevant for effective mastery in all sorts of domains of life. Among them

are (1) a good self-esteem, (2) a solid but flexible self, (3) positive beliefs in one's potential (also called self-efficacy or agency), (4) a positive and optimistic orientation toward the future and the subsequent stages of life, and (5) the emergence of knowledge about such concepts as wisdom and moral behaviour.

Each of these five components has its foundational origins in childhood and adolescence. It is possible to acquire and refine them later in life, but it makes for easier and earlier progress if they are built up early. What is occasionally difficult for adolescents is that they, in their wants to be independent and different from their parents or the current "establishment," see these components as parts of the conventional order of society and what parents want. It is later in life, however, that the insight arises that having these building blocks is in their own best interest as adolescents as well. What I as a researcher hope is that adolescents can do both: gain their autonomy including critical thinking but also the pool of resources that propels them forward to pursue their own and the common good.

of compensation are the substitution of means or the use of external aids (e.g., obtaining the help of a tutor). When compensatory efforts fail or their costs outweigh their gains, the more adaptive response to loss or decline in resources might be to restructure our goal hierarchy (e.g., place academics ahead of music), to lower our standards (e.g., settle for practising music without a band), or to look for new goals (**loss-based selection**; make academics a higher priority goal instead of a means).

To summarize, *selection* refers to the development of preferences or goals, the construction of a goal hierarchy, and the commitment to a set of goals or areas of preferred functioning. *Optimization* denotes the investment of goal-related resources in order to achieve higher levels of functioning. *Compensation* refers to the process involved in maintaining a given level of functioning in the face of loss or decline in goal-related resources.

Although it is possible to differentiate these components of SOC, successful development encompasses their coordinated integration (Freund & P. Baltes, 2000; Marsiske et al., 1995). For instance, optimization efforts most likely only lead to higher levels of functioning when they are focused on a small number of domains of functioning instead of diffused among many domains. Similarly, selection per se does not ensure high achievement if no goal-relevant resources are applied (e.g., wanting to have high peer status but using no means—neither athletic nor academic success—to attain it).

Finally, the adaptiveness of compensation needs to be seen in the context of the entire set of an adolescent's goals (e.g., how many other goals are there that need resources for optimization? how important, relative to other goals, is a threatened goal?) and the availability of resources. It does not appear to be adaptive to put a lot of one's resources into a relatively unimportant domain of functioning at the cost of having to neglect more important goals (Freund, Li, & P. Baltes, 1999). Meet the Researcher Box 2.3 discusses some of the other conceptual and empirical contributions of Paul B. Baltes to the understanding of adolescent development.

Conclusions

There exists a diverse array of theories with which to study development. Although these theories differ in regard to the way they approach the nature-nurture issue in the study of development, they are similar in one important respect. Each theory is an attempt to enhance understanding of the course of adolescence (i.e., how, across this period of life, youth act, why they act in particular ways, and the implications of these actions for healthy, adaptive development).

Although all theories have important uses for an advancing understanding of adolescence and, as well, even though *no* theory is free of limitations (Lerner, 2001), strong interaction theories such as those of Bronfenbrenner and of Baltes and Baltes appear most useful at this point in the history of the study of adolescence (Lerner, 1998a, 1998b). These theories integrate all levels of organization that are part of a young person's life (biology through society, culture, and history), stress the relative plasticity and diversity of development, and offer an active and optimistic approach to applications aimed at promoting healthy and successful adolescent development. Accordingly, as we consider the features of adolescent development in the following chapters, we find that strong interaction theories are useful for appreciating the diversity of development, the role of the context in adolescent development, and the several ways in which healthy development of youth can be furthered by positively integrating young people and their ecologies.

Summary

- The key challenge for adolescents is to discover what they can do to develop successfully in their context, given their biological, psychological, and social characteristics.
- An essential task for theories of adolescence is to understand adolescents' *selection* of goals,

their *optimization* of their abilities to meet these goals, and their *compensation* for failures to meet their goals.
- Theories of adolescence must explain how an individual adolescent interacts with his or her context.
- Contemporary theories of adolescence stress that development occurs as a consequence of relations among "multiple levels of organization," such as biological, psychological, societal, and cultural.

Loss-based selection When compensatory efforts fail or their costs outweigh their gains, individuals restructure their goal hierarchy, lower their standards, or look for new goals.

- Developmental systems theories stress that development occurs as a result of organized and mutually influential relations among the various levels of organization.
- The developmental contextual approach to life-span development suggests that to understand adolescence, influences from multiple disciplines must be considered in an integrated manner, systematic change or development must be considered, and the individual must be seen as an active agent in his or her own development.
- To study adolescents, multivariate, longitudinal, and multilevel research should be used.
- The goal of applied developmental science is to use knowledge about adolescent development, diversity, and context to design interventions to prevent problems and to promote positive development.
- Person-context interactions are plastic (they show systematic change), and future developmental pathways can be constructed that are discontinuous from previous ones, as well as continuous.
- The nature-nurture controversy pertains to whether behaviour and development derive from heredity, maturation, and genes (nature) or environment, experience, and learning (nurture).
- The developmental contextual approach stresses dynamic interaction between nature and nurture such that biological and contextual variables influence each other over the course of life.
- Genes and environment are equal forces in the determination of development and they are completely fused in life.
- The diversity of possible developmental outcomes is constrained by the individual's characteristics and context despite *relative* plasticity of human development.
- No two people have the same fusion of genes and environment across their lives.
- Differences in genotypes and environments, and the fusion of the two, underscore the error in making global characterizations of entire groups of people.
- The large number of potential human genotypes makes the possibility of any two people ever having the same genotype (excluding multiple, identical births) next to impossible.
- Genes must be fused with the environment if any human physical or behavioural characteristics are to be developed.
- Nature and nurture are inextricably linked and one cannot exist independently of the other.
- Although G. Stanley Hall's *specific* nature theory was not adopted, he had an influence in developing scientific concern with human development and a general nature perspective.
- Boyd R. McCandless's drive theory of human behaviour states there are several drives in the person that are energizers of behaviour. His theory is a nurture theory because he believes a person will learn from society that certain behaviours will reduce drive states, which is rewarding to the person.
- McCandless points to adolescence as a special time because of the emergence of the sex drive. Society does not reward males and females for the same sex-drive-reducing behaviours. This could be a period of undiminished drives for the adolescent, and thus it is a nurture explanation of "storm and stress."
- A weak interaction theory places the stress primarily on nature *or* nurture as the source of development. A moderate interaction theory places equal stress on nature and nurture but sees them as independent of each other. A strong interaction theory places the stress on nature and nurture, and views them as reciprocally related.
- Sigmund Freud's theory of psychosexual development is a weak interaction theory. He believed human life is governed by the libido, which moves throughout the body over the course of development, determining what type of stimulation is gratifying.
- Freud proposed five stages of psychosexual development: oral, anal, phallic, latency, and genital. The stages correspond to localization in the body of the libido.
- Freud's ideas were critiqued because he worked with adult neurotic patients who were attempting to reconstruct their childhood. Freud did not check for memory lapses or distortions of early memories. He also worked at a time when views of sexuality were repressed. Other psychoanalytically oriented thinkers accepted most of Freud's ideas as correct, but incomplete.
- Erik Erikson created a weak interaction theory of psychosocial development focusing on the

contributions of the ego to development, and on what the ego must do to adapt to reality.

- Erikson's theory proposes stages of psychosocial development that present capabilities the ego must develop to meet societal demands. Development will proceed even if the capability is not achieved, but the ego will not be optimally developed.
- There are eight stages of psychosocial development and each presents a crisis of development.
- Erikson's stage theory is consistent with a life-span perspective, and although it has some of the same limitations as Freud's theory, it is a major basis for research about human development.
- Anna Freud and her father believed there were three structures of personality: the id (the initial source of libido), the ego (developed to deal with reality), and the superego (the conscience) that are present and balanced by the end of the phallic stage.
- The id only wants pleasure, the superego cares nothing of pleasure and is the conscience, and the ego is the balance between the two, caring only about survival.
- The unconscious contains material most difficult to bring into awareness. The ego uses defence mechanisms to take pressures imposed by the id and place them into the unconscious. The superego's pressures are not defended against because they represent the rules of society and placing this in the unconscious would mean losing morality.
- Anna Freud believes the balance among the superego, id, and ego is destroyed in adolescence because of new pressures on the ego.
- Anna Freud associated special alterations in adolescence—alterations in drives, ego organization, object relations, and ideals and social relations—that make adolescence a time of imbalance and upheaval.
- Anna Freud's theory was criticized because she did not acknowledge the plasticity within people and the differences between people and she characterized adolescence as inevitably stormy and stressful.
- Jean Piaget's theory of cognitive development is an example of a moderate interaction theory. He believed cognitive development arose from the action of the organism on the environment and from the action of the environment on the organism, but there is not as full a consideration of

environmental or experiential changes as there is of organism changes.

- Piaget proposed that cognition develops through four universal stages in an unvarying sequence: sensorimotor, preoperational, concrete operational, and formal operational. Movement through these stages represents a person's attempt to maintain equilibrium using assimilation and accommodation.
- A special type of egocentrism characterizes adolescence. The adolescent believes that others are as preoccupied with him or her as he or she is (imaginary audience) and the adolescent comes to believe he or she is a special, unique person (personal fable).
- Lawrence Kohlberg developed a theory of moral development from a cognitive development viewpoint that has been the impetus for much research and discussion.
- Kohlberg described a progression of moral development starting with preconventional morality, moving to conventional morality, and ending with postconventional morality.
- Kohlberg's theory is a moderate interaction theory because it did not sufficiently deal with what is claimed to be the source of development, person-environment interactions. His theory focused almost exclusively on person processes to the exclusion of environmental processes.
- Urie Bronfenbrenner proposed a strong interaction theory of development, arguing that human development needs to be understood as it occurs in its real-world setting, or ecology.
- Bronfenbrenner believes that human development occurs in four distinct, although interrelated, settings: the microsystem, the mesosystem, the exosystem, and the macrosystem.
- There are many theories of adolescent development, which differ in regard to their treatment of the nature-nurture debate; however, they are all attempts to understand how and why youth act across adolescence, and what the implications of these actions are for adaptive development.
- These actions involve selection, optimization, and compensation and are discussed by Paul B. Baltes and Margret M. Baltes (1990) in their selection, optimization, and compensation (SOC) model.
- In the SOC model, selection refers to the development of preferences or goals, the construction

of a goal hierarchy, and the commitment to a set of goals or areas of preferred functioning. Optimization denotes the investment of goal-related resources in order to achieve higher levels of functioning. Compensation refers to the process involved in maintaining a given level of functioning in the face of loss or decline in goal-related resources.

Discussion Topics

1. Guided by developmental systems theory, how might you design efforts to support adolescents who exhibit problem and/or risky behaviours?
2. How do you think your particular genes and life contexts have determined your developmental outcome—the person you are today? Do you feel your genes or your life contexts have been more influential in that determination?
3. What might studies of fraternal and identical twins add to the nature-nurture debate?
4. Compare and contrast the theories of Hall and McCandless, focusing specifically on their conceptions of adolescence.
5. Why might the three psychoanalytic theories presented in the chapter be considered examples of weak nature-nurture interaction?
6. Why might Piaget's theory of cognitive development and Kohlberg's theory of moral reasoning be considered a moderate nature-nurture interaction theory?
7. Why might Bronfenbrenner's approach be considered a strong nature-nurture interaction theory?
8. Think of an example in your development to which you could apply the SOC model. What selections did you make? How did you optimize your chances of attaining, refining, and/or coordinating those selections? How did you compensate if and when you faced failure? Based on this example, would you describe the Baltes and Baltes model as a strong approach to the nature-nurture debate? Why?

Key Terms

accommodation, p. 47
adulthood, p. 45
anal stage, p. 41
anal musculature stage, p. 44
applied developmental science,
   p. 31
assimilation, p. 47
castration anxiety, p. 42
compensation, p. 50
concrete operational stage, p. 47
conscience, p. 42
conventional morality, p. 48
critical period, p. 44
defence mechanisms, p. 45
developmental system theories,
   p. 29
diversity, p. 30
Down syndrome, p. 36
drive state, p. 40
dynamic interaction, p. 33
ecological milieu, p. 39
ecological validity, p. 38
ecology, p. 49

ego, p. 43
egocentrism, p. 47
ego ideal, p. 42
Electra complex, p. 42
equilibration, p. 47
exosystem, p. 49
fixation, p. 41
formal operational stage, p. 47
genital locomotor stage, p. 44
genital stage, p. 42
genotype, p. 36
id, p. 43
imaginary audience, p. 47
intellectualization, p. 46
interventions, p. 31
latency, p. 44
latency stage, p. 42
libido, p. 41
longitudinal research/studies,
   p. 30
loss-based selection, p. 52
macrosystem, p. 49
maturity, p. 45

meiosis, p. 36
mesosystem, p. 49
microsystem, p. 49
moderate interaction theory,
   p. 41
monozygotic (MZ) twins, p. 35
multilevel research/studies, p. 30
multiple levels of organization,
   p. 29
multivariate research/studies,
   p. 30
nature-nurture controversy,
   p. 29
Oedipus complex, p. 42
ontogeny, p. 38
operation, p. 47
optimization, p. 50
oral stage, p. 41
oral sensory stage, p. 44
penis envy, p. 42
personal fable, p. 47
phallic stage, p. 41
phenylketonuria (PKU), p. 37

3

Puberty, Physical Development, and Health

"Mom, I just can't go to the dance. I look so gross in a dress and heels!"

"Tina, you look lovely," her mother insisted. "I'm sure you'll look as nice as any of the other Grade 6 girls."

"No I won't," Tina pleaded. "I'm too tall already and these shoes make it worse. None of the boys will want to come close to me." Tears began to fill her eyes.

"Honey, at your age girls are often taller than boys. Believe me, I'm sure that a few centimetres won't stop them from asking you to dance. You're so pretty, you'll have a line of them asking you."

"Oh sure, and you're not biased. I'm so pretty and I just happen to be your daughter."

"Well dear, you are my daughter, but that does not mean I can't see that . . ."

"But Mom," Tina interrupted, "the boys already make fun of me. They make me feel so uncomfortable because I'm bigger than the other girls in my grade. This doesn't hide anything."

"Oh," her mother said softly, "I understand, but you know you can wear a shawl and . . ."

"No, Mom, you don't understand! I feel ugly and wearing a dress makes me feel even worse. I just don't want to go any place where I have to wear one."

Learning Objectives

1. To understand adolescents' perceptions of pubertal changes.
2. To define the three stages of adolescence and their corresponding ages.
3. To understand the three phases of pubertal maturation and what occurs during those stages.
4. To understand the role of hormones in pubertal maturation.
5. To define puberty and to understand the difference between puberty and pubertal maturation.
6. To understand the differences between primary and secondary sexual characteristics.
7. To understand the causes and effects of variations in the speed and timing of pubertal maturation and how the effects are influenced by the social context, including history (the secular trend).
8. To understand how adolescents' behaviours influence their health.
9. To understand some of the physical problems related to pubertal changes.
10. To appreciate how psychological and contextual influences, as well as adolescents' preoccupation with their bodily appearance, can lead to eating behaviours that are detrimental to their health.
11. To name and describe some eating disorders and their implications.

This interaction between Tina and her mother is all too typical during adolescence, especially during its early phases. The physical and physiological changes of adolescence involving **pubertal maturation** bring the young person from looking like a child to appearing like an adult.

Many adolescents report that they are not fully prepared for pubertal changes or fully informed about what will happen to them and how they should think and feel about these changes. In one study of about 150 Grade 9 girls, the participants reported a need to receive emotional support and assurance that menstruation is normal and healthy rather than bad, frightening, or embarrassing (Koff & Rierdan, 1995). They stated they would have liked to receive information about menstrual hygiene and about how they would actually feel

Pubertal maturation Process through which the primary sexual characteristics develop into adult form and the secondary sexual characteristics associated with puberty emerge and develop.

Concerns about appearance and grooming are important parts of life for many adolescents.

across their menstrual cycles. The girls also noted that they talked about menstruation with their mothers but were unlikely to have similar discussions with their fathers. They were uncomfortable talking with their fathers about menstruation and many felt that their fathers should be supportive but silent (Koff & Rierdan, 1995).

Among younger (Grade 6) girls from Australia, participants had only limited knowledge about menarche (the beginning of the first menstrual period) and much of it was incorrect or reflective of negative myths (e.g., menarche is a source of shame and anxiety linked to periods of incapacity and illness) (Moore, 1995). The girls' attitudes about

menstruation were characterized by embarrassment, discomfort, and ambivalence about growing up (Moore, 1995).

Both male and female adolescents find it useful to have accurate information about the nature and implications of pubertal change (Brooks-Gunn & Petersen, 1983). It is important to stress that emotions and thoughts often do not develop at the same pace as one's physical characteristics and that because of the relations among biological, psychological, and social functioning, **puberty** can have profound implications for both physical health and behaviour. In this chapter we discuss both of these implications of puberty.

Characteristics of Pubertal Maturation

ISSUES TO CONSIDER

- What are the three phases of pubertal maturation, and what are their general characteristics?
- What is the physiological process that leads to pubertal maturation and bodily changes?
- What is puberty? How is it different from pubertal maturation?
- What are primary and secondary sexual characteristics?

The physical and physiological changes of adolescence typically span the second decade of life, involving early adolescence (around years 10 to 14 or 15), middle adolescence (years 15 to 17), and late adolescence (years 18 to 20). Although within these stages of adolescence, bodily and psychological changes do not proceed uniformly, a general sequence for these changes applies to most people (Katchadourian, 1977; Tanner, 1991).

The bodily changes of adolescence relate to both primary and secondary sexual characteristics. Bodily changes affect height, weight, fat and muscle distribution, glandular secretions, and both primary and secondary sexual characteristics. Pubertal maturation and physiological changes involve changes in the particular chemicals released from certain organs within the body. These organs are **endocrine glands**, and the chemicals they release into the bloodstream are termed **hormones.**

Puberty Period during which the primary sexual characteristics develop into adult form and the secondary sexual characteristics are emerging and developing and the capability to reproduce is attained.
Endocrine glands Ductless glands, such as the pituitary gland, that secrete their content into the bloodstream.
Hormones Chemicals released into the bloodstream that have specific regulatory effects on the activity of certain organs.

Pubertal maturation begins when a portion of the brain, the hypothalamus, produces "luteinizing hormone releasing hormone" (LHRH), a chemical that stimulates the secretion of hormones from the pituitary gland. These hormones are termed gonadotropins, luteinizing hormone (LH), and follicle-stimulating hormone (FSH). These hormones stimulate other endocrine glands, the gonads (ovaries in females, testes in males), to secrete **sex steroids** (**estrogens** in females, **androgens** in males). It is these sex steroids that produce the physical and physiological changes of pubertal maturation.

Adolescence is a period during which the person reaches an adult level of reproductive maturity. However, puberty, the point at which the person can reproduce, is not synonymous with all maturational changes (Schonfeld, 1969). Puberty is not synonymous with menarche in females or with the first ejaculation (the release of semen) in males. Typically, the initial menstrual cycles of females are not accompanied by ovulation. Similarly, for males there is a gap between the first ejaculation, which usually occurs between 11 and 16 years of age (Kinsey, Pomeroy, & Martin, 1948), and the capability to fertilize.

Primary sexual characteristics are present at birth and involve the internal and external genitalia (e.g., the penis in males and the vagina in females). **Secondary sexual characteristics** are those attributes that develop during the prepubescent through postpubescent phases (e.g., breast development in females and pigmented facial hair in males).

Puberty is just one event within a series of changes that bring the adolescent from childhood to adulthood. Adjusting to these internal and external bodily changes represents a developmental task of adolescence. In order to understand the nature of this physiological developmental task, we discuss the three phases involved in adolescent physical maturation. Given the vast number of bodily changes that adolescents must adjust to, we can appreciate the difficulty they face in formulating and maintaining a consistent sense of self.

Phases of Pubertal Maturation

ISSUES TO CONSIDER

- What are the characteristics of the prepubescent phase for males and females?
- What are the major events that occur in the pubescence phase of development?
- What are the major bodily changes in the postpubescence phase?

Prepubescence begins with the first indication of sexual maturation. It ends with the initial appearance of pubic hair. Prepubescent changes typically begin an average of two years earlier in females than in males. For females, this phase includes enlargement of the ovary and the ripening of its cells (primary sexual characteristics). Secondary sexual characteristics include rounding of the hips and the

Figure 3.1

Stages of pubic hair development in adolescent girls. (1) early pubescent (not shown) in which there is no true pubic hair; (2) late prepubescent/early pubescent in which sparse growth of downy hair is mainly at sides of labia; (3) pigmentation, coarsening, and curling with an increase in the amount of hair; (4) adult hair, but limited in area; (5) adult hair with horizontal upper border.

(*Source:* Redrawn from J. M. Tanner, 1962.)

Sex steroids Sex hormones (androgens in males and estrogens in females) that control development of physical and physiological changes associated with pubertal maturation.

Estrogens Female sex hormones associated with the development of secondary sexual characteristics in girls.

Androgens Male sex hormones associated with the development of secondary sexual characteristics in boys.

Primary sexual characteristics Physical attributes present at birth that involve internal and external genitalia (e.g., the penis in males and the vagina in females).

Secondary sexual characteristics Physical attributes that develop during puberty (e.g., breast development in females and pigmented facial hair in males).

Prepubescence Stage in pubertal maturation during which some of the bodily changes associated with adolescence (e.g., changes in height, weight, fat and muscle distribution, glandular secretions, or sexual characteristics) have begun.

Figure 3.2
Stages of pubic hair development in boys.
(1) early prepubescent (not shown) in which there is no true
pubic hair; (2) late prepubescent/early pubescent in which
sparse growth of downy hair is mainly at base of penis;
(3) pigmentation, coarsening, and curling, with an increase
in amount of hair; (4) adult hair, but limited in area; (5) adult
hair with horizontal upper border and spreading to thighs.

(*Source:* Redrawn from Tanner, 1962.)

appearance of the breast *bud* (elevation of the areola
surrounding the nipple producing a small conelike
growth [Schonfeld, 1969]).

In males, there is a continuing enlargement of the
testicles, an enlargement and reddening of the scrotal sac, and an increase in the length and circumfer-
ence of the penis (Schonfeld, 1969). Downy pubic
hair may be present for both males and females.

The onset of **pubescence** occurs with the appearance of pubic hair and ends when pubic hair devel-

Figure 3.3
Stages of male genital development.
(1) prepubescence, in which the size of the testes and penis is
like that in early childhood; (2) testes become larger, and scrotal
skin reddens and coarsens; (3) continuation of Stage 2, with
lengthening of penis; (4) penis enlarges in general size, and
scrotal skin becomes pigmented; (5) adult genitalia.

(*Source:* Redrawn from Tanner, 1962.)

opment is complete (Schonfeld, 1969). Figure 3.1
shows the changes involved in pubic hair development for adolescent females, and Figure 3.2 shows
these changes for adolescent males.

The peak velocity (speed) of growth in height
and weight occurs during this phase. The adolescent
growth spurt occurs about two years earlier in
females than in males. Menarche occurs in females
about 18 months after the maximum height increase
of the growth spurt (Schonfeld, 1969).

Primary sexual characteristics include enlargement of the vulva and clitoris of the female, and of
the testes, scrotum, and penis in the male (Schonfeld,
1969). The changes in males are illustrated in Figure
3.3.

In regard to secondary sexual characteristics, in
females there is a change from having breast buds to
having the areola and nipple elevated to form the
primary breast (Schonfeld, 1969). These changes are
illustrated in Figure 3.4. For males there is a deep-
ening of the voice and pigmented axillary and facial
hair appear, usually about two years after the emergence of pubic hair (Schonfeld, 1969).

Postpubescence starts when pubic hair growth is
complete, when there is a decrease in the rate of
growth in height, when there is completion of most of
the changes in the primary and secondary sexual characteristics, and when the person is fertile and he or she
can reproduce (Schonfeld, 1969). However, changes
in the primary and secondary sexual characteristics
continue. In males, the beard usually starts to grow in
this phase, and in females there is further growth of
axillary hair and breast development.

Conclusions About the Characteristics of Pubertal Maturation

ISSUE TO CONSIDER

● What are the limitations and variations in pubertal
development?

The physical and physiological changes characterizing
adolescence involve much more than just puberty. They
include also changes spanning perhaps an entire decade
of the life span and involving at least three phases of

Pubescence Stage in pubertal
maturation during which most
of the bodily changes associated with adolescence have
been initiated.

Postpubescence Stage in
pubertal maturation during
which the bodily changes
associated with adolescence
are completed.

Figure 3.4

Stages of breast development in adolescent girls.
(1) prepubescent flat appearance; (2) small, raised breast bud;
(3) general enlargement and raising of breast and
areola; (4) areola and nipple form contour separate from
that of breast; (5) adult breast—areola is in the same contour
as breast.

(*Source*: Redrawn from Tanner, 1962.)

certain diseases. Eating disorders are a major example (discussed further on in the chapter).

Second, although all males and females go through the changes of pubertal maturation in much the same sequence, people vary in the speed they mature. Some adolescents mature earlier than their peers; others mature later than the rest of their group. What is the basis of such differences? Does such variation matter for the individual's development? Does such variation complicate the nature of the physiological developmental task the adolescent must meet? If so, do the developments that occur correspond in any way to the stereotype that adolescence is a period of inevitable storm and stress (see Chapter 1), one linked (as hypothesized by Anna Freud, 1969; see Chapter 2) to the universal changes of puberty?

The following sections address these questions. Consistent with the themes of diversity and context stressed in this book, there is little if any support for the stereotype of adolescence or for the view that pubertal change creates a necessary disruption in healthy psychological and social behaviour. Instead, there are a range of behavioural and social implications of pubertal change, some negative and some positive. This variation is associated with the different peer group, familial, socioeconomic, and even historical contexts of the developing adolescent.

Social and Cultural Differences in the Timing of Pubertal Change

ISSUE TO CONSIDER

- What variables influence the timing and speed of pubertal maturation?

Early maturers develop faster than their same-age peers. They go through the periods of adolescent bodily change faster than average. **Late maturers** develop more slowly than do most of their same-age peers. They pass through the periods of adolescent bodily change slower than average. There are also youth who are **on-time maturers**, passing through the periods of bodily change at an average rate. In essence, then, although of the same age, the early

bodily change. It is important to recognize two points, however. First, the growth gains involved in pubertal maturation do not exist independently of limitations. Accompanying this growth is an increased risk for

Early maturers Adolescents who attain the physical maturation characteristics of puberty earlier than the rest of their same-age peers.

Late maturers Adolescents who attain the physical maturation characteristics of puberty later than the rest of their same-age peers.

On-time maturers Adolescents who attain the physical maturation characteristics of puberty at the same time as most of their same-age peers.

maturer is accelerated in bodily growth and the late maturer is delayed.

Differences in rate of development lead to quite distinct differences in bodily appearance. As seen in Figure 3.5, all the females are of the same age, but "1" has the characteristics of prepubescence, "2" of pubescence, and "3" of postpubescence. Similar differences are seen with the three identically aged males shown in this figure.

Different rates of bodily change found in regard to pubertal maturation occur as a consequence of genetic differences (Comite et al., 1987; Surbey,

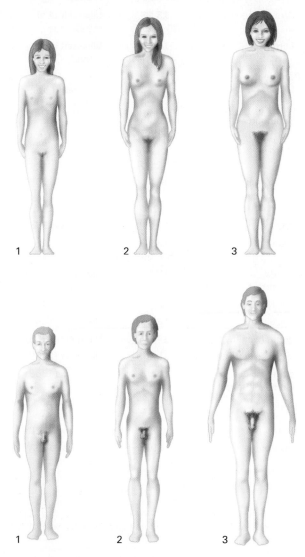

Figure 3.5
Variations in pubescent development.
All three females are 12¾ years old, and all three males are 14¾ years old, but they are in different phases of change.
(*Source:* Tanner, 1973.)

1990) and in relation to social and cultural differences. To illustrate, consider one aspect of bodily change—menarche.

As shown in Table 3.1, there is a vast difference in the age of menarche in different cultures and in different social classes within a culture. The median age at menarche for Greek adolescents is 12.27 years, the lowest age listed in Table 3.1, and the median age for people of the Bundi tribe of New Guinea is 18.8 years, the highest age shown.

These differences in age of menarche might relate to nutritional or health care differences associated with various social or cultural settings. For instance, differences in age of menarche within the same country are often seen between urban and rural areas. Tanner (1970, 1991) reports that in Romania the average age of menarche is 13.5 years in towns and 14.6 years in villages. Corresponding differences between town-reared and rural-reared children have been found in the former Soviet Union (13.0 and 14.3 years, respectively), and in India (12.8 and 14.2 years, respectively). In all of these countries, nutritional resources were less abundant in the rural setting.

The different availability of resources in different classes within a society is also associated with variation in the age of menarche. In Hong Kong, the age at menarche is 12.5 years for children of the rich, 12.8 years for those of average income levels, and 13.3 years for children of poor families (Tanner, 1970, 1991). In European countries, the range of socioeconomic status from rich to poor is associated with a range of about two to four months in age of menarche (Katchadourian, 1977). Furthermore, the mean age of menarche in India varied from 13.08 in Assam in the eastern region to 18.2 in the high-altitude region of Nepal (Sharma, 1990). Again poor nutrition and low socioeconomic status were suspected to be causal here, although Sharma suggested that the low oxygen pressure of the atmosphere and excessive physical activity may also play a role. Different studies of the relation between age of menarche and social class define social class differently. Although there is often a situation where the "poor" in one country may be starving while the poor in another society may have relatively adequate nutrition (Katchadourian, 1977), a relation between socioeconomic status and menarche is typically found.

Menarche Beginning of the first menstrual cycle.

Table 3-1 Median Age at Menarche in Several Populations

Population or location	Median age, years	Source	Population or location	Median age, years	Source
Greece	12.27 (SD 1.13)	Papadimitriou et al. (1999)	Ontario, Canada Total sample	13.00 (SD 1.32 yrs)	Surbey (1990, personal communication, 2002)
Edmonton, Canada	12.3 (SD 0.97)	Kieren & Morse (1995)	Both parents present	13.07 (SD 1.31 yrs)	
Cuba	12.4	Hiernaux (1968)	Father absent	12.71 (SD 1.29 yrs)	
Black	12.4		London, U.K.	13.1	Hiernaux (1968)
White	12.4		Indo-Pakistani	13.06 (SD 0.20)	Ulijaszek et al (1991)
Mixed race	12.4				
Rio de Janeiro, Brazil	12.4	Kac et al. (2000)	Afro-Caribbean	13.18 (SD 0.11)	Ulijaszek et al (1991)
Florence, Italy	12.5	Hiernaux (1968)	European	13.59 (SD 0.37)	Ulijaszek et al (1991)
Wroclaw, Poland	12.6	Hiernaux (1968)			
Wroclaw, Poland	13.16 (SD 1.05)	Hulanicka & Waliszko (1991)	Cameroon Urban	13.18 (SD 1.08)	Pasquet et al. (1999)
Poland (cities)	12.9	Hulanicka & Waliszko (1991)	Suburban	13.98 (SD 1.55)	
Poland (villages)	13.6				
Glasgow, Scotland, U.K.	12.7 (SD 1.20)	Okasha et al. (2001)	Rural	14.27 (SD 1.65)	
Spain (city)	12.79 (SD 1.04)	Marrodain et al. 1999)	Assam, India (city dwellers)	13.2	Hiernaux (1968)
Madrid (rural)	12.90 (SD1.03)		Assam	13.08	Sharma (1990)
Budapest, Hungary	12.8	Hiernaux (1968)	Burma (city dwellers)	13.2	Hiernaux (1968)
California, U.S.	12.8	Hiernaux (1968)	Oman	13.3 (SD .09)	Musaiger (1991)
China Urban	12.8 (SD 0.9)	Tomkins (2002)			
Rural	13.2 (SD 1.0)	Tomkins (2002)	Uganda (wealthy Kampala)	13.4	Hiernaux (1968)
Hong Kong (wealthy Chinese)	12.5	Hiernaux (1968)	Oslo, Norway	13.5	Hiernaux (1968)
Colombo, Ceylon	12.8	Hiernaux (1968)	France	13.5	Hiernaux (1968)
Australia	12.9 (SD 1.2 yrs)	Magarey et al (1999)	Nigeria (wealthy Ibo)	14.1	Hiernaux (1968)
Iran	12.91 (SD 1.23)	Ayatollahi (2002)	U.S.S.R. (rural Buriats)	15.0	Hiernaux (1968)
Río Negro, Argentina	13.0	Crognier et al. (1996)	South Africa (Transkei Banfu)	15.0	Hiernaux (1968)
Bangladesh	13.0 (SD 0.89 yrs)	Chowdhury et al (2000)	Rwanda Tutsi	16.5	
			Hutu	17.1	Hiernaux (1968)
Moscow, U.S.S.R.	13.0	Hiernaux (1968)	New Guinea (Bundi)	18.8	Hiernaux (1968)
Tel Aviv, Israel	13.0	Hiernaux (1968)			

Note: SD represents standard deviation.

Sources: Ayatollahi, 2002; Chowdhury et al., 2000; Crognier et al., 1996; Hiernaux, 1968; Hulanicka & Waliszko, 1991; Kac et al., 2000; Kieren & Morse, 1995; Magarey et al., 1999; Marrodain et al., 2000; Musaiger, 1991; Okasha et al., 2001; Papadimitriou et al., 1999; Pasquet et al., 1999; Sharma 1990; Surbey, 1990; Surbey, 2002; Tomkins, 2002; Ulijaszek, Evans, & Miller 1991.

There is some evidence that family composition and stress are related to age of menarche. Surbey (1990) found that adolescent girls in Hamilton, Ontario, who were parent or father absent reached menarche at a significantly younger age than those who lived with both parents throughout their lives. Evolutionary psychology suggests that delayed menarche may be adaptive in that it prevents any

Predictors of Pubertal Timing and Its Psychological and Social Effects

Michele Surbey is an evolutionary psychologist currently teaching in the School of Psychology, James Cook University, Queensland, Australia. She taught evolutionary psychology in Canada for 10 years before moving to Australia. She conducts research in three areas: evolution of development, human mate selection, and the evolution of self-deception.

My interest in the antecedents and consequences of the timing of puberty in humans stems from my background in animal behaviour and evolutionary psychology. I thought that considering human development from these perspectives was a useful means to gaining a broader understanding of the physiological and psychological changes occurring during adolescence.

Pubertal timing is an important life history trait that has presumably been shaped by natural selection over many generations and varies between species and individuals in nonrandom ways. Humans are a long-lived species with a relatively late age of puberty compared with other mammals. People usually think that puberty "just happens" and they aren't often aware of what causes variations in pubertal timing. For example, Canadian girls experience menarche (the first menstrual period) between 9 and 18.5 years of age—a range of almost 10 years, of which only a small proportion is accounted for by heredity. As an undergraduate, I became aware of how the social environment can affect development and reproductive function in nonhuman animals. For example, did you know that female mice exposed to unrelated adult males or their odours mature earlier than those living in all-female groups? This phenomenon is referred to as the Vandenberg Effect and is just one of the fascinating ways in which pubertal timing is altered in nonhumans. When I became a graduate student, I set out to extend some of this nonhuman work into the human sphere by examining the antecedents of human pubertal timing. My goal was to determine if variations in human pubertal timing fit into a broader evolutionary model viewing alterations in individual development as adaptive responses to particular environmental events.

In addition, I thought it was important to understand the sources of variation in pubertal timing because puberty is a significant psychological, as well as biological, event in our species, and is accompanied by changes in self-concept and social behaviours. Developmental psychologists have noted that especially early or late puberty may be problematic and associated with negative outcomes in adolescence. For example, early puberty in girls is a good predictor of early sexual activity, pregnancy, and delinquency, and may increase a girl's vulnerability to anorexia nervosa and sexual abuse. An understanding of the antecedents of pubertal timing might shed light on its effects and inform intervention strategies, such as those intended to reduce the number of teenage pregnancies where high rates are associated with personal and societal hardship. For example, early pregnancy tends to be associated with increased risks for children, and often eclipses a mother's educational and occupational choices.

In the 1980s, guided by evolutionary notions and findings in the nonhuman literature, I began to study the factors associated with either an acceleration or delay in puberty in girls. I surveyed over 1000 women in eastern Canada and found that women who reported the absence of a biological father and high levels of stress during childhood experienced menarche about half a year earlier than other women. Related to the Vandenberg Effect, I also found a tendency for girls with stepfathers in the home to mature earlier than those without stepfathers. These findings have been replicated, in whole or in part, by others and there has been some debate regarding the evolutionary significance of them. The association between the absence of a father and early menarche is partly accounted for by the mother's age at puberty. Women who develop early tend to marry early and produce father-absent children, because early marriages are more likely to end in divorce than later

marriages. Increased exposure to stress may also partly explain the relationship between the absence of a father and early menarche. However, stress usually results in a delay in puberty or a shutdown in reproduction in females as a means to synchronize reproduction with good environmental conditions.

So why would stress be related to an acceleration of puberty? One possibility is that exposure to stress might trigger a compensatory response, such as the "catch-up growth" observed in children who have been ill or malnourished but then recover, thus accelerating puberty. This might be a way for an individual to compensate for early periods of deprivation and get back on track developmentally. I have been exploring this possibility and the hormonal correlates of pubertal timing in a longitudinal study of more than 200 children. Preliminary analyses suggest that, as predicted, girls' reproductive development and endocrine profiles are more highly associated with environmental and psychological stress than are boys'. Continuing examination of other potential predictors of pubertal timing, such as parental influences, birth order, and family size, may eventually result in a general model of the nonrandom variation in human developmental rate. Such a model would presumably increase our ability to predict which children will mature unusually early or late and intervene before puberty and any negative consequences are manifested.

Adolescents of the same age may vary in their respective levels of physical maturity.

temptation of incest between father and daughter. When the biological father is no longer in the house, there is no need to delay puberty. One possible explanation is that, similar to the animal kingdom, a chemical signal or pheromone delays the onset of puberty. Another possibility is that stress during childhood (e.g., parental conflict, absence of the father) may lead to early menarche, as those adolescents in Surbey's sample who scored high on a measure of stressful life events had significantly earlier menarche than those with few such life events. The finding by Turner, Runtz, and Galambos (1999) that girls who were sexually abused experienced menarche a full year earlier than nonabused adolescents lends support to this notion. A final possibility is suggested by the finding that the mothers' age at menarche was significantly correlated with the daughters' age at menarche, and that there was a tendency for mothers of father-absent adolescents to have an earlier age at menarche than other mothers. Early menarche tends to be associated with early dating and sexual experiences, early pregnancy and early marriage. These in turn are associated with higher rates of divorce. Thus, genetics may be the reason why early menarche occurs among adolescents in father-absent families.

Secular trend Variation of adolescent bodily changes across history.

The Role of Historical Differences in the Timing of Pubertal Change

ISSUE TO CONSIDER

• What is the secular trend, and what has the trend been in regard to adolescent bodily changes?

Adolescents seem to have matured at different rates in different historical periods. This relation between history and adolescent bodily changes is termed the **secular trend** (Garn, 1980; Katchadourian, 1977; Tanner, 1991). Since 1900, changes in height and weight occurring during the adolescent growth spurt have involved gains of 2.5 centimetres and 2.5 kilograms, respectively (Falkner, 1972; Katchadourian, 1977).

As shown in Figure 3.6a, there has been a historical trend downward in the average age of menarche. Among European samples of youth there was a decrease of about four months per decade from about 1840 to about 1950 (Tanner, 1962, 1973, 1991). Although this rate of decrease seems to have slowed down in some countries, it may not have stopped (Marshall & Tanner, 1986; Tanner, 1991). However, as revealed in Figure 3.6b, in some countries the secular trend seems to have levelled off or even reversed. Within samples in the United States, the decline in age of menarche seems to have stopped around 1940. Since that time, 12.5 years has been the expected age for menarche among European American, middle-class adolescents in the United States. In Japan the most dramatic secular trend was evidenced. From the immediate post–World War II years until about 1975, there was a decline of 11 months a decade in the average age of menarche (Marshall & Tanner, 1986). As suggested, the secular trend in menarche is generally explained by the improved health and nutrition of children and adolescents, influences moderated by historical, cultural, and socioeconomic variables affecting a given society or group. There is also some suggestion that greater exposure to estrogens (e.g., from hormones added to beef) may be a reason for the secular trend (Duplisea, 2001, Huen, Leung, Lau, Cheung, Leung, & Chui, 1997). Although a feasible hypothesis, there is little published data as yet to evaluate it.

The bodily changes of adolescence vary in relation to social, cultural, and historical settings. Given such variation, we may expect differences among adolescents in their rate of physical maturation. But if the pubertal changes of adolescence are so dependent on

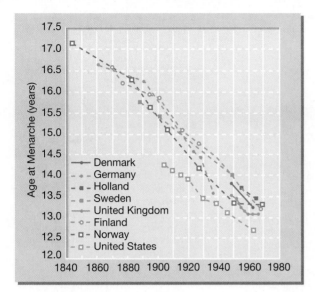

Figure 3.6a
Historically declining age of menarche.
(*Source:* Tanner, 1973)

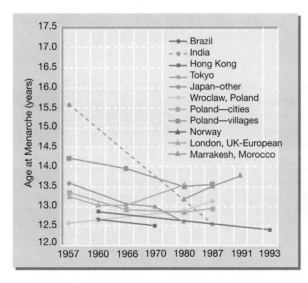

Figure 3.6b
Updated historically declining age of menarche.
(*Sources:* Kac et al., 2000; Sharma, 1990; Hiernaux, 1968; Huen et al., 1997; Hoshi & Kouchi, 1981; Tsuzaki et al., 1989; Hulanicka & Waliszko, 1991; Rosenberg, 1991; Ulijaszek, Evans, & Miller, 1991; Loukid & Hilali, 1996.)

social, cultural, and historical conditions, may it also be the case that the implications of these biological changes for psychological and social development are also contextually influenced?

Implications of Differences Among Adolescents in Their Pubertal Maturation

ISSUE TO CONSIDER

● How is the influence of the hormonal changes of puberty consistent with the developmental systems idea?

The influence of the hormonal changes of puberty on psychological and social behaviour and development during adolescence occurs in a manner consistent with the integrative developmental systems ideas we discussed in Chapters 1 and 2. The biological influences in adolescence occur in relation to physiological and social influences (Susman, 1997).

The research of Elizabeth J. Susman has been central in understanding these relations. Some of her recent research is presented in Meet the Researcher Box 3.2.

Research About Puberty and the Developmental System

ISSUES TO CONSIDER

● How does pubertal change and pubertal timing affect behaviour? What is the interacting variable that causes pubertal influences on behaviour?

● How does pubertal change and timing alter the relationship with the family?

Research aimed at understanding whether or how pubertal maturation influences an individual's development has taken one of two general approaches. First, studies have tried to determine whether pubertal change per se affects emotional and/or cognitive changes (Hill & Holmbeck, 1987; Hill et al., 1985a, 1985b; Papini & Datan, 1983; Steinberg, 1981) and, second, the effects of timing of pubertal maturation have been investigated (Brooks-Gunn, Petersen, & Eichorn, 1985). The second idea has been to determine if maturing earlier or later than is normative for one's sex-specific age group is associated with psychosocial functioning. One rationale for studying potential effects of pubertal timing is that, by assessing the extremes of normal variation, we may obtain a clearer view of more subtle effects associated with normative or on-time pubertal change.

One conclusion that can be drawn from these studies is that there exist few consistent (e.g., Nottelmann et al., 1987) direct effects of puberty or pubertal timing on emotional or cognitive function-

Successful Passages Through Puberty and Pregnancy During Adolescence

Elizabeth J. Susman is the Jean Phillips Shibley Professor of Biobehavioral Health at The Pennsylvania State University. She was a co-editor of *Journal of Research on Adolescence* and participates in many U.S. government and foundation-sponsored activities related to health and development in adolescents.

The biological transitions that occur in development, like puberty and pregnancy, bring both opportunities for independence and new roles and risks for new problems. These changes may be welcomed by some adolescents but may lead to problems in others. In the case of puberty, rapid and pervasive changes occur in chemical messengers, called hormones, and in physical growth. For decades, scientists, parents, and adolescents have pondered whether changes in hormones and growth, like increases in height, weight, and body proportions, are related to changes in moods and behaviour, like depression and anxiety and aggressive behaviour.

My colleagues and I have studied hormone change related to pubertal development and hormones secreted when adolescents are feeling stressed. The hormones that bring about pubertal development include estrogen and testosterone. The hormone secreted under stressful conditions is cortisol. When hormones were measured in adolescents during puberty, the hormones estrogen and testosterone were lower in boys with aggressive behaviour than in boys who were not aggressive. In girls, estrogen was related to expressing anger toward parents, attempting to dominate parents, and other problem interactions with parents. In another aspect of the study, my colleagues and I showed that as testosterone levels increased, boys' ability to solve spatial problems also

increased. To assess how the stress hormone cortisol changed during a challenging situation, it was measured at three different times when blood was being obtained for the hormones just mentioned. The stress of having blood drawn can change cortisol levels. Adolescents who increased in cortisol level during the challenging situation later developed more behaviour problems and symptoms of depression than adolescents who showed no change in levels or who decreased in cortisol levels. An increase in cortisol levels during a stressful event is considered a risk factor for problems. In summary, the hormones that increase at puberty are related to aggressive behaviour and emotions during adolescence. These findings do not mean that these behaviours or emotions are abnormal or that all adolescents have difficulty interacting with their parents during puberty. But hormones do appear to make a difference in the lives of adolescents at puberty.

My colleagues and I also have studied hormones and emotions in pregnant adolescents. As discussed for puberty, scientists and individuals responsible for the health care of adolescents have wondered whether the hormone changes that occur during pregnancy are related to moods in pregnant adolescents. The moods that adolescents sometimes experience, like depression, anger, and anxiety, are likely to become even more intense during pregnancy because of the hormone

changes that occur as well as the changes that adolescents must make in their social lives while pregnant. Much to our surprise, the emotions of pregnant adolescents did not differ from emotions in adolescents of the same age who were not pregnant. As in the case of pubertal age adolescents, increases in cortisol levels in a challenging situation were related to emotions, in this case depression. Although change in cortisol level is considered a risk factor for problems, cortisol changes did not predict problems in the infants of these teens.

There is still much to be learned about how hormones affect emotions and behaviour and even more to be learned about how behaviour affects hormones and other physiological substances. Scientists from many different fields now are conducting research in the field of hormones, behaviour, and brain development. This work is important and exciting as the findings will likely give insights into why some adolescents become depressed or aggressive whereas other adolescents experience no behaviour problems or problematic changes in emotions.

ing (e.g., Crockett & Petersen, 1987; Petersen, 1985, 1987) and certainly no strong effects (Linn & Petersen, 1985). Although some relationships between puberty and the development of problems such as depression, eating disorders, and norm-breaking behaviours have been identified (Alsaker, 1995), these associations have been linked to the developmental system of the adolescent.

To illustrate the nature of the links between

puberty and psychological and social functioning, consider the findings of a study of more than 400 mostly European American students in Grades 5 through 9 living in the suburbs of Chicago. For girls, there was no relationship found between puberty and their moods or their mood changes (Richards & Larson, 1993). For boys, there were small relationships between being in a more advanced stage of puberty and positive mood, better attention, feelings of strength, and increased feelings of tension (Richards & Larson, 1993).

In contrast, in a sample of more than 1000 girls and more than 1200 boys from Bergen, Norway, adolescents' *perceptions* that they were early maturers (relative to their peers) were related in girls in Grades 6 through 8 to poor body image and negative self-evaluation (Alsaker, 1992). In boys, the perception of late maturation was associated with negative self-evaluations, whereas early maturation was related to more positive self-evaluations (Alsaker, 1992). In a study of 52 young adolescent girls living in a midwestern suburban community of the United States, girls who felt they were experiencing pubertal change reported more negative moods and nervousness, and more variation in their negative moods, than did prepubertal girls (Buchanan, 1991).

Associations found between puberty level and change and emotional functioning vary from study to study for both boys and girls. Thus there is little if any support that emotional and cognitive changes are invariant, direct outcomes of puberty. To illustrate, consider some results of two major longitudinal studies of early adolescence, the Petersen Early Adolescence Study (EAS), an investigation of youth in Grades 6 through 8 growing up in the suburbs of Chicago (Crockett & Petersen, 1987; Petersen, 1987), and the Lerner and Lerner Pennsylvania Early Adolescent Transitions Study (PEATS), an investigation of Grade 6 youth from a semirural area of northwestern Pennsylvania (Lenerz et al., 1987). These studies measured a number of psychosocial variables longitudinally, ranging from school achievement and cognitive ability to temperament, self-perceived competence, and behaviour. For the boys in the Petersen study, only 2 of 12 variables showed **statistically significant** relationships with age. For girls, 5 of the 12 variables were statistically significant.

Results from the Lerner and Lerner study of children from the beginning, middle, and end of the Grade 6 school year also found most relations studied to be nonsignificant (only 8 of 30 variables for boys across the school year showed significant change; 2 of these variables showed significant change for girls). The few relations that are statistically significant do not appear to be systematic or repeatable across studies. It might be concluded that pubertal change has little to do with an adolescent's psychological or social functioning, that the physiological developmental task is not so complicated after all, and, despite the vast number of bodily changes that

occur in adolescence, there is little of importance to threaten or challenge the adolescent's sense of who he or she is.

Such conclusions would be incorrect. Pubertal change and pubertal timing do have fairly consistent and in many cases strong relationships with behaviour. These relationships do not involve the *direct*, intrapsychic, inevitably stormy and stressful associations predicted in the stereotype of the period (A. Freud, 1969; Hall, 1904). The influence of an adolescent's pubertal characteristics on behaviour involves interactions with his or her particular social context.

Influences of the Context on Puberty-Behaviour Relations

ISSUE TO CONSIDER
• How does the social context influence the relation between puberty and adolescent behaviour?

Several studies indicate that pubertal *change* can alter adolescents' social interactions and relationships with parents. Other studies suggest that pubertal *timing* may also influence young adolescents' relationships with parents (e.g., Clausen, 1975; Petersen, 1985; Savin-Williams & Small, 1986; Steinberg, 1987).

To illustrate these associations between puberty and family functioning, note that in some types of families more conflict and greater emotional distance is seen in relation to an adolescent's pubertal changes (e.g., Hill & Holmbeck, 1987; Hill et al., 1985a, 1985b; Papini & Datan, 1983; Steinberg, 1977, 1981, 1986; Steinberg & Hill, 1978). In a study of 85 mostly European American two-parent families with adolescents in Grades 5 through 9, more advanced physical maturation in the youth was associated with the expression of *negative* affect by both mothers and fathers (Montemayor, Eberly, & Flannery, 1993). The level of parental and adolescent *positive* affect was not related to pubertal status.

These associations between adolescent pubertal change and relationships with parents may not necessarily be generalized to families of all racial/ethnic backgrounds. Among samples of primarily Mexican American boys and their families, pubertal

Statistical significance
Statistical significance is reached when the results could not have been caused by random chance alone.

maturation brought youth *closer* to their parents (Molina & Chassin, 1996). Puberty among these Latino youth is associated with greater parental social support and less intergenerational conflict than is the case for corresponding samples of European American samples of youth.

Steinberg (1981, 1988) found that increases in pubertal maturation were associated with different changes in "emotional distance" (that is, increased conflict and decreased closeness) between sons and their parents depending on the sex of the parent. Increased maturation in boys was associated with fewer interruptions of and more deference toward their fathers, with an increase in the tendency for boys to interrupt their mothers during conversations and with a decrease in deference to their mothers.

Indicative of increased conflicts in the mother-son relationship during periods of pubertal growth, Steinberg found that mothers showed a tendency to increasingly interrupt their sons during conversations. However, mothers' deference to sons increased after the boys reached the height of their pubertal maturation (Grotevant, 1998; Steinberg, 1981, 1988). In contrast, among Grade 7 girls menarche was followed by a withdrawal of positive affect and a temporary period of conflict, especially between daughters and mothers (Holmbeck & Hill, 1988; Grotevant, 1998).

Despite such implications of pubertal maturation on adolescent-parent relationships, Grotevant (1998) notes that the relationship between the biological changes of adolescence and the relationships of youth with their parents often involves quite contradictory behaviours. Grotevant notes that there is both distancing from parents and a tendency for youth to use their parents as a "buffer" (as a source of support and protection) against some of the potential social pressures that may be linked to looking and feeling more physically mature. For instance, among Grade 7 males and females, increases in pubertal maturation were generally associated with decreased attachments to mothers and fathers; however, higher levels of attachment to mothers and fathers were linked to lower levels of depression and to lessened social anxiety (Papini, Roggman, & Anderson, 1991).

There have been repeated demonstrations that the social context influences the relation between puberty and adolescent behaviour and development in numerous ways. In regard to pubertal change, the research of Simmons and her colleagues (e.g., Simmons & Blyth, 1987; Simmons, Carlton-Ford,

Although adolescents may at times distance themselves from parents, they also typically remain attached to them.

& Blyth, 1987) has shown that the relationship between pubertal changes in girls and their self-esteem involves the co-occurrence of contextual change, that is, the transition to junior high school (see Chapter 11 for a fuller discussion of the relations between school transitions and adolescent development). The research of Dornbusch and his colleagues (e.g., Dornbusch et al., 1981) indicates that the social context can moderate any potential effect of puberty on behaviour. Social norms regarding the appropriate age for dating, rather than pubertal maturation, determined adolescents' heterosexual dating behaviours.

The research of Brooks-Gunn (1987) indicates that the particular social context within which an adolescent functions moderates the link between pubertal timing and behaviour. Brooks-Gunn studied adolescent girls who were enrolled in highly competitive and physically strenuous schools for ballet and a comparison group of adolescent girls enrolled in a regular school setting. Within the ballet schools, extremely strong pressures existed for especially thin body builds, whereas no such intense pressures existed in the social contexts of the comparison group girls. Brooks-Gunn (1987) expected that in the comparison group, neither late nor on-time maturation would be related to a measure of body image, even though on-time maturation was related to high body weight in both groups. Brooks-Gunn also predicted that the pressures of the dancers' social context would mean that late maturation would be related to a better body image than would be the case with on-time maturation. These predictions were supported by Brooks-Gunn's findings.

The pressures of competing, for example, in ballet, may complicate the ability of the adolescent to cope with the physical transitions of puberty.

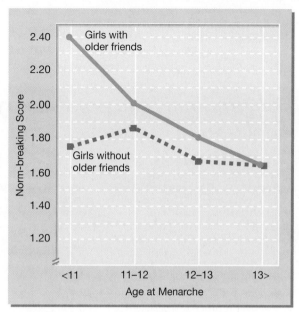

Figure 3.8
Relation between norm-breaking and menarcheal age for girls with and without older friends
(*Source:* Magnusson et al., 1986)

Magnusson and his colleagues (e.g., Magnusson, Stattin, & Allen, 1986; Stattin & Magnusson, 1990) found that the relation between girls' early maturation and their problem behaviours was moderated by the specific characteristics of their peer context. Early maturing girls with older friends tend to break more norms (see Figure 3.7) and expect fewer sanctions from peers if they break norms than is the case for early maturing girls without older friends (see

Figure 3.8). Meet the Researcher Box 3.3 presents more information about the work of David Magnusson.

In a four-year longitudinal study of about 200 girls, early maturation was associated with more psychological distress than was the case in regard to on-time or late maturation (Ge, Conger, & Elder, 1996). The early maturing girls were more vulnerable to prior psychological problems, deviant peer pressures, and hostile feelings from their fathers. However, the association between maturational timing and distress was linked to the nature of the girls' peer groups. If early maturing girls had peer groups during Grades 7 through 9 composed of both boys and girls, they were more distressed in Grade 10 than were early maturing girls who had peer groups in earlier grades composed only of girls (Ge et al., 1996).

Conclusions About the Implications of Puberty for Psychological and Social Behaviour

Adolescents vary in their rate of physical maturation. Although this variation influences their personality

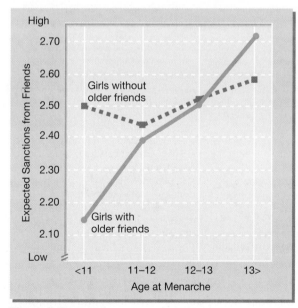

Figure 3.7
Relation between expected peer sanctions for norm-breaking and menarcheal age for girls with and without older friends
(*Source:* Magnusson et al., 1986.)

MEET THE RESEARCHER   Box 3.3   David Magnusson

Longitudinal Study of Puberty and Adolescent Development and Adaptation

David Magnusson is Olof Eneroth professor emeritus of psychology at the Department of Psychology, Stockholm University. He is the author of *Individual Development from an Interactional Perspective* (1988). As vice president of the European Science Foundation, he initiated and chaired the European Network on Longitudinal Studies on Individual Development, from which eight volumes on developmental issues were published during the years 1988 to 1993.

My own interest in research on adolescence has two roots. Substantively, it emanates from my experiences as an elementary school teacher and as a school psychologist responsible for a class of male and female problem youngsters in a Stockholm suburb in the mid-1950s. In terms of research strategy and methodology, my interest stems from my dissatisfaction with the kind of knowledge about adolescence that the literature offered at that time and from my experiences of teaching psychometrics at the university.

When I had to deal with and sometimes make decisions about young people in real-life situations—not as an observer in the lab—I asked myself, over and over again, questions like these: Why do some girls who mature earlier biologically than their age-mates often show what adults call norm-breaking behaviour? Does this behaviour have long-term effects on their life careers? What is the developmental background of deviant behaviours among male youngsters and what are the implications for the future? Why is it that most of the boys who come from so-called risky home environments do not become criminals and/or alcoholics? What are the protective factors that lead to a positive rather than a negative development?

In order to contribute empirical answers to these questions in the framework of knowledge about the processes involved in individual development in general, I initiated the longitudinal research program IDA (Individual Development and Adaptation), in which the first data were collected in 1965. The main cohort consisted of all boys and girls, about 1300 at an average age of 10, attending the general school system in a community of reasonable size in central Sweden. The program is still active, since 1996 under the leadership of Lars R. Bergman.

Two issues pertaining to puberty and adolescence have been the foci of studies under the program in collaboration with colleagues and students. The first is the timing and synchronization of girls' mental, biological, and behavioural aspects and the sociocultural demands in terms of rules, regulations, and role expectations that a girl has to handle and master during this period and the long-term implications of the way these problems are solved. At present, female life careers, focusing on the developmental background of adult mental and physical health, are being studied after the collection of relevant data for the females at the age of 43 to 44. These data now provide a unique opportunity to study the role for the adult life situation of the girl's transformation from a girl into a woman during puberty and early adolescence.

The second focus was, for a long time, the role of psychological, biological, and social factors in the developmental background of deviant behaviours among male youngsters and young adults. Recently, my own interest has been extended to include the study of what promotes human strengths and positive development. In theoretical terms, the design, implementation, and interpretation of studies within the program have been guided by the proposition that an individual functions and develops as an integrated, indivisible organism, intentionally involved in reciprocal, dynamic interaction with the environment. At present I am concerned with the processes involved in the very early establishment of the integrated individual system of mental, biological, and behavioural aspects that form the platform for further developmental processes through childhood, puberty, adolescence, adulthood, and aging.

In planning the longitudinal program and in designing, implementing, and interpreting studies on specific developmental issues, I have gained from my early psychometric work and from teaching psychometrics at the university. My experiences of how psychometric methods were used and misused in experimental and applied settings taught me the importance of applying methods that match the character of the developmental processes in which we are interested. This issue has occupied much of my time and does so still. Good solutions to this matching issue are, to my mind, one of the most important tasks for further progress in research on puberty and adolescence.

and social behaviour, it is not a direct influence. Indirect, mediated, or interactive pubertal effects exist through their relation and moderation of the social context (Lerner, 1985, 1987; Petersen, 1985, 1987). The adolescent meets the developmental task of dealing with his or her changed body and physiology through interaction with the social context. Some of these interactions between puberty and psychological and social functioning may be adaptive, but others may cause problems for adolescents.

Adolescent Health Issues Associated with Pubertal Change

ISSUES TO CONSIDER
- What is resiliency?
- What is the prime influence on adolescent health problems?
- How does the sleep cycle change in adolescence, and how does it affect adolescent behaviour?

Generally, adolescence is a period of health (Koch, Maney, & Susman, 1993; Pattishall, 1984). It is a time relatively free from disease (Koch et al., 1993). As well, adolescents possess considerable physical and physiological ability during this period to overcome adversity, or to be *resilient.*

Indeed, even chronically ill adolescents may show considerable **resiliency** to the stress of their disease. In fact, adolescents with chronic disease can be remarkably like their healthy peers. For instance, Italian adolescents with thalassemia major (a type of blood disorder) have normal psychological and social development and self-esteem as high if not better than their healthy peers (Zani, Di Palma, & Vullo, 1995). In turn, the experience of life stressors or of variation in social support by adolescents with juvenile rheumatic disease is unrelated to the outcomes of the disease on their health (Timko et al., 1995), although—as with healthy adolescents—increases in negative life events, life stressors, and problematic social support does impact their psychological and social functioning.

Moreover, adolescents may benefit psychologically when they pursue healthy lifestyles. For example, valuing health and positive health behaviour was related to self-esteem among 12- to 13-year-old and 16- to 17-year-old Spanish youth (Torres, Fernandez, & Maceira, 1995). In turn, adolescents' views about health may be influenced by their families. For instance, adolescent self-reported physical health is linked to their parents' levels of education (Wickrama et al., 1998).

Of course, adolescents are also confronted with serious challenges to their health (Koch et al., 1993; Millstein, 1989; Pattishall, 1984). The adolescent's own behaviour is the major influence on these health problems. Consistent with the selection, optimization, and compensation (SOC) model (Baltes, 1987; Baltes & Baltes, 1990; Freund & Baltes, 1998) of adolescent behaviour discussed in Chapter 2, youth select courses of action that influence their

adaptation and health. Accidents (e.g., via motor vehicles), suicides, substance use and abuse, unsafe sexual behaviours, violence to and by adolescents, eating disorders, and even insufficient rest are examples of adolescent health problems affected by the youths' behaviour. In later chapters, we discuss many of these problems (for example, in Chapter 10 we discuss problems relating to adolescent sexuality and in Chapter 13 we review problems linked to substance use and to crime and violence). Nevertheless, it is useful here to illustrate how adolescent behaviour may influence adolescent health. In turn, it is important in the present chapter to discuss health problems linked to pubertal change.

To begin to illustrate, then, the association between adolescent behaviour and health, it is useful to note that sleep and waking cycles change significantly during adolescence (Wolfson & Carskadon, 1998). Many of these changes are due to choices made by the adolescent. In a study of more than 3000 Rhode Island high school students, self-reported total sleep time on both school and weekend nights decreased by about 50 minutes from age 13 to age 19 (Wolfson & Carskadon, 1998). The decrease in sleep was associated with later bedtimes rather than earlier wake-up times. Students with better grades got, on average, more sleep and went to bed earlier than students who were doing poorly in school. However, all adolescents, despite their grades, did not get enough sleep, and this lack of sleep interfered with their daytime functioning (Wolfson & Carskadon, 1998). Habekothe and Van Den Wittenboer (2000) reported that 43% of the early adolescents they studied in Amsterdam had difficulties getting up in the morning and that 25% did not feel rested at school. Quality of sleep in their study was related to school functioning, particularly achievement motivation. Carskadon (1999) suggested that schools may want to consider changing the hour that they begin the school day, as junior high and high school tend to start earlier than elementary schools, yet adolescents seem to need to sleep later in the mornings than do younger children.

Resiliency Presence of considerable physical and physiological ability to overcome adversities.

Puberty and Health

ISSUE TO CONSIDER

• What are some examples of physical problems that can result from pubertal changes?

Beyond the influences of the behavioural choices made by adolescents, pubertal changes can also impact adolescent health. Variations in the rate of bodily changes in adolescence can be sufficiently extreme to affect the health of the young person. For example, **delayed puberty** and **precocious puberty** are related to the insufficient production or the early production of hormones (Cutler, 1991). These disorders are elicited by early or late hormone production. However, although primarily biological in origin, whether they are treated or whether they cause long-term problems for the person depends on the availability in society of the necessary medical treatments (Comite et al., 1987).

Initially, pubertal changes that cause physical problems may be known only to the adolescent. Painful menstruation, known as **dysmenorrhea**, and the failure to menstruate, known as **amenorrhea**, may have both medical and emotional causes. Other physical disorders are noticeable to others. Acne (a skin condition characterized by blackheads, pimples, and cysts) causes great concern to adolescents because it is visible to others. It is the most common medical condition during this period of life. About 85% of adolescents have acne at least some time during the adolescent period (Pattishall, 1984).

As a consequence of pubertal change, there are variations in height, weight, and muscle and fat distributions and adolescents often become preoccupied with their own bodies (Elkind, 1967; Lerner, 1987; McCandless, 1970; Perkins & Lerner, 1995). As illustrated by the conversation between Tina and her mother that opened this chapter, this preoccupation can result in particularly trying problems for parents. Changes in the adolescent's bodily appearance may puzzle and challenge a parent, particularly when their child(ren) are just beginning to undergo the changes of puberty. Implications for Parenting Box 3.1 describes these challenges for parents and suggests ways in which they may deal with their adolescents' bodily changes.

Body Image

Girls' dissatisfaction with their bodies seems to increase over the course of adolescence. A Health Canada survey (1998) found that the proportion of girls who were on a diet or felt they should be on one rose from 28% in Grade 6 to 41% in Grade 8 to 44% in Grade 10. In a sample of adolescent girls from Ontario, disturbed eating attitudes or behaviours were found to increase from 13% of 12- to 14-year-olds to 16% of 15- to 18-year-olds (Jones, Bennett, Olmsted, Lawson, & Rodin, 2001). Bingeing and purging also increased with age in these Ontario adolescents, from 18.8% of 12- to 14-year-olds to 26% of 15- to 18-year-olds. This increase may be related to pubertal status, as Thompson and Chad (2000) from the University of Saskatchewan found that the proportion of girls who were dissatisfied with their body shape grew from 34% among prepubescent girls to 36% among early pubescent girls and 76% among postpubescent girls in their sample of 7- to 16-year-old girls.

Although three-quarters of the participants in a province-wide survey of children in Grades 7 through 12 in British Columbia were deemed by the researchers to be of healthy weight, only half perceived themselves to be so (the McCreary Centre, 1999b). Forty-one percent of girls reported themselves to be overweight; 27% of boys reported themselves to be underweight. No tests of statistical significance were presented in these reports.

Adolescents' concerns with their own bodily changes can result in problems for youth. Adolescents are preoccupied with their weight and with controlling their appearance through their eating behaviours. These behaviours may involve not only unnecessary dieting but also problems of eating that are detrimental to their health and may even threaten their lives. Adolescent girls are more likely than adolescent boys to have eating disorders such as **anorexia nervosa** or **bulimia**. However, both sexes may show attitudes toward food and to eating

---

Delayed puberty Being behind schedule, for a given age group, in reaching puberty.
Precocious puberty Early or premature puberty.

Dysmenorrhea Difficult or painful menstruation.
Amenorrhea Failure to menstruate.

Anorexia nervosa Eating disorder characterized by low body weight due to a person's misperception of his or her body image and by the

mistaken belief that he or she is overweight.
Bulimia Eating disorder characterized by self-induced binge eating and purging behaviour.

My Body Is So Ugly!

With the bathroom door locked, 12-year-old Anya carefully examines her still shower-damp body. She pokes disgustedly at her stomach. A year ago, her body felt comfortable and familiar. But the one in the mirror has new curves, and hair she isn't sure she likes. Maybe she should try that diet Becky told her about. Sighing, Anya pulls on her oversize black sweatshirt.

To their parents, it often seems as if young teenagers and preteens such as Anya are obsessed with their bodies, and that they are determined that their weight, height, and shape be regarded as desirable, or at least acceptable, to their peers. In fact, by age seven—if not sooner—children know which body shapes are considered best. By the early teens, the forms that children's bodies take become crucial to their sense of who they are.

All children this age will complain from time to time about being the wrong size or shape, even when they seemingly fit well within the norm for their peer group or their family. When a child becomes obsessed with appearance, however, there is genuine cause for concern. This is particularly true for young girls: because of the pressure they feel to remain slim in order to be considered attractive, they suffer from body-image problems more often than boys do.

In general, your best response to these complaints is to listen and then to reassure your child that everyone's body goes through awkward changes around this age. Make sure, though, that you don't supply your child with so much sympathy that you make the problem bigger than it is. For example, if your daughter is upset because she looks "dumpy" in a dress she likes, you can commiserate with her briefly by saying, "I remember how frustrating it was when my body was changing. We all grow out of it, though, thank goodness. In the meantime, let's try to find a dress that is better suited to your figure."

Girls' early maturity can cause anxieties

Much of the confusion preteens feel about their bodies has its origins, unsurprisingly, in puberty. On average, the first period for a girl arrives when she is between 12 and 13 years old, with changes in body hair and shape, including breast development, starting even earlier. Because girls typically start puberty two years earlier than boys, most 10- or 11-year-old girls are bigger and taller than their male counterparts—ironically enough, just at the time when boys begin really wanting to be taller, and girls trimmer.

While the changes that come with puberty often make life difficult for girls, with boys the reverse is frequently true. Puberty, for them, means more weight and bigger muscles, in addition to sexual development—all physical qualities that we are taught to admire. Therefore, boys who mature early tend to be popular and are more likely to be seen as leaders by peers and adults.

Although these social advantages may last throughout life, it is also often the case that early maturers, by the time they're finished growing, are no bigger or stronger than the late bloomers; the Grade 7 sports hero isn't necessarily destined for the National Hockey League.

But how can you prepare your early-blooming athlete for a more competitive future without deflating his pride at his accomplishments? You might try saying something along the lines of, "I'm very proud of what a good football player you are. But, you know, other boys are going to catch up to you in size eventually, so if you want to continue to be a strong competitor, you have to keep practising."

Late-blooming boys need your reassurance

If your son is distressed because—for the time being, at least—he's shorter and less muscular than his peers, you can help him in several ways. First of all, you might tell him something like, "You know, it's normal for some boys to mature more slowly than others. I realize that it's hard to be patient sometimes, but your time will come, and if you practise and exercise now, it will really pay off later on."

Meanwhile, build your son's self-confidence by encouraging activities that set his intellectual or artistic abilities to good advantage while also promoting sports that are appropriate to his body build. Gymnastics and soccer are often well suited to shorter boys, whereas tall, slim boys often excel at track and field or basketball.

While puberty is often at the root of differences in body build among children this age, other factors such as obesity can play a harmful role. Research shows that preteens see being fat as a greater physical obstacle to popularity even than missing an arm or a leg. In one landmark study, youth were shown drawings of children who were disabled along with children who were obese: youth consistently chose the fat children as the ones they would least like to be, or to be friends with.

Unfortunately, although researchers aren't exactly sure why, a majority of preteen girls want their weight to be below average, and therefore are often unhappy with themselves for having what medical experts consider a normal, healthy weight.

Diet-conscious girls need your attention

If your daughter is constantly dieting, chances are good that she's not getting the nutrients she needs for a body that is still growing. She may also be forming a pattern of dieting and bingeing that will carry into adulthood, with adverse long-term health consequences. Should she frequently complain of being overweight when she clearly is not, or should there be a sudden, unexplained shift in her eating habits accompanied by changes in her mood, then she may be having problems accepting her weight.

How can you help her? Start by examining your own attitudes and habits. Do you often complain of feeling fat, or compare your figure unfavourably with those of models in magazines or on television? Do you fluctuate between restricting your diet and indulging yourself? If so, without realizing it, you may be encouraging your child to dislike her post-puberty body.

Whether your child imagines that she is heavy or is genuinely overweight, you

>

> can best address the problem by focusing not on her eating habits but on your family's. Stick to a sensible, nutritious meal plan, and keep the emphasis on health rather than weight so that your daughter can think of changing her body in positive terms rather than negative

ones. If you criticize her eating choices too often, or forbid her to eat certain foods, you'll only create power struggles that won't do either of you any good.

Finally, keep reminding your preteen that her body is still working toward its eventual shape, and that

while her body's shape and size are hard to control at this time in her life, she still has control over something that's much more important—her good health.

Source: Lerner, R. M., & Olson, C. K. (1995, February). My body is so ugly! Parents, pp. 87–88.

behaviours that are dangerous. These problematic attitudes may exist even at elementary school levels and are often predictors of disordered eating. Disordered eating is associated with other unhealthy behaviours, such as smoking, use of drugs or alcohol, and depression (Jones et al., 2001; the McCreary Centre, 1999b). The McCreary Centre's survey (1999b) found that 3% of the 13- to 17-year-old girls and 1% of the boys in their sample reported self-induced vomiting. A higher number (15% of the girls and 9% of the boys) admitted binge eating at least twice a month. A small percentage reported using diet pills or laxatives (3% of girls and 2% of boys) in the week prior to the survey.

Health Canada (1998) found that 16% of 15-year-old girls were on a diet at the time of its study. However, a comparison with 10 other countries revealed that many have greater ratios of dieters. Only Sweden, at 8%, had a lower proportion of girls on diets. Switzerland and Denmark had rates similar to that of Canada. Norway, at 28%, had the greater proportion dieting, followed by the United States, with 25%.

In a sample of more than 500 adolescent 13- and 14-year-olds from Spain, 12.4% of the girls and 8.3% of the boys had risky attitudes toward eating (Canals et al., 1996). For both boys and girls, low self-esteem and high anxiety were related to problematic attitudes about eating. The attitudes of the girls, however, were more prototypic of pathological eating disorders than was the case for the boys' attitudes (Canals et al., 1996). Heavy and obese male

and female adolescents were at high risk of having an actual eating disorder.

Although more rare among males than females, boys do exhibit eating disorders (R. Olivardia, H. G. Pope, Jr., B. Mangweth, & J. I. Hudson, 1995). However, males are more likely to perceive themselves as being underweight than overweight. For example, college men in Austria, France, and the United States preferred a body shape that was about 13 kilograms more muscular than their own shape (Pope, Gruber, Mangweth, & Bureau, 2000). Donald McCreary at the Regina Health District and Doris Sasse from Brock University created the Drive for Muscularity Scale (2000) that found that boys had a stronger drive for muscularity than girls. For boys (but not girls), a high drive was associated with low self-esteem and depression. Adolescents who had such a drive engaged in more weight training and a high-calorie diet in an attempt to gain weight.

Dissatisfaction with their bodies leads some males to develop "muscle dysphoria," a body image so distorted that they are driven to exercise (e.g., lifting weights) to the point of hurting themselves, and may abuse **anabolic steroids** (Choi, Pope, Olivardia, & Cash, 2002). In fact, a survey of 1800 adolescents in one Ontario school district found that 7% of boys in Grade 11 were taking steroids (Haldimond-Norfolk Health Unit, 2002). A Canadian national survey of students from Grades 6 to 12 found a slightly lower percentage; 2.8% reported using anabolic steroids in the year prior to the survey (Melia, Pipe, & Greenberg, 1996). Steroids are addictive and withdrawal can be unpleasant (Alberta Alcohol and Drug Abuse Commission, 2000). Melia et al. (1996) found that students in their survey reported using a number of other substances in an attempt to improve their athletic performance. Twenty-seven percent of their sample reported using caffeine for this reason; 27% used extra protein,

Anabolic steroids Synthetic derivatives of testosterone, the primary natural androgen that is responsible for androgenic (masculinizing) and anabolic effects.

8.6% tried alcohol, 9% used painkillers, and 3.1% used stimulants.

A recent report from Statistics Canada (Che, 2002) revealed that 35% of girls aged 15 to 19 were actually underweight, according to their Body Mass Index (BMI). Another 22% of boys this age were also underweight. Thirty-three percent of individuals of all ages who were underweight were also smokers as opposed to 29% of those whose weights fell within healthy range. Che suggested that smoking may have been used as a method of weight control.

Eating Disorders

ISSUES TO CONSIDER
- What are some examples of eating disorders?
- What are the implications of having an eating disorder?
- What are some factors that may influence the existence of an eating disorder?

Obesity can be an outcome of a type of eating disorder that affects a significant minority of adolescents. When a person is 20% above the average weight associated with others of his or her height, he or she can be classified as obese (Katchadourian, 1977). An international study revealed that in Canada, 6% of males and 8% of females aged 18 to 24 were obese (Macdonald, 1999). There is no known cure for obesity, although increasing regular physical activity and following a moderately low-calorie diet may help an adolescent maintain normal body fat levels (Freedland & Dwyer, 1991). Unfortunately, many North American youth, particularly females, follow rather sedentary lifestyles (Freedland & Dwyer, 1991). A 1998–99 Statistics Canada survey confirmed this. Among 12- to 14-year-old boys, 16.6% exercised less than three times per week. This rose to 23.5% of 15- to 19-year-old boys. For girls, 20.4% of the younger group and 35.6% of the older group exercised less than three times weekly. This is important because a province-wide survey of children in Grades 7 through 12 conducted by the McCreary Centre (1999a) in British Columbia found that body image was related to physical activity. Of those who were satisfied with their bodies, 73% exercised at least three times per week (as opposed to 60% of dissatisfied youth). Looking more specifically at adolescents' feelings about their weight (as opposed to general body dissatisfaction), those who believed they were very overweight or very underweight were more likely than those who felt their weight was fine to report having exercised less than three times in the week before the survey (40% versus 27%).

Less frequent, but even more severe in their effects than overeating and not exercising are anorexia nervosa and bulimia. Girls are 10 times more likely to be affected by these disorders than are boys (Litt, 1991). In industrialized nations, the rates of anorexia nervosa and bulimia have increased about 400% over the last 20 years (Litt, 1991). Anorexia nervosa involves severe loss of weight (a 25% loss of normal weight is not unusual) with no known medical explanation. However, recent work has focused on the possibility of a genetic component (e.g., Sissingh, 2002) or birth complications (Cnattingius, Hultman, Dahl, & Sparen, 1999) as possible causes. Surbey (1987) proposed an ethological perspective that suggested that some girls who are prone to early menarche develop anorexia as a means of delaying their reproductive capability. One of the primary symptoms of anorexia is delayed menarche or amenorrhea. Other female mammals suppress reproduction by a variety of means including delayed puberty when in stressful conditions or poor physical shape. This is thought to occur if giving birth at that time would be more risky to the offspring's survival than giving birth at a later date when conditions have improved. In many cases human females stop menstruating when under stress or when heavy exercise has severely reduced the proportion of fat on their bodies, conditions that may not be conducive to the survival of a child.

Anorexia may involve up to 1% of the total adolescent population (Pawluck & Gorey, 1998). Bulimia, a disorder characterized by uncontrolled binge eating and purging behaviours, has a reported prevalence among adolescent females of about 3%. But it is difficult to determine the prevalence of bulimia because it is harder to detect. Bulimia is not typically accompanied by severe weight loss. It may not be until the problem has existed for some time, that is, at a point where binge-purge episodes may occur as often as 10 to 12 times a day (Leon, 1991), that signs (such as gastrointestinal problems and tooth decay) become evident. Both anorexia nervosa and bulimia can cause severe medical problems and result in death. In advanced anorexia nervosa, heart muscle tissue begins to metabolize, which can cause heart attacks. The mortality rate for anorexia nervosa is estimated to be between 5% and 23% (Leon, 1991).

Obesity Condition characterized by an excessive accumulation of fat in the body.

Researchers at the University of Toronto found that adolescents with eating disorders have lower global self-esteem than other adolescents, and their feelings about their weight affect their self-esteem in the areas of appearance, social relationships, and performance at school or work (McFarlane, McCabe, Jarry, Olmsted, & Polivy, 2001).

There are both psychological and contextual influences on eating disorders. In addition to influences from attitudes and body appearance that were noted earlier, family variables can influence eating disorders in adolescence. Relationship and interaction patterns of the individuals within families of girls with bulimia show less attachment and less autonomy among family members than is the case within families with an adolescent daughter without bulimia (Ratti, Humphreys, & Lyons, 1996). Among adolescents with anorexia nervosa, as compared to normal adolescents, there is a greater likelihood of a history of family depression and alcohol or drug abuse or dependence and feelings of personal ineffectiveness than among adolescents without anorexia nervosa (Lyon et al., 1997).

Family influences on adolescents' eating problems occur in relation to the influences of peers. In a study of more than 800 Japanese adolescent girls in Grades 7 through 11, influences of both parents and peers were found (Mukai, 1996). During earlier grades, maternal influences were greater than peer influences. At higher grade levels (Grades 10 and 11), peer interactions had the most influence on girls' eating problems. Among 12- and 13-year-old girls, dating is associated with both dieting and disordered eating, especially among youth who recently experienced menarche (Cauffman & Steinberg, 1966).

The media may have some influence on the development of poor body image and eating disorders. The University of Alberta's Health Centre (2001) reported that fashion models weigh 23% less than the average woman. This has increased from 8% less than average in the mid-1970s. Fouts and Burggraf (1999) reported that 33% of female leads in situation comedies were underweight, whereas only 25% of the general population of women that age were underweight. Men in men's magazines (*GQ*, *Rolling Stone*, and *Sports Illustrated*) have become more muscular over the years, becoming more lean and "V-shaped" since the 1960s (Law & Peixoto Labre, 2002).

Conclusions

In adolescence, people experience the physical and physiological changes of puberty. The timing of puberty is influenced by the social, cultural, economic, medical, and historical contexts of youth. The implications of pubertal change for the health of the adolescent and for his or her psychological and social functioning occur in relation to the complex developmental system within which the young person is embedded. Puberty does affect psychological and social life, but the behavioural choices made by youth and the influences of their peers, parents, and culture also affect the presence and impact of puberty.

Summary

- Many adolescents feel unprepared for pubertal changes and report a need for more information about the nature and implications of pubertal change.
- Three stages of adolescence span the second decade of life: early adolescence (from 10 to 14 or 15 years of age), middle adolescence (from 15 to 17 years of age), and late adolescence (from 18 to 20 years of age).
- The prepubescent phase is when some of the physical and physiological changes of adolescence have begun, but most are yet to occur. The pubescent phase is when most of the bodily changes that will occur have been initiated. The postpubescent phase is when most of the bodily changes have already occurred.
- Prepubescence begins with the first indication of sexual maturation and ends with the first appearance of pubic hair. Pubescence occurs with the appearance of pubic hair and ends when pubic hair development is complete. Postpubescence starts when pubic hair growth is complete and

ends when the person is fertile and can reproduce.

- Pubertal maturation and bodily changes involve changes in hormones that are released from endocrine glands. When hormones are released, they stimulate the secretions of sex steroids, which results in the physical and physiological changes of pubertal maturation.
- Puberty is the point at which a person can reproduce, but it is only one event in the pubescent phase, which brings the person from childhood to adulthood.
- Primary sexual characteristics are present at birth and involve internal and external genitalia. Secondary sexual characteristics develop during the pre- through postpubescent phases.
- There is variation in the speed of pubertal maturation. A person can be an early maturer, an on-time maturer, or a late maturer. The different rates of development occur because of genetic, social, and cultural differences.
- The secular trend is the relation between history and adolescent bodily changes.
- Biological influences in adolescence occur in relation to physiological and social influences.
- There are few, if any, consistent direct effects of puberty or pubertal timing on emotional or cognitive functioning. The effects of pubertal change and timing are influenced by the adolescent's social context.
- Adolescents as a group are resilient and have physical and physiological abilities to overcome adversity.
- Adolescents' behaviours are the major influence on their health problems. Sleep and waking cycles also change significantly during this period, and adolescents do not get enough sleep.
- Pubertal changes can lead to physical problems, such as dysmenorrhea (painful menstruation), amenorrhea (a failure to menstruate), and acne.
- Adolescents as a group are preoccupied with their bodily appearance, which can lead to disordered eating behaviours or other behaviours harmful to their health.
- Examples of eating disorders include overeating to the point of obesity, anorexia nervosa, and bulimia.
- Eating disorders can lead to severe medical problems, and even death.
- There are both psychological and contextual influences on eating disorders, such as attitudes, body appearance, and family variables.

Discussion Topics

1. Why is it important for adolescents to be better prepared for the changes associated with pubertal maturation? How can this preparation occur?
2. Why might the vast bodily changes associated with pubertal maturation create difficulty in meeting the developmental task of defining the self?
3. Do you think the effects of the variation in the speed and timing of pubertal maturation are the same for males and females? Do you think the differences are more difficult for one gender or the other?
4. What is the relationship between the social context of adolescents, pubertal maturation, and behaviour? Give examples.
5. How might the knowledge that context influences the relation between pubertal maturation and behaviour be used to help prepare adolescents and their parents for the many changes that can occur?
6. How does the adolescent's behaviour affect his or her health? What interventions can be done to promote healthy development? Why should parents try to encourage adolescents to sleep more?
7. Pubertal changes can lead to physical problems that are known only to the person or that are noticeable to others. Do you think one is worse than the other? Why or why not?
8. What are some of the social/cultural contexts that can lead to eating disorders?
9. In today's society, do you think males have similar issues with body image that are manifested in eating disorders? Do you think the issues might manifest themselves in a different way? Why is it more of a current issue?
10. Why do you think obesity as an outcome of an eating disorder gets less attention from the media?
11. What various selection, optimization, and compensation behaviours might an adolescent with an eating disorder go through?

Key Terms

amenorrhea, p. 74
anabolic steroids, p. 76
androgens, p. 60
anorexia nervosa, p. 74
bulimia, p. 74
delayed puberty, p. 74
dysmenorrhea, p. 74
early maturers, p. 62
endocrine glands, p. 59
estrogens, p. 60

hormones, p. 59
late maturers, p. 62
menarche, p. 63
obesity, p. 77
on-time maturers, p. 62
postpubescence, p. 61
precocious puberty, p. 74
prepubescence, p. 60
primary sexual characteristics,
 p. 60

pubertal maturation, p. 58
puberty, p. 59
pubescence, p. 61
resiliency, p. 73
secondary sexual characteristics,
 p. 60
secular trend, p. 66
sex steroids, p. 60
statistical significance, p. 69

4

Cognitive Development

Mr. Stevens thought he had made a neutral observation. The arrangements his daughter Jennifer was making to get herself and Sheila from the mall to Stefanie's house and then to the party at Gloria's that evening seemed unnecessarily complicated. There was no reason, he commented, that the girls had to stop first at Stefanie's. It would require that he do all sorts of criss-crossing around town. Why not just meet Stefanie at the party?

His daughter could not believe her father had interjected himself into the situation with such a stupid comment as that. "Dad, you just don't seem to understand," she sighed with exasperation.

"But Jennifer, honey, I . . ."

"Stop," Jennifer shouted. "You always do this. Why don't you just admit that you're wrong?" Jennifer turned away from her father and stomped angrily to her room.

Mr. Stevens sat there not understanding what had just happened.

In the early portions of adolescence, interactions between youth and their parents seem to be marked by disagreement and conflict. As illustrated by the interaction between Jennifer and her father, these types of exchanges involve adolescents' beliefs that what they know differs from what their parents know. These differences in knowledge, or cognition, are associated with often intense emotions on the part of the young person and with behaviours that reflect assertiveness and social independence.

The adolescent years involve intertwined changes in cognition and personality, and there exist important individual differences in key features of adolescent development. This variation is influenced by the social, cultural, and broader ecological context within which the adolescent lives.

Some of the diversity that exists in adolescence is associated with problems in development, especially when there are problems as well in the settings within which adolescents live. Programs that address problems associated with adolescent cognition and personality development have to be designed to be responsive to the particular contextual circumstances of the diverse youth that may participate in them. These emphases on diversity and context help frame a discussion of the cognitive processes involved in adolescent development.

Learning Objectives

1. To recognize that, in adolescence, cognition changes in two ways: Adolescents have more quantitative knowledge, and they think about their world in qualitatively different ways.
2. To understand that standardized tests and the IQ scores associated with them have been developed and widely used to assess intelligence quantitatively.
3. To identify the bases of debates about what psychological characteristics are actually measured by intelligence tests and what the results are useful for.
4. To recognize that variation in quantitative intelligence is influenced by the social domain and that qualitative features of cognition constitute a key dimension of cognitive development.
5. To recognize that academic achievement (grades attained in school) is a factor that influences cognitive competence and academic achievement and is itself affected by multiple levels of the international and Canadian context of human development.
6. To appreciate that the academic achievements of youth from different cultural and linguistic backgrounds differ due, primarily, to socialization experiences beginning in childhood, and that family and peer variables have an influence on academic achievement.
7. To understand that, in Piaget's theory, cognitive development involves the relation between the person and the context and that the person-context relation involves two processes: *assimilation* and *accommodation*.
8. To understand that, to Piaget, the goal of cognitive development is to create an *equilibration* between assimilation and accommodation.
9. To understand the basis of egocentrism and recognize that overcoming the egocentrism

prototypic of each stage of cognitive development leads the person to attain the cognitive development most central to that stage and that the cognitive attainment of one stage leads the person to the egocentrism of the next stage.

10. To understand the defining characteristics of formal operational thinking, especially the INRC group.

11. To understand characteristics of adolescent egocentrism such as the *imaginary audience* and the *personal fable*.

12. To recognize that, across the formal operational stage, social thought becomes less egocentric and more responsive to societal conventions and the particular social audience or context to which it is directed and that it is increasingly more reflective of abstract principles of social organization.

13. To recognize that it is through interaction with peers and elders, and, most importantly, with the assumption of adult roles and responsibilities, that the adolescent decentres and the egocentrism of this stage diminishes.

Dimensions of Adolescent Cognitive Development

ISSUE TO CONSIDER

• How does cognition change during the adolescent period?

In adolescence, cognition changes in at least two ways. First, adolescents know *more* about their world. Increases in how much adolescents know, as measured by changes in their scores on tests of mathematics, reading, or spatial reasoning, reflect quantitative alterations in adolescents' knowledge. They may know more math, moving from algebra, to geometry, to calculus. Second, there are also *qualitative* changes in adolescents' cognition. Rather than being limited to concrete thinking, they begin to think abstractly. A problem of government (e.g., how to create a new law) may be decided by thinking about the particular system of representative democracy that exists in Canada, or it might be dealt with by imagining that a completely different form of government (e.g., a constitutional monarchy) could be used.

Both the quantitative and qualitative changes that occur in regard to adolescent cognition are discussed in this chapter. Both discussions highlight the importance of individual differences in cognitive development, the way that the context influences cognition, and the links between cognition and other individual characteristics of youth development.

The Quantitative Study of Adolescent Cognition

ISSUE TO CONSIDER

• What is an "intelligence quotient"? How is it measured?

A key means to assess cognition quantitatively is by administering a standardized test such as the Stanford-Binet test or the Wechsler Intelligence Scale for Children. Intelligence tests quantify a person's knowledge relative to others of a similar age by computation of an intelligence quotient (**IQ**) score. To compute an IQ score, mental age (e.g., how much you know) is divided by chronological age (e.g., how much is known on average by others of your age) and multiplied by 100 (to eliminate fractions).

For at least half a century, researchers have studied the course of IQ changes from infancy through adolescence (e.g., Bloom, 1964). IQ scores remain fairly consistent across the adolescent period. The stability of IQ scores means that you can predict an 18-year-old person's IQ score with a good deal of accuracy by knowing his or her score in the early adolescent period. But what is being predicted when we predict IQ? What precisely is being measured by standardized intelligence tests and expressed as an IQ score?

Dimensions of Intelligence

ISSUES TO CONSIDER

• Why might a single IQ score not be useful?
• How does the social context influence cognition?

Across the 20th century there were debates about what psychological characteristics are actually measured by IQ tests (e.g., Gould, 1981; Lerner, 1976, 1986, 2002). Spearman (1927) hypothesized that one general intellectual factor—termed "g" (for "general intelligence")—was being measured, and Guilford (1967) theorized that over 100 different abilities could be measured by intelligence tests. Other scholars have also proposed that different aspects of cognition are assessed by intelligence tests (Fitzgerald, Nesselroade, & Baltes, 1973). To the extent that intelligence is expressed through multiple

IQ The intelligence quotient. A numerical scale measuring level of intelligence. For example, to compute an IQ score, mental age (i.e., how much you know) is divided by chronological age (i.e., how much is known on average by others of your age) and multiplied by 100 (to eliminate fractions).

dimensions, the usefulness of a single score, such as IQ, is diminished.

Current Canadian and international research lends support to the multiple dimensions viewpoint. Among both normal adolescents and youth with psychiatric problems, four distinct intellectual factors (verbal comprehension, perceptual organization, processing speed, and freedom from distractability) are measured by the current form of the Wechsler Intelligence Scale for Children (4th Edition) (WISC-IV; Wechsler, 2003). Additional evidence for the presence of four intellectual factors exists. Among 1100 children and youth, aged 6 to 16, who participated in the Canadian norming study (Wechsler, 1996), these factors also were identified (Roid & Worall, 1997). Several different facets of both perceptual and reasoning ability were found among about 850 Grade 8 and 9 youth from the United States, Japan, and China (Li, Sano, & Merwin, 1996).

It should also be noted that quantitative differences on intelligence tests are apparent between children and youth in Canada and the United States. Canadian youth have consistently and significantly higher full-scale IQ scores, as well as all index scores for all four factors on the WISC (Beal, Dumont, Cruse, & Branche, 1996) than their American counterparts. What this means is that a youth's intelligence and index scores will be lower using Canadian norms than American norms for the same test. Differences may be due to social, cultural, or environmental factors that are known to affect performance on intelligence tests. For example, in their study of North American Native/non-Native IQ score differences, Beiser and Gotowiec (2000) reported that biopsychosocial variables including maternal and child health, socioeconomic status, parental attitudes toward school and cultural separation, as well as children's English-language skills accounted for more than half of the difference in scores.

Additionally, the number of different intellectual abilities may remain consistent throughout the adolescent years. Studies of youth from Grades 7 to 12 found the same number of mental abilities (four) to exist at all grade levels (Fitzgerald, Nesselroade, & Baltes, 1973). These abilities related to verbal intelligence, numeric intelligence, reasoning, and spatial ability.

This research underscores the importance of developing educational curricula to support the diverse dimensions of intellectual development

Formal operational thought involves scientific, logical thinking.

among youth. Such findings, especially those of Matthews and Keating (1995), point to the significance of the social domain in the cognitive development of adolescents. In a longitudinal study of about 190 youth from late childhood/early adolescence (i.e., ages 8 to 12 years) through late adolescence/young adulthood (i.e., 17 to 23 years), cognitive competence was linked to three domains of functioning in the early developmental period: academic achievement, social competence, and conduct. Among 121 juvenile offenders in Alberta followed up 10 years after their confrontation with the law, verbal intellectual skill deficits predicted their involvement in a serious offence and incarceration as young adults (Anderson & Walsh, 1998).

The social context is not only an important part of the content of cognitive functioning, but it also influences the course of cognitive development. Among approximately 400 young adolescents from a predominantly poor rural area in the United States, both family and community factors influence academic achievement (Felner et al., 1995). As compared to adolescents from families in which adults were employed in semiskilled or skilled professional occupations, youth from families in which adults were employed in low-income unskilled jobs had lower school performance and academic achievement. When youth lived in families in which neither parent was a high school graduate, there was less likelihood of academic and socioemotional adjustment than when adolescents lived in families with parents who had higher educational levels (Felner et al., 1995).

In sum, studies of the quantitative features of adolescent cognition underscore the idea of multiple dimensions of adolescent cognitive development. Social functioning and the social context constitute significant domains of and important influences on cognitive development. Achievement in both academic and social arenas is an important part of cognitive development. Academic achievement and its relation to the context of human development is discussed next.

Academic Achievement: Diversity and Context

ISSUES TO CONSIDER

- How does culture influence academic achievement?
- How do peers influence academic achievement?
- What are their differences in achievement for adolescents with different self-perceptions?
- What other factors can lead to diversity in academic achievement? What can be done to raise achievement of adolescents?

Academic achievement is affected by multiple levels of the context of human development, ranging from the most macro cultural influences to micro interpersonal influences involving peers and family members. Although there appear to be differences in academic achievement, the motivational profiles of some diverse groups of students appear to be more similar than different. A study of approximately 1400 students in Grades 7 to 11 in Australia, the United States, and Canada examined differences between students from a non-Western indigenous minority background and those from a Western cultural background on their educational goals (McInerney, Roche, McInerney, & Marsh, 1997). The results indicated that achievement variation was attributable to the same narrow range of educational goals and sense-of-self measures shared between groups. It appears that achievement differences have more to do with the prevalence and not the type of educational goals in youth. For example, intergroup differences regarding academic goals were found in a study of more than 25 000 Grade 7 to 12 students in British Columbia (McCreary Centre, 2000). About three-quarters (76%) of Chinese Canadian youth expected to graduate from university in comparison to only about half (56%) of their non-Chinese Canadian peers.

Many of the academic achievements of youth from different cultural backgrounds may be based on socialization experiences beginning in childhood. In a longitudinal study of 475 North American, Chinese, and Japanese youth from Grade 1 through middle adolescence, consistent relationships were found across time in all cultures among family socioeconomic status, cognitive abilities, and academic achievement (Chen, Lee, & Stevenson, 1996).

An orientation toward academic achievement may remain with youth despite emigration to another country. A common cultural stress on education, shared by youth, their peers, and their families, seemed most critical to the greater achievement of 1100 adolescents from first- and second-generation immigrant families than immigrant peers with longer residency in the United States (Fuligni, 1997). It is possible that these factors also account for the variation in achievement among 150 refugee students in Montreal-area high schools, whose mental health was not found to be highly predictive of academic difficulties (Rousseau & Drapeau, 2000).

English-language proficiency appears to be associated with higher academic achievement among immigrant Canadian students (Chow, 2000). The father's level of education was the strongest predictor of adolescent English-language proficiency among almost 370 Chinese immigrant students in public Toronto high schools (Chow, 2001a). In a study of more than 500 Chinese adolescents attending Chinese language schools in Calgary, age at immigration was positively associated with retention of mother tongue (Chow, 2001b). Adolescents who immigrated as small children were more likely to lose their mother tongue than those who immigrated as older children.

Canadian research linking socioeconomic status (SES) to academic achievement suggests that lower family SES is related to lower achievement by youth. It appears that parental job insecurity affects school performance for older adolescents (Barling & Mendelson, 1999), perhaps through the effects of beliefs in an unjust world and negative mood.

Negative family attitudes and beliefs about schooling and learning are associated with low achievement (Ma & Klinger, 2000), and not with variations in family structure (e.g. number of parents and siblings). Additionally, it should be noted that grades assigned by teachers do seem to be affected by contextual variables, such as the student's SES (Wilson & Martinussen, 1999).

Some variation in academic achievement may be attributable to differential parental expectations and type of relationship with the school, even for youth within the same family. In a sample of approximately 300 Grade 4, 6, 8, 10, and 12 students in Ontario, the importance assigned to educational goals by youth and their parents, across the grades, was very consistent (Bigelow & Min Zhou, 2001). Within a sample of Quebec adolescents aged 14 to 16, females had higher grades, spent more time on homework, and had higher educational goals than males (Deslandes, Bouchard, & St. Amant, 1988). Time spent on homework and grades in French were attributable to different types of home-school relationships for General and Special Education students in Quebec (Deslandes, Royer, Potvin, & Leclerc, 1999). Peers can also have a facilitative influence on academic achievement. Working with peers when trying to solve a problem enhances the ability to succeed in such tasks (Dimant & Bearison, 1991). Peers seem especially useful when the interactions an adolescent has with them are relevant to the particular problem at hand, but even engaging in general games with peers or with interactive computers can facilitate cognitive performance. Playing video games, such as Tetris, can enhance an adolescent's ability to rotate figures mentally and to visualize objects in space (Okagaki & Frensch, 1994).

Although it may enhance peer popularity, spending a lot of time in casual or romantic peer interactions appears to have a negative impact on academic achievement. Research on Grade 9 inner-city youth in the United States (Luthar, 1995) finds that high sociability ratings from peers is linked to lower academic competence. A study of a group of more than 300 Grade 7 students from Quebec indicated that females who were in a romantic relationship did not achieve as highly as their unattached peers (Brendgen, Vitaro, Doyle, Markiewicz, & Bukowski, 2002).

In a study of ethnically diverse young adolescents (Graham, Taylor, & Hudley, 1998), girls of all ethnic backgrounds and European American boys were found to value high-achieving female classmates, while ethnic minority boys placed little value on high-achieving male peers. All youth believed that both academic disengagement and social deviance were associated with being male, a low achiever, and a member of an ethnic minority (Graham et al., 1998).

It may be that some instances of low achievement are related to adolescents' own characterization of themselves. Their self-categorizations or labels of themselves may be self-handicapping in regard to their achievement. High-achieving matriculation students and low-achieving general diploma students in northwestern Alberta high schools were found to differ in respect to locus of control (internal versus external control of their achievement in school) and academic self-concept (McLean, 1997).

Some youth use "self-handicapping strategies" (Midgley, Arunkumar, & Urdan, 1996) to account for their poor academic performance. Work avoidance in high school seems to be associated with low control and competence (Siefert & O'Keefe, 2001). By engaging in procrastination, fooling around in class, and intentional reduction in effort, students can provide for themselves causes for their poor academic achievement (Midgley et al., 1996). Adolescents can also develop self-enhancing strategies. Self-confidence beliefs may be a basis for these strategies; they were identified as a protective factor in the transition for youth moving from Grade 6 to a Grade 7 in junior high school (Bouffard, Boileau, & Vezeau, 2001), and served as a successful buffer against negative effects of failure on an academic task for first-year university students (Johnson, Vincent, & Ross, 1997). Motivation was more highly related to personal adjustment and achievement for students in a first-year university course than intelligence (Cote & Levine, 2000). Developing an ability to delay gratification facilitates cognitive and academic competence in adolescence (Shoda, Mischel, & Peake, 1990). Delay of gratification ability also enhances the capacity to cope with both frustration and stress (Shoda et al., 1990).

Both IQ scores and academic performance are related to three aspects of social competence among 12- and 13-year-olds: showing socially responsible behaviour; receiving positive appraisals by peers; and having the ability to regulate oneself socially, to set goals, solve problems, and elicit interpersonal trust (Wentzel, 1991). Adolescent girls who have high mastery of academic subjects also have the ability to seek and obtain appropriate help in solving a task (Nelson-Le Gall, 1990).

Building Programs to Counter Illiteracy and Its Associated Problems

Neither a country, its communities, nor its citizens can prosper unless they possess the knowledge and skills necessary to contribute to the global village and compete in the global marketplace. For these reasons programs are being developed around the world to counteract illiteracy and to diminish, or even prevent, the problems associated with it.

Here, two such programs are described, one from Dhaka, Bangladesh, and the other from Salvador, Bahia, Brazil.

Increasing Literacy Rates Among Rural Youth in Bangladesh: The "Non-Formal Primary Education Program" of Dhaka, Bangladesh

Equal access to education is a human right, reaffirmed by international acceptance at the United Nations Convention on the Rights of the Child. Yet almost 100 million children in the developing world were given no opportunity to attend school in 2001, a majority of which were girls.

In Bangladesh, the problem is especially severe with 35% of young people never learning how to read or write. In response to the educational needs of rural youth in particular, the Bangladesh Rural Advancement Committee (BRAC) created its Non-Formal Primary Education Program (NFPE) in 1985.

Through this program, BRAC recruits and trains paraprofessional teachers, 97% of which are women, and places them in one-room schoolhouses within their own community. These schools provide four years of primary education for 8- to 10-year-olds who have never attended school, or have dropped out. A similar program exists for older children providing the same curriculum but spread across three years of schooling. Special attention is paid to the needs of girls who make up 65% of those enrolled.

In the 15 years since its inception, BRAC has achieved remarkable success, expanding from a base of 22 schools to nearly 34 000. Dropout rates are less than 7%, compared with 35% in the overcrowded formal school system. Over 90% of students graduating from BRAC's Grade 5 class have gained admission into formal government schools.

The BRAC experience is testimony to the fact that poor rural families want education for their children. It has also demonstrated that motivated paraprofessional teachers can be trained quickly and successfully.

Studies have shown repeatedly that on completion of BRAC's schooling, students from poor homes with illiterate parents are only marginally behind middle class families of government schools. Tests revealed that children from BRAC schools gained equal scores to their government counterparts in reading and writing skills and slightly lower scores in mathematics and social studies.

A team of international education experts is currently evaluating the program to help improve its curriculum and teaching methods.

Increasing School Opportunities Among Brazilian Youth: The "Community Public Schools" (CECUP) Program of Salvador, Bahia, Brazil

In the 1970s, residents of poor neighbourhoods in Bahia began organizing to secure land titles, electricity, water, and other basic services. Education was, and remains, a high priority due to their children's lack of access to basic education. Community organizing unfolded in an environment marked by sharp class distinctions, a skewed distribution of income, and racial discrimination. In Bahia, the state in which Salvador is located, an estimated 50% of school-age children are not enrolled in school and adult illiteracy (15 years and older) hovers around 50%. In Salvador alone, an estimated 220 000 school-age children are not in school. These statistics bode poorly for Brazilian children in terms of their health, future employability, income-earning capacity, and overall quality of life. In Brazil, the chief problems are low enrollment and high attrition rates, particularly in the first years of primary school. Causal factors include poor teaching and weak curricula; parents' inability to provide books and uniforms; children's lack of readiness to learn when they enter Grade 1; inadequate educational materials and facilities; and lack of communication between schools and parents. In response to the absence of viable educational opportunities, associations of low-income residents throughout the city took matters into their own hands and established their own schools.

Over 10 000 low-income children and youth, ages 5 through 18, benefit from 62 community-built and community-run schools in poor neighbourhoods of Salvador. To combat low levels of literacy among the city's poor, CECUP works closely with community organizations and teachers to improve the quality of education through teacher training, the development of curricula and educational materials, and cultural enrichment activities.

CECUP and its teachers incorporate elements from the children's Afro-Brazilian culture and daily experience into the educational process. In bridging the gap between school and the children's living environment, parents support their children's education. The dropout rate among the community public school children is low.

Source: International Youth Foundation, 2001.www.iyfnet.org

For some students, low achievement is related to a learning disability. Learning disabled youth encounter difficulty in inhibiting incorrect responses in academic situations (Barrouillet, Fayol, & Lathulière, 1997). In such circumstances, family support such as parental expectations for the child's academic achievement and the young person's awareness of these expectations influence academic achievement among youth, even those varying along a learning disabled and nonlearning disabled continuum (Patrikakou, 1996).

There are numerous interventions, beyond those associated with parental support, that can enhance academic achievement among youth. Many of these efforts involve community-based programs aimed at enhancing academic functioning and alleviating other interrelated problems of youth development (e.g., see Dryfoos, 1990, 1994, 1995, 1998).

In a report about the Chicago Longitudinal Study of the role of extended early childhood intervention in school achievement (Reynolds & Temple, 1998), about 560 low-income inner-city African American youth were followed from early childhood to Grade 7. Program participation for two or three years after preschool and kindergarten was associated with higher reading achievement through Grade 7 and with lower rates of grade retention and placement into special education classes. This study provides important longitudinal evidence of the benefits of a large-scale community-based program of extended early childhood intervention for adolescent academic achievement (Reynolds & Temple, 1998).

Being literate is a key requirement for academic achievement and success in life, especially in a world growing more dependent on technology and thus on the ability to speak, read, and write. Adolescents' literacy skills can affect not only their own life chances but those of others in their social world. Among African American children of adolescent mothers, differences in preschool cognition and behaviour were related to literacy in late adolescence and young adulthood. Variations in maternal education, the size of the family during early childhood, the marital status of the mother, and family income in middle childhood and in early adolescence also influenced literacy (Baydar, Brooks-Gunn, & Furstenberg, 1993).

Given the developmental and generational significance of literacy, it is understandable that numerous programs exist worldwide designed to enhance literacy among youth. Applications Box 4.1 describes some of these programs. The programs typically have to attend simultaneously to several literacy-related problems to be effective.

Conclusions About Quantitative Features of Adolescent Cognitive Development

The quantitative characteristics of adolescent cognition show both consistency and change in patterns of development that are influenced by the context within which they occur. Such development in context provides the underpinnings of diversity in the course of cognitive development and promotes the link between cognition and other aspects of the individual's psychological and social functioning. These themes are not exclusive to the quantitative dimension of adolescent cognition. They apply as well to the qualitative one. There are important changes during adolescence in the quality of thinking.

The Qualitative Study of Adolescent Cognition

The way an adolescent thinks about the world differs from the type of thought shown by infants and children. Differences in "kind" or "type" are **qualitative differences**. Numerous scholars of human development in general, and adolescence in particular, have studied the qualitative changes that characterize cognitive development (Mitchell, 1996, 2001; Overton, 1991, 1998). Historically, the most important approach to adolescent cognition was presented by Jean Piaget (1896–1980). Today, even though Piaget's (1970, 1972) approach is no longer the only one or even the central approach, most other perspectives take Piaget's views into account (e. g., Elkind, 1967, 1980; Feldman, 2000; Keating, 1991; Neimark, 1979; Overton, 1991; Overton & Byrnes, 1991). Because of this continuing salience, it is important to describe Piaget's ideas about adolescent cognition.

Qualitative differences (in cognition) Differences in "kind" or "type" of thought shown by a person.

Table 4-1 Stages of Cognitive Development in the Theory of Jean Piaget

Stage	Approx. Age Range	Major Cognitive Achievements	Major Cognitive Limitations
Sensorimotor	0–1	Scheme of object permanency	Egocentrism: Lack of ability to differentiate between self and external stimulus world
Preoperational	2–6 or 7	Systems of representation. Symbolic functioning (e.g., language, symbolic play, delayed imitation)	Lack of conservation ability. Egocentrism: Lack of ability to differentiate between symbol and object
Concrete operational	6 or 7–12	Ability to show experience/ independent thought (reversible, internalized actions)	Egocentrism: Lack of ability to differentiate between thoughts about reality and actual experience of reality
Formal operational	12–adulthood	Ability to think hypothetically, counterfactually, and propositionally	Egocentrism: Imaginary audience, personal fable

Source: Adapted from Lerner, 1986.

Adolescence and the Formal Operational Stage

ISSUES TO CONSIDER

- What are the achievements and limitations of the formal operational stage?
- Describe how knowledge is attained through the processes of assimilation, accommodation, and equilibration.
- According to David Elkind, what is egocentrism and why is it important?

As described in Chapter 2, the infancy and childhood portions of life are associated with the first three stages of Piaget's (1970) theory, and adolescence and adulthood are associated with the fourth. Table 4.1 presents the four stages of Piaget's theory: the sensorimotor, the preoperational, the concrete operational, and the formal operational stages. The cognitive achievements and limitations involved in each of these stages within Piaget's theory are included in the table as well.

Note that in all periods of development within Piaget's (1970) theory, cognitive development involves the relation between the person and the context. The person-context relation discussed by Piaget involves two processes. First, knowledge is built by the person taking in information from the world around him or her and fitting it into his or her existing cognitive organization or structure. This changing of the world outside the person (the "object") to fit the structure of the person (the "subject") is termed **assimilation**. Second, knowledge is also built by the person (the "subject") changing his or her cognitive structure to adapt to new information ("object") in the world. This process is termed **accommodation**.

Piaget proposes that the goal of cognitive development is to create a balance (an equilibrium) between assimilation and accommodation. Piaget calls the process of maintaining this balance **equilibration** and notes that equilibrium is hard to maintain. The world is constantly presenting new information, and a person initially tries to deal with it by treating it as something he or she already knows and trying to assimilate it (a process that Piaget terms **reproductive assimilation**). When this attempt occurs, equilibrium is lost. Assimilation outweighs accommodation because there is more of a cognitive focus on the subject than on the object. Eventually, the person needs to accommodate to bring his or her cognitive structure back into balance. This process of falling out of and moving into equilibration is the means through which the

Assimilation Process during which a person modifies his or her external world to fit into the already existing cognitive schemas (structures) of the person (the subject).

Accommodation Process during which a person (the subject) modifies his or her cognitive schemas (structure) to conform with new information (the object) in the external world.

Equilibration Process of reaching a balanced relationship between assimilation and accommodation.

Reproductive assimilation When a person initially tries to deal with new information by treating it as something he or she already knows.

Linguistic skills are important facets of the mental abilities assessed on intelligence tests.

person moves from one level, or stage, of cognitive development to the next.

When the person is centred on his or her own cognitive structure, there is more of a concern with the perspective of the subject than with the actual details of the object, and the person is said to be egocentric (Elkind, 1967). As illustrated in Table 4.1, each stage of cognitive development within Piaget's theory has a type of **egocentrism** prototypic of it. According to David Elkind (1967), the scholar most instructive about the nature of cognitive egocentrism, overcoming the egocentrism prototypic of each stage of development leads the person to attain the cognitive development most central to that stage. At the same time, the cognitive attainment of one stage leads the person to the egocentrism of the next stage (Elkind, 1967).

The processes involving assimilation, accommodation, equilibration, reproductive assimilation, **disequilibration**, egocentrism, and eventual re-equilibration leads eventually to the attainment of the last stage of Piaget's (1970, 1972) theory: formal operations. It leads to the emergence of a type of egocentrism prototypic to the adolescent period. To understand this development, let's focus first on the characteristics of **formal operational thinking.**

Features of Formal Operational Thought

ISSUES TO CONSIDER

- What are the characteristics of formal operational thought?
- What is the INRC group? How is it important for formal operations?
- What does the *structural whole* in regard to formal operations mean? Does it exist?

When children attain the ability to see that reality and their thoughts about reality are different and can generate and recognize hypotheses about reality, they have reached the formal operational stage in Piaget's theory.

Formal operations begin at about 11 or 12 years of age and continue for the rest of life (Piaget, 1972). Because, in both theory and research, the lower age limit typically associated with this stage corresponds to the years associated with early adolescence (see Keating, 1991; Neimark, 1979; Overton, 1991; Overton & Byrnes, 1991), the study of the qualitative aspect of adolescent cognition is associated with the evaluation of formal operational development.

The concrete operational child can only form abstractions relevant to events or problems that exist. As a consequence, thoughts about a given topic cannot be integrated with potentially relevant but hypothetical aspects of the problem. The child cannot reach solutions to problems by means of general theories or by the postulation of all possible solutions to a problem (Overton & Byrnes, 1991; Wadsworth, 1971). The formal operational child shows these attributes of thought.

Egocentrism When the person is centred on his or her own cognitive structure/s and unable to differentiate between one's own point of view and the views of others; when there is more concern with the perspective of the subject than with the actual details of the object (i.e., the world surrounding the subject). **Disequilibration** Cognitive process that occurs when our cognitive schemas (structures) are not in an agreement with one another, when there is an imbalance between assimilation and accommodation. **Formal operational thought** Fourth stage of Piaget's theory of cognitive development, when a person attains the ability to see that reality and his or her thoughts about reality are different, and when the person can generate and recognize hypotheses about reality.

Researching Adolescent Cognition: Puzzlement and Vexation

John J. Mitchell is Professor of Education at Okanagan University College and Professor Emeritus, University of Alberta.

I have been investigating the thinking habits of adolescents for the past 25 years. During this time I have looked into how thinking changes during adolescence—especially the dramatic changes that take place between early and late adolescence. I have also looked into how adolescent thought is propelled by reason, but at the same time, by the irrational, the mystical, and the eternal.

My current research focuses on some of the unsolved mysteries of the adolescent thought process—and there are many. The common thread connecting these mysteries is that during adolescence intellectual efficiency fluctuates tremendously from problem to problem, from mood state to mood state, and from social setting to social setting within the same individual. As a result, adolescent thinking is neither constant nor uniform; rather, it is an unsettled brew of sophisticated *and* primitive analysis, effective *and* inept problem solving, clever *and* dopey calculations. This is a disconcerting state of affairs for teachers, parents, and for adolescents themselves.

Two parallel questions guide my current research. First, "Can we predict when adolescent thinking will operate smoothly and efficiently?" Second, "Can

we predict when it will operate clumsily and inefficiently?" It now appears that "clumsy and inefficient" is far easier to predict than "smooth and efficient." This puzzlement of adolescent thought is investigated at great length in *The Mental and Emotional Lives of Teenagers* (Mitchell, 2001).

These vexations are no small matter! North American teens routinely encounter real-life situations where their ineffective thinking leads to pregnancy, sexually transmitted disease, vehicular death, drug overdose, incarceration, school expulsion. Avoiding these damaging consequences is a profound challenge faced by all youth in our culture, yet each year millions of North American teens fail it, and for many of them their failure is caused by a failure of thinking.

I also am intrigued by the gap between ability and performance—which is considerable during adolescence. This gap is widened by a basic principle of adolescent intelligence—thought is rendered less competent whenever the thinker is (a) emotionally aroused, (b) egocentrically preoccupied, or (c) narcissistically charged. My research suggests that these phenomenological states are quite common during adolescence, and, as a

result, their thinking is cloudy and imprecise more frequently than most psychologists recognize.

One question I have recently been investigating is the degree to which adolescent intellectualism is susceptible to erosion and deterioration. By this I mean how adolescent thought shifts from critical to noncritical, from reality-based to narcissistic-based, and from altruistic to egocentric with abrupt swiftness. An adolescent thought sequence that starts off as reasoned and measured may hastily shift to ill-reasoned and disproportional. This inconsistency of adolescent thought is a source of rich research possibilities for those of us who investigate cognition.

My future research topics include a look into the adolescent's ability to understand propaganda, hate-speech, love-talk, and other forms of emotionally charged language. Further, I am engaged in trying to discover why so many early adolescents *believe* they can effectively negotiate the demands of drug use and sexual intimacy, when, as a rule, they cannot.

In the formal operational stage, thought becomes hypothetical in emphasis (Overton & Byrnes, 1991). The child comes to recognize that his or her thoughts about reality have an element of arbitrariness about them, that they may not actually be real representations about the true nature of experience. The child's thoughts about reality take on a hypothetical characteristic. In forming hypotheses about the world, the child's thought can be seen to correspond, at least in part, to formal, scientific, logical thinking (Linn, 1991). Meet the Researcher Box 4.1 presents the work of John J. Mitchell in regard to how thinking changes during adolescence.

To be able to deal with all potentially relevant aspects of a problem, we must be able to transform

the problem so as to contend with all its possible forms. The cognitive structure that characterizes formal operations, termed the **INRC group** by Piaget, allows such complete transformations (Inhelder & Piaget, 1958). All transformations of a problem may be obtained through the application of the components of this group: identity, negation, reciprocal, and correlative transformations. We can think of all aspects of a problem by recognizing the problem in

INRC grouping Cognitive structure that characterizes formal operations and implies that all solutions to a problem may be obtained through the application of four components: *i*dentity, *n*egation, *r*eciprocity, and *c*orrelation.

terms of its singular attributes (an **identity transformation**), by cancelling the existence of the problem (a **negation operation**), by taking its opposite (a **reciprocal transformation**), or by relating it to other problems (a **correlative transformation**). Only the coordinated use of all these transformations allows all potentially applicable aspects of a problem to be solved. Not until the INRC group is established do we possess a cognitive structure appropriate for dealing with pure abstractions.

To illustrate, Piaget and Inhelder (1969) describe a problem in which a youth is presented with five jars, each containing colourless liquids. Combining the liquids from three particular jars will produce a colour; any use of the liquids from either of the other jars will not produce a colour. The child is shown that a colour can be produced but is not shown which combination will do this. Concrete operational children typically try to solve this problem by combining liquids two at a time, but after combining all pairs, or possibly trying to mix all five liquids together, their search for the workable combination usually stops. The formal operational adolescent explores all possible solutions and, typically, tests all possible combinations of two and three liquids until a colour is produced.

As another example, consider the following verbal problem: "If Jane is taller than Doris and is shorter than Francine, who is the shortest of the three?" (Wadsworth, 1971). Concrete operational children may be able to solve an analogous problem (e.g., one dealing with sticks of various lengths when the sticks are physically present). However, abstract verbal problems such as this one are usually not solved until formal operations have emerged.

Formal operational thinking increases substantially in early adolescence, between Grades 6 and 8 (Petersen, 1987). A central aspect of formal operational thinking, **conditional reasoning**, increases across adolescence (Overton, Byrnes, & O'Brien, 1985). This reasoning involves the idea that "if p, then q," and is the logical statement in scientific hypotheses. Also related to scientific reasoning is the ability to make valid inferences, for example, if and only if p, then q. The competence to make valid inferences emerges in and continues to develop throughout adolescence

During adolescence, thought changes from being predominantly concrete to being predominantly abstract.

(Moshman & Franks, 1986). Strategies for remembering (Bray, Hersh, & Turner, 1985), particularly in familiar contexts (Ceci & Bronfenbrenner, 1985), develop in adolescence as well.

Formal operational development tends to occur in respect to certain cognitive competencies and not others (Keating, 1991; Kuhn, 1991; Kuhn, Amsel, & O'Loughlin, 1988; Leadbeater, 1991). It occurs for those competencies for which the person has a particular interest and/or specialized experience or training (Piaget, 1972). The essence of formal operations is abstract thought. This type of thought develops in a manner that includes both general and specific components (Marini & Case, 1994). Similarly, understanding of particular topics, for instance, aspects of social roles such as job responsibility, develops in diverse ways (Warton & Goodnow, 1991). This research suggests that formal operations do not exist as a "structural whole" (Kuhn, 1991; Kuhn et al., 1988) and implies that universal stagelike structures may not likely be found (Keating, 1991).

In summary, formal operational thought is no longer dependent on concrete reality. The child can now think not only in the "if . . . then" manner, but also counterfactually and abstractly. These mental abilities continue to characterize thought in the adolescent years and beyond. However, several qualifications of these conclusions are necessary.

Identity transformation Process of approaching a problem by recognizing the problem in terms of its singular attributes.
Negation operation Process of approaching a problem by cancelling the existence of the problem.
Reciprocal transformation Process of approaching a problem by considering and taking its opposite.
Correlative transformation Process of thinking of all aspects of a problem by relating them to other problems.
Conditional reasoning Type of deductive reasoning, characterized by "if p, then q" statements.

Development Across the Period of Formal Operations

ISSUE TO CONSIDER
• What change marks the movement from concrete operations to the formal reasoning ability of formal operations?

Willis F. Overton and his colleagues have conducted a series of studies investigating the individual and contextual bases of the development of cognition during adolescence (e.g., Foltz, Overton, & Ricco, 1995; Reimer et al., 1996). Researchers hypothesized that the acquisition of competence in formal reasoning ability would be marked by a transition from inductive to **deductive reasoning** (Foltz et al., 1995). This hypothesis is based on the understanding that in the concrete operational stage youth are overly centred on existing phenomena, on the world as it was empirically given to them (Elkind, 1967), and use reasoning to confirm that their specific observations reflect the general state of affairs of the world. They therefore *induce* that what is observed is prototypic of the general nature of existence.

Foltz et al. (1995) conclude that a cognitive developmental progression exists, one that involves the adolescent moving from inductive to deductive reasoning strategies. By late adolescence, youth are highly efficient at using deduction to reduce or eliminate alternative solutions in problem-solving situations (Drumm & Jackson, 1996). This conclusion is based on the study where 100 adolescents were given both a problem-solving and a reasoning task (Foltz et al., 1995). They were given a toy wooden boat, were shown it could float on water, and were then asked to demonstrate that wooden boats, and only wooden boats, could float on water. Foltz et al. found that nonformal operational thinking was associated with **inductive reasoning** strategies, by attempts to verify their ideas through generating redundant information. Here, adolescents might place other wooden objects into the water to see if they too could float. However, formal reasoning was associated with attempts to prove one's ideas via "falsification" strategies, that is, by trying to identify information that would disconfirm one's ideas (Foltz et al., 1995).

If the boat task was involved in an adolescent's attempts to use **falsification strategies**, for example, then the young person might attempt to place toys made of materials other than wood into the water to see if they could float.

Other research confirms that cognitive development during adolescence involves changes in the use of inductive reasoning. In a study of more than 2000 Hungarian youth from Grades 3, 5, 7, 9, and 11, six tests of inductive reasoning (number analogies, verbal analogies, number series, verbal series, coding, and exclusion) were administered (Csapó, 1997). The major increase in inductive reasoning occurred between Grades 5 and 9, with only small changes in such reasoning after Grade 9 (Csapó, 1997), when deductive reasoning typically increases dramatically (Foltz et al., 1995).

During the portion of adolescence when deductive reasoning predominates there may not only be attempts to confirm existing beliefs, but also it may be the case that adolescents will evaluate arguments and evidence in a manner that maintains their already formed beliefs. For example, in one study, adolescents were presented with "scientific" information that either confirmed, disconfirmed, or was irrelevant to their existing religious beliefs (Klaczynski & Gordon, 1996); however, each presentation contained some problematic reasoning/evidence that contradicted the information. Adolescents were most likely to detect problems in evidence that was inconsistent with their religious preferences. This bias in reasoning was not related to the intellectual ability of adolescents (Klaczynski & Gordon, 1996). Other research indicates that the development of formal operational thinking during adolescence is not related to quantitatively assessed intellectual abilities (Pulos, 1997).

Deductive reasoning Type of reasoning that begins with a set of statements (premises) used to infer if another statement (conclusion) is valid.

Inductive reasoning When reasoning inductively we use our observations and experiences to draw conclusions about the general truth of a particular statement.

Falsification strategies Proving one's ideas by trying to identify information that would disconfirm these ideas.

Diversity and Context in Formal Operations

ISSUE TO CONSIDER

- Why can't generalizations be made about the emergence and course of formal operations?

Evidence indicates that the emergence of formal operational thought is not characteristic of all youth. Studies done with older adolescents and adults in Western cultures show that not all individuals attain formal operations (e.g., Kuhn, 1991; Kuhn et al., 1988). Estimates are that only about 40% to 60% of samples of university students from Western countries show appropriate performance on tasks requiring formal operational thinking (Neimark, 1979). Adolescents may be competent to reason formally, but they may not have developed the strategies to show this competence (Overton, 1990, 1991). Thus education is important for such cognitive performance (Kuhn et al., 1988).

Generalizations about the course of formal operations across the life span within a culture must be made with caution. Although evidence shows that some aspects of cognition (e.g., the ways in which youth justify their beliefs) are generalizable across cultural settings (Kitchener & Wood, 1987), people in many cultural settings do not attain formal operational abilities at the same average time in life that it occurs within Western cultural settings. For example, American adolescents (13- and 15-year-olds) are more advanced in formal operations than Hong Kong Chinese youth of corresponding ages (Douglas & Wong, 1977). In fact, in some non-Western groups there is a failure ever to attain such thinking ability. Piaget (1969, 1972) himself noted such failures.

Reasons for these differences have been suggested to lie in the different experiences of youth from rural and urban settings (Peluffo, 1962; Youniss & Dean, 1974), in type of school experiences (Goodnow, 1962; Goodnow & Bethon, 1966; Kuhn, 1991; Kuhn et al., 1988; Peluffo, 1962, 1967), and in the sorts of parent-child relations experienced (Jacobsen, Edelstein, & Hoffmann, 1994). For example, Icelandic youth with a secure attachment to their parents performed better on both concrete and formal operational tasks than did youth with insecure attachments (Jacobsen et al., 1994).

Although these explanations might lead us to expect socioeconomic or educational differences to be associated with formal operational attainment, the data do not support such a view. Neimark (1975,

With the emergence of formal operations, many adolescents spend a lot of time immersed in their own thoughts.

1979) found that socioeconomic status had no effect on the development of formal thought, and only very profound differences in education seemed to be associated with differences in the development of formal thought. IQ score differences do not relate to differences in formal operational development either (Kuhn, 1976). After some minimal level of psychometric intelligence is reached, variables other than those associated with IQ scores contribute to formal operational development (Neimark, 1975).

Formal operational thought does not represent a level of cognitive functioning reached universally by all people in all cultures. However, for many adolescents, formal operations represent a stage of thought that is reached. Although the abstract thinking associated with this type of thought is an asset to the young person, formal operational thinking also has limitations.

MEET THE RESEARCHER Box 4.2 David Elkind

Perceptions of Adolescents

David Elkind is professor of child development in the Eliot-Pearson Department of Child Development at Tufts University. He is perhaps best known for his more popular books, *The Hurried Child, All Grown Up and No Place to Go,* and *Miseducation.*

The adolescent is a gift of nature, but our perception of adolescence is always a social construction. As a social construction, adolescence always reflects the values, roles, and perceptions of the prevailing society. When these values, roles, and perceptions change, so too does our manner of viewing adolescence. Much of my current research is an attempt to describe society that had its onset around mid-century.

Up until mid-century, our society was provincial in the sense that there was a great deal of ethnic, religious, and racial clannishness with many social taboos for dating and wedding outside of these rigid boundaries. In addition, male and female roles were sharply defined with little overlapping between what were regarded as appropriate activities for men and women. Finally, children were perceived as innocent and in need of protection and adolescents were perceived as immature and in need of adult guidance and protection. In turn, modern adolescents have been looked upon as needing to experiment, to try things out with a moratorium during which they were free from adult responsi-

bilities. Starting with World War II, and followed by the women's movement, the civil rights movement, and the Vietnam War, there was a strong reaction against authority, particularly as it was exercised by white males. It resulted in a new cosmopolitanism in American society. For example, there is now much greater acceptance and valuation of the achievements of different ethnic, racial, and religious groups as well as of women. Increased intermarriage among those of different racial and ethnic backgrounds reflects this cosmopolitanism. In the same way, gender roles have become more loose and overlapping; women now engage in many previously male occupations and males are now free to show their more sensitive, nurturant sides. Finally, today's children are seen as more competent, ready, and able to deal with whatever our postmodern society has to throw at them. In their turn, adolescents are now viewed as sophisticated and knowledgeable about technology, drugs, and sex.

My own research has focused on how the postmodern perception of adolescence

maps onto the biological and psychological characteristics of adolescents that have remained unchanged. Much of our work suggests that it is the mismatch between our new postmodern perception of adolescents and the real developing need of young people that helps account for at least a part of the disturbed behaviour among them. As just one example, body piercing, tattooing, and hair dyeing are adolescent-created markers of their marginal status that replace societal markers, rites of passage, that have been taken away from them. Our task is to shape our postperceptions of adolescents in such a way that they reflect both the changes in society and the abiding needs, interests, and abilities of the young.

Adolescent Egocentrism

ISSUE TO CONSIDER

• What are the two components of adolescent egocentrism?

As noted previously, the scholarship of David Elkind (1967) allows us to understand the special characteristics of the egocentrism of the formal operational period. Some of Elkind's recent work is featured in Meet the Researcher Box 4.2.

As Elkind (1967) explains, adolescent egocentrism is complicated by the physiological, emotional, and social changes involved in this period of life. Because anything and everything can become the object of adolescents' newly developed abstract and hypothetical cognitive ability, they may recognize their thoughts as only one possible interpretation of reality. Adolescents also may come to view reality as only a possible instance of a potentially unlimited number

of possible realities. The concrete predomination of what is real is replaced in adolescence by the abstract and hypothetical predomination of what can be real. All things in experience are thought about hypothetically, and even adolescents' own thoughts can become an object of their hypothesizing.

In other words, adolescents can now think about their own thinking. Because young people spend a good deal of time using these new thought capabilities, their preoccupation, or **centration**, on self leads to egocentrism within the formal operational stage, a development that limits the newly developed formal

Centration In Piaget's theory, a focus on one's own point of view, which involves therefore a lack of balance between assimilation and accommodation.

operational thought. Elkind (1967) labels the egocentrism of this stage **adolescent egocentrism** and sees it as having two components.

① First, because adolescents are preoccupied with their thinking, they fail to distinguish, or discriminate, between their thoughts and the thoughts of other people. Because adolescents are so preoccupied with their own appearance and behaviour, and fail to make this discrimination, they come to believe that others are as preoccupied with their appearance and behaviour as they are. Thus adolescents construct an **imaginary audience** (Elkind, 1967).

You can see an illustration of the functioning of the imaginary audience and of some emotional concomitants of this cognitive development if you think back to your days of early adolescence. Assuredly some new fad, perhaps in regard to a particular style of clothing, sprang up among your peers. Some adolescents you knew perhaps were stuck wearing the outdated style and were literally afraid to be seen in public. Because they were so aware of their absence of fitting in, they were equally sure that everyone was immediately aware of their shortcomings.

② A second component of adolescent egocentrism also exists. The adolescent's thoughts and feelings are experienced as new and unique. Although to the adolescent they are in fact new and unique, the young person comes to believe that they are historically new and unique. The adolescent constructs a **personal fable**, the belief that he or she is a unique, one-of-a-kind individual, a person having singular feelings and thoughts.

Here, too, it is easy to think of an illustration of the personal fable. We can think back to our early adolescent years and our first "love affair." No one ever loved as deeply, as totally . . . no one had ever felt such intense passion, devotion, the longing, the overwhelming fulfillment that we felt for this, our one true love. . . . Then remember a few days or week later when the relationship ended, when it was "over!" The pain, the depression, the agony . . . no one had ever suffered so deeply, no one had ever been so wrongfully abused, so thoroughly tortured, so spitefully crushed by unrequited love. . . . We sat in our rooms, unmoving, and our mothers would say, "What's wrong with you? Dinner is ready. Come and eat." Our inevitable answer: "You don't understand. What do you know about love?"

Clearly, then, adolescent egocentrism is a feature of cognitive functioning that has both emotional and social components. Indeed, this may be especially true for girls. A heightened sense of imaginary audience is associated with depression among girls, but not boys (Schonert-Reichl, 1994). High egocentrism among girls is associated with their perceptions of being at high risk for problems (Dolcini et al., 1989). Sexual behaviour among adolescents has some associated risks due to adolescent egocentrism. One approach used to challenge the perception among youth that pregnancy and parenting only happen to others is the "Baby Think It Over" program (Jurmaine, 1994). It was found that 14- to 19-year-old youth who spent between two to three days and nights with an infant simulator that required attention and care were more likely to accurately assess their risk for unplanned pregnancy than their peers who did not participate in the program (Out & Lafeniere, 2001).

From the perspective of the parent of an adolescent, having a young person in the midst of adolescent egocentrism presents a formidable challenge for child rearing. Implications for Parenting Box 4.1 describes the impact of adolescent egocentrism on parents and suggests ways for coping with a youth in this period of development.

Research about the nature and importance of adolescent egocentrism continues (e.g., Elkind & Bowen, 1979; Enright, Lapsley, & Shukla, 1979; Enright, Shukla, & Lapsley, 1980; Lapsley, 1991; Schonert-Reichl, 1994). There seem to be rich implications of adolescent egocentrism for adolescent cognitive, personality, and social development. For instance, adolescent egocentrism is highly related to **social cognition** (e.g., Vartanian & Powlishta, 1996). As discussed next, many of the features of the development of social cognition during adolescence are marked by egocentric thinking, especially at the beginning of this period.

Adolescent egocentrism Term introduced by Elkind in 1967 to label problems in adolescents' thoughts; the belief that others are preoccupied with them and that they are unique individuals.

Imaginary audience When adolescents become preoccupied with self, they come to believe that others are as preoccupied with their appearance and behaviour as they are.

Personal fable Belief that one is a unique, one-of-a-kind individual; the idea that one is a singular person having singular feelings and thoughts.

Social cognition Thinking about interpersonal relationships and the social world.

Why Every Young Adolescent Sees Himself or Herself as the Centre of the World

Thirteen-year-old Alexandra picks at her dinner, rolling the peas around her plate, not saying a word to anyone. Afterward, when her father invites her to join the rest of the family for a rental video and a bowl of popcorn, she instead barricades herself in her room.

There, overwhelmed by her feelings, she sulks and thinks about Sam, the guy who sits across from her in math class. How could he have ignored her sitting at the same table at lunch, especially when he *must* know how she feels about him? How could he *not* know? It doesn't occur to her that she has never said so much as "hello" to Sam.

Alexandra cannot imagine that anyone, ever, has felt so much or so deeply. Those who study adolescent behaviour call this a "personal fable," the child's belief that she is, for better or worse, utterly different from everyone else. To a parent, such preteen—and even teenage—behaviour appears self-centred, even grandiose. But it is absolutely normal, and quite different from being selfish or putting on airs.

But how can you help your child get through this period of egocentrism, especially when it is frequently so difficult to communicate with her? You can start by maintaining your patience and empathy—and a good memory of your own adolescence.

By the preadolescent years, a child's emotional and mental sophistication has grown to the point that she is quite comfortable with thinking abstractly. She asks new questions: "What if I try acting like this instead?" If I dress that way, what will happen?" Her sudden discovery of all these new alternatives is exhilarating, but with it comes profound uncertainty about making the right choices.

Within your family, your child often displays this uncertainty by questioning the house rules. Although being challenged by your preteen can be trying, remember that the questioning comes not out of disrespect but because, for the first time, your child envisions a range of alternatives.

At the same time that they are moving rapidly toward maturity, young teens are still in many ways children. They have a tendency to focus almost exclusively on their own ideas, feelings, and behaviour. Assuming that they are as central in the thoughts of others as they are in their own, children this age often feel as if an imaginary audience is continually observing and judging everything they say, do, feel, and wear.

That's why 13-year-old Tom flushes with embarrassment and fury when his mother volunteers to chaperone a school dance. Even if he doesn't attend, he'll be humiliated because everyone will know that his mother is there. Reminded that there will be 10 adult chaperones and, therefore, 9 other classmates in the same boat, Tom responds, "Well, they don't care as much about what their parents do." As far as he is concerned, his own shame is uniquely awful.

Preteens tend to feel that their problems are more obvious and important than those of other people. Sally, 11, feels sure that everyone can tell she's wearing a tampon. And 12-year-old Richard sits at his desk, head tucked into his arm, convinced that the new pimple on his cheek is the object of everyone's disgusted gaze.

The worst thing you can do when your child's outsize emotions are on display is to dismiss them. They may seem silly to you, but they are all too real to her. If she broods for days about whether she said the right thing to a boy she met at a party, or insists on a certain style of shirt, don't make fun of her or say that her worries aren't important. Doing so will only reinforce her sense that no one understands her.

Don't dismiss a child's need to be accepted.

And be tolerant of the fact that, because your child feels so utterly different from everyone else, fitting in with his peers becomes a top priority in his life. Accept his need to be accepted. If he spurns your peck on his cheek as you're

dropping him off at school and says, "You're embarrassing me in front of all my friends," it won't help for you to point out that no one can see inside the car.

Your wisest course of action in such cases is to talk about his concerns and to negotiate solutions that both of you can live with. For example, you might express your willingness not only to stop kissing him when you leave him at school but also to drop him off around the corner and out of sight—if he is willing to offer you a hug when he gets home. It should be added, however, that acknowledging your child's need to be part of the crowd does not require that you accept open rudeness or give in to demands for the most expensive sneakers in the store.

You can't banish your preteen's self-consciousness, but you can help him see that although others think and care about him, they also have other things on their minds. One way to accomplish this is to share your own adolescence with him. (This is where a good memory—or a high school yearbook—can come in handy.)

Think back to your own adolescent crises. In describing to your child how embarrassed you were the time you had to take a shower after gym class, or how hopelessly in love you were after your first date, you can help him understand that he is not alone in his feelings. Focus on how you felt at the time, not on how "everything worked out fine."

If your daughter is among the first girls in her class to start developing breasts, acknowledge how embarrassing that can be, and then talk about the ways that other kids in her class stand out. How might another girl feel about being the tallest or the only one with braces? Help your child see that all of her peers are different in some way, and that this difference is not necessarily bad.

Outside pursuits get kids outside themselves.

Another way that you can give your preteen a less egocentric perspective on the world is by encouraging her to be involved with a range of activities and

>

people. Playing multiple roles in sports, joining arts groups, or even being with peers who share a hobby can shift your child's focus outside herself.

As your child gets older, she'll begin to realize that her thoughts and emotions are not as odd or unique as she once believed. Of course, most of us keep traces of our youthful egocentrism; we all feel that we're the ones who always get the parking ticket or pick the slowest line at the store. But adults have realized that their imaginary audience is just that—imaginary. Be patient; your preteen will realize it too.

Source: Lerner, R. M., & Olson, C. K. (1994, February). The imaginary audience. *Parents*, pp. 133–134.

Social Cognition During Adolescence

ISSUES TO CONSIDER

- What are the characteristics of adolescent social cognition?
- How does social cognition differ between younger and older adolescents?

Formal operational thinking may be applied to any content area, including mathematics or the social world. This latter content area is termed social cognition. Such thought may involve virtually any aspect of the adolescent's social life. The development of social cognition occurs in a manner consistent with changes that are associated with formal operational development more generally.

Young adolescents, who are at the threshold of their formal operational period, may make decisions about social issues in a manner that is more egocentric than would be the case among youth at later points in their formal operational period. In a study of youth ranging in age from 6 through 18 years (Dyl & Wapner, 1996), younger individuals were more egocentric than older ones in their thoughts about cherished social objects (e.g., emphasizing the personal enjoyment provided by such possessions). Older youth thought about such valued possessions in a manner that reflected their understanding of the social relationships involved with one's possessions.

Social cognition among older youth typically involves the use of social principles. In a study of 120 Latino and European American Grade 5, 8, and 11 students (Phinney & Cobb, 1996), youth were asked to respond to a dilemma in which a student from one ethnic group wished to join an exclusive club of the other ethnic group. Although three-quarters of the participants made judgments to include the student, and neither ethnicity, grade, nor gender was related to these judgments of inclusion, older youth more often cited abstract social principles, as compared to individual welfare, as the basis for their decisions

(Phinney & Cobb, 1996). In a study of the strategies 10-, 12-, and 14-year-olds use to present themselves socially, youth were asked about their willingness to portray themselves as diligent and as making a lot of effort to work hard in school (Juvonen & Murdock, 1995). Adolescents in the two younger age groups wanted to present themselves as effortful to both teachers and peers. However, in light of a changing idea about the social value of achievement among one's peers and of the tactics one must use for successful self-presentation to friends, the older adolescents were more reluctant to convey to their popular peers that they were diligent students (Juvonen & Murdock, 1995).

Adolescents who are at the beginning of their formal operational period may not make decisions about social issues in as differentiated a manner as occurs later in their formal operational period. In a study of students from Grades 4, 6, and 8, youth were asked about the role a peer plays when the peer witnesses an act of aggression perpetrated by either a sibling or by a friend (Tisak & Tisak, 1996). The younger participants tended to think that bystanders should intervene and in fact would intervene. The older participants indicated that there is more of an expectation to intervene when the perpetrator is a sibling, and it would be more wrong not to intervene when the aggressor was a sibling than a friend (Tisak & Tisak, 1996).

Other evidence suggests that older adolescents possess a differentiated social cognitive structure. In two studies of about 350 late adolescents enrolled in university, evidence was found for several distinct components of social cognition (e.g., social perception, social knowledge, and social insight) (Wong et al., 1995). Other evidence indicates that such a differentiated intellectual orientation to the world is used when youth make social decisions. Adolescence is a time of choices involving self-definition and social roles (topics discussed in Chapters 6 and 7). Young people must

The choices adolescents make are facilitated by their capacities for hypothetical and propositional thought.

make decisions about what sorts of activities they will undertake, both in the present and in the future. In one study of such decisions (Finken & Jacobs, 1996), 18- to 20-year-old adolescents were presented with four topic areas (abortion, medical issues, future plans, and interpersonal relations) and asked to select the people they would turn to for advice. Consistent with the presence of a differentiated cognitive structure, one in which different social issues are understood in their specific context, adolescents indicated they would consult with different groups for the different topics. For example, although abortion decisions may involve medical procedures, adolescents indicated they would prefer to consult with different people for advice about abortion than for advice about general medical issues (Finken & Jacobs, 1996). Similarly, with increasing development, individuals reason about gender roles, social conventions, and moral rules with greater flexibility (Levy, Taylor, & Gelman, 1995).

Social cognition develops across the formal operational stage in a manner reflective of other cognitive changes of this stage. Social thought becomes less egocentric and more responsive to societal conventions. It becomes more differentiated and more attuned to the particular social audience or context to which it is directed, and it is also increasingly more reflective of abstract principles of social organization.

Conclusions About Formal Operations

Egocentrism of the formal operational stage diminishes over the course of the person's subsequent cognitive functioning. According to Piaget (Inhelder & Piaget, 1958), the adolescent "decentres" through interaction with peers, elders, and, most importantly, with the assumption of adult roles and responsibilities: "The focal point of the decentering process is the entrance into the occupational world or the beginning of serious professional training. The adolescent becomes an adult when he or she undertakes a real job" (Inhelder & Piaget, 1958, p. 346).

Quite interestingly, Piaget sees the end point of adolescence as the adoption of a role in society, an idea consistent with what we will learn (in Chapter 6) is formulated by Erikson (1959, 1963). Thus within different theoretical perspectives the linkage of adolescents with their society through the processes of role search and attainment is a core component of development (Kahlbaugh & Haviland, 1991). Indeed, formal operations are related to adolescent identity resolution (Leadbeater & Dionne, 1981). Some scholars (e.g., Wagner, 1987) have posited that formal operations are necessary for identity achievement in adolescence.

What, then, does the achievement of formal operations give adolescents? How does it help them deal with the developmental tasks imposed by their changed body? How does it help them find an appropriate niche in the social world? Being able to think hypothetically allows adolescents to imagine what their life would be like if they chose one or another life path: "Would I, given my physical characteristics, my beliefs, my values, and my hopes, be able to be a salesclerk, a day care worker, an athlete, or a parent? Would I be more happy doing one or the other of these things?" Formal operational thinking gives adolescents the ability to see themselves as workers, as parents, and as citizens. Given their understanding of their physical and psychological characteristics, formal thought enables adolescents to make plans and to establish goals and priorities.

For example, a tall, big-boned girl may understand that she would not do well in a career as a ballet dancer; but perhaps she would succeed in, and could plan for, sports such as basketball. In turn, a boy who understood that he liked helping others, enjoyed working with people, but did not prefer highly technical or scientific endeavours, could plan to enter the field of social work (as opposed to medicine or nursing).

Accordingly, formal thought allows adolescents to plan and to obtain the knowledge and skills for entry into the world of work, and to fit their individual characteristics with available or possible social roles. Formal thought allows adolescents to meet their psychological developmental tasks of understanding self and defining self appropriately and to move in the direction of becoming an independent adult. Adolescents will be able to be autonomous, self-governing people to the extent that they know who they are, know what they want, and can plan accordingly.

Conclusions

Formal thought allows people to demonstrate planful responsibility for their future, to plan to prepare themselves to merge with the social world as responsible partners in the enterprise of advancing self and their society. Such responsible partnership with the social world gives adolescents an important sense of morality (Kohlberg, 1978). It gives them a sense that an implicit, mutual contract exists between adolescents and their society. Society will provide a role that will allow adolescents to exercise their individuality, particular interests and abilities, and the opportunity to test this role. In turn, adolescents will responsibly perform these roles and be, for instance, productive workers, good parents, and participating citizens. In its most general sense, formal operations ability enables adolescents to organize a belief system involving self and society. It gives them a life plan, an ideology, and a moral code by which to live.

In short, a key contribution of cognitive development to adolescent functioning is the potential role it may play in allowing the young people to exist as moral members of society. We explore this potential contribution in the next chapter.

Summary

- The adolescent years involve changes in cognition and personality that influence each other and are influenced by the social, cultural, and broader ecological contexts.
- Cognitively, adolescents have more quantitative knowledge and think about their world in qualitatively different ways.
- There are debates about what psychological characteristics are actually measured by intelligence tests. Spearman hypothesized that one general intellectual factor ("g") is being measured. Guilford theorized that over 100 different abilities can be measured by intelligence tests. Intelligence tests with Canadian norms are available.
- Other scholars propose that different aspects of cognition are assessed by intelligence tests and that the distinct dimensions of quantitative intelligence remain consistent across the adolescent years.
- Qualitative features of cognition constitute a key dimension of cognitive development.
- Academic achievement is affected by multiple levels of the context of human development, ranging from the most macro cultural influences to micro interpersonal influences involving peers and family members.
- The academic achievements of youth from different cultural backgrounds differ due, primarily, to socialization experiences beginning in childhood.
- Family and peer variables have an influence on academic achievement.
- Peers have a facilitative influence on academic achievement. The use of peers seems especially useful when the interactions with them are specifically relevant to the particular problem at hand. Spending a lot of time in informal peer interactions appears to have a negative impact on academic achievement—high sociability ratings from peers is linked to lower academic competence.
- Some instances of low achievement are related to adolescents' own characterization of themselves. "Self-handicapping strategies" are associated with self-deprecation, negative attitudes toward education, and low grades.
- Self-enhancing strategies such as the ability to delay gratification in preschool facilitates cognitive and academic competence in adolescence.
- There are numerous interventions that enhance academic achievement among youth and the interrelated problems of youth development.
- Adolescents' literacy skills can affect their own life chances as well as others in their social world.
- In Piaget's theory, cognitive development involves the relation between the person and the context. The person-context relation involves two processes: *assimilation* and *accommodation*.
- Piaget proposes that the goal of cognitive development is to create an *equilibration* between assimilation and accommodation.

- When the person is more concerned with the perspective of the subject than with the actual details of the object the person is said to be *egocentric.*

- Overcoming the egocentrism prototypic of each stage leads the person to attain the cognitive development most central to that stage.

- In the formal operational stage, the child's thoughts about reality take on a hypothetical "if . . . then" characteristic.

- The cognitive structure that characterizes formal operations is termed the *INRC group* by Piaget. All transformations of a problem may be obtained through the application of the components of this group: identity, negation, reciprocal, and correlative transformations.

- Conditional reasoning increases across adolescence, involving the idea that "if p, then q"— the logical statement in scientific hypotheses.

- A cognitive developmental progression exists, one that involves the adolescent moving from inductive to deductive reasoning strategies.

- The emergence of formal operational thought is not a characteristic of all youth. Not all individuals attain formal operations.

- People in many cultural settings do not attain formal operational abilities at the average time in life that it occurs within Western cultural settings.

- Egocentrism coincides with the emergence of adolescence and is complicated by the physiological, emotional, and social changes involved in this period of life.

- With adolescent egocentrism, the adolescent's own thoughts come to predominate his or her thinking. The adolescent constructs an *imaginary audience.* The adolescent's thoughts and feelings are experienced as new and unique. The adolescent constructs a *personal fable.*

- Across the formal operational stage, social thought becomes less egocentric and more responsive to societal conventions.

- Through interaction with peers, elders, and, most importantly, with the assumption of adult roles and responsibilities, the adolescent decentres and the egocentrism of this stage diminishes.

- Piaget sees the end point of adolescence as the adoption of a role in society. Formal operations enables the adolescent to organize a belief system involving self and society.

Discussion Topics

1. Think of some experiences from your own childhood. Do you remember having an argument or disagreement with your parent(s) that at the time was very important and relevant to your life but now seems to be what you might define as typical teenage behaviour? Why, at the time, were you so devoted to your side of the argument? Does your response include multiple life contexts and reasons? Why?

2. Why is it appropriate to use Canadian norms to determine the IQ of a Canadian youth?

3. How does the fact that IQ remains relatively stable throughout life colour your view on the value of standardized tests and the courses and curricula designed to "teach to the test"?

4. Give an example of how an elementary school child and a high school child think differently about a specific emotional situation and about a specific academic experience.

5. How have your ecological contexts impacted your academic achievement?

6. How might an adolescent's ability to think hypothetically add to his or her conflict resolution skills?

7. How has your specific cultural socialization impacted your academic achievement and cognitive competence?

8. Why is it important for educational institutions to recognize and appreciate the cultural variations inherent in approaches to academic achievement?

9. What are some of the challenges facing refugees to Canada that affect their academic achievement?

10. How have your peers helped or hindered your cognitive development?

11. Why do some adolescents adopt self-handicapping strategies and some self-enhancing? Are

there certain individual and/or contextual assets or risks that lead some teens to adopt more harmful/less supportive learning traits?

12. Were the programs offered by your high school designed to support those with learning disabilities and/or life circumstances that compromise academic achievement? Why or why not?

13. Do you believe your literacy skills were predetermined by the literacy achievement of your parent(s)?

14. Give an example of a memory of a concept that went through the equilibration process—that was assimilated and accommodated to. For example, as a school-aged child you thought one way about a concept and as a teenager you were able to realize there were many more "sides to the coin."

15. How do you feel adolescent egocentrism limits and defines the thought processes of teenagers? Specifically, did the imaginary audience and personal fables of your life limit your experiences and understandings? How?

16. Why might a simple concept such as the "if . . . then" logic of thinking expand your world and cognitive competence?

17. Think of an example to which you could apply the INRC grouping to explain the characteristics of formal operational thought.

18. Cite evidence to prove that formal operations do not exist as a "structured whole." Can you be "advanced" in one content area and "behind" in others?

19. Why might not formal operational thought be universal? Can you make assumptions about those who do not attain formal operational thought? Are those assumptions qualified? Must you be cautious in making those assumptions? Why or why not?

20. How might formal operational thought prepare you to be a participating member of society?

21. How has interaction with peers, elders, and, most importantly, the assumption of adult roles and responsibilities, helped to diminish any sense of egocentrism you may have experienced as an adolescent?

Key Terms

accommodation, p. 89
adolescent egocentrism, p. 96
assimilation, p. 89
centration, p. 95
conditional reasoning, p. 92
correlative transformation, p. 92
deductive reasoning, p. 93
disequilibration, p. 90

egocentrism, p. 90
equilibration, p. 89
falsification strategies, p. 93
formal operational thought, p. 90
identity transformation, p. 92
imaginary audience, p. 96
inductive reasoning, p. 93
INRC grouping, p. 91

IQ, p. 83
negation operation, p. 92
personal fable, p. 96
qualitative differences, p. 88
reciprocal transformation, p. 92
reproductive assimilation, p. 89
social cognition, p. 96

5

Moral Development Behaviour, and Civil Society

Scott thought Mr. Simpson was a terrific teacher, perhaps the best he had had in his four years at Pathground High. Mr. Simpson made the honours calculus course come alive. Even though it was really hard for Scott, and his grade in the course was still dependent on the final, Mr. Simpson's love for math was infectious. He conveyed enthusiasm to his students and generated in them an excitement for learning. He was also nice, approachable, and always willing to spend as much time as necessary to help his students. When Scott had asked him to write letters of recommendation for university, Mr. Simpson did not flinch—even when Scott said that he was applying to 10 universities, each needing a letter.

Scott also thought Mr. Simpson was one of the most disorganized people he had ever known. He always seemed to misplace things and, because he never remembered to check his daily calendar or wear a watch, he was inevitably running late for appointments.

As Scott knocked on the door to the teacher's lounge, to meet Mr. Simpson and give him copies of the final two forms he needed to complete the letters of recommendation, Scott was not surprised to hear a frazzled-sounding Mr. Simpson tell him to come in. "Hi, Mr. Simpson," Scott said, as he saw Mr. Simpson rushing to gather papers off the table in front of him and balance them under his arm atop of the books and folders he was also carrying. "I've brought the two copies of the forms I need you to fill out for me."

"Thanks, Scott. Please just stick them on top of this pile here under my arm. I'll be sure not to lose them this time. I'll put them in a folder as soon as I get to my next class."

"Are you sure, Mr. Simpson?" Scott asked. "It looks like you have a lot of papers there and they might get mixed in with them. I could just follow you to class and help you get organized and then put the letters in the folder for you."

"No, that won't work, Scott. These are copies of the honours calculus final exam. My first section of the course takes the exam this next period. Since you won't be taking the exam until last period, I don't think it's a good idea for you to help me organize these papers."

"Oh, sure. I agree. I didn't know what you were carrying,"

"I know, Scott. No problem. I'll be careful with the letters this time. Just stick them under my arm . . . Thanks."

Scott placed the letters on top of the pile and Mr. Simpson hurried out of the door and down the hall. Scott followed him out and saw him start a sprint down the corridor. As the bell to start the period sounded, Mr. Simpson moved the books and papers under his arm to the front of his body in order to cradle them with two hands as he continued his run.

A paper flew out from the pile and landed behind the now rapidly receding Mr. Simpson. Scott ran to get the paper, certain that it must be one of his letters. The long hall was now empty as Scott caught up to the fallen paper. Scott picked the paper up. It was not one of his letters. Typed across the top of the paper was the title "Honours Calculus: Final Exam."

Mr. Simpson would never know that he had lost this one copy of the exam, and no one would know that Scott had found it. He could, unbeknownst to anyone else, spend the rest of the day preparing the answers to the exam, ace it, and be sure that a great grade in an honours course would be reported to university admissions' offices. Or, he could simply destroy the copy and not even look at it. Or, he could just give it back to Mr. Simpson, and hope he would believe Scott had not looked at it. What should he do?

Learning Objectives

1. To understand what civil society is and how it can be promoted.
2. To appreciate why the study of moral development is important.
3. To understand Lawrence Kohlberg's framework for studying moral development and to describe his levels and stages of moral development.

4. To recognize that individual and contextual factors influence levels of moral reasoning.

5. To understand how war and social conflict can influence moral reasoning.

6. To understand the development of prosocial behaviour and the influences on it.

7. To appreciate the need for "youth charters" that create partnerships in the promotion of civil society.

8. To identify the 20 internal and 20 external developmental assets of youth and how these assets correlate with positive youth development.

9. To understand the model for promoting civil society through enhancing positive youth development and how this model may influence future generations.

10. To identify the "five Cs" related to positive developmental outcomes that can be attained from appropriate policies and programs.

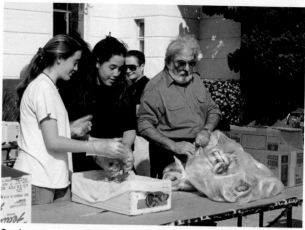

One key component of positive youth development is caring (or compassion) for others.

ISSUES TO CONSIDER
• What is civil society? How is it maintained?
• What is the relation between civil society and adolescent moral development?

For any society to maintain and perpetuate itself over the course of generations, it must become committed to promoting the healthy, productive, and successful development of self, family, and society. Such a commitment by youth constitutes an allegiance to **civil society**, that is, to society's nongovernmental and governmental institutions (including cultural and political values) that provide rights to people and require responsibilities of individuals (Lerner, Fisher, & Weinberg, 2000a). Civil society balances the rights "granted to individuals in free societies and the responsibilities required by citizens to maintain those rights" (O'Connell, 1999, pp. 10–11).

For civil society to exist, individuals must believe in and hold values that support a just, democratic social order. In both their personal lives and their roles as citizens, individuals must support justice and act to maintain governmental institutions and laws, and nongovernmental organizations that promote social justice, equity, and democracy.

Within the context of civil society, morally developed youth think and behave in ways that maintain and enhance a just social order. Moral development involves thinking and behaving **prosocially**, in ways that allow society to create a just and equitable system. Given the crucial importance of the survival of a civil society, and of the quality of life of citizens within such a society, the study of moral development

continues to be a central concern of scholars of human development and of adolescence in particular.

As noted in Chapter 2, Piaget (1932/1965), in *The Moral Judgment of the Child*, provided an important theoretical foundation for this topic. He discussed the development of moral reasoning and stressed that the child initially judges right and wrong solely on the basis of the objective outcomes of a behaviour. For example, if the child's behaviour resulted in a broken cup, the child is bad. At a subsequent point in development, the child makes judgments based on intentions. For example, if the child broke the cup intentionally, the child would be judged as bad; but if the act was an accident, no negative judgment would be made.

Building on Piaget's work, Lawrence Kohlberg (1958, 1963a, 1963b, 1976, 1978), Elliot Turiel (1969; Nucci & Turiel, 1993), Nancy Eisenberg (1986, 1991; Carlo, Eisenberg, & Knight, 1992), Paul Mussen (Eisenberg & Mussen, 1989; Mussen et al., 1970), William Damon (1997), Anne Colby (1978; Colby et al., 1983), and Lawrence Walker (Walker & Taylor, 1991; Walker & Henning, 1999) have extended the study of moral development in several significant ways. Today, the study of adolescent moral functioning

Civil society Society in which cultural and political values, as well as all nongovernmental and governmental institutions, both provide rights to people and require responsibilities of individuals.

Prosocial behaviour Behaviour that allows society to create a just and equitable system; individuals act in a way that contributes to a just social order.

focuses on both moral thinking or reasoning *and* moral behaviours, especially prosocial behaviours, that is, behaviours that *benefit* society. The study of moral development has also been extended to include an interest in how the strengths of the developing adolescent may be integrated with the assets of communities to enhance the likelihood that young people will develop the cognitive, emotional, and behavioural attributes necessary for contributing to civil society.

In this chapter we discuss all three of these topics: the development of moral reasoning, the character and bases of prosocial behaviour, and the ways that youth and community assets may be combined to further civil society. Building on the discussion of cognitive development in adolescence (Chapter 4), we begin this presentation with a discussion of the development of moral reasoning.

Chapter 2 introduced the general characteristics of Kohlberg's theory of moral reasoning development. In the relatively recent history of the study of moral development, Kohlberg's theory and research has been most influential. We present more details of his work in order to provide a framework for discussing what is known about adolescent moral functioning.

Lawrence Kohlberg's Theory of the Development of Moral Reasoning

ISSUES TO CONSIDER

- What is the focus of Kohlberg's theory of moral development?
- What are Kohlberg's three levels and six stages of moral development?

Kohlberg (1958, 1963, 1978) proposed that a theory of moral development should focus on the reasons for moral behaviour, rather than moral behaviour itself. Two people could show similar moral behaviour, but the reason for their behaviour can be very different. For example, one person could refuse to steal because he or she was afraid of being caught and punished. The second could say one should not steal because such behaviour violates principles of mutual trust. Kohlberg devised a way to ascertain the reasons underlying moral behaviour through the construction of a moral development interview. Information derived from this interview provided the data for his theory.

Kohlberg's Method of Assessing Moral Reasoning

To understand the reasons for a person's moral behaviour, Kohlberg devised a series of stories, each presenting an imaginary moral dilemma. Here is an example:

One day, air raid sirens began to sound. Everyone realized that a hydrogen bomb was going to be dropped on the city by the enemy, and that the only way to survive was to be in a bomb shelter. Not everyone had bomb shelters, but those who did ran quickly to them. Since Mr. and Mrs. McKay had built a shelter, they immediately went to it where they had enough air inside to last them for exactly five days. They knew that after five days the fallout would have diminished to the point where they could safely leave the shelter. If they left before that, they would die. There was enough air for the McKays only. Their next-door neighbours had not built a shelter and were trying to get in. The McKays knew that they would not have enough air if they let the neighbours in, and that they would all die if they came inside. So they refused to let them in.

So now the neighbours were trying to break the door down in order to get in. Mr. McKay took his rifle and told them to go away or else he would shoot. They would not go away. So he either had to shoot them or let them come into the shelter.

This story is a moral dilemma because it presents a conflict to the listener. In this particular story the conflict involves the need for making a choice between two culturally unacceptable alternatives: killing others so that you might survive or allowing others and yourself and family to die. The story presents a dilemma because it puts the listener in a conflict situation such that any response is clearly not the only acceptable one. For Kohlberg, the particular response is irrelevant, but what is of concern is the reasoning used to resolve the conflict. Thus Kohlberg asks the listener not just to tell him what Mr. McKay should do but why Mr. McKay should do whatever the listener decides.

Kohlberg would first ask, "What should Mr. McKay do?" Next he would ask, "Does he have the right to shoot his neighbours if he feels they would all die if he let them in because there would not be enough air to last very long? Why?" Then, "Does he have the right to keep his neighbours out of his shelter even though he knows they will die if he keeps them out? Why?" And finally Kohlberg would ask, "Does he have the right to let them in if he knows they will all die? Why?"

Table 5-1 **Levels and Stages in Lawrence Kohlberg's Theory of Moral Reasoning**

Level 1: Preconventional

Stage 1. Heteronomous morality.	"Egocentric point of view." The person does not consider the interests of others or recognize that they differ from the actor's. The person does not relate two points of view. Actions are considered physically rather than in terms of the psychological interests of others. There is a confusion of authority's perspective with one's own.
Stage 2. Individualism, instrumental purpose, and exchange.	"Concrete individualistic perspective." The person is aware that everybody has interests to pursue and that these can conflict. What is right is relative (in the concrete individualistic sense).

Level 2: Conventional

Stage 3. Mutual interpersonal expectations, relationships, and interpersonal conformity.	"Perspective of the individual in relationships with other individuals." The person is aware of shared feelings, agreements, and expectations, which take primacy over individual interests, and relates points of view through the concrete "golden rule" and putting oneself "in the other guy's shoes." The person does not yet consider generalized system perspective.
Stage 4. Social system and conscience.	"Differentiates societal point of view from interpersonal agreement or motives." At this stage, the person takes the point of view of the larger system that defines roles and rules and considers individual relations in terms of play in the system.

Level 3: Postconventional, or Principled

Stage 5. Social contract or utility and individual rights.	"Prior-to-society perspective." The rational individual is aware of values and rights prior to social attachments and contracts. Such a person integrates perspectives by formal mechanisms of agreement, contract, objective impartiality, and due process; considers moral and legal points of view; and recognizes that they sometimes conflict and finds it difficult to integrate them.
Stage 6. Universal ethical principles or principled morality.	Self-chosen ethical principles. This stage involves abstract moral guidelines of universal justice. When laws violate ethical principles, a person at this stage acts according to the principles. The individual responds in a way to avoid self-condemnation.

Source: Adapted from Kohlberg, 1976; Schonert-Reichl, 2001.

On the basis of an elaborate and complicated system for scoring, the reasons people give to questions about this and other dilemmas (Kohlberg, 1958, 1963a; Kurtines & Greif, 1974) have evolved into a system that has undergone considerable revision (Colby, 1979). Kohlberg classifies people into different reasoning categories. This classification led him to formulate the idea that a sequence exists in the types of reasons people offer about their responses to moral dilemmas. He believed that the types of moral reasoning people use pass through a series of qualitatively different stages. Kohlberg (1976, 1978) and his collaborators (Colby, 1978, 1979) specify five stages of moral reasoning. The first and second stages, and the third and fourth stages, are associated with two distinct levels of moral thought, respectively. The

fifth stage is associated with a third level. There was a sixth stage, but this was achieved so rarely that eventually it was removed from the model and considered a hypothetical stage. Only 10% to 15% of people even reach stage five, and this rarely happens before young adulthood (Schonert-Reichl, 2001). Kohlberg's levels and stages are shown in Table 5.1.

Heteronomous morality Form of moral reasoning in which the person does not consider the interests of others or recognize that the interests of others differ from his or her own.

Developmental Sequences in Moral Reasoning

ISSUE TO CONSIDER

● What evidence exists that there is a progression in the development of moral reasoning?

Kohlberg and his colleagues (e.g., Kohlberg, 1958, 1963a, 1963b, 1971, 1976; Colby et al., 1983) investigated whether moral reasoning progresses through a sequence akin to that suggested by his theory. Other researchers have also investigated how both moral reasoning and moral behaviours develop. Taken together, this research indicates that there is some sequence to moral reasoning development.

Data collected in a longitudinal study by Kohlberg and his colleagues (Colby, 1979; Colby et al., 1983) provide the strongest support of the view that from late childhood to the early part of the middle adult years, people go through the stages of moral reasoning in the manner Kohlberg specifies. Other data also suggest a developmental progression toward using principles or intentions to judge whether a person's behaviours are moral (Lourenço, 1990; Walker & Taylor, 1991). For example, final-year university students showed a higher level of moral reasoning than first-year students when asked about behaviours that could lead to the transmission of sexually transmitted diseases (STDs) (Jadack et al., 1995). In a longitudinal study of elementary and high school students' reasoning about moral dilemmas, elementary school children's reasoning tended to be pleasure or approval oriented, stereotyped, interpersonally oriented, or concerned about others' needs (Eisenberg-Berg, 1979). Each of these indicates lower levels of moral reasoning than that exhibited by the high school students. The high school students expressed more empathy in discussing the moral dilemmas. The moral judgments showed that as children get older, they are more likely to internalize values just as Kohlberg predicted.

Other studies indicate that adolescents use a variety of reasons to support their moral judgments. Early in adolescence, youth use reasons that reflect narrow or selfish concerns as well as concerns about care (wanting others not to suffer) and justice (using principles such as the "golden rule") (Perry & McIntire, 1995). Although all types of reasons are used by both males and females, boys were more likely than girls to use "narrow," selfish reasons (Perry & McIntire, 1995). Although in early adolescence girls are more advanced in their moral reasoning, by late adolescence and adulthood, sex differences in level of moral reasoning disappear (Basinger, Gibbs, & Fuller, 1995; Jadack et al., 1995).

Diversity and Context in Moral Development

ISSUE TO CONSIDER

● Why do individual differences and context need to be considered when studying moral development and behaviour?

Moral development involves an orientation of a person toward others in his or her world. This underscores the social relational character of morality and why society deems morality so integral to maintaining the quality of life in a community. However, not all youth have similar levels of moral reasoning. This variation seems to be associated with gender and with different types of social experiences. Most of these experiences relate to interactions with models of moral behaviour, including family members and people in the community (Camino, 1995). Individual differences and context need to be taken into account in understanding both the development of moral reasoning and of moral behaviour. Walker (1991) cautions that culture needs to be considered when attempting to apply Kohlberg's theory. For example, many of his participants in China noted that the dilemma about stealing a drug to save someone's life was characteristic of capitalistic societies and would not arise in countries that had public ownership of the medical system.

Gender Differences

ISSUE TO CONSIDER

● What differences exist in moral reasoning and behaviour between males and females?

There is some evidence of gender differences in the development of moral reasoning. Carol Gilligan (1982) argues that approaches such as Kohlberg's stress the male "voice" of moral reasoning, a voice focused on "justice," rather than the female voice of reasoning, a voice focused on "care." Although not all research supports Gilligan's viewpoint (e.g., Brabeck, 1983; Walker, 1984), there are findings consistent with her perspective (e.g., Pratt, Golding, Hunter, & Sampson, 1988).

Adolescent girls, more so than adolescent boys, show a care-based morality that involves caring for other people (Skoe & Gooden, 1993). Girls also have more personal, real-life dilemmas, whereas boys have more impersonal ones. Girls' emotions are often related to their interpersonal caring and their involvement in the problems of other significant people in their lives (Gore, Aseltine, & Colten, 1993). Girls tend to be more concerned about hurting others and maintaining friendships; boys are more likely to be concerned about leisure activities and avoiding trouble (Skoe & Gooden, 1993). The extent to which gender differences exist may depend on the age of adolescents as well as on culture. For example, Skoe, Morch, and Bakke (1999) found that when tested on the Ethic of Care Interview (a measure created to assess "care-based morality"), no gender differences were found for North American late adolescents or young adults. However, when Canadian early adolescents (aged 11 to 13) were tested, girls scored significantly higher than boys and provided more relational dilemmas when asked to report a personal moral conflict. Yet no such gender differences were found for similar aged Norwegians. The authors suggested that possible differences in gender role expectations between the two countries could explain the different results. The findings of stronger gender differences at younger ages in Canada support the gender intensification hypothesis, which suggests that societal pressure to be masculine or feminine is greatest during early adolescence (see Chapter 7).

Although not associated with Gilligan's (1982) ideas, other research does suggest gender differences in moral reasoning. From childhood through adolescence and into adulthood, women's overall prosocial moral reasoning increases more so than is the case for men (Eisenberg et al., 1995). However, for both women and men there are relations among prosocial reasoning, feelings of sympathy, the cognitive ability to take another person's perspective, and prosocial *behaviour* (Eisenberg et al., 1995). The prosocial behaviour of both men and women is related to having socially integrative goals, as compared to self-enhancing goals (Estrada, 1995).

There are also gender differences in ideas about punishments for violating behavioural rules. Young adolescent boys see punishment for cheating as more acceptable than for breaking classroom rules about talking or getting out of one's seat (Bear & Stewart, 1990). Girls are more accepting of applying discipline for any infraction of rules.

There is diversity in moral reasoning, moral behaviour, and in other morality-related thoughts and feelings (e.g., perspective taking, judging rule

Prosocial behaviour in adolescence may involve caring for others.

violations, empathy, and caring) linked to variation across development and to gender. This variation is also associated with contextual effects involving social interactions of several types.

Contextual "Models" of Moral Behaviour

ISSUES TO CONSIDER
- How can modelling promote moral development in youth?
- What other contextual factors can influence moral functioning?

For more than 30 years, research has demonstrated that moral reasoning and behaviour does not just naturally unfold. Rather, people in a youth's life shape his or her morality. The fact that modelling positive, or prosocial, moral behaviour can help develop it in others has resulted in several programs being designed worldwide to instill a prosocial orientation in youth. Given the investment all societies have in socializing the next generation to maintain and enhance the social fabric of their nation, and the increasing economic, technological, and ecological interdependence of all nations, it is likely that such programs will become even more important in the future. The programs discussed in Applications Box 5.1 illustrate the nature and scope of current efforts to foster moral leadership values and citizenship skills among today's youth.

Parents and peers can influence the moral development of adolescents. For instance, young adolescent girls who show high levels of honesty and altruism have warm, intimate interactions with their mothers and high self-esteem. For boys, honesty is negatively related to gratifying relationships with parents and peers and to self-esteem (Mussen et al., 1970).

Creating Character, Caring, Competence, and Community Commitment Among Diverse Youth

Every society in the world needs a younger generation committed to and capable of moral, compassionate, intellectually sound, and productive leadership. The individuals, families, and communities of any nation will be healthier, and provide a more wholesome and higher quality of life, when its youth have such capacities.

Around the world, organizations and programs are striving to develop such youth community leadership. Three such programs, one involving more than 30 nations around the globe, one centred in Canada and one in the United States, are described.

A School-Based Approach to Learning Life Skills: The Quest International "Skills for Growing, Skills for Adolescence and Skills for Action" Programs of Maryland, United States

Founded in 1975, Quest International is an organization dedicated to the positive development of young people. Since its inception, Quest has recognized the need for children and youth to grow up and learn in healthy, safe, and nurturing environments. In its work with schools, community agencies, and youth-serving organizations worldwide, Quest has transmitted its belief that young people must be provided guidance so they may embrace positive values such as honesty, integrity, respect for self and family, and service to others.

As a youth advocacy organization, Quest has joined over the years with like-minded partners to ensure that our schools become caring and nurturing environments, free of violence, weapons, and alcohol, tobacco, and other drugs. Joined in common purpose with its partners, Quest advocates a spirit of increased cooperation between families, schools, and other caring adults to meet the educational, physical, and emotional needs of youth. Throughout its existence, Quest has provided the tools and training to assist and empower parents, teachers, and community members in teaching children to make healthy decisions.

Lions Clubs International, an international service organization, has joined with Quest and other partners in the development of its programs aimed at positive youth development. These programs, *Skills for Growing*, designed for 5- to 10-year-old children, *Skills for Adolescence*, used with children 10 to 14 years of age, and *Skills for Action*, for 15- to 19-year-olds, focus on the importance of acquiring key life skills such as decision making, goal setting, knowledge about the danger of alcohol and drugs, self-confidence, and problem solving necessary for success in adult life.

Quest's programs are designed to involve the home and community in assisting young people to make the necessary connections between knowledge and responsible behaviour. In cooperation with its many partners representing service organizations, parent and community agencies, and professional societies, Quest's life skills programs are used by more than 300 000 educators in more than 30 countries. As a measure of its mission to serve youth worldwide, Quest has partners in the United States, Canada, New Zealand, Sweden, Argentina, Denmark, Finland, Germany, Iceland, India, Italy, the Netherlands, Norway, Pakistan, South Africa, Sri Lanka, and Thailand.

In a world full of danger and challenges, Quest's programs have made a difference in the lives of millions of young people in communities around the globe.

Katimavik

Katimavik is a seven-month long Canadian program for 17- to 21-year-olds. It is a national youth service learning program that aims to foster personal, social, and professional development by engaging youth in volunteer community work, training, and group interaction. The name means "meeting place" in Inuktitut. Emphasis is placed on leadership, second-language attainment, cultural discovery, environmental protection, and adoption of a healthy lifestyle. There are 11 participants in each group, which lives in three different regions during the program. Each group is deliberately made up of individuals from different regions of the country.

A recent evaluation of the program (Étude Économique Conseil [EEC], 2002) revealed that the proportion of participants who rated their leadership skills as "good" or "very good" increased from 44% before entering the program to 87% after finishing the program. The majority of participants (67%) agreed that Katimavik had beneficial effects on their plans for a career. Of the partner organizations involved with Katimavik, 92% agreed that the participants helped improve the quality of services provided to the community. The evaluation concluded that $1.49 was returned to Canadian society for every dollar spent on the Katimavik program.

Helping Youth Develop a Stronger Community: The "YouthBuild USA" Program of Massachusetts, United States

In the United States, there are 5.4 million young people between the ages of 16 and 24 who either have dropped out of school without a diploma or completed high school but are nonetheless unemployed. There are approximately 2 million homeless people and countless government-owned properties in need of rehabilitation and construction. These are some of the grim facts that prompted the establishment of the YouthBuild program.

Founded in 1988, YouthBuild USA is committed to creating and sustaining a broad-based national movement to enable young people to assume leadership, rebuild their communities, gain an education, and lead responsible lives. YouthBuild is a comprehensive youth and community development program that has been designed by community activists with considerable contribution from young people over more than 20

>

years. In 2001, there were 165 YouthBuild programs operating in 43 states.

Young people interested in renewing their communities are trained in construction skills for 12 to 18 months. During their training, they rehabilitate abandoned buildings to provide affordable permanent housing for the homeless or very low-income people. In rural areas, because there are few abandoned buildings, they construct new housing. Besides weeks of on-site supervised construction work, they enrich their knowledge base with off-site academic and job skills training and counselling for half the program time. They receive a weekly stipend of US$150. Upon completion of the YouthBuild program, graduates usually pursue a university education or obtain unsubsidized jobs in the construction industry where they earn between US$6 and US$18 per hour.

YouthBuild USA acts as a catalyst for positive change in the larger community by creating affordable housing; responding to the needs of homeless people and various community needs; creating access to well-paying, long-term, substantive jobs for young people; advocating for expanded resources for low-income communities and youth; providing and developing visible role models; and stabilizing and strengthening the economic fabric of local communities by fostering entrepreneurship and individual residential home ownership.

The YouthBuild program is operating in both urban and rural communities throughout the United States. Statistics collected each year since 1993 show that an average of 60% of students complete the program, and 85% of these go on to university or jobs with wages averaging $7.60 an hour. This is especially noteworthy since 89% of the students had previously dropped out of school and most have enormous obstacles to overcome in their personal lives.

Sources: International Youth Foundation, 2001. www.ifynet.org; Katimavik. Retrieved from: www.katimavik.ofg/internet/kati_english.htm; Étude Économique Conseil (EEC, 2002). Evaluation of the economic and social impacts of the Katimavik program. Retrieved from: www.katimavik.org/internet/kati_english.htm.

Other research indicates that parents' moral judgments are associated with adolescents' moral reasoning, especially for girls (Speicher, 1994). Walker's work at the University of British Columbia with 6- to 16-year-olds illustrates the role of parents. When parents are authoritative and ask the child for his/her opinions, help the child think through issues, and ensure that the child understands items under discussion, children are presented with opportunities to grow in moral reasoning (Walker & Henning, 1999). When they are engaged with their youth in a morally relevant discussion, parents adjust their moral reasoning to the level of their adolescents (Walker & Taylor, 1991). Parents' use of Socratic questioning, supportive interactions, and moral reasons higher than those of their offspring is associated with enhanced adolescent moral development (Walker & Taylor, 1991). Boyes and Allen (1993), at the University of British Columbia, and Pratt, Arnold, Pratt, and Diessner (1999), at Wilfrid Laurier University, found a positive relationship between authoritative parenting and the level of moral reasoning demonstrated by adolescents. Authoritative parenting may allow more sharing of perspectives between parents and children, helping to develop moral reasoning. In contrast, children who have parents who are opinionated, hostile, critical, defensive, and rigid are less likely to develop advanced moral reasoning (Walker & Henning, 1999).

The structure of the family, and the style of parent-child interaction, can influence moral functioning among youth. Young adolescents living in a divorced family report more family-related moral dilemmas than youth living in married families (Breen & Crosbie-Burnett, 1993).

Religiosity, perhaps especially in the home (McAdoo, 1995), can influence the development of moral reasoning and behaviour. In a Canadian national survey of 15- to 19-year-olds (Bibby, 2001), adolescents who attended religious services weekly were more conservative in their attitudes about sexual activities than were adolescents who did not attend services this often. A study of students at Catholic high schools in Winnipeg found that religiosity was related to prosocial values for boys but not for girls (Schludermann, Schludermann, & Huynh, 2000). Boys high in religiosity also had more positive attitudes about school, their families, their lives, and themselves in comparison to boys low in religiosity.

The community surrounding the adolescent and his or her family is linked to moral functioning as well. For instance, youth from several different religious communities—Amish-Mennonite, Dutch Reform Calvinist, and Conservative and Orthodox Jewish—were found to differentiate between moral and nonmoral religious issues (Nucci & Turiel, 1993). Moral rules and some nonmoral ones were seen as not alterable by religious authorities. In all groups of youth, judgments regarding moral issues were justified in terms of justice and human welfare.

Social leadership in a community is also associated with morality. Youth who were perceived as community leaders described themselves as more moral and had more goals related to morality than youth not having such commitments. They also had better senses of the past and of their futures and believed their behaviours incorporated both their ideas and their images of their parents. Although they did not differ from other youth in stage of moral reasoning, the youth leaders had ideas about themselves that stressed the importance of personal beliefs and of philosophy in governing one's life (Hart & Fegley, 1995).

Values of Canadian Adolescents

A Canadian national survey of 15- to 19-year-olds (Bibby, 2001) asked adolescents which items from a list of 27 were "very important" to them. As shown in Table 5.2, "friendship" and "freedom" were endorsed most frequently (each was endorsed by 85% of the sample). Fifty-nine percent rated "family life" as "very important" and 44% endorsed "what your parents think of you." Asked about personal values, these youth reported that honesty and humour were the most important to them. Seventy-three percent of the sample rated each of these as "very important" (see Table 5.2).

Just 10% of Bibby's sample described religious group involvement as being "very important" to them (although 29% rated "spirituality" as "very important"). Yet 40% reported that "God or some other supernatural force" had at least "quite a bit" of influence on their lives. (To help put this into perspective, 91% agreed that the way they were brought up had "quite a bit" of influence, and 15% stated this of the Internet.)

Nationally, 45% of Bibby's adolescents reported that being a Canadian is "very important." However, this was lower in Quebec, where 37% of anglophones and 15% of francophones endorsed this as "very important." Quebec adolescents were slightly more likely than adolescents in the rest of Canada to endorse bilingualism as "very important" (83% of Quebec anglophones, 80% of Quebec francophones, and 70% of the rest of Canada). Opposition to a "melting pot" of cultures was considered a significant issue by 66% of the national sample (70% of Quebec anglophones and 59% of Quebec francophones).

Bibby's survey found that 22% of 15- to 19-year-olds attended religious services at least weekly. A

Table 5.2 Values Rated "Very Important" by Canadian Adolescents

Value	Percentage
Friendship	85%
Freedom	85%
Family life	59%
What your parents think of you	44%
Religious group involvement	10%
Spirituality	29%
Honesty	73%
Humour	73%
Being a Canadian	45%
Quebec anglophones	37%
Quebec francophones	15%
Bilingualism	70%
Quebec anglophones	83%
Quebec francophones	80%
Attendance at Religious Services	**Weekly**
15- to 19-year-olds	22%
	Monthly
15- to 24-year-olds	26%
25- to 34-year-olds	24%
Canadians aged 15+	34%

Sources: Based on Bibby, R. W. (2001). *Canada's Teens: Today, Yesterday, and Tomorrow.* Toronto: Stoddart; Clark, W. (2000). Patterns of religious attendance. *Canadian Social Trends*, 59, 23–27 Statistics Canada, Catalogue No. 11-008

Statistics Canada national survey in 1998 revealed that 26% of 15- to 24-year-olds attended church or another religious institution at least once a month for the year prior to the survey (Clark, 2000). The rate for these youth is slightly higher than that for the age group with the lowest rate of attendance, which was for those aged 25 to 34 (24% attended on a monthly basis). This compares to a rate of 34% for all Canadians aged 15 or older.

Effects of War and Social Conflict on Moral Reasoning and Behaviour

ISSUES TO CONSIDER

- How do war and social conflicts influence moral reasoning and behaviour in youth?
- What can mediate the effects of war and social conflict on the development of moral behaviour?

Not all community or broader social contexts can facilitate the development of moral reasoning and behaviour. At some points in history and in some societal settings, the institutions of civil society may be so weak or so damaged that any potential positive contribution of community context to moral development is lost. Periods of war or of sustained social conflict may be such contexts. A growing body of research describes the risks to healthy youth development, and especially to the attainment of the moral orientation to contribute to civil society, which may occur in such contexts (e.g., Cairns & Dawes, 1996).

In a study of war experiences and psychosocial development of children in Lebanon (Macksoud & Aber, 1996), the traumas associated with growing up in a country torn by war were assessed among more than 200 10- to 16-year-olds. The more traumatic the war events, such as living through battles, kidnapping, torture, injury, mutilation, death of loved ones, separation from parents, or forced resettlement, the greater the likelihood of problems of adjustment and mental health, such as **post-traumatic stress disorder (PTSD)** or depression (Macksoud & Aber, 1996). In a sample of 170 Cambodian youth, an association between PTSD symptoms and war traumas was found (Sack, Clarke, & Seeley, 1996). In a study of 150 Palestinian youth living amid the Intifada (uprising) in the West Bank, the number of risks present in the child's life due to the social strife of his or her context was related to the likelihood of the child having behavioural problems (Garbarino & Kostelny, 1996). Under conditions of high community risk (e.g., high level of political violence in the community), boys more than girls, and younger children more than older children, are at heightened behavioural risk (Garbarino & Kostelny, 1996). Among samples of youth living in South Africa during different periods of high violence, intracommunity violence was seen as the most significant problem for their adjustment (Straker et al., 1996). Finally, among a sample of Guatemalan Mayan Indian youth living in refugee camps in the Mexican state of Chiapas, positive maternal mental health was linked to good mental health among the youth and depressive symptoms in girls were related to the poor health status of their mothers (Miller, 1996).

Ideological or moral commitment to the political values involved in the conflict in one's society has been studied as a possible factor in moderating the effects of war on the behavioural development of youth (e.g., Covell, 1996; McLernon, Ferguson, & Cairns, 1997; Punamäki, 1996; Wainryb, 1995). For instance, in a study of 385 Israeli young adolescent girls and boys (Punamäki, 1996), exposure to political hardship and violence was associated with problems of anxiety, insecurity, depression, or with feelings of failure among youth with weak ideological commitment to the Israeli political cause. Among youth with a strong ideological commitment, these problems were not associated with the experience of political violence. That the buffering from the effects of war is due to political ideology, as contrasted to more general cultural differences between groups of youth in Israel, is supported by other research (Wainryb, 1995).

The specific national orientation to war can become a major part of the ideology of youth. Canadian youth tend to possess attitudes reflective of the peacekeeping emphasis of Canada, whereas youth from the United States show attitudes prototypic of the interventionist policy orientation of the United States (Covell, 1996). In a study of about 100 14- to 15-year-olds from Northern Ireland, concepts of war as static and unchanging diminished after the country had committed itself to a cease-fire and to engagement in a peace process (McLernon et al., 1997).

Conclusions About the Individual and Contextual Bases of Moral Development

Considerable variation may exist in the development of moral reasoning and in behaviours that may reflect moral thought and support a society that has a moral stance reflective of social justice and civil society. By not giving young people the opportunity to develop in a community and societal context that supports the development of behaviours which advance civil society, the positive development of children and society is at risk. There is considerable social value to understanding the bases of the development of prosocial behaviour among children.

The Development of Prosocial Behaviour

ISSUES TO CONSIDER
- What developmental pattern exists for prosocial behaviour?
- What factors influence the likelihood of prosocial behaviour?

Nancy Eisenberg and her colleagues (e.g., Eisenberg et al., 1995; Eisenberg & Fabes, 1998) have studied

Post-traumatic stress disorder (PTSD) Psychological disorder experienced by individuals who have gone through some major traumatic experiences, such as a serious accident or war.

Emotion and Its Regulation: Contributors to Development

Nancy Eisenberg is Regents' Professor of Psychology at Arizona State University. She has been the editor of *Psychological Bulletin* and associate editor of *Personality and Social Psychology Bulletin* and *Merrill-Palmer Quarterly*.

Children and adolescents who get along with others and behave in a socially appropriate manner differ from their less prosocial peers in a variety of ways. One important difference is in regard to how they express and handle their emotions. My interest is in the emotions children and youth express, the variety of ways they manage these emotions, and the factors that contribute to their success or failure at doing so.

In our work, which is supported by the U.S. National Institutes of Mental Health, we are following two samples of children from early school age into adolescence. We examine differences among the children in their tendencies to experience or express negative emotions such as sadness and anger, and their tendencies to regulate themselves by shifting their attention, focusing their attention, and inhibiting their behaviour. For example, if a girl is angry, she can manage the anger by shifting her attention to other thoughts and control her facial and behavioural expression of anger (e.g., suppress facial expressions and aggressive responding). Children who are able to manage their attention and behaviour in these ways tend to be socially competent and low in aggression and related problem behaviours, even if they are quick to anger. Moreover, they tend to be resilient to stress, sympathetic, and helpful to others. We are finding that differences in children's emotional responding and regulation predict how socially competent and adjusted they are, not only at the time, but years later.

Because of the importance of the regulation of emotions and emotionally driven behaviour for children's development, we also are interested in why children differ in these aspects of their functioning. We believe that both socialization experiences and biologically based differences in temperament contribute to how children experience and manage emotions. Our data are consistent with the view that parents can help children learn ways to cope with their emotions and regulate their emotion-related behaviour. For example, if parents respond punitively to children's expression of negative emotions such as sadness and embarrassment, their children tend to be relatively unregulated. Moreover, parents who express hostile negative emotions toward or in view of their children tend to have children who are less regulated and more prone to problem behaviours.

Currently, my colleagues Tracy Spinrad, Richard Fabes, and I, along with our students, are examining issues such as how differences in children's emotionality and regulation, and parents' expression and socialization of their children's emotional responding, relate to adolescents' adjustment, sympathy and social competence, and conflict with friends and parents. We also are examining stability and change in children's tendencies to express negative emotions and regulate themselves over six or more years. Findings from this work help us to understand stability and change in how children and youth deal with emotions and factors that contribute to healthy development. Moreover, in related work with

Laurie Chassin funded by the National Institute of Drug Abuse, I am examining the relation of differences among children in their emotionality and regulation to familial risk for alcoholism (e.g., alcoholism in parent or grandparents) and behaviours associated with later alcoholism (e.g., antisocial behaviour).

In addition to our work on emotion regulation, I study the development of sympathy and a prosocial orientation (i.e., the tendency to assist others). We have a longitudinal study in which a group of children have been studied from age 4 to 5 to age 25 to 26. We have found, for example, that children who spontaneously shared in preschool—that is, shared without being asked—were more helpful and sympathetic in childhood, adolescence, and even early adulthood. Their reasoning about why people help changed greatly over the years, and their thinking about this issue has been related to their tendencies to help and sympathize with others. In our view, prosocial development is an important aspect of successful social development. By studying a variety of factors contributing to social and emotional functioning, we hope to develop a richer, more nuanced picture of the complex process of social development.

extensively the development of prosocial reasoning and behaviour. In a 15-year longitudinal follow-up of a study of the development of the reasons youth used for behaving in a prosocial manner, a complex pattern of prosocial moral reasoning was observed, one in which several distinct patterns of change were seen in regard to different types of prosocial reasoning (Eisenberg et al., 1995). Needs-oriented and stereotypic reasoning increased until mid-childhood/early adolescence and then declined in subsequent years. Hedonistic reasoning declined in use across childhood and into adolescence but then began to increase into early adulthood. Direct reciprocity and approval reasoning did not decline between mid-adolescence and early adulthood, but higher-level reasoning increased in use across adolescence and into early adulthood. Overall, females' prosocial reasoning was higher than that of males (Eisenberg et al., 1995). Some of the recent work of Nancy Eisenberg is presented in Meet the Researcher Box 5.1.

Kim Schonert-Reichl (2001) at the University of British Columbia found correlations between moral reasoning and prosocial behaviour among adolescents. This relationship held for both boys and girls. However, in a 1999 study, she found that for boys, antisocial behaviour (as rated by their peers) was also associated with high moral reasoning, possibly because the peers perceived these boys as engaging in positive or instrumental aggression (fighting for the right reason).

Fabes and Eisenberg (1996) conducted an analysis of 179 studies of prosocial behaviour. This analysis confirmed the general trend for higher prosocial moral reasoning across adolescence. The results also indicated that characteristics of the person in need of help influence the likelihood of prosocial behaviour. For example, adolescents are more likely to act prosocially when the person in need is a child rather than an adult.

Psychological and contextual characteristics also play roles in prosocial behaviour (Eisenberg & Fabes, 1998). In a study of about 90 high school students, cognitive understanding of a situation, the ability to take the perspective of other people, and sympathy were related to prosocial behaviour, in response to distress in friends (Estrada, 1995). Higher levels of prosocial behaviour were associated with sympathy for one's friend as opposed to one's own personal distress (Estrada, 1995).

Empathy, as well as sympathy, may be linked to prosocial behaviour. For instance, among 5-, 9-, and 13-year-olds, empathy among boys was related to prosocial behaviour (Roberts & Strayer, 1996), whereas in girls it was related to prosocial behaviour with friends but not to cooperation with peers in general (Roberts & Strayer, 1996).

In addition to the peer group, the family, workplace, and school may provide contexts that influence the expression of prosocial behaviour. In a study of 1000 Minnesota youth, helpfulness in the home and in paid work settings was assessed (Call, Mortimer, & Shanahan, 1995). Among girls, helpfulness in the home was related to responsiveness to needs within the family, and helpfulness at work was related to behavioural competence. For both boys and girls, the occurrence of helpfulness depended on the adolescent's motivation and on how meaningful the act of helping would be in the situation (Call et al., 1995).

Whether young adolescents did or did not cheat in a science class depended on whether the youth perceived their classrooms and schools as being extrinsically focused on performance and external rewards (Anderman et al., 1998). Such perceptions were associated with cheating, as were worries about school and the use of "self-handicapping" classroom behaviours (e.g., partying the night before an exam in order to have something on which to blame poor exam performance) (Anderman et al., 1998). Other, longitudinal research finds that either rule-breaking or rule-abiding conduct may remain relatively continuous from childhood through late adolescence, and that rule breaking undermines both academic achievement and job competence (Masten et al., 1995).

There is evidence that a youth's expression of prosocial behaviour may be continuous, if not increasing across life (Fabes & Eisenberg, 1996). Such behaviour may be applied across the key settings of life—peer group, family, school, and workplace—albeit in complex ways (Eisenberg & Fabes, 1998). The absence of prosocial behaviour may disrupt a young person's development across childhood and adolescence (Masten et al., 1995), and competence in key contextual settings and the quality of the adolescent's experiences in these settings will be diminished. The nature of the development of prosocial behaviour underscores the importance of moral development for civil society and the reason why communities find it crucial to invest their assets in the promotion of morally committed, competent youth.

Promoting Civil Society for Youth

Morally developed youth think and act in ways that maintain and enhance civil society (cf. O'Connell, 1999). Given the importance of moral development in support of civil society, at least two key questions suggest themselves as important. First, does adolescent cognitive development and/or moral reasoning development reflect attributes of thought pertinent to civil society? Second, is there any way in which the context in which adolescents live may foster the development of moral reasoning and prosocial behavioural orientations in support of civil society? Data suggest that the answer to both of these questions is "yes."

Moral Reasoning Development and Civil Society

ISSUE TO CONSIDER
• Are there data supporting the idea that adolescents' cognitive and moral development support civil society?

Several studies of youth have investigated adolescents' concepts of the components of civil society. In a study of adolescents in the U.S. ranging in age from 12 to 19 years, civil liberties such as freedom of speech and religion were conceived of as universal rights (Helwig, 1995). Another U.S. study of about 170 youth, ranging in age from 8 to 16 years, investigated the understanding of nurturance and of self-determination rights (Ruck, Abramovitch, & Keating, 1998). Younger children (8- to 12-year-olds) were less likely than older youth (14- to 16-year-olds) to see these rights as important. Whereas reasoning about nurturance did not show an age-related progression from concrete to abstract, reasoning about self-determination did show such a change.

In a U.S study of 6- to 11-year-olds developing ideas about democratic and nondemocratic systems of government and freedom of speech (Helwig, 1998), notions of political fairness were present among all youth and were used to evaluate the range of political systems presented to them. These notions were used to reject the appropriateness of the nondemocratic alternatives. However, there were important age group differences among the youth (Helwig, 1998). The older children, more so than the younger, considered the practical and moral consequences of the different systems of government presented to them. The older children were also more likely to use a broad set of rationales to justify the importance of freedom of speech (Helwig, 1998).

Additional data indicate that the growth of moral reasoning is consistent with the support of civil society. Adolescents enrolled in college or university demonstrate less of a capacity for interpersonal forgiveness than do their same-sex parents (Subkoviak et al., 1995). However, tolerance for people who transgress (if not their acts of transgression per se) does increase across age. In a study of 160 youth ranging in age from 7 to 10 years (Wainryb, Shaw, & Maianu, 1998), all participants were more tolerant of dissenting beliefs than dissenting behaviours. They were also more tolerant of persons engaged in acts based on dissenting beliefs than they were of the acts themselves. Symbolic of an increase in the orientation to diversity of perspectives in society, tolerance of nonconforming beliefs and speech increased with age (Wainryb et al., 1998).

Among adolescents developing within North America, and, one may speculate, for youth developing within other democratic societies, there are cognitive changes consistent with a greater understanding of the features of civil society. In the next section we consider how such developmental changes may become associated with the furthering of civil society.

Enhancing Behaviour That Promotes Civil Society

ISSUES TO CONSIDER
• What is the purpose of William Damon's "youth charter"? How does it work in a community?
• What is the relationship between positive youth development and the 40 developmental assets identified by Search Institute?

What is required for the promotion of civil society by young people? William Damon (1997) has envisioned the creation of a **youth charter** in each community in the world. The charter consists of a set of rules, guidelines, and plans of action that each community can adopt to provide their youth with a framework for developing in a healthy manner. Damon (1997) describes how youth and significant adults in their community (e.g., parents, teachers, clergy, coaches, police, and government and business leaders) can create partnerships to pursue a common

Youth charter A set of rules, guidelines, and plans of action that each community can adopt to provide their youth with a framework for developing a healthy manner.

Adolescents' participation in democratically run organizations may facilitate the development of their moral reasoning abilities.

MEET THE RESEARCHER | Box 5.2 | William Damon

Adolescent Moral Identity

In the early part of my career, I spent years trying to figure out—without much success—how a person's moral judgment (what the person would say when asked "what if" questions about right and wrong) was connected to the person's actual social conduct in real life. Then I came on the idea of "moral identity," and it occurred to me that this might be the key explanatory concept we had been missing.

Moral identity is how a person answers the question, "What difference does acting in a good rather than a bad way make to the kind of person I am, as well as to the kind of person I want to be?" It occurred to me that the way a person answers this question could be more indicative of how the person will behave in real life than any other measure that psychologists had been using.

And this is indeed what Anne Colby and I found when we conducted a study of extraordinary people who had spent their lives doing good work (Colby & Damon, 1992). We found that these people had a strong sense of themselves as moral people, indicating a high level of moral identity. They did *not* show a tendency to score especially high on standardized moral judgment measures. Colby and I concluded that "people who define themselves in terms of their moral goals are likely to . . . take responsibility for the actual solution of moral problems" (Colby & Damon, 1992, p. 282). In contrast to such people, those who do no more than mouth high-minded principles cannot be relied on to act in a moral manner when the chips are down.

Adolescence is a key time for the formation of moral identity. In studies with Dan Hart (Damon & Hart, 1988), we found that during adolescence, self-identity is marked by small gradual increases in the use of moral concepts such as "kind," "fair-minded," and "honest." Adolescents who describe themselves *primarily* in terms of moral goals are exceptionally committed to voluntary service and other prosocial activity. This is true even in the most disadvantaged communities (Hart & Fegley, 1995).

In order to promote the development of adolescent moral identity, I have been helping schools and communities create youth charters. A youth charter is a consensus of clear expectations shared by a young person and all the important people in the young person's life. A youth charter evolves through discussions between young people and their parents, neighbours, teachers, friends, coaches, and other community members. It covers deep moral and spiritual issues such as the purpose of life. It also deals with practical problems such as cheating in school, alcohol and drug abuse, and hostile relations among peer groups.

In our beginning efforts with the youth charter approach (Damon & Gregory, 1997), we have led town meetings in a number of communities. In one place, parents were upset about an epidemic of binge drinking, especially at teen parties. They organized a town-wide forum to create a community youth charter. The youth charter discussions led to many constructive actions, such as building a substance-free coffeehouse, run by the

William Damon is professor of education and director of the Center on Adolescence at Stanford University. For more than 20 years, Damon has studied moral development at all ages of human life. Damon's books include *The Moral Child* (1990), *Greater Expectations* (1995), and *The Youth Charter* (1997). Damon is editor-in-chief of *New Directions for Child and Adolescent Development* and *The Handbook of Child Psychology* (1998).

youth, where young people can have a good time without drugs or alcohol. Some other issues that were addressed included fostering a positive, character-building approach to youth sports; mitigating the pressures of academic competition; promoting spiritual understanding; and developing engaging service programs.

Youth charters are communication devices. They can help young people anticipate and understand the reactions of others to their behaviour. When a teacher is disappointed in a student's performance, or when a neighbour calls the local police on a miscreant teenager, a youth charter can turn the youngster's shame or outrage into a constructive developmental experience. A youth charter can define high moral standards for adolescent conduct. It can provide a conduit for regular feedback among a young person, peers, and the adult world, thereby facilitating the formation of the young person's moral identity.

ideal of positive moral development and intellectual achievement.

Embedding youth in a caring and developmentally facilitative community can promote their ability to develop morally and to contribute to civil society. In a study of more than 3100 students in their final year of high school (Youniss, Yates, & Su, 1997), the activities engaged in by youth were categorized into (1) school-based, adult-endorsed norms; or (2) engagement in peer fun activities that excluded adults.

Youth were then placed into groups that reflected orientations to (1) school-adult norms, but not peer fun (the "School" group); (2) peer fun but not school-adult norms (the "Party" group); or (3) both "1" and "2" (the "All-around" group). The School and the All-around groups were both high in community service, religious orientation, and political awareness.

Damon (1997) envisions that by embedding youth in a community where service and responsible leadership are possible, the creation of community-specific youth charters can enable adolescents and adults, together, to promote systematically positive youth development. Youth charters can create opportunities to actualize both individual and community goals to eliminate risk behaviours among adolescents and promote in them the ability to contribute to high-quality individual and community life. Through community youth charters, youth and adults may work together to create a system in which civil society is maintained and perpetuated (Damon, 1997). Features of Damon's recent scholarship are presented in Meet the Researcher Box 5.2.

What, precisely, must be brought together by such charters to ensure the promotion of such positive youth development? Peter L. Benson and his colleagues at Search Institute in Minneapolis, Minnesota, believe that what is needed is the application of **assets** (Benson, 1997; Benson et al., 1998; Leffert et al., 1998; Scales & Leffert, 1999). That is, they stress that positive youth development is furthered when actions are taken to enhance the strengths of a person (e.g., a commitment to learning, a healthy sense of identity), a family (e.g., caring attitudes toward children, rearing styles that both empower youth and set boundaries and provide expectations for positive growth), and a community (e.g., social support, programs that provide access to the resources for education, safety, and mentorship available in a community) (Benson, 1997).

Accordingly, Benson and his colleagues believe there are both internal and external attributes that comprise the developmental assets needed by youth. Through their research they have identified 40 such assets, 20 internal ones and 20 external ones. These attributes are presented in Table 5.3.

Benson and his colleagues have found that the more developmental assets an adolescent has, the greater is his or her likelihood of positive, healthy development. For instance, in a study of 99 462 youth in Grades 6 through 12 in public and/or alternative schools from 213 U.S. cities and towns who were assessed during the 1996–1997 academic year for their possession of the 40 assets presented in Table 5.3, Leffert et al. (1998) found that the more assets present among youth, the lower the likelihood of alcohol use, depression/suicide risk, and violence.

Assets (Developmental assets) Resources of a person (e.g., commitment to learning), a family (e.g., caring attitudes toward children), and a community (e.g., social support) that are needed for positive youth development.

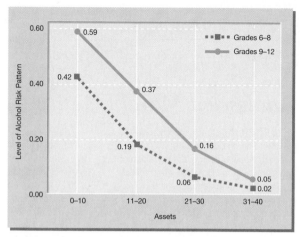

Figure 5.1
Changes in level of alcohol risk in relation to the possession of developmental assets.

(*Source:* Leffert et al., 1998.)

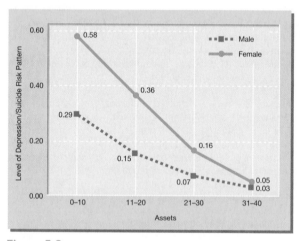

Figure 5.2
Changes in level of depression/suicide risk in relation to the possession of developmental assets.

(*Source:* Leffert et al., 1998.)

Figures 5.1 and 5.2, taken from the research of Leffert et al., present some of these findings.

For instance, Figure 5.1 displays the level of alcohol use risk for youth in Grades 6 through 8 combined and for youth in Grades 9 through 12 combined; as shown in this figure, in both grade groupings alcohol risk decreases with the possession of more assets. Youth with 0 to 10 assets have the highest risk, followed by youth with 11 to 20 assets, youth with 21 to 30 assets, and youth with 31 to 40 assets. Thus, consistent with Benson's (1997) view of the importance of developmental assets for promoting healthy behaviour among young people, both the trend lines

Table 5-3 The 40 Developmental Assets Proposed by Search Institute

External Support
1. *Family support*—Family life provides high levels of love and support.
2. *Positive family communication*—Young person and his or her parent(s) communicate positively, and young person is willing to seek advice and counsel from parent(s).
3. *Other adult relationships*—Young person receives support from three or more nonparent adults.
4. *Caring neighbourhood*—Young person experiences caring neighbours.
5. *Caring school climate*—School provides a caring, encouraging environment.
6. *Parent involvement in schooling*—Parent(s) are actively involved in helping young person succeed in school.

Empowerment
7. *Community values youth*—Young person perceives that adults in the community value youth.
8. *Youth as resources*—Young people are given useful roles in the community.
9. *Service to others*—Young person serves in the community one hour or more per week.
10. *Safety*—Young person feels safe in home, at school, and in the neighbourhood.

Boundaries and Expectations
11. *Family boundaries*—Family has clear rules and consequences and monitors the young person's whereabouts.
12. *School boundaries*—School provides clear rules and consequences.
13. *Neighbourhood boundaries*—Neighbours take responsibility for monitoring young people's behaviour.
14. *Adult role models*—Parent(s) and other adults model positive, responsible behaviour.
15. *Positive peer influence*—Young person's best friends model positive, responsible behaviour.
16. *High expectations*—Both parent(s) and teachers encourage the young person to do well.

Constructive Use of Time
17. *Creative activities*—Young person spends three or more hours per week in lessons or practice in music, theatre, or other arts.
18. *Youth programs*—Young person spends three hours or more per week in sports, clubs, or organizations at school and/or in community organizations.
19. *Religious community*—Young person spends one or more hours per week in activities in a religious institution.
20. *Time at home*—Young person is out with friends "with nothing special to do" two or fewer nights per week.

Internal Commitment to Learning
21. *Achievement motivation*—Young person is motivated to do well in school.
22. *School engagement*—Young person is actively engaged in learning.
23. *Homework*—Young person reports doing at least one hour of homework every school day.
24. *Bonding to school*—Young person cares about his or her school.
25. *Reading for pleasure*—Young person reads for pleasure three or more hours per week.

Positive Values
26. *Caring*—Young person places high value on helping other people.
27. *Equality and social justice*—Young person places high value on promoting equality and reducing hunger and poverty.
28. *Integrity*—Young person acts on convictions and stands up for his or her beliefs.
29. *Honesty*—Young person "tells the truth even when it is not easy."
30. *Responsibility*—Young person accepts and takes personal responsibility.
31. *Restraint*—Young person believes it is important not to be sexually active or to use alcohol or other drugs.

>

Table 5-3 **The 40 Developmental Assets Proposed by Search Institute (continued)**

Social Competencies	32. *Planning and decision making*—Young person knows how to plan ahead and make choices.
	33. *Interpersonal competence*—Young person has empathy, sensitivity, and friendship skills.
	34. *Cultural competence*—Young person has knowledge of and comfort with people of different cultural/racial/ethnic backgrounds.
	35. *Resistance skills*—Young person can resist negative peer pressure and dangerous situations.
	36. *Peaceful conflict resolution*—Young person seeks to resolve conflict nonviolently.
Positive Identity	37. *Personal power*—Young person feels he or she has control over "things that happen to me."
	38. *Self-esteem*—Young person reports having high self-esteem.
	39. *Sense of purpose*—Young person reports that "my life has a purpose."
	40. *Positive view of personal future*—Young person is optimistic about her or his personal future.

Source: Benson et al., 1998.

represented in the figure and the fact that the last group has the lowest level of risk show the importance of the asset approach in work aimed at promoting positive development in children and adolescents. This strengthens the argument for the critical significance of developmental assets in the promotion of positive youth development and, as such, in the enhancement of the capacity and commitment of young people to contribute to civil society.

Other data by Benson and his colleagues provide direct support for this argument. Scales et al. (2000) measured a concept termed **thriving** among 6000 youth in Grades 6 to 12, evenly divided across six ethnic groups (American Indian, African American, Asian American, Latino, European American, and multiracial). Thriving was defined as involving seven attributes: school success, leadership, valuing diversity, physical health, helping others, delay of gratification, and overcoming adversity. Most, if not all, of these attributes are linked to the presence of prosocial behaviour (e.g., helping others, delay of gratification) and to the behaviours essential for contributing to civil society (e.g., valuing diversity, leadership, overcoming adversity). The greater the number of developmental assets possessed by youth,

the more likely they were to possess the attributes of thriving. Figures 5.3, 5.4, and 5.5 indicate that as developmental assets increase from the lowest to the highest level, thriving in regard to helping others,

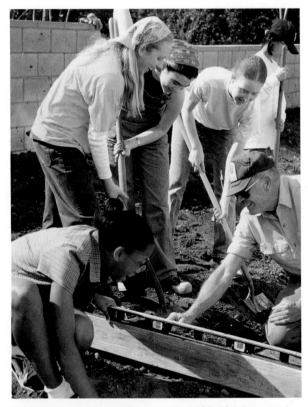

Civic engagement and contributions to the welfare of their communities are associated with positive youth development.

Thriving Concept defined and measured by Scales et al. Thriving is defined as involving the following seven attributes: school success, leadership, valuing diversity, physical health, helping others, delay of gratification, and overcoming adversity.

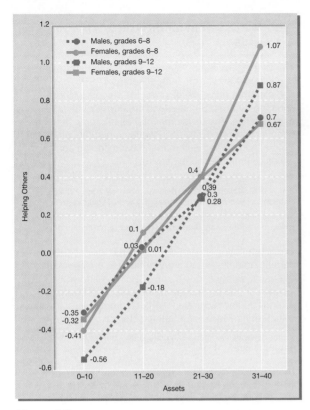

Figure 5.3
Changes in helping others in relation to the possession of
developmental assets.

(*Source:* Scales et al., 2000.)

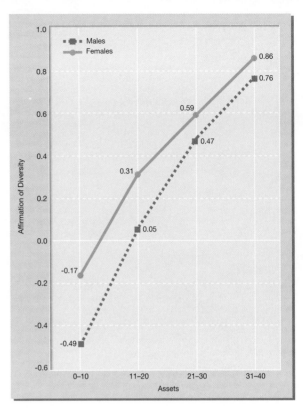

Figure 5.4
Changes in affirmation of diversity in relation to the possession
of developmental assets.

(*Source:* Scales et al., 2000.)

valuing diversity, and leadership increases. Peter
Benson's perspective about his work is presented in
Meet the Researcher Box 5.3.

Other data support the importance of focusing
on developmental assets both in understanding the
bases of positive youth development and in using
that knowledge to further civil society. Luster and
McAdoo (1994) sought to identify the factors that
contribute to individual differences in the cognitive
competence of African American children in early
elementary grades. Consistent with an asset-based
approach to promoting the positive development of
youth (Benson, 1997; Scales & Leffert, 1998), they
found that favourable outcomes in cognitive and
socioemotional development were associated with
high scores on an **advantage index**. This index was
formed by scoring children on the basis of the
absence of risk factors (e.g., pertaining to poverty or
problems in the quality of the home environment)
and the presence of more favourable circumstances
in their lives.

Several communities in Canada have adopted the
developmental assets approach (see Table 5-4 for a
description of some Canadian projects). The Boys and
Girls Club of British Columbia (2003) reported findings from an evaluation of training workshops. This
evaluation, undertaken by Anne Matheson of the
College of the Rockies, revealed that 46% of participants reported a change in behaviour or attitude
toward assisting young people's development. (Only
12% reported that the workshop had no impact on
them; the remaining 46% stated that the workshop
reinforced their current beliefs and behaviour.)

There have been a number of other Canadian
initiatives that aim to promote behaviours that
enhance civil society. Many of these are new and have

Advantage index Index formed
by scoring children on the
basis of the absence of risk
factors (such as factors pertinent to poverty) and the
presence of more favourable
circumstances in the children's lives.

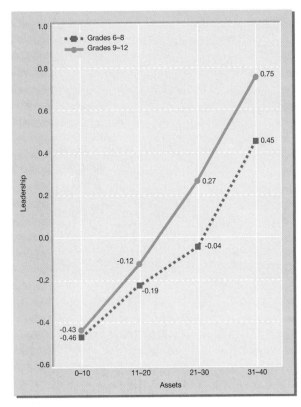

Figure 5.5
Changes in leadership in relation to the possession of developmental assets.

(*Source:* Scales et al., 2000.)

yet to be fully evaluated. For example, the Calgary Board of Education designed a program entitled "It's My World" to inform students throughout the school system about how to be good citizens (Jeary, 2001). The program is tailored to each grade, but the approach at all ages is to have students reflect on their own personal relationships. They can then generalize from their family, friends, and peers to the importance of human rights for all individuals.

The Canadian Policy Research Networks (CPRN; 2001) suggests that organized recreational activities provided by school or other institutions can have a great impact on citizenship development for young people. Along with helping youth to learn to deal with conflict, become tolerant of individual differences, appreciate rules, and improve communication skills, CPRN claims that participation also decreases the chances that adolescents will leave school early.

Hebert and Page (2000) reported on a nationwide group of professionals meeting to share research with the aim of developing educational policy and practice for citizenship education. The Citizenship Education Research Network (CERN) meets at least two times per year. Sample projects stemming from this have

Box 5.3   Peter L. Benson

Unleashing the Power of Communities for Raising Healthy Children and Adolescents

Peter L. Benson is president of Search Institute, Minneapolis, an independent applied research organization specializing in child and adolescent development. Trained as a social psychologist and the author of 10 books, he speaks and lectures widely about the natural and inherent power of communities in raising successful, competent, and caring youth. He was visiting scholar at the William T. Grant Foundation in New York City.

Many of the efforts taken to improve the health and well-being of children and adolescents are organized to *reduce* the rate and incidence of health-compromising behaviours. For decades, Canada and the United States have invested people and resources in tackling such problems as alcohol, tobacco, illicit drugs, violence, teen pregnancy, and delinquency. These efforts are often orchestrated through federal and provincial or state initiatives and led by professionals trained in these areas.

In the late 1980s, I decided to go down a different path. Looking through a different lens, I asked this question: What opportunities, resources, and experiences do children and adolescents need in order to thrive? Asking the question in this way leads to a focus on the essential building blocks of human development that we need to *promote*.

I began to construct a taxonomy of positive building blocks by synthesizing decades of research. I also sought to identify those experiences and resources that were health promoting for all youth regardless of race, ethnicity, gender, or family income. This search for "universal" building blocks was fed by an instinct that naming a common core of experiences that are good for all youth would be helpful, ultimately, for uniting communities to take action on behalf of all youth.

This work led to the concept of developmental assets, a framework of 40 "molecules" of healthy development that communities have within their control. The assets are organized into eight categories: support, empowerment, boundaries, structured time use, educational commitment, positive values, social competencies, and identity.

With my colleagues at Search Institute, we have developed a survey tool to help cities understand how they are doing in building these developmental assets. More than 1000 cities have developed this profile of assets. A remarkable thing happens when local leaders and citizens look through the developmental asset lens. They rediscover a great deal of community capacity, often dormant in cities, to mobilize asset-building power. That's because inherent in the developmental asset model is the fact that developmental assets emerge significantly and powerfully from human relationships—from people, whether neighbours, teachers, employers, parents, youth leaders, coaches, members of congregations, or just passersby on the street—attending deeply to knowing, naming, engaging, and connecting to the youth of a city.

We now do a great deal of publishing, speaking, training, and consulting to ignite community-wide asset-building initiatives. As of the end of 2002, about 700 communities have launched these efforts. Imagine the new challenge of learning the processes and dynamics of growing asset-building communities, with more than 700 "petri dishes." We've decided that the best way to grow knowledge about community change is to position ourselves as co-learners with all of these communities, asking them to teach us what they are learning about transforming neighbourhoods, businesses, schools, families, congregations, and youth organizations into a vibrant, connected team of systems all seeking to build developmental strengths. Part of our scientific challenge now is to invite all of these communities to be part of the learning effort, synthesize the lay findings, feed back what we learn, and then loop through this process again and again, with the hope that all of us can become wiser about holding up and supporting the developmental journey of all children and adolescents.

included the development of a conceptual framework relating to identity, rights, and citizenship, research comparing conceptions of citizenships among anglophone and francophone students in Quebec, New Brunswick, and Alberta, and studies of the effectiveness of the Social Studies curriculum in British Columbia in developing tolerance, appreciation of others, and other attitudes underlying good citizenship.

Covell and Howe (2001) reported on a six-month long unit for children in Grade 8 in Nova Scotia that focused on children's rights and responsibilities as defined by The United Nations Conventions on the Rights of the Child. In comparison to a matched control group, these adolescents reported higher levels of self-esteem, support from peers and teachers, and attitudes that respected people's rights. Three of the five classes receiving the unit created projects involving community service.

A Model for Promoting Civil Society Through Enhancing Positive Youth Development

ISSUES TO CONSIDER

- How can civil society be promoted by linking youth, families, and society?
- What should be the focus of public policies and programs in the promotion of civil society?
- What positive developmental effects should be seen from public programs?
- How does the promotion of civil society maintain itself over generations?

Consistent with the perspective forwarded by Benson (1997), and the data provided by Leffert et al. (1998) and by Luster and McAdoo (1994, 1996), the individual and contextual assets of youth are linked to their positive development. These data confirm the idea that the enhancement of such assets will be associated with the promotion of positive youth development. How may such enhancement result in the promotion of civil society?

Figure 5.6 provides a model that links youth with the family and the community in ways that, over time, result in the promotion of civil society. Key to the model is the ability of the family to nurture and socialize youth effectively. The model summarizes the results of several studies and scholarly essays (e.g., Benson, 1997; Benson et al., 1998; Damon, 1997; Dryfoos, 1998; Leffert et al., 1998; Scales & Leffert, 1999; Scales et al., 2000; Schorr, 1997). This literature describes the essential functions needed for families to promote positive development in their children, the resources necessary for families to transform their functional characteristics into valued child outcomes, and the elements of these positive youth outcomes.

As indicated in Figure 5.6, the enhancement of civil society feeds back to influence the family and the young people reared within it. As young people grow up in families providing the orientation to self and society, they take on the behaviours that the policies and associated programs were designed to instill. As the model indicates, through facilitating the nurturing and socialization of families, the growth of civil society occurs.

Figure 5.6

A model of national youth policy: The integration of families, children, and civil society.

(*Source:* Lerner et al., 2000b.)

Figure 5.6 further indicates that **public policies** (discussed in more detail in Chapter 14) should be aimed at ensuring that families have the capacity to provide children with boundaries and expectations, fulfillment of physiological and safety needs, a climate of love and caring, the promotion of self-esteem, the encouragement for growth, positive values, and positive links to the community. The programs that derive from these policies should ensure that the resources are available for families to nurture and socialize children in these ways. These resources would give children a healthy start, a safe environment, caring and reliable adults, an education resulting in marketable skills, and opportunities to "give back" to their communities by volunteering and serving.

Although they may be difficult to create in practice, if programs are effective, several positive developmental outcomes can become evident among children. These outcomes can be summarized by **Five Cs**: Competence, Connection, Character, Confidence, and Caring (or Compassion) (Carnegie Council on Adolescent Development, 1989; Lerner, 1995; Little,

Public policy Standards, or rules, for the conduct of individuals, organizations, and institutions.

Five Cs Five attributes (Competence, Connection, Character, Confidence, and Caring) representing positive developmental outcomes in youth.

1993). These five attributes represent five clusters of individual attributes, for example, intellectual ability and social and behavioural skills (competence), positive bonds with people and institutions (connection), integrity and moral centredness (character), positive self-regard, a sense of self-efficacy and courage (confidence), and humane values, empathy, and a sense of social justice (caring/compassion). When these five sets of outcomes are developed in youth, civil society is enhanced. Through the intergenerational effect these youth may initiate in rearing of their own children, these youth can positively affect the rearing of subsequent generations (Bornstein, 1995).

Conclusions

As with cognitive development, the development of moral reasoning and behaviour is associated with other individual characteristics and with different instances of the social context surrounding the adolescent. These associations promote general characteristics of moral reasoning development and a change from judging a behaviour based on the consequences of an act to judging whether an actor intended the consequences of the act to occur. These associations also foster diversity in moral functioning, especially those prosocial behaviours that with the community strengthen civil society.

The fact that the context, and specifically people in it, can model moral functioning and promote moral commitments and behaviours among youth is a key basis of applications aimed at developing a next generation of youth community leaders and citizens contributing to the maintenance and perpetuation of civil society.

Diversity and context are key themes useful in understanding moral development and behaviour in adolescence. How adolescents through their unique combination of cognitive, emotional, behavioural, and contextual characteristics contribute in healthy ways to self and to society depends critically on understanding the individuality of their selves and of their contexts. This understanding involves adolescents' self-definitions and their attainment of personal identities. We consider the development of self-definition and identity in the next chapter.

Summary

- Moral development involves thinking and behaving *prosocially*. For any society to maintain and perpetuate itself over the course of generations, its youth must develop as individuals committed to promoting the healthy, productive, and successful development of self, family, and society.

- Although Kohlberg's work is widely used as the basis for most theories dedicated to moral development, today the study of adolescent moral functioning focuses both on moral thinking or reasoning *and* on moral behaviours, especially those that *benefit* society.

- Kohlberg proposed that a theory of moral development should focus on the reasons for moral behaviour, rather than moral behaviour. He devised a way to ascertain the reasons underlying moral behaviour through the construction of a moral development interview. Kohlberg found that the types of moral reasoning people used passed through a series of five qualitatively different stages, with a sixth hypothetical stage.

- Overall, research indicates that individual differences and context need to be taken into account in understanding the development of both moral reasoning and moral behaviour. Not all youth have similar levels of moral reasoning. Variation seems to be associated with gender (see, for example, Gilligan's work) and with different types of social experiences. Most of these experiences relate to interactions with models of moral behaviour, including family members and people in the community.

- Modelling prosocial, moral behaviour can help develop it in others. This information has resulted in several worldwide programs designed to promote a prosocial orientation among youth. Both "experimentally created" and naturally occurring models (parents and peers) can promote moral thought and action.

- There are risks to healthy youth development, and especially to the attainment of the moral orientation to contribute to civil society in contexts, such as war, in which the institutions of civil society are weak and/or damaged. Society risks the generation of behaviourally and emotionally problematic children by not affording young people the opportunity to develop in a community and broader societal context that supports the development of behaviours which advance the institutions of civil society.

- In addition to the peer group, the family, workplace, and school may provide contexts that influence the expression of prosocial behaviour. Prosocial behaviour may be applied across the key settings of life. The absence of prosocial behaviour may disrupt a young person's development across childhood and adolescence. In such instances, competence in key contextual settings will be decreased and the quality of the adolescent's experience in these settings will likely be diminished.

- To promote civil society in young people, William Damon (1997) envisions the creation of a youth charter in every community. Living and working under the guidelines of a youth charter, communities can create partnerships to pursue a common ideal of positive moral development and intellectual achievement and, thereby, create a system wherein civil society is maintained and perpetuated.

- Positive youth development is furthered when actions are taken to enhance the strengths of a person, a family, and a community. Benson and his colleagues have identified 40 developmental assets, 20 internal ones and 20 external ones that comprise the resources needed for the healthy development of youth.

- Because the individual and contextual assets of youth are linked to their positive development, it makes sense to assume the enhancement of such assets will be associated with the promotion of positive youth development. Key to models that link youth with family and the community in manners that result in the promotion of civil society is the ability of the family to nurture and socialize youth effectively.

- Public policies should be aimed at ensuring that families have the capacity to provide for children. If programs are effective in delivering resources to families, several positive developmental outcomes will be evident among children. When "five Cs," competence, connection, character, confidence, and caring (or compassion), are developed in youth, civil society is enhanced. As young people grow up in families providing the orientation to self and society, they may take on the behaviours that the policies and associated programs are designed to foster.

Discussion Topics

1. Within the context of civil society, morally developed youth think and behave in ways that maintain and enhance a just social order. Moral development involves thinking and behaving *prosocially*. What prosocial actions do you and/or your peers take to help maintain and support civil society?

2. Do you agree with the widely held belief that youth of today lack the moral principles practised and promoted by your parents' and grandparents' generations? If so, why? If not, why not?

3. Based on your knowledge of the work of Jean Piaget, how does his conception of moral development mirror his theory of cognitive development? Give examples to back up your claims.

4. Look back on the Kohlberg moral dilemma story presented in the chapter. How would you resolve the dilemma? Is your response contingent on who you are culturally, ethnically, racially? Is it easy or difficult for you to resolve the dilemma? What is the basis behind your reasoning? Is it easy or hard for you to understand the reasoning of those who might solve the dilemma differently? Do you feel your gender may impact the way you resolve moral issues? If so, why? Does your age impact your resolution? Can you imagine that you would or will respond differently to the dilemma at different times in your life?

5. Individual differences and context need to be taken into account in understanding the development both of moral reasoning and of moral behaviour. Who in your life impacted your moral development? Is there a specific life context that was significant in this development? In what ways do you feel you have contributed to the moral development of your siblings and/or peers?

6. Carol Gilligan contends that there are important differences in moral reasoning and behaviour among males and females and that certain approaches, such as Kohlberg's, stress the morality of "justice" rather than the morality of "care." The latter type of morality provides the

"voice" of females' moral reasoning. What is she referring to in this distinction? Do you believe the moral reasoning of women is expressed in terms of relationships and responsibilities? Is the distinction between the moral reasoning of men and women all that clear and defined to you? Or can women, like men, resolve dilemmas based on issues of equity and justice? Why or why not?

7. Can you see the neighbourhood in which you were raised creating a youth charter? What would it look like? Who would be involved (both individual members and businesses and institutions)? How would the charter support the moral development of its youth? What roadblocks might the community run into in establishing and maintaining the goals set forth by the charter?

8. With the asset model of Benson and colleagues as a guide, how much does socioeconomic status determine developmental outcome? Race? Gender? Are there some assets you feel are more significant and important than others in promoting positive youth development? What are they, and why do you feel they are so significant?

9. With an understanding that positive youth development is furthered when actions are taken to enhance the assets of a person, a family, and a community, how might you design a youth charter that met the needs of impoverished communities?

10. What do you know about local policies and programs designed to support families in your area? Do they support the promotion of developmental assets and, in so doing, do they promote the moral development of youth?

11. In what ways did your parents promote in you the "five Cs" of competence, connection, character, confidence, and caring (or compassion)? Do you believe there are intergenerational effects inherent in this promotion—that civil society will be enhanced as youth initiate the positive moral behaviour instilled in them by their parents in the rearing of subsequent generations of citizens?

Key Terms

advantage index, p. 121
assets, p. 118
civil society, p. 105
five Cs, p. 124

heteronomous morality, p. 107
prosocial behaviour, p. 105
post-traumatic stress disorder (PSTD), p. 113

public policy, p. 124
thriving, p. 120
youth charters, p. 116

6

Identity: The Search for Self-Definition During Adolescence

Garrett was nervous. The Grade 7 dance was starting in less than an hour and he still wasn't 100% sure if he was ready to go.

He wanted to look good but he didn't want to appear that he wanted to look good. When he walked into the gym he wanted people to look at him but he also wanted to fit in. He wanted his classmates to see him as special, but not in a bad way. Cool, but not different, was what he was after.

"Garrett, are you ready yet?" his dad shouted up the stairs to him. "I have to pick up two of your friends on the way and the traffic is going to be terrible tonight. I don't want to be stuck in it longer because we left late."

"Yeah, Dad, I'm coming in one more minute," Garrett called back. He turned from the door of his room to face the mirror over his dresser. One last check and he guessed he'd be ready to go. In any case, he knew he'd have to be.

His new runners were loosely laced. His pants were belted slightly below his waist and his extra-large flannel shirt was unbuttoned, its untucked tails hanging almost to his knees. It was opened wide enough so the logo on his T-shirt could be clearly seen. He was not sure his hair looked good but, as he placed his baseball cap carefully on his head, he decided it would not matter. He'd just keep his hat on all night.

"Garrett!" The tone of his dad's voice told him that the time for self-reflection was over.

"Yes," he said to himself in the mirror, "you do look good." "I'm ready," he yelled out. He sprinted from his room and down the stairs. This was who he was and he and the kids at the dance would have to deal with it.

Learning Objectives

1. To define identity.
2. To learn what society expects from adolescents and how this relates to identity.
3. To understand the characteristics and importance of a role.
4. To understand what occurs if the adolescent does not resolve the identity crisis by early adulthood.
5. To understand the process of identity development through person-context interactions.
6. To describe Erik Erikson's theory of ego development.
7. To appreciate the role self-esteem plays in identity development.
8. To learn what self-regulation is and how identity is an instrument of self-regulation.
9. To appreciate the major instances of diversity in adolescent self-conception.
10. To understand the four identity statuses described by James Marcia.
11. To understand contextual influences on identity development.
12. To define ethnic identity and its importance to an adolescent's identity.
13. To understand there may be gender differences in identity development.

Parents often feel that each week they encounter a new person living in the body of their teenager. At least from the parents' perspective their adolescent's interests and emotions seem to rapidly change from one activity to another. Adolescence is a period of major change in body, mind, and behaviour. The basis of adolescent self-definition lies in the combination of these major changes.

The combination of changes involved in adolescence leads to an alteration in how one looks, feels, and thinks. The **developmental task** involved in these alterations is to understand who one is in the face of these changes. If this task is dealt with successfully, it will result in a new definition of the self as a particular individual with specific competencies, a personal life plan, and a niche in the world. This revised self-definition constitutes an alteration in personality. It represents a psychological and social adjustment to the physiological and psychological changes of adolescence. This adjustment is one based on the abstract self-understanding of the individual way these changes have affected the adolescent and the implications of the changes for the life directions he or she desires to take (Damon, 1991; Damon & Hart, 1988; Harter, 1986, 1988, 1998).

Accomplishing the task of self-understanding is not easy. The host of major biological, psychological, and social changes that characterize adolescence presents the young person with a serious emotional challenge. A young adolescent has developed a specific sense of self, as well as a sense of his or her self-competence and what he or she can do (e.g., in regard to school performance, social relationships, or athletics). At the beginning of adolescence this knowledge of self is challenged. The far-reaching bodily changes of this period (see Chapter 3) are accompanied by equally dramatic changes in thoughts (see Chapter 4). The assumptions adolescents held about their "selves" in the earlier stages of their lives may no longer be relevant to the new individuals they find themselves to be. The process involves, as described by Boyes and Chandler (1992, p. 283), a period of "epistemic development aimed at eventually allowing young persons to act with confidence in a newly created world of wholesale uncertainty."

William Damon (1991; Damon & Hart, 1988) notes that prior to adolescence people view themselves in terms of their bodily characteristics (e.g., their height), their actions (e.g., playing video games, skateboarding), their membership in particular groups (e.g., their school class or 4-H program or scouting group), or the state of their moods at a given moment. With the transition into the beginning of adolescence and the emergence of formal operational

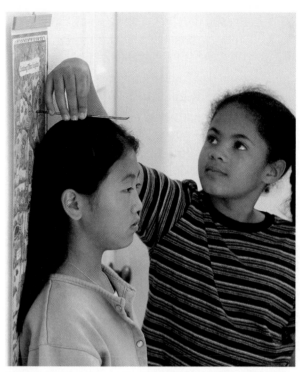
Physical characteristics are often a key part of an adolescent's identity.

thinking (see Chapter 4), youth define themselves in enduring and general terms (Damon, 1991). They see themselves as possessing specific personality traits that apply across time and situations.

Young adolescents may apply contradictory traits to themselves, for instance, labelling themselves as both "smart" and "dumb" (Harter, 1988). It is not until the latter portion of adolescence, in fact, that a systematic and integrated sense of self develops (Damon, 1991; Harter, 1986). Often, youth use their moral ideas (see Chapter 5) in order to attain this integrated and coherent sense of self.

A coherent sense of self is necessary for functioning productively in society (Archer & Waterman, 1991; Erikson, 1968). As a consequence of their biological and psychological changes, and of society's pressure to have them make a useful contribution to the world, during adolescence young people ask themselves the crucial psychological question: "Who am I?" While trying to answer this question the adolescent may experience an **identity crisis** (Erikson, 1959). This crisis occurs because, at the same time adolescents feel unsure about who they are, society begins to ask them questions related to their self-definitions.

Social and behavioural scientists believe this crisis is the central issue in understanding personality and social development in adolescence. The need

Developmental task Challenge to healthy or positive development that exists at a particular point in life; a challenge that must be met for development to proceed optimally.

Identity crisis Crisis between identity and role confusion elicited by the emotional upheaval provoked by the personal and social mandate to adopt a role in adolescence.

to resolve the crisis is another way to understand the key self-definitional developmental task of this period. To understand this issue, it is important to understand the meaning of the term *identity*.

Defining Identity

ISSUE TO CONSIDER

● How is identity defined?

Do you have a sense of your own attitudes and values? Do you know how you feel about things— about ideas (e.g., democracy, civil rights), people (your friends, parents, politicians, particular rock or movie stars), or activities (skiing, chatting online with friends, studying all night for exams)? Can you describe how you behave generally (e.g., in regard to how physically active you like to be, how much you enjoy being in social groups versus spending time alone, how much sleep you need) and in specific situations (e.g., when you are stuck for a long time in traffic, when you have too many things to do at one time, when you meet a particularly attractive person)? Would you guess that if you gave your best answers to these questions people who knew you well would agree you had described yourself accurately?

If your answers to all these questions are "yes," then you have described your identity. **Identity** is the "distinctive combination of personality characteristics and social style by which one defines him- or herself and by which one is recognized by others" (Grotevant, 1998, p. 1119). A person's identity is the set of the thoughts, feelings, values, attitudes, and behaviours that define his or her "self." It is the conception of who you are that you use to govern your present interactions with the world and navigate your life into the future. Identity also involves the feeling of self-continuity, that the self persists over time (Lalonde, Chandler, Hallett, and Paul, 2001). Identity means accurately knowing one's attitudes and values, how one feels about things, and how one behaves generally and in specific situations.

Why Do Adolescents Need an Identity?

ISSUES TO CONSIDER

● Why is an identity necessary for adolescents?
● What does society expect from adolescents? How does this relate to identity?
● What influence does the resolution of an identity crisis have on development during adulthood?

Much is asked of an adolescent by his or her family, teachers, and even friends that is not asked of children. Adolescents are expected to make the first steps toward career objectives (Castellino & Lerner, 1999; Perron, Vondracek, Skorikov, Tremblay, & Corbiere, 1998; Vondracek, 1994; Vondracek, Lerner, & Schulenberg, 1986) by making educational choices that will lead them toward or away from particular vocational or professional objectives (Greenberger & Steinberg, 1986; Vondracek, 1999). Adolescents are also expected to develop intimate and/or romantic relationships (see Chapter 10), and they are given more responsibility for managing their time and finances.

Through such changed expectations, society is asking adolescents what roles they will play as adults. Society wants to know what socially prescribed set of behaviours adolescents will choose to adopt. In other words, a key aspect of the adolescent dilemma regarding self-definition or identity is that of finding a role. A general commitment to a role is taken to be the outward expression of an adolescent's identity.

A **role** provides a self-definition, which coordinates for the adolescent his or her biological and psychological characteristics with a set of activities deemed useful by society (Baumeister, 1986, 1991; Erikson, 1968). A role typically cannot be something that is self-destructive or socially disapproved (e.g., criminal behaviour).

In the search for an identity, adolescents must discover what they believe and what their attitudes and ideas are. Commitment to a role entails commitment to a set of values (Erikson, 1959). An identity crisis may be elicited by the emotional upheaval provoked by this strong societal and personal mandate for role adoption, if it occurs at a time in the person's life when he or she cannot find a role that fits (Baumeister, 1986; Erikson, 1959, 1968). In order to resolve this crisis and achieve a sense of identity, the adolescent must find an orientation to life that not only fulfills the changing biological and psychological attributes of the self but one that is also consistent with what society expects of a person.

Resolution of the adolescent identity crisis has a profound influence on development during later adulthood. If the identity crisis is not resolved by the

Identity Set of thoughts, feeling, values, attitudes, and behaviours that defines a person's self.

Role Socially prescribed set of behaviours to which the person can show commitment.

time the adolescent enters adulthood, he or she will feel a sense of **role confusion** or **identity diffusion** (Archer & Waterman, 1991; Erikson, 1968). Some young adults waver between roles in a prolonged **moratorium** period in which they avoid commitment (Marcia, 1980). Others **foreclose** on a socially approved, easily available identity and avoid the crisis altogether (Marcia, 1980). Others resolve their crises by adopting an available but socially disapproved role or **ideology**. Called **negative identity formation**, it is often associated with delinquent behaviour (Erikson, 1959; Kennedy, 1991).

Accordingly, for the person experiencing the changes of adolescence, the definitional challenge that must be met has implications for health and success for much of the rest of life. Thus it is crucial for the adolescent to deal adequately, and in many ways this means *integratively*, with the changes of biology, psychology, and the social world confronting him or her. For successful (healthy, or positive) development to occur, a role cannot be chosen that (1) ignores one's biological attributes, assets, or limitations (e.g., males cannot choose the role of "mother," and people of short stature would be ill-advised to aspire to a career in professional basketball); (2) does not consider one's psychological characteristics (e.g., people with high activity levels and who find themselves easily distracted would not fit well with the job demands of an air traffic controller); or (3) is independent of societal needs or constraints (e.g., the profile of socially prescribed roles differs between industrialized and preindustrialized nations; Whiting & Whiting, 1991). The adolescent must go through a process that allows him or her to develop a healthy identity and the capacities for interacting successfully with society. Chandler and Lalonde (1998) warn that dramatic personal or cultural change can destabilize a person's identity. Adolescents are more likely than individuals at other ages to experience such upheaval, and thus may be at greater risk for suicide.

The Process of Identity Development

ISSUE TO CONSIDER

● How does identity develop through person-context interactions?

An identity allows you to explore your world in ways specific to your particular abilities, thoughts, feelings, and interests. It allows you to cull from your experiences with such interactions those "things" (e.g., activities, jobs, people) that fit with your self and that you will want to keep as a part of you in the future (e.g., "I seem to like skiing and will want to do more of this again"). In other words, identity develops through a process of person-context interactions in which you explore your world and evaluate and integrate the reactions you have to your explorations (Grotevant, 1998).

Given its person-context relational character, identity can change whenever there are significant alterations in the context (e.g., moving from elementary school to middle school; Simmons & Blyth, 1987) or in the person (e.g., involving puberty, and an ensuing spurt in height and weight that allows one to play basketball with a new ability; Graaffsma et al., 1994). Taylor (1997) argues that identity development of members of minority cultures, such as the Inuit in Canada, is more difficult because not only is their heritage culture poorly defined (due to the impact of **colonization** ["unequal relations involving a 'mother country' that exploits the labor power or natural resources of an external 'subject country' or colony," (Taylor, 2002, p. 72)]), but their role in mainstream culture is also poorly defined (due to being deprived of many of the benefits mainstream culture provides those in the mainstream). Similarly, culture affects the way youth explain self-continuity. Lalonde et al. (2001) found that the majority of Canadian youth use an "essentialist" approach, which involves finding underlying commonalities among the self that continue to exist over time. In contrast, Native youth are more likely to adopt a "narrative" approach, which relates past and present selves through creation of a story.

Role confusion Feeling an adolescent gets if he or she cannot find a role that fits his or her biological, psychological, and social characteristics.
Identity diffusion Feeling an adolescent gets if he or she cannot resolve the identity crisis. The defining characteristic is a lack of commitment, about which the adolescent is not concerned.
Moratorium Period in which an adolescent avoids commitment.

Foreclosure Adopting a socially approved, easily available role and thereby avoiding the identity crisis.
Ideology Set of attitudes, beliefs, and values that serves to define a role.

Negative identity formation Resolving the identity crisis by adopting an available but socially disapproved role or ideology.
Colonization Subjugation of another group's culture.

The former approach tends to resist the notion of change while the latter approach accepts change.

Identity is a concept that reflects many of the theoretical ideas about person-context relations we discussed in other chapters, including the classical theory of Erik H. Erikson (see Chapter 2) as well as more contemporary approaches.

Erikson's Theory of Ego Development in Adolescence

ISSUES TO CONSIDER

- What is Erik Erikson's theory of ego development?
- How can an identity crisis be resolved?
- What is the relation between an ideology and identity development?
- What occurs if an adolescent cannot show commitment to a role?
- How does self-esteem relate to identity development?

Erik H. Erikson's (1959, 1964, 1968) richly evocative descriptions of the changes involved in adolescent ego development have fired the imaginations and energies of many scientists studying adolescents, perhaps more so than any other theorist. As such, his ideas provide a useful frame for our discussion of the emotional and self-definitional changes of adolescence. Erikson (1959) proposed a theory of development that encompassed the entire human life span. As shown in Table 6.1, he divided the course of life into eight stages.

In each of the stages of development, Erikson saw development as involving the emergence of a new capability of the ego. However, such a gain in capacity comes at a price—there is the emergence of an emotional crisis and the risk of developing ego limitations as well. In fact, Erikson (1959, 1963) believes that within each stage of life, development involves a synthesis of a new ego capacity with a new type of incapacity. This synthesis of gain and loss in adolescence involves the concepts of ego identity, on the one hand, and role confusion, on the other.

We introduced Erikson's theory of psychosocial development in Chapter 2. We noted that Erikson sees the changes of puberty as presenting the adolescent with serious problems. If development was successful throughout the stages leading to adolescence, an adolescent will have developed more trust than mistrust, more autonomy than shame and doubt, more initiative than guilt, and more industry than inferiority. All the feelings that have developed have given the youth a feeling about who he or she is and of what he or she can do. In adolescence, this knowledge is challenged. Adolescents now find themselves in a body that looks and feels different and find they are thinking about this body, and all things, in a new way.

It is at this time of life that a great disparity between the "real self," the person an adolescent believes himself or herself to be, and the "ideal self," the person he or she wants to be, may be felt (Harter, 1988; see too Damon, 1991). This disparity is greatest in the area of physical appearance (Harter, 1988), especially for young adolescent girls (Koff, Rierdan, & Stubbs, 1990; Simmons & Blyth, 1987), who are less secure than are boys of this age about their physical appearance. It may be for this reason that young adolescent girls tend to have lower self-esteem than young adolescent boys (Harter, 1988; see too Simmons & Blyth, 1987).

Because all past associations the adolescent has had about the self may now be irrelevant, the adolescent feels the need to develop a coherent and adaptive sense of self. The adolescent asks the crucial psychosocial question, "Who am I?"

Table 6-1 Erikson's Theory of the Eight Stages of Ego Development

Psychosocial stage	Bipolar emotional crisis		
	A sense of	versus	A sense of
1. Oral sensory	basic trust	———————————	mistrust
2. Anal musculature	autonomy	———————————	shame, doubt
3. Genital locomotor	initiative	———————————	guilt
4. Latency	industry	———————————	inferiority
5. Puberty and adolescence	identity	———————————	role confusion
6. Young adulthood	intimacy	———————————	isolation
7. Adulthood	generativity	———————————	stagnation
8. Maturity	ego integrity	———————————	despair

Source: Lerner, 1986, p. 353.

As already noted, at precisely the time when the adolescent feels unsure about himself or herself, society begins to ask related questions about the adolescent. For instance, we have observed that in our society the adolescent must now begin to make the first definite steps toward career objectives (Vondracek, 1994, 1999; Vondracek et al., 1986). For example, students have to make a decision about whether or not they will enter into university preparatory courses.

Thus society asks adolescents what role they will play in society. Society wants to know how these soon-to-be-adult persons will contribute to its maintenance. Society wants to know what socially prescribed set of behaviours, useful for the effective maintenance of society, will be adopted. Yet how can one know what one can do, and what one wants to do, to contribute to society and meet its demands, if one does not know who one is?

In essence, then, the question *Who am I?* is basically a question of self-definition; it is necessitated by the emergence of all the new bodily changes, feelings, and capabilities arising during adolescence (e.g., the sex drive and formal thought), and by the new demands placed on the adolescent by society. The adaptive challenge to find a role one can be committed to, and thus to achieve an identity, is the most important task of adolescence. The emotional upheaval provoked by this crisis is termed by Erikson the *identity crisis*.

To achieve identity adolescents must, therefore, discover what they believe in, and what their attitudes and ideals are. Along with any role, there is an ideology, or set of attitudes, beliefs, and values, that serves to define it. These factors, which can be said to define our ideology, provide an important component of our role. When we know who we are, we know what we do, and when we know what we do, we know our role in society.

Along with any role (e.g., wife, father, student, teacher) goes a set of orientations toward the world that serves to define that role. These attitudes, beliefs, and values give us some idea of what a person engaged in a particular role in society thinks of and does. Thus an *ideology* serves to define a societal role. We know fairly well what the ideology of a Catholic priest is and how it is similar to and different from the ideology associated with a military general, or a professional artist, or a professional politician. The point is that along with any role goes a role-defining ideology. To solve our identity crisis, we must be committed to a role, which means showing commitment toward an ideology. Erikson (1963) calls such an emotional orientation **fidelity**.

If adolescents find their role in society, and show commitment to an ideology, they will have achieved a sense of identity. If adolescents do not find a role to play in society, they will remain in the identity crisis. In an attempt to resolve this crisis, adolescents might try many roles and, perhaps, be only temporarily successful investing the self in any one.

Erikson maintains that if adolescents are unable to show commitment to a role and thereby do not resolve the identity crisis, they will feel a sense of role confusion, or identity diffusion. In short, the terms *crisis* and *commitment* become hallmarks of the fifth stage of psychosocial development in Erikson's theory.

Yet the adaptive struggle in this stage is not only preceded by events in earlier ones but also is influenced in its outcome by them. As Constantinople (1969, p. 358) pointed out,

> In order to achieve a positive resolution of the identity crisis, the adolescent must sift through all of the attitudes toward himself and the world which have occurred over the years with the resolution of earlier crises, and he must fashion for himself a sense of who he is that will remain constant across situations and that can be shared by others when they interact with him.

The identity the adolescent attains as a consequence of the psychosocial crises preceding and during adolescence influences the rest of the life span. To Erikson, **self-esteem** is a feeling about the self, which tends to remain constant across life and gives the person a coherent psychological basis for dealing with the demands of social reality. In one essay (1959) in which he cast the notion of identity in terms of self-esteem, Erikson says,

> Self-esteem, confirmed at the end of a major crisis, grows to be a conviction that one is learning effective steps toward a tangible future, that one is developing a defined personality within a social reality which one understands. (p. 89)

Constantinople (1969, p. 358) elaborates,

> This self-esteem is the end product of successful resolutions of each crisis; the fewer or the less satisfactory the successful resolutions, the less

---

Fidelity Emotional orientation toward showing commitment to a role and ideology.

Self-esteem Degree of positive or negative feelings one holds about the self.

self-esteem on which to build at this stage of development, and the greater the likelihood of a prolonged sense of identity diffusion, of not being sure of who one is and where one is going.

Where we go from adolescence is the early portion of adulthood. During this period, we face another psychosocial crisis. Successful resolution of this crisis and the remaining crises of the adult years rests on the attainment of an adequate identity. Chapter 15 discusses the transition from adolescence to adulthood. Here, we turn to some concluding comments about Erikson's ideas about adolescence and then to a discussion of other theories of identity development.

Conclusions About Erikson's Theory

Erikson believes the identity crisis of adolescence is provoked by individual and societal changes and can only be resolved through commitment to a role, which balances the individual and social demands raised by these changes. The crisis of this stage comes from the emotional turmoil triggered by adolescent pubertal change, and the commitment of this stage arises due to the need to establish a new definition of the self that settles the emotional upheaval.

This viewpoint raises, however, what we have discussed as the "lore of adolescence" (Chapter 1). As epitomized in the theory of Anna Freud (1969; see Chapter 2), the changes of puberty are thought to initiate the alterations in body, emotions, and thought that precipitate this crisis of self-definition. Thus the identity crisis, at least insofar as its initial

stages are concerned, would seem to be a phenomenon of the early portions of the adolescent period. By the latter portion of adolescence, as we make the transition into early adulthood, we need to resolve the crisis of identity if successful transition to and development within young adulthood are to occur. Therefore, the portion of adolescence in which we would expect to see most ego identity development occurring is early adolescence. To determine if research evidence supports this type of development of identity, it is important to review other theories.

Contemporary Theoretical Views of Identity Development

ISSUES TO CONSIDER
- What is self-regulation? How does it relate to identity?
- How are assimilation and accommodation related to identity?

The work of Michael Berzonsky and his colleagues (1993, 1997; Berzonsky & Neimeyer, 1994) emphasizes that a person's developing identity is a feature of the individual that results from past, and contributes to future, person-context relations. As such, identity is an instrument of **self-regulation** (see Chapter 2). For example, it is the feature of adolescent psychological functioning and social life that allows the individual to *select* the paths he or she will pursue in life, to find the means to attain the goals that are chosen (*optimization*), and to cope with failures or losses in the means to reach goals (*compensation*).

As well, regulation of one's relations with the context involves figuring out how the context (e.g., the crowd of peers in one's high school) may be adapted or modified (e.g., through choosing a subset of peers with whom to form a clique) in order to fit or meet one's goals (e.g., the attainment of friendship or popularity). Assimilation (Chapter 4) may be involved in such selection and optimization actions. In turn, a youth may find that he or she cannot completely alter the context (e.g., the attitudes of the peer group about what looks "cool") while trying to reach a goal (e.g., popularity), and that one must change the self (e.g., adopt a different style of dress to fit in better) in order to reach the goal. Thus accommodation (Chapter 4) is part of the process of

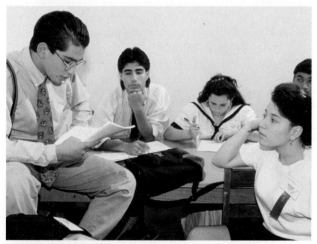

Identity may involve understanding how the self fits into particular peer, school, or community settings.

Self-regulation Feature of adolescent psychological and social functioning that allows the individual to select goals, find the means to attain those goals, and cope with failures or losses to reach these goals.

Contexts That Support or Hinder Adolescent Identity Development

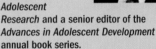

Gerald R. Adams is a professor of family relations and human development at the University of Guelph, Ontario. He is the current editor of the *Journal of Adolescent Research* and a senior editor of the *Advances in Adolescent Development* annual book series.

Most teenagers grow up in supportive families, attend good schools, have a part-time job, date a little, or even have a serious girlfriend or boyfriend. So life is good for most teens. But for a few, life is less than kind. Some youth come from dysfunctional homes, live in poverty, and attend decaying and old schools where teachers are trying hard to work with little financial resources or operating money. The neighbourhoods are often in rapid decline. The local role models are often involved in criminal or social deviance (drug dealers, prostitutes, etc.).

No matter if teens live in an advantaged or disadvantaged context, they share the same challenge of formulating a sense of self and constructing a sense of identity. For several years, I have been studying the patterns of identity development and the contexts that support or hinder identity formation.

As one example, our research team has been using the National Longitudinal Survey of Children and Youth, the first such study in Canada, to identify what family processes support children's academic success in school. Being a good or poor student in school is in part development of an identity as a student. We are observing a complex web of connections between family life and school success. Let me briefly describe for you one set of linkages. Higher income families have a wider number of family support systems. This is important because social support helps to diminish parent depression, where depression predicts higher family dysfunction (quarrelling, fighting, disagreeing). So how does this relate to school success? Well, family dysfunction is associated with hostile and ineffective parenting behaviours that lower a child's academic interests and skills. And lower academic interest and skills result in lower academic grades. So we are finding that income, family support, parental depression, family dysfunction, and hostile or ineffective parenting are important factors in predicting a teen's interest and success in school and their sense of academic identity. The web of interpersonal and social influences are complex and very interactive, as this book is demonstrating to you.

I have also been very interested in the role of identity in understanding problems like runaway behaviour or bulimia. I believe that society sets certain expectations during the adolescent years to formulate a sense of self. With funding from the Social Science and Humanities Research Council of Canada, I have been able to study the nature and form of identity formation. Our research team is finding that we can identify three basic types of identity. The *empty self* is a teenager who avoids, procrastinates, and fails to make identity commitments, even in the face of societal pressure to do so. The *prefabricated self* involves using social conventions and parental role models to imitate and provide the structure and values that the teenager accepts is true of him or her. The *constructive self* includes teenagers who seek out information, analyze choices for work, values, and commitments, and select only those that fit the emerging construction of self-identity.

In our research programs we are finding the empty self is associated with many social problems, including running away, eating disorders, conduct disorders, and inattention in school settings. Escaping the developmental task of identity formation is diminishing the resources or human capital that teenagers should be making to help guide and direct them into adulthood. To this point in time, we are finding that escaping the self leaves an empty sense of identity that may make a teen and perhaps an adult susceptible to social deviance and identity disorders.

compensation in such a situation (Berzonsky, 1993, 1997; Berzonsky & Neimeyer, 1994; Grotevant, 1997, 1998). Berzonsky (1989) has studied the processes that adolescents use in developing an identity. Individuals who are information-oriented make decisions about their identities by seeking out useful information. Individuals characterized as having a diffuse/avoidant identity orientation tend to procrastinate in making decisions. People who show the normative identity orientation tend to conform to others' expectations. These identity orientations seem to remain fairly stable (Kier & Berzonsky, 2003).

Other scholars also stress that identity development involves relations between the person and the social/cultural context (Adams & Marshall, 1996; Côté, 1996; Goossens & Phinney, 1996) and that it involves the regulation of these relations (Adams, 1997; Baumeister & Muraven, 1996; Berzonsky, 1997; Grotevant, 1987, 1997; Kerpelman, Pittmann, & Lamke, 1997). The ideas of one leading researcher, Gerald R. Adams, are presented in Meet the Researcher Box 6.1.

As we discussed in Chapter 2, the regulation of our relationship with the social world, through, for instance, the processes of selection, optimization, and compensation (Baltes & Baltes, 1990; Freund & Baltes, 1998), or through other attempts to control the relationships we have with the social context (e.g., Kerpelman et al., 1997), allows us to adapt to the context, and "adaptation may be the best way to conceptualize the complex, multilateral relationship between individual identity and sociocultural context, because it recognizes the causal importance of culture yet also recognizes individual choice and change" (Baumeister & Muraven, 1996, p. 405).

Much of this research has been based on adolescents from individualistic cultures, particularly the United States. However, there is evidence to suggest that there are differences among individualistic cultures in the emphasis placed on valuing, recognizing, and rewarding individual achievement. For example, U.S. university students had higher self-esteem scores and rated competence and achievement values as more important in comparison to students in Canada or Australia (Feather, 1998). They also rated conformity values (being polite, responsible, self-controlled, obedient, forgiving, clean) as more important than did Canadian students. The Canadians rated affiliative values (happiness, loving, mature love, true friendship, inner harmony, cheerfulness, family security) as less important than did the American students (and Australian students). Thus it is important to examine research from a diverse array of countries.

Several studies provide empirical support for the theory of the role of identity in regulating links between the adolescent and the sociocultural context. In a study of the influence of culture on adolescent coping behaviour (Oláh, 1995), involving more than 700 male and female 17- and 18-year-olds from India, Italy, Hungary, Sweden, and Yemen, both cultural differences and similarities in regulative behaviour were seen. When needing to cope with stresses from the context, youth from European countries were more likely to use assimilation as a strategy, whereas youth from India and Yemen preferred emotion-focused solutions. Youth from all cultural settings, if they possessed high levels of anxiety, coped with stresses by showing avoidance behaviours.

There are also cultural differences between youth within a geographic region related to regulation. German youth prefer a more active approach to reaching the developmental goals they select than

Polish youth, and Polish youth extend their goals for later in their development than German adolescents (Schönpflug & Jansen, 1995). There are within-nation differences as well. Younger German youth (11- to 16-year-olds) use both behavioural approach and avoidance coping strategies, whereas older German adolescents (17- to 19-year-olds) show both behavioural and cognitive forms of approach (Kavsek & Seiffge-Krenke, 1996). In a longitudinal study of more than 3200 Swiss adolescents, aged between 14 and 20 years, youth saw two general domains of the context over which they needed to exert control—the personal/social domain and the society domain (Grob, Flammer, & Wearing, 1995). Finally, in a sample of about 350 Korean adolescents in Grade 12, problem-solving and information-seeking approaches to coping were associated with a lower likelihood of depression, and physical symptoms were associated with a coping style that involved discharge of emotions.

In short, the concept of identity is central to the understanding of adolescence and the theoretical ideas about the regulation of person-context relations. Given this centrality, it may be surprising to learn there are relatively few studies of the behavioural correlates or developmental consequences of identity development (Grotevant, 1998). Although Erikson (1968) emphasized that identity development is a process involving *the core of the individual and . . . the core of his* [or her] *communal culture*" (p. 22), there have also been relatively few studies of the influence of the context on identity development (Goossens & Phinney, 1996). It is important to review what the research about identity development has focused on and what it says about the character of self and identity during adolescence.

How Does Identity Develop in Adolescence?: Research Directions

For at least the last 30 years scholars have conducted hundreds (and perhaps thousands) of investigations of identity during adolescence. This emphasis is not surprising, given the importance of this concept in (potentially at least) explaining how young people may or may not become healthy, contributing members of society. What may be surprising, however, is that still, after all this research, there remain relatively few sound studies that actually measure identity development across the span of adolescence (Grotevant, 1998).

Instead, beginning in the late 1970s and early 1980s, much of the research about identity focused on different statuses an adolescent may attain during the identity crisis—status that, as we discuss later, may involve the attainment of an identity (in at least one of two different ways), remaining in a state of crisis, or being actively engaged in a search for identity (Marcia, 1980). Research has also focused on the different domains within which identity may be expressed, for instance, in regard to one's ethnicity or gender and/or in relation to one's interpersonal relationships with family members and peers (Grotevant, 1998). Accordingly, in order to appreciate contemporary understanding of the nature of identity in adolescence it is important to discuss research that has tested Erikson's theory and, in turn, research about the developmental and contextual bases of identity development. This latter research involves also a consideration of the influence of characteristics such as ethnicity and gender on individual differences (diversity) in such development.

Research About Erikson's Theory of Ego Development

ISSUES TO CONSIDER

- During what period of adolescence should research on identity development focus on? Why?
- Does contemporary research support Erikson's theory of ego development?

Despite the theoretical importance attached to the emergence of the identity crisis in adolescence in Erikson's theory, little research has been reported about the study of ego identity in *early* adolescence. Most of the research activity has been directed at the late adolescent period, when we would expect most of the changes that should have occurred to have been completed (e.g., Archer & Waterman, 1991; Marcia, 1980, 1991; Schiedel & Marcia, 1985; Waterman, 1982). Meet the Researcher Box 6.2 presents the work of Sally L. Archer, a leading researcher in this area.

This research has typically provided interesting and useful information about the search for a role (see Archer & Waterman, 1991; Marcia, 1991) and about how the family context and interactions with parents facilitate the exploration of roles (Adams & Jones, 1983; Grotevant, 1998; Grotevant & Cooper,

1985). However, this research has been focused too much on late adolescence. As a result, there is a lack of data pertinent to early adolescence.

Moreover, the findings that exist about ego identity in late adolescence indicate that theoretically surprising identity change rather than stability seems to be the rule (Archer & Waterman, 1991). For example, in a large and classic study involving an assessment of the presence of stagelike qualities in adolescent development, Constantinople (1969) tested more than 900 male and female students from the University of Rochester. There were consistent increases in the successful resolution of identity from the first year to the final across participants and from one year to the next within groups of participants. However, only males showed consistent decreases in the scores for identity diffusion. Changes in scores for the other crises did not always decrease or increase in accordance with Erikson's theory. Thus Constantinople's (1969) data provide, at best, only partial support for Erikson's theory of ego development.

Other data also contradict Erikson's theory. For instance, by the end of their college or university experience, and the presumed beginning of their early adulthood stage of psychosocial development, college or university students do not invariably show stable identity achievement (Archer & Waterman, 1991; Waterman, 1982). Adolescents' feelings and ideas about themselves seem to change in several directions. In the Early Adolescence Study (Petersen, 1987), some aspects of self-esteem increase across early adolescence, others decrease, and still others show curvilinear changes across age.

Either the purported identity crisis of early adolescence does not develop until the late adolescent/young adult years or Erikson's theory and the lore of adolescence must be revised to encompass all of this period and the next one as well. In either case, and as we have seen, too, in respect to the issue of storm and stress and to pubertal change (Chapters 1 and 3, respectively) and to cognitive development (Chapter 4), the lore of adolescence—as a period of upheaval, general maladjustment, and interpersonal conflict—finds no support.

Whether we view Erikson's theory as valid or not (e.g., see Lerner, 1986; Muuss, 1996), Erikson undoubtedly provided a service in directing the study of personality development in adolescence to a focus on the self, self-concept, and self-esteem. Much contemporary research, both consistent with and

MEET THE RESEARCHER   Box 6.2   Sally L. Archer

Does Commitment Guarantee Implementation of Identity Choices?: Barriers to Living One's Choices

Sally L. Archer is a professor of developmental psychology at The College of New Jersey. She is on the editorial boards of *The Journal of Early Adolescence* and *Identity: An International Journal of Theory and Research.* She is a founding member of the Society for Research on Adolescence and the Society for Research on Identity Formation.

As you have noted in this chapter, one of the ways we investigate the formation of one's identity is to examine the processes of exploration and commitment. Individuals who are knowledgeable, engaged in relevant activity, and can envision this choice as part of their future are seen as having a self-defined identity in this area of their life. As examples, one may have a committed identity pertaining to a career, religious beliefs, parenting, or so forth.

In earlier research, I documented the serious concern expressed by a majority of Grade 12 women regarding making their personal identity decisions about the priorities of career and family for their future. The next step in this dilemma was to investigate how one makes decisions regarding the implementation of these potentially conflicting choices. Toward that end I have developed a course on career decision-making in psychology for second- and fourth-year university students. These students have made the commitment to their major and are searching for a specific career and/or the continuance of study at the graduate level. "How do they proceed to implement their commitment to career, given their potential plans for family?" I have been using a variety of techniques to measure this process, such as identity interviews, a cognitive career block instrument, autobiographical life-lines of important events from birth to the present to retirement, professional autobiographical essays, and practical professional preparation. One of the challenges is to distinguish between issues of career implementation and family/career conflicts that block movement toward that implementation.

The university men (of the 1990s) recognize the issue of conflict in the priorities of career and family to a far greater extent than did Grade 12 men (of the 1980s). But in common between the two age groups, there is little concern about how one might integrate the two major areas of career and family into their lives. They are comfortable making the self-definitional commitment to both identity areas and can envision both in their future, but they give little thought to their implementation. Thus plans for a family are not a barrier to plans for career implementation. University women, who make the commitment to both areas, attempt to visualize the implementation of the two in far greater detail than do the men. As a consequence, they experience major cognitive and emotional blocks to decisions regarding the implementation of the career component of their identities. This has serious implications for their ability to live the life that most fully expresses their potentials and sense of self. Do they choose careers that require major commitments in order to advance in or impact on their field? How much do they invest in graduate school, if they plan to have families and perhaps take time to remain home with their infants? These are not issues for the vast majority of these university men who also profess commitment to career and family and state that they believe in shared family responsibilities.

At the present, I am working on obtaining a more representative sample. My subsequent goal will be to address the implications of such findings for our university advisement process. Have you thought about these issues and spoken with your faculty about the impact of a "potential" family on career alternatives?

---

independent of Erikson's ideas, focuses on changes in the self during adolescence. This research demonstrates both the considerable diversity in the development of the self during adolescence and the important role of the social context in influencing this development. It is useful to consider first the diversity that exists in the development of the self.

Research on the Definition of Self During Adolescence

ISSUES TO CONSIDER

- What are the major instances of diversity in adolescent self-conception?
- What are two types of identity crises? How do they differ by gender?

Researchers concerned with the central issue of how adolescents define themselves have studied several variables related to the self, including self-concept, self-esteem, perceived self-competence, and ego development. Despite the particular variable of interest in a given study, research shows that major instances of diversity in adolescents' beliefs about themselves occur in regard to differences in developmental pathways and contrasts between males and females.

In a longitudinal study of developmental changes in self-esteem from early adolescence through late adolescence to early adulthood, males and females were found to have distinct developmental trajectories (Block & Robins, 1993). The self-esteem of males tended to increase from early adolescence through early adulthood; that of females tended to decrease. In another longitudinal study of male and female adolescents, sex differences in using concepts of masculinity to define the self increased between Grades 6 and 8 (Galambos, Almeida, & Petersen, 1990); however, there were no sex differences in the use of concepts of femininity across this portion of adolescence.

Images of one's body and its capabilities are also part of the adolescent's sense of self (Perkins & Lerner, 1995), which differs between males and females. Females have more differentiated and males more global body images (Koff et al., 1990). That is, this research found that females' body images tend to involve ideas about many separate features or parts of their bodies, whereas males' body images tend to reflect a more general, overall impression of their bodies. The research found also that male adolescents are more positive about their bodies than are female adolescents.

Other developmental differences occur in regard to self-development. Longitudinal research has found that children define themselves in regard to three dimensions of self-competence: academic achievement, social competence, and conduct (Masten et al., 1995). Adolescents, however, use these dimensions and two others—romantic competence and job competence—to define themselves. Similarly, from childhood through early and late adolescence, youth become more flexible in the roles they associate with the two genders (Katz & Ksansnak, 1994). Adolescents show more flexibility in regard to the particular roles they adopt—showing a greater willingness to adopt behaviours that may typically be associated with the other gender (see Chapter 7 for a discussion of such gender role flexibility). In addition,

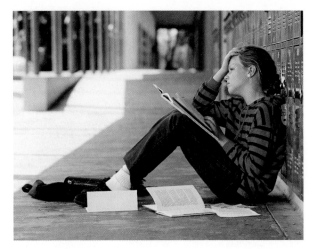

The stress of searching for an identity may elicit emotional turmoil or a sense of crisis in an adolescent.

they show greater tolerance about other people showing such flexibility (Katz & Ksansnak, 1994).

Diversity in the nature of the ego identity crisis has also been found by researchers (Archer & Waterman, 1991; Marcia, 1964, 1966, 1980, 1991), and, once again, gender differences are part of this diversity. For instance, Baumeister (1986; Baumeister, Shapiro, & Tice, 1985) found that at least two types of identity crisis exist. One type is labelled an **identity deficit**. Here the person cannot resolve his or her identity crisis because of an inability to make decisions (e.g., role choices). The second type of crisis is labelled **identity conflict**. In this type of crisis the person makes incompatible decisions (e.g., choosing roles that require different, almost mutually exclusive behaviours). For instance, the person might decide to be a parent who stays at home to raise children *and* a Ph.D.-level scientist, a role that requires several years of postgraduate training. Baumeister (1991) reports that crises involving identity conflict seem to be an important part of the ego development of girls more so than boys.

Research on Identity "Status" During Adolescence

ISSUES TO CONSIDER

• What four identity statuses have been identified? What are some features of these identity statuses?
• Does gender play a role in the likelihood of being in any of the four ego identity status categories? If so, how does gender play a role?

A series of provocative studies of different identity statuses among adolescents is related to research that

Identity deficit Identity crisis in which the person fails to resolve the identity crisis because of an inability to make decisions.

Identity conflict Crisis in which the person is uncertain of how to define self and is not sure about the role he or she wants to play in society.

focuses on differences between youth in how they define their selves during adolescence. James Marcia (1964, 1966, 1980, 1991) hypothesized that resolutions of the adolescent identity crisis involve more than just identity versus role confusion (or identity diffusion). Marcia believed that a more diverse pattern exists, and that to ascertain the adolescent's identity status accurately, a youth's feelings of both crisis and commitment to a role should be measured.

Marcia (1966) found evidence for four identity statuses (see Table 6.2). As Erikson (1959, 1963, 1968) said, two of these statuses are held by adolescents who achieve *identity* or those who are in a state of *identity diffusion*. The former group has a crisis period but then shows a commitment to an occupation and to an ideology. The latter group may or may not have a crisis, but their defining characteristic is their lack of commitment, a lack about which they are not concerned.

The third status Marcia identified is labelled *moratorium*. Although adolescents in moratorium are in a crisis and have, at best, a vague commitment to an occupation or to an ideology, they are actively trying to make commitments. The last identity status Marcia identified is termed *foreclosure*. Adolescents in this status never experience a crisis, yet are highly committed. Marcia found that they adopt the identities their parents want them to take, and they do so with little or no question and with no crisis. James Marcia describes his work in Meet the Researcher Box 6.3.

Marcia (1991) summarized the evidence in support of the existence of the four identity status categories (e.g., from Marcia et al., 1985/1992). He notes that current research evidence indicates that identity achievers are cognitively flexible, have higher levels of moral reasoning, and are more capable of intimate relations than youth in the other ego identity status categories. These youth are also less neurotic and more extroverted and conscientious than those in other identity categories (Clancy & Dollinger, 1993). They are also more attached to their

mothers (but not their fathers) than are other youth (Benson, Harris, & Rogers, 1992).

Youth in the moratorium category have conflicting needs to conform and to rebel, have ambivalent relationships with their parents, and are seen by other people as intense, often annoyingly so (Marcia, 1991). Adolescents who are actively engaged in identity exploration are likely to be characterized by self-doubt, confusion, and conflicts with parents (Kidwell et al., 1995).

Youth in the foreclosure category are high in authoritarianism, enmeshed in their families, and cognitively rigid (Marcia, 1991). They are also not open to new experiences (Clancy & Dollinger, 1993) and tend to have an extrinsic religious orientation (Markstrom-Adams & Smith, 1996). Youth who maintain their foreclosure status over a two-year period of their late adolescence have been found to seek a lot of nurturance from others and to have many memories of seeking security early in their lives (Kroger, 1995).

People in the identity diffusion status have lower levels of moral reasoning than youth in other categories, feel alienated from their parents, and are less capable of intimate relations than are youth in the other categories. In addition, a study of youth in Edmonton found that those who adopt a diffused-avoidant identity style (which most often is associated with identity diffusion status) are more likely to have conduct disorder or hyperactivity than other youth (Adams, Munro, Doherty-Poirer, Munro, Petersen, & Edwards, 2001). It was also associated with binge-eating in a sample of undergraduates in Ontario (Wheeler, Adams, & Keating, 2001).

Both these youth and those in moratorium are more neurotic and less conscientious than youth in other identity categories (Clancy & Dollinger, 1993). Both moratorium and diffusion youth are less likely to be attached to their mothers and fathers (Benson et al., 1992).

Although the likelihood of being in any of the four ego identity status categories specified by Marcia (1991) does not differ between males and females (Archer, 1991), there are gender differences that occur in regard to the domains of social behaviour that contribute to a person's identity status (Archer, 1985, 1989; Whitbourne & Tesch, 1985). Archer (1985) finds no gender differences in regard to the domains of vocational choice, religious beliefs, and sex role orientation, but in regard to political ideology, males are more likely to be in a foreclosed status and females in a diffusion status. In regard to family and career

---

Table 6-2 Different Identity Statuses Identified by Marcia

Identity achievement
Identity diffusion
Moratorium
Foreclosure

Source: Marcia, 1980.

The Development of Identity Statuses

The identity research began as the result of a clinical error and an academic necessity. During my internship at Massachusetts Mental Health Center (Harvard Medical School), I was assigned to do a diagnostic work-up on a 16-year-old boy. My supervisor, Dave Guttman, and I agreed that his projective test responses suggested a schizophrenic process. However, six months later, he was discharged from hospital much improved. Not what one would expect from such a diagnosis. At that time, Dave was a teaching assistant for Erik Erikson at Harvard and he gave me *Identity and the Life Cycle* to read. It was clear that our hospitalized young man was in a severe identity crisis and not schizophrenic. More personally relevant, I knew that I had to complete a doctoral dissertation back at Ohio State upon my return from internship. I wanted to do something that would be both interesting and a real contribution to knowledge. My professors at Ohio State (among them George Kelly and Julian Rotter) had claimed that there were few ideas in personality theory that could not be empirically tested using the method of construct validity. I took them up on that and, after three rather "bloody" research team meetings, came up with a method for measuring and validating Erikson's fifth psychosocial stage of identity versus identity diffusion. Doug Crowne very generously agreed to be my senior supervisor on a project that some of my peers at the time felt to be somewhat of a fool's errand.

I chose a semistructured interview with a scoring manual as my measure of identity. Although this is a labour-intensive way of going about research, it seems to me both to do justice to the complexity of Erikson's construct as well as allowing the investigator to explore thoroughly participants' identity formation process. In pilot work, after interviewing about 20 persons, it became clear to me that there were more styles of identity resolution than just the two that Erikson had proposed. Erikson had largely emphasized occupational and ideological *commitment* as central to identity formation. However, there seemed to be different ways in which commitment could be arrived at (hence, the variable of *exploration*), as well as different meanings for a lack of commitment. Identity could be self-constructed after a period of exploration

(achieved) or just adopted (foreclosed). As well, if no commitment were present this could be because the person was in an identity crisis (moratorium) or just unable or unwilling to make commitments (diffused). In the initial studies, I chose dependent variables with which to validate the newly minted "identity statuses" that seemed consistent with Erikson's theory and ego psychoanalytic theory in general. I was lucky in both this initial study and a subsequent one; most of my predictions were confirmed.

The initial identity studies had been conducted with university men and we used the life areas of occupational choice and ideological (politics and religion) position within which to assess identity development. When we began studying women, five years after the initial research with men, we realized that relationships were also central to identity development, and we added the areas of sexuality, later expanded to include sex roles, as well for both men and women. Subsequently, in looking at adult identity development, we expanded the areas to include marriage and family issues. Throughout the multiplication of these interview areas, our focus has remained always on the *process* (exploration and commitment) of identity formation, rather than on the particular *content* of an individual's beliefs.

The subsequent series of identity studies, conducted by myself, my students, and, now, a growing number of colleagues whom I had never met, focused on accumulating additional evidence for the validity of the identity statuses as a measure of Erikson's identity construct. Our research turned next to looking at antecedent conditions to identity development such as family variables as well as consequences such as intimacy development. As more and more identity status studies entered the literature (to date, there are more than 500 studies using the identity status approach), researchers in other countries, as well as many graduate students doing dissertations, picked up the approach and expanded its application, both in empirical and applied contexts. Although it might appear that the identity statuses are "mine," in fact, their accumulated validity represents the hard work of many others in many different settings.

The work has not been without its critics. Some of the criticisms have been that the

James Marcia is professor emeritus of psychology at Simon Fraser University. Dr. Marcia obtained his Ph.D. (1965) in clinical psychology from Ohio State University. His publications include two co-authored books on identity research as well as numerous journal articles, book chapters, and encyclopedia pieces dealing largely with construct validity of Erikson's psychosocial developmental theory.

identity statuses underrepresent Erikson's construct, that they are not "truly developmental," that they do not focus sufficiently on individual experience, and that they are tied too closely to a Western technological context. All of these criticisms have been answered more or less satisfactorily, depending, of course, on whether one is the critic or the respondent!

Current research has involved validation of four other Eriksonian stages: industry (Andrea Kowaz), intimacy (Jay Orlofsky), generativity (Cheryl Bradley), and integrity (Simon Hearn and Gary Saulnier). I have mentioned only the names of researchers working in our setting. Others, in other places, have also made significant research contributions, especially on the last three stages. I mention this here in order to point to the amenability of Erikson's theory to empirical validation. I am not suggesting that the work is easy. Erikson was more a poetic theorist and clinician than he was a researcher. But we have good evidence that operational definitions of at least the stages of industry through integrity can be constructed, measures developed, and construct validity established.

What would I say to young researchers beginning their careers or thinking about a research career in psychology? Pick a topic that is personally engaging; be as careful as you can about formulating a theoretically consistent and, within reasonable constraints, a tight research design; be prepared for lots of hard work on numerous projects. And don't be deterred by others who say, "It'll never fly." I wish you as good fortune, good students, and good colleagues, as I have had.

priorities and sexuality, females are more likely to be in either the identity achievement or the moratorium categories, whereas males are more likely to be in the foreclosure or the diffusion categories.

In short, then, differences in ego development are associated with differences between male and female adolescents and, as well, with variation in several domains of cognition, behaviour, and personality. Similarly, differences in personality characteristics are associated with variation in dimensions of adolescent self-definition other than ego identity.

For instance, feelings of low self-worth are linked to feelings of depression among young adolescents (Harter & Jackson, 1993). Moreover, low ego development in adolescence is linked to anger and sadness (Hauser & Safyer, 1994); in turn, high ego development is associated with enthusiasm, affection, and low anxiety. Similarly, among Norwegian 10- to 15-year-olds, negative self-esteem is associated with high social anxiety (Alsaker & Olweus, 1986); in addition, negative self-esteem is related to peer harassment. Because self-esteem level remains relatively constant across the adolescent years for these Norwegian youth, especially among older adolescents (Alsaker & Olweus, 1992), these associations are likely to remain important parts of their development.

Conclusions: Diversity in Adolescent Self-Definition and Identity Status

Constructs related to self-esteem, self-concept, perceived self-competence, body image, and ego identity vary across the adolescent years. This diversity, associated with gender, developmental change, and individual psychological characteristics pertinent to cognition and personality, is influenced by several features of the adolescent's context. The contextual influence on identity development is now discussed.

Identity Development: Diversity and Context

ISSUES TO CONSIDER
- What are some contextual influences on identity development?
- What research supports these contextual influences?

Considerable research links the general course of adolescent self-development to the context. Identity development is related to varying contexts, ranging from those general socialization experiences that vary

across history and culture to quite specific effects of the family and the school setting.

The Historical Context of Adolescent Identity Development

Perhaps the best example of how the changing historical context provides a basis of individual development is derived from a study by Elder (1974; see too Elder, 1980, 1998, 1999). Elder (1974, 1999) analyzed longitudinal data about the development of people who were children and adolescents between 1929 and 1941, the years of the Great Depression in the United States. He found that among a group of 84 males and 83 females born in 1920 and 1921, characteristics of the historical era produced alterations in the influence that education had on achievement (Elder, 1974, 1999).

The historical context of their adolescence continued to influence people in their subsequent adult years. Later adult health was affected among youth from working-class families who suffered hardships during the Depression, and the importance of children in later adult marriages was enhanced among these youth (Elder, 1974, 1999).

Influences of the Sociocultural Context

As suggested by the research described above that demonstrates a link between cultural context and processes of person-context regulation during adolescence, sociocultural context influences identity development (Nurmi, Poole, & Kalakoski, 1996). A study of 680 younger (13- to 14-year-old) and older (16- to 17-year-old) boys and girls from either urban or rural areas in Australia or Finland assessed the processes of identity exploration and commitment. Older youth living in Australian urban settings possessed higher levels of exploration and commitment in regard to both future occupation and education than did younger urban youth. There were no age differences among rural Australian adolescents or among the urban and rural Finnish youth (Nurmi et al., 1996).

In a study comparing identity development among approximately 200 American late adolescent youth and approximately 100 similarly aged Finnish youth (Nurmi et al., 1997), comparable relationships in both groups were found between identity and self-esteem. Youth with an information-oriented identity style had higher self-esteem than other individuals,

U.S. study

whereas youth with diffuse or avoidant identity styles were most likely to be depressed (Nurmi et al., 1997).

Within a culture there are also important contextual influences on identity development. These influences are associated with family, peers, school, sports/athletics, social support, neighbourhood/community, and the social, political, and economic structure of a society (e.g., DuBois et al., 1996; Grotevant & Bosma, 1994; Paschall & Hubbard, 1998).

Family Influences

Parents and family can play a direct role in the socialization of differences in self-definition. For instance, in terms of gender differences, more girls than boys have parents who do not let them out of their homes after dark (Simmons & Blyth, 1987). Independent of the socialization of gender differences, parents and family provide contextual influences that influence self-development in adolescence. For example, authoritarian parenting style is associated with foreclosed identity, authoritative parenting is associated with achieved identity, and permissive parenting is associated with diffused identity (Adams & Côté, 2002). Among African American youth, high self-esteem is associated with the acceptance and warmth received from parents and other family members (Luster & McAdoo, 1995). Self-esteem among these youth is also linked to the completion of high school and to movement to economic independence. For a group of 13- to 15-year-old girls in Ottawa, maternal (but not paternal) authoritative parenting was correlated with high self-worth (Pychyl, Coplan, & Reid, 2002). This was not found for boys. Girls with high self-esteem were less likely to procrastinate than other girls.

As the research implies, family influences on adolescents' self-development appear most pronounced when specific types of parent-child interactions occur in the context of particular emotional exchanges in the family. For example, adolescent ego development and self-esteem increase when fathers challenge the autonomy and relatedness of their youth and when they express to them their feelings about the importance of being independent and involved in family life (Allen, Hauser, Bell, & O'Connor, 1994; Allen, Hauser, Eickholt, Bell, & O'Connor, 1994; Hauser et al., 1991; Powers et al., 1983).

Other research confirms the importance of the role for self-development of adolescents being urged to be both individuals and connected to the family (Cooper, Grotevant, & Condon, 1983; Grotevant,

1994; Grotevant & Cooper, 1983). The work of Harold Grotevant and Catherine Cooper (e.g., Cooper, 1994; Grotevant, 1998; Grotevant & Cooper, 1983, 1985, 1986, 1998) has been central in specifying that individuality and connection to parents are not opposing orientations in the world of adolescents. Rather, both of these orientations are important for healthy adolescent development.

Youth who live in families in which there is an opportunity and the support for expressing and developing their own viewpoints show high levels of identity explorations (Grotevant, 1998; Grotevant & Cooper, 1998). Although emotional detachment from parents is detrimental to the psychological adjustment of adolescents when they live in such supportive families, such detachment is adaptive in less supportive families (Fuhrman & Holmbeck, 1995). Several characteristics of family interaction (enduring engagement of youth by parents, parental self-disclosure and sharing, tolerance of novelty and uncertainty, and tolerance of unwanted/unexpected emotions) is linked to enhanced ego development among youth (Hauser, Powers, & Noam, 1991).

Relations Between Family and Peer Influences

Of course, the family and other portions of the social context can interrelate in influencing self and identity development. Chapters 8 and 9 illustrate the combined contributions of the family and of peers, respectively. Here, we may note that these combined influences occur in regard to identity and self-development. For instance, Cooper (1994) has shown that close relationships—with peers as well as with family members—provide an important link in a causal chain between the broader sociocultural context (e.g., opportunities available to youth from particular ethnic, racial, or socioeconomic groups) and identity development.

Other studies find an influence of both parents and peers on identity development. For example, in a nationally representative study of Dutch adolescents, aged 12 to 14 years, both peers and parents contributed positively to identity development (Meeus & Dekovic, 1995).

In a study of young adolescents (Harter, Stocker, & Robinson, 1996), youth who based their self-worth on peer approval were more preoccupied with such approval than were adolescents who maintained that their self-worth existed prior to any approval they received from peers. The group preoccupied with peer approval was also more likely to be distracted from their schoolwork by peers, to show more fluctuations in both classmates' approval and their self-worth, and to have lower levels of classmate approval than the other group of youth (Harter et al., 1996). In a study of adolescent self-worth and relations to parents, teachers, male peers, and female peers, about 75% of youth reported differences in self-worth across the four contexts. High self-worth in one relational context was related to overall self-worth (Harter, Waters, & Whitesell, 1998).

Support from the social context in general may be linked to the development of a positive sense of self (e.g., Gray-Little & Carels, 1997). Adolescents' perceptions of approval from others, especially a general peer reference group such as classmates, is strongly related to self-worth among adolescents (Robinson, 1995). The school context is also important to consider as an influence on the development of self.

The Influence of the School Context

The family and the peer group provide contexts that influence the development of the self in adolescence in often complex ways. Corresponding conclusions can be drawn about the influence of the school context. In a study of approximately 2000 children and adolescents, young adolescents, in comparison to 8- to 11-year-old children, showed more self-consciousness, greater instability of self-image, and slightly lower self-esteem (Simmons, Rosenberg, & Rosenberg, 1973). However, context, rather than age, seemed to account for these findings (see, too, Simmons & Blyth, 1987). Upon completion of Grade 6, one portion of the young adolescent group had moved to a new school, typically a local junior high school, and the remaining portion of the young adolescents stayed in the same school, which offered Grade 7 and 8 classes. The group of young adolescents who changed their school setting showed a much greater incidence of the above-noted changes in self than did the group that remained in elementary school. Variables related to the school context, and to school transitions more specifically, therefore seem to influence self-development in adolescence.

Other research is consistent with this view. Although children's self-esteem does not seem to decrease during elementary school, it does show such change following the transition to junior high school

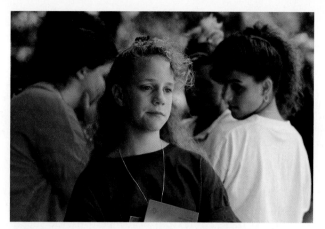

Social interactions in school can influence identity development in adolescence.

(Wigfield & Eccles, 1994). In a study of almost 2000 young adolescents, self-esteem declined across the transition to junior high school but increased during Grade 7 (Wigfield et al., 1991). If an adolescent is young relative to classmates accompanying him or her in the transition to junior high or middle school, the detrimental effects on self-esteem seem to be increased (Fenzel, 1992).

The influence of school transition on self-esteem occurs in many countries. Japanese adolescents were more pessimistic and less optimistic about their future personal success in Grade 7 (beginning of junior high school) than in Grade 6 (the end of elementary school) (Kozumi, 1995).

School transition is not the only way the school context influences the development of self during adolescence. Adolescents' educational plans and self-image have been found to be lower among youth living and going to school in rural communities (Sarigiani et al., 1990). It may be that the quality of teaching the adolescent experiences can protect against such influences. For instance, adolescents enrolled in middle schools that provide interdisciplinary teaching teams have higher self-concepts than youth who attend schools where such instruction is not emphasized (Stefanich, Wills, & Buss, 1991). Youth with low self-esteem can show significant improvement in their self-regard if they have physical education instructors who are reinforcing and encouraging of their efforts at sports (Smith & Smoll, 1990).

In fact, youth who experienced positive social interactions in their school have been shown to undergo marked enhancement in their perceived self-competence, and this influence can occur even among youth who are already quite advanced in their capacities

(Kramer, 1991). Indeed, adolescent self-worth is predicted by social approval, especially from one's classmates (Robinson, 1995). In short, then, there may be features of the context that can have a positive effect on virtually any youth.

Conclusions About Diversity and Context in Adolescent Identity Development

Multiple levels of the context are influential in the promotion of identity development during adolescence. If these contextual influences provide social support for young people, then they should be satisfied with who they are and who they are becoming. Such youths should develop a positive regard for their "self." If so, then, in a sense, they should find themselves "good company." They should enjoy spending time with themselves.

Research supports this possibility. About 500 European American adolescents in Grades 5 through 9 reported on their feelings when alone (Larson, 1997). Time spent alone became more voluntary across this age period, and for the youth in Grades 7 through 9, solitude had a positive effect on emotional state (Larson, 1997). This finding suggests that spending time alone has a useful influence in the development of the person during early adolescence.

Adolescents can typically decide if and when they want to be alone. To some extent they can make decisions about other contextual influences, such as peer groups, sport/athletic activities, and/or joining in on other community contexts (e.g., clubs or organizations). However, certain variables cannot be selected by the adolescent: Variables such as race, ethnicity, and gender are among such potential influences. It is important to understand their role in identity development.

Ethnic Identity in Adolescence

ISSUES TO CONSIDER
- What is ethnic identity? Why is it important to adolescent identity formation?
- What influences on ethnic identity exist?

Ethnic identity involves defining one's self in terms of one's membership in a particular racial group (e.g., African American) or as having a specific ethnic heritage (e.g., Chinese Canadian). A youth's racial or ethnic group membership often plays a central part in the formation of identity (Spencer, 1990, 1991; Spencer & Dornbusch, 1990; Spencer & Markstrom-

Adams, 1990). Ethnic group membership provides a youth with a cultural identity, a sense of belonging and group pride, and a set of prescribed norms, values, and social behaviours. These attributes help give the youth a role to couple with his or her identity (Spencer, 1991). Racial pride acts to support the youth's self-respect, self-concept, and the ethnic or racial component of his or her identity and role. Taylor (2002) stressed the importance of collective identity among various ethnic groups and cultures. He suggests that colonization has negatively affected the collective identity of many ethnic groups such as Aboriginals. Some poignant examples provided by Taylor include the presence of yellow school buses and "storm watchers" in isolated Inuit villages. These were modelled, respectively, after schools in the mainstream culture in which yellow buses transport children to school and meteorologists suggest when schools should be closed due to inclement weather. However, aside from the fact that the Inuit were traditionally nomadic cultures and rarely settled in permanent villages, the presence of these mainstream practices threatens a part of the Inuit's collective identity: the ability to adapt to harsh environments. Being transported to school (instead of walking short distances in the small villages) avoids the need to dress for the weather, as does the cancellation of school due to heavy snowfall. While these may be perceived as minor examples, they illustrate the challenges to collective, ethnic identity. More about Taylor's work can be found in Meet the Researcher Box 6.4.

Data indicate that ethnic identity increases with age. Among about 550 adolescents from three ethnic groups (African Americans, Latinos, and Asian Americans) such an age trend was noted (Phinney, Ferguson, & Tate, 1997). Increases in ethnic identity were associated with positive attitudes among the youth toward their ethnic group (Phinney et al., 1997). Perron et al. (1998) found that ethnic identity increased over time for adolescents in a minority ethnic group but decreased over time for adolescents in the majority ethnic group (those who described themselves and their parents as "Québécois" or "Canadian"). In a study of identity among African American young women ranging in age from 12 to 22 years (Shorter-Gooden & Washington, 1996), several domains of identity were found (race, gender, sexual orientation, relationships, career, religious beliefs, and political beliefs). The domain of racial identity was the most important to these women. In turn, however, among 14- to 18-year-old adolescents from Jamaica (Smith &

Self-Concept or Group Identity?

Donald M. Taylor is a professor of psychology at McGill University. He has published many articles on the quest for identity in the *Canadian Journal of Native Studies* and in the *Canadian Journal of Behavioural Science*, as well as for the American Psychological Association. In 2002, he published *The Quest for Identity: From Minority Groups to Generation Xers.*

Ten years ago, developing a theory centring on the self-concept was the furthest thing from my mind. Ten years ago I would have told you that as a social psychologist interested in the plight of young people from society's most disadvantaged groups, I would reject any concept that had the word "self" in it. The reason? For years I had been committed to overturning psychology's bias of focusing on individual processes to the neglect of group-based processes. I mean if Aboriginals, certain other visible minority groups, and street youth are suffering academic underachievement and social dysfunction, then surely we need to focus on their shared group-based experiences rather than look to individual psychological processes for the key. And so my theory and research concentrated on the impact of prejudice and discrimination on young people from these different groups.

Try as I might, however, there was one individual process that I could not escape. Self-esteem was the theoretical construct that purported to explain every malaise, and surely young people who are victims of group-based discrimination will suffer low self-esteem. Imagine my shock when two prominent social psychologists (Jennifer Crocker and Brenda Major) published a seminal article detailing how members of stigmatized groups have a self-esteem that is at least as high, and sometimes higher, than members of society's advantaged groups.

This insight was indeed challenging. For years, every disadvantaged school I worked in was totally committed to the idea that the key to their students' academic success and psychological well-being was rooted in raising their self-esteem. Indeed so pervasive was the belief in self-esteem that a 1990 California task force that was formed to promote self-esteem concluded that "self-esteem might function as a social vaccine to inoculate individuals against the lures of crime, violence, substance abuse, chronic welfare dependency and educational failure. The lack of self-esteem is central to most personal and social ills plaguing our state and nation."

But now the whole idea that members of stigmatized groups suffered from low self-esteem had been called into question. I was intellectually liberated. I wanted nothing to do with individual processes like the "self," and now the one "self" process I couldn't avoid had been called into question. I was now free to pursue my theoretical bias, the search for group processes that might explain the difficulty that young disadvantaged group members were having.

But research is more than concocting rigorous experimental designs and testing formal hypotheses; it requires commerce with young people. So whether it was a First Nations reserve, a remote Inuit community, an inner-city school, or an all-night van cruising the inner city to feed homeless youth, I spent a lot of formal teaching time and down time with young people. And the more time I spent, the more the topic of identity became central. They worried about their own identity and even more about their group identity. What it means to be Mohawk, or Inuit, or black, or a "street kid," consumed them, and these were their issues that required no prompting from me.

Was I being sucked back to individual processes in general and the "self" in particular? Identity is very much a self theme, but our conversations revolved around group identity. For Aboriginal people it was about restructuring their heritage culture. For blacks it was about having their own unique style of speech and their own dress code. Even "street kids" embraced that label and their dress style, tattoos, and body piercing were worn proudly. Maybe because it was *group* identity and not individual identity, I became convinced that I was being educated by these young people about a very fundamental process.

In workshops and courses I began asking, "What does it mean to be _____ (Mohawk, Inuit, black, a street kid)?" The answers were never satisfying. For example, I would ask, "Would you still be Inuit if you had short curly hair, or couldn't speak your heritage language fluently, or didn't hunt on the land, or moved to a big city?" The answer was invariably YES. So what is the essence of Inuit group identity?

Formal and informal interaction with disadvantaged young people compelled me to conclude that the self and identity were the essence of effective human functioning and that group identity had a special status. Specifically, I came to believe that the self-concept arises out of the uniquely human capacity for self-reflection and it is the most important cognitive process that allows for effective interaction with the social environment and thereby well-being. I had to conclude that the self-concept is experienced as something very personal. But I was convinced that in order to develop a healthy personal identity, an individual needed a clearly defined group identity against which to understand her- or himself personally. How do I know if I am tall if I have no concept of my group's average height?

And that's when it hit me. Groups of young people who are struggling are those that have had their group identity destroyed. Colonization destroyed Aboriginal group identity and slavery robbed the black community of its heritage group identity. Without a clearly defined cultural group identity, individual group members have no anchor point for developing a clear personal identity. What could be worse than a personal identity vacuum? I believe this to be the malaise we have imposed on minority young people, and I believe we are seeing signs of the same malaise among more advantaged young people.

Having proposed the theory, the challenge is to test it. That is what I and my dedicated students are pursuing now both in the laboratory and the community. I only hope we can capture the voice of those threatened with losing their group identity.

Part of identity development involves understanding where one fits into one's society or culture.

Muenchen, 1995), gender and age were the major bases of differences in definitions of self in regard to domains such as morals, social relationships, sexual attitudes, mastery of the external world, vocational and educational goals, and emotional health.

It may be that the ethnic composition of the community within which youth live accounts for some of the above-noted differences across studies in the importance of ethnicity in the identities of youth. Research indicates that ethnic identity is influenced by community and family context. For an ethnic minority group in Norway, the Sami, having both parents of Sami background was associated with a Sami ethnic identity only among youth whose families lived in the highland areas of northern Norway (Kvernmo & Heyerdahl, 1996). When youth with two Sami parents lived in coastal communities, settings characterized by great assimilation and integration, they identified themselves as either bicultural or as Norwegian. Youth with only one Sami parent identified themselves strongly as Norwegian when living on the coast and as bicultural when living in the highlands (Kvernmo & Heyerdahl, 1996). Similarly, a comparison of adolescents who had been born in China but moved to Canada after age six with Chinese adolescents who had been born in Canada found that the Canadian-born youth were more likely to describe themselves as Chinese Canadian (rather than "Chinese"), and were less likely to mention their ethnicity in assessments of their identity. China-born adolescents had high self-esteem when they valued aspects of collective self-esteem. This was not found for the Canadian-born adolescents (Lay & Verkuyten, 1999).

The neighbourhood context also contributes to ethnic identity. For example, in the Toronto area,

Jewish adolescents who lived in neighbourhoods in which Jewish people were the largest ethnic group showed higher ethnic identity and a lower likelihood of ideological identity diffusion than Jewish adolescents who lived in neighbourhoods in which Jewish people were among the smallest ethnic groups (Markstrom, Berman, & Brusch, 1998).

Mexican American and African American adolescents showed three types of ethnic identity patterns in regard to their two reference groups, their ethnic one and their American one. These identity patterns were blended bicultural, alternating bicultural, and separated (Phinney & Devich-Navarro, 1997). In a study of about 100 Native American male and female students from Grades 9 and 12, youth in a high school with a predominantly Native American student body demonstrated more ethnic identity exploration and commitment than did Native American youth in a high school with a predominantly European American student body (Lysne & Levy, 1997).

As with other aspects of identity, there are contextual influences on ethnic identity, and the family is one key context. The self-esteem of African American adolescents is associated with positive relationships with their parents and with the perceptions that their families approved of them and of what they were doing (Luster & McAdoo, 1995). In regard to such family influences, African American parents discuss prejudice with their adolescents more often than do Japanese American or Mexican American parents (Phinney & Chavira, 1995). However, Japanese American and African American parents emphasize adaptation to society more than Mexican American parents (Phinney & Chavira, 1995). Among about 200 Korean American youth living in California, about three-quarters expressed a concern about their parents' limited English proficiency (Park, 1995). Although most of these youth were well adjusted to their parents' way of life and to the social patterns they encountered in their schools, more than half of them were concerned about their schoolwork and about a third were worried about their facility with the English language (Park, 1995).

The school context can also affect an adolescent's ethnic identity. First- and second-generation Muslim students who had been living in Canada for at least 10 years found that Muslim Student Associations in high schools helped students to develop social networks (Zane, 2001). Because these students or their parents came from a variety of countries (South Asian, Caribbean, Arab, and Somali), their identity development involved coordinating influences from their religion, their ethnicity, and the majority culture. Positive peer support was related to their ability to maintain their Islamic identity. In Zane's investigation, many students also reported a lack of understanding from other students and their teachers about Islam. For example, some teachers asked whether a female Muslim student had a head injury or was bald when they first saw her hijab (head scarf). Other students reported being placed in low academic streams despite getting high marks and others were placed in English as a Second Language (ESL) classes, despite being born in Canada and having English as their only language. These experiences contributed to low self-esteem and well-being of these minority students.

Gender Differences

ISSUE TO CONSIDER

• What gender differences exist in identity development?

Identity may develop in different ways for boys and girls. Several studies confirm this possibility. In a four-year longitudinal study, which started with youth at the beginning of Grade 9, of about 170 youth, girls had lower self-esteem than boys (Chubb, Fertman, & Ross, 1997). In a representative sample of 12-, 13-, and 14-year-old male and female adolescents from Lausanne, Switzerland (Bolognni et al., 1996), girls were found to have poorer self-esteem than boys across all domains of self-definition (e.g., in regard to appearance, scholastics, and athletic performance). These differences, and self-esteem in general, showed no major changes across the age range (Bolognni et al., 1996). Note, however, that as time goes on the situation may change. For example, Bosacki, Innerd, and Towson (1997) found no gender differences in self-esteem among the 11- and 12-year-olds they studied in Ontario.

In a longitudinal study of Finnish males and females between 11 and 15 years of age (Lintunen et al., 1995), self-perceptions became increasingly fixed across the four-year span, particularly for boys. Among girls, but not boys, there was a decrease in their perceptions of self-attractiveness with age (Lintunen et al., 1995). In a study of about 270 Turkish youth ranging in age from 14 to 17 years, symbolic items (e.g., relationships, happiness) and artistic and creative endeavours were more important

in the identities of girls than boys, whereas material items (TV, sports equipment) and athletic activities were more salient to boys (Yildirim, 1997).

Of course, not all boys and girls embrace the general pattern of malelike or femalelike identity. Rather, there seem to be differences in adjustment associated with variation in gender identity. For instance, in a longitudinal study of about 160 adolescents, studied first between the ages of 13 and 18 years and then assessed again about six years later, males who showed coping behaviours associated with feminine gender roles showed poor adaptation in adulthood (Feldman et al., 1995). For females, coping behaviours associated with feminine gender roles was associated with good adaptation in adulthood (Feldman et al., 1995).

Conclusions About the Role of the Context: Promoting Positive Selves to Further Civil Society

People—parents, peers, and teachers, for instance—and institutions—for example, schools or the media—can influence the development of the self during adolescence. Such influences can promote either positive or negative changes among youth. Given the importance for society of having adolescents incorporate commitments to useful roles in society in their self-definitions, numerous programs around the world are aimed at promoting positive identity among youth. As shown in Applications Box 6.1, these programs seek to instill in youth identities that involve a commitment to the institutions and organizations of civil society (see Chapter 5).

As illustrated by the programs described in Applications Box 6.1, the range of possible contextual influences on positive identity development among youth provides a reason for optimism about finding combinations of people and settings that can improve human development. At the same time, the combinations of individuals and contexts that will detract from healthy development must be identified and eliminated or prevented. As demonstrated by the thought and richness of the youth programs discussed in the applications box, the combined challenge of "promotion" and "prevention" is being addressed around the globe. The potential for civil society can only be enhanced by these efforts.

To the extent that such initiatives are successful, youth will find roles in a society that enable them to contribute to their societies with enthusiasm and skill. In such a society youth will find identities that seamlessly blend what they do with what they believe. Their roles will work for them and for their society. Conversely, their work will involve a role that is useful to them and to their social world. In Chapter 7 we consider the nature of the relationship in adolescence between role development and work.

Promoting Self-Development, Promoting Civil Society

To maintain and perpetuate its institutions, society needs youth to develop in manners that reflect a commitment to civil society. For society to continue to function well in the present and the future it needs citizens committed to playing roles that society values. Across the world, communities and governments create programs aimed at promoting such identities among youth.

The programs described here represent a range of exemplary programs.

Boys' Society of Sierra Leone, Freetown, Sierra Leone

In the 1960s, increased urbanization and deteriorating economic conditions in Freetown, Sierra Leone, resulted in more and more young people living and working on the streets. Seeking to reduce the number of marginalized youth, an American professor convened a prominent group of area leaders to identify a solution. The result of their efforts is the Boys' Society of Sierra Leone, a multifaceted program providing youth from low-income families with vocational training, community service activities, and assistance with schoolwork.

The Boys' Society concentrates its efforts on boys (72%) and more recently girls (28%) between the ages of 8 and 18. Its offices and skills training program are housed in a downtown facility. The society also operates a working farm on 25 hectares outside the city, where young people help to raise pigs and grow rice and vegetables. The goal of the farm is to generate financial resources while providing youth with training in animal husbandry and small-scale production. A production and training centre located in a former auto service station provides youth with hands-on training in mechanics, metal work, spray painting, body work, and electronics.

The society reaches young people throughout Freetown through the establishment of clubs or "zones." Today, more than 400 disadvantaged youth participate in club activities ranging from community betterment projects to vocational training. The zones function like surrogate extended families, generating a sense of camaraderie, peer support, identity, and belonging.

In preparing youth to enter the work force, the society operates a Job Placement Program in which young people serve as apprentices to small businesses throughout Freetown. Of the 90% of young people who enroll and complete the program, 50% find jobs and 50% start their own businesses. Through this and other activities, the society fosters a feeling of "belonging" among youth who have grown alienated from their family and community.

With 44% of the population of Sierra Leone currently under the age of 15, the society's role is as vital today as ever.

Duke of Edinburgh's International Award Program, London, England

This program originated in a secondary school in Scotland, the brainchild of a headmaster with a belief in the importance of physical fitness in promoting confidence and the holistic development of young people. Officially launched in 1956, the Duke of Edinburgh's International Award Program encourages personal growth and discovery, self-reliance, responsibility, and community service among young people.

The Award Program is implemented by government agencies, nonprofit institutions, public and private schools, and independent groups of adult volunteers within individual countries. The program is based on individual development, not competition. To earn an award, young people, ages 14 to 25, work with adult volunteers to build a personal development program that includes four distinct activities: service, expeditions, skills, and physical recreation. Medals are awarded to those who successfully complete all four sections over a set period of time— 6 months designates a bronze medal, 12 months a silver, and 18 months a gold. The criteria for granting an award are individual effort and self-improvement.

Service activities can include helping an individual in need, learning first aid, conservation work, fund-raising for charity, or other activities that meet community needs. The expeditions section encourages a spirit of adventure and self-discovery. Participants plan, train for, and undertake a venture with a clearly defined purpose—whether on foot, cycle, horseback, or on water. The skills component is designed to develop personal interests and practical skills in fields such as agriculture, computer science, music, and arts and crafts. And finally, the physical recreation section encourages participation in athletic endeavours. Participants may choose from activities such as team sports, martial arts, swimming, yoga, and dance.

The Award Program has been successfully adapted to more than 100 countries, both developing and industrialized. Although the basic structure of the program remains the same, activities differ from country to country. In the past, local projects have included AIDS awareness programs in Uganda, fruit production and forestry in the Gambia, environmental protection in Sri Lanka, and Dragon Boat Teams in Hong Kong. In 1990–1991, there were 130 152 young people participating around the world, half girls and half boys.

>

Adolescent Development Program (Servol), Port-of-Spain, Trinidad

This program started in 1970 as a result of a widespread government protest against the desperate economic conditions of the poor in Trinidad. The uprising failed, but its message left a strong impression on Father Gerard Pantin. Father Pantin, a Roman Catholic priest, left his job as a schoolteacher and started talking to people about their problems and hopes for the future.

Rather than wait for change, Father Pantin soon realized that individuals and communities must take it upon themselves to create change. In bringing this theory to life, he founded "Service Volunteered for All," soon known as Servol. In the more than 30 years since it began, Servol has grown into an internationally recognized organization, providing training for youth educators throughout the Caribbean and Central America, and even as far as South Africa, while working to empower citizens and communities in Trinidad and Tobago to help themselves.

In fostering positive attitudes among community members, Servol focuses much of its attention on the youngest members of society. To date, it has helped establish more than 184 preschools throughout Trinidad and Tobago. Teachers within the schools take part in an intensive preschool training program in which they are taught how to better interact with students and their parents. The schools are designed to encourage healthy youth development right from the start.

In addition, thousands of young people have benefited from participation in Servol's Adolescent Development Program (ADP). The program works to foster a positive self-image among teenagers. Classes include instruction on nutrition, health and sex education, sports and drama, drug prevention, craftmaking, self-awareness, spirituality, and community service. They focus on spiritual, emotional, creative, intellectual, physical, and social development (SPICES). Parenting classes are also offered as a means of preparing young people to be better parents themselves.

In partnership with the national government, Servol has helped build more than 30 "Life Centres," providing young people with valuable skills training in such areas as welding, plumbing, woodwork, pottery, painting, and child care. Through training, young people develop marketable skills they can use to get jobs, or in some cases, to start their own small businesses. More importantly, however, they grow to have faith in themselves and their abilities.

Since 1994, Servol, with a grant from the InterAmerican Development Bank, has set up three technology centres providing training in computer literacy, electronics, computer repairs, and computer-controlled electronics for its trainees. These courses are being complemented by an enhancement course preparing them for the world of work.

Since 1981, Servol has trained more than 450 early childhood educators, 33 field officers, and 125 adolescent instructors throughout Trinidad and Tobago. Its approach has been replicated in a number of countries throughout the region and in Ireland and South Africa.

Mobility International

An estimated 1 out of 10 people in the world have a disability of one form or another. Mobility International USA (MIUSA) was founded in 1981 to expand opportunities for people with disabilities in international exchange, leadership, community service, and disability rights training.

Since it was started, MIUSA has helped young people from the U.S. and 80 other countries to develop leadership and organizational skills, gain a crosscultural perspective, and experiment with independent living in foreign settings. As its name denotes, Mobility International USA works to eliminate the barriers that have traditionally prevented people with disabilities from participating in exchange programs and other crosscultural learning experiences.

MIUSA's international exchange programs for youth last from two to four weeks and are held during the summer in the United States and abroad. Activities include living with homestay families, leadership seminars, disability rights workshops, crosscultural learning, and team building activities such as river rafting and challenge courses. Participants develop strategies for making changes both within themselves and in their communities. MIUSA is able to offer Youth Leadership programs as funding is available.

MIUSA has received positive responses from participants, many of whom note that they were challenged in a positive way and were empowered to effect changes in their own lives and communities. Participation in the program has enabled many to overcome feelings of isolation and helplessness as they discover through sharing and their own actions what they are capable of. For some participants, the catalyst for empowerment is the simple act of using public transportation or boarding a jet for the first time. Others acquire confidence by learning to communicate in another culture. Still others grow by working together with other disabled youth to build a ramp, organize a public rally, or talk with local politicians about the rights of young people with disabilities.

MIUSA assists other organizations throughout the world to include youth with disabilities in all their existing and future programs. This is done through the National Clearinghouse on Disability and Exchange (NCDE) with its free information and referral services. NCDE is managed by MIUSA and sponsored by the Bureau of Educational and Cultural Affairs of the United States Department of State.

CelebrateYouth!, Albuquerque, New Mexico

The state of New Mexico has been found to have some of the highest rates of school drop-outs, poverty, unemployment, and youth substance abuse in the United States. The percentage of youth suffering the devastating effects of such problems is particularly high in minority areas. A 1991 study by the Center for the Study of Social Policy found New Mexico to be one of the worst places to raise a child in the United States, particularly with respect to its commitment of resources to children.

Added to this are the pervasive problems of alienation from learning and from self, racism and sexism, lack of integration between ages and between parents and children, between individuals and communities, and among various groups. Such problems create confusion

>

and despair among children and youth of all classes and backgrounds.

To nurture the talents of the state's at-risk youth in particular, CelebrateYouth! was established in 1988. Although originally created as a drug prevention program, its focus shifted within a year to education and youth development. As such, its philosophy is based on promoting young people's strengths rather than overcoming their problems.

The focus of the program is on the pursuit of knowledge to foster personal and social development; the creation of new ways for young people to relate while recognizing their differences; and, most importantly, on building a human culture that places human development so high on its list of priorities that in any given exchange each person's dignity, integrity, and ethics come first in importance.

Through the program, young people, ages 9 to 18, work for a year with volunteer mentors on projects in dance, literature, theatre, music, visual arts, history, chess, psychology, and other areas of interest. Each summer, their work is showcased during a three-day festival attended by more than 1000 people.

In 1992, more than 450 young people, 200 mentors, and 150 other volunteers participated in the program. CelebrateYouth! reflects the region's rich ethnic diversity, including young people from the state's varied cultural and economic groups. More than 50% of program participants are from minority groups.

Outside studies of CelebrateYouth! have found the program to be successful in building self-esteem and promoting self-directed learning and meaningful sharing among diverse groups of young people, parents, and volunteers.

Source: International Youth Foundation, 2001. www.iyfnet.org

Summary

- Identity is the set of thoughts, feelings, values, attitudes, and behaviours that defines a person's self.
- Adolescents need an identity so they can coordinate their biological and psychological characteristics with a set of activities deemed useful by society.
- A commitment to a role is an outward expression of an adolescent's identity.
- If an adolescent cannot find a role that resolves the emotional upheaval which results from the strong societal and personal mandates for role adoption, an identity crisis may result.
- If the identity crisis is not resolved by the time adolescents enter adulthood, they will feel a sense of role confusion or identity diffusion.
- Some young adults waver between roles in a prolonged "moratorium" period, some "foreclose" on a socially approved, easily available identity and avoid the crisis, and others adopt an available but socially disapproved role or ideology or go through "negative identity formation."
- Identity develops through a process of person-context interactions in which adolescents evaluate and integrate reactions to the explorations of their world.
- Erikson sees the changes of puberty as presenting the adolescent with serious problems and bringing about the crisis between identity and role confusion. To resolve the crisis, it is necessary in Erikson's view to attain a complex synthesis between psychological processes and societal goals and directives.
- To resolve the identity crisis, the adolescent must be committed to a role and the accompanying ideology.
- Self-esteem grows out of the successful resolution of crises and is a confirmation that one is learning effective steps toward the future and developing a defined personality.
- Self-regulation allows the individual to select goals to pursue, to find means to attain those goals (optimization), and to cope with failures to reach goals (compensation).
- Erikson's theory predicted an invariant identity achievement in late adolescence, but research has shown that there continues to be important changes in ego identity throughout adolescence.
- Other data show that although Erikson would predict stable identity achievement by early adulthood, university or college students do not invariably show stable identity achievement.
- The major instances of diversity in adolescent self-conception occur in regard to differences in developmental pathways and gender differences.
- Baumeister found two types of identity crises: identity deficit, when a person cannot resolve

the crisis because of an inability to make decisions, and identity conflict, when the person makes incompatible decisions when trying to resolve the identity crisis.
- Crises involving identity conflict are a more important part of ego development for girls than for boys.
- Marcia believed that the resolution of the identity crisis involves more than just identity versus role confusion, and that a more diverse pattern exists of adolescent's identity status.
- The four statuses Marcia identified are identity achievement, having a crisis period but then showing a commitment to a role or ideology; identity diffusion, having or not having a crisis,

but lacking commitment and not being concerned about it; moratorium, having a vague commitment but being in active search; and foreclosure, never experiencing a crisis, yet being highly committed.
- If contextual influences provide social support for young people, they should be satisfied with who they are or who they are becoming.
- Ethnic identity involves defining one's self in terms of one's membership in a particular racial group or as having a specific ethnic identity.
- Research indicates that identity may develop in different ways for boys and girls, and differences in adjustment are associated with variation in gender identity.

Discussion Topics

1. As a young adolescent do you remember how you felt emotionally as you began to experience changes in your body? Did you welcome those changes? How were your bodily changes regarded and responded to by those of your social world? Do you feel their reactions and involvement impacted your identity development? If so, how, and if not, why not?
2. Many adolescents experience an identity crisis as they attempt to answer the defining question, "Who am I?" Why are adolescents so self-reflective? What are the primary factors in an adolescent's life that may cause him or her to feel helpless in the face of this question?
3. How did you define your identity as a young adolescent? How would you define your identity today? How and why are these two definitions similar and different? How have the ecological contexts of your life influenced these definitions?
4. How did the adults in your world, such as parents and school guidance counsellors, impress on you the importance of selecting a role as an adolescent? Do you believe your social contexts were supportive of your quest to select a role or more harmful in the pressure they applied?
5. As adolescents, many of us are known to say, "When I grow up, I will be completely different from my parents." Now that you are a bit removed from the heart of the adolescent years, do you feel their involvement in your life was effective, appropriate, and supportive? What

would you have done differently as a parent of an adolescent who was trying to select a role?
6. Do you feel the commitment you made to a role(s) as an adolescent enabled you to feel more at ease, stable, structured, and focused? Why or why not?
7. What ideology defined the role you chose as an adolescent? Are those attitudes, beliefs, and values still important to you today? Why do you believe they were important to you during your adolescent years? Do you feel they may change again if and when you decide to become a parent? Why is there often not complete fidelity to role ideologies throughout the life span?
8. Do you remember feeling as if your self-esteem increased throughout your high school years? If so, what factors influenced this change? Did your transition to university or college challenge your self-esteem? What have been some of the primary forces of your life that impact the self-esteem you have today?
9. What memories do you have of junior high and high school in which you had to assimilate or accommodate to your social contexts? Are you better able to adapt to your environment today? Why is adaptation generally less difficult as an adult?
10. What do you believe are some of the factors that might cause the developmental trajectories of adolescent self-esteem to differ for males and females?

11. What impact on development will the historical context of the years you spent as a child and adolescent have on you and the next generation? For example, do you believe that growing up in a generation when the "working mom" was an expected role will impact the way you parent?

12. Do you believe the way you were raised by your parents was heavily influenced by your gender? If so, in what ways? If not, do you believe they made conscious decisions to raise you in a gender-neutral fashion?

13. In what grades did your schools make the transitions from elementary to junior high and junior high to high school? What do you believe would be the ideal grades for schools to make these divisions and why?

14. How were your ethnic and racial identities supported or not supported in your social contexts as an adolescent? Do you believe the level of support you received influenced your personality development? If so, in what ways? How might schools do a better job of instilling ethnic and racial pride in their students?

Key Terms

colonization, p. 132
developmental task, p. 130
fidelity, p. 134
foreclosure, p. 132
identity, p. 131
identity conflict, p. 140

identity crisis, p. 130
identity deficit, p. 140
identity diffusion, p. 132
ideology, p. 132
moratorium, p. 132
negative identity formation,
     p. 132

role, p. 131
role confusion, p. 132
self-esteem, p. 134
self-regulation, p. 135

7

Role Development and Work in Adolescence

As Jean pulled his car carefully into the open space in front of the field house, he could not help but notice the wide-eyed stares of his teammates.

"Hey, man," François exclaimed with obvious admiration, "where did you get that car?"

"I bought it," Jean said. He carefully removed his helmet, pads, and skates from the backseat. He wanted to be certain that he did not soil the new upholstery.

"Yeah, with what money?" Don asked with evident sarcasm. "Who'd you have to rob?"

"No one," Jean replied. "I earned the money this summer."

"If you worked this summer, what are you doing here at hockey practice?" Don asked. "I thought you had to make up two courses in summer school to be eligible for the team."

"Well, I took the classes and I got Bs in both courses," Jean explained with obvious pride.

François became skeptical. "So you took classes all day, studied all night, and still found time to work enough to get money for this car? I guess that means you haven't slept since June," he said.

"Nope. I slept plenty *and* worked plenty. It's just that I was able to study while I worked," Jean explained.

"What were you, a night watchman or something like that?" François asked.

"Well, sort of . . .," Jean replied.

"So what is it?" François asked. "What did you do to earn the money for the car?"

"Well," Jean explained, "when I knew I had to study every night and that I wouldn't be able to get a day job, I put up a poster in the community room of my apartment building. I advertised myself as a babysitter and said I would be available on any night, including weekends."

"From construction work last summer to babysitting this summer," François laughed. "So much for the rough, tough hockey player."

"Well, François," Jean said with a broad smile, "who is still taking the school bus and who is driving his own car? Maybe you should start thinking about becoming a babysitter yourself."

Learning Objectives

1. To understand the current patterns of work for adolescents.
2. To describe the positive impact work can have on adolescent development.
3. To be aware of the possible negative impact that work can have on an adolescent's life.
4. To understand differences in school performance between working and nonworking students.
5. To learn how gender is related to differences in the experience of a part-time job.
6. To understand gender role stereotypes and how they represent a significant influence on the social context and on youth development.
7. To understand why both flexibility and use of stereotypes exist in regard to work and gender roles.
8. To describe the gender intensification hypothesis and provide research evidence for it.

ISSUES TO CONSIDER

- What are some of the ways in which socially and culturally defined gender roles may direct adolescents' selection of employment?
- How might adolescents' decision to be employed affect their identity development?

The establishment of one's identity involves finding a **role**—a socially prescribed set of behaviours—to play in life (see Chapter 6). In actuality, a person's identity is a synthesis of several different roles. There are **gender roles**, a socially and culturally defined set

Role Socially prescribed set of behaviours.

Gender roles Socially and culturally defined set of behaviours linked to being a male or a female in a given society.

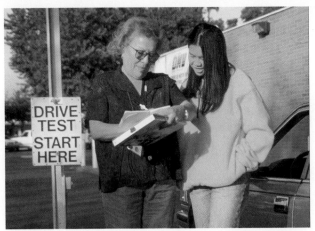

An important role transition in adolescence involves obtaining a driver's licence.

of behaviours linked to being a male or a female in a given society. There are sets of behaviours linked to being a student, to being a student athlete, or to being a student leader (see Chapter 12). Of course, in addition, the type of work one does (e.g., being a sales clerk, a chef, or an auto mechanic) and/or the type of career one enters (e.g., lawyer, physician, engineer, teacher) are associated with specific sets of behaviours. Similarly, and on a more abstract level, roles such as "son," "daughter," or "citizen" also have behavioural expectations associated with them, although perhaps less explicit ones than those linked to being a chef or a mechanic.

As a consequence of their search for identity (see Chapter 6), youth develop roles that have several components (Vondracek, 1994; Vondracek et al., 1995). These components indicate to adolescents and to those with whom they interact what the adolescents will do in their world as workers, as men or women, and as members of the community.

Serious commitments to career are usually reserved for young adulthood (see Chapter 15) when, after high school or college/university, the adolescent chooses a specific occupation to pursue and makes choices regarding intimate relationships, marriage, and family. The selections made and the experiences that occur during the adolescent period shape and prepare young people to meet the challenges they will encounter when they make the transition from adolescence to young adulthood (see Chapter 15). For instance, in integrating their biological, psychological, and social characteristics, adolescents will make decisions about the extent to which they feel comfortable with adult roles that are traditional or nontraditional for their genders. To illustrate, an electrical

engineer or a preschool teacher are roles traditionally associated with males and females, respectively. Yet women may enter into electrical engineering as a career and men may become preschool teachers. However, this is still rare. While the number of women entering engineering and applied sciences increased by 109% from 1986 to 1996, they still only represented 22% of university graduates in these areas (Canadian Council on Social Development, 1998). Women continued to predominate in stereotypical feminine fields of educational, recreational, and counselling services (73% of university graduates) but also were the majority in health professions, sciences, and technologies (72%). Côté (2003) suggests that gender stereotypes about cognitive ability have led advisers to steer women toward fields that require verbal ability (e.g., education, library science) and away from occupations involving math or science. Gender stereotypes often produce beliefs and expectations about what males and females "should" and "should not" be like (Heilman, 2001). Heilman (2001) claims that gender bias in the workplace means that competent women will not receive as high a promotion as equally competent men, especially if the women work in male-dominated fields in which they exhibit traits traditionally considered "masculine." What adolescents decide to do in regard to their role choices will be influenced by their willingness to depart from traditional gender-linked roles (or, in turn, to be flexible in regard to the gender roles).

Several other factors influence how youth approach the world of work. Do they see themselves as involved in roles that require little or no education or training past high school or are they oriented to roles that require considerable postsecondary education? Cognitive abilities, personality, family,

During high school, many adolescents have part-time jobs.

and peers are important influences on role selections. Part-time work during adolescence is increasingly a key influence on the role choices of youth.

In this chapter we discuss the influences of work on adolescent development and role behaviours. The characteristics of gender role development are focused on, as are the nature and implications of traditional and nontraditional gender role selections during adolescence.

Work During Adolescence

ISSUES TO CONSIDER

- How frequent is part-time work during adolescence?
- What are some of the influences affecting whether or not adolescents work?

Many adolescents in Canada and the United States work outside the home during their high school years and continue earning a salary during their postsecondary years. In fact, by the time they have completed high school, the majority of North American adolescents have worked (Barling, Rogers, & Kelloway (1995; Kunz & Schellenberg, 1998; Mortimer, Shanahan, & Ryus, 1994).

Data from 1996 (Kunz & Schellenberg, 1998) revealed that 26% of 15-year-olds in Canada had some paid employment in the year prior to the study. This rose to 78% of 19-year-olds. On average, adolescents worked 14 hours per week (Covell & Howe, 1999). The rate of working is lower among youth born outside of Canada than among Canadian-born youth. According to the Canadian Institute of Child Health (2001), 62% of 15- to 16-year-olds born in Canada never had paid employment. However, 77% of those born outside of Canada never had paid employment. The gap is even wider for older adolescents (aged 17 to 19). While only 25% of Canadian-born older adolescents had never had paid employment, the proportion rises to 51% of immigrant youth.

The employment rate is also higher among adolescents living in middle- and upper-class homes than for those living in lower-income families (Kunz & Schellenberg, 1998). Lower-income youths may have parents with fewer contacts and may find accessing transportation to the job to be more difficult. Similarly, adolescents residing in small communities seem to have an easier time finding jobs than do those in large urban areas (Canadian Council on Social Development, 1998).

Youth employment rates vary across the country. For example, in 1996, 77% of 15- to 16-year-olds in Quebec had never had paid employment as opposed to 49% in the Prairie provinces (Kunz & Schellenberg, 1998). Regional unemployment rates for youth parallel those for adults. These reflect local labour market conditions (Human Resources Development Canada [HRDC], 2000a).

After a peak of about 45% in the early 1990s, employment among 15- to 19-year-old students declined steadily across the country, reaching 35% in 1997 (Jenkins, 1998). Kunz and Schellenberg (1998) attributed this to economic factors. In the late 1980s Canada had a strong economy, the unemployment rate was low, and the number of working youth rose. However, when the economy weakened in the 1990s, so did the proportion of working youth. At the same time, the school dropout rate for Canadians decreased (17.1% in 1990 versus 11.9% in 1999; HRDC, 2000b). The males who dropped out were more likely to have been working more than 20 hours per week than were other males (HRDC, 2000a). The school dropout rate seems to vary based on the employment rate and changes in minimum wage, at least for males. For females, dropping out is more related to having children than to minimum wage. Youth who leave high school early tend to have lower levels of literacy than those who graduate. They also tend to be less literate than dropouts in other countries that belong to the Organization for Economic Co-operation and Development (OECD) (HRDC, 2000a).

Unfortunately, 10% of 15- to 19-year-olds in 1999 were neither in school nor in the labour force (HRDC, 2000a). Not completing high school puts people at risk for unemployment, as a skilled workforce is in demand. Negative correlates of adolescent unemployment include little spending money, more difficulty finding jobs later on due to lack of experience, greater mental health problems, and increased risk of criminal activity (Canadian Council on Social Development, 1998).

The situation is even more difficult for Aboriginal youth as they tend to achieve lower educational levels than other youth and obtain lower quality jobs than others with a similar level of education (HRDC, 2000a). Aboriginal students were three times as likely as other students to drop out of school and half as likely to have completed postsecondary education, according to 1996 census data (HRDC, 2000a). HRDC (2000a) states that Aboriginals who hold university degrees obtain jobs as favourable as those of other graduates. However, a report by the Canadian Race Relations Foundation (2000) reveals that Aboriginal university graduates are four times as likely as Canadian-born nonminority university graduates to be unemployed. Different sample sizes, methods of data collection, and definitions may explain the discrepancy, but more research needs to be conducted in this area. For the Aboriginal population to be as highly employed as the national average, more than 80 000 jobs would need to be found (Watkins, 1997).

Unemployment is related to education level; the less education the higher the unemployment rate (Canadian Policy Research Networks [CPRN], 2000). Due to their limited work experience, youth tend to be among the first people laid off when companies downsize (HRDC, 1996).

Although working during adolescence is not as prevalent in other industrialized nations, such as Japan (Mortimer et al., 1994), considerable numbers of young people in these nations do work during their student years (e.g., Hagström & Gamberale, 1995; McKechnie et al., 1996; van der Velde, Feij, & van Emmerik, 1998). Evidence indicates that working during the adolescent years is linked to valuing work intrinsically (e.g., for its contributions to enhancing one's competence as a person) and not just for its extrinsic value (i.e., for its link to obtaining money). Youth from the Netherlands show increases in the intrinsic value of work across their late adolescent and young adult years (van der Velde et al., 1998) and, among Swedish youth, intrinsic work goals are seen as more important than are the economic benefits of employment (Hagström & Gamberale, 1995).

Employment rates for 15- to 24-year-olds are similar across Canada, the United States, Australia, and New Zealand, ranging from 62% to 66% for females and 65% to 71% among males (Statistics Canada, 1999). Thus, among contemporary youth, employment during the student years is a widespread phenomenon. Moreover, there is some evidence that such activity is regarded by youth as being of primary importance because it helps make them better people—for instance, by giving them experiences and competencies that will enhance their future, adult lives.

Volunteer work also helps prepare adolescents for the future. Not only may volunteering provide young people with skills, contacts, and/or "look good" on a résumé, but when volunteers obtain paid positions they receive 7% higher incomes over those who do not volunteer (Day & Devlin, 1998). Youth aged 15 to 24 provided 15% of all volunteer hours in Canada in 2000 (Pickering, 2003). Twenty-four

percent of volunteers this age believed that volunteering had played a part in landing a job at some point in their lives (Hall, McKeown, & Roberts, 2001). Thirty-seven percent of 15- to 19-year-olds engaged in volunteer work, which is higher than the national average (26%; Pickering, 2003). On average the adolescents devoted 136 hours per person that year, mostly organizing or supervising events and fundraising (Pickering, 2003). The volunteer rate among youth doubled from 1987 to 1997, partly due to an increase in volunteering among full-time students (Dreessen, 2000). Some of this volunteer work has been part of a school project. For example, the province of Ontario now requires that students do 40 hours of volunteer community service in order to graduate from high school (Ontario Ministry of Education, 2000). The importance that volunteering has for civil society (see Chapter 5) has been described by the Government of Canada (1999, as cited in Dresson, 2000, p. 23):

Voluntary activity encompasses economic, social, cultural and environmental perspectives. Many view the sector as not only strengthening, but as embodying civil society. The sector plays an important role in reinforcing social trust, educating the public, providing support for individuals, families and communities in transition, and reinforcing common values and a sense of common purpose that binds communities and gives them the resilience to cope with change.

Before concluding that work during adolescence is of unequivocal benefit to young people, note that some data suggest such benefits may not be certain, or that benefits of work can be outweighed by the negative influences of work on adolescent development. It is therefore important to understand the positive and negative impacts of work on adolescent development and under what conditions work may be beneficial to adolescents.

Positive and Negative Consequences of Adolescent Employment

ISSUES TO CONSIDER
• What characterizes employment opportunities most readily available to youth and why may these opportunities be considered a good challenge for identity development of youth?
• What are some of the positive and negative consequences of work for adolescents' academic and personal development?

- How does the intensity of employment interact with adolescents' intrinsic motivation for school?
- In what way may adolescents' employment influence their relationship with parents?

Covell and Howe (1999) warn that most data on the effects that working has on adolescent development comes from the United States. They suggest that these results be treated with caution when considering Canadian adolescents, as a smaller proportion are working and they tend to work fewer hours. Adolescent employment may have several possible positive implications for youth development. Working may give adolescents a basis for new identities, new expectations of responsibility and independence from parents, and a new high status among peers (Mortimer et al., 1994). Cooperative education (combining work and study) seems to have positive benefits for adolescents. For example, graduates from cooperative education programs in the Maritimes (Newfoundland, New Brunswick, and Nova Scotia) were more likely to be employed, to earn a higher wage, and to have a smaller student loan than students from the same schools who did not engage in cooperative education (Canadian Council on Social Development, 1998). These programs aim to help students learn about teamwork and communication, as well as stimulate reflective and critical thinking by having students report on their work experiences.

Working adolescents may encounter working peers and adults in their jobs, and these people may provide new models of adult behaviour and new reference groups (Mortimer et al., 1994). Of course, these new groups may serve as either good or bad influences on the adolescent.

Indeed, working may not only offer positive benefits to adolescents. In fact, it can often have a negative impact on their lives. For example, working can take time away from school, diminishing the opportunity to participate in extracurricular activities or the time available for homework.

Moreover, the kinds of employment opportunities most readily available to youth are the same work activities that have the most negative consequences for adults. That is, most youth work in the retail and service sectors and are given jobs with high turnover, low pay, little authority, and low prestige (Mortimer et al., 1994). Adults in such jobs are often displaced by such roles because of these work characteristics and because such positions involve simple, repetitive tasks (e.g., "flipping burgers") that require very little

or no special training or skills (e.g., "Here is the hamburger. Flip it over when it is brown. Don't touch the hot stove").

It may be the case that such jobs are invariably boring and undesirable to most adults, who, if they find themselves in such roles, will feel that their future prospects are dim. Nevertheless, it is possible that even such tasks may be new and challenging activities to a young person. Someone who has never worked outside the home, and never been asked to be productive for pay, may be more excited by the opportunity to be involved in the world of work than displeased by the particular activities he or she finds available in this setting (Mortimer et al., 1994). The amount of autonomy and role clarity of the job can make a difference in the adolescent's response to part-time work (Barling et al., 1995).

Thus there is a range of possible positive and negative influences of work on adolescent development. It may be that the issue is not one of deciding whether work is or is not beneficial. Rather, it may be a matter of learning under what circumstances work may have either a positive or a negative effect. Several major research projects have been conducted that are pertinent to the role of work in adolescent development.

Kuntz and Schellenberg (1998) reported on the behaviours of Canadian 15- to 19-year-old workers. They found that the school performance of these students was not affected, as long as they worked less than 20 hours per week. Similarly, they were not more likely to drop out of school than nonworking students.

In a major research project, Greenberger and Steinberg (1986) studied youth employment among students in four California high schools. The students reported that their employment was associated with their being punctual, dependable, and personally responsible. Among girls, employment was also linked to reports of self-reliance (Greenberger, 1984). But employed adolescents were more frequently late for school, showed poorer school performance, engaged in more substance use, had fewer contacts with their family, and had more cynical attitudes toward work than was the case with nonemployed youth (Greenberger & Steinberg, 1986).

Another study of the implications of work for youth development involved a longitudinal assessment of approximately 1000 American adolescents in Grades 9 and 10 conducted by Mortimer, Shanahan, and their colleagues (e.g., Mortimer et al., 1994, 1996). Less than 20% of the adolescents indicated that their jobs provided them with knowledge about topics studied in school or reported that their work experiences gave them information they could contribute to class discussions. Correspondingly, a survey by Krahn, Lowe, and Lehmann (2002) of more than 2000 Grade 12 students in Alberta found that adolescents felt that school didn't relate well to their needs on the job. They indicated that part-time paid work better prepared them for the job market upon graduation than did school in that they developed people skills, business skills, and work attitudes and behaviours from their employment. Work experience programs also taught them people skills, job preparation, and business skills. Even their volunteer work helped them learn more people skills, business skills, work attitudes and behaviour, and citizenship skills than they acquired from their formal education.

Consistent with the earlier findings of Greenberger and Steinberg (1986), as well as those of other researchers (e.g., Kuntz & Schellenberg, 1998; McKechnie et al., 1996; Mihalic & Elliott, 1997), Mortimer et al. (1994) found that working had some negative implications for the academic and personal development of youth. For instance, 43% of the adolescents reported that working decreased the time they had available for their homework, and about 50% of the students reported that being a worker and a student simultaneously was stressful. Many students in the study also reported positive characteristics associated with working while being a high school student. For example, about 48% of the students indicated that their job taught them the importance of obtaining a good education, and approximately 33% of the students reported that working helped them identify the courses in high school they liked or did not like. By Grade 10, 42% of the boys and 52% of the girls in this study were employed (Mortimer et al., 1994). Consistent with what was found when the students were in Grade 9, no overall difference existed in Grade 10 between working and nonworking students in time spent on schoolwork, in the time devoted to extracurricular activities, or in their grades (Mortimer et al., 1994). Overall work status was not related to the incidence of school behaviour problems (Mortimer et al., 1994). Working at a low intensity (i.e., few hours per week) was linked to lower dropout rates (Mortimer et al., 1994).

Furthermore, no difference was found between working and nonworking students in their *intrinsic* motivation for school, that is, in the degree to which they wanted to do well in school because of internal

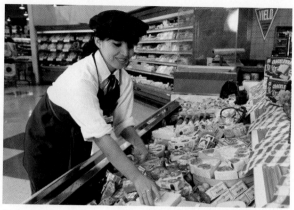
By Grade 10, a majority of adolescent girls work in part-time jobs.

standards of excellence and personal values for achievement—as compared to wanting to achieve in school because such attainment is associated with rewards from parents, teachers, or society. Furthermore, the number of hours per week a student worked was also not systematically related to such motivation (Mortimer et al., 1994). For instance, the highest intrinsic motivation for school existed among students who worked relatively few hours a week (i.e., 1 to 5 hours) and among youth who worked in excess of 25 hours a week.

Accordingly, as compared to the conclusions associated with the research of Greenberger and Steinberg (1986), the findings reported by Mortimer et al. (1994) suggest no link between student employment—even when it exists at a high number of hours a week—and risk of poor school attitudes, diminished time devoted to homework, lessened involvement in extracurricular activities, or low school grades. Instead, for the youth in the Mortimer et al. (1994) study, evidence indicates that young people could "do it all," or—at least—could maintain their involvement and achievement in school and participate in the work force. Indeed, although the amount of work stress did have a negative impact on the schoolwork of these youth, the quality of the work environment (e.g., the menial nature of the roles youth were assigned at work) was not associated with their grades or their participation in extracurricular activities.

Similarly, working did not seem to have an effect on the levels of physical activity of the 15- to 19-year-old working Canadians studied by Kuntz and Schellenberg (1998). In fact, more female working students than nonworking students reported exercising at least three times a week (70% versus 54%). The authors suggested that working adolescents may have a larger social circle than those who don't work, so they may have had more opportunities to engage in sports. Another possible explanation was that adolescents who both work and go to school have learned time management skills and thus are able to fit exercise into their routine. Their final suggestion was that the employment experience helped develop a sense of responsibility in these individuals, which included the responsibility of taking care of themselves. (However, it is possible that a sense of responsibility encouraged adolescents to take on employment in the first place.)

Having a sense of responsibility could not explain Kuntz and Schellenberg's (1998) findings that working adolescents use alcohol and smoke more than do nonworkers (50% of workers drink alcohol at least once a month versus 25% of nonworkers; 28% of workers smoke versus 22% of nonworkers). In addition, working students are more likely to have engaged in binge drinking (having five or more drinks in a row) in the previous year. More than 62% of working students reported binge drinking, while 44% of nonworking students had this experience. Mortimer et al. (1996) also found that students in their American sample who worked at high intensity engaged in more alcohol use. Kuntz and Schellenberg (1998) suggested that, in part, this may be because working students have more access to alcohol at work.

In addition to not negatively influencing activities in extracurricular contexts, work can have a beneficial influence on behaviour in particular settings. For instance, in a longitudinal study of youth from rural Iowa between Grades 7 and 10 (Shanahan et al., 1996), earnings from paid labour spent on nonleisure activities was associated with more positive parent-adolescent relationships, with more time spent with the family, and with less parental monitoring of the youth. For girls, opportunities for skill development at work increased their intrinsic motivation for schoolwork (Mortimer et al., 1994). In a study of helpfulness at home and at work, both boys and girls adapted their helpfulness at home in response to family need. In addition, for girls, helpfulness at work increased their overall behavioural competence, and their increasing behavioural competence furthered the girls' tendencies to be helpful at work (Call, Mortimer, & Shanahan, 1995).

Work therefore has several beneficial effects for youth development in regard to personal abilities, school performance, and family relations. Some of these influences, including those pertinent to development into adulthood, are discussed by Jeylan Mortimer in Meet the Researcher Box 7.1.

There are important gender differences in the effects of work experiences on youth and, more generally, on the character of role development in adolescence. We discuss the dimensions and bases of these gender differences next.

Gender Differences in Work and Role Development

ISSUE TO CONSIDER
- How might gender affect the experience of adolescent employment?

For most adolescents in North America, entry into the workplace begins in middle or late adolescence and usually involves experience with a part-time job (Camarena, Stemmler, & Petersen, 1994). However, there are usually gender differences in this experience (Camarena et al., 1994). For instance, boys are more likely to work for an employer and girls are more likely to do odd jobs for different people (Canadian Council on Social Development, 2002). Volunteer work may be more likely among girls, according to the Nova Scotia School to Work Transition project (Thiessen & Nickerson, 1999).

Although both boys and girls are typically given jobs that involve little skill, training, or initiative, the precise assignments they are given often vary along gender-stereotypical lines (Camarena et al., 1994). For example, although boys and girls might both get a job in a department store, boys may be more likely to be assigned to duties in the stock room or mailroom and girls may be more apt to be assigned duties as sales clerks. For 15- to 16-year-old Canadians, 41% of boys worked in services and sales in 1997 (Kuntz & Schellenberg, 1998), compared to 55% of girls of that age. In contrast, 45% of boys versus 15% of girls worked in blue-collar jobs (e.g., manufacturing, manual labour). The same gender division can be found among 17- to 19-year-olds. For boys, 49% of workers had jobs in sales, service, or clerical areas and 44% were in blue-collar jobs. Among the working females, 73% had jobs in services, sales, and clerical areas while only 11% were blue-collar workers.

The gender stereotypes reflected in such job assignments may signify society-wide beliefs that males and females are fundamentally different in their capacities, behaviours, and interests. Gender-stereotypical job assignments do not seem to change during adulthood. Theissen and Nickerson (1999)

MEET THE RESEARCHER | Box 7.1 | Jeylan Mortimer

Youth Work Experience and the Transition to Adulthood

Jeylan Mortimer is professor of sociology, director of the Life Course Center, and principal investigator of the Youth Development Study at the University of Minnesota.

Combining the roles of paid worker and student is very common in North America. However, adolescent employment is a neglected context in the study of development. Some believe that extensive early work is detrimental because it imposes stressors and responsibilities for which the teenager is not yet ready. This "developmental readiness" or "stress sensitizing" hypothesis may be contrasted with a more sanguine "steeling" or "stress resilience" model. According to the second point of view, early work experience fosters coping skills that allow more effective response to subsequent stressors and better performance of adult roles. It has also been suggested that adolescents who have more work experience "grow up faster," acquiring adultlike identities and leisure time pursuits at an earlier age than those who invest less time in work while in high school, and make a more rapid transition to adulthood. Such "growing up" may take both negative—for example, alcohol use and smoking—and positive forms. Positive effects of employment on early adult development can be anticipated as a result of experiences in the work setting that develop both human and social capital.

To address these questions, I initiated the Youth Development Study with my colleague Dr. Michael Finch in 1987. Because a large project like this requires the involvement of many people, we are joined by many other researchers, including Kathleen Call, Monica Johnson, Sabrina Oesterle, Michael Shanahan, and Christopher Uggen. We have followed 1000 Grade 9 students through high school and into their late 20s (with support from the National Institute of Mental Health). This is the only longitudinal study in the United States focused on part-time labour force participation (and other forms of work) during high school. With this data set, we can examine the effects of working on adjustment during high school, as well as the establishment of adult work and family roles.

We find that the quality of work experience, especially the rewards, opportunities, and stressors encountered in the work sphere, has important consequences for youth mental health (e.g., depressive affect, sense of mastery, or control orientation) and behavioural adjustment, as indicated by school problem behaviour and substance use. Positive work experiences and supervisory relations buffer the effects of problems in the family, lessening depressive affect, declines in school achievement, and other negative responses to familial distress. Working during adolescence is also formative with respect to vocational development.

The "growing up faster" model is only partially confirmed. Youth's early involvement in the labour force is a precursor to earlier initiation of alcohol use, but not more use in the long term. Early investment in the labour force, as measured by hours of work, also precedes more rapid transition to full-time employment and higher earnings in the years following high school. However, attachment to work during high school appears to be associated with normative (not premature) timing of transition to family roles.

"Balanced early employment," work that is stable but limited to less than 20 hours per week, has advantages in terms of postsecondary educational achievement, especially for youth who, when they initially entered high school, indicated little educational promise (e.g., they had little interest in school, poorer grades, and relatively low educational aspirations). In contrast, youth who worked more than 20 hours per week obtained fewer months of postsecondary education and were less likely to receive BA degrees. Our future research will address the mechanisms through which early work produces such advantage and disadvantage, and longer term consequences that only become manifest after education is complete and occupational careers are established.

reported that of the top 10 jobs held by women, only 1 (retail salesperson) overlapped with the top 10 jobs held by men. The women's jobs held less variability and involved lower skills. Men aged 15 to 24 earned higher wages than women the same age (Canadian Council on Social Development, 2002). In addition, as will be discussed later, women are underrepresented in many fields, or are underrepresented at the highest levels.

To understand gender differences in work and role development we must understand the nature of gender role stereotypes and how they may represent a significant influence on the social context of youth development.

Gender Role Stereotypes

ISSUES TO CONSIDER

- In what way might societal gender-bound beliefs regarding a person's capacities, behaviours, and interest be reflected in a person's job assignment?
- How do stereotypical gender role attributes differ for males and females?
- How might an adolescent's flexible personal orientation toward work defy a stereotyped view of gender roles?

Across history and in contemporary society, men and women do not engage with equal frequency in the various social roles present in a given culture (Block, 1973; Camarena et al., 1994). Some roles are traditionally associated with men (e.g., working outside of the home in gainful, salaried employment) and some with women (e.g., being a homemaker and caring for children). These traditional divisions between the genders in the roles they play in society may, over time, become regarded as gender role stereotypes in a given society.

A *stereotype* is an overgeneralized belief. It is an *attitude*—that is, some combination of cognition and feeling—about a social stimulus, for instance, a person. A stereotype is an attitude that invariantly characterizes a person as possessing specific attributes. A stereotype allows for little exception (Allport, 1954). Because of this rigidity, a social stereotype is relatively resistant to change and, as such, may become accepted as always true in a given society. For more than a quarter century, scholars have indicated that gender role stereotypes exist in North American society (Block, 1973; Worell, 1981). These stereotypes are learned at a very young age, perhaps as early as age two (Serbin, Poulin-Dubois, & Eichstedt, 2002). From birth girls and boys are treated differently. Fathers stay in the delivery room longer and make more comments about the baby if it is a boy (Woollett, White, & Lyon, 1982; as cited in Lewis, 1987). Differential treatment of the sexes continues at home. Boys aged 5, 13, and 25 months have more sports equipment, tools, and vehicles in their bedrooms than do girls (Pomerleau & Bolduc, 1990). Bedrooms of infant girls, on the other hand, have more dolls, furniture, and toys that can be manipulated than do boys' bedrooms. Boys have more blue pacifiers and blue bedding; girls have more pink pacifiers and pink clothing. Pomerleau and Bolduc (1990) suggested that these sex-stereotyped environments may influence gender-typed abilities and choice of activities. Later in life, differential treatment continues. Adolescent boys are expected to do more outside chores and girls are expected to do more inside chores (Peters, 1994). Parents enforce curfews more strictly with adolescent girls than boys, and are more lenient with lending the car to their sons than their daughters (Peters, 1994). Peters (1994, p. 913) concluded, "It is

evident from the perspective of the teenager, that stereotypical gender roles are being perpetuated in North American home life."

A gender role may be defined as a socially defined set of prescriptions for behaviour for people of a particular sex group. **Gender role behaviour** may be defined as behavioural functioning in accordance with the prescriptions, and **gender role stereotypes** are the generalized beliefs that particular behaviours are characteristic of one sex group as opposed to the other (Lerner, 1986; Worell, 1981). Table 7.1 presents the findings of a well-known study (Broverman et al., 1972) of the gender role attributes associated stereotypically with males and females by male and female university students. Included in the table are data from a partial replication of the study by Broverman and colleagues conducted by Nesbitt and Penn (2000) with male and female university students in San Diego. The table illustrates changes over time in university students' perceptions of gender role stereotypes. Notable from the table is that more gender stereotypes were identified in 1972 than in 2000 (41 versus 19). Also notable is that 7 of these 19 stereotypes are new in 2000. Nesbitt and Penn commented that, in one significant change, participants in the

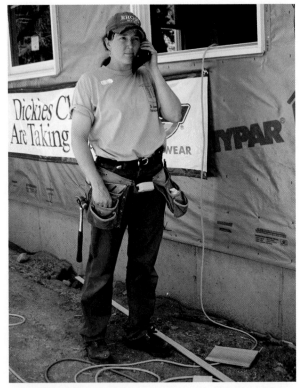

Adolescent girls often engage in jobs that are not stereotypically associated with women.

Gender role behaviour
Behavioural functioning in accordance with the prescriptions set by the society one lives in.

Gender role stereotypes
Generalized beliefs that particular behaviours are more characteristic of one sex group than the other.

Table 7-1 Gender Role Stereotypes of Male and Female American University Students

Competency cluster (masculine pole is more desirable)

Feminine	Masculine	Nesbitt & Penn (2000) agreement
Not at all aggressive	Very aggressive	Yes
Not at all independent	Very independent	Yes
Very emotional	Not at all emotional	Yes
Does not hide emotions at all	Almost always hides emotions	Yes
Very subjective	Very objective	No
Very easily influenced	Not at all easily influenced	No
Very submissive	Very dominant	Yes
Dislikes math and science very much	Likes math and science very much	No
Very excitable in a minor crisis	Not at all excitable in a minor crisis	No
Very passive	Very active	No
Not at all competitive	Very competitive	No
Very illogical	Very logical	No
Very home oriented	Very worldly	No
Not at all skilled in business	Very skilled in business	No
Very sneaky	Very direct	No
Does not know the way of the world	Knows the way of the world	No
Feelings easily hurt	Feelings not easily hurt	Yes
Not at all adventurous	Very adventurous	No
Has difficulty making decisions	Can make decisions easily	No
Cries very easily	Never cries	Yes
Almost never acts as a leader	Almost always acts as a leader	No
Not at all self-confident	Very self-confident	No
Very uncomfortable about being aggressive	Not at all uncomfortable about being aggressive	No
Not at all ambitious	Very ambitious	No
Unable to separate feelings from ideas	Easily able to separate feelings from ideas	No
Very dependent	Not at all dependent	No
Very conceited about appearance	Never conceited about appearance	No
Thinks women are always superior to men	Thinks men are always superior to women	No
Does not talk freely about sex with men	Talks freely about sex with women	No. Males more proud of sexual ability

Warmth-expressiveness cluster (feminine pole is more desirable)

Feminine	Masculine	Nesbitt & Penn (2000) agreement
Doesn't use harsh language at all	Uses very harsh language	Yes
Very talkative	Not at all talkative	No
Very tactful	Very blunt	No
Very gentle	Very rough	Yes
Very aware of feelings of others	Not at all aware of feelings of others	Yes
Very religious	Not at all religious	No
Very interested in own appearance	Not at all interested in own appearance	No
Very neat in habits	Very sloppy in habits	No
Very quiet	Very loud	Yes
Very strong need for security	Very little need for security	No

>

Table 7-1 Gender Role Stereotypes of Male and Female American University Students (continued)

Warmth-expressiveness cluster (feminine pole is more desirable)

Feminine	Masculine	Nesbitt & Penn (2000) agreement
Enjoys art and literature Easily expresses tender feelings	Does not enjoy art and literature at all Does not express tender feelings at all easily	No Yes Females more kind Females more mature Females more understanding of others Females more warm in relationships Females less careless Females less reckless

Note: Broverman et al.'s results are based on the responses of 74 university men and 80 university women. Nesbitt and Penn's results are based on the responses of university men and women aged 18 to 26. The number of these students was not specified, but they were selected from a sample of 83 men and 165 women ranging in age from 18 to 70 years.

Source: Adapted from Broverman et al., 1972, p. 63 and Nesbitt & Penn, 2000, pp. 498–499.

original study viewed masculine traits as more socially desirable than feminine ones; however, the situation was reversed in the recent replication.

Broverman et al. (1972) found that these gender role stereotypes were held fairly consistently across sex, age, and educational levels within society. In addition, other classic research indicates considerable cross-cultural consistency in these stereotypes. In a study of six countries (Norway, Sweden, Denmark, Finland, England, and the United States) cross-cultural consistency in these stereotypes was found to exist (Block, 1973). Similarly, a study of Inuit adolescents (Condon & Stern, 1993) revealed that masculine traits included the terms "bully," "scary," "aggressive," "hard-working" (i.e., in physically demanding jobs), "show-off," "dirty," "drunkardly," and "mean." Feminine traits included terms such as "sexy," "shy," "clean," "quiet," "friendly," and "nice." Yet there is evidence that stereotypes can vary among cultures. For example, Gross (2003) reports that compassion is considered a masculine trait and wisdom is considered a feminine trait by Tibetan Vajrayana Buddhists.

In short, stereotypes exist specifying that different sets of behaviours are expected from males and females. The male gender role in North America is associated with individual effectiveness, independent competence, and agency. The North American female role is associated with interpersonal warmth, expressiveness, and communication. A sample of university students from Ontario and New York revealed that males (but not females) believed that to be a successful manager a person would need "male traits" (Norris & Wylie, 1995).

Gender stereotypes may lead to bias and inequality in the workplace. For example, Hughes and Lowe (1993) found that despite similar sociodemographic characteristics, faculties, educational attainment, and grades, one year after graduating from university, females from Edmonton, Toronto, and Sudbury earned 83% of the males' net weekly salary. They also felt they had a lower chance for promotion. The Canadian Council on Social Development (1998) revealed that female high school graduates earn 26% less than males. Among university graduates, women continue to earn 15% less than men.

Although the existence of these stereotypes means that people may believe males and females generally differ in these ways, the existence of the stereotypes does not necessarily mean males and females *actually* behave differently along these dimensions. Moreover, in regard to issues of work and role development in adolescence, although these stereotypes may represent sources of bias in the job opportunities made available to male and female youth, the existence of the stereotypes may not mean

Adolescent boys often engage in nontraditional male roles, such as child-care worker.

boys and girls actually take jobs during adolescence that are consistent with the stereotype.

Perhaps most importantly, the presence of the stereotypes may not mean that adolescents plan to pursue jobs in later life that are gender stereotyped. Youth may hold a more flexible personal orientation to work. As opposed to a fixed or stereotyped view about what males and females are capable of doing and about what they might be "allowed" by society to do, youth might believe that males and females can (in regard to capacities) and may (in regard to societal opportunities) pursue the same set of work roles. Erickson, Albanese, and Drakulic (2000, p. 1) claim that "Using broadly defined groupings of occupations, gender segregation has declined modestly in recent decades." Yet, these authors continue, there are still jobs that are considered "women's work" and others that are considered "men's work." They point out that 86% of women who are employed work in the service industry whereas only 64% of

employed men do so. Similarly, while 30% of employees and supervisors are women, only 9% of managers are women. The variety of jobs held by women is much smaller than that held by men, and women are more likely to be in lower skilled jobs (Thiessen and Nickerson, 1999). For example, while women represent half of students in medical school in Canada, there are no women deans in medical schools (Cohen, 1997). Similarly, in 1990, only 3% of engineers were women, and two-thirds of these were working in jobs that had a low level of responsibility (Taylor, 1995). Women judges have reported that they are more likely to be assigned cases involving family law rather than other types of cases (Taylor, 1995). Similarly, data from 1985 reveal that there were no women chief executive officers in the top 500 Canadian companies (Peitchinis, 1989; as cited in Thiessen & Nickerson, 1999). While women comprise more than half of the 1600 employees in the Department of Foreign Affairs and International Trade, only one of six ministers and parliamentary secretaries and two of eight assistant deputy ministers in the department are women (Grams, 2003). Women in senior positions (but not chief executives) in Canadian companies believed that gender stereotypes held them back from promotion (Thiessen & Nickerson, 1999). The limitations faced by female workers are not exclusive to Canada. For example, the first female chief executive of a Financial Times (FT-SE) 100 firm in Britain was not hired until 1997 (Adler, 1999), and 1996 data reveal that only 2.4% of chairmen and chief executive officers in U.S. Fortune 500 firms are women (Himelstein, 1996; as cited in Adler, 1999). The nature of work orientation and gender differences in role development in adolescence is discussed next.

Gender Roles: Stereotypes or Flexibility?

ISSUES TO CONSIDER

- In what way may the nature of parental employment affect an adolescent's perception of different gender-bound roles at work and his or her flexibility to hold those roles?
- What characterizes the role strain experienced by an increasing number of adolescent females?

Although the gender role stereotypes of the 20th century are still very much a part of the landscape of North American culture, the influence of the stereotypes is waning. The evidence indicates that society is at a point of historical transition from stereotypes to flexibility in the nature of the roles seen as appropriate, possible, and desirable for men and women. In almost every aspect of research pertinent to work and gender roles, both use of stereotypes and flexibility exist simultaneously. For example, some researchers are studying individuals who have both masculine and feminine traits, considered to be "androgynous" in their roles. Morgan and Ness (2003) found that first-year university students in Manitoba who were androgynous or had a high number of masculine traits (regardless of their biological sex) had fewer difficulties in decision making and higher self-efficacy regarding career decisions than students who were either high in feminine traits or who had a small number of either gender's traits. Among undergraduate business students at a university in western Canada, groups that were highly androgynous made higher quality decisions than groups that were mostly masculine or mostly feminine (Kirchmeyer, 1996). Furthermore, androgyny levels of women and members of ethnic minority groups were more important to quality of decision making than was the androgyny level of white males from European backgrounds. September, McCarrey, Baranowsky, Patent, and Schindler (2001) found that among their sample of university students in central Canada, more women scored as androgynous than as expressive (feminine). Expressive students reported lower well-being than androgynous and instrumental (masculine) students. McCarrey et al. concluded (p. 226), "These findings reflect a shift away from stereotypic gender roles, particularly among university women (at least in Canada and, perhaps, elsewhere), thereby challenging previous conceptualizations of instrumental traits as being associated primarily with men."

Although having a mother who works outside of the home is the typical experience for most North American children and adolescents (Hernandez, 1993; J. Lerner, 1994), the meaning attached by youth to parental employment continues to show evidence of the influence of the gender stereotypes described above (Camarena et al., 1994).

Consistent with the stereotype, work outside the home (being the "breadwinner") is seen traditionally as the central domain of males, and family life is regarded as the central domain of females (who are regarded as the "homemakers") (Camarena et al., 1994). In this context, work is defined as earning a salary, whereas family is equated with housework (Camarena et al., 1994). This is in spite of the fact that the proportion of working mothers has increased from 45% in 1976 to 68% in 1991 (Statistics Canada, 1991, as cited in Norris & Wylie, 1995).

Consistent with a stereotyped division of labour between males and females, Looker's (2000) study of 17-year-olds in Ontario and Nova Scotia revealed that more of the boys (80% versus 20% of girls) believed they would definitely work while their (future) children were preschoolers, despite the fact that both sexes expected to obtain professional or managerial jobs when they completed their education. Thus it seems that adolescents' expectations of the balance of work and family life falls along gender stereotypes. Further evidence for this comes from the findings that more boys than girls placed owning their own home and "earning a lot of money" as very important to them while more girls than boys valued family, friends, and marriage as very important. Although more girls than boys felt having children was very important, this difference did not reach statistical significance. A five-year follow-up again found that 58% of males believed it was a good idea to work while their children were preschoolers while only 25% of the females felt this way. The females who were open to the idea of working while their children were young had mothers who had worked when they had preschool children. Looker suggested that lifestyle expectations are often based on what "people like me" are doing, so that rather than falling back on gender stereotypes, females with mothers as role models may feel that their mothers are "like me." Girls from the working class are particularly likely to believe that the job they would *prefer* to have is not the job they *expect* to have (Looker & Thiessen, 1999).

Although an increasing number of adolescent females aspire to succeed in labour areas traditionally associated with males (Camarena et al., 1994), there has not been a corresponding investment in family work on the part of adolescent males (Camarena et al., 1994). McLaren (1996), in her interviews with British Columbian students in their final year of secondary school, found that girls anticipated that they would be full-time mothers for a period of time, partly due to their belief that men wouldn't be capable of raising children. The boys in the sample had given little thought to the effect that children might have on their careers. When questioned, some of them assumed that their (future) wives would engage in childcare and their own careers would not be affected. Accordingly, for the older adolescent female, the need to integrate work and family may influence significantly the choice of her vocation or the timing of marriage. In addition, the more flexible role orientation of females—in regard to balancing family and work roles—may place more strain on them in regard to enactment of overall role behaviours than would be the case for men who opt to devote most of their effort to enacting their work roles (J. Lerner, 1994). According to McLaren (1996), what may make it especially difficult for girls is the fact that schools prepare students for work, citizenship, and individualism, but they neglect the development of care, concern, and connection, traits that are related to caregiving: "Schools tend to align their goals and structures with those of the workplace. Young women are compelled to negotiate between the desire for employment (which is validated by these two institutions) and the desire for mothering (which is not). It is a cruel irony that educational and occupational reforms which encourage girls and women to aspire to 'unfettered' careers are all based on assumptions of gender, social class, race, and other privileges" (p. 92).

The basis of role strain may begin in adolescence (Camarena et al., 1994). Although boys' attitudes toward women's roles changed more than did girls' attitudes to the work and family roles of men and women, across grades girls' attitudes were more positive and open than was the case with boys (Camarena et al., 1994).

Among the Inuit studied by Condon and Stern (1993), modernization has affected gender roles for boys (although not for girls). Adolescent girls continue to take care of their younger siblings and do almost as many household chores as adult women do, especially if their mothers are working. However, the adolescent boys have few responsibilities. Although they learn traditional hunting and trapping skills, these are no longer needed on a daily basis and the boys are allowed to spend their days in sporting and other leisure activities.

Evidence exists for the presence of both stereotypes and flexibility in work and gender roles. Given this evidence, it may be reasonable to ask why these two contradictory trends exist. One hypothesis is that although society enunciates ideals about gender equality, and even promotes public policies and programs in support of such values, it also includes some countervailing influences. It may be that institutions of society, such as the family and media, socialize youth to become more gender stereotyped in their personal behaviours. Such socialization has

been termed the **gender intensification hypothesis**. It is useful to consider whether there is evidence in support of this idea.

The Gender Intensification Hypothesis

ISSUES TO CONSIDER

- What are some of the examples in support of the gender intensification hypothesis?
- Why might it be important to understand conditions during adolescence under which gender intensification occurs?
- What might contribute to adolescents' development of flexible attitudes toward stereotypical gender role behaviours?

The gender intensification hypothesis rests on the idea that a key component of the social context of youth involves the socialization experiences an adolescent receives as a consequence of being male or female. That is, it is believed that adolescents experience quite different worlds by virtue of being either male or female. For instance, there may be increasing pressure by key socializing agents—for example, peers, media, and even family members and school personnel—for boys to act more masculine and for girls to act more feminine, that is, to show behaviours consistent with the stereotypes summarized in Table 7.1 (e.g., Bakan, 1966; Galambos, Almeida, & Petersen, 1990). For instance, it is believed that independence is encouraged in boys and compliance is encouraged in girls (Crouter, Manke, & McHale, 1995).

Such differential socialization is summarized around the concept of *gender intensification* (Hill & Lynch, 1983; Lynch, 1991), and the hypothesis associated with this concept is that these contrasting experiences will result in emerging or increasing differences between males and females during the early portion of adolescence. The belief is that, as the youth progresses through puberty, changes in physical appearance and in sexual maturity influence self-expectations and the expectations of other people about the adolescent (Lynch, 1991).

There are data consistent with such contextual effects. In addition, there are data that do not support the presence of gender intensification. For example,

Gender intensification hypothesis Adolescents' socialization by institutions of society, such as the family, aimed at making the youth more gender stereotyped in their personal behaviour. The hypothesis rests on the idea that adolescents experience quite different socialization by virtue of being either male or female.

Côté and Allahar (1994) argue that gender intensification is an outmoded artifact from a time when women did not tend to work outside the home. They suggest that businesses benefit from selling products to enhance femininity and masculinity, so that it is in their favour to promote gender differences. As we discuss, and as was the case with stereotypes versus flexibility in work and gender roles, the issue becomes one of understanding the conditions under which gender intensification occurs during adolescence.

To illustrate the nature of the evidence pertinent to gender intensification, we may note that in a major U.S. longitudinal study of young adolescents, males and females showed increased concerns about gender roles, about body image, and about the perceived importance of popularity (Simmons & Blyth, 1987). Both boys and girls showed an increase after Grade 6 in feeling that it was important *not* to act like members of the opposite sex.

During the middle of the adolescent period both boys and girls engage in high levels of gender-typed activities and possess gender-typed interests (Ruble & Martin, 1998). There is also some evidence that girls show a relative preference for stereotypically feminine versus stereotypically masculine high school subjects (Archer, 1992).

Evidence shows that gender intensification occurs in regard to the incidence of psychiatric disorders among young adolescents (Brooks-Gunn, 1989). In girls, there was an increase in eating disorders (e.g., anorexia and bulimia; see Chapter 3) and in depression. In boys, there was an increase in conduct disorders.

But recent evidence indicates that during the middle portion of adolescence there may be an increasing willingness for both boys and girls to depart, respectively, from stereotypically masculine or feminine role behaviours, and to adopt more flexible views of role behaviours. For instance, from middle childhood through early adolescence, gender preferences become less stereotyped and more flexible (Etaugh & Liss, 1992; Katz & Ksansnak, 1994).

It is not certain if boys and girls differ in regard to the flexibility of their gender preferences. Some evidence indicates that this increase in flexibility may occur primarily, or perhaps even only, for girls (Archer, 1984, 1992; Ruble & Martin, 1998). However, there is also research that shows an increase through late adolescence in the flexibility of gender role preferences among both males and females (Katz & Ksansnak, 1994) and that contemporary adolescents have a more flexible attitude toward female gender roles than do

members of older generations (Mills & Mills, 1996).

In a U.S. longitudinal study of 144 adolescents between the ages of 9 and 11 years, three aspects of the purported differential socialization for gender intensification were studied: (1) adolescents' participation in "feminine" or "masculine" household chores; (2) parental monitoring; and (3) adolescents' involvement in paired activities with mothers or fathers (Crouter et al., 1995). Evidence for socialization consistent with gender intensification occurred only in regard to the third aspect of family functioning. Over time, girls became increasingly involved with their mothers and boys with their fathers, especially when the adolescents had a younger sibling of the opposite sex (Crouter et al., 1995).

To the extent that gender intensification occurs, it may be likely to take place in such one-to-one mother-daughter or father-son activities (Witt, 1997). In a longitudinal study of paternal involvement and gender role development among about 2000 male and female youth, ongoing relationships with fathers were more important for sons' than for daughters' gender role development (Hardesty, Wenk, & Morgan, 1995).

Conclusions About Gender Role Development and the Importance of Work in Adolescence

Work represents an essential part of the life of all people. What we do to contribute to our own quality of life and to the health and prosperity of our family and community is vital to individual welfare and to societal maintenance and perpetuation. The vocation or career we select in life and the orientation toward work we develop during youth are crucial parts of identity development and the transition to adulthood (Vondracek, 1994; Vondracek et al., 1995).

Although the data are not unequivocal, most information currently available indicates that work during adolescence has a beneficial influence on adolescent development. Work experiences during adolescence help prepare youth for successful adult careers—a point we emphasize again in Chapter 15 when we consider the nature of the transition from adolescence to young adulthood.

Whereas in the past, society has not maximized the potential contributions of its citizens because of the restrictions on equal role opportunities provided to men and women, there is more recent evidence of a greater presence of individual and social flexibility in gender roles. Even though evidence indicates that in adolescence socialization pressures exist for boys to engage in traditionally masculine roles and for girls to engage in traditionally feminine roles, there is also information indicating that gender intensification is far from a universal feature of adolescent development. Many of the aspects of family life do not socialize youth to become more stereotyped in their gender role behaviour (Crouter et al., 1995).

Because of the evidence for a growing flexibility among youth and their social worlds in regard to the work and career roles associated with males and females, there is optimism that future decades will bear witness to greater opportunities for male and female adolescents to explore and use the full range of the competencies and interests they possess. Due to the importance of such flexibility for the health of individual development and for the welfare of society, numerous programs around the world are aimed at improving the life chances of young people and, especially in contexts where gender role stereotypes have been markedly prevalent, among women in particular. Applications Box 7.1 describes several of these programs.

APPLICATIONS : Box 7.1

Overcoming Traditional Gender Role Restrictions in the Work and Careers of Women

Daughter's Education Program (DEP)

In the Northern province of Chiang Rai, Thailand, exploitation of girls is rampant. Poverty and the prevailing view of females as subservient encourage the sale of girls for commercial sex. The Daughter's Education Program (DEP) was established in 1989 to prevent elementary and high school aged girls from being forced into the sex trade. An internationally supported effort of the Development and Education Program for Daughters and Communities, DEP improves the employment prospects of girls through a residential education program that provides basic schooling and access to vocational training. Such training is offered in weaving, sewing, handicrafts, and computer operation. Equally important, the program reaches out to community members and educates them about alternatives to prostitution. Youth serve as spokespersons and role models and also work in the centre in administrative roles. DEP is currently working with more than 250 elementary and high school girls in the region and, since its inception, has saved nearly 600 from sexual exploitation. The vast majority of those who complete the program find permanent employment, many becoming educators in the community.

Programa de Alfabetización Intergeneracional (Intergenerational Literacy Program)

Programa de Alfabetización Intergeneracional (Intergenerational Literacy Program) was begun in 1991 to improve the standard of living among Ecuador's villagers, primarily through greater literacy. The program uses the Total Language Approach that has been successfully tested in Australia and the United States. It trains mothers and youth to read to—and write stories and songs for—young children as a way of cultivating their own literacy skills. In the community's day care centre, mothers and youth receive training in infant and child care and preschool development. Once trained, mothers work at the centre where they read aloud books, folk tales, and other literature. Youth write and distribute a monthly newsletter. Employment skills are also strengthened through workshops on income-earning activities such as weaving, sewing, and electrical repair. Program results have been positive, including increased knowledge of childcare, awareness of good nutrition, and enhancement of trade skills. To date, over 100 women and children have participated, and 60% of the mothers and youth report receiving economic benefits from skills learned in the program.

Junior Achievement International (JAI)

Junior Achievement International (JAI) was created to empower students with the knowledge, skills, and social awareness needed to participate in the global marketplace. The program aims to provide young people with skills in business management and economics as well as with self-confidence and the leadership skills required in the workplace. This is not done through job training or counselling, but through young people's exposure to business and economic concepts, their interactions with businesspeople, and the opportunity for them to run small businesses. JAI's approach is based on "learning by doing." As such, it is team-based, interactive, and practical. Enlisting volunteers in the business field, JAI teaches the fundamentals of business and applied economics, and fosters the development of democratic decision-making and entrepreneurial skills through a variety of projects for youth, ages 5 to 22. The program's impact on youth includes better comprehension of business fundamentals, as well as greater self-esteem, increased job readiness, and teamwork. JAI has also shown effectiveness in adapting to various cultural contexts, operating in 108 countries; the materials are available in 36 languages.

Source: International Youth Foundation, 2001. www.iyfnet.org

Summary

- Working can give adolescents a basis for new identities, new expectations of responsibility and independence, and a new high status among peers.
- Work can take time away from school, diminish the opportunity to participate in extracurricular activities, and limit the time available for homework.
- High turnover, low pay, little authority, and low prestige often characterize adolescent jobs.
- Working students have reported that their employment was associated with being more punctual, dependable, and personally responsible. However, working adolescents have been found to be more frequently late to school and engaged in more deviant behaviour (such as smoking and drinking) than their nonworking peers.
- Working status is not associated with differences in time spent in schoolwork, time spent in extracurricular activities, or grades. It is also not related to incidence of school behaviour problems. Working a low or moderate number of hours was associated with lower dropout rates than working more than 20 hours per week.
- There is no difference in intrinsic motivation for school between working and nonworking students and no systematic relation between intrinsic motivation and the number of hours worked.
- Male and female adolescents are both typically given jobs that require little skill or training; however, precise job assignments often vary along gender-stereotypic lines.

- A gender role is a socially defined set of prescriptions for the behaviour of a gender group. Gender role behaviour is acting in accordance with this set of prescriptions.
- Research has shown that men and women hold gender stereotypes, with men typically being described as more aggressive and independent, and women being described as gentle, aware of others' feelings, and needing security.
- Gender role stereotypes are held fairly consistently across sex, age, educational levels, and cultures.
- The existence of gender role stereotypes may be a source of bias in the job opportunities made available to male and female adolescents.
- Despite the existence of gender stereotypes, youth may hold a flexible personal orientation to work and pursue jobs in later life that counter the stereotypes.
- Although an increasing number of females aspire to succeed in labour areas, there has not been a corresponding increase in male investment in family work.
- The gender intensification hypothesis rests on the idea that adolescents experience different socialization, depending on whether they are male or female.
- The differences in socialization result in emerging or increasing differences between males and females during the early portions of adolescence.
- To the extent that gender intensification occurs, it is likely to take place in mother-daughter or father-son activities.

Discussion Topics

1. What roles define(d) your life as an adolescent? Of these roles, are any of them considered by your culture to be stereotypical of your gender? Did the various social contexts (i.e., family, peers, school) of which you are/were a part influence which roles you adopted? If so, how?
2. If you worked as an adolescent, in what ways did your position influence you—what were the positive and negative influences? Looking back on it now, did the intrinsic values you gained

from the experience outweigh the extrinsic value of the job? Why or why not?
3. Do you believe that male and female adolescents suffer under societal gender stereotypes? What aspects of their lives are affected by gender biases? Did your social world make efforts to offer gender-neutral opportunities to you throughout your development? If so, what efforts were made and how did the efforts impact your development? If not, how did gender stereotypes present

during your adolescence impact the roles that now define you?

4. Do you think both mothers and fathers should work outside of the home? Why or why not? What if the family only needs to rely on one income—should the mother be the one to stay home with the child? Why or why not? Do you think the choices your parent(s) made in terms of working will affect the decisions you will make as a parent in terms of working or staying home to care for the children? If so, how?

5. In what ways did/do your peers and/or overall school environment intensify the pressure you felt/feel as an adolescent to hold to some gender stereotype?

6. If you worked or volunteered during high school, did your experience impact the career path you see yourself on at this time? If so, how?

Key Terms

gender intensification hypothesis, p. 169

gender roles, p. 156
gender role behaviour, p. 164

gender role stereotypes, p. 164
role, p. 156

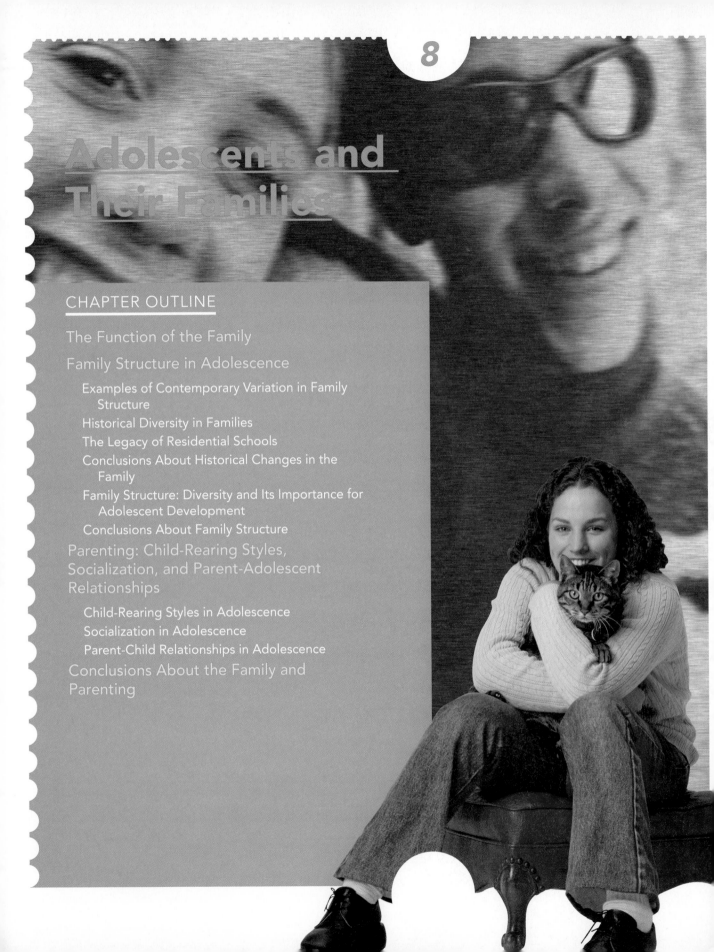

8

Adolescents and Their Families

"Jimmy, come out of your room. Dad and I are ready to go out to dinner."

There was no answer.

"Jimmy, I'm calling you . . . Jimmy. JIMMY!"

"What?" The reply came from inside Jimmy's room.

"Jimmy, I'm not going to shout through a door to you," she said, recognizing that this was precisely what she was doing.

"What, Mom? Do you want me?"

She caught her breath. If she didn't want him, why would she be calling? "Jimmy, your dad and I are ready to go out for dinner now. Are you ready?"

"Mom, I don't want to go. I thought I would have Rohan and Blair over and we'd watch a movie. I'll just make a sandwich or something."

"Jimmy, I'd rather you went out with us. You can see your friends after dinner."

"Mom, I don't want to eat what you guys like. And I'd rather spend time with my friends."

Learning Objectives

1. To understand that the family is the most important component of an adolescent's social world.
2. To understand the changes that have occurred over time in regard to family structure in North America.
3. To understand why diversity in family structure is important to adolescent development.
4. To understand how poverty, and economic hardship more generally, influence youth development, and how despite these influences, positive development can be promoted.
5. To understand the roles grandparents, marital quality, divorce, adoption, and maternal employment play in the social and emotional development of youth.
6. To realize that unsupervised time can promote problem behaviour in youth and that parents can exert some control over the decisions youth make during this time and, as well, that effective and available community youth programs can offer youth rich experiences and promote fewer life problems.
7. To recognize that adults differ in the ways they enact their roles as a parent and that parenting style is associated with differences in adolescent behaviour and development.
8. To recognize that cultures differ in what they determine to be a well-socialized individual and that parents can help to model and shape the cognitive, emotional, and behavioural attributes they hope to see develop in their adolescent.

The changes young people undergo during adolescence are linked to changes that occur in the context, particularly the family, the peer group, and the school. These three social institutions and the social relationships that occur within them provide the key contextual influences across adolescence. The diversity that characterizes the structure and function of these contexts is associated with diversity in developmental changes across adolescence.

In several ways, the social context of adolescence differs significantly from the context surrounding the person at earlier periods of development. The adolescent's social world is broader and more complex than that of the infant and the child. The most notable social phenomenon of adolescence is the emergence of the marked importance of peer groups (see Chapter 9 and, as well, Chapter 10, in regard to sexual relationships). The adolescent comes to rely heavily on the peer group for security and guidance. This is a time when the young person may feel that such peer support is urgently needed, perhaps because the adolescent thinks that only others experiencing the same transition can be relied on to understand what is being experienced. Nevertheless, the family still remains the most important component of the social world of adolescents.

The Function of the Family

ISSUES TO CONSIDER
- How is the family the most important influence on adolescents' social development?
- What is the key function of the family?

Contrary to a common cultural stereotype about adolescence, the family is quite influential for adolescents (Adelson, 1970; Bengtson & Troll, 1978; Lerner, Sparks, & McCubbin, 2000; Steinberg, 1991). Families create caring people through modelling and establishing bonds of social and emotional attachment, through fostering healthy peer and other interpersonal relationships, and through instilling in youth prosocial behaviour and empathy (see Chapter 5), and agency and self-control (see Chapter 6). The family is the major institution of society that fosters the development of caring individuals (Chase-Lansdale, Wakschlag, & Brooks-Gunn, 1995), and promotes civil society (Lerner et al., 1999, 2000b; see also Chapter 5). This chapter discusses the diverse structure and function of families, both as they have changed historically and as they exist in contemporary society.

Despite the diverse structures and functions of the family context, and the historical changes that have occurred in these attributes of the family (e.g., Hernandez, 1993; Milan, 2000), the essential point on which to focus is the continual influence of the family on the development of the young person. Due to this constancy of influence, the family is, and has always been, the key institution of society charged

with creating a new generation of citizens committed to maintaining and furthering the social order (Chase-Lansdale et al., 1995; Elder, Modell, & Parke, 1993; Lerner et al., 2000b). As such, *parenting* is the core function of the family. Feeling connected to family (as well as school) is related to adolescent resilience and involvement in the community (McCreary Centre, 1999). The nature and effects on youth of child-rearing behaviour is the focus of our discussion of the functions of families. It is possible to evaluate the success of any particular family structure by ascertaining the quality of development of the youth living within it. Any family structure can be appraised in regard to how well it produces healthy, able, and productive youth.

After a discussion of the nature and diversity of family structures, we consider the differences in family functioning that influence an adolescent's development. This presentation involves a discussion of the different styles parents have of rearing children, and of how these styles relate to **socialization**—the process by which one generation (the parental one) influences another (the adolescent one) to adopt the values, beliefs, and desired behaviours of society. In addition we discuss how the development of adolescents is influenced by the diversity of parent-child relations that exist as a consequence of parents' rearing styles and socialization patterns.

Family Structure in Adolescence

What is a family? Who are the people who comprise it? How does that structure relate to what a family does, how it functions, how parenting affects children? Across history, there has always been diversity in both family structure and parenting, and thus in the sort of parent-child relationships that occur within families. Understanding this historical and contemporary variation in family structure and function is important for appreciating ways in which parenting occurs, its influences, and the nature of parent-adolescent relationships. Understanding this diversity also helps us appreciate other family (e.g., sibling, grandparent) and nonfamily (e.g., peer) relationships associated with the developing adolescent. These relationships, and the family structures with which they are associated, shape adolescent development. In the next section we describe contemporary and historical diversity in the structure of the family.

Socialization Process by which one generation (the parental one) influences another (the adolescent one) to adopt the values, beliefs, and desired behaviours of society.

Examples of Contemporary Variation in Family Structure

ISSUE TO CONSIDER

- What changes have occurred in regard to Canadian and U.S. and family structure over time?

Many of us grew up at a time when the stereotypic North American family was a **nuclear family**, with two biological parents and two or three children (named either David and Ricky, or Bud, Kitten, and Princess, respectively). Yet, today, in the U.S. only one in five married couples with children fits this still popular stereotype of living in what has been termed the "Ozzie and Harriet" family (i.e., the never-divorced, two-parent-two-child family) (Ahlburg & De Vita, 1992; Hernandez, 1993). As shown in Table 8.1, at any one time children and parents may live in several quite different family contexts (see Allison, 1993). Yet, in Canada, 87% of adults report no change in family structure (from their child's or children's birth to the age of 15, Williams, 2001).

The cross-sectional location of people in one of the family contexts noted in Table 8.1 is complicated by the fact that such settings may change longitudinally over the course of the lives of children and parents, and thus across generations (that is, over the course of history). This observation raises the need for a historically sensitive analysis of the social contexts within which youth find themselves (Allison, 1993; Featherman, Spenner, & Tsunematsu, 1988; Hernandez, 1993).

Children and adolescents may find themselves in more than one family during their socialization. In Canada, lone-parent families make up 18.5% of all families with children (Ondercin-Bourne, 2003). Among 15- to 19-year-olds, 16% were living in lone-parent families in 1991 (Lindsay, Devereux, & Bergob, 1994). The proportion of Aboriginal children under age 15 living with one parent is almost 33% (Vanier Institute of the Family, 2000). There are a substantial number of single-parent families, and many children and adolescents live in families with two adults, but only one biological parent. These variations in living arrangements and family status come about partly as a result of the high rates of marital dissolution found in North America. Divorce and remarriage are common in the United States today, with about two out of every five marriages involving recently married persons expected to end in divorce (Demos et al., 2000). Rates of divorce in Canada have been lower than those in the U.S. (LeBourdais and

Marcil-Gratton, 1996). It wasn't until the 1968 divorce law that divorce became common. Whether Canada's rate will eventually increase to match that of the U.S. or whether it will level off is unknown. Using data from 1998, Statistics Canada estimated that 36% of marriages end in divorce within 30 years of marriage and 39% of marriages end in divorce within 50 years of marriage (*The Daily*, 2000). About 75% of the persons involved in divorce eventually remarry, and those who remarry do so, on the average, about three years after the divorce. As many as 45% of children and adolescents can expect to live in a family setting without one of their biological parents for a period of time before they reach adulthood. Also, 24.2% of women in Canada have chosen to have children without getting married. Some are heading lone-parent households, but many are living with a partner (Ondercin-Bourne, 2003). Statistics

---

Table 8-1 Examples of Contemporary "Family" Contexts of Children and Youth

Married or cohabiting nuclear (and biological)

Single parent (biological)

Married or cohabiting nuclear (adoptive)

Single parent (adoptive)

Married or cohabiting (blended)
  {heterosexual; homosexual}

Single parent (step)

Intergenerational

Extended, without parent
  {e.g., child-aunt}

Same-sex parents

In loco parentis (in the position or place of a parent)
  families/institutions
    Foster-care homes
    Group homes
    Psychiatric hospitals
    Residential treatment facilities
    Juvenile detention facilities

Runaways

Street children/youth
  {e.g., adolescent prostitutes}

Homeless children/youth

Source: Adapted from Lerner et al., 1995.

Nuclear family Family characterized by the presence of both biological parents and one or more children.

Canada began keeping track of common-law families in the 1981 census. At that point, 6% of all families were common-law families. This increased to 12% of all families in 1996 (Jenson, 2001). In addition, while the numbers are small, there is increased recognition that children may be raised with two parents of the same sex (0.5% of couples were of the same sex in the Canadian 2001 census, the first year such couples were counted). For female-female couples, 15% of these unions included children; 3% of male-male unions included children (*The Daily*, 2002). The three-generation household remains, but also is not common. According to Rosenthal and Gladstone (2000), only 2.7% of Canadian households consist of children living with parents and a grandparent. This arrangement appears to be slightly more common in the U.S. (4.7% of adults live in a house with three or more generations (Szinovacz, 1998, as cited in Rosenthal & Gladstone, 2000).

Social class and the financial resources differentially available to youth living in different types of families (J. Lerner, 1994) structure the large majority of the societal resources and cultural values influencing families. The magnitude of change in regard to family social class and parental structure underscores the need to appraise the diversity of youth-family relations **longitudinally** (historically) as well as **cross-sectionally** (at any one point in time).

Historical Diversity in Families

ISSUES TO CONSIDER

• What are the major changes in the lives of North American children and adolescents across the 20th century?
• What do these changes mean in terms of parent-child relations and history?

Family researchers (e.g., Hernandez, 1993 in the U.S.; Milan, 2000 and the Vanier Institute of the Family, 2000 in Canada) have identified several quite profound changes that have characterized the life courses of children, adolescents, and their families over the last 50 to 150 years.

Hernandez (1993) has adopted a perspective consistent with the stress in developmental contextualism on integrated relations between people and the multiple levels of the context within which they live. He argues that a person's life trajectory is constituted by, and differentiated from, those of others on the basis of (1) the specific order, duration, and timing of the particular events and resources experienced in life; and (2) by the number, characteristics, and activities of the family members with whom the person lives.

The Disappearance of the Two-Parent Farm Family and the Growth in the One-Parent Family Between the late 18th century to almost the end of the 19th century, the majority of children between the ages of birth and 17 years in the United States lived in two-parent farm families (Hernandez, 1993). In 1990, fewer than 5% of America's children lived, during the first 17 years of their lives, in two-parent farm families. The move from rural to urban areas can be seen in Canada as well. In 1900, 60% of Canadians lived in rural areas. Farming was the major occupation for 45% of individuals. In the year 2000, less than 3% of Canadians lived on farms (Vanier Institute of the Family, 2000). Among adolescents (aged 15 to 19), 4% lived on rural farms and 21.9% lived in rural nonfarm areas. The remaining 74.1% lived in urban areas (Lindsay et al., 1994). Fewer than 30% of children under 17 in the U.S. in 1990 lived in married nonfarm families in which the father was the breadwinner and the mother was the homemaker. Rather, about 70% of all U.S. children in this age range lived in either dual-earner nonfarm families or in one-parent families. Indeed, about 25% lived in one-parent families.

The increase in one-parent families over the course of the 20th century was coupled with a decrease in the presence of a grandparent in the home. Although 48% of three-generation households in Canada in 1996 included a lone parent, these types of households composed less than 3% of all families (Che-Alford & Hamm, 1999).

The Decrease in the Number of Siblings in the Family As shown in Table 8.2, there have been dramatic changes over the last 100 or so years in the percentage of children living in families with large numbers of siblings. In 1890, 46% of children in the U.S. lived in families with eight or more siblings. In contrast, Hernandez (1993) found that only 7% of American children lived in families having just one or two siblings.

In 1990, only 1% of U.S. children lived in families with eight or more siblings and only 5% of U.S. children lived in families with five to seven siblings. In Canada, too, families have decreased in size over

---

Longitudinal study Study that assesses a particular variable (e.g., sibling relationships) repeatedly over time.
Cross-sectional study Study that assesses a particular variable (e.g., youth-parent relations) at one point in time (e.g., during the year 2000). Often, different age groups are studied at this point in time.

Table 8-2 A Century of Changes in the Percentage of Children Living in Families with Eight or More Siblings (U.S.) and in the Average Number of Siblings (Canada)

United States		Canada	
Year	% of Families	Year	Average No. of Siblings
1890	46%	1851	5.6
1940	10%	1937	1.6
		1959	2.9
1990	1%	1997	0.6

Source: Based on Hernandez, 1993; Milan, 2000.

the past century. The birth rate has declined from 116 births per 1000 women (1921) to 44 per 1000 women in 1997 (Ondercin-Bourne, 2003). In 1993 less than 1% of children were born to mothers who had six or more previous children, whereas 43% of children were firstborn and 35% were second-born children (Grindstaff, 1995). One reason for smaller families is that women are waiting longer before having children, so they have less time to produce big families. The availability of contraception and greater involvement of mothers in the labour force have also contributed to this trend.

The Growth of Mothers in the Labour Force
As shown in Table 8.3, the percentage of children with mothers in the labour force in the U.S. increased dramatically in the last half of the 20th century

(Hernandez, 1993; J. Lerner, 1994), and the same pattern appears to be true for Canada. Moreover, in 1991 65% of husband-wife families (including those without children) consisted of two workers. This is in contrast to almost 40% of families in 1981, and only 20% of families in 1961 (Ondercin-Bourne, 2003).

Changes in Fathers' Full-Time Employment
As shown in Table 8.4, the marked growth in maternal employment since 1940 has been coupled with the fact that between the 1940s and the 1980s many children in the U.S. lived with fathers who were not employed full-time year round (Hernandez, 1993).

Between 1950 and 1980, the 8% decrease in children living with fathers who did not have full-time employment was offset by an 8% increase in children who did not have a father in the home (Hernandez, 1993). Given the percentage of American children that lived in such father-absent homes during this period, a phenomenon discussed later, from the 1950s to the 1980s only about 60% of America's children lived with fathers who worked full time throughout the year (Hernandez, 1993).

The Growth of Single-Parent, Female Head-of-Household Families
As noted, the last half of the 20th century saw a dramatic increase in the percentage of North American children living in single-parent homes with their mothers (Hernandez, 1993) (see Table 8.5). As stated earlier, 18.5% of all families with children were headed by a female single-parent (Ondercin-Bourne, 2003). This has more than

Table 8-3 Percentage of Children with Mothers in the Labour Force

United States		Canada Percentage of mothers with children over age 6		Canada[3] (all ages) Percentage of mothers with children (all ages)
Year	Percentage	Year	Percentage	Percentage
1940	10%			
1950	16%			
1960	26%			
1970	36%	1975	——	48.2%[1]
1980	49%	1981	55.0%	44.6%
1990	59%	1991	71.6%	65.3%
		1996	——	78.5%[2]

[1] Children aged 6–15 years

[2] Youngest child 6–14 years

[3] Canadian data were not available for 1940, 1950, 1960, 1970, 1980, or 1990.

Source: Based on Hernandez, 1993; McVey & Kalbach, 1995. Statistics Canada. (1987). Vanier Institute of the Family (2000).

Consequences of Welfare Reform for Children, Adolescents, and Their Families

Donald J. Hernandez is a professor in the Department of Sociology and Center for Social and Demographic Analysis at the State University of New York in Albany. He is responsible for developing the U.S. Census Bureau's Survey of Program Dynamics, which is the federal survey for assessing the effects of welfare reform, particularly for children and adolescents, and he directed the study reported in *From Generation to Generation: The Health and Well-Being of Children in Immigrant Families* and in *Children of Immigrants: Health, Adjustment, and Public Assistance.*

The survival, comfort, and self-respect of children and adolescents depend on having access to adequate levels of nutrition, clothing, housing, health care, and other amenities of modern life. The market economy and government are the two society-wide institutions that provide access to these essential goods and services. From the market economy, persons with jobs obtain income in return for work they perform in the labour market. From government, individuals can obtain access to essential goods and services through social welfare programs that provide economic resources in the form of cash, or in the form of quasi-cash benefits such as food stamps.

Children are legally barred from most jobs; few adolescents can earn enough from paid work to support themselves; and children and adolescents are usually not directly eligible for social welfare benefits. Therefore, children and adolescents depend mainly on parents to ensure their economic well-being. But parents' economic resources are obtained, originally, from either the economy or government. A major goal of government welfare programs, historically, was to provide resources to families with low incomes. U.S. welfare reform in 1996 introduced new goals that include forcing welfare recipients off welfare and into the labour force and discouraging out-of-wedlock childbearing, especially among teens.

Proponents argue that children and adolescents will benefit from these reforms in several ways. Parents who are economically self-sufficient workers, instead of dependent on government welfare, will serve as better role models; their children will see work rather than welfare as a way of life. Working parents can obtain higher incomes for their families. Adolescents who do not bear children out of wedlock are less likely to drop out of school and more likely to become self-supporting. But, based on past research, critics argue that many parents who receive welfare are already working and are not qualified for jobs that pay well enough to lift them, and their families, out of poverty. They also argue that adolescents often drop out of school because of a lack of economic opportunities, and that adolescents and young adults who bear children out-of-wedlock do so because their potential spouses are not able to find work that would allow them to contribute significantly to the support of a family.

I am using the U.S. Census Bureau's Survey of Program Dynamics, and other data sources, to study effects of welfare reform for children, adolescents, and their families. I am seeking answers to the following questions. Are parents working more, or less, as a result of welfare reform? Is self-esteem increasing among parents because they are becoming self-sufficient, or, alternatively, is stress increasing because of greater difficulties in juggling family responsibilities with additional hours of work? What are the consequences for the well-being of their children? Are children and adolescents experiencing increases in family income or increases in family poverty? Are children and adolescents receiving better care because their parents have more money to pay for higher quality child care and after-school learning opportunities, or are they receiving less attention because parents have less time to spend with them and to monitor their activities? What are the consequences of teen childbearing?

All children and adolescents share the same basic needs. But welfare reform is particularly significant for those in immigrant families, because the law has made them or their parents ineligible for many welfare benefits. Of all the children and adolescents in the United States, those in immigrant families are the fastest growing group. During the seven years from 1990 to 1997, the number of children and adolescents in immigrant families grew by 47%, compared to only 7% for other children and adolescents. By 1997, one of every five children and adolescents under age 18 lived in an immigrant family. Because of these trends, children and adolescents in immigrant families are a major focus of my research.

Will the massive welfare reform initiated in 1996 lead to better or worse lives for children and adolescents? Preliminary results indicate that major social welfare programs acted to reduce child and adolescent poverty prior to welfare reform, but since welfare reform they are less effective in reducing poverty. But many additional consequences may flow from welfare reform, and we have only begun to measure these effects. Our hope is that this research will increase scientific knowledge about the effects of recent reforms and lead in the future to additional reforms that will increase the well-being of children and adolescents.

Across history, families have often included siblings of a wide age range.

Table 8-4 Percentage of U.S. Children Living with Fathers Not Employed Full Time Year Round

Year	Percentage
1940	40%
1950	32%
1980	24%

Source: Based on Hernandez, 1993.

doubled since 1961, when 9% of families with children were lone-mother households (Ondercin-Bourne, 2003). However, it is important to note the historical and social context of one-parent families. For example, as stated by the Vanier Institute of the Family (2000), "Many marriages collapsed in the 19th century because of the voluntary separation of

Table 8-5 Percentage of Children Living in Lone-Parent, Female Head-of-Household Families (U.S.); Percentage of Lone-Parent Households (Canada)

United States Lone-parent females		Canada Lone parent, both sexes		Canada Lone-parent females
Year	Percentage	Year	Percentage	Percentage
1940	6.7%	1931	12%	——
1950	6.4%	——	——	——
1960	7.7%	——	——	——
1970	11.8%	1971	9.4%	7.4%
——		1976	9.8%	8.1%
1980	16.2%	1981	11.3%	9.3%
——		1986	12.7%	10.4%
——		1991	13%	10.7%
1990	20.0%	1996	15%	——

Source: Based on Hernandez, 1993; La Novara, 1993; Milan (2000).

Table 8-6 Reasons for Lone Parenthood (Canada)

Unmarried Woman (Including Cohabitation)		Marriage breakdown		Widowhood	
Year	Percentage	Year	Percentage	Year	Percentage
1931	<0.5%	1931	24%	1931	75%
1941	4%	1941	25%	1941	73%
1981	16.7%	1981	58%	1981	33%
1996	22%	1996	58%	1996	20%

Sources: Burke, 1986; Jenson, 2001; Milan, 2000.

spouses, the departure of one spouse from the marital home, or the death of a spouse. The result was that there were almost as many single-parent families in Canada in 1901 as there were at the end of the 20th century." See Table 8.6 for the different reasons for the formation of lone-parent households over the years.

The Disappearance of the "Ozzie and Harriet" Family (the Married, Never Divorced Two-Parent-Two-Child Family) Over the course of the 20th century, North America experienced a disappearance of the stereotypically predominant married, two-parent family, in which the father is the breadwinner, the mother is the homemaker, and two to three children either spend their lives in socioeconomic and personal security or are faced with problems that require only about 30 minutes (the time of the typical American television situation comedy) to resolve. Not only are such stereotypic families largely absent in North America, but, since the 1940s, a decreasing minority of children have been born into such families (Hernandez, 1993).

The changing percentages of children born into "Ozzie and Harriet" type families are presented in Table 8.7. In addition to the trend illustrated in the table, few North Americans spend their entire childhood and adolescent years in these family settings. Note that Table 8.7 reveals that even at the peak rate (1950) less than half of all U.S. families fit this stereotypic family type. As Ondercin-Bourne (2003) argues, this illustrates that the traditional "Ozzie and Harriet" family may have never been the norm. "The traditional family is an idea, not a fact," he claims (p. 228). In 1920, only 31% of children and youth in the U.S. lived their first 17 years in these types of families. This percentage fell to 16.3% by 1960, and estimates for succeeding decades have fallen to less than 10% (Hernandez, 1993).

The Reappearance of Widespread Child Poverty Between 1940 and 1980 there was a substantial increase in the proportion of adolescents living in demographically advantaged families in the United States (Cornwell, Eggebeen, & Meschke, 1996).

However, during the 1980s, the percentage of children living in poor families returned to the comparatively high level seen in 1949 (Hernandez, 1993). The percentage of children living in "middle-class comfort" decreased between 1969 and 1988 from 43% to 37% (Hernandez, 1993). Poverty among the general population of Canadians has increased over the decades as well. According to the "low-income cutoff" (spending more than 58.5% of income on food, shelter, and clothes), 14% of individuals were living in poverty in 1991. This shows

Table 8-7 Percentage of Children Living in "Ozzie and Harriet" Type Families: Father Is the Breadwinner, Mother Is the Homemaker (U.S.); Percentage of Families in Which Husband Is the Breadwinner, Wife Is the Homemaker (Canada)

United States (% of children)		Canada (% of families; with and without children)	
Year	Percentage	Year	Percentage
1940	40.8%	——	
1950	44.5%	——	
1960	43.1%	1967	58%
1970	37.3%	——	
1980	27.4%	1986	27%
——		1991	19%
——		1996	14%

Source: Based on Hernandez, 1993; Moore, 1989; Oderkirk, Silver, & Prud'homme, 1994; Vanier Institute of the Family, 2000.

an increase from 11.8% of the population in 1986 and from 12% of the population in 1981 (Ondercin-Bourne, 2003). Twenty percent of all Canadian children lived in poverty in 1997 (Jenson, 2001).

The Legacy of the Residential Schools

From 1883 until the mid-1970s, the Canadian government operated schools for First Nations children. The aim of these schools was to assimilate Aboriginal children into the majority culture (Morrissette, 1994). As stated by the Department of Indian and Northern Affairs (2000, p. 1), "Church and government leaders had come to the conclusion that the problem (as they saw it) of Aboriginal independence and 'savagery' could be solved by taking children from their families at an early age and instilling the ways of the dominant society during eight or nine years of residential schooling far from home." The aims of many government policies have been to undermine Aboriginal cultures and to stifle Aboriginal identity (Department of Indian and Northern Affairs, 2000). These policies of cultural genocide have had multigenerational effects on families and communities. Though unsuccessful in their intent to destroy traditional ways of life, these policies have most certainly forced many unwanted changes that continue to negatively affect Aboriginal people in Canada.

Children were targeted as the best way to assimilate Aboriginal people because they were seen to be more amenable to change than adults (Bedwell, 1999). They were removed from their parents and their traditional way of life to attend schools often located far away from their homes. It has been revealed that many of these schools were staffed by people who physically and sexually abused the children and punished them severely for speaking their own language. In addition, the children were often malnourished (Morrissette, 1994).

The banning of their cultural practices led to a feeling of disconnection with their families (Morrissette, 1994). The oral tradition of learning from elders was stymied, so children in residential schools often felt a loss of identity (Ing, 1991). They were taught that their language and culture were inferior to that of the majority culture, which caused them to suffer low self-esteem and to undervalue their people. Residential schools were not successful in instilling the values, skills, language, culture, and religion of the European majority culture, but children returning to their homes did

not initially share the values of their communities, either. This resulted in parent-child conflict (Ing, 1991).

Because children were taken away from their parents at such a young age and for such a long period of time, they never experienced healthy parenting or good role models (Bull, 1991; Ing, 1991). They learned little about child-rearing. When children of residential schools had children of their own, the only model they had to follow was the dysfunctional one they experienced at the residential schools. Thus, this generation experienced difficulties in their parenting roles. For example, disciplining their own children was difficult for them because they associated discipline with the lack of caring they experienced when they were growing up.

Parents who had themselves been raised in residential schools were unable to pass on traditions to the next generation because they were not given the opportunity to learn these and were punished for engaging in them while living in the residential schools. Some children were afraid to speak their original language even after they left the schools (Ing, 1991). This may also have resulted in a lack of communication among extended family members, who were then less able to be a part of the lives of children and youth. Thus, when the next generation became parents, they too faced challenges with parenting and were disconnected from their language and traditions.

Not only were the rights of parents to care for their children taken away but the rights of entire communities who would have helped raise these children were robbed by the residential schools. Traditional ways of self-governance that maintained community well-being were replaced by external systems (e.g., health, social services, justice), resulting in compartmentalized service delivery mostly in urban centres, far from home communities (e.g., Dyck, 1997). The lasting effects of these dramatic changes to community life and school experiences can be seen in high rates of internalizing and externalizing problems in the next generations. Substance abuse (Gfellner & Hundleby, 1991) and suicide (Health Canada, 1994; Sakinofsky & Leenaars, 1997) are examples of problems disproportionately affecting Aboriginal youth in Canada.

Conclusions About Historical Changes in the Family

Many family researchers (e.g., Hernandez, 1993; Milan, 2000; the Vanier Institute of the Family, 2000) embed the child-parent relation within a changing set of variables involving family structure and function and other key institutions of society (e.g., the educational system and the economy). The importance of this scholarship is that, at any given time, parent-child relations and the diversity in these relations are products of multiple historical changes in the contexts of family life. In other words, historical variation provides a basis for the diversity of parent-child relations that exists at any point. In addition, the nature of the changes that characterize the family over time makes clear the diversity of family structures and functions that exist in society and the implications of this diversity for differences in family-child relations and adolescent development.

Families differ in their size. Some families consist of two parents in the home and others have one. Some may have one or two children and others may have many more. Some exist in densely populated urban centres and others are found in sparsely populated rural settings. How families function to rear youth varies also. In some families, adherence to rules of conduct is stressed for youth, and other families emphasize sports and/or academic achievement. In some families, parents' job responsibilities require a youngster to take on numerous household duties often assumed by adults (e.g., shopping for food for the family, preparation of dinner for the family); in other families, adolescents are assigned few tasks. In some families, parents and adolescents interact in warm and almost peerlike ways, whereas in other families the roles of parent and child are kept quite distinct.

The diversity in the structure and function of the family context fosters variation in parent-child relations and in adolescent development. To understand these influences let's begin by discussing the role of family structure in adolescent development.

Family Structure: Diversity and Its Importance for Adolescent Development

ISSUES TO CONSIDER

- How do the variations in family structure influence the way parents interact with youth and how the youth behaves?
- What impact does the relation between family diversity and other contextual factors have on adolescent development?

As shown in Table 8.1, adolescents live in different family structures. This variation influences both the way parents interact with youth and how the adolescent behaves. In a study of urban African American adolescents living in either single-mother, stepparent, dual-parent, mother-with-extended-family (e.g., grandparents, aunt, uncle), or extended-family-only settings (e.g., only an aunt is present), the social support provided to youth was generally the same across family types, with one exception: Youth living in single-mother families were given *more* support than the youth in the other four family types (Zimmerman, Salem, & Maton, 1995).

Support to mothers, especially when provided by relatives, can enhance adolescent and maternal adjustment and improve the mother's parenting skills (Taylor & Roberts, 1995). Among 14- to 19-year-old African American youth, social support from kin was related to self-reliance and good school grades. When kinship support was low, the youth experienced feelings of distress (Taylor, 1996). Although differences in regard to academic achievement and high school grades are slight among youth living in either married, single-parent, or remarried families, large differences exist in regard to school dropout (Zimiles & Lee, 1991). Students from married families are least likely to drop out. Youth from such families are also less likely to experiment with drugs than are adolescents from single-parent families (Turner, Irwin, & Millstein, 1991).

When variation in family structure occurs in relation to other contextual factors—relating to parental education, family social support, parental mental health, and poverty, for instance—influences on the adolescent may be more pronounced. IQ scores for youth are lower in larger families, in which the mother's educational attainment and the family's social support are low and the family is of minority background and poor (Sameroff et al., 1993; Taylor, 1996).

Many youth enjoy the support provided by a large nuclear and extended family network.

Poverty Effects A family challenged by the economic stresses of poverty places its children at risk for problems of behaviour and health (Farran & Margolis, 1987). These implications of financial stress on youth development exist for families living in both rural and urban areas. Parents from farm families report higher levels of family financial stress and of depression than do parents from nonfarm families (Clark-Lempers, Lempers, & Netusil, 1990). In both farm and nonfarm families, however, financial stress felt by parents is related to depression among adolescents. Youth living in poor, rural families have more social and emotional problems and poor academic adjustment and school performance than do adolescents living in less financially disadvantaged households (Felner et al., 1995). In a study of poor families who either did or did not receive welfare benefits (Kalil & Eccles, 1998), there was little evidence that welfare receipt has a negative impact on parent-child interactions (although mothers on welfare do show less effective strategies for managing the behaviour of their youth).

The influence of economic hardship on youth development appears to occur through a process involving feelings of economic pressure by parents (e.g., the inability to pay monthly bills), which result in parents feeling depressed and demoralized. These feelings are associated with marital conflicts and disruptions of skillful parenting, which eventuates in problems of adolescent behaviour (Conger et al., 1992). Problematic outcomes of this process include the use of alcohol, antisocial behaviour, depression, anxiety, and/or hostility among young adolescents (Conger et al., 1991; Ge et al., 1992).

Despite the negative outcomes of poverty (Schorr, 1988, 1997), parents in even the poorest families can promote positive outcomes in their children (McAdoo, 1998, 1999; Spencer, 1995).

Among poor African American families, social support to mothers from their kin was associated with adolescent and maternal well-being and with higher quality parenting practices (e.g., firm control and monitoring) (Taylor & Roberts, 1995). A study of about 250 urban African American adolescent males found that these youth, living in single-parent, female head-of-household homes, reported more parental support than did youth living in stepparent, dual-parent, mother-and-extended-family, and extended-family-only households (Zimmerman, Salem, & Maton, 1995).

Although family poverty is a significant structural variable affecting youth development, other structural characteristics of the family are important to note as well. Some of them are discussed next.

The Role of Grandparents Grandparents have always been important parts of families, especially for families living in rural areas (Hernandez, 1993). Even today, grandchildren in farm families live closer to their grandparents and have more contact with them than is the case with nonfarm rural youth (King & Elder, 1995). Grandparents still often play an important role in the lives of grandchildren living in urban areas. They often live within driving distance of their grandchildren (Vanier Institute of the Family, 2000). In a Canadian study of university students (Boon and Brussoni, 1996), many young people reported feeling close to their grandparents, particularly their maternal grandmother, even though half of the sample had grandmothers who did not live in the same province. Individuals who reported a close relationship with a grandparent also felt that the grandparent was influential in their lives in terms of family ideals, moral beliefs, and work ethic (Brussoni and Boon, 1998).

Grandparents play an important role in single-parent families, especially in those headed by a female adolescent. In such contexts, grandparents provide critical social support to the mother (Spieker & Bensley, 1994). Grandfathers, in particular, have been found to enhance the quality of life in such families (Clingempeel et al., 1992; Oyserman, Radin, & Benn, 1993).

Marital Quality Conflicts and disagreements are typical parts of life. All individuals, couples, and groups can expect to have negative interactions from time to time. Of course, it is possible to have an over-

Grandparents are significant parts of contemporary family life.

all high-quality relationship despite occasional conflicts. However, when conflicts—arguments, fights, or even physical abuse—predominate in a relationship, the quality of the relationship tends to be quite poor. There is a negative impact of such relationships on the people in them and on the people living within the context in which they observe such a relationship.

When the parents of adolescents have a low-quality marriage, youth are adversely affected. In a longitudinal study of Grade 7 adolescents in the rural Midwestern United States, marital conflict was related to the presence of what are termed **internalizing problems** (e.g., depression or anxiety) and **externalizing problems** (e.g., aggression) among youth (Harold & Conger, 1997). Parents not only showed negative behaviours to each other, but also showed hostility toward their adolescent children (Harold & Conger, 1997). In another study of youth from Utah and Tennessee, parental conflict and hostility were associated with youth problem behaviours (Buehler et al., 1998).

In a study of Japanese youth and their families (Gjerde & Shimizu, 1995), parent disagreement in regard to how the adolescent should be socialized was related to adjustment problems among youth. In addition, boys who were more closely aligned with their mothers' points of view were most likely to have adjustment problems (Gjerde & Shimizu, 1995).

Whereas poor marital quality can negatively impact adolescents, good marital quality can be a positive influence. In a longitudinal study of adolescent boys, parents' satisfaction with their marriage was related to good peer relations (Feldman & Wentzel, 1995). When mothers and fathers share equal levels of family power, there are positive influences on youth emotional adjustment (Wentzel & Feldman, 1996). However, for male adolescents, when mothers have more power in the marriage than do fathers, there is a likelihood that depression will occur in the adolescent (Wentzel & Feldman, 1996).

The positive benefits on adolescents of parental marital satisfaction may extend into adolescents' adulthood. In a longitudinal study of youth first studied when they were 13- to 18-year-olds and then

again when they were between 18 and 25 years of age, marital satisfaction, especially for mothers, was related to the emotional and physical health of the young adults (Feldman, Fisher, & Seitel, 1997).

In sum, marital quality is associated with adolescent behaviour and development. However, marital quality can have other ramifications. When the quality of a marriage is poor, parents may obtain a divorce, a transition that impacts youth behaviour and development.

Influences of Divorce About 50% of all marriages in the United States and 36% of all marriages in Canada that began over the last quarter century will end in divorce (Hetherington & Clingempeel, 1988; Sessa & Steinberg, 1991), and as many as 60% of American children born in the 1990s will live for a time in a single-parent family (Bumpass & Sweet, 1989; Furstenberg & Cherlin, 1991; Simons et al., 1994). Some studies suggest that divorce may not have an influence on particular instances of adolescent development. For example, decisions made by adolescents or their parents about health and safety do not differ between married and divorced families (Jacobs, Bennett, & Flanagan, 1993). Some studies of adolescents from divorced families find no difference in self-esteem (Clark & Barber, 1994), self-image, depression, or anxiety (Dunlop & Burns, 1995), although most research does find differences. Some studies of older adolescents find more similarities than differences between those who have been brought up with divorced versus married parents. For example, in a study of McGill University students, Bolgar, Zweig-Frank, and Paris (1995) found no group differences in six of eight scales assessing interpersonal problems. Differences that were found were in the areas of control (individuals from divorced families were more likely to describe themselves as too controlling of others) and in difficulty in being submissive (individuals from divorced families tended to describe themselves as having more difficulty in collaborative working relationships).

Divorce can have negative effects on an adolescent. Most research indicates that divorce is associated with social, academic, and personal adjustment problems, including those associated with early initiation of sexual behaviour (e.g., Brody & Forehand, 1990; Carson, Madison, & Santrock, 1987; Demo & Acock, 1988; Doherty & Needle, 1991; Hetherington, 1991; Hetherington, Cox, & Cox, 1985; Simons et al., 1994; Whitbeck, Simons, &

Internalizing problems
Behaviour problems not expressed toward one's environment but rather directed to one's mental or emoting functioning (e.g., depression or anxiety).

Externalizing problems
Behaviour problems expressed through actions toward one's environment and, thereby, easily visible to others (e.g., aggression).

Kao, 1994; Zaslow, 1988, 1989). Ambert (1998) reported that 65% of young offenders in Montreal had divorced parents. Adolescents who experienced the divorce of their parents were less likely to finish high school than their peers in two-parent families (Frederick & Boyd, 1998; as cited in Ambert, 1998). In a longitudinal study involving over 17 000 youth from Great Britain (Chase-Lansdale, Cherlin, & Kiernan, 1995), parental divorce was found to impact adult mental health. Although most individuals did not experience serious emotional disorders after divorce, the risk of having such problems did increase (Chase-Lansdale et al., 1995).

Parent-child relations in divorced families are less hierarchical and children are encouraged to grow up faster (Smetana, 1993).

Whereas conflictual parent-child relations are not the norm in adolescence, such problematic interactions tend to occur more often in single-parent families and stepfamilies (Demo & Acock, 1996; Montemayor, 1986; Steinberg, 1991). Divorced families and stepfamilies have higher levels of mother-adolescent disagreement, lower levels of parental supervision, and lower levels of mother-adolescent interaction than do first-married families or families headed by continuously single mothers (Demo & Acock, 1996); however, this may depend on the length of time since separation or remarriage (e.g., Hetherington, Anderson, & Hagan, 1991).

The period following separation and divorce seems to be particularly stressful for youth (Doherty & Needle, 1991), especially if the adolescent is caught between divorced parents engaged in continuing, conflictual, and hostile interactions (Brody & Forehand, 1990; Buchanan, Maccoby, & Dornbusch, 1991). Adolescents who felt close to their parents were less likely to feel caught between them (Galambos & Ehrenberg, 1997). In the period immediately after a divorce, there are numerous instances of behavioural disruption and emotional upheaval (Hetherington, Anderson, & Hagan, 1991). Increases occur in aggression and noncompliance with rules, decreases occur in academic achievement and school adjustment, and there are problems that occur in peer interactions and in sexual behaviour (Hetherington et al., 1991). It may take two years or more for the family to establish a new equilibrium (Hetherington et al., 1985).

The effects of divorce seem to be more pervasive, problematic, and long lasting for boys than for girls (Beaty, 1995; Hetherington et al., 1991). Although girls tend to react more negatively than boys prior to the parents' separation, they also tend to adapt better than boys after the divorce (Doherty & Needle, 1991; Hetherington et al., 1985). Girls from single-mother, divorced homes have problematic sexual and heterosexual behaviours. They are more likely to marry early, be pregnant at the time of their marriage, and wed immature men (Hetherington, 1989). Given that, after divorce, 90% of children are in mother-custody homes (Hetherington et al., 1991), these problems related to girls may be quite widespread. However, as with other historical changes, this pattern may vary over time.

In a study following young adolescents into their young adulthood (Summers et al., 1998), individuals from divorced families had less secure romantic attachments in young adulthood than did youth from nondivorced families. However, a study conducted at the University of Victoria (Walker & Ehrenberg, 1998) found that whether or not young adults developed secure romantic relationships depended on their perceptions of the reasons for the parental divorce. They reported that adolescent perception of overt anger expressed by the parents, extramarital affairs, and involvement of children in the parental decision to divorce distinguished young adults with secure versus insecure attachment styles.

Remarriage can lead to additional problems for youth. There is evidence that both male and female adolescents may have difficulty interacting with stepfathers, although girls may have particular problems (Lee et al., 1994; Vuchinich et al., 1991), possibly because their mothers relied on them as confidants and advisors prior to the remarriage. Both male and female adolescents show no improvement in their relationship with their stepfather or in behaviour problems (e.g., regarding school grades) associated with the divorce two years or more after the remarriage (Hetherington, 1991; Lee et al., 1994). However, living with a stepfather, as compared to living with a stepmother, is associated with more positive self-esteem among both male and female adolescents (Fine & Kurdek, 1992). A study of Montreal university students provided some evidence that a stable remarriage can have positive long-term results (Bolgar, Zweig-Frank, & Paris, 1995). These individuals had fewer problems with intimacy or over-control (they were no different from peers brought up with both biological parents) than a group whose mothers never remarried or who had remarried several times.

In turn, living under the custody of one's biological father is linked to problems for both male and

Teens in Divorcing Families: Adolescents' Perceptions of What Helps and Hinders

Marion Ehrenberg received her Ph.D. in clinical psychology from Simon Fraser University in 1991. She is currently an associate professor and the director of Clinical Training in the Department of Psychology at University of Victoria.

Many adolescents are affected by their parents' separation and divorce. Teens who experience their parents' break-up during childhood are faced with a subsequent family transition, such as one or both of their parents remarrying, during adolescence. It is well known that adolescents who have experienced their parents' divorces and other family transitions are, on average, at greater risk for difficulties in social, emotional, behavioural, cognitive, and school adjustment. Although these potentially negative effects of family change on adolescents may be long lasting, it is also known that the majority of children and adolescents in divorcing families achieve positive health outcomes in the long term.

While the identification of risk factors for children and adolescents in divorcing families has been a long-standing priority for family researchers, it is only more recently that an emphasis on protective factors and positive coping has been incorporated into research. At the Families in Motion Research and Information Group (www.uvic.ca/psyc/fmric), we are particularly interested in psychosocial factors that influence positive coping and outcomes for adolescents affected by family changes.

In a recent study, we considered that health opportunities might be evident in support- and help-seeking efforts exercised by teens faced with changing family systems. Although a literature demonstrating the effectiveness of psychoeducational and supportive groups for children and parents in divorcing families has accumulated, we also know that the majority of adolescents in need of help do not seek, or receive, any type of formal assistance. We were interested in learning more about the attitudes, perceptions, and experiences of help-needing and help-seeking teens in divorcing families. We also kept in mind that there is a developmental literature that suggests that adolescents are more likely to seek support from their friends than from adults. We wanted to answer questions about where teens go for support when faced with family stresses. Do they turn to each other? If they need more than peer

support, what helps them to get this additional assistance? What gets in the way of them accessing this help, if they want it?

We surveyed a representative sample of 3198 adolescent boys and girls, between the ages of 11 and 19 years, enrolled at nine secondary schools in British Columbia. The schools were selected to reflect a diversity of urban and rural communities, socioeconomic circumstances, and independent and public school systems. Of the surveyed adolescents, 29% had experienced their parents' marital separation and divorce, which is what one would expect based on current statistics. Interestingly, there was a great deal of variability in the extent to which parental divorce was relatively rare (just over 10%) to very common (over 50%) within a given school and neighbourhood. We developed an "Adolescent Divorce Questionnaire" that used open-ended questions, such as "Where would be the best place to go if you wanted help figuring out your feelings about your parents' separation or divorce or knowing what to do in that situation?" Developing a reliable coding system to accurately capture the teens' written responses is a time-consuming task, but we felt it was important to do so in trying to "look through the eyes" of these adolescents, in their own language and terms. We also included rating scale questions to give a balanced qualitative and quantitative methodology.

Seeking an adult helping professional, leaning on friends, talking to extended family members, and just "getting away" from the family problems were seen as the top-ranking options for adolescents in divorcing families. This was true of adolescents regardless of age or gender, but girls did emphasize seeking help from a knowledgeable adult or talking to friends more strongly than did boys. For those adolescents who wish to receive assistance about difficult family matters, adolescents perceived that peer support, recognition that one needs the help, personal strength, and family support were instrumental in getting a young person to take steps toward actually getting this assistance. What is likely to hold an adolescent needing help back from accessing that

help? Adolescents perceived that feeling overwhelmed and immobilized by negative feelings about the parents' separation was the most important obstacle in getting help. Negative peer influences, such as being teased about wanting to get help, having a negative view of the help-seeking process, being "in denial" about one's situation, and not wanting to add to the family's problems were viewed as other key hindrances.

In focusing on the adolescents who had actually sought help about their parents' divorces we learned that, consistent with our thinking, the majority of adolescents (79%) had talked to friends and found this to be helpful. Of these help-seeking-experienced teens, 42% had talked to their mothers about their feelings (regardless of age or gender), but only 8% had talked to their fathers. It is important to remember that the majority of children and adolescents in divorced families live with their mothers and have varying degrees of contact with their fathers. More than one-third of the adolescents who had experienced a family disruption had seen an adult therapist or counsellor and, consistent with findings from another of our recent studies, siblings were also very important confidants. As was our emphasis in this study, the majority of our respondents demonstrated an optimistic, open, and trusting orientation toward reaching out to others at times of family stress, with female adolescents reflecting this orientation more strongly than male adolescents. We are trying to use our findings to develop a model of help-seeking among adolescents, as well as prevention and intervention programs for teens in divorcing families, that fully incorporate their natural coping orientation and developmentally relevant help-seeking options illuminated in this study.

female adolescents (Lee et al., 1994). Adolescents living with their fathers adjust more poorly than youth living in other arrangements. This reaction seems to be due to the closeness they have with their father, and the monitoring provided by him (Buchanan, Maccoby, & Dornbusch, 1992). The risk of drug use is also increased among youth living in father-custody families (Hoffmann & Johnson, 1998).

Effects of Maternal Employment The majority of North American mothers work outside the home. They do so for personal, social, and economic reasons (Hernandez, 1993; J. Lerner, 1994). Regardless of their reasons for working, maternal employment generally has not been found to have adverse effects on the personal or social development of youth (J. Lerner & Galambos, 1985, 1991). There are also some benefits to having two working parents.

Adolescents whose mothers work outside the home do not differ from youth with nonemployed mothers in regard to variables such as adjustment (Armistead, Wierson, & Forehand, 1990; Galambos & Maggs, 1990), the nature of the mother-adolescent relationship (Galambos & Maggs, 1990), adolescent responsibility and self-management (Keith et al., 1990), and adolescent sexual attitudes and behaviours (Wright, Peterson, & Barnes, 1990). There also does not appear to be a difference among adolescents with full-time, part-time, or nonemployed mothers in regard to conflict or social interactions (Laursen, 1995). However, and independent of employment status, youth in single-mother households do have more conflict with their mothers than is the case with youth in two-parent families (Laursen, 1995). Thus single parenthood, and not employment, predicts youth problems.

In turn, in a study of the relation between maternal employment and mathematics achievement among approximately 14 000 American youth, unsupervised time after school, rather than maternal employment, was the major determinant of achievement (Muller, 1995). Overall, youth with nonemployed mothers did slightly worse than did youth with mothers who worked either full time or part time.

Maternal employment can create a sense of **role strain** in some mothers. A working mother may find it difficult to balance the demands of her role of worker with the demands of her role as mother, or she may feel dissatisfied with her role. Such role strain occurs when the mother feels there is a poor match between her aspirations or education and her job duties (Joebgen & Richards, 1990) or when she

is in the midst of work transitions (Flanagan & Eccles, 1993). Because of the nature of her multiple roles, the mother feels stress, and when such stress or role strain is experienced, a negative influence on adolescent adjustment can occur (Galambos et al., 1995; J. Lerner, 1994; J. Lerner & Galambos, 1985, 1991). However, when mothers find they can handle the stress associated with their work overload, the influence on their adolescents' adjustment is improved (Galambos et al., 1995). A similar finding occurred among working fathers and their adolescents. When fathers felt stressed by being overloaded at work there was more conflict between parents and adolescents, and thus also more adolescent problem behaviour. When both mothers and fathers were highly stressed, parent-adolescent conflict was particularly high. However, the effects of this conflict on adolescent problem behaviour was buffered if the mother and adolescent had an accepting relationship (Galambos & Ehrenberg, 1997).

Aside from the risks to adolescent development, Galambos and Ehrenberg (1997) pointed out some advantages of dual working parents. For example, when parents were able to provide material as well as emotional support for an adolescent's talent (e.g., music lessons, sports equipment), this talent was able to thrive. However, when this support was unavailable, the adolescent often lost the talent (Csikszentmihalyi, Rathunde, & Whalen, 1993, as cited in Galambos & Ehrenberg, 1997). An employed mother may also become a role model and break down sex-role stereotypes and serve to model a strong work ethic (Galambos & Ehrenberg, 1997). Father-adolescent relationships have an opportunity to improve when mothers are working, as fathers tend to spend more time in child-care activities when mothers work. Those fathers who are more involved with their adolescents (driving them places, taking care of them, spending time with them) tend to be more accepting of them six months later (Almeida & Galambos, 1991, as cited in Galambos & Ehrenberg, 1997).

Parental Work and Adolescents in Self-Care For many youth, when their parents are at work, there is no adult in the home. Indeed, a mother's time

Role strain Often associated with maternal employment, the difficulty of balancing the demands of one's role as a worker and the demands of being a parent.

at work is associated with the amount of unsupervised time a youth experiences after, and sometimes before, school (Muller, 1995; Richards & Duckett, 1994). Unsupervised time, especially between the hours of 3 p.m. and 8 p.m., represents a problem period for youth. During these times, they often do not spend their time profitably (e.g., they just "hang out"), or they engage in high risk and/or illegal behaviours (Carnegie Corporation of New York, 1992). Problems are especially high if adolescents spend this time with peers. However, if parents have an authoritative parenting style (warm and nurturing while exerting firm control), "latch-key" adolescents do not engage in problem behaviour (Galambos & Ehrenberg, 1997). The lack of supervision during this time and not maternal employment is the source of these difficulties for youth.

Effective community programs for youth, such as 4-H or Boys and Girls Clubs, and community athletics, can provide youth with positive and productive ways to spend their time. Current opinion among leaders of youth-serving organizations is that if such community programs are strengthened, young adolescents will have richer experiences and fewer life problems (Carnegie Corporation of New York, 1992).

Families with Adopted Adolescents As is the case for other families, families with youth who have been adopted try to create strong and healthy connections between the adolescent and his or her family and the larger community (Grotevant, 1997). These families strive to regulate the adolescent's behaviour in appropriate ways, and to instill in him or her the capacity for autonomy and the basis for a healthy identity (see Chapter 6) (Grotevant, 1997).

In a study of about 700 adoptive families in the United States, comparisons were made among adoptive adolescents and "birth" adolescents (i.e., youth

Conflict is an inevitable part of family life.

born into their families) (Sharma, McGue, & Benson, 1998). Scores of the adopted youth on various psychological tests were also compared to the norms (i.e., expected average scores) on these tests. The results of these comparisons indicated that in some cases adopted adolescents had higher adjustment scores than the comparison groups (e.g., for adopted boys in regard to withdrawn behaviours and for adopted girls in regard to withdrawn behaviours and social problems), whereas, in other cases the adopted youth had lower scores (e.g., for adopted girls in regard to delinquent behaviours and externalizing behaviours) (Sharma et al., 1998). A similar pattern of positive and negative differences was found in a study of adopted adolescents in the Netherlands (Hoksbergen, 1997).

Given the presence of these contrasting implications for adolescent adjustment, we should not make any generalization about whether adoption results in problems or benefits for adopted youth (Sharma et al., 1998). Instead, it is important to conduct additional research to discover how families of adopted youth can best pursue their goals of promoting positive development and preventing negative outcomes among these adolescents (Grotevant, 1997; Sharma et al., 1998).

Conclusions About Family Structure

Neither across history nor within contemporary society do we find one structure of the family. Families are diverse, and this diversity may be associated with either positive *or* negative developments in adolescence. It is simply not the case that one family structure is ideal for all people, living under all conditions, at all points in time.

The important issue for science is what sorts of family structures are associated with what types of family functions and how these links between structure and parenting influence adolescent development. The key issue for the application of developmental science is how to maximize the probability of healthy adolescent development, given the family structures and parenting experiences that youth encounter.

To address these key issues of science and application it is important to understand the central role of the family: parenting. Parents of adolescents use quite different styles of behaviour to rear their offspring. This variation is associated with differences in the success of parents in socializing their youth and with diversity in the sorts of relationships parents have with their adolescent children. All this variation creates considerable diversity in adolescents' development.

Parenting: Child-Rearing Styles, Socialization, and Parent-Adolescent Relationships

ISSUE TO CONSIDER
• What are the key functions of parenting?

The key function of a child's family is to raise the young person in as healthy a manner as possible (e.g., see Bornstein, 1995). Although there is variation in different cultures in the family structures used to serve this function (e.g., Harrison et al., 1997), the caregiver's role is always to provide the child with a safe, secure, nurturant, loving, and supportive environment, one that allows the child to have a happy and healthy youth. This sort of experience allows youth to develop the knowledge, values, attitudes, and behaviours necessary to become an adult who makes a productive contribution to self, family, community, and society (Lerner et al., 1995).

What a parent does to fulfill these duties of his or her role is called *parenting*, a term that summarizes behaviours used by a person, usually, but not exclusively, the mother or father, to raise a child. Parenting is both a biological and a social process (Lerner et al., 1995; Tobach & Schneirla, 1968). Biologically, parenting summarizes the set of behaviours involved across life in the relations among organisms who are usually **conspecifics** (members of the same species), and typically members of different generations or, at the least, of different birth cohorts. Parenting interactions provide resources across the generational groups and function in regard to domains of survival, reproduction, nurturance, and socialization.

Parenting is a complex process, involving much more than a mother or father providing food, safety, and comfort to an infant or child. Parenting involves bidirectional relationships between members of two or more generations and can extend through all or major parts of the respective life spans of these groups. It may engage all institutions within a culture (including educational, economic, political, and social ones), and is embedded in the history of a people, as that history occurs within the natural and the designed setting within which the group lives (Ford & Lerner, 1992).

Adults differ in the ways in which they enact their role as parent. They show different styles of raising their children. Differences in child-rearing styles are associated with important variation in adolescent development.

Child-Rearing Styles in Adolescence

ISSUES TO CONSIDER
• What are the various parenting styles as defined by both Baumrind and Maccoby and Martin?
• How does specific parenting style impact adolescent development?

The classic research of Diana Baumrind (1967, 1971) resulted in the identification of three major types of child-rearing styles: **authoritative, authoritarian**, and **permissive**. The authoritative style of rearing is marked by parental warmth, the use of rules and reasoning (induction) to promote obedience and keep discipline, nonphysical punishment (e.g., using "time out" or "grounding" instead of physical punishment), and consistency between statements and actions and across time (Baumrind, 1971; Lamborn et al., 1991). Authoritarian parents are not warm, stress rigid adherence to the rules they set (obey—just because we, the parents, are setting the rules), emphasize the power of their role, and use physical (corporal) punishment for transgressions (Baumrind, 1971; Belsky et al., 1984). Permissive parents do not show consistency in their use of rules, they may have a laissez-faire attitude toward their child's behaviours (i.e., they may either not attend to the child or let him or

Conspecifics Organisms that are members of the same species.
Authoritative parenting Parenting marked by parental warmth and the use of rules and reasoning to promote obedience and keep discipline.

Authoritative parents use nonphysical punishment and maintain consistency between their statements and actions across time.
Authoritarian parenting Parenting marked by lack of warmth and rigid adherence to

the rules set by parents. Authoritarian parents emphasize their power in the family and tend to use physical punishment.
Permissive parenting Parenting marked by lack of consistency in parents' use of rules.

Permissive parents tend to have a laissez-faire attitude toward their child(ren)'s behaviours. The parents often overindulge their child(ren)'s requests and act more as a peer or an independent observer.

her do whatever he or she wants), and they may give the child anything he or she requests; their style may be characterized as being either more of a peer or, instead, an independent "observer" of their child. Indeed, because of the diversity of behavioural patterns that can characterize the permissive parenting style, Maccoby and Martin (1983) proposed that this approach to parenting can best be thought of as two distinct types: **indulgent** (e.g., "If my child wants something, I give it to her") and **neglectful** (e.g., "I really don't know what my child is up to. I don't really keep close tabs on her").

Whether the three categories of rearing style originally proposed by Baumrind (1967, 1971), the four categories suggested by Maccoby and Martin (1983), or other labels are employed, the use of different parenting styles is clearly associated with differences in adolescent behaviour and development (Lamborn et al., 1991; Mboya, 1995; Smetana, 1995). In a study of more than 4000 14- to 18-year-olds, adolescents with authoritative parents had more social competence and fewer psychological and behavioural problems than youth with authoritarian, indulgent, or neglectful parents (Lamborn et al., 1991). Youth with neglectful parents were the least socially competent and had the most psychological and behavioural problems of any group of adolescents in the study. In turn, youth with authoritarian parents were obedient and conformed well to authority, but had poorer self-concepts than other adolescents. Youth with indulgent parents had high self-confidence, but they more often abused substances, misbehaved in school, and were less engaged in school.

In a study of about 10 000 high school students, adolescents whose parents were accepting, firm, and democratic achieved higher school grades, were more self-reliant, less anxious and depressed, and less likely to engage in delinquent behaviour than were youth with parents using other rearing styles (Steinberg et al., 1991). This influence of authoritative parenting held for youth of different ethnic and socioeconomic backgrounds and regardless of whether the adolescent's family was married. Similarly, a group of Ontario high school students who described their

parents as authoritative were more likely than other high school students to respond to parental advice with understanding and respect (Mackey, Arnold & Pratt, 2001). Adolescents with authoritative parents are also more likely to have well-rounded peer groups, that is, groups that admire both adult as well as youth values and norms (e.g., academic achievement/school success and athletics/social popularity, respectively) (Durbin et al., 1993). Youth with uninvolved parents had peer groups that did not support adult norms or values, and boys with indulgent parents were in peer groups that stressed fun and partying (Durbin et al., 1993).

A great deal of research has assessed the link between parenting styles and school behaviours and achievements. For example, among 14- to 16-year-old rural and urban Quebec students, supervision and psychological autonomy-granting predicted higher grades for male students and parental warmth predicted higher female students' grades (Deslandes, Bouchard, & St. Amant, 1998). In a longitudinal study of adolescents from California and Wisconsin, non-authoritative parenting was associated with youth attributing academic outcomes to external causes or to low ability (Glasgow et al., 1997). Nonauthoritative parents, whose styles are either unengaged or authoritarian and directive, have youth who score poorly both in regard to measures of academic achievement in college and in respect to measures of personality, adjustment, and substance use (Weiss & Schwarz, 1996). First-year Canadian university students adapted better if they had been parented in an authoritative style (Wintre & Yaffe, 2000).

When parents are connected to and involved with their adolescents, better educational outcomes are seen (Herman et al., 1997). In a longitudinal study of about 350 Grade 7 students, parenting practices fostered change in adolescents' academic accomplishments (Melby & Conger, 1996). When mothers and fathers set and reinforced appropriate behaviours in their adolescent children, academic performance improved. If parents were hostile to their adolescents, academic performance decreased (Melby & Conger, 1996). In a longitudinal study of adolescents in the United Kingdom (Shucksmith, Hendry, & Glendinning, 1995), authoritative parenting was related to both school integration and mental well-being. Furthermore, in a study of 10 000 high school students, parental involvement in their adolescent's schooling was associated with better school performance among youth (Bogenschneider, 1997).

Indulgent parenting Parenting marked by overly permissive and condoning behaviour toward one's child (e.g., "If my child wants something, I give it to him").

Neglectful parenting Parenting marked by inattentive, careless behaviour toward one's child (e.g., "I really don't know what my child is up to. I don't really keep close tabs on her").

Monitoring by parents seems to be an especially important feature of authoritative parenting. Among approximately 900 African American youth living in Alabama or New York City and Latino youth living in Puerto Rico or New York City, higher levels of parental monitoring were related to lower levels of adolescent problem or deviant behaviours (Forehand et al., 1997). Among more than 600 pairs of European American mothers and adolescents and more than 500 pairs of European American fathers and adolescents, more parental monitoring and less parental psychological control was related to adolescent academic and psychosocial competence (Bogenschneider, Small, & Tsay, 1997).

Considerable additional research confirms the generally positive influence on adolescent development of authoritative parenting and the developmental problems that emerge in youth when parents are authoritarian, permissive, indulgent, or uninvolved (e.g., Almeida & Galambos, 1991; Baumrind, 1991; Brown et al., 1993; Feldman & Wood, 1994; Melby & Conger, 1996; Paulson, 1994; Simons, Johnson, & Conger, 1994; Wentzel, Feldman, & Weinberger, 1991). Poor parental discipline is linked to problems in adolescent adjustment among both rural Iowa youth and urban Oregon youth (Conger, Patterson, & Ge, 1995). In a longitudinal study of about 500 adolescents, harsh discipline by parents was associated with stress and depression among youth (Wagner, Cohen, & Brook, 1996). Warm parenting was linked to lower depression (Wagner et al., 1996). Among Australian adolescents, punitive discipline styles in parents is related to delinquency among boys (Peiser & Heaven, 1996), and authoritative (inductive) parenting is related to low levels of delinquency (Peiser & Heaven, 1996). Disruptive boys in a Montreal sample were followed from kindergarten to age 13; those whose mothers parented in an authoritarian style were more likely to develop early onset substance abuse than those whose mothers parented in a nonauthoritarian style (Dobkin, Tremblay, & Sacchitelle, 1997).

One especially problematic feature of ineffective parenting styles such as authoritarian ones appears to be the use of physical (corporal) punishment. In a nationally representative sample of 1042 boys and 958 girls between the ages of 10 and 16 years in the United States, parental use of corporal punishment was related to adolescent depression and distress (Turner & Finkelhor, 1996). In a study of about 4400 couples, corporal punishment was found to be linked to subsequent aggression in youth and to an increased likelihood of future, marital violence (Straus & Yodanis, 1996). Because corporal punishment is used in more than half of the families in the United States, such relationships between this type of punishment and adolescent outcomes is alarming (Straus & Yodanis, 1996).

Finally, the research on parenting styles confirms that the positive influences of authoritative parenting extend to the adolescent's choice of and involvement with peers (e.g., Brown et al., 1993). As discussed in Chapter 9, the influence of parents is often highly consistent with the influence of peers among adolescents (Lerner & Galambos, 1998).

Socialization in Adolescence

ISSUES TO CONSIDER
- How do different cultures define a socially successful individual?
- What are the different ways of identifying if and how society has been successful in socializing youth?
- How do parents influence the socialization process?

Whatever style parents use to rear their adolescents, the goal of parenting is to raise a child who is healthy and successful in life, who can contribute to self and to society, who accepts and works to further the social order. The behaviours used over time to reach these goals are termed *socialization*. Although all societies socialize their youth (in order that, as future contributors to society, the society can survive and prosper), there are marked differences in what different societies, or groups within society, want to see in a youth who has been "successfully" socialized. Said another way, there is great diversity in the specific approaches and goals parents have in socializing their youth.

There are differences between approaches in individualist and collectivist cultures regarding the communication of values to children. Studies of immigrants to Canada from more collectivist cultures highlight these differences. Egyptian Canadian adults who were first or second-generation immigrants were found to differ from Anglo Canadian adults on the importance of power in the role of parent, but not in terms of warmth, negative attributions about children, or flexibility in parent-child problem-solving. (Rudy & Grusec, 2001). In a study of the social experiences of 15- to 17-year-old second-generation South Asian immigrants in Montreal, participants reported differential treatment of boys and girls at home, with girls given less decision-making power and less control over their opposite-sex associations (Talbani & Hasanali, 2000).

One way of illustrating this contextual variation and of judging whether parents and society at large have been successful in shaping youth to accept social values is to ask youth what it means to be a good or a bad child. In one study (Crystal & Stevenson, 1995) that took this approach, American, Japanese, and Chinese adolescents were asked, "What is a bad kid?" In the United States, youth answered that a lack of self-control and substance abuse were the marks of being bad. In China, a youth who engaged in acts against society was judged as bad. In Japan, a youth who created disruptions of interpersonal harmony was regarded as bad.

Another way of understanding the socialization process is to see how immigrants to a new country give up the values and customs of their country of origin and adopt those of their new country—a set of changes termed **acculturation**. In a study of Chinese migrant high-school students in Canada it was found that adaptation to the new country was affected by societal, situational, and individual variables (Leung, 2001). During the resettlement process, Southeast Asian refugee youth in Toronto aged 15 to 20 years struggled with language barriers at school and at home, with high parental standards for achievement, and with fitting into a peer group (Hyman, Vu, & Beiser, 2000). They also reported a need to express gratitude to their parents or repay them for the sacrifices they made in order to provide a better life for their children in Canada. Their respect for parental values and a desire to maintain their ways of life sometimes collided with an attraction to some incompatible Canadian values and practices, such as self-fulfillment and what they described as an "open" style of communication observed in Canadian families. Furthermore, a different study found that Canadian youth who were recent immigrants reported a greater emphasis on faith than their Canadian-born peers and less participation in religious activities over time as they became more integrated into their new country (cited in Canadian Council on Social Development, 1999).

Another approach to understanding socialization is to appraise whether different groups within a society direct their youth to comparable developmental achievements. Research in Israel, for instance, suggests that youth from Arab Israeli families are raised to view the father as having more power than the mother. Conversely, Jewish Israeli youth see more maternal than paternal power (Weller, Florian, & Mikulincer, 1995). In Japan, problems of adolescent adjustment are most likely to occur for boys who are aligned with their mothers, but whose mothers and fathers disagree about socialization practices (Gjerde & Shimizo, 1995). Male and female adolescents who emigrated from developing countries to Norway differ in their attitudes toward acculturation (Sam, 1995). Although both groups place a lot of importance on maintaining their cultural heritage, boys favour acculturation more than girls. Differences in socialization practices can be seen cross-culturally. A comparison of Canadian, Belgian, and Italian youth in their home countries found that family plays the most central role in the relational world of Italian adolescents, peers play the most central role for Canadian adolescents, and Belgian adolescents were between the extremes (Claes, 1998).

Whereas in the United States there is evidence of consistency in some socialization practices across diverse groups (e.g., in regard to the development of mental health among Latino and European American youth; Knight, Virdin, & Roosa, 1994), there is also research indicating that practices vary in different American groups. For instance, African American parents more frequently discuss prejudice with their adolescent children than is the case for Japanese American or Mexican American parents (Phinney & Chavira, 1995); in addition, both African American and Japanese American parents emphasize adaptation to society more so than is the case with Mexican American parents.

How successful are parents' attempts at socialization? By virtue of the fact that society continues to evolve and is not characterized by intergenerational warfare or revolution, and that the vast majority of youth become contributing adults to society, we can conclude that socialization "works," that the "apple does not fall far from the tree" (Adelson, 1970; Lerner, 1986). Indeed, during adolescence very few families—estimates are between 5% and 10%—experience a major deterioration in the parent-child relationship (Steinberg, 1991). Not only do parents expect to see change in their sons' and daughters' behaviours as they socialize them during adolescence (Freedman-Doan et al., 1993), but, through their

Acculturation Process of cultural change during which a member/group of one culture gives up his or her/their own values and customs and adopts those from a different culture.

interactions on a day-to-day basis, parents can also model and/or shape the cognitive, emotional, and behavioural attributes they desire to see in their offspring (e.g., Eisenberg & McNally, 1993; Grotevant, 1998; Larson & Richards, 1994; Simons, Finlay, & Yang, 1991; Whitbeck, 1987). It is through the relationships that parents and their adolescent children have that the most immediate bases of youth behaviour and development are provided.

Parent-Child Relationships in Adolescence

Anyone who has ever been entertained by a stand-up comic knows that at some point in the performance, his or her parents will be blamed for one or even a host of psychological and social ills besetting the performer. However, you do not have to dig very deep under the surface of the monologue to realize that in addition to the comic's parents being a source of humour, they are also a source of love and admiration. The reason that such comic routines are so frequent and so popular is that they reflect a virtually universal reaction to our parents: ambivalence. We love and respect our parents and yet we often are frustrated by them and/or angry with or exasperated by them. Mark Twain's famous observation—that at age 14 he could not believe how stupid and embarrassing his father was but that, at age 21, he was amazed to see how much the old man had learned in just seven years—perhaps captures for all of us the often mixed reactions we have about our parents.

Such reactions mirror the nature of research findings about parent-child relations in adolescence. A

Parent-child conflict may occur when adolescents try to exert their independence in ways unacceptable to parents.

range of behaviours and associated emotions are exchanged between parents and their adolescent offspring. Some of these exchanges involve positive and healthy behaviours and others not. Some of the outcomes for adolescent development of these exchanges reflect good adjustment and individual and social success, whereas other outcomes reflect poor adjustment and problems of development. As is true for all facets of human development, there is diversity in the nature and implications of parent-child relations in adolescence.

Parent and Adolescent Expectations About Their Relationship Collins (1997; Collins et al., 1997) has noted that the relationships between adolescents and their parents involve the expectations that youth have about their parents (e.g., my parents will support my interest in sports; my parents will ground me for a week if I break my curfew) and the expectations that parents have about their adolescent children (e.g., I don't want to see your involvement in sports interfere with your doing your homework or your getting good grades; I expect that you will know enough not to go to a party where kids are drinking). Both youth and their parents expect that across the adolescent age period young people will become more autonomous, that is, able to make their own decisions about their behaviour (e.g., when to go to bed, how long to talk on the phone, if and at what time a curfew should be set, and food choices).

Often, however, parents and youth disagree about the age at which such transitions from parent-determined behaviours to adolescent-determined behaviours should occur. For example, at what age should a parent allow his or her child to decide when to come home from a date? In a study of mothers and their 10- through 17-year-old adolescents, most discrepancies in opinions about the timing of these transitions to autonomous behaviour occurred for 13- to 15-year-old youth (Collins et al., 1997).

There are often differences between what people expect others to do and how, in fact, others behave (Grotevant, 1998). During adolescence, such differences occur in relation to the young person's increasing maturation and changes in social relationships (e.g., involving greater participation in peer activities than family activities; despite parental expectations adolescents may attend peer gatherings where alcohol is being used) (Collins, 1997). These differences between expected and actual behaviours can result in conflicts between youth and their parents, can change expectations (e.g., "Son, I guess you can't be trusted to go to parties where no alcohol is being used"), and can alter family relationships ("From now on, son, I will have to approve every party you go to." "Dad, you're just unreasonable. You can't control all the kids in my high school, and if you won't let me go out just because there is a chance someone might be there with beer, then I will never be able to go out!") (Collins, 1997; Grotevant, 1998).

Moreover, youth and their parents have different expectations about when during adolescence it is appropriate for particular transitions (e.g., staying home in the evening without parental supervision, going out on a date with one person instead of with a group) to occur (Collins et al., 1997). Nevertheless, decisions about what to do and when it is appropriate to do it are increasingly made by adolescents as opposed to their parents (Grotevant, 1998). For example, in their study of Montreal elementary and high school students, Lieberman and her colleagues (Lieberman, Doyle, & Markiewicz, 1999) found that while perceptions of parental availability did not change between childhood and adolescence, dependence on parents decreased. Across the adolescent years the number of issues youth perceive as within their control, and not the control of their parents, increases (Smetana, 1988; Smetana & Asquith, 1994). As a consequence of these changes in expected control of their own behaviours, adolescents are often in a position of having to renegotiate the rules their parents ask them to live under (Smetana, 1995). In other words, part of parenting a child across adolescence is to have one's authority continually challenged (Grotevant, 1998; Smetana, 1995).

In sum, adolescents and their parents often have different expectations about youth behaviour and, as well, their respective expectations vary across adolescence. In addition to expectations, there are behavioural components of parent-adolescent relationships. These components can involve either positive or negative behaviours.

Parent-Adolescent Relationships Involving Supportive Behaviours and Positive Emotions

Life always presents challenges and obstacles. Healthy, adaptive development involves being able to solve the problems life presents, for example, by making wise decisions about how to spend our money, juggling multiple demands on our time, or resolving interpersonal conflicts.

For this reason, many researchers study family interaction patterns of youth and parents in the context of family problem solving or decision making (e.g., Jory et al., 1996; Lamborn, Dornbusch, & Steinberg, 1996); they try to determine the bases of successful and/or productive, or of unsuccessful or destructive, problem-solving styles.

Several studies have found that, among North American youth, warm parental interactions are associated with effective problem-solving ability in both the adolescent and the family as a whole; however, hostile interactions are associated with destructive adolescent problem-solving behaviours (De Wit, Embree, & De Wit, 1999; Ge, Best, Conger, & Simons, 1996; Rueter & Conger, 1995b). Moreover, problem solving is worse when adolescents do not join parents in the problem-solving process (Vuchinich, Angelelli, & Gatherum, 1996). In turn, among German adolescents, parental behaviours marked by approval and attention to the positive behaviour of the youth are associated with an adolescent who feels he or she is capable of controlling events that can affect him or her (Krampen, 1989); however, when parental behaviours disparage the child and fail to attend to his or her specific behaviour, the adolescent feels that chance determines what happens to him or her in life.

As illustrated by these studies, warmth, nonhostility, and closeness seem to be characteristics of parent-adolescent interaction associated with positive outcomes among youth. Indeed, adolescents who are in relationships with parents that are marked by good connections show less anxiety and depression than is the case among youth who are detached from their parents (Delaney, 1996). For example, maternal warmth was found, in a Montreal sample of 12- to 15-year-old girls, to negatively predict self-handicapping behaviour (Greaven, Santor, Thompson, & Zuroff, 2000). Self-handicapping behaviour (see Chapter 11) is the manipulation of a situation so that obstacles to performance can be blamed for potential failure.

Other research confirms these links between the quality of parent-adolescent relationships and youth development (e.g., Lau & Lau, 1996; Phares & Renk, 1998). For example, in a study of 984 children and their parents in Alberta, family harmony and adult-child synchrony were related to adolescent emotional and behavioural adjustment (Barber, Bolitho, & Bertrand, 2001).

Positive parent-adolescent relationships may be expected to involve feelings of attachment or closeness on the part of the young person to his or her parents. Such feelings may be beneficial to both parents and adolescents. For instance, feelings of closeness in the parent-adolescent relationship are related to parents' views of their parenting as satisfying to them and to the youth's self-esteem and to his or her participation in family activities (Paulson, Hill, & Holmbeck, 1991).

Similarly, when adolescents feel secure in their attachments to parents, they are more competent with peers, have fewer internalizing problems, and fewer deviant behaviours (Allen et al., 1998). Moreover, poor attachment (e.g., anger about their relationships with their parents) is associated with the adolescent showing internalizing problems and behavioural deviance (Allen et al., 1998). Moreover, parent-child relations marked by attachment are associated with high self-perceived competence among youth, especially across the transition to junior high school, and with low feelings of depression or anxiety (Papini & Roggman, 1992). The benefits of secure attachment relationships with parents appear to extend to the transition to university for Canadian adolescents. Attachment to parents during the transition to university from high school among a group of students in Quebec City did not change (Larose & Boivin, 1998), with those who reported a higher level of security having more positive expectations of support in university as well as better socioemotional adjustment.

Furthermore, North American adolescents who are close to their parents are more self-reliant and competent and have better self-esteem and school achievements, and fewer problem behaviours (e.g., drug use, depression, and deviant behaviour) than is the case with adolescents who do not have close relations with their parents (Doyle, Markiewicz, Brendgen, Lieberman, & Voss, 2000; Barnes, 1984; Maccoby & Martin, 1983; Montemayor & Flannery, 1991; Steinberg, 1991). Similarly, parents who encourage their adolescent children to express their own feelings and ideas have youngsters with high levels of ego development (Hauser et al., 1984).

Positive attachment involves in part warmth and acceptance by parents of their children. Other data indicate that nonhostile parent-adolescent relations are associated with better adjustment by the adolescent to the transition to middle school and greater peer popularity (Bronstein et al., 1993); nonhostility is also related to a better self-concept for girls and better classroom behaviour for boys. In addition, parent-youth relationships improve over the course

of adolescence in warm supportive families, whereas relationships deteriorate in hostile and coercive families (Reuter & Conger, 1995a). Moreover, in the former (positive) type of parent-adolescent relationship problem-solving effectiveness improves, whereas the latter type of relationship is associated with destructive problem-solving styles (Reuter & Conger, 1995b).

When parents are attuned to their child's development and support his or her autonomy in decision making, the youth is better adjusted and *gains* in self-esteem across the junior high school transition (Lord, Eccles, & McCarthy, 1994). Similarly, parental support is associated with life satisfaction among youth (Young et al., 1995). Furthermore, parental religiosity, cohesive family relationships, and low interpersonal conflict are associated with low levels of problem behaviours and with self-regulation among rural African American youth (Brody, Stoneman, & Flor, 1996).

The characteristics of parent-child interaction associated with positive outcomes for the adolescent are similar in that they reflect support for and acceptance of the developing youth. Parental patterns of support and acceptance, as expressed for instance in their willingness to grant independence to their children, varies by family race/ethnicity and by youth age and gender (Alnajjar, 1996; Bulcroft, Carmody, & Bulcroft, 1996). Nevertheless, in general, when parent-adolescent relationships provide support for the youth's behaviours, interests, and activities, numerous positive developmental outcomes are likely to occur. For instance, support has been associated with consistent school goals (Bigelow & Zhou, 2001); better school grades and scholastic self-concept (DuBois, Eitel, & Felner, 1994); with perceiving that social relationships could be more beneficial to one's development than risky (East, 1989); with being more satisfied with one's life (Young et al., 1995); and with a decreased likelihood of involvement in drinking, delinquency, and other problem behaviours (Barnes & Farrell, 1992).

Family relationships involving siblings are influential as well (Stocker & Dunn, 1991). Although 10- to 14-year-olds spend only about 5% of their time alone with their siblings—compared to about 20% alone with peers and about 6% alone with parents (Raffaelli & Larson, 1987)—77% of high school students report that their siblings are important influences in their lives (Blyth, Hill, & Thiel, 1982). However, if parents treat their children differently rather than similarly, then conflictual and rivalrous sibling relationships tend to occur (Hetherington, 1989, 1991; Stocker & Dunn, 1991). Relationships with siblings were found to be associated with late adolescents' experiences of loneliness in university (Ponzetti & James, 1997). Those who reported greater closeness with less rivalry and conflict were found to be less lonely.

In sum, then, parent-child relationships, and family relationships more generally, that are marked by behaviours supportive of the youth and by positive feelings connecting the generations are associated with psychologically and socially healthy developmental outcomes for the adolescent. However, some families do not have parent-child relations marked by support and positive emotions; and no family has such exchanges all the time. Families experience conflict and negative emotions. Such exchanges also influence the adolescent; but, as we might expect, the outcomes for youth of these influences differ from those associated with support and positive emotions.

Parent-Adolescent Relations Involving Conflict and Stress

As noted, family conflicts are inevitable (Fisher & Johnson, 1990). At the least, conflicts are a ubiquitous part of all families at some times in their history. Just as the reasons for conflicts between individuals, on the one hand, or nations, on the other, vary, so too do the reasons for conflicts in families. For example, adolescents report that conflicts often arise because they feel parents are not providing the emotional support they want, or because youth or parents believe the other generation is not meeting the expectations held for them, or because of a lack of consensus about family or societal values (Fisher & Johnson, 1990). Moreover, when adolescents and parents have discrepancies in their perceptions of family functioning (e.g., regarding the cohesiveness or closeness in the family), there is a greater likelihood of adolescent depression or anxiety, particularly for girls (Ohannessian et al., 1995). In addition, adolescents' negative beliefs about their mothers are associated with negative communications with them (Reed & Dubow, 1997).

It seems that parent-adolescent conflicts mainly concern everyday matters. In a survey of 3500 high school students across Canada, Bibby (2001) found that disagreements with parents "very often" or "fairly often" concerned jobs around the house (58%), school (55%), safety (49%), parental authority (44%), when the youth came in at night (40%),

and money (39%); disagreements also occurred over parental concerns about their adolescents staying out of trouble (36%), having appropriate friends (25%), drinking (23%), dating (21%), drugs (20%), appearance (20%), and sex (18%). Similarly, among Chinese youth living in Hong Kong, conflicts also occurred in the main over everyday issues (Yau & Smetana, 1996). As discussed in Chapter 1, similar findings were reported in research conducted a generation earlier (Lerner & Knapp, 1975), suggesting that the nature of parents' views of reasons for arguing with their children may not change very much across time.

While only a small proportion of Canadian adolescents (15%) reported daily arguments with parents, a majority reported arguing more than once a week (40%), and very few said that they rarely (17%) or never (5%) had an argument with their parents (Bibby, 2001). In a U.S. study, European American parents reported more conflict than Latino and African American parents (Barber, 1994).

Moreover, although other research reports that adolescents and their parents are in conflict about the same sorts of issues—chores, appearance, and politeness—there is a decrease in arguments about these issues as the adolescent develops (Galambos & Almeida, 1992); however, conflict over finances tend to increase at older age levels. In turn, as youth develop, they are less likely to concede an argument to parents; as a result conflicts may be left unresolved, especially it seems in families with boys (Smetana, Yau, & Hanson, 1991).

The presence of conflicts between youth and parents is, then, a fact of family life during adolescence. Arguments with their youngsters are events parents must learn to cope with. Parenting Box 8.1 presents letters sent to Lerner and Hoopfer from parents. In these letters parents ask questions about the nature of the conflicts they have with their adolescents. In their responses to these questions, Lerner and Hoopfer provide suggestions about how parents may deal with these unpleasant interactions with their child.

Canadian adolescents were asked how parents should respond to their teenagers when they've done something wrong (Bibby, 2001). The majority of youth favoured talking it out or removing privileges: give them a "good talking to" (29%), discussion without discipline (23%), take away privileges (25%), or grounding (5%). A minority of adolescents endorsed physical discipline: a discussion with discipline (5%) or physical discipline (4%). Almost 10% of adolescents noted that a combination of responses was best.

Nevertheless, despite its developmental course, the presence of conflict at any point in the parent-adolescent relationship may influence the behaviour and development of the youth. For instance, family conflicts may lead the adolescent to think negatively about himself or herself, and can even eventuate in his or her thinking about suicide (Shagle & Barber, 1993). In addition, conflict is associated with "externalizing" problems (e.g., such as hostility) among youth (Mason et al., 1996). In adolescent girls, the experience of menarche (see Chapter 3) is associated with increased conflict, especially in the mother-daughter relationship, and as a consequence less positive emotions and more negative ones characterize adolescent-parent exchanges (Holmbeck & Hill, 1991; Steinberg, 1987).

In addition, psychological control (e.g., exerting control through inducing guilt) by parents (and siblings) is associated with adjustment problems and lowered self-confidence among youth (Conger, Conger, & Scaramella, 1997). Moreover, in a study of about 3200 young adolescents, lack of cohesion in the family was associated with depression (McKeown et al., 1997). In short, then, conflicts in the parent-adolescent relationship result in problems in youth development (Rubenstein & Feldman, 1993). A vicious cycle may be created in that, in turn, adolescent problems can increase parent-adolescent conflicts (Maggs & Galambos, 1993).

Moreover, the negative emotions exchanged between adolescents and their parents can themselves result in problems for the youth. For instance, Canadian parents' feelings of stress are associated with adolescents' emotional and behavioural problems (Galambos, Sears, Almeida, & Kolaric, 1995) and, as well, maternal stress is associated with "internalizing" problems (e.g., anxiety, depression) in adolescent boys and with poor school grades for adolescent girls (Compas et al., 1989).

The process through which parents' stress is linked to adolescent problems seems to involve the experience of depression in parents as a consequence of their stress, which, in turn, disrupts effective parental discipline and leads to adolescent problem behaviours (Conger, Patterson, & Ge, 1995). Other research finds that parental depression is associated with depression in youth (Gallimore & Kurdek, 1992), and that ineffective parenting behaviours (e.g.,

low self-restraint among fathers) eventuate in problem behaviours in their offspring (Baumrind, 1991; D'Angelo, Weinberger, & Feldman, 1995; Feldman & Weinberger, 1994; Simons, Finlay, & Yang, 1991).

Furthermore, parents of Grade 10 students with conduct problems are more hostile than parents of Grade 10 students with depression (Ge, Best, et al., 1996); parents of Grade 10 students who are both depressed and showing problem behaviours had high levels of hostility and low levels of warmth when their children were in Grades 7, 8, and 9. Similarly, depression among both European American and Asian American adolescents is associated with family relations marked by low warmth and acceptance and high levels of conflict with mothers and fathers (Greenberger & Chen, 1996). In turn, maternal depression adversely influences daughters' educational expectations (Silverberg, Marczak, & Gondoli, 1996). In addition, anger, hostility, coercion, and conflict shown by both parents and siblings have a detrimental effect on adolescent adjustment (Pike et al., 1996).

Clearly, then, parents' negative emotions can lead, through the creation of problematic parenting behaviours, to negative outcomes in adolescent development. Moreover, the presence of problem behaviours in parents per se is linked to problems in adolescent development. For instance, psychiatric disorders among parents are related to the occurrence of antisocial and hostile behaviours among adolescents (Ge, Conger, et al., 1996). As well, problematic alcohol consumption—problem drinking or alcoholism—in parents is associated with alcohol use and abuse problems in their adolescent offspring, a relation that occurs in Canadian families, both Aboriginal and non-Aboriginal (De Wit, Embree, & De Wit, 2001). Similarly, parental drug use results in a host of behavioural, cognitive, and self-esteem problems in their offspring (Kandel, Rosenbaum, & Chen, 1994). Maternal smoking is associated with smoking in their adolescent children (Kandel & Wu, 1995), and in fact parental substance use in general is linked to numerous problems, including experience with the substances (drugs, alcohol, cigarettes, etc.) used by parents (e.g., Andrews et al., 1993; Stice & Barrera, 1995). Moreover, when fathers have an emotionally distant relationship with their wives, and as a consequence turn to their adolescent daughters for intimacy and affection, the daughters show depression, anxiety, and low self-esteem (Jacobvitz & Bush, 1996).

Teens and Tweens: Questions Parents Ask About Their Adolescents

Question: My 10-year-old daughter seems obsessed with Beverly Hills, 90210 and has crushes on some of the characters. Should I be concerned?

Answer: In most cases crushes like your daughter's are perfectly normal. In fact, they may be a way for her to begin to act out her romantic notions in a safe, nonsexual way. Preteen crushes are like imaginary dates—unthreatening ones, since the preteenager will not have to deal with the consequences of her romantic feelings.

Question: Over the past year, our usually sweet 12-year-old son has started to argue with my wife and me about anything and everything. What's happening?

Answer: In the early part of the teen years, kids develop different ways of thinking about the world. They imagine new ways of behaving, question parental rules and wonder whether things could be different. Although they may test out their ideas on their friends, there is probably nobody safer to argue with than a parent. Kids know that by and large their parents will continue to accept and love them no matter how many arguments they have. Your child probably enjoys using his new thinking skills and has

found that it is safe to argue with you. Use the best listening skills that you have, and let him know you are interested in hearing his ideas, although you don't always agree with him.

Question: Our 13-year-old insists on wearing old shirts hanging out over torn jeans. We can't get him to dress up without an all-out war. What can we do?

Answer: An important goal of adolescence is to understand who you are as an individual, and one of the easiest ways to declare who you are—especially as a person different from your parents—is through your clothing. Over time your child will find other ways to define his identity. Until then, try to quietly tolerate some differences of opinion about dress standards. However, let your son know that while he can choose his everyday clothes, you have veto power over the choices for special occasions.

Question: My husband and I work full time. Our 15-year-old spends four to five hours alone before we get home. She says she likes it, but we're worried.

Answer: The issue is not about how much time your daughter spends by herself, but what she does with it. If she sits around

watching television or engaging in aimless activities and doesn't do her homework, for example, then the time alone can be negative. First, leave numbers where you can be reached, and make it a practice to check in with her at regular times. Make it clear that you are checking in—not checking *up* on her. Talk to her about what you hope she will be accomplishing while you are gone. In addition, find out whether there is an after-school program for teens available in your community. This would provide your daughter with adult supervision and give her the opportunity to make new friends.

Question: My 10-year-old daughter is a bit chubby and she gets picked on at school. How can I help her feel good about herself and lose weight without making her too concerned about looks?

Answer: Work with your daughter to find things that she can be proud of about her appearance. Can she find a way to do her hair that she is excited about? Does she have some clothes that she thinks are really neat? Tell her that the whole family should and will find ways to eat well to maintain a healthy body. Don't *put* her on a diet, but provide healthful food that will promote weight control.

Source: From Lerner, R. M., & Hoopfer, L. C. (1993, October). Teens and tweens. *Family Circle*, p. 43.

Conclusions About the Family and Parenting

Parents are charged with an awesome responsibility by society. The role of parents is to develop future generations to carry society forward into the future. The children that the parents rear are the future. Society expects parents to do a good job in creating healthy and productive citizens. Although most parents fulfill this expectation, there are failures as well.

Parents vary in their rearing styles, the directions in which they socialize their youth, and the types of relationships they have with, and behaviours and emotions they show to, their offspring. A good deal of this diversity is healthy and necessary to maintain

the richness of culture and experience that enhances human life. But other levels of diversity involving, for instance, indulgent, neglectful, or authoritarian rearing styles, or hostile interactions marked by negative emotions, or the display of problem behaviours, can result in significant problems for youth.

The diversity in family functioning, coupled with the diversity in family structure, has pervasive implications for adolescent development. Families, in their structure and function, influence virtually all facets of the youth's psychological and social functioning, not only during adolescence but well into adulthood. The key social contexts affected by family structure and function are the peer group and the school. These contexts are discussed in Chapters 9 and 11.

Summary

- Families create caring young people through fostering healthy interpersonal relations and through promoting prosocial behaviour, empathy, agency, and self-control in their children.
- The family is the major institution that fosters the development of caring individuals and promotes civil society and is charged with creating a new generation of citizens committed to maintaining and furthering the social order.
- In the 1950s, almost half of all families were nuclear families, with two biological parents and two to three children. Today, only one in five U.S. families still fits this structure. The family context in which youth grow up is much more diverse today.
- Children and adolescents today may find themselves in more than one family structure during the course of their socialization.
- The variation in family structures in which adolescents live influences both the way the parents interact with youth and how adolescents behave.
- A family under stress from poverty places its children at risk for problems of behaviour and health. Parents may feel pressured, depressed, and demoralized by their financial situation.
- Forced attendance of Aboriginal children at residential schools over a number of generations has lasting negative effects on today's adolescents.
- Parents can promote positive development in their children by receiving social support that promotes higher quality parenting practices.
- Grandparents can play an important role for families, especially those headed by a female single-parent adolescent.
- When parents have a low-quality marriage, youth are adversely affected.
- Good marital quality can positively influence adolescent development and be related to positive peer relations and emotional adjustment.
- Most research finds that divorce has negative effects on adolescent development in social, academic, and personal adjustment realms, but there are many exceptions.
- Gender differences are associated with the effects of divorce on adolescent development, the effects of remarriage on the adolescent, and the effects of living with the biological father after divorce.
- Maternal employment does not have any direct adverse effects on the social and emotional development of youth.
- Adolescent adjustment may be related to having a mother who can adequately handle the stress of role strain.
- Unsupervised time can promote problem behaviours in youth.
- Research on adoptive families should concentrate on how the youth who are adopted and their families can best achieve goals and strategies that ensure positive development and prevent negative outcomes.
- Adults differ in the ways they enact their roles as a parent. Parenting style is associated with differences in adolescent behaviour and development.
- Cultures differ in what they determine to be a well-socialized individual.
- In North America, parents and adolescents expect that adolescents will become more autonomous across the adolescent period.
- Parents and youth often disagree about the age at which certain role transitions should occur.
- Warm parent-child relationships tend to foster effective problem-solving strategies and positive outcomes among youth.
- Adolescents often argue with their parents about everyday matters such as chores, appearance, and politeness. The number of conflicts tends to decrease over the course of adolescence.

Discussion Topics

1. In what ways are you significantly different from your close friends? How much of this variation is due to the influence of your family on your development?

2. Has the structure of your family changed throughout your life? How did the timing of these changes impact your development? For example, if you lived in a two-parent family until

your parents divorced in adolescence, how did the timing of the divorce impact you?

3. What are some of the main causes and effects of the decline of the two-parent family?

4. How do you feel about mothers and fathers choosing to work soon after the birth of a baby? How do their decisions impact the development of their child? Do you believe one parent is more responsible for the caregiving and the other for the financial responsibilities of the family? Why or why not?

5. Do you believe North American society will ever view the caregiving and breadwinning responsibilities of the family to be shared, 50/50, between two partners? Why or why not?

6. If a single, financially able woman came to you for advice on whether or not she should decide to have a baby on her own, what would you say? What are the bases for your advice?

7. What are some of the reasons behind the decrease in the birthrate in the United States and Canada over the course of the 20th century? How does the number of children in a family serve as both risk and protective factors in a family's welfare?

8. How has the increase of women in the work force impacted society?

9. Why might youth living in single-mother families be given more support than youth in the other nonnuclear family structures?

10. What are the potential reasons behind the finding that nonfarm poor adolescents suffer from fewer cases of depression than poor families who live on farms? What protective factors might influence the nonfarm youth as opposed to the farm youth?

11. How financially stable was your family throughout your childhood? How did your parent(s) influence your understanding of finances and its

impact on your life? Were finances a significant issue of stress in your family, and, if so, how well did your parent(s) cope with those stresses?

12. Today, many grandparents are partially or fully responsible for raising children. What are some ways that society can better recognize and support their efforts? For example, how might schools and service organizations reach out to these grandparents?

13. How did the quality of your parents' marriage impact your development?

14. Why do you believe children of divorce tend to have higher rates of adjustment problems than children in two-parent families? How can parents who divorce support their child's social and emotional development?

15. If there were unsupervised blocks of time that you spent as an adolescent, how was that time spent? Why was there no adult monitoring your time? How do you feel this time impacted your development? How can communities better support adolescents and children who go home to empty houses after school and during the summer?

16. What is the sign of a successful parent? Is your answer culturally determined?

17. What parenting style defined your parent(s)? Using Bronfenbrenner's ecological model as a guide, how did your parents' life contexts impact their parenting style?

18. What socially derived expectations did your parent(s) have for you during your adolescence? What rules were set? What role did you have in creating these rules? How well did you follow those rules and live up to their expectations? Do you believe adolescents should have some say in the rules they live by? Why or why not?

19. How has the pattern of resolving conflicts established between you and members of your family impacted your social and emotional development?

Key Terms

acculturation, p. 194
authoritarian parenting, p. 191
authoritative parenting, p. 191
conspecifics, p. 191
cross-sectional study, p. 178

externalizing problems, p. 186
indulgent parenting, p. 192
internalizing problems, p. 186
longitudinal study, p. 178
neglectful parenting, p. 192

nuclear family, p. 177
permissive parenting, p. 191
role strain, p. 189
socialization, p. 176

9

The Adolescent Peer Group

"Francisco, come inside," Mrs. Garcia called to her son.

Francisco stopped shooting the basketball at the hoop in the driveway long enough to answer. "Why, Mom?"

"First, because I said so, and second because your father just called. He'll be home in about 30 minutes and would like to go out tonight for a family dinner."

Francisco moaned. He carried the ball to the back door where his mother was standing. As he walked, he thought quickly. There were several reasons he did not need to go with his parents.

"Jaime is coming over and we were going to play basketball for a while. Can't you just take Rosita with you? It's Friday night, I have been in school all week, and I just want to do something with my friends."

"Well, your dad and I have worked all week and it would be nice to see you and your sister."

"Okay, I guess . . ." He paused for a moment until an idea came to him. "Why can't we eat at home? I don't really feel like going to a restaurant."

"Well, your parents don't feel like cooking, and if we eat at home you and your sister will disappear from the table in five minutes and so much for having a family dinner."

"But Mom, Jaime will be here in a minute."

"Good. Then after you wash up and change your shirt you and he can talk for a while until your father and I are ready to leave."

"But Mom," Francisco pleaded, "I'll be bored."

"Then you'll be bored. Now get in the house, get ready, and stop arguing."

Francisco knew he had lost the debate. He began to walk slowly into the house, but then he stopped and smiled.

"Okay, Mom, I'll go. But can we invite Jaime to come to dinner with us?"

Learning Objectives

1. To appreciate the different peer group structures that exist in adolescence and how they function.
2. To understand how peer status is determined, what types of peer statuses exist, and their effect on adolescent development.
3. To understand the components of friendship.
4. To appreciate how the nature of friendships changes across adolescence.
5. To learn how parents influence an adolescent's choice of friends.
6. To understand the broader peer context within which youth are embedded.
7. To define what a clique is and how it functions in adolescence.
8. To understand how peer status and peer relations are related to adolescent adjustment.
9. To learn the three dimensions of friendship that affect the course of adolescent development.
10. To appreciate the individual and contextual variables that shape the formation of friendships and the importance of friends for development in adolescence.
11. To learn how feelings of closeness to parents and peers develop across adolescence.
12. To understand how the amount of time spent with parents and peers changes across adolescence.
13. To understand how adolescent, parental, and peer values converge.
14. To learn how parents and peers can work together to promote positive youth development.

The adolescent's social world is broader and more complex than that of the infant or the child. The most notable social phenomenon of adolescence is the emergence of the marked importance of peer groups. The adolescent comes to rely heavily on the peer group for security and guidance. Adolescence is a time when such support is urgently needed, perhaps especially from others who are experiencing the same transition and can understand what is being experienced.

To understand adolescent development, it is important to review the nature and structure of peer relationships in adolescence, and to discuss the influence of peer relationships on adolescent behaviour and development. Because of the continued importance of the family during adolescence (Adelson, 1970; Bengtson & Troll, 1978; Steinberg, 1991), it is also important to review the relationships an adolescent has with both parents and peers during this time, and the relative influence each has on the adolescent.

The Nature of Peer Relationships During Adolescence

ISSUES TO CONSIDER
- How are social interactions different from social relationships?
- What are social groups?

Consistent with developmental systems perspectives such as developmental contextualism, Rubin, Bukowski, and Parker (1998, p. 623) note that the experience of youth with peers "can best be understood by referring to several levels of social complexity: within individuals, within interactions, within relationships, and within groups." Rubin et al. (1998) explain that **interactions** integrate "the behaviours of two individuals into a social exchange of some duration"(p. 624). Social **relationships** rest on a commitment of the members of the relationship to each other and "involve a succession of interactions between two individuals known to each other. Importantly, because the individuals are known to each other, the nature and course of each interaction are influenced by the history of past interactions between the individuals as well as by their expectations for interactions in the future" (p. 625).

Rubin et al. (1998) note that a **group** "is a collection of interacting individuals who have some degree of reciprocal influence over one another. Groups often form spontaneously out of common interests or circumstances, but they are also established formally, the most ubiquitous example being the school class" (p. 626). Different groups may have distinct rules or standards for behaviour, that is, different norms for what is regarded as appropriate behaviour (Rubin et al., 1998). Such norms may serve as a basis for identifying distinct crowds "within the network of relationships among children in high school" (Rubin et al., 1998, p. 626). Several different types of relationships may exist among the youth that comprise the peers of adolescents.

Peer Group Structures

ISSUES TO CONSIDER
- What different types of social networks exist during adolescence? How do they function?
- How is peer status determined? What does peer status mean for an adolescent?

Several types of peer groups exist in adolescence and these diverse structures are associated with important variations in adolescent behaviour and development. Adolescents' peer relationships may be divided into several types of distinct groups of young people, or **social networks**. These groups include best friends, close friends, cliques (or small groups of friends), social crowds, and sometimes romantic relationships (Urberg et al., 1995).

Although boys and girls possess all of these social networks, girls typically have more intimate relationships than boys (Urberg et al., 1995). Girls also have more positive network interactions and are bothered more by negative interactions than boys (Gavin & Furman, 1989). However, for both boys and girls there is "fluidity" in their social networks; that is, where a particular peer may be in the youth's set of networks (whether the peer is a best friend, a close friend, or an object of romance) may change relatively rapidly, over even a period of a few weeks (Cairns et al., 1995).

Nevertheless, the *status* youth have—for instance, as popular or unpopular—does remain relatively stable. This status not only reflects the social

---

Interactions Integration of the behaviours of two individuals into a social exchange of some duration.
Relationships Succession of interactions between two indi- | viduals known and committed to each other, which is influenced by the past interactions between the two individuals and by their expectations for the future. | **Group** Collection of interacting individuals who have influence over one another and who have relationships based on common interests or circumstances. | **Social networks** Distinct groups of relationships such as best friends, close friends, cliques, crowds, and romantic relationships.

Many adolescents spend time with their friends at shopping malls.

status of a youth in his or her broad peer group, but also marks the sorts of interactions he or she may have with peers. Perhaps most importantly, an adolescent's peer group status is related to both current and later life behaviour and development.

Peer status can be determined for a particular youth by asking the members of his or her peer group to "nominate" or name people in their group (e.g., in their school or neighbourhood) who have particular positive characteristics (e.g., well liked, chosen for games, would want to be with at a party) and particular negative characteristics (e.g., disliked, left out of games, would not want to be with at a party). An adolescent's status can be determined by counting the number of positive and negative nominations he or she receives from the peer group.

Various types of peer status exist. **Popular** youth are those adolescents who have a lot of positive nominations and few negative ones. **Rejected** adolescents have few positive nominations and a lot of negative ones. **Neglected** youth have very few nominations at all, either positive or negative, and **controversial** youth receive a lot of positive and a lot of negative nominations. Finally, **average** youth do not show extreme numbers of either type of nomination ("by definition," they have average numbers).

Regardless of his or her peer status, a given adolescent can have a certain type of peer relationship, a **friendship**. Just as youth having different status in their peer group differ in their personal and social behaviour, youth with different patterns of friendship also show contrasting behaviour.

The Nature of Friendships

ISSUES TO CONSIDER

- What are the components of a friendship?
- How does the nature of friendships change across adolescence?

A friendship constitutes a special type of relationship within the groups formed by adolescents. According to Rubin et al. (1998, pp. 625–626), a friendship has at least four specific components:

1. A friendship involves a reciprocal relationship acknowledged by the people in it;
2. There is reciprocal affection in a friendship;
3. Friendships constitute voluntary associations between individuals; there is no obligation to be someone's friend; and
4. Friendships exist within a network of other relationships, for instance, involving peer cliques or crowds and family relations.

The nature of friendships develops during adolescence. Adolescents think about friendships differently than younger children (Selman & Schultz, 1990). Whereas young adolescents describe friends by noting their specific behavioural characteristics (e.g., "Ted is a terrific skateboarder" or "Anita sings great"), older adolescents depict their friends through descriptions of their personalities and values (e.g., "Crystal is so generous" or "Mohammad seems shy until you get to know him") (Rubin et al., 1998).

There are also behavioural differences between adolescents and younger children in regard to the character of their respective friendships. In contrast to younger children, adolescents have fewer friends and same-sex friends become more important; friends equal or exceed parents as sources of social support and advice; friendships tend to be relatively stable;

Popular status Peer reputation characterized by receiving many positive nominations and few negative ones.
Rejected status Peer reputation characterized by receiving few positive nominations and many negative nominations.

Neglected status Peer reputation characterized by receiving very few nominations, either positive or negative.
Controversial status Peer reputation characterized by receiving a lot of positive nominations and a lot of negative nominations.

Average status Peer reputation characterized by not showing extreme numbers of either positive or negative nominations.
Friendship Voluntary and reciprocal relationship between individuals acknowledged by the people in it, with reciprocal affection and

existing within a network of other relationships.

and intimacy and self-disclosure are the hallmarks of friendships (Rubin et al., 1998).

Parental Influences on Adolescent Friendships

ISSUE TO CONSIDER

• How do parents influence adolescent friendships?

Friendships are relationships based on personal choice (Hartup, 1996; Rubin et al., 1998), but parents still influence a youth's choice (Grotevant, 1998). Parents exercise great influence over their adolescent's peer relations in general and friendships more specifically (e.g., Parke et al., 1994). Through their socialization practices and child-rearing styles, parents instill in their children values and attitudes that influence their friendship selections.

Parents also supervise much of their adolescent's time, especially during early adolescence (Grotevant, 1998; Parke et al., 1994). They serve as chauffeurs to and from parties and trips to the mall, and they may initiate (and pay for) their child's involvement in activities such as piano lessons, ballet classes, gymnastics, or hockey.

The relationship that adolescents have with their parents also seems to be related to their peer relationships. For example, Ducharme, Doyle, and Markiewicz (2002), in their study of more than 100 15- to 16-year-olds in Montreal, found that adolescents who were securely attached to their fathers had fewer conflicts with their peers in comparison to adolescents without this secure attachment. Quality of attachment to mothers did not relate to peer interactions. A possible reason for this may be that since the father-child relationship tends to be more distant than the mother-child one, interaction with the father is more similar to the adolescent's relationships with people outside the family. Also, the father's role in the family tends to be that of a playmate (rather than a primary caregiver), which may generalize better to the relationships that adolescents have with peers. Lieberman, Doyle, and Markiewicz (1999) reported similar findings with younger adolescents: 12- to 14-year-old Montrealers who felt they could rely on their parents, especially their fathers, to be available to them had lower conflict in their peer relationships. They may have learned conflict resolution skills in the family that transferred to their other relationships. Another finding was that adolescents who had closer, more supportive, and more secure peer relationships tended to feel that their mothers were available to them but

Parents may support their adolescents' social activities by attending their sporting events.

were not overly dependent on their mothers. A positive attachment to both parents was related to positive friendships' qualities of helpfulness, closeness, and security. Thus, parents have both direct and indirect influences on their adolescents' peer relationships.

Friendships and Crowds

ISSUES TO CONSIDER

• What is the broader social context of the adolescent?
• What are the characteristics of a crowd?

The transformation across the adolescent period in what being or having a friend means to a person occurs in relation to the youth's broader peer context (Grotevant, 1998). For example, building on the scholarship of Brown (1990), Rubin et al. (1998) defined a **crowd** as "a reputation-based collective of similarly stereotyped individuals who may or may not spend much time together" (p. 643). Across adolescence, young people become enmeshed in crowds or "liaisons," that is, groups made up of often quite different youth (e.g., "jocks," "populars," and "brains") who are still in at least a loose sense affiliated with each other (England & Petro, 1998; Henrich et al., 2000). Crowds or liaisons may be identified on the basis of the attitudes or activities shared by their members (Rubin et al., 1998).

These attitudes and behaviours constitute the **stereotypes**—the overgeneralized beliefs—(Allport, 1954) that people viewing a crowd ascribe to them.

Crowd (liaison) Collective group of similarly stereotyped individuals who may or may not spend time together.

Stereotype Overgeneralized belief.

Table 9-1 Examples of Adolescent Crowds or Liaisons

Brains
Burnouts
Druggies
Eggheads
Greasers
Grungers
Jocks
Loners
Nerds
Populars
Punksters

Source: Based on Brown, 1990, and Brown et al., 1987.

For example, people may believe all the members of one crowd ("jocks") place a high (if not the highest) value on athletic participation and achievement and engage in behaviours (e.g., weight training) that facilitate their ability to perform in a manner consistent with this value. Numerous such crowds exist among Canadian and American high school students. Brown and his colleagues (1990; Brown, Clasen, & Neiss, 1987) have identified some of the labels associated with these different crowds. As indicated in Table 9.1, these labels include brains, burnouts, druggies, eggheads, greasers, grungers, jocks, loners, nerds, populars, and punksters.

Cliques

ISSUES TO CONSIDER

- What is a clique and how does it function in adolescence?
- How does an adolescent's social context develop across adolescence?
- How can crowds help adolescents understand the nature of social relationships?

Within a group there may be significant subdivisions. One key subdivision is a **clique**, a set of usually three or more young people who are in a tightly knit group. Clique members see themselves as mutual or reciprocating friends (Henrich et al., 2000) and are seen by others as having a key common identity or interest (e.g., athletics, socializing, music, academics). Cliques have a sort of impermeable "social membrane" around the youth in them. Youth within

the clique hang out together and there is a degree of exclusivity of membership within a clique (cf. Rubin et al., 1998).

Cliques serve an important function in adolescence. Although membership in cliques decreases from early to late adolescence, across adolescence membership in a clique is associated with psychological well-being and the capacity to cope with stress (Rubin et al., 1998).

Grotevant (1998) notes that the larger groups of crowds and cliques within which adolescent friendships exist develop across this period. During the early portions of adolescence, friendships are structured in regard to crowds (Urberg et al., 1995), and tend to be predominantly same-sex groups (Hartup, 1993). By the beginning of high school most youth are in cliques, although there continue to be crowds and youth who are isolated and do not belong to any identifiable friendship group (Ennett & Bauman, 1996; Henrich et al., 2000).

All youth have one or another of these friendship types. For instance, hearing-impaired adolescents form friendships as do nonhearing-impaired youth; however, hearing-impaired youth tend to interact more with other hearing-impaired youth than with their hearing peers (Stinson, Whitmire, & Kluwin, 1996). Moreover, hearing-impaired youth tend to form emotional bonds with their hearing-impaired peers as opposed to their hearing peers.

The crowds within which adolescents exist may help the adolescent understand the nature of social relationships. For instance, building on the work of Brown, Mory, and Kinney (1994), Grotevant (1998, pp. 1115–1116) notes, "first, crowds and the stereotypes associated with them ("brains," "jocks," etc.) help adolescents understand alternative social identities available to them; second, crowd affiliations channel interaction such that relationships among some individuals are more likely than among others; third, crowds themselves vary in how relationships are structured in features such as closeness and endurance over time."

Functions of Peers During Adolescence

ISSUE TO CONSIDER

- How do peer relations influence adolescent development and behaviour?

Adolescents' relationships with their peers have a profound influence on their behaviour and development,

---

Clique Subdivision of a crowd in which a set of three or more people with a key common identity or interest form a tightly knit and often exclusive group.

second only, perhaps, to the significance family relationships have in their lives. Good peer relationships are a mark of a youth's social competence (Morison & Masten, 1991); in addition, and underscoring the important connections that exist among the key contexts of adolescence, good peer relations are related as well to academic competence (Hartup, 1993; Morison & Masten, 1991) and enjoyment of school (Health Canada, 1999).

Good peer relationships in adolescence are predictive of healthy development in adulthood (Parker & Asher, 1987). Adolescents who are disliked by peers, who are aggressive and disruptive, and who cannot establish good friendships are at risk for developing significant problems in adulthood. Youth with poor peer relationships are more likely to drop out of school, to engage in criminal behaviour, and to experience mental or behavioural problems than are youth with good peer relationships (Morison & Masten, 1991; Parker & Asher, 1987).

Youth agree that a good peer group and strong friendships are valuable. For instance, when engaged in competitive activities (e.g., sports or games), friends are seen to offer supportive evaluations (e.g., to cheer you on, to say "you can do it"); in noncompetitive activities, they are seen to provide inclusion in a group, common interests, acceptance, and help with schoolwork (Zarbatany, Ghesquiere, & Mohr, 1992). Moreover, youth report that it is very valuable to them to be in a popular group (Gavin & Furman, 1989).

In turn, not only are peers perceived by the adolescent to be influential, they may in fact have an important influence on the adolescent's behaviour. For instance, adolescents who report they have a good friend also tend to have good self-esteem and behavioural competence (e.g., Buhrmester, 1988; Bukowski & Newcomb, 1987). Among early adolescents in western Canada, having a large number of close friends is related to a higher level of moral reasoning compared to having a smaller number of close friends. This may be because a greater circle of friends allows more opportunities to engage in role-taking, which can serve to promote higher levels of moral development (Schonert-Reichl, 1999). In turn, not being accepted by friends is related to school dropout, to delinquency and criminality, and to poor personal adjustment (Hartup & Overhauser, 1991; Parke & Asher, 1987). Indeed, Coates (1991) notes that having a social network during adolescence has the primary purpose of providing social support, that is, a group of peers that may buffer the youth from

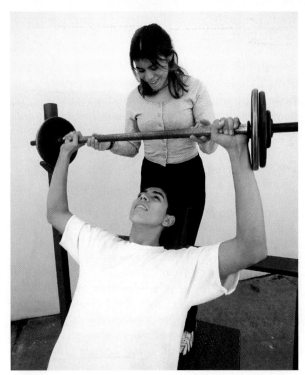

Peer interactions often occur in the context of shared recreational or athletic activities.

experiencing the problems associated with lack of friendship (East, 1991). Bukowski, Hoza, and Boivin (1993) suggest that friendship and peer status serve different purposes for adolescents. Popularity may provide a sense of belonging or fitting in. Friendships provide closeness and security, and thus ward off feelings of loneliness.

Fortunately, at least insofar as it has been studied among middle-class youth, most adolescents (about 80%) have a "best friend" and five or more "good friends" (Hartup & Overhauser, 1991). In fact, fewer than 10% of youth have no contact with friends outside of school (Crockett, Lossoff, & Petersen, 1984).

Although, as we have noted, girls' friendships are more intimate than those found among boys (Bukowski & Kramer, 1986), adolescents of both sexes tend to choose friends of similar age and sex (Hartup & Overhauser, 1991). Moreover, in early adolescence, youth make friends with others who share their attitudes and values regarding schooling, drug use, and alcohol consumption (Epstein, 1983; Kandel, 1986).

In short, when an adolescent is popular with his or her peers, he or she is both sociable and has the ability to lead others (East, 1991). In addition, such youth tend to be physically attractive, intelligent, and successful in athletics (East, 1991). In turn, rejected youth tend to be physically and verbally aggressive and off-task and disruptive in the classroom (East, 1991). Understandably, these adolescents tend to perform poorly in school. Given this significance of peers in the lives of adolescents, it is useful to understand the function of these groups.

Peer Status, Peer Relations, and Adolescent Adjustment

ISSUE TO CONSIDER

• How are different peer status categories related to adolescent development and behaviour?

Although positive peer relations are associated with healthy development in adolescence and later life (Hartup, 1993), not all youth have positive peer relations and not all youth are popular with other adolescents. Peer status influences development. Youth in different peer status categories behave differently, and these behavioural differences exist in comparable manners in different countries (Hatzichristou & Hopf, 1996; Luthar & McMahon, 1996). Peer status tends to remain fairly continuous across adolescence. Placement in a given status category (e.g., rejected) at one age by peers tends to be associated with being placed in that same category by peers at a later age (Merten, 1996).

Many different variables are associated with placement in a given peer category. Physical characteristics, as well as personality attributes and social skills, combine to influence peer rejection or acceptance (Brown, 1996). Youth who differ in physical attractiveness, especially facial attractiveness, enjoy different levels of peer acceptance. Higher physical attractiveness is linked to greater peer popularity (Adams, 1977; Perkins & Lerner, 1995).

Whatever physical, personality, or social attributes adolescents have that lead them to be placed in a given category tend to be repeated or carried over when youths enter a new setting. This carryover can be either negative (e.g., in the case of rejected youth) or positive (e.g., in the case of popular youth). For instance, adolescents who have best friendships characterized by positive features are accepted more readily in new groups they join (e.g., at a summer camp) than are youth whose best friendships are negative in character (Hanna & Berndt, 1995).

Differences in peer status category are associated with different behaviours and adjustment outcomes.

This diversity in peer status category, behaviour, and adjustment is influenced by individual and contextual factors. For example, popular youth show signs of good adjustment. Although there are a few studies that do not find such a link between peer group status and indicators of good adjustment, such as high self-esteem (e.g., Bishop & Inderbitzen, 1995), a great majority of studies do. Positive peer status is associated with good social and athletic competence, high academic performance, few symptoms of behavioural problems, and a positive sense of well-being (Morison & Masten, 1991).

Both neglected boys and neglected girls have been found to have good academic profiles, especially when compared to average status youth (Wentzel & Asher, 1995). They also have been shown to have greater motivation, higher levels of self-regulation as learners, more prosocial and compliant behaviour, and were better liked by teachers (Wentzel & Asher, 1995). Among adolescent girls, both popular and neglected youth feel less stressed than controversial, rejected, or average girls.

Rejected youth have problematic academic records. Peer rejection and academic failure are not only closely related, but together they are associated with a youth becoming engaged with antisocial peers (Dishion et al., 1991). When rejected children are also aggressive, they do more poorly in the school context than do rejected but nonaggressive youth. Rejected

Youth who are rejected by their peers may engage in a range of problem behaviours.

youth also receive the least social support and have a higher rate of adjustment problems than do youth in other status categories (East, Hess, & Lerner, 1987), even though the levels of social support they receive can vary from time to time across all peer status groups (Munsch & Kinchen, 1995).

Finally, young adolescent girls who have a controversial status are more likely to become teenage mothers than are other girls (Underwood, Kupersmith, & Coie, 1996). In one U.S. study of 285 girls (Underwood et al., 1996), 50% of girls who were controversial in early adolescence eventually became adolescent mothers, whereas the base rate for teen motherhood in the sample was 26%. Similar findings occurred in regard to girls who had been aggressive in early adolescence. Controversial and aggressive girls both gave birth earlier in their adolescence than did girls in other status or behavioural groups (Underwood et al., 1996).

In sum, differences in adolescent peer status associated with a range of positive through negative personal and social characteristics are influenced by both individual and contextual variables. These influences on peer status and adjustment represent important potential sources for the application of knowledge about youth development. Knowledge about what influences peer status is vital in order to enhance the lives of youth through improving the quality of their peer relationships.

Influences on Peer Status and Friendship

ISSUES TO CONSIDER
- What are the three dimensions of friendship that affect the course of adolescent development?
- What individual and contextual variables shape the formation of friendships in adolescence?
- What characteristics of a friendship can be linked to positive or negative development in adolescence?

Not a lot of theoretical attention has been paid to conceptualizing what individual and contextual variables enhance the quality of an adolescent's peer status, or how to help adolescents build healthy and supportive friendships (Furman, 1993). However, research does indicate that three dimensions of peer relationships, or friendships, affect the course of youth development: simply having friends, who one has as a friend, and the quality of the friendship (Hartup, 1983). Variation along all three of these dimensions is related to differences in the adjustment of youth (Bukowski, Hoza, & Borvin, 1993).

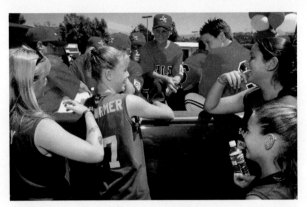
Adolescents' interactions with their peers often occur in large groups or crowds.

Adolescents form friendships more often with members of their own crowds than with members of other crowds (Urberg, Degirmencioglu, & Tolson, 1998; Urberg et al., 2000). The friendships formed within different types of adolescent groups—not only crowds but, as well, cliques, pairs, or other instances of social networks—tend to be relatively stable, for example, a best friend in the fall of a school year is likely to remain a close friend (if not still a best friend) in the spring of the year (Degirmencioglu et al., 1998).

Unless one has a friend, the other influences of friendship on adolescent development cannot act. A diverse set of individual and contextual variables shapes the formation of friendships in adolescence.

Friendships are formed more readily by youth who are more age-mate oriented than family oriented in their attempts to establish new social relationships with peers (Takahashi & Majima, 1994). The ability to take the perspective of other people is important in establishing new friendships in adolescence (Vernberg et al., 1994). Knowledge of what are appropriate versus inappropriate strategies that can be used in making friends is important in establishing acceptance by peers (Wentzel & Erdley, 1993). Knowledge of such strategies as well as perspective-taking ability can be quite useful because being able to fit one's style of behaviour to those desired by peers is a key basis of having positive peer relations (East et al., 1992).

Useful strategies in establishing friendships include managing conflicts in manners that avoid any disruption in the relationship and using **display behaviours** to enhance one's attractiveness to others

Display behaviours Actions designed to enhance one's attractiveness to others.

(Kolaric & Galambos, 1995). Because physical attractiveness is linked to better peer relations in both boys and girls (Lerner et al., 1991), each gender may use a set of behaviours they believe is associated with greater physical attractiveness. For instance, in order to try to appear more attractive, girls have been found to display chin strokes, hair flips, head tilts, coy looks, and movements to try to appear physically smaller (Kolaric & Galambos, 1995).

To the extent that these behaviours and characteristics are successful in forming a friendship, *and* if the adolescent can then become engaged in a friendship that is marked by the qualities of (1) stability (duration over time); (2) engagement (i.e., being involved in activities with a best or close friend); and (3) lack of deviance in the friend (that is, a friend who does not get into trouble; a friend who has behaviours and attitudes that are socially positive), then it is likely that positive self-esteem will develop in the youth (DuBois & Hirsch, 1993; Gillmore et al., 1992; Juvonen, 1991; Keefe & Berndt, 1996).

However, not all friendships are formed with youth who are engaged in positive behaviours and who avoid trouble and deviance. When friendships are formed with youth having such negative characteristics, the implications for adolescent development are not favourable. For instance, when a youth's friends engage in antisocial behaviour or in disruptive behaviour, it is likely the youth will follow course (Berndt & Keefe, 1995; Dishion, Andrews, & Crosby, 1995). Furthermore, Brendgen, Vitaro, and Bukowski (2000) found that adolescents in northwestern Quebec who maintained friendships with delinquent peers from age 12 to age 13 engaged in delinquent behaviour themselves at age 14. The level of delinquent behaviour was much higher than for adolescents who maintained friendship with a nondelinquent peer over that time.

Moreover, there can be a congruence in the feelings of internal distress among youth and their friends (Hogue & Steinberg, 1995), and such personality characteristics can be associated with both adolescent and peer substance abuse (Dobkin et al., 1995). Indeed, involvement with deviant peers and feelings of depression increase the likelihood that the adolescent will use drugs (Simons, Finlay, & Yang, 1991). Moreover, changes in youths' grades and drug use are linked to these same changes in their friends (Mounts & Steinberg, 1995).

Bullying A way of attaining power through aggression.

Such associations may develop through a process involving both hostile and low reciprocity relationships with a close friend, occurring in relation to feelings of depression and self-destructive behaviours in a youth (Windle, 1994). Such a process is related to high levels of alcohol use among adolescents.

A range of types of friendships exists in adolescence. As with peer relations in general, there are specific implications for youth behaviour and development of the type of friendships they possess.

Bullying

ISSUE TO CONSIDER
• Does bullying change form at adolescence?

Peer relations are not always positive at adolescence. Pepler, Craig, and Conolly (1997) define **bullying** as a way of attaining power through aggression. As many as 20% of Canadian children and adolescents have experienced being bullied by a peer (Craig, Pepler, Connolly, & Henderson, 2001). Bullying is higher at early adolescence than during preadolescence or late adolescence, as 11- to 12-year-olds reported engaging in bullying more often than did 9- to 10-year-olds and 13- to 14-year-olds (Craig, Pepler, & Connolly, 1997). Reports of being a *target* of bullying decreased from 26% of children in Grades 1 to 3, to 15% of children in Grades 4 to 6, to 12% of children in Grades 7 to 8. Children in the younger grades are often bullied by older children, which may account for this decrease (Craig et al., 1997). Although bullying tends to decrease after early adolescence, the experience leaves many feeling anxious and lonely (Boivin, Hymel, & Hodges, 2001), and may affect their self-esteem and achievement at school. Furthermore, an Australian study (Rigby & Slee, 1999) found that suicidal thoughts were more prevalent among adolescents who experienced bullying, especially if they had little social support.

Bullying may change form in early adolescence, with indirect aggression (gossip, exclusion) (Tremblay, Boulerice, Haren, McDuff, Perusse, Pihl, and Zoccolillo, 1995) or sexual harassment taking its place. It also tends to expand to include taunts from opposite-sex peers in addition to those from the same sex (Craig et al., 2001). For example, in a Canadian sample of youth in Grades 5 through 8, Connolly, Pepler, Craig, and Taradash (2000) found that bullies started dating earlier than other youth and were more likely to report social and physical aggression with their boyfriend/girlfriend.

There may be long-term correlates to being a bully. Lisa Serbin and her colleagues at Concordia University conducted follow-up studies of girls in Montreal who were identified by their peers as being aggressive when they were in Grades 1, 4, or 7 (e.g., Serbin, Moskowitz, Schwartzman, & Ledingham, 1991; Serbin, Cooperman, Peters, Lehoux, Stack, & Schwartzman; 1998). When they reached adolescence, these girls were more likely than the comparison group of nonaggressive girls to have gynecological problems, to contract sexually transmitted diseases, to become pregnant, and to leave school early. In addition, when aggressive girls became parents, they showed poorer parenting skills and their preschool children made more visits to the emergency room than those individuals who were not rated as aggressive in their youth. Further follow-ups may shed light on whether bullying continues throughout the life span. Pepler, Craig, and Connolly (1997) suggest that it may begin with physical aggression on the playground during childhood, but may expand to sexual harassment, dating violence, and perhaps gang assaults during adolescence. In adulthood, bullying may continue with violence toward the spouse, child abuse, workplace harassment, and elder abuse.

Friendship Quality and Behaviour

ISSUES TO CONSIDER

- How does friendship quality influence adolescent development and later life?
- How do school friendships influence adolescent behaviour and development?

Friendships are generally beneficial (Hartup, 1993; Henrich et al., 2000). For instance, "being liked" or "being disliked" by peers is related to an adolescent's social competence (Hartup, 1996). Also, who one has as a friend (e.g., a youth with positive attitudes to school and society versus a youth who behaves in aggressive or delinquent manners) and the quality of that friendship (e.g., whether one enjoys continuous or stable support from one's friends, whether the friendship is marked by the reciprocal exchange of positive regard and cooperation) are significant as well (Hartup, 1996).

When friendships are marked by positive, healthy behaviours, they are associated with comparable behaviour and development in adolescence (Shulman & Knafo, 1997). When high-quality friendships are stable during adolescence, youth show positive self-esteem (Keefe & Berndt, 1996). Such close friendships are also related to an adolescent's social skills (Berndt & Keefe, 1995).

Positive friendships during adolescence can have beneficial effects during later life. In a study of young adults who either had a stable and reciprocal best friend during adolescence or who had been chumless during this period, friendship was associated with higher levels of feelings of self-worth in adulthood (Bagwell, Newcomb, & Bukowski, 1998).

Friendships in school may be particularly useful in promoting positive development in adolescence. Positive school friendships can enhance a young person's academic performance and quality of school behaviours, including prosocial behaviours (Cairns & Cairns, 1994; Henrich et al., 2000; Wentzel & Caldwell, 1997).

Different types of school friendships are associated with differences in the behaviour and development of youth. For instance, students aged 9 to 15 years who are more popular with the opposite sex hold attitudes about lifestyle (e.g., having an after-school job or avoiding smoking) that differ from those held by youth less popular with the opposite sex (Harton & Latané, 1997). Membership in a clique in Grade 6 is associated with better grades in both Grade 6 and 8 (Wentzel & Caldwell, 1997).

However, because there is a great deal of consistency (homogeneity) in the behaviours of clique members, clique membership, as well as friendship per se, can be associated both with positive behaviours (good school grades, classroom involvement) and with negative behaviours (e.g., substance use, cognitive distortions, lower problem-solving ability, aggression, or delinquency) (Berndt & Keefe, 1995; Cairns & Cairns, 1994; Dishion, Andrews, & Crosby, 1995; Grotpeter & Crick, 1996; Henrich et al., 2000; Hunter, Vizelberg, & Berenson, 1991; Marcus, 1996; Vitaro et al., 1997). Being an isolate is also a potential basis of negative behaviours (e.g., substance use) (Ennett & Bauman, 1993; Henrich et al., 2000).

In a study of about 500 Grade 6 and 7 European American, African American, and Latino youth, isolation from school-based friends was associated with poor adjustment among both boys and girls (Henrich et al., 2000). For girls, membership in a clique or in a crowd was related to positive peer relationships, fewer behaviour problems, and better school adjustment. Such associations were not present for boys (Henrich et al., 2000).

Conclusions About the Functions of Peers in Adolescence

As is also true of families, peer relationships can enhance or detract from healthy adolescent development. Despite the diversity that exists in the influence of the peer context, most youth peer relationships function to help bridge a successful path from adolescence to adulthood. This positive contribution of the peer group to adolescent development may occur because there is a great deal of consistency between the influence of peers and the influence of the family.

This congruence between the role of parents and peers is not a recent phenomenon. The consistency of the results of research conducted over the course of more than a quarter century suggests that such congruence may be a general feature of the relationships among generations.

Influences of Peers and Parents on Adolescent Development

No social institution has as great an influence throughout development as does the family (Lerner & Spanier, 1978). Studies across a 30-year period indicate that most adolescents have few, if any, serious disagreements with parents (e.g., Douvan & Adelson, 1966; Laursen, 1995; Laursen, Coy, & Collins, 1998; Lerner & Knapp, 1975). As noted earlier, during adolescence very few families—estimates are between 5% and 10%—experience a major deterioration in the quality of the parent-child relationship (Steinberg, 1991). Furthermore, Galambos and Almeida (1992) found that parent-child conflict actually decreased in certain areas (but increased or showed no change in others). In choosing their peers, adolescents typically gravitate toward those who exhibit attitudes and values consistent with those maintained by the parents. These attitudes and values ultimately are adopted by the adolescents themselves (Foster-Clark & Blyth, 1991; Guerney & Arthur, 1984; Kandel & Andrews, 1987). However, culture seems to affect the influence of parents versus peers. For example, Claes (1998) found that friends played a more important role in the lives of adolescents (aged 11 to 18 years) in Canada than in the lives of adolescents in Italy, whereas parents were

more involved with Italian youth than with Canadian youth. In addition, the Italian adolescents reported a greater number of close friends (4.19) than did the Canadians (3.02), but the Canadians engaged in more shared activities with their friends than did either Italian or Belgian adolescents.

Attitudes About and Emotions Expressed to Peers and Parents

ISSUES TO CONSIDER
- How do feelings of closeness to parents and peers develop across adolescence?
- How is this intimacy related to adolescent behaviour?

Feelings of closeness to parents and peers develop in similar ways across adolescence, and these feelings are associated with the adolescent's behaviour. From Grades 8 to 12, male and female adolescents' feelings of intimacy with their parents tended to increase, but somewhat more so for boys than for girls (Rice & Mulkeen, 1995), perhaps because they started off at a lower point and had more room for development. Although both boys' and girls' intimacy with their best friends also increased across grades, the increases were greater for boys (Rice & Mulkeen, 1995). A study by McNelles and Connolly (1999) followed Toronto students from Grade 9 to Grade 11. They also found that intimacy with friends increased over time for both sexes. However, girls tended to establish intimacy by discussion and self-disclosure whereas boys developed intimacy through shared activities. These findings are contrary to studies that report that boys do not reach the level of intimacy attained by girls (e.g., Bukowski & Kramer, 1986; Urberg et al., 1995), perhaps due to different definitions or ways of measuring intimacy. Adolescents who have high intimacy with both their mothers and fathers have higher self-esteem, lower depression, and lower scores for risk taking. Adolescents who have same-sex friends and greater intimacy with their mothers report greater interest in school. High intimacy with parents may be associated with a desire to please the parents, thus the lower risk taking and higher interest in school shown by these adolescents (Field et al., 1995). High intimacy with parents may reflect parental warmth, support, and a feeling of belonging. This may serve as a buffer for depression and low self-esteem.

The attachment of adolescents to their parents remains strong in 16- and 17-year-old adolescents and is related to attachment to peers, particularly for girls (O'Koon, 1997). Attachment to parents is also associated with youth involvement in extracurricular peer group activities (Schneider & Younger, 1996). Harmonious relations between adolescent girls and their mothers are characterized by attributes (e.g., similar needs, needs being met) that correspond to the ones found in harmonious relationships between adolescent girls and their best friends (Gavin & Furman, 1996).

Time Spent with Parents and Peers

ISSUES TO CONSIDER

- How does the time adolescents spend with parents and peers change across adolescence?
- How does the provision of support change across adolescence?

Despite the high-quality relationships maintained between most adolescents and their parents, across the adolescent years there is a dramatic decline in the amount of time adolescents spend with parents and a marked increase in the time spent with peers, especially for girls (Larson & Richards, 1991). In order to study how adolescents spend their time, Csikszentmihalyi and Larson (1987) and Larson and Richards (1991, 1994) have ingeniously capitalized on adolescents' interest in electronic equipment and invented a new way of observing adolescent behaviour. Termed the experience sampling method (ESM), youth are given electronic pagers (beepers) to carry. Youth are paged from time to time and asked to respond to a short set of questions such as "Where are you?" "What are you doing?" "Who are you doing this with?" and "How do you feel right now?" Because they also carry a set of these questionnaires with them, they can respond to repeated beeps over the course of a day or week.

Using ESM, Larson and Richards (1991) found that across the 9- to 15-year-old age range, there was a decreasing likelihood that male and female adolescents would be in situations with their parents when paged. For boys, the tendency to spend time alone increased, and for girls, there was an increased tendency to spend time either alone or with friends. A Statistics Canada study found that 13- and 14-year-olds spend approximately 2 hours and 40 minutes per day with both parents (Statistics Canada, 2000). This includes time spent together on errands and chores.

Larson, Richards, and their colleagues have traced longitudinally the changes in the distribution of time adolescents direct to peers and parents. For instance,

four years after a group of Grade 5 to 8 adolescents were initially studied, the now Grade 9 through Grade 12 youth showed several changes in the way they apportioned their time with friends (Richards et al., 1998). Thinking about the opposite sex occurred before youth reported that they actually spent time with members of the opposite sex (Richards et al., 1998), and both thinking about the opposite sex and spending time with them increased over the course of adolescence. Girls spent more time with the opposite sex, and both girls and boys reported that spending time alone with the opposite sex was positive. As the youth developed, however, they regarded time spent thinking about the opposite sex as less positive. This may have been because they felt lonely without the person present or because they had time to reflect on the negative aspects of the relationship (Richards et al., 1998).

Across time, there were also changes in same-sex relationships. Girls spent more time thinking about both same-sex and opposite-sex peers (Richard et al., 1998). In addition, in a study of about 2000 Grade 7 and 9 students, girls reported that spending more time alone or in conversation per week than did boys (Smith, 1997). In a study of adolescent girls, Beaumont (1996) found that girls' conversations with friends tended to be more involved and friendly than their conversations with their mothers.

Given such developmental changes in time youth spend with their peers, it is not surprising that between early adolescence (about 10 years) through mid-adolescence (about 15 years) there is a decrease of about 50% in the time spent with parents (Larson & Richards, 1991). Between Grade 5 and Grade 12 the amount of time spent with the family decreases from 35% to 14% of waking hours (Larson et al., 1996). In addition, whereas mothers and fathers are seen as the most frequent providers of support in early adolescence, same-sex friends are regarded to be as supportive as parents in middle adolescence and as the most frequent providers of support by late adolescence (Furman & Buhrmester, 1992). The effects of mothers on daughters' sexual behaviour is strongest in Grades 9 and 10, whereas the influence of friends is higher starting in Grade 11 and continuing into the postsecondary years (Treboux & Busch-Rossnagel, 1995).

Despite the greater attention paid to peers over the course of adolescence, as will be discussed, considerable data indicate that the influence of parents not only remains strong but shapes and reinforces the effects of peers on youth development. Despite the decrease in the amount of total time adolescents spend with their parents, there are no changes in the proportion of time youth spend talking with parents about interpersonal issues, and this stability is especially true for girls (Larson et al., 1996).

Attitudes and Values

ISSUE TO CONSIDER

• How do adolescent, parent, and peer values converge?

As already emphasized, adolescents typically select peers who have attitudes and values consistent with those maintained by the parents. Perhaps not surprisingly, there is great agreement among adolescents in their attitudes and values. For instance, in one study involving about 3500 youth from five nations (Israel, Costa Rica, the Philippines, Scotland, and the United States), youth showed significant agreement across both age and sex in their attitudes about the transition to adulthood (Seltzer & Waterman, 1996). Such high levels of similarity among adolescents do not contradict the fact that there is also congruence between youth and their parents. All three groups, adolescents, adolescents' peers, and adolescents' parents, tend to have comparable attitudes and values.

Given this consistency, it is not surprising that parents' opinions are the beliefs ultimately adopted by the adolescents themselves (Foster-Clark & Blyth, 1991; Guerney & Arthur, 1984; Kandel & Andrews, 1987). For example, a Reader's Digest poll of more than 1000 16- to 18-year-old Canadians revealed that 98% agreed that their parents had set a good example of "right and wrong" (Kiener, 2000). Adolescents' endorsement of conventional values (i.e., values pertinent to maintaining society, values about helping others) is associated with their identification with their parents and their parents' support of these values and with a lessened probability of selecting friends with socially deviant behaviours (Whitbeck et al., 1989).

Although peers affect adolescents in regard to such issues as educational aspirations and performance, in most cases there is convergence between family and peer influences (Brittain, 1963; Foster-Clark & Blyth, 1991; Kandel & Andrews, 1987). Adolescents and parents can have somewhat different attitudes about issues of contemporary social concern (drug use, sexuality, style of dress), but most of these differences reflect contrasts in attitude intensity rather than attitude direction. Rather than adolescents and parents standing on opposite sides of a particular issue, most generational differences simply involve different levels of

support for the same position (Lerner & Knapp, 1975). For example, in regard to the statement, "Birth control devices and information should be made available to all who desire them," one study found that adolescents showed strong agreement with the item and their mothers showed moderate agreement with the item (Lerner & Knapp, 1975).

Adolescents tended to see their own attitudes as lying between those of others of their own generation and those of their parents' generation (Lerner et al., 1975). They placed their own positions between the "conservative" and the "liberal" end of a conservative-liberal attitude continuum. They put their parents toward the conservative end and their peers toward the liberal end. In reality, therefore, adolescents think their peers are more liberal than they actually are, which means, for example, that adolescents think their friends are using more drugs and having more sex than is actually the case.

If closeness and intimacy characterize adolescent peer relationships, there is correspondence between the educational aspirations of the adolescent and his or her peers (Kandel & Lesser, 1969), and most adolescents (57%) have educational plans that agree with both peers and parents. Among those adolescents who disagree with their parents, there is also a great likelihood (50%) that they disagree with peers as well. When there is a discrepancy between parent and peer orientations, it is most likely that the parental orientation will prevail (Kandel & Lesser, 1969).

Corresponding findings occur in other studies, including those conducted relatively recently (e.g., Laursen, 1995; Laursen et al., 1998). Brett Laursen's work pertinent to adolescent-parent and adolescent-peer relations is discussed in Meet the Researcher Box 9.1.

Most adolescents perceive their parents as more influential than their peers in adjustment to school, and relatively few adolescents believe that peers are important at all in shaping school adjustment (Berndt, Miller, & Park, 1989). For other critical developmental issues such as deciding who to turn to for help when faced with a substance abuse problem, adolescents are more at risk if they turn to peers instead of to parents for help (Windle et al., 1991).

The data suggest that adolescents and their parents do not have many major differences in attitudes and values. Adolescents tend to perceive that their values lie between those of their parents and peers. Apparently, the impact of the intragenerational and intergenerational social contexts is often compatible.

MEET THE RESEARCHER   Box 9.1   Brett Laursen

Understanding How Closeness and Conflict in Parent-Child and Peer Relationships Influence Adolescent Adjustment

Brett Laursen is a professor of psychology at Florida Atlantic University. He received his Ph.D. in 1989 from the Institute of Child Development at the University of Minnesota. He is a member of the Steering Committee of the International Society for the Study of Behavioural Development and a consulting editor for *Child Development*, the *Merrill-Palmer Quarterly*, and the *Journal of Research on Adolescence*.

Closeness and conflict are part and parcel of all interdependent relationships. When it comes to the adolescent years, however, most of the research attention seems to focus on the downs rather than the ups. In the past, experts tended to reinforce the conventional wisdom about adolescence, namely, that it is an altogether disagreeable period of life. But is this really the case?

My research—supported by the U.S. National Institute of Child Health and Human Development and by the Johann Jacobs Foundation—is aimed at better understanding the positive and negative interchanges that adolescents have with their mothers, fathers, friends, and romantic partners. The ultimate goal of this work is to determine how relationship closeness and conflict shape the social and academic outcomes of individual adolescents.

It is important to remember that there is no such thing as an objective participant in the exchanges that take place in an interpersonal relationship. Two people can have completely different perceptions of the same interaction. In terms of effects, what may be gleaned by an observer is probably of less importance than what the participants themselves think and feel about the interaction. Simply put, if you want to know how experiences in a particular relationship affect an adolescent's well-being, then you have to ask the adolescent to recount the events and their consequences. In my

research, we do this by having participants describe all their disagreements from the previous day. We ask them to tell us about every little quibble, not just about the major confrontations.

The findings may surprise you. On average, adolescents report between 5 and 10 disagreements every day across all relationships. This may sound like a great deal, but it really isn't when you consider that youth spend around 12 hours a day in social interaction. That works out to something like one disagreement for every two hours of interaction. Furthermore, the vast majority of these conflicts mean little or nothing to the adolescent. Angry feelings are reported in just 25% of the disputes. Few disagreements with family members are perceived to have any consequence for the relationship and, among friends, disagreements are as likely to make things better as make things worse. The *bottom line* is that most adolescents report only one or two substantive conflicts per day, typically one with their mother and perhaps another with a sibling or a friend.

These figures are averages, but we all know that there is no such thing as an average child. There are huge individual differences in interpersonal conflict. Some youth report no disagreements of any type with anyone; a few report 30 or 40 over the course of an average day! How do these different experiences impact development? Data from an ongoing longitudinal study suggest that the

influence of conflict depends on the perceived closeness of the relationship in which it arises. When relationships with friends and parents are not close, more frequent conflicts are associated with lower school grades and more behaviour problems. When relationships with friends and parents are close, the effect of perceived conflict is a little more complicated: Adolescents with no conflicts and those with many conflicts have worse school grades and more behaviour problems than adolescents reporting just a few conflicts. Apparently, relationship closeness operates as a buffer that permits adolescents to explore some differences in a beneficial manner; those who have no conflicts miss this opportunity for growth, and those with many conflicts overload the system. Take away the closeness in a relationship, and conflict is an increasingly detrimental experience. These findings have important implications for our understanding of the role of relationships in development because they suggest that under conditions of closeness, disagreements can promote positive outcomes.

Interactions Between Peer and Parent Contexts

ISSUES TO CONSIDER

• How can parents and peers work together to promote positive youth development?

• What are some programs that allow for facilitative contributions by peers?

Although peers gain in their influence on adolescence, their influence does not replace the influence of parents. Peer and parent contexts can work together to support healthy behaviour and development. Both can be sources of positive interaction, and in supporting positive behaviour, one context can compensate for the other when necessary.

To illustrate how the contexts can contribute to similar outcomes, consider the findings of one longitudinal study, the Maryland Adolescent Growth in Context (MAGIC) study. This study of about 1400 African American and European American adolescents and their families assessed the quality of social interaction in the home, in school, and in peer groups (Eccles et al., 1997). Youth with positive interactions in one context were also likely to have positive interactions in the other contexts (Eccles et al., 1997).

The power of peers to facilitate success of youth in the multiple contexts within which they function can be used as a basis for building programs to promote positive experiences among young people and the enhancement of their contexts. Applications Box 9.1 illustrates these facilitative contributions of peers by describing three innovative programs. Children's Express involves youth and their peers in a nonprofit news service. The program uses 14- to 18-year-old editors in the training of 13-year-old or younger reporters, and provides youth with experiences and skill development in language use, writing, interpersonal relationships, and journalism. Youth as Resources helps groups of young people to form partnerships with institutions in their community (e.g., day care centres, nursing homes, community centres) in order to enhance the welfare of the community and to further civil society (see Chapter 5). Child to Child is based in Oaxaca, Mexico, and is a trainer program aimed at improving the health of youth and their communities. Youth community leaders train their younger peers to educate other young people and adults in their community in how to act to promote health and to prevent disease.

Given the role of peers in facilitating youth development and in making contributions to key contexts of their lives, it is not surprising that peers can enhance the functioning of youth in school. Among Grade 6 students, adjustment to school is related to quality of parenting (e.g., supervision, acceptance, and autonomy granting) *and* to peer group orientations (e.g., the presence of peer norms supporting academic excellence) (Kurdek, Fine, & Sinclair, 1995). Other studies confirm that peers and parents contribute to positive behaviour among students in Grade 6. Among such students, peer support was associated with pursuing prosocial goals, and parent support was related to school-related interests and

goals (Wentzel, 1998). In a study of African American, Latino, and European American families, the social support provided by peers emerged as significant in all groups during adolescence (Levitt, Guacci-Franco, & Levitt, 1993). This change was coupled with the significance of close family ties remaining strong from childhood through early adolescence within all the ethnic groups.

Other studies illustrate how one context can counteract the shortcomings of the other setting. In a study of 900 children in Grades 5 and 8, problems of social interaction and problems in the family, peer, or school contexts were compensated for by experiences in the other contexts (Barber & Olsen, 1997). In the families of African American adolescents, high-quality parenting can play a small but significant role in compensating for the negative influence on youth of having problematic peers (Mason et al., 1996). Maternal responsiveness and paternal monitoring have been found to decrease adolescents' orientation to substance-using peers and to result in reduced adolescent substance use (Bogenschneider et al., 1998).

As another illustration of compensating influences among contexts, when adolescents lack a close friend healthy adjustment can still occur if the adolescent has an adaptive and cohesive family (Gauze et al., 1996). In turn, if family adaptability and cohesion are low, healthy adolescent adjustment is associated with having a close friend (Gauze et al., 1996).

When parents show effective parenting practices—for example, authoritative child-rearing styles (see Chapter 8)—the convergence between family and peer influences may be maximized. When parents' authoritative parenting extends to the youth's choice of peer network and his or her behaviour in this network, several positive outcomes of youth development occur. These positive outcomes include lower levels of delinquency, substance use, and school misconduct for boys, and greater psychological and social competence and lower psychological distress for girls (Fletcher et al., 1995). Parenting practices that differ from authoritative ones (e.g., authoritarian styles) can create less positive outcomes for youth, and, in some cases, can result in adolescents being more oriented to peers than parents for support (Fuligni & Eccles, 1993).

Promoting Adolescents' Positive Contributions to Their Context Through Peer Relations

Peers are a key influence in the lives of youth. This influence can be used to promote positive development in young people. Numerous community-based programs throughout the world rely on the peers of adolescents to act as facilitators of their healthy development. Three exemplary instances of such programs are described here.

Providing Young People with Valuable Skills and a Voice on Issues Affecting Them

Children's Express Worldwide News Network, Washington, D.C.

Since it was founded in 1975, Children's Express (CE) has trained thousands of young people as reporters. More importantly, CE has given them a means through which to express their ideas and develop opinions on critical issues impacting their lives—from violence, divorce, and dropping out of school to domestic and international events.

Headquartered in Washington, D.C., but with offices in the United Kingdom and Japan, CE is a nonprofit, international news service run by student reporters 13 years of age and under who are assisted by teen editors ages 14 to 18. CE is based on the premise that young people not only understand but have valid perspectives on social, economic, and political issues. Through covering current events, CE promotes the written and verbal skills of participants, their critical thinking, and their awareness of national and international issues.

Currently, CE serves close to 1000 youth annually from its 10 bureaus and affiliated bureaus. In addition to its U.S. operations, CE has bureaus in Tokyo, Japan; CE United Kingdom operates bureaus in London, Newcastle, and Belfast, Northern Ireland, and satellite bureaus in a number of small towns in the U.K. Applicants are chosen on a first come, first served basis. CE reporters choose their own topics and which individuals to interview. Teenage editors then assist them in writing, editing, and producing their stories for publication.

In addition, participants and the young people they interview are urged to take part in roundtable discussions and workshops on specific social and political issues. Such meetings often include professional news anchors, educators, and policy analysts.

Through CE, young people gain skills in journalism and exposure to different views and ideas. The program has proven successful in promoting values such as patience, teamwork, tolerance, and compromise. A number of its graduates have gone on to pursue careers in professional journalism.

Involving Youth in the Design and Implementation of Community Service Projects

Youth as Resources, Washington, D.C.

Developed in 1987, Youth as Resources (YAR) views young people as valuable assets and provides youth with a means to contribute to the welfare of their communities. In the process, youth gain decision-making and other life and leadership skills.

The key components of the YAR model are youth-adult partnership in governance, youth as grantmakers, and youth-led service. YAR programs, governed by local youth-adult boards, award grants to youth volunteers to design and carry out community service projects.

YAR is unique because youth, not adults, research, plan, and lead the projects. Youth receiving grants require a sponsoring local nonprofit organization to serve as a conduit for grant funds and an adult volunteer to help with troubleshooting and general oversight of the project while still allowing the youth to be in charge.

Now in over 70 communities in the United States as well as Canada, New Zealand, and Poland, YAR programs have involved more than 200 000 youth ranging in age from 5 to 21 in contributing to positive change in their communities. YAR programs engage young people in a wide range of settings, including community-based organizations, faith-based institutions, public housing, schools, and juvenile justice facilities.

Projects can last anywhere from several days to months. Examples of YAR projects include middle school students who provided tutoring to 21 classmates for whom English was not a first language, high school students who performed puppet skits with an antidrug message, and other young people who offered companionship to seniors and assisted them with their chores.

An outside evaluation of the program found YAR participants to have developed more caring attitudes and a greater stake in the well-being of their communities. The Center for Youth as Resources in Washington, D.C., serves as the umbrella organization for YAR. Through instructional materials, technical assistance, and training conducted by experienced youth and adults, CYAR helps local YAR programs start, develop, and expand.

Youth Community Leaders Promoting Health Among Their Peers

Child to Child, Oaxaca, Mexico

The Child to Child program began in Oaxaca, Mexico, in 1989. The program is an instance of an international effort, begun in 1979 in London, England, as part of the celebration of the International Year of the Child, and has the goal of promoting health and preventive health care among youth.

The program is based on the philosophy that youth are a resource in the promotion of the health of other young people and of the community more generally. The program uses youth leaders in a community to attract children and adolescents to participate in an effort to learn to analyze health problems in the community, to study them, to act to solve them, and ultimately to evaluate the results of their actions.

Using youth leaders from the community (termed "guides"), groups of about 10 youth, usually ranging in age from 8 to 12 years, are formed. Using activities that are fun for young people and build on their creativity (for example,

>

involving drawing, theatre, and the construction and use of puppets in puppet shows), the groups participate in "train the trainer" programs. The youth leaders train the young people in their group to act as trainers of other youth and of adults in their community in regard to healthy behaviours.

For example, many youth and families in Oaxaca suffer from malnutrition, and the youth are trained to instruct their peers and the adults in the community in the principles of good diet and nutrition. Education is provided about how to develop a family garden in which nutritious foods are grown. In addition, the youth get trained in and then teach basic first aid skills. Other activities involve the cleaning up of the rivers and streams in a community.

Currently the Oaxaca Child to Child program involves about 380 youth and about 100 guides from almost 30 communities in its "train the trainer" groups. These groups are reaching approximately 1500 youth in these communities. All youth who work in the program are volunteers, and all activities pursued by the youth groups use recyclable materials (cardboard, newspapers, and plastic) or materials indigenous to the communities (e.g., corn husks, clay, or dried flowers).

Source: International Youth Foundation, 2001. www.iyfnet.org

Conclusions About Adolescent Peer Groups

The peer group context provides an important source of the person's behaviour, both during adolescence and into adulthood. As is the case with the family, this influence of peers can be negative or positive. Much of this influence is shaped not by the peer group alone, but by how the family and peer group contexts combine to influence adolescent developmental outcomes.

As emphasized throughout this chapter and across this textbook, the developmental system within which youth exist must always be considered.

We cannot fully understand the impact of peers on the development of youth without also understanding the impact of the family and the other components of the adolescent's social world (e.g., his or her school, the media, and technology). Outcomes of the relations between the developing person and his or her context can show considerable diversity in relation to the particular set of individual and social variables encountered at a particular time in life. In the case of peer relations, it appears that characteristics of the individual's peer status, characteristics of the peer group, and characteristics of the family need to be considered to understand how relationships with peers influence developmental outcomes for youth.

Summary

- Peer experiences can be understood by referring to several levels of social complexity within individuals, within interactions involving social relationships, and within groups.
- *Interactions* integrate the behaviours of two people in a social interaction, *relationships* involve a succession of interactions between two individuals committed to each other, and *groups* are a collection of interacting individuals who influence one another.
- Adolescents' peer relationships can be divided into several distinct groups of social networks: best friends, close friends, cliques, crowds, and romantic relationships.
- Peer status can be determined by asking adolescents to nominate peers for certain positive or negative characteristics. Various types of peer statuses include popular, rejected, neglected, controversial, and average.
- Peer status remains relatively stable across adolescence. Peer group status is related to current and later life behaviour and development.
- A friendship involves a reciprocal relationship acknowledged by the people in it and with reciprocal affection. Friendships are voluntary and they exist within a network of other relationships.
- As compared to younger adolescents, older adolescents have fewer friends, same-sex friends become more important, and friends equal or exceed parents as sources of support and advice.
- Parents impart values and attitudes to their children that influence their friendship selections.

Parents also provide supervision to their adolescents and peers through chauffeuring and involving their children in activities.

- Across adolescence, youth become involved in crowds, or liaisons, of loosely affiliated youth based on a similar stereotype.
- A clique is a set of usually three or more people in a tightly knit, somewhat exclusive, and mutually reciprocating friendship based on a key common interest or identity.
- During early adolescence, friendships are structured around crowds and tend to be predominantly same sex. By the beginning of high school, most youth are in cliques, although crowds still exist.
- Good peer relationships are a mark of social competence, related to academic competence, and predictive of healthy development in adulthood.
- Youth with poor peer relationships are more likely to drop out of school, engage in criminal activity, and experience mental or behavioural problems.
- Adolescents with good friends tend to have high self-esteem and good behavioural competence; not having good friends is related to school dropout, delinquency and criminality, and poor personal adjustment.
- The three dimensions of friendship are simply having friends, who one has as a friend, and the quality of the friendship.
- Friendships marked by stability, engagement, and lack of deviance allow positive self-esteem to develop in the adolescent.

- Friendships with youth who have negative characteristics and who engage in antisocial or disruptive behaviours often lead the adolescent to do the same.
- Bullying seems to peak at age 11-12, but may change into sexual harassment.
- Feelings of closeness to parents and peers develop in similar ways across adolescence. Intimacy with both parents and peers increases across the high school years. High intimacy with parents can be related to higher self-esteem, lower depression, greater interest in school, and involvement in extracurricular activities.
- Across adolescence there is a large decrease in time spent with parents and a large increase in time spent with peers. Thinking about the opposite sex and spending time with them increases across adolescence.
- As adolescents typically select peers who have attitudes similar to those maintained by their parents, there is great concordance among adolescent friends in their attitudes and values. Most adolescents have educational plans that are consistent with both parents and peers.
- Parents and peers can work together to support healthy behaviour and development, and when there is a problem in one context, the other can compensate.

Discussion Topics

1. Why do girls tend to have more intimate social relationships than boys? Why are girls more bothered by negative interactions with their peers than boys? Think back on your close friendships as a young adolescent. What traits were the most important and defining in terms of whom you became close to? Did those traits maintain their importance in late adolescence? Do they hold importance now? If you have experienced a change in the traits you value most, what factors and experiences in your life influenced that change?

2. Why do we so naturally define/limit people to one status or another? Can status be supportive of one's development? Or, alternatively, must

status always be considered destructive? Why is it so difficult to change one's status in high school and why is it so common for one's high school status to influence behaviour in later life?

3. What traits defined the popular adolescents in your high school? The rejected ones? The neglected? The average? At your fifth year high school reunion, do you believe those reputations will still be warranted? What influences your response? Did your status in high school fairly describe you or your status among your peers? Does it stand up to the image you hold of yourself now?

4. When you were in high school, how did your parents influence your choice of friends? Did you respond well to their involvement? Why or why

not? When you look back on it now, can you better appreciate their influence and input? How does their previous involvement in your friendship choices impact the choices you make now?

5. The term *clique* is often associated with negative, exclusive behaviours among adolescents. Despite this association, research finds that one's membership in a clique is actually related with psychological well-being and is, therefore, a positive attribute. If you were a member of a clique in high school, do you recall behaving in ways that may have been harmful to your classmates? What was the impetus behind this behaviour? Did the feeling of membership you gained from your clique support your social and emotional development? If so, in what ways?

6. In light of the growing presence of violence in schools, school personnel need to make every effort to reach out to all students and make them feel welcome and accepted. Think back to your high school years and the students who were either rejected or neglected. How did their status influence their experiences at school? Were any attempts made by students or the school administration to reach out to these adolescents? If so, what efforts were made and were they successful? Based on what you know about the tendency and desire to identify with and rely on cliques and crowds in adolescents, what factors would you have to consider if you were to design a school mission statement that would empower and be accepted and practised by all students?

7. What was your main focus in high school, academics or social relationships? How did one impact the other?

8. Did you ever have to alter your own behaviours to fit in with your peer group? How comfortable were you with those changes? Did your popularity increase among your peer group as a result of these changes? How did the changes impact your relationship with your parents? Your siblings? Do you at all regret altering your behaviour patterns to fit in?

9. Of the friendships you shared in adolescence, how would you describe the nature of the friendship that most supported the development of your self-esteem? Did it have a positive or a negative impact? How, if at all, has that relationship impacted your later development and the relationships you presently seek to maintain?

10. How many close friends of the opposite sex did you have in high school? How did your personality, self-esteem, and life experiences determine your interactions with the opposite sex during those years? How do your experiences from adolescence impact relationships that you currently share with the opposite sex?

11. During adolescence, how well did the attitudes your parent(s) held about adolescent high-risk behaviour correspond with the attitudes of your friends? Whose attitudes were more influential in terms of impacting the daily decisions you made? Who did you typically turn to for advice? Did it depend on the topic you sought advice about? Why did you feel more comfortable seeking out one party (friend or parent) over the other? Given the chance, is there advice you would like to offer your parents now regarding their openness and ability to discuss certain topics?

12. If, during your adolescent years, there was a part of your social context that had a negative impact on your development, how well did your other social contexts compensate for these negative influences?

Key Terms

average status, p. 206
bullying, p. 212
clique, p. 208
controversial status, p. 206
crowd (liaison), p. 207

display behaviours, p. 211
friendship, p. 206
group, p. 205
interactions, p. 205
neglected status, p. 206

popular status, p. 206
rejected status, p. 206
relationships, p. 205
social networks, p. 205
stereotype, p. 207

10

Sexuality in Adolescence

Sabrina looked at her reflection in the mirror. She turned her mouth up in a half smile and made sure her lipstick was evenly applied. Turning slightly, she looked at her profile. She smoothed her shirt over her skirt and pulled at the sleeves.

"I have to look perfect for Anthony," she said to herself.

Tonight was the first night Sabrina and Anthony were going out and she wanted to make sure she looked nice. As Sabrina was putting away her lipstick the doorbell rang. Sabrina quickly flipped her hair, grabbed her coat, and ran down the stairs. She took a deep breath and opened the door to see Anthony smiling at her.

"You look great. Ready to go?" he asked, giving her a big smile.

"Yep," she replied, blushing a little.

They got into his car and started driving. Sabrina was not sure where they were going, but she didn't really care. Anthony reached over and placed his hand on her knee. Sabrina felt her stomach do a flip-flop. A few minutes later they pulled into a deserted park. Anthony turned off the car and turned toward Sabrina. Sabrina's palms were sweating and she twitched nervously.

Anthony reached over and lifted her face up to his. She looked at him and he moved in to kiss her. Sabrina moved away. This was not what she had thought her first date with Anthony would be like. Anthony moved in again, and this time they kissed and he put his hand on her chest. Sabrina pushed his hand away but he persisted.

"Aw come on," he whined.

"Please don't," she said quietly.

"You expect me to stop when you show up looking like that?" he retorted as he continued to kiss her.

Sabrina admitted to herself that she had dressed to get Anthony's attention. But this was not the attention she wanted. She didn't know what to do.

Learning Objectives

1. To recognize the ways that male and female adolescents differ in their conception of romance and dating.
2. To understand what influences adolescents' styles of sexual behaviour.
3. To understand why research on adolescence should address the complexity of developmental contexts and issues experienced by homosexual youth.
4. To understand the ways in which heterosexism and homonegativity represent important obstacles to healthy development for homosexual youth.
5. To understand some of the sexual problems and risks faced by contemporary adolescents.
6. To learn the prevalence of STDs in Canada and the United States and the behaviours that increase adolescents' risk of contracting HIV infection and/or other STDs.
7. To understand what contributes to the effectiveness of AIDS intervention programs that address problem behaviours involved in contracting HIV infection.
8. To understand the conditions under which adolescents usually experience unwanted sex.
9. To understand how pubertal maturation, fantasies about sexual experiences, role expectations, attitudes regarding sex, and societal norms influence adolescents' sexual behaviour.
10. To understand the characteristics of the community context that might influence adolescent attitudes toward sexual activity.

What do Sabrina and other adolescents in her situation do? What about Anthony? What can be expected in regard to sexual behaviours among contemporary youth?

This chapter addresses these questions and explains why sexuality and dating are some of the greatest concerns of adolescents and of the adults who worry about them. Given the importance attached to sexuality in contemporary society, the attendant pleasures, and the dangers ranging from sexual abuse and violence, exploitation, disease, to unwanted pregnancy and childbirth, it is obvious why there is so much concern about adolescent sexuality.

As noted in Chapter 3, the adolescent's hormonal balance changes throughout this period. The genitals develop to their nearly adult form. Both males and females begin to experience new feelings, including new bodily functions such as menstruation for females and ejaculation of seminal fluid for males. Perhaps more important than these physical changes, however, are the social and psychological changes that accompany adolescence. Given the cognitive changes that occur during adolescence (see Chapter 4), it is not surprising that sexual behaviour and sexual interaction take on new meanings as the adolescent begins to think about social events in school, parties outside of school, love, and dating.

Dating and Romance

ISSUE TO CONSIDER

• In what ways do male and female adolescents differ in their conception of romance and dating?

The character of romantic relationships changes across adolescence (Furman & Brown, 1999). A key facet of this development involves developing the skills to regulate the intense emotions associated with these relationships (Larson, Clore, & Wood, 1999). Support derived from other close, loving relationships, for instance with parents, may aid this regulation (Gray & Steinberg, 1999).

During adolescence, especially in its early and middle years, most youth have dating experiences that are brief in duration but intense in regard to the frequency of contact (Feiring, 1996). Feelings of affiliation rather than attachment characterize young adolescents' conceptions of romance, with girls stressing the interpersonal qualities of those with whom they are romantically involved and boys emphasizing the importance of physical attraction (Feiring, 1996).

In a study of sexual behaviours and attitudes among high school students with a steady dating partner in the Kingdom of Swaziland, in southern Africa, "traditional" gender differences were found (McLean, 1995). Although most youth were sexually active by the age of 16, girls stressed the importance of demonstrating affection more than boys and were less supportive of multiple sexual partners.

A study of 12- to 19-year-olds in the United States indicates that the ages of *acceptable* dating

Dating and romantic relationships are important parts of adolescents' sexual development.

partners among male and female adolescents range from partners who are about their own age (for girls dating boys) or slightly younger (for boys dating girls), to partners who are somewhat above their own ages (Kenrick et al., 1996). Males, however, reported that their *ideal* attractive partners would be several years older than themselves (Kenrick et al., 1996).

Across adolescence, especially during the early portions of this period, adolescents' romantic inclinations are not always directed exclusively to people they know personally. Adolescents often have relatively brief romantic attractions—crushes, if you will—to movie or music stars or to other people falling into the category of teenage idols. Parents often get concerned about such crushes, but, as explained in Parenting Box 10.1, attractions to teenage idols may serve very useful functions in the development of romantic emotions in adolescence.

Given this diversity in adolescents' ideas about dating and romance, it is not surprising to learn there are also differences among youth in the sorts of sexual behaviours in which they engage. These behaviours influence the person's emotions, social relationships, and often health throughout adolescence and may often have important implications for the rest of the adolescent's life, especially when problems of sexuality arise.

Adolescent Sexuality Today

The nature and extent of adolescent sexual activity clearly have changed in recent years. Several different patterns, or styles, of sexual behaviour characterize contemporary adolescents. Many of these styles are linked to sexual activity that places the young

Teen Idols: Celebrity Crushes Actually Help Your Child Learn About Love

When 11-year-old Ming broke her arm, her parents' biggest worry was getting her to the hospital as fast as possible. Ming's greatest concern, however, was not the pain, nor even the disruption the injury would cause to her sports schedule. "Promise me you won't forget!" she pleaded with her parents in the emergency room. "You *have* to tape *Friends!*"

How much does the show mean to Ming? Only everything. Its characters are central to the lives of her group of friends. Posters of the cast members cover much of the available space on their bedroom walls, and the girls pass along fan magazines offering glimpses into the actors' lives. They debate which of the guys is the cutest and fantasize about meeting them face-to-face.

All this can be tough for a parent to endure. If you've ever spent an evening listening to the stereo in your daughter's room play the same Eminem song over and over (and over), or if you've ever wished that your son spent more time studying and less time mooning over the *Sports Illustrated* swimsuit issue, you know what we mean. But your preteen's fixation on a teen idol is more than just a drain on the allowance; it provides a safe stepping-stone on the path to adult feelings and roles.

Girls Develop Celebrity Crushes Before Boys Do

You may notice your child's devotion to a certain pop-culture figure as early as 8 or 9 years of age; girls, who generally mature a couple of years sooner than boys, likewise tend to develop crushes earlier. However, it's generally not until the early teen years, when an interest in romantic relationships collides with a developing skill in abstract thought, that the swooning really begins.

Being infatuated with an idol offers a young teen a number of advantages over a relationship that involves actual dating. A real-life failure would be devastating to a child this age, but by imagining how attractive and witty she would be with her renowned crush, she boosts her self-esteem without risk of public deflation.

In addition, your child's fixation on a persona shaped by popular culture can offer her social benefits; if all your 13-year-old's friends like the same rock group or the cast of a particular television show, the conversation naturally turns to such hallowed questions as "Which one do you like best?" Chatting about their idols and acquiring photos, T-shirts, and tapes of them offers teens a common interest.

Talking about the doings of the cute and famous also allows the participants to share and test their values ("I heard he was arrested for drunk driving." "That *has* to be a lie! I *know* he doesn't drink!") And it gives a child the chance to assert that she's her own person. When The Beatles were popular in the 1960s, Paul McCartney was almost universally regarded as "the cute one"; announcing Ringo as her favourite was one way for a girl to show her independence. (It also meant less competition for her idol's imagined attention.)

Finally, a crush on an idol—like a crush on a "real" but unattainable person, such as a teacher or a popular older teen—helps prepare a teen for age-appropriate dating. She can rehearse how she might feel, act, and talk, as well as the responses she might get from her idealized date. (Of course, if she really met her idol, she'd be dumbstruck.)

All these are perfectly good reasons *not* to belittle your child's lovestruck extremes, no matter how patience-testing they become. Instead, acknowledge her feelings. Tell her about your own preteen crushes. ("I remember seeing *The Way We Were* 13 days in a row, just to see Robert Redford.") Let her know how you felt ("I thought, 'Humph. He'd drop Barbra Streisand in a minute for me.'")

Granted, it's harder to foster a sense of shared experience when your child's teen idol's hairstyle, behaviour, or song lyrics are abhorrent to you. But saying, "How can you *like* someone like that?" won't get you anywhere. And, tempting as it might be, taking away the posters and CDs won't take away the fantasy. Instead, ask your child what she likes about her celebrity crush. If possible, mention something you like about him ("He *does* have a cute smile, and he's a good dancer") before mentioning specifics that concern you ("I really don't like the way he treats the women in his videos"). Again, sharing your memories may help—perhaps you adored Mick Jagger, and felt betrayed after his arrest for drug possession.

Your Child's Choice of Idols Can Be Revealing

You might also ask your child how he'd feel if a girl he dated did some of the things his idol does on her show—a question that could lead to a discussion of what qualities he finds attractive in girls. Although you may not change his mind about his idol, you'll have given him food for thought. *And* you will have shown him that you respect his feelings and views. In general, infatuation with teen heartthrobs wanes as your child gets a social foothold in high school, although it's normal to maintain some fantasies about famous people into adulthood—witness the middle-aged Fabio fans. Although an occasional teenage crush is both common and healthy, you should be concerned if your preteen's infatuation is interfering with friendships or is leading to problems with schoolwork. If that's the case, your child may need some professional help in developing his social skills or addressing some other underlying problem.

Source: Adapted from Lerner, R. M., & Olson, C. K. (1995, September). Teen idols. *Parents,* pp. 91–92.

person at risk of experiencing health, psychological, and social problems. The characteristics of contemporary adolescent sexual behaviour and the nature and bases of the problems adolescents encounter in the expression of their sexuality are covered further on. This discussion focuses on the diversity of patterns of sexual behaviour that develop during adolescence, the role of the context in influencing this diversity, and the importance of the relations that adolescents have with their contexts in fostering both problems of sexual behaviour *and* solutions to these problems.

Styles of Adolescent Sexual Behaviour

ISSUE TO CONSIDER
• What influences adolescents' patterns of sexual behaviour?

Today, adolescents develop many different patterns of sexual behaviours. For instance, Australian youth in Grades 10 through 12 cluster into five different sexual style groups: sexually naive, sexually unassured, sexually competent, sexually adventurous, and sexually driven (Buzwell & Rosenthal, 1996). Youth in some of the style groups (e.g., adventurous, driven) take more risks in regard to sex with both casual and regular partners (e.g., in regard to the number of sexual partners they had in the six months prior to the study or the number of "one-night stands") (Buzwell & Rosenthal, 1996).

Youth in other nations and/or from diverse ethnic backgrounds also develop particular styles of sexual behaviours. Among youth living in Norway, the development of sexuality is marked by slow growth and experimentation (Jakobsen, 1997), whereas Mexican adolescents working in factories are more sexually active and less likely to use contraception than are adolescents enrolled in schools (Huerta-Franco, Diaz de Leon, & Malacara, 1996).

Adolescents' family relationships and family communication patterns are often associated with the sexual styles they develop. In a study of about 750 adolescents and their mothers in the United States, little agreement was found in regard to level of shared communication about sex, satisfaction with the parent-child relationship, maternal disapproval of adolescent sexual activity, and adolescent sexual behaviour (Jaccard, Dittus, & Gordon, 1998). Mothers tended to underestimate the sexual activity of their daughters, and adolescents tended to underestimate their mothers' level of disapproval for engaging in sexual

behaviours (Jaccard et al., 1998). Given these differences in communication and perception, it is perhaps understandable that the adolescents' reports, as compared to mothers' reports, were more associated with adolescent sexual behaviours (Jaccard et al., 1998). In a similar study among Mexicans, the communication pattern that 12- to 19-year-old adolescents had with their mothers was related to the initiation of sexual relations, contraceptive use, and pregnancy (Pick & Palos, 1995).

In another study of about 1800 junior high school students in the United States, girls saw parents as less approving of sex than boys did, and yet girls were more likely than boys to discuss sex and dating practices with parents (De Gaston, Weed, & Jensen, 1996). Females reported more often than boys that parents had more rules, were more likely to believe that parents were unfair, and were more apt to report they had violated parental rules (De Gaston et al., 1996). In a related U.S. study of more than 8300 youth raised in families that belong to the Seventh-Day Adventist religion, engagement by youth in behaviours discouraged by their family's religion (e.g., going to a movie theatre or participating in competitive sports) was associated with early sexual activity (Weinbender & Rossignol, 1996). Hampton, Jeffery, Smith, & McWatters (2001) found that among 2000 Regina, Saskatchewan adolescents in Grades 10 and 12, those who had so far abstained from intercourse were more likely to believe that their parents would not approve of it. Similarly, surveys of adult Canadians suggest they are more comfortable with sexual activity among adolescents age 16 and over than they are with adolescents under age 16, and this is the pattern of sexual behaviour among adolescents (Maticka-Tyndale, 2001).

In essence, adolescents show different patterns of sexual behaviour. Some behaviours (e.g., early, unprotected sex) are linked to the problems and risks to their health and positive development more so than other behaviours (e.g., dating). These problems and risks are discussed later in this chapter.

Although, in terms of proportions, a logical assumption might be that most of the youth involved as participants in the just noted research on adolescent sexuality are heterosexual and that most of the styles of sexual expression among these youth involved members of the opposite sex, many adolescents have homosexual sexual orientations or are bisexual in their sexual orientation.

Romance and dating are significant features of relationships among gay and lesbian youth.

Homosexuality in Adolescence

ISSUE TO CONSIDER

- Why should current research on adolescence address the complexity of developmental contexts and issues experienced by homosexual youth?

Many of the studies of the development of sexuality during adolescence do not explicitly investigate whether the youth being studied are heterosexual or homosexual. As Grotevant (1998, p. 1116) has explained, many summaries of research knowledge about the development of adolescent sexuality "generally carry the presumption that these emerging sexual relationships are heterosexual"; this reflects the **heterosexism** of North American society ("an ideology that excludes reference to gay people, effectively making them invisible"; Alderson, 2002, p. 4). However, according to Grotevant (1998, p. 1116),

> awareness of gay, lesbian, and bisexual identities and relationships is growing in the popular culture and the research literature as well (D'Augelli &

Heterosexism Ideology that excludes reference to gay people, effectively making them invisible.

Patterson, 1995; Herdt, 1989; Oswald, 1994; Savin-Williams, 1990, 1994).

Developmental challenges facing gay or lesbian youth are multifaceted and illustrate the need to understand adolescent development in context. Their erotic fantasies and experiences typically do not mesh with the messages they see portrayed in the media; they may feel isolated from peers and unable to discuss their feelings with family members; their sense of identity involves coming to terms not only with this sexual identity but also with how it relates to other identity domains; their emerging sexual orientation may clash with their racial, ethnic, or religious affiliations in such a way that they must hide their true feelings; and their behaviour may put them at high risk for exposure to AIDS or drug use. Although there has been a significant increase in research activity relating to the development of homosexual behaviour and identity, much work remains to be undertaken.

Savin-Williams (1999) agrees with the need for research and argues that both scholars and society must enhance their understanding of the complex developmental situation for gay, lesbian, and bisexual youth that Grotevant (1998) describes. He notes, "Investigators often explore the effects of gender, social class, religion, race, intelligence, and countless other human qualities in their empirical investigations, but rarely is sexual orientation or identity included" (Savin-Williams, 1999, pp. 151–152). He emphasizes,

> Few sexual minorities want special rights, only adequate rights. They want the right not to be psychologically and physically harmed. They want to lead their lives as we all do. They want to see the murders of young people stopped, regardless of the victim's sexuality, race-ethnicity, social class, or sex. As professionals, we are afforded an invaluable opportunity to contribute to the struggle for justice by the way we conduct research, teach courses, and confront heterosexism and homonegativity. (Savin-Williams, 1999, p. 154)

In 1981 the Charter of Rights and Freedoms took a step to create these rights requested by Savin-Williams. The Charter enshrines a number of rights such as freedom of religion, life, liberty, and security, and the right to legal protection regardless of race, national or ethnic origin, skin colour, religion, sex, age, or mental or physical disability. The courts have read in sexual orientation as one of the grounds entitled to legal protection (World Wide Legal Information Association, 1996). All provincial and federal laws must conform to the Charter.

MEET THE RESEARCHER

Box 10.1

Ritch Savin-Williams

The Development of Youth Who Experience Same-Sex Attractions

Ritch Savin-Williams is a professor in the Department of Human Development and Family Studies in the College of Human Ecology at Cornell University.

In my research, teaching, and clinical practice during the last two decades I have explored the developmental milestones of youths with physical and romantic attractions for members of their own sex. It should be understood that many youths who experience same-sex attractions and sexual behaviour never identify themselves as a sexual minority. Indeed, fewer than 2% of all adolescents classify themselves as lesbian, gay, or bisexual, although far more might were it not for negative societal stereotypes and discrimination.

Through in-depth interviews conducted over more than 10 years, these youths have shared with me experiences of their first awareness that they might be different from other youths because they have sexual desires toward their own sex. This early awareness can begin with first memories that emerge on average in Grade 3. Awareness proceeds through self-recognition, self-labelling, disclosure of this information to friends and family, sexual and romantic encounters, and a sense of resolution. This process can occur over a few years or a lifetime. When these milestones are reached and how they are negotiated differ based on a youth's gender, personality, family history, and life experiences.

One of the most striking changes that has occurred during the past few years is the earlier age of reaching these milestones, including disclosing to family members, often while still living at home. This contrasts markedly with earlier cohorts of youths, most of whom remained safely hidden and tightly closeted until they moved into their own apartment or dorm room. Thus adolescents are coping with family reactions earlier, more immediately, and for longer periods of time than those who grew up during any previous generation. A second noteworthy lesson from the youths' narratives is that many of the developmental issues they face as sexual-minority adolescents are the same ones faced by other youths regardless of their sexual orientation: concern with being popular, having an early curfew, engaging in sexual relations, relating to parents, and selecting a university or college to attend. A third discovery is that their lives are diverse and complex. There is no one way "to be gay" or to have a "gay lifestyle." Some youths are troubled and some are resilient, but most are ordinary. This full spectrum of sexual-minority youths has seldom been acknowledged or celebrated. I have written about these issues in the lives of youths in *"...And Then I Became Gay": Young Men's Stories* (1998, Routledge) and *"Mom, Dad, I'm Gay." How Families Negotiate Coming Out* (2001, APA Press). The third book in this trilogy will focus on the life stories of young women. The experiences of girls appear to differ markedly from most boys. For example, many young women first recognize their same-sex attractions through crushes and infatuations with other girls, and not through physical cues, and tell a best friend as soon as they become aware of their romantic attractions.

I am equally fascinated by the ways in which sexual-minority youth cope with peer victimization and harassment, societal condemnation, and family disappointment to become healthy, resilient individuals who develop romantic relationships, raise children, and are major contributors to our culture. Sexual-minority youth are fabulously successful navigating the terrains of their sexuality to become healthy, well-functioning adults. This resiliency—a necessary adaptation to living in heterocentric and homonegative environments—is generally not recognized in the popular media, which tend to emphasize the "doom and gloom" of gay youths. The visibility given to same-sex attracted individuals, however, has helped by giving adolescents positive role models to emulate and pride with being associated with such individuals. They thus learn to refute societal and religious stereotypes to experience the joy and diversity of life.

Nearly every junior high school student today knows what homosexuality is and most families have a sexual-minority member or know someone who is. It is nearly impossible not to see homosexuality portrayed on television or in the movies or written about in magazines or newspapers. Individuals might attempt to deny its existence, but this is becoming increasingly difficult with each gay pride march held or denied, each law passed or rejected, or each adoption granted or refused. Indeed, it is now possible to be young, gay, and proud and to live an ordinary life as someone who falls in love with someone of his or her own gender.

Ritch Savin-Williams continues his research on gay, lesbian, and bisexual youth. His work is presented in Meet the Researcher Box 10.1.

Homosexuality in Adolescence: Definitions and Prevalence Scholars who define homosexuality refer to one or more components of sexual

In Search of Sexual Orientation

Kevin Alderson recently became assistant professor of counselling psychology at University of Calgary, after working at Mount Royal College's counselling centre for 16 years. His developing specialty is in the area of sexual orientation, gay studies, and human sexuality. He has written two books: *Beyond Coming Out: Experiences of Positive Gay Identity* (2000) and *Breaking Out: The Complete Guide to Building and Enhancing a Positive Gay Identity for Men and Women* (2002). He is currently working on a third book looking at same-sex marriage.

I remember all too well my own arduous journey of coming out as a gay man. Life was so complicated then. I was a successful 36-year-old psychologist, and very married with two beautiful children. I came to a point where I couldn't deny my feelings any longer, feelings that I had harboured in silence ever since I could remember. Coming out was an explosion, one that even today deeply intrigues me.

In July 2001, I became a professor at the University of Calgary, a position that allows me to focus on my concern, passion, and study of those who belong to sexual minorities. I knew then how deeply I wanted to have a societal, if not global, impact. I needed to create a stronger voice for myself and for others like me.

In psychology, it seems that **social constructionism** is the movement that has collected the most moss. Its growth continues, despite the limited data supporting its "truth" in all areas of human behaviour. One such area is sexual orientation.

We all have notions about what sexual orientation is. Alfred Kinsey defined it as a combination of sexual behaviour and psychic reaction. *Psychic reaction* is analogous to sexual attraction and sexual fantasies. Kinsey developed his famous seven-point Likert scale, with zero representing total heterosexuality and six representing total homosexuality. Although the Kinsey scale is overly simplistic, it is still the one most commonly used in research.

Can sexual behaviour be modified? Of course—most of us make a conscious decision about whom we have sex with. Can psychic reaction be modified? At least in the short term, this appears to be possible. There are some mental health professionals in the United States who continue to believe that homosexuality is pathological, unhealthy, and inferior compared to heterosexuality. Their views are nothing new. Homosexuality was included as a mental disorder in the American Psychological Association's *Diagnostic and Statistical Manual* nomenclature prior to 1973. These therapists have come to be known as *conversion therapists*, or *reparative therapists*.

I was shocked when I read some of their published articles suggesting that they have been successful in helping a percentage of their gay clients become fully functioning heterosexuals. Some of these converts have even gone on to become married. It wasn't clear in their articles what they meant by sexual orientation. I assumed they were referring to Kinsey's conception of sexual orientation as being a combination of sexual behaviour and psychic reaction.

If this is true, they have lost the forest for the trees. I believe sexual orientation is about the heart, about who we have the propensity to fall in love with romantically. I wasn't the first to postulate this. Researcher John Money made it clear that this is what he believed in his works. If you can only fall in love romantically with someone of the same gender, that defines you as having a homosexual orientation. If you can fall in love with people of both genders, that defines you as having a bisexual orientation.

I believe all good research begins with our own convictions, as I suspect it does for the conversion therapists. But now I need to prove them wrong. When I was younger, I was disappointed that I could never fall in love with a woman no matter how hard I tried. I married because I was following the societal script of the day. I didn't marry because I had fallen in love. I believe it would be a real shame for others to marry because they feel obligated to do so, and I suspect that those who have married after conversion therapy have done so because their religious, cultural, social, and/or familial beliefs pushed them to marry, as such beliefs did for me. I also acknowledge that some people with bisexual orientations may not know this when they are young. After all, it takes time for true love to develop.

My research begins with working on developing a new sexual orientation scale. This is not an easy task, and it may in fact lead to a redefinition of sexual orientation. I think that would be a good thing. Once the scale is developed, I intend to begin a longitudinal study looking at the stability of sexual orientation over a 5- to 10-year period, comparing Canada to the Netherlands. If sexual orientation is a multidimensional construct, which aspects of it change naturally over time, and which aspects remain stable? By comparing two cultures, this should help to draw out those aspects that are socially constructed.

But I believe we will have something left which is not socially constructed. I've learned during my 46 years of life that you have to listen to the heart. Somewhere in there, I believe, resides the deepest connection to our soul. I don't think any person should tamper with that.

Social constructionism
A school of thought now dominant in women's studies and gay studies that holds that categories of gender and sexuality like masculine/feminine and heterosexuality/homosexuality derive from cultural influences, not from essential features of an individual's biology or psychology.

sexual

orientation, that is, emotional attraction, behaviour, self-definitions, targets of sexual fantasies, and affiliation in a given social community (Remafedi, 1985, 1991). **Homosexuality** may be defined as the orientation of such components to people of the same sex as oneself (Remafedi, 1991). The classic interviews conducted by Kinsey and his colleagues (Kinsey, Pomeroy, & Martin, 1948; with Gebhard, 1953) are still useful in providing estimates of the incidence of homosexuality. Kinsey et al. reported that about 37% of males and 13% of females had at least one homosexual experience that resulted in orgasm. However, many youth who have homosexual experiences do not identify themselves as gay or lesbian. Rather than homosexual behaviour, a propensity to fall in love with a person of the same sex may provide a useful definition (Alderson, 2002). Kevin Alderson discusses his work on definitions of sexual orientation in Meet the Researcher Box 10.2.

According to Kinsey and colleagues, 8% of adult men and about 1% to 3% of adult women were reported to be exclusively homosexual. A survey by the McCreary Centre (Youthquest! 2002) found that 6% of adolescents in British Columbia were unsure of their sexual orientation, 1.6% identified themselves as bisexual, and less than 1% stated they had a homosexual orientation. However, the survey noted that respondents may have been reluctant to admit they were not heterosexual and that it may take time to recognize one's sexual orientation. Adolescents reported that they recognized their gay, lesbian, or bisexual orientation at about age 14, and that if they came out to others, it was usually about a year later. Although most people reacted in a supportive fashion, 8% of respondents stated that their parents tried to find professional help to get them to change their sexual orientation.

Homosexuality and Individual and Social Development During Adolescence

There is variation in the implications of homosexuality for adolescent psychosocial development (Remafedi, 1991). As with all youth, the sense of self for homosexual youth is influenced by many factors. In a U.S. study of 85 lesbian adolescents and 87 gay male adolescents, variables important for the males' identities included political ideology, socioeconomic status, heterosexual friends, and gender nonconformity (Waldner-Haugrud & Magruder, 1996). For females, key variables were religion and the importance of school (Waldner-Haugrud & Magruder, 1996). In a related U.S. study of adolescent male

homosexuals ranging in age from 16 to 21 years, all participants reported that they understood their sexual minority status and were comfortable with their sexual identities (Edwards, 1996). Despite the fact that, at the time of the study, all participants were living their lives as heterosexuals (Edwards, 1996), the youth had positive perceptions of themselves (Edwards, 1996). In fact, many gay and lesbian individuals develop positive identities and are proud of who they are (Alderson, 2000).

Homosexual adolescents may face obstacles to healthy development as a consequence of their sexual orientations. As Savin-Williams (1999) has explained, key bases of these obstacles are heterosexism and **homonegativity**. In a study of more than 1000 youth in Grades 10 through 12 from Newfoundland and Labrador, male adolescents were more likely than female adolescents to possess homonegative attitudes, as well as gender-stereotypic attitudes and erroneous beliefs about sexual coercion (Morrison et al., 1997). Lower grades for both male and female adolescents also were associated with more homonegativity, gender stereotypes, and erroneous beliefs about sexual coercion. Morrison et al. suggested that people with low academic achievement may have difficulty integrating individual rights with societal responsibilities, so they take a viewpoint on sexuality that is less intellectually challenging. This would involve a conservative sexual ideology.

Homonegative attitudes are all too often translated into violence against gay and lesbian youth (Savin-Williams, 1999; Van de Ven, 1995). Adolescent perpetrators of such violence have attitudes toward gays and lesbians that, in addition to their homonegativity, may be characterized by ambivalence, defensiveness, and adherence to myths and stereotypes about gay and lesbian lifestyle (Van de Ven, 1995). Alderson (2002) suggests that homonegative attitudes may be less strong in Canada than in the United States: Kiener (2000, as cited in Alderson, 2002) found that 67% of Canadian adolescents versus 45% of adolescents in the United States supported laws allowing same-sex marriage. However, this does not mean that lesbian and gay youth have an easy time in Canada. For example, the McCreary Centre found that nearly one in five lesbian and gay youth in British

---

Homosexuality Sexual orientation to people of the same gender as oneself. Propensity to fall in love with a person of the same sex.

Homonegativity Expressing negative attitudes toward homosexuals.

Columbia had been physically assaulted at school in the year prior to the study (Sims, 2000). In addition, two-thirds had heard fellow students make homophobic remarks. In fact, 28% reported that their teachers had made homophobic comments (Youthquest!, 2002). Many of these youth (37%) felt like outsiders at school (Sims, 2000), so it probably is not surprising that across the adolescent age range there are some indications of poor adjustment (e.g., suicide attempts; Hershberger, Pilkington, & D'Augelli, 1997) that occur more among homosexual youth than among heterosexual youth (Remafedi, 1991). And when the obstacles to healthy development affect gay, lesbian, and bisexual youth, younger adolescents may be particularly at risk for problems of psychosocial adjustment (Remafedi, 1991).

In a U.S. study of about 200 gay, lesbian, and bisexual youth aged 15 to 21 years (Hershberger et al., 1997), youth who had made suicide attempts were more likely than youth who had not made suicide attempts to have disclosed their sexual orientations to others in a more complete manner. The former group of youth had lost more friends due to their disclosures and had experienced more victimization due to their sexual orientation (Hershberger et al., 1997). The suicide attempters also had lower self-esteem and more mental health problems than did the youth who had not attempted suicide (Hershberger et al., 1997). Substance use and abuse was found to be prevalent among gay, lesbian, and bisexual youth, with lesbian youth particularly at risk for substance abuse (Rosario, Hunter, & Gwadz, 1997).

As discussed in further detail later, substance abuse, particularly intravenous drug use (Rotheram-Borus & Koopman, 1991), is linked to other risks during adolescence. Although a risk to all adolescents practising unsafe sex and/or drug practices, particularly for gay, lesbian, and bisexual youth, a major risk during adolescence is **AIDS (Acquired Immune Deficiency Syndrome)**. During the 1980s and 1990s AIDS became a major problem among homosexual youth (Sussman & Duffy, 1996), with about 80% of AIDS cases in homosexual youth resulting from unsafe sexual practices (Remafedi, 1988, 1991). Gay and lesbian youth may be less

likely to use protection against AIDS when having sex compared to heterosexual youth (the McCreary Centre Adolescent Health Survey, as cited in McKay, 1999; Youthquest!, 2002). As a consequence, preventive educational interventions, as well as testing for the **HIV** antibody, are recommended for all youth, but particularly for homosexual youth who engage in unsafe sexual practices and substance abuse involving intravenous drug use (Remafedi, 1991; Rotherman-Borus & Koopman, 1991; Sussman & Duffy, 1996).

Unfortunately, homonegativity and heterosexism are associated with barriers to the receipt of effective services by gay and lesbian youth (Travers & Schneider, 1996). Youth attempting to receive treatment for addictions report feeling marginalized, harassed, and misinformed by treatment facility staff (Travers & Schneider, 1996). The sample of lesbians interviewed by Barbara, Quandt, and Anderson (2001) reported concern about the quality of health care they would receive if they revealed their sexual orientation to homophobic health care providers. However, if they chose not to reveal their sexual orientation, they were hesitant to trust the health care provider's judgment. This distrust may lead to avoidance of the health care system.

Conclusions About Contemporary Adolescent Sexuality

Today's adolescents express their sexuality in diverse ways. Many of these styles of expression are associated with positive engagement with peers, dating, romance, and the building of a foundation for later adult sexuality. For some youth, expressing their sexuality involves risky sexual behaviours (e.g., adventurous sexual actions, early initiation of sexual intercourse) as well as other types of behavioural risks (e.g., substance use and abuse). Because contemporary adolescence can be fraught with problems associated with sexual behaviour, we discuss the nature and extent of these relationships next.

AIDS (Acquired Immune Deficiency Syndrome) Condition of acquired deficiency of the immune system caused by the presence of a retrovirus.

HIV Type of retrovirus (human immunodeficiency virus) responsible for AIDS.

Contemporary Problems of Adolescent Sexual Behaviour

ISSUES TO CONSIDER

- What are some of the sexual problems and risks faced by contemporary adolescents?
- What are some of the implications of these problems?

Depending on personal values, the definition of what constitutes a sexual problem may vary from person to person. Most researchers who study adolescent sexuality would, however, now agree on at least one fact: A greater number of unmarried adolescents have sexual intercourse before reaching adulthood than at any previous time in North American history. Although adolescents are biologically ready to engage in sexual intercourse and childbearing, they may not be socially or cognitively ready to do so (Maticka-Tyndale, 2001). Most agree that when adolescents are forced to have sex they do not want, have unwanted pregnancies, bear children they are neither emotionally nor financially capable of supporting, or contract

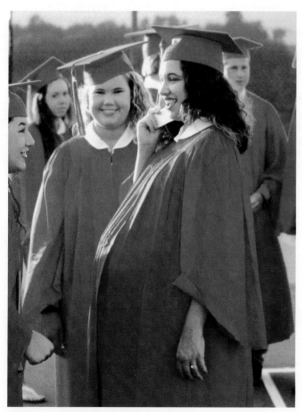

Teenage pregnancy is a significant life event for many adolescents.

sexually transmitted diseases, their sexuality is associated with problems and risk for their future healthy development.

Numerous illustrations indicate the presence of such sexual problems and risks among contemporary adolescents. However, Maticka-Tyndale (2001) cautions that Canada lags behind a number of countries in conducting national research on sexual practices. She states (p. 7), "We tend to use data from other countries (usually the United States) and assume it applies to Canadians. That is not good practice since it leads to invalid conclusions." She suggests that Canada is more similar to Great Britain, Australia, and France in terms of statistical indicators of sexual health. Thus, more research needs to be conducted in Canada; the following points highlight the Canadian situation where such data exist. You can read about Maticka-Tyndale's work in Meet the Researcher Box 10.3.

- About every minute, an adolescent in the United States has a baby (Children's Defense Fund, 1995). However, Canadian adolescents are more likely to use contraception than U.S. adolescents, and their pregnancy rate is lower (Bala & Bala, 1996). According to Martin and Zheng (2000, p. 68), referring to people of all ages, "The level of overall contraceptive practice (including nonreversible methods) in Canada in 1984 was among the highest in the world. . . ." However, these authors went on to say that the situation changed over the next 10 years so that in 1995 "Canada now ha[d] one of the lowest levels of contraceptive use. . . . Prevalence is even lower than in the United States; this is surprising, given that Canada's universal health care system provides Canadians with free access to medical services, including contraceptive prescriptions and sterilization procedures, while the United States has no universal health care system" (p. 76). One explanation for the discrepancy in these findings is that Martin and Zheng's data were for individuals aged 15 to 49, and it was people in the older age range who were using less contraception than in previous years, possibly due to increased sterilization for medical reasons (which also served to prevent pregnancy).

- A comparison of 46 countries (Singh & Darroch, 2000) revealed that the birthrate for 15- to 19-year-olds in Canada is 24.2 per 1000 adolescents, considered "moderate" by

MEET THE RESEARCHER   Box 10.3   Eleanor Maticka-Tyndale

The Effects of Social Policy on Sexuality

Eleanor Maticka-Tyndale, Ph.D., has one of the scarce and prestigious Tier 1 (i.e., senior) Canada Research Chairs in Social Justice and Sexual Health at the University of Windsor. Born in New York, she now enjoys living in a country known for peacekeeping, high-quality social programs, and a strong sense of respect for the diversity of its peoples.

The motivation behind my research and teaching originally came from years of experience as a community activist working to improve access to sexual health services and information. From these experiences and from my training as a sociologist, my research gaze has been set on understanding how social and cultural contexts influence the expression and experience of sexuality. We often think of the immediate, or what have been referred to as proximal, influences on human behaviour. Thus we turn to interpersonal relationships, attitudes, and values when we want to explain or influence how sexuality is expressed or what the sexual health outcomes are. My own work, however, turns to what many consider the more distant, or distal, influences of social and economic policies, particular historical moments, the intersections between cultural groups, and the environments in which we live, work, socialize, and "play." This has taken me to different countries, to research with different cultural groups, and to different environmental settings within my own country. What I have found is that what often are considered to be *distant* influences have comparatively *immediate* effects. For example, a recent change in Canadian government policy that made paternity leave available to fathers of young children on much the same grounds that maternity leave has been available to mothers (i.e., by using employment insurance provisions) produced a sharp increase in the percentage of men who opted to stay at home with their young children within a year of the legislative change. The change

occurred across the country. Contrast this relatively rapid and widespread change to the results of programs focusing on the more individual level. For example, programs designed to teach young men to take more time with their young children are useful, but have a limited capacity to create social change. By providing all mothers and fathers with the economic means to actively parent their young children, more children can have mommy and/or daddy providing them with primary care, for nearly two full years of their lives. Similarly, in a recent comparison of countries that share relatively similar economic and social profiles (the United States, France, Great Britain, Sweden, and Canada) it was differences in social, educational, economic, and family-related policies that demonstrated a stronger association with teen pregnancies and sexually transmitted infection (STI) rates than did the actual sexual behaviours of teens. It appears that when these policies and their related programs provide teens with the tools they need to take responsibility for their own sexuality they are less vulnerable to unwanted outcomes such as early pregnancy and sexually transmitted infection. But not all policies benefit sexual health. There are at least as many, and perhaps more, examples that illustrate how policies can contribute to sexual vulnerability rather than promoting sexual health and resilience. For example, policies of vacation and holiday resorts that cater to youth and promote high alcohol consumption and the celebration of sexuality without concern for health effects, as well as policies of

governments and schools that deny youth access to sexual information and services based on the belief that this will keep them from engaging in sexual activity, increase the vulnerability of youth to poor sexual health outcomes. Similarly, government and church policies in several African nations that forbid teaching children that condoms can protect them against the spread of HIV, rather than encouraging abstinence as the only way to protect against HIV, are leaving sexually active youth without any defence against the virus and contributing to rising rates of infection among the very young.

As I continue my research, the power of social policy to influence sexual health and well-being becomes eminently clear. What is also apparent is that policies don't necessarily work the way that those who frame them wish they would. For me this highlights the importance both of research that can guide policy formation and a willingness on the part of policymakers and the public to listen to what the research tells us.

Singh and Darroch. Rates were highest in the Northwest Territories (104.5 births per 1000 adolescents) and lowest in Quebec (17.4 per 1000; Cheesbrough, Ingham, & Massey, 2002). The birthrate among Aboriginal adolescents may be higher than that of the national average. For example, the British Columbia Ministry of Children and Family Development (2002) reported that the rate

among Aboriginal teens had been 4.5 times higher than the rest of B.C. teens from 1991 to 1998. One reason for this may be similar to the explanation given by Taylor (1995) about the high birthrate among the Inuit in the Eastern Arctic; that is, the great value placed on children in the Inuit culture. This esteem for children means that sexual activity and pregnancy among adolescents is not looked down upon and is not considered to be a disgrace.

- In both Canada (Maticka-Tyndale, Barrett, & McKay, 2000) and the U.S. (Coontz, 1992) the teen pregnancy rate and birthrate are lower than they were in 1974. (However, fewer adolescent mothers are married now.) The lower birthrate over the years could be due to more abortions, better sex education, more information given by health care providers, and/or more available contraception (Maticka-Tyndale, 2000).

- By age 24, 31% of unmarried Canadian females who have had sexual intercourse experience an unplanned pregnancy (Fisher & Boroditsky, 2000). The proportion of females giving birth before age 20 in Canada is half that of the United States (11% versus 22%; Darroch, Singh, & Frost, 2001). In 1995, Canada's rate was 23.6 per 1000 adolescents (Singh & Darroch, 2000). Singh and Darroch (2000) suggest that one reason for higher rates in the U.S. is the large proportion of adolescents who live in low-income families there. Low socioeconomic status is related to early sexual activity, pregnancy, and childbirth. The education level of the parents and the adolescent him/herself also are related to these behaviours (Singh & Darroch, 2000). The motivation to avoid pregnancy may be less strong among these individuals (Cheesbrough, Ingham, & Massey, 2002).

- National data suggest that on average, in 1995, experience of intercourse was virtually identical for Canada and the U.S. (37.4% of Canadians versus 38.3% of Americans aged 15 to 17 had had intercourse at least once, and 70.9% of Canadians versus 70.7% of Americans aged 18 to 19 had had intercourse; Darroch, Singh, & Frost, 2001). Maticka-Tyndale (2000) suggests that girls may now be having their first sexual experience at an earlier age than boys. Data from 1996 reveal that 25.6% of Canadian girls and 19.5% of Canadian boys had intercourse by their 15th birthday (Maticka-Tyndale, 2000). Intercourse before age 15 is more common among adolescents from families with the lowest incomes (Maticka-Tyndale, 2000). Less than 2% of Canadians had intercourse before age 14 (Maticka-Tyndale, 2001).

- Canadian data on condom use during most recent intercourse showed that 81% of low-income 15- to 19-year-olds and 76% of high-income 15- to 19-year-olds used condoms (Singh, Darroch, & Frost, 2001). Similarly, 80.8% of Canadian 15- to 19-year-old boys and 69.8% of girls reported the use of a condom during their most recent intercourse (Maticka-Tyndale, Barrett, & McKay, 2000). Among gay male adolescents, 38% used a condom the most recent time they had sex with a male (Youthquest!, 2002). Darroch et al. (2001) concluded that the rate of nonuse of contraception was quite high in the United States, quite low in Europe, and that Canada fit somewhere in between. Individuals (of all ages) with high education and low religious attendance (or no religious affiliation) were more likely to use contraception than other individuals (Martin & Zheng, 2000).

- Among Canadians aged 15 to 19, 36% of the males and 24% of the females who were sexually active had more than one partner in the year prior to the study (Marticka, Barrett, & McKay, 2000). This was more true for those in lower income families than for those in higher income brackets.

- The Canadian birthrate for adolescents aged 10 to 14 is more than five times lower than that of the U.S. (Cheesbrough, Ingham, & Massey, 2002). One reason for this is that a greater proportion of Canadians aged 10 to 14 abort their pregnancies (Cheesbrough, Ingram, & Massey, 2002).

- In Canada in 1993, 46% of pregnant adolescents under age 20 had an abortion (Cheesbrough, Ingham, & Massey, 2002). The proportion was 36% in the U.S. (Singh & Darroch, 2000). The abortion rate has increased in Canada since 1980 but has decreased in the U.S. during that time (Singh & Darroch, 2000).

- In 1989, 2.2% of Canadian pregnant unmarried women below age 25 chose to put their child up for adoption. This represents a decrease from 1981 (when 5.1% chose adoption; Daly & Sobol, 1994).

- One-quarter of Canadian adolescent mothers had a partner at least six years older than themselves. Of mothers aged 15 to 17, 54% had partners aged 20 or older (Cheesbrough, Ingham, & Massey, 2002).

■ In Canada, teen mothers account for 3% of all single mothers who receive social assistance (Bissell, 2000).

■ Despite the popular belief that giving birth during adolescence generates a life of poverty, a 10-year follow-up study of mothers in Nova Scotia (Nova Scotia Department of Community Services, 1991, as cited in Bissell, 2000) found that marital status seemed more related to poverty than did age at child bearing: among unmarried women, 54% of those who gave birth in their 20s and 52% of those who gave birth before age 20 experienced poverty, as opposed to 16% of those who were married and in their 20s when giving birth and 29% of those were married but under 20 years of age at the time of the birth.

Another Canadian study using 1981 census data (Grindstaff, 1988) found that regardless of their age at the birth of their first child, by the time they reached age 30, 54% to 58% of mothers were in the labour force and 65% to 68% were working full-time. Economically, by the age of 30, women who had given birth as teenagers were no worse off than those who had their first child between the ages of 20 and 24. However, women who gave birth before age 25 were less likely to obtain a university degree than women who waited until after 25 to have children (5% versus 25%).

The scope and variation of the problems just noted as pertinent to contemporary adolescent sexual behaviour may seem staggering. The magnitude and diversity of the manifestation of these problems is challenging educational, health care, and social service systems.

A full appreciation of the breadth and complexity of any of these problems of adolescent sexuality requires greater depth of discussion. In all cases, such discussion indicates that the adolescent's relations to his or her context is both a basis of the problems of adolescent sexuality and a potential route to addressing the problems.

Accordingly, to illustrate the person-context relational character of the problems of adolescent sexuality, we discuss three key problems. One problem is that AIDS and other sexually transmitted diseases cannot only diminish the adolescent's life chances but can also eliminate his or her chances of even *having* a life. A second key problem is sexual abuse, involving unwanted sex and date rape in particular. Sexual abuse may profoundly impact the safety and self-esteem of the young people involved in this problem. Finally, prostitution is discussed as a problem facing adolescents.

AIDS and Other Sexually Transmitted Diseases (STDs)

ISSUES TO CONSIDER

● How prevalent are STDs in Canada and the United States?
● Why must we take into account the latency period for HIV when talking about the prevalence of AIDS among adolescents?

The U.S. CDC (Centers for Disease Control) estimates that about 12 million cases of **STDs (sexually transmitted diseases)**, and **STIs (sexually transmitted infections)**, occur each year in the United States, and approximately two-thirds involve people younger than 25 years of age (Boyer, Shafer, & Tschann, 1997). Adolescents usually have higher rates of STDs than other age groups (Maticka-Tyndale, 2000; St. Lawrence et al., 1995a), perhaps because they are less likely to be married, are more likely to have multiple partners, and are more likely to neglect using protection. They may also have less information and access to services (Panchaud, Singh, Feivelson, & Darroch, 2000). Rates of STDs are much higher in the United States than in Canada (Panchaud, Singh, Feivelson, & Darroch, 2000). (See Table 10.1 to compare rates.) Differences in policies and screening programs may account for some of the differences in rates (Panchaud, Singh, Feivelson, & Darroch, 2000). In addition, 15- to 19-year-olds in the U.S. are more likely to have multiple partners than are 15- to 19-year-olds in Canada (50.8% of males and 46.5% of females in the U.S. versus 32.1% of males and 23.9% of females in Canada), which may make them more vulnerable to STDs (Darroch, Singh, & Frost, 2001).

Regardless of where they live, adolescents who live in poor economic conditions have higher rates. This may be because they may have difficulty accessing adequate medical care (Panchaud, Singh, Feivelson, & Darroch, 2000).

STD (sexually transmitted disease) or **STI (sexually transmitted infection)** Disease, such as HIV or gonorrhea, that is transmitted by sexual contact.

Table 10-1 **Rates of STIs Among Adolescents in Canada and the United States**

| | TYPE OF STI | | |
	Syphilis*	Gonorrhea	Chlamydia
Canada	0.6	59.4	563.3
United States	6.4	571.8	1131.6

*per 100 000 individuals

Source: Panchaud, Singh, Feivelson, & Darroch, 2000.

In Canada, rates of gonorrhea have increased since 1998, especially among males under age 30 (Sarwal, Wong, Sevigny, & Ng, 2003), and especially for those living in Nunavut (Ferry, 1999). Although the rates of gonorrhea are lower here than in the United States, parts of Europe have practically eradicated the disease (Maticka-Tyndale, 2001). Rates of chlamydia are highest among 15- to 24-year-olds, especially females (Maticka-Tyndale, Barrett, & McKay, 2000). Because no symptoms are shown for a long time, chlamydia can cause tubal infertility and ectopic pregnancies before the infected person is aware of the infection (Maticka-Tyndale, 2001). Human papilloma virus (HPV) is another STD of concern, as it may be related to cervical cancer (Maticka-Tyndale, 2001).

The best current predictor of the spread of AIDS among adolescents is their rate of STD infection (St. Lawrence et al., 1995a). AIDS was first recognized as a separate disease in 1981 (Boyer & Hein, 1991). Over the past two decades AIDS has become an epidemic throughout the world, particularly in developing nations (e.g., in Africa; Araoye & Adegoke, 1996).

Because no precise studies have examined the prevalence of AIDS across the general adolescent population (St. Lawrence et al., 1995a), the exact number of adolescents infected with the human immunodeficiency virus (HIV) causing AIDS is unknown (Rotheram-Borus & Koopman, 1991). Although the relative number of reported cases of AIDS among adolescents is small (e.g., only 1392 individuals out of over 51 000 Canadians who tested positive for HIV were under age 20; Health Canada, 2002), the disease is probably much more prevalent during adolescence. HIV has a long **latency period** (that is, a long period between infection and appearance of symptoms), averaging about eight years (Boyer & Hein, 1991). Therefore, many of the AIDS cases that appear among people in their 20s probably

involve infection during adolescence (St. Lawrence et al., 1995a). Aboriginal youth tend to be diagnosed with AIDS at younger ages than other youth, especially in areas where there are high levels of poverty, violence, drug abuse, and alcoholism (Health Canada, 1999). Aboriginals are overrepresented in AIDS cases in Canada; they make up 3.3% of the Canadian population but 5.3% of AIDS cases in which ethnicity is reported (Health Canada, 2003). Similarly, blacks represent only 2.2% of the population, yet make up 13.9% of AIDS cases in which ethnicity is known. Not all provinces request data on ethnicity, and those that do tend to have a high proportion of Aboriginals, so these figures may be imprecise.

Preventing HIV Infection and AIDS Medical advances continue to be made in the treatment of HIV infection and AIDS. However, because at this writing, there is still no cure for the disease, preventing infection remains the best way to avoid the spread of AIDS (Boyer & Hein, 1991).

HIV infection, as well as the contraction of STDs, occurs in relation to other behaviours that place the adolescent at risk. Chapter 13 focuses on the nature of and interrelation among risk behaviours in adolescence. Note that HIV infection is related to engaging in unsafe sexual practices (e.g., failure to use a condom during intercourse), intravenous drug use, and delinquent behaviours such as running away from home (Rotheram-Borus & Koopman, 1991; St. Lawrence et al., 1995b). Runaway youth often engage in unsafe sex, prostitution, and intravenous drug use. Each year thousands of infected individuals are going out onto the streets of North American towns and cities and spreading a disease that will kill them and the other people with whom they engage in unsafe sexual and drug use–related behaviours. Partner notification is neither systematic nor compulsory in Canada, so diseases have the potential to spread (Panchaud, Singh, Feivelson, & Darroch, 2000).

Programs that seek to prevent AIDS need to direct their efforts to the cluster of problem behaviours involved in HIV infection, and not just to AIDS prevention per se (Boyer & Hein, 1991; Dryfoos,

Latency period Incubation period of a disease (period between the time an infection takes place and the time first symptoms of the infection appear).

1990; Lerner, 1998). When these intervention programs involve attempts to promote multiple changes in youth, such as better knowledge *and* more skills, they appear to be more effective than efforts directed at changing only one feature of adolescent behaviour and development. Skill training appears to be especially useful. Applications Box 10.1 describes the results of several intervention programs aimed at changing risky behaviour and knowledge about HIV and AIDS through education or skill training.

Sexual Violence: Unwanted Sex and Date Rape

ISSUES TO CONSIDER

- How is the experience of sexual abuse related to later behaviour problems?
- Under what conditions do adolescent girls usually experience unwanted sex?
- In what way may family and peer contexts increase a girl's likelihood of experiencing unwanted sexual activity?

APPLICATIONS Box 10.1

Preventing HIV Infection and AIDS Through Intervention Programs Involving Education or Skill Training

Numerous programs have been developed to use education as a means to increase knowledge about HIV/AIDS and to reduce behaviours that place an adolescent at risk for contracting HIV (Grunseit et al., 1997). Providing youth with accurate information about AIDS is obviously important. For instance, two one-hour sessions with 111 Grade 9 students in Ontario were sufficient to increase HIV/AIDS prevention knowledge, prevention attitudes, self-efficacy, and behavioural intentions in comparison to the 49 Grade 9 students in the school who did not receive these sessions (Dunn, Ross, Caines, & Howorth, 1998).

Although there has been criticism that education programs actually increase the sexual behaviours they are intended to prevent (e.g., some people claim that educating youth about safe sex "puts ideas in their heads" about sexuality that they would otherwise not have), there is little evidence of such an influence (Grunseit et al., 1997). In fact, an analysis of the effectiveness of 47 HIV/AIDS and sexuality education programs by the World Health Organization indicated that more than half of them (25 of 47) neither decreased sexual activity nor rates of STDs or pregnancy (Grunseit et al., 1997). Although three programs did report that education was associated with an increase in sexual behaviour, about a third (17) reported that education delayed the onset of sexual activity,

resulted in a reduction in the number of adolescents' sexual partners, and reduced STD and unplanned pregnancy rates (Grunseit et al., 1997).

Programs that employ just education as their mode of intervention have not met with overwhelming success. In response, many people trying to prevent HIV infection and AIDS have sought to combine education that enhances knowledge with education that improves the behavioural skills of youth regarding unsafe sexual practices. For example, a group of substance-dependent youth in the United States who received training in skills to avoid HIV risk behaviours showed greater knowledge about HIV/AIDS, more favourable attitudes about condom use, a greater sense of internal control and self-efficacy, increased recognition of HIV risks, and decreased high-risk sexual behaviours than did substance-dependent youth who received only education about HIV risks (St. Lawrence et al., 1995b).

McKay (2000) suggests that sex education programs have the most success when they encourage delay of first intercourse as well as provide information and skill development about preventing HIV.

Using peer educators may be a promising way forward in prevention programs. The Ontario program described above by Dunn et al. (1998) compared intervention sessions facilitated by trained peers versus

community health nurses. While both resulted in greater knowledge about HIV prevention in comparison to the nonintervention group, students in peer-led sessions retained even more information than did those in the community health nurse group.

Similarly, a community-based intervention program in Nigeria involving more than 1800 14- to 20-year-olds that included peer educators along with school health clubs, public lectures, and training of STD treatment providers (including informal health providers who had no formal medical education) found that after 11 months significantly fewer students reported STD symptoms than students who had not received the intervention (Okonofua, Coplan, Collins, Oronsaye, Ogunsakin, Ogonor, Kaufman, & Heggenhougen, 2003). They were also more likely to seek formally trained private physicians (rather than informal health providers) for help after the program. In comparison to youth who had not experienced the intervention, these youth had more knowledge about STDs and slightly but significantly higher condom use. This is despite the fact that the schools did not allow encouragement of or distribution of condoms as part of the program. Although the authors were unable to tease out which component(s) of the intervention package were most effective, they noted that peer educators were one of the main sources of information about condom use.

Sexual harassment, sexual abuse, and violence toward youth are all too common in North America. Sexual harassment (unwanted sexual comments, looks, gestures, or name-calling) among 12-year-olds in Ontario reached 48% (McMaster, Connolly, Craig, & Pepler, 1997; as cited in Craig, Pepler, & Connolly, 1997). The British Columbia Ministry of Children and Family Development (2002) found that 54% of female students had received unwanted sexual comments in the year prior to the study. This rose to 60% of Aboriginal females. Berman, McKenna, Arnold, Taylor, and MacQuarrie (2000) noted from their focus groups with 33 girls from Ontario aged 11 to 16 that the girls felt that school staff did not do enough to protect them from the harassment. Reports suggested that when girls tried to take the situation into their own hands (e.g., by "fighting back"), they often faced detentions themselves while the harasser did not receive any consequences. The authors suggested that the continued presence of sexual harassment and the implied message that it should be tolerated or ignored serves to decrease girls' confidence and prevents gender equality.

About 23% of adolescent girls in Grades 7 through 12 in Alberta experienced sexual assault (including sexual touching, sexual threats or remarks, or an incident of indecent exposure; Bagley & Bolitho, 1997). Bagley, Wood, and Young (1994) found that 15.6% of a random sample of 750 males aged 18 to 27 in Calgary had experienced unwanted sexual contact before the age of 17. Price et al. (2000) surveyed 1700 New Brunswick students in Grades 7, 9, and 11. Of those who had started dating, 19% of girls and 4% of boys had experienced an "upsetting sexually coercive experience." Furthermore, these researchers found that while most students were not accepting of dating violence (sexual, physical, or psychological), boys were more accepting than were girls. A study of 111 undergraduates at a western Canadian university revealed that 35% of the women and 14% of the men had been sexually victimized during their adolescence (i.e., verbally, physically, or forcefully coerced into sex play or intercourse; Murray & Henjum, 1993). In British Columbia, 35% of non-Aboriginal female students and 46% of Aboriginal female students had experienced unwanted sexual touching in the year prior to the study (The British Columbia Ministry of Children and Family Development, 2002).

Newton-Taylor, DeWit, and Glicksman (1998) reported that 15% of 6000 female university students

from six Ontario universities had been sexually assaulted during the year prior to the study. Sexual assault included date rape and having been coerced into engaging in sexual activities when they did not want to.

Weir (2001) suggests that the use of drugs in date rape cases is becoming more common. Flunitrazepam (Rohypnol) and gamma hydroxybutyrate acid (GHB) can be added to a person's drink when she or he leaves it to dance or for other reasons. These drugs are colourless, odourless, and mostly flavourless and seem to have effects similar to alcohol intoxication. The results are that, due to sedation and amnesia, targets may be unable to defend against or even be aware of a sexual assault.

These experiences have profound impacts on the behaviour and development of young people. The experience of sexual abuse, especially when coupled with physical abuse, was linked to problems such as binge drinking and suicidal thoughts, gestures, and attempts (Bagley & Bolitho, 1997; Luster & Small, 1997). The negative outcomes of sexual abuse were lessened by high levels of parental monitoring and of support from at least one parent (Luster & Small, 1997).

Given these patterns of sexual violence involving youth, it may be expected that many adolescent girls experience unwanted sex or even date rape. Data support this conjecture. For example, in the U.S., 75% of girls under the age of 14 who have had sexual relations are victims of sexual assault (di Mauro, 1995). The Carnegie Corporation of New York (1995) concluded that sex is usually forced among young adolescent girls. Murray and Henjum (1993) suggested that much adolescent sexual activity among girls in Canada may occur against their wills, based on the high amount of sexual abuse during adolescent dating reported by women in their sample.

A study of a small community in British Columbia revealed that 26% of the 165 13- to 18-year-olds in the sample had experienced unwanted sexual activity on a date (defined as kissing, touching, fondling, removal of clothing, and sexual intercourse; Rhynard & Krebs, 1997). The authors commented that unwanted sexual experiences are not limited to adolescents living in big cities.

In a four-year longitudinal study of young, rural adolescent girls in the United States (Vicary, Klingaman, & Harkness, 1995), 23% had unwanted sexual experiences by the end of the four-year period. Instances included forced touching, intercourse, and oral sex. Fifteen percent of the girls had been raped by their dates. Girls who had been early maturers, who already had been sexually active, who had sexually active friends, who had poor peer relations, and/or who had emotional problems were more likely to have these experiences.

Family and peer contexts also influence the likelihood that adolescent girls will experience an incident of unwanted sexual activity (Small & Kerns, 1993). Most of the unwanted experiences were initiated by boyfriends, dates, friends, or acquaintances (in this order). A girl's history of sexual abuse, a tendency to conform to peers, and having parents whose parenting style is either authoritarian or reflective of low monitoring are predictive of her being a target of an unwanted sexual advance.

Family and peer contexts may also have an influence on whether an individual attempts to force unwanted sexual activity on another person. A questionnaire study of Canadian male university students by Lackie and de Man (1997) found that high scores on sexual aggression were correlated with high scores on physical aggression, sex-role stereotyping, and fraternity involvement.

Youth do not necessarily feel helpless in the face of unwanted sex. Although both adolescent girls and boys find it easier to encourage than to discourage sex (Rosenthal & Peart, 1996), in a study of about 2400 U.S. adolescents in Grade 10, girls were more likely than boys to believe they could say no to unwanted sex (Zimmerman et al., 1995). In addition, youth who had a less permissive attitude toward sex and who placed less importance on peer influence were also more likely to believe they could decline unwanted sex (Zimmerman et al., 1995). For girls, a sense of self-efficacy was particularly important in regard to their believing they could say no to sex (Zimmerman et al., 1995). Girls report that the presence of others is a useful strategy to avoid engaging in unwanted sexual behaviour (Rosenthal, Lewis, & Cohen, 1996).

As illustrated by the vignette about Sabrina and Anthony that opened this chapter, there exist tendencies in North American society to blame the victim in cases of sexual assault. These tendencies can be found among both male and female youth. Adolescent girls may take actions that place them "in harm's way" in regard to experiencing unwanted sex and/or being blamed for it if it in fact occurs. For example, evidence shows that both male and female adolescents perceive a girl who experiences date rape when dressed provocatively as more responsible for her assailant's behaviour than a girl who dresses conservatively (Cassidy & Hurrell, 1995). In addition, provocative dressing was associated with youth believing the male's behaviour was justified or that the unwanted sexual intercourse was not sexual assault (Cassidy & Hurrell, 1995).

Prostitution

Another contemporary problem faced by adolescents is prostitution. Although it is unclear how many prostitutes in Canada are adolescents, the mean age of starting in the sex trade is 14 to 15.4 years (Bagley, 1999; Nadon, Koverola, & Schludermann, 1998), with a large range (e.g., 9 to 18 years; Schissel & Fedec, 1999). This suggests that a large number of prostitutes are children or adolescents.

Context, particularly family influences, seems to affect adolescent participation in the sex trade. A history of sexual abuse is one factor that many prostitutes seem to have in common. For example, Bagley (1999) reported that in a sample from Calgary, 73% of prostitutes versus 29% of a community mental health comparison group experienced sexual abuse during their childhood. Schissel and Fedec (1999) found that among a sample of young offenders in Saskatchewan, prostitutes were more likely to have experienced childhood sexual abuse than were other young offenders. Schissel and Fedec (1999) suggest that early sexual victimization makes individuals more vulnerable to being exploited in the future, partly because abuse is now seen as normal behaviour. Kingsley and Mark (2000) have suggested that the step from engaging in unpaid sexual abuse to paid sexual abuse may be a small one, especially for

Many adolescents are victims of unwanted sexual advances.

adolescents who run away from home. Referring specifically to Aboriginal prostitutes, who often drop out of school, Kingsley and Mark (2000, p.9) describe common experiences:

> Having nowhere to go, most youth who find themselves in this situation are also lacking integral life skills and have few, if any, chances for meaningful employment. Their situation becomes one of survival, and the deprivation of the basic necessities of life ensures that the exchange of sex for money, food, shelter, or clothing becomes a decision about day-to-day existence. Without safe places for them to frequent and/or live, consistent support from caring individuals, tailored life skills, educational and employment programs, financial support, commercially sexually exploited Aboriginal children and youth have few alternatives for physical and economic survival, and little opportunity to reintegrate themselves into the larger communities, both Aboriginal and non-Aboriginal.

Although childhood sexual abuse may be a common factor among prostitutes, many individuals have this experience yet don't enter the sex trade (Bagley, 1999; Nadon, Koverola, & Shludermann, 1998). Some researchers have found that the severity and extent of the abuse are important factors (Bagley, 1999), but others have found that this does not make a difference (Nadon, Koverola, & Shludermann, 1998). Schissel and Fedec (1999) reported that severity of abuse was related to prostitution for non-Aboriginals, but not for Aboriginals. Further research is needed to clarify the effects of childhood sexual abuse.

Other aspects of the context, such as running away and being homeless (Bagley, 1999; Kingsley & Mark, 2000; Nadon, Koverola, & Shludermann, 1998; Schissel & Fedec, 1999), dropping out of school (Bagley, 1999), having an alcoholic parent (Bagley, 1999; Kingsley & Mark, 2000), having low self-esteem (Kingsley & Mark, 2000; Schissel & Fedec, 1999), having friends in the sex trade (Kingsley & Mark, 2000), or craving the acceptance and feeling of belonging the sex trade community provides (Kingsley & Mark, 2000) help determine whether an adolescent will turn to prostitution.

Youth who are involved in prostitution are exposed to a number of dangers. They often are exposed to violence, especially Aboriginal women (Schissel & Fedec, 1999). Kingsley and Mark (2000) report that prostitutes in Canada are 160 times more likely to be killed than other women. They are at risk for developing an STD (Kingsley & Mark, 2000) and may be inclined to attempt suicide (Schissel & Fedec, 1999).

Several programs exist to aid youth prostitutes. For example, in Victoria, the Prostitute Empowerment Education and Resource Society (PEERS) is an agency of ex-prostitutes who help create a safe working environment for those currently in the sex trade (Rabinovitch & Lewis, 2001). They also work to decrease the stigma associated with prostitution and to help youth leave prostitution if they choose to do so. Several provinces have adopted the attitude that youth prostitutes are victims rather than criminals and have taken steps to "rescue" youth by using "secure care" programs (Bittle, 2002). For example, Alberta has enacted the Protection of Children Involved in Prostitution (PCHIP) Act, which allows authorities to confine young prostitutes to a safehouse for up to five days (longer with extensions) in order to allow social workers to help get them off the streets.

Conclusions About Problems of Adolescent Sexuality

The problems adolescents experience in regard to their sexual behaviours are complex. This complexity is due, at least in part, to the connection of these problems to other risk behaviours in adolescence and to the numerous individual and contextual influences on adolescents, such as their peers, families, and communities (Small & Luster, 1994). Whether we seek to understand the bases of problems of sexuality or of the adolescent's resilience to such problems, we need to appreciate the diversity of adolescent sexual behaviour and of the contextual influences on it.

Diversity of, and Contextual Influences on, Sexual Behaviours

Individual variables involving biology, cognitions, emotions, and behavioural characteristics, and contextual variables linked to peers, family, and the community, influence adolescent sexual behaviours and the problems associated with these behaviours. Although it is useful to introduce the influence of these individual and contextual variables separately, a clear theme evident in the research is that these individual and contextual variables act together within the developmental system to affect adolescent development.

Both individual and contextual variables often coincide not only with the presence or absence of problematic sexual behaviours but also with other risks or problem behaviours. When the developmental system involves multiple risks, the likelihood of problematic sexual behaviours increases (Jessor, 1987, 1992; Jessor, Donovan, & Costa, 1991; Jessor & Jessor, 1977; Ketterlinus & Lamb, 1994; Lerner, 1998). Accordingly, we discuss sexual behaviours in a special context: the context of multiple risks and problem behaviours.

Individual Influences

ISSUES TO CONSIDER

- In what way are adolescents' attitudes regarding sex and societal norms associated with the adolescents' sexual behaviour?
- How is pubertal maturation linked to adolescents' sexual behaviour?
- What role do expectations and fantasies about sexual experiences play in the adolescents' sexual behaviour?
- What are some of the individual characteristics associated with teenage parenting?

Attitudes are mental structures that have both an emotional component (e.g., attitudes reflect one's likes and dislikes about some topic, thing, or person) and a cognitive component (e.g., attitudes involve beliefs about and/or some knowledge of the topic, thing, or person in question). Ambivalent attitudes toward childbearing, contraception, contraceptive efficacy, and abortions are related to adolescent childbearing (Zabin, Astone, & Emerson, 1993). Similarly, a U.S. study found that when combined with nonconforming behaviour, possession of attitudes that reject societal norms is associated with early initiation of sexual intercourse among adolescents (Costa et al., 1995). Among both male and female adolescents, poor psychological adjustment is linked to early initiation of sexual intercourse (Bingham & Crockett, 1996).

Pubertal maturation may also be related to adolescents' sexual behaviours. Among gay and bisexual male adolescents, pubertal maturation is associated with age of first orgasm and first homosexual activity and with frequency of orgasms during junior high school (Savin-Williams, 1995). Other individual variables, if shown by gay adolescents, may not bode well for their adjustment. A U.S. study of gay and bisexual adolescent males found that sexually risky attitudes, coupled with substance abuse, conduct problems, and emotional distress, are associated with the likelihood that this set of problems will remain stable for the youth (Borus et al., 1995). In fact, across a two-year period only about 20% to 30% of youth changed their pattern of problem behaviours.

Expectations and fantasies about sexual experiences also play a role in the adolescent's sexual behaviour. Adolescents who have not yet initiated sexual activity may have unrealistic expectations about how it will make them feel. They may, for example, overestimate how positive they will feel about sexual activity. In a study of about 1300 high school students from Miami, Florida, the degree to which virgins predicted they would feel better after first experiencing sexual intercourse was much *less* than that which nonvirgins reported actually feeling about the event (Langer, Zimmerman, & Katz, 1995). Male nonvirgins felt better about their first sexual experience than did female nonvirgins, and the more sexual partners youth had, the more positive were their reported feelings (Langer et al., 1995).

There are also behavioural characteristics of youth whose sexuality has resulted in childbearing that appear to be associated specifically with their status as teenage parents. U.S. studies have found a number of poor outcomes for the children of adolescent mothers (e.g., Broman, 1979; Field, 1991; Osofsky & Eberhart-Wright, 1988). However, a substantial portion of these families was doing well 18 years after the adolescent mothers first gave birth. The key factor here seemed to be the overall level of education obtained by the mothers (Furstenberg, Brooks-Gunn, & Morgan, 1987). The situation doesn't seem to be as dire for adolescent mothers and their children in Canada. A 10-year follow-up study of mothers in Nova Scotia (Nova Scotia Department of Community Services, 1991, as cited in Bissell, 2000) found that children born to adolescent mothers were no different from those born to older mothers on a number of different indicators. Similarly, Maticka-Tyndale (2001) reported on a national study (Dryburgh, 2001) that found no differences in adjustment between preschoolers born to adolescent mothers and preschoolers born to older mothers.

In regard to teenage fathers, little research has been conducted in Canada. However, U.S. studies

Attitudes Mental structures that have both an emotional and a cognitive component.

have found that youth who father a child during adolescence are less likely than nonteenage fathers to complete high school and that they attain fewer years of education than do nonteenage fathers (Pirog-Good, 1996). Overall, teenage fathers are more likely to use drugs, engage in crime, and initiate these problems at earlier ages than youth who are not teenage fathers (Pirog-Good, 1996). Teenage fathers are more likely than nonteenage fathers to come from minority, poor, and single-parent households (Pirog-Good, 1996; Thornberry, Smith, & Howard, 1997). Moreover, the members of the households of teenage fathers are less educated than family members of nonteenage fathers (Pirog-Good, 1995).

In sum, the individual characteristics associated with adolescent sexuality and with teenage parenting combine with contextual variables to shape the implications of the adolescent's sexuality for his or her current behaviour and later development. As we consider contextual influences on the adolescent's sexuality, the continued combined impact of individual variables is apparent as well.

Contextual Influences

ISSUES TO CONSIDER

- In what ways do family and peers represent contextual variables that influence adolescents' sexual behaviour?
- How might the presence of an older sibling impact younger siblings' sexuality during adolescence?
- What characteristics of community context might influence adolescent attitudes toward sexual activity?

Both families and peers of adolescents influence their sexuality. For instance, although adolescents' reports of their age at first intercourse are not particularly reliable (Capaldi, 1996), several contextual variables—and some individual ones as well—influence whether youth (report that they) initiate sexual intercourse early or late in adolescence (Murray, 1996).

Studies have linked peers with sexual activity. In a U.S. longitudinal study of about 75 boys from Grade 6 through Grade 10 (Feldman et al., 1995), both peer rejection *and* peer acceptance were associated with the number of sexual partners a youth had four years later. Rejected youth were low in self-restraint and were involved in misconduct. This pattern of behaviour was linked to the number of sexual partners a youth had four years later (Feldman et al., 1995). Connolly, Pepler, Craig, and Taradash (2000) found that bullies of both sexes in Grades 5 through 8 started dating earlier and engaged in more types of dating activities

than other adolescents. However, they rated these relationships as being less intimate, less affectionate, and less durable than did nonbullies. The bullies also rated their friendships as being less intimate and less durable than did other adolescents.

Peers are also important influences in the lives of adolescents whose sexual activity has resulted in pregnancy and childbirth. Peers provide more emotional support to adolescent mothers than do family members and interfere less than family members do in the life of the teenage mother (Richardson, Barbour, & Butenzer, 1995). Siblings are both peers and family members, and they have important influences on adolescent sexuality. Having an older sister who is a teenage mother is associated with childbearing among younger sisters (East, 1996). Younger sisters of childbearing adolescents differ from younger sisters of nonchildbearing youth in that they are more accepting of nonmarital adolescent childbearing, more pessimistic about their school and career chances, and more likely to have engaged in problem behaviours such as smoking cigarettes and skipping school (East, 1996). In addition, these younger sisters were likely to be nonvirgins (East, 1996). Moreover, the number of sexually active girlfriends that an adolescent female has, as well as the number of her sexually active sisters and whether she has an adolescent childbearing sister, are linked to her possessing permissive sexual attitudes, having positive intentions for future sex, and being more likely a nonvirgin (East, Felice, & Morgan, 1993). Some of the work of Patricia L. East on this topic is presented in Meet the Researcher Box 10.4.

Siblings as well as teachers, but not, it seems, parents, are cited by youth as major sources of accurate information about sexuality (Ansuini, Fiddler-Woite, & Woite, 1996). Reliance on siblings for accurate knowledge may at times be appropriate because, in some cases, mothers have been found unable (or perhaps unwilling because embarrassed) to define sexual development terms adequately (e.g., ejaculation, hormones, menstruation, ovulation, puberty, semen, and wet dreams) to their adolescent children (Hockenberry-Eaton et al., 1996).

Thus both peer and family contexts can combine to influence adolescent sexuality. This point is underscored by other research. Having a girlfriend or a boyfriend was associated with being sexually active (Scott-Jones & White, 1990). One's educational expectations and the educational background of one's mother and father were also associated with being

The Sisters of Pregnant and Parenting Teens at High Risk for Early Pregnancy

Patricia East is an associate research scientist in the Department of Pediatrics at the University of California, San Diego Medical Center. She has been on the editorial boards of the *Journal of Research on Adolescence*, the *Journal of Youth and Adolescence*, *Developmental Psychology*, and the *International Journal of Behavioral Development*, and on several grant review committees for the National Institutes of Health.

In the late 1980s, my colleagues and I noticed that in the University of California San Diego Medical Center adolescent health clinic, many of our current pregnant teenage patients were the *younger sisters* of our *former* pregnant teenage patients. Although many doctors across the country had also recognized this as a clinical phenomenon, research on the younger sisters of pregnant teens, at that point, was very sparse.

In 1992 Dr. Marianne Felice and I published a literature review of the studies that had been done on the sisters of pregnant and parenting teens. These studies showed that, when compared to same-age women of comparable race, ethnicity, and economic status, the sisters of teenage mothers had as much as six times higher teenage childbearing rates, four times higher teenage sexual activity rates, were significantly younger at their first pregnancy, and were significantly more likely to be sexually active during early adolescence, or by age 12 or 13.

Why would the sisters of pregnant and parenting teens be especially vulnerable to an early pregnancy? We believe two general sets of factors predispose the sisters of pregnant and parenting teens to early pregnancy. The first set of factors derives from the sisters' shared background. These factors include sisters' shared economic situation, their shared race and ethnicity, living within the same family and neighbourhood, and being parented by the same parents. Much research has shown that these kinds of factors increase one's risk for a teenage pregnancy.

The second set of factors, we think, results directly from the teen's pregnancy and birth and the impact they have for the teen's family and siblings. Close to 80% of teenagers continue to live with their

families one year after they give birth. So it is very likely that a teenager's childbearing would have a profound impact on all the siblings within the household.

How does a teen's childbearing affect her family and siblings? Unfortunately, not much research has been done on this subject, but findings from a few studies are beginning to provide some answers. For example, I studied a group of pregnant teenagers and their mothers and followed them until about a year after the teenager had her baby. In all of these families, no other child had ever been pregnant, so the teen's family had not been previously "exposed to" a teen's birth. Results showed that, after the teen gave birth, the mothers reported being less strict with their other children, talking less with their other children, and monitoring their other children less carefully. Mothers also reported being more accepting of teenage sex after the older daughter gave birth. These findings are important because they show how a teen's pregnancy and birth affect her mother and, consequently, how they impact the other children in the household. The particular changes that the mothers in the study underwent are important because they indicate that the teen's family may be changed in ways that make siblings in the household more susceptible to early sexual activity and, thus, early pregnancy.

There are many other plausible ways that a teenager having a baby could affect her brothers and sisters. For example, it could expose the girls in the family to a role model of "mother" that appears attractive because of its associated status, femininity, and attention. Teenagers who are mothers often receive a lot of attention and are sometimes treated as adults, both within the immedi-

ate family and within the community. Thus mimicking their sister's pregnancy may be very seductive for girls because they see their sisters achieve adult status and recognition through motherhood instead of through school or job achievements.

One of the most positive things that has been accomplished by my research was that a new program was started in California called the Adolescent Sibling Pregnancy Prevention Program. This program started in 1996 and has provided pregnancy prevention services to approximately 4000 siblings of pregnant and parenting teens throughout California. This is a very important program because it serves a group known to be at high risk for teen pregnancy. This is also a unique program, being the first of its kind to focus specifically and exclusively on the siblings of pregnant and parenting teens. It is hoped that this program will be permanently legislated within California, as well as serve as a model program for other states that wish to launch similar pregnancy prevention initiatives. In the meantime, continued research on the siblings of pregnant and parenting teens will help us understand how these siblings are affected by their sisters' giving birth and how they themselves become at risk for early pregnancy.

sexually active (Cheesbrough, Ingham, & Massey, 2002; Scott-Jones & White, 1990). In divorced families, a mother's dating behaviour and her possession of sexually permissive attitudes influence the sexual

activity of both daughters and sons (Whitbeck, Simons, & Kao, 1994).

The community context also is related to adolescent sexuality. In poor communities, youth have higher rates of abortion and lower rates of marriage (Sullivan, 1993). Among female adolescents in the U.S., living in a socially disorganized, low-income community (one in which family planning services are not readily available) is associated with the initiation of sexual intercourse and with the young women's subsequent sexual activity. In sum, sexual behaviours are related to several different individual and contextual variables. There are conditions under which the expression of an adolescent's sexuality in the context of particular individual or contextual variables will involve either healthy sexual behaviours (e.g., avoidance of early initiation of sexual activity) or risky ones (e.g., early initiation of sexual intercourse). However, when sexuality is expressed in the context of other behaviour risks, it is very likely that problems in sexual behaviour will be seen.

Influences of Other Risk Behaviours

ISSUE TO CONSIDER

- What are some additional individual and contextual risk factors influencing adolescent sexual activity?

Some of the individual and contextual variables linked to adolescent sexual activity involve risk or problem behaviours other than sexual ones (Fortenberry et al., 1997). For instance, in a study of about 1000 U.S. high school students, sexually active males used alcohol more often, had higher stress levels, were less likely to use seat belts, were more likely to engage in physical fights, and (understandably) were more likely to worry about AIDS than were males who had never engaged in intercourse (Harvey & Spigner, 1995). In turn, sexually active females used more alcohol and cigarettes and had higher stress levels than did females who had never had sexual intercourse (Harvey & Spigner, 1995).

Engaging in unconventional behaviour (e.g., rejecting social norms, showing nonconformist behaviours) is also linked to sexual activity in youth (Costa et al., 1995). For instance, in a longitudinal study of more than 1300 urban male and female middle school and high school students in the U.S., unconventionality was associated with early initiation of sexual intercourse (Costa et al., 1995). Additional risk factors related to sexuality are antisocial and delinquent behaviour. These behaviours, as well as early pubertal maturation and substance use, were associated with early initiation of sexual intercourse among Oregon youth in Grades 7 through 12 (Capaldi,

Crosby, & Stoolmiller, 1996). In turn, anxiety was associated with the delay of first intercourse (Capaldi et al., 1996). Other U.S. studies (e.g., Tubman, Windle, & Windle, 1996) also find a link between delinquency and early onset of sexual intercourse, as well as with such behaviour problems as poor school grades, early alcohol use, and antisocial behaviour. Repeat pregnancies among adolescent mothers are associated with many of the same variables in what appears to be a "cluster" of problem behaviours (Jessor, 1987, 1992; Jessor, Donovan, & Costa, 1991; Jessor & Jessor, 1977), that is, school problems, substance use and abuse, and violence/delinquency (Gillmore et al., 1997).

Given that teenage sexual intercourse, pregnancy, and childbearing occur in the context of other problem behaviours, interventions that are most effective in preventing the problems of adolescent sexuality focus on these clusters of behaviours and not just on sexual behaviour alone (e.g., Allen et al., 1997). Chapter 14 presents a fuller discussion of the importance of a multi-problem focus on interventions aimed at preventing unhealthy/undesirable behaviours in adolescence.

Conclusions About Adolescent Sexuality

The breadth and depth of the problems associated with the sexual behaviour of today's youth exist at historically unprecedented levels. Not only do these problems arise from a diverse set of individual and contextual influences but they also impact the adolescent's social world (e.g., his or her peers, family of origin, and, with increasing probability, his or her own children).

To address the problems of adolescent sexuality requires an approach that considers the entire system of influences involved in the youth's development. This need to devise programs that bridge sexual and other risk behaviours in manners that are sensitive to the diverse contexts of youth is no less true in other nations than it is in Canada. Issues of youth sexuality are present and pressing ones around the world. Applications Box 10.2 provides details about three effective programs in other nations—in Gaborone, Botswana, in Recife, Brazil, and in Jamaica, West Indies—and illustrates the common need for all effective youth programs to address the complex system of individual and contextual variables affecting youth development.

The influences on problems of adolescent sexuality and the sorts of systems change needed to address them are similar to those found in regard to other problems of adolescent development. In Chapters 8 and 9 we discussed the multiple individual and contextual bases associated with both negative and positive development in the family and peer contexts. These themes will be evident again in Chapter 11 in a discussion of adolescence and school and the nature, bases, and implications of school underachievement, failure, and dropout.

APPLICATIONS ⋮ Box 10.2

Addressing the Complex Problems of Adolescent Sexuality Around the World

Problems of teenage sexuality exist in all nations of the world. These problems may be manifested through issues of emotional distress in sexually active youth; in health problems, such as sexually transmitted diseases and AIDS; in teenage prostitution; in teenage child-bearing; in losses to the educational and economic system, arising because teenage parents cannot go to school or prepare for jobs; and in weakened families, arising when a generation of children themselves bear and rear children. Even when only a subset of issues applies in a country, these problems nevertheless involve multiple facets of the young person's individual, interpersonal, and institutional (family, community) world.

Successful programs effecting positive changes in adolescents' sexuality engage as many of the relations between youth and their contexts as possible, given their available financial and personnel resources (Benson, 1997; Dryfoos, 1990; Lerner, Sparks, & McCubbin, 2000). The three programs described here are illustrative of this attempt to change the system of influences within which youth are embedded.

Increasing Opportunities for Pregnant Teenagers

The Educational Centre for Adolescent Women/Peer Counselling by Teens Program, Gaborone, Botswana

Since gaining independence from Britain in 1966, Botswana has experienced rapid development and social change, including advances in education, health, and communications. Traditional family and community structures no longer control sexuality and reproduction. Youth are sexually active from a very

early age, often have multiple sex partners, and frequently use no protection against pregnancy and sexually transmitted diseases.

In response to high rates of teenage pregnancy in Botswana, the YWCA initiated two programs aimed at educating teen mothers and adolescents at risk of becoming pregnant. Established in 1989, the Educational Centre for Adolescent Women (ECAW) provides pregnant women and new mothers with a place they can go to continue their education and learn about motherhood. It fills a critical gap in services for pregnant teens in that many are forced to leave school for at least a year after becoming pregnant and find it difficult to return due to lack of space and other reasons. ECAW courses include family and sexuality education, baby and child care, individual and group counselling, and academic subjects. A craft component was introduced in 1990 whereby teen mothers learn sewing, dressmaking, and knitting skills so that those who do not continue with their education can be self-supporting.

The Peer Counselling by Teens (PACT) program is based on the notion that young people are more apt to trust and listen to each other concerning their sexuality than older, authority figures. PACT trains youth to act as peer counsellors to their friends and classmates. Each year, the program trains five boys and five girls from each of Gaborone's nine secondary schools to be Peer Counsellors. These 90 students, ages 12 through 19, meet regularly to learn about human sexuality, HIV, AIDS, and other sexually transmitted diseases and receive training aimed at increasing their self-esteem, confidence, and communication

skills. Afterward, each is expected to share the information they have learned with their friends and classmates.

Both programs build on one another's efforts. Through ECAW, PACT counsellors learn the circumstances and influences behind teenage pregnancies. By focusing on preventive efforts, PACT aims to reduce the number of teenage pregnancies in Gaborone in the future. Because of its impact on behavioural change and self-assurance among young people, PACT is in demand and has spread countrywide.

Providing Street-Based Girls with Health Care Education and Training

The "Casa de Passagem" Program, Recife, Brazil

In Recife, the capital of Northeast Brazil, the poorest region in the country, more than 700 children and adolescents live on the streets. Many of these children and adolescents maintain contact with their families, but poverty does not permit them to live as a family unit. To survive, many girls become involved in prostitution, leading them to a world of drugs and often death. In addition to the sexual violence that they suffer in the streets, many of these girls also suffer sexual abuse in their families.

Founded in 1989, Casa de Passagem (Passage House) works through an educational process so that the girls recognize themselves as people with rights. For this, it is necessary to work on their self-esteem, to help them see themselves as citizens—with rights—and to help them see their individual talents and develop other strategies for survival. In little more than 10 years, Casa de Passagem has served

>

10 000 girls directly and, through them, around 60 000 others indirectly.

Casa de Passagem has become so well known that the street girls come to the centre to participate in the programs of their own accord. Casa de Passagem's services are delivered through three basic programs that include self-esteem building and counselling, community training and assessment, and job placement. The program also offers a primary health clinic.

In addition, Casa de Passagem trains young girls and adolescents to serve as peer educators that reach out to other adolescents and community members. The peer educators work on issues ranging from family planning to drug prevention to prevention of STDs.

Casa de Passagem also plays an important advocacy role, working with other institutions to advocate for improved policies benefiting young girls, particularly in the areas of preventing domestic violence, sexual abuse, and the imprisonment of girls by the police.

Providing Teens with Life Skills Training and Sex Education
The YWCA NEET Project, Jamaica, West Indies

Teenage pregnancy is a serious problem in Jamaica, where in 1988 23% of all births were to teenage mothers. With 40% of the country's population currently under the age of 15, the problem is expected to worsen. Factors contributing to the rise in teenage pregnancies include poverty, high school dropout rates, few employment opportunities, and an increase in single-parent, female-headed households.

In an effort to reverse this trend, the YWCA initiated the NEET ("teen" spelled backward) program in 1980. The goals of the program are to reduce the incidence of teenage pregnancy and help teens prepare for the responsibilities they will face in adulthood.

NEET provides education and services to young men and women aged 12 to 19. Regular educational sessions are conducted in participating schools following a curriculum developed by NEET. The curriculum includes discussion topics on physical and emotional growth and development, conception and contraception, health, and social issues.

In addition, NEET offers workshops on family life and sex education and a peer counselling training program in which young people are instructed in how to provide other young people with accurate sex information. With many young people hesitant or fearful to discuss personal issues with adult authority figures, NEET's peer counselling program provides them with support and a much-needed outlet. To date, more than 250 young people have been trained through NEET as peer counsellors.

Between 1987 and 1991, over 26 500 young people received instruction and training through NEET in their schools or through youth groups. Participating schools report improved discipline and fewer dropouts due to pregnancy. Student participants report a better understanding of reproduction, heightened awareness of themselves, enhanced self-esteem, and increased ability to perform leadership roles.

Source: International Youth Foundation, 2001. www.iyfnet.org

Summary

- Girls tend to stress the interpersonal qualities of their romantic partners, and boys are apt to emphasize the importance of physical attraction. Girls also stress the importance of demonstrating affection and are less supportive of multiple sexual partners.

- Diversity in ethnic backgrounds, adolescents' family relationships and communication patterns, and religion all influence the development of particular styles of adolescent sexual behaviours.

- Because of the complex and multifaceted developmental challenges facing gay and lesbian youth, there is a great need to understand adolescent development in context and to explicitly investigate through research the developmental situation for gay, lesbian, and bisexual youth.

- About 37% of males and 13% of females have had at least one homosexual encounter that has resulted in orgasm, and estimates are that 8% of men and about 1% to 3% of women are exclusively homosexual.

- Political ideology, socioeconomic status, heterosexual friends, and gender nonconformity for males, and religion and the importance of school for females, influence a homosexual adolescent's sense of self.

- Homonegative attitudes can lead to violence against homosexuals, and the perpetrators of such violence often have attitudes characterized by ambivalence, defensiveness, and adherence to myths about homosexual lifestyles. Homonegativity and heterosexism are obstacles to healthy development and lead homosexual youth to be at greater risk for psychosocial adjustment problems.

- Some of the sexual problems facing adolescents today include forced sex, unwanted pregnancies and the birth of children that cannot be supported, prostitution, and sexually transmitted diseases.

■ The U.S. Centers for Disease Control estimates that three million cases of sexually transmitted diseases occur each year within the United States to adolescents between the ages of 15 and 19. Rates are lower in Canada, but chlamydia and human papilloma virus (HPV) are of increasing concern.

■ AIDS is probably more prevalent in adolescence than statistics might show because there is a long latency period for HIV.

■ Programs that focus on the cluster of problem behaviours involved in HIV infection and attempt to promote multiple changes in youth are most effective in preventing HIV and AIDS.

■ Sexual abuse, especially when combined with physical abuse, is linked to problems such as binge drinking and suicidal thoughts.

■ A girl's history of sexual abuse, a tendency to conform to peers, and having parents whose rearing style was authoritarian or reflective of low monitoring raise her likelihood of being a victim of an unwanted sexual advance.

■ Teenage fathers are less likely to complete high school than nonteenage fathers. Teenage fathers also tend to have low self-esteem, an external locus of control, and conservative sex role attitudes, and are more likely to use drugs and engage in crime.

■ Family and peers have a great influence on adolescent sexuality, for instance, in regard to time of first intercourse and the number of sexual partners per year. Peers are also important influences in the lives of teenage parents.

■ Living in poor communities is linked to higher rates of abortion and lower rates of marriage, as well as to the initiation and continuance of sexual activity.

■ Adolescent sexual behaviour is associated with the use of alcohol and tobacco, levels of stress, involvement in physical fights, and worrying about AIDS.

■ Antisocial and delinquent behaviour, as well as pubertal maturation and substance abuse, are linked to early initiation of sexual intercourse.

Discussion Topics

1. Do you remember when your age-mates started to first express romantic interests in others? How old were you? Were you a leader in being one of the first to express these emotions or did these feelings take longer to develop in you than in your friends? How did the timing of your romantic and/or sexual emotions influence you and your friendships? When you first started having these feelings, did you share them with anyone? If you could describe now the feelings you felt then, what would you describe? Were those feelings typical for your gender and age?

2. What was it about the people you were romantically attracted to or involved with as an adolescent that drew you to them? Are you still attracted to those same qualities? If not, what caused your change in interests and/or what determined your interests as an adolescent?

3. Did your parent(s) ever sit down with you and have the "birds and the bees" discussion? If so, how did this discussion affect you and the decisions you made and make about sexual involvement? If not, do you think such a discussion would have made a difference in the decisions you make? Why or why not?

4. How accepting was your high school of individuals whose life experiences and expressions were outside of the so-called norm? Were there any homosexuals at your school? Do you think it was easy to be open about one's sexual orientation at that time? Was there a gay/lesbian support group at your school? How were the experiences of gay and lesbian students different from those of heterosexual students in terms of feeling and expressing emotions for same-sex classmates?

5. Look back over the illustrations of risks and problems related to adolescent sexual experience. Which findings are the most surprising to you? What factors have led to the increase in the last decades in the rate of sexual intercourse among adolescents?

6. Did you know any teenage mothers as an adolescent? How were the lives of teen parents influenced by this life change? Can you identify any contextual variables that might have been

potential risk factors leading to the early pregnancies? How were the adolescent parents supported (by their families, friends, communities) once the babies were born?

7. What reasoning and rationales do teenagers tend to employ when discussing the use of contraceptives? What information were you supplied with as a teenager? Was this information available from parents, siblings, peers, and/or school? How open were you to this information? Why do so many adolescents believe they will not be affected by high-risk sexual behaviours?

8. Data show that up to one in five adolescent girls are victims of unwanted sex. Despite the fact that sexual experimentation during adolescence is often experienced by youth as occurring too early and therefore as lacking in pleasure and enjoyment, there is still great pressure on adolescents to become sexually experienced. Why? How might one's peer group influence the occurrence of unwanted sex? When an adolescent is a victim of unwanted sex, he or she often has no one to turn to. Why is being a victim such a taboo?

9. Think back on the adolescents in your high school and, specifically, those teenagers you believed were involved in high-risk sexual behaviours. What about these teenagers made you think they were sexually active? What was their overall reputation in school? How do you think their sexual behaviours impacted this reputation? Can you identify any commonalities in the contexts of these youth that might stand out in terms of being predictors for unwanted sex and/or teenage pregnancy?

10. If you were ever in a situation where you found yourself needing to discourage sexual activity, what strategies did you employ? How well did those strategies work? Looking back on the experience now, how might the situation have been avoided? Did you change your behaviours and interactions once this experience occurred? In what ways?

11. Do you believe girls and women who dress provocatively and behave flirtatiously deserve the potential unwanted attention they get? Why or why not? Is your answer influenced by your gender or by your own experiences or the experiences of those close to you?

12. Research shows that individual and contextual influences predict sexual activity. What personal characteristics and environmental factors influenced the choices you made about sexual behaviour?

13. How would you describe your generation's attitude about sex? How has the media affected that attitude? How has the prevalence of AIDS affected that attitude?

14. What makes someone ready to have sexual intercourse? Is your response different now from what it would have been in high school? Do your personal experiences with sex affect your response?

Key Terms

AIDS (acquired immune deficiency syndrome), p. 232
attitudes, p. 242
heterosexism, p. 228
HIV, p. 232

homonegativity, p. 231
homosexuality, p. 231
latency period, p. 237
social constructionism, p. 230

STD (sexually transmitted disease), p. 236
STI (sexually transmitted infection), p. 236

11

Schools and Education During Adolescence

Jacques had not seen Marc for a long time, not since they had been in gym class together during their first year in high school. Now, as Jacques entered the tuxedo rental store, there was Marc standing behind the counter.

"Hey, Marc, what's up?" Jacques said, extending his hand in greeting. The two young men shook hands warmly.

"Hey, man, good to see you. Nothing much. Are you here to rent a tux?"

"Yes, I am renting one for grad. I'm taking Marie Lalonde. You remember her, don't you?"

"No. No, I don't think so," Marc responded matter-of-factly.

Jacques sensed a bit of unease creeping into Marc's demeanour. "Oh, well, anyway, you must be able to get a great deal on tux rentals since you work here."

"Yeah, I suppose," Marc shrugged. "But I don't really ever rent them."

"I don't much either, just for graduation. You'll need one for grad too, though, I guess."

"No, no I won't," Marc explained. "I'm not going to the graduation ceremony."

"Why not?" Jacques blurted out. But as soon as the question left his mouth he saw that it pained Marc. He regretted asking him.

"Hey, man, don't you know? I'm not in school anymore. I dropped out at the end of last year."

Learning Objectives

1. To understand the types of functions that schools perform.
2. To appreciate how the structure of the school can influence youth.
3. To understand how teachers' attitudes, expectations, and behaviours can influence adolescent development and behaviour.
4. To understand the factors associated with the achievement of diverse students.
5. To appreciate how parents, peers, and the neighbourhood or community can affect the academic performance of youth.
6. To learn how extracurricular activities are associated with school-related behaviours.
7. To understand the individual and contextual variables linked to school dropout and to other school problems and risks related to youth development.
8. To learn the approach that effective school dropout prevention programs take.
9. To understand the individual bases of school problems in adolescence.
10. To appreciate how a return to school affects teenage mothers.
11. To learn why schools are being charged with providing services that were previously provided by other social institutions.
12. To understand why schools are failing to provide a goodness of fit with the social, health, and cognitive needs of adolescents.
13. To understand different kinds of classroom and school organizations (e.g., full-service schools) and the effects they have.
14. To understand how school transition affects adolescents.
15. To understand how pubertal change and school transition are related.

At the beginning of adolescence, virtually all boys and girls in North America attend school. This enrollment can be attributed to the high value placed on education and the compulsory laws of school attendance. In most Canadian provinces and territories, however, a student is no longer compelled to attend school upon reaching his or her 16th or 17th birthday. As a consequence, by the end of the high school years, many adolescents have left school early. Canada's 1998 graduation rate was 72%, comparable to the United States (74%), but both were far behind other industrialized countries such as France (87%) and Japan (96%) (Clark, 2000).

Discontinuing school attendance does not necessarily mean that a young person becomes gainfully employed. About three-quarters of 18- to 20-year-old early school leavers in Canada were working (57% full-time and 20% part-time). The remainder (23%) were without a job in 1999 (Bowlby & McMullen, 2002).

This chapter discusses the bases and implications of failure to complete high school and the successful outcomes for adolescents of their educational experiences. Again we emphasize the connections between the development of adolescents and their key contexts. This chapter focuses on the school and other contexts in influencing adolescent development and in fostering either academic success or academic problems.

The School Context and Adolescent Development

A lot of development occurs in schools. Growth in academic abilities is a key instance of this development. The capacity of the young person to be socially competent with peers and with adults develops, and athletic and health-maintaining abilities can advance. Self-esteem and personal perceptions of competence also develop by virtue of changes in all these facets of academic, social, and physical growth.

Variables from the school context as well as from the family and the peer group are linked to a diversity of developmental outcomes. The school functions alone and in combination with other key contexts of adolescence to affect adolescent development.

Maintenance-actualization
Function of schools in which students are both made happy about their current status and yet challenged to do better.

Training-acculturation
Function of schools in which students are taught particular behaviours and values of the surrounding culture.

Functions of the School

ISSUES TO CONSIDER
- What types of functions do schools perform?
- What types of schools and unique issues are there in Canada?
- How can social status be earned through school attendance?
- How can the structure and climate of school be nonbeneficial to some youth?
- How does the school culture and climate influence adolescent behaviour and development?

Schools perform many functions. A long tradition views schools as training institutions (e.g., Ausubel, Montemayor, & Svajian, 1977; McCandless, 1970), as agents of cultural transmission designed to perpetuate and improve a given way of life, and as a means to instill both knowledge and values. They also serve a number of latent functions including "babysitting" teens, giving them a place to socialize, and preparing future workers for the job market. Schools have been regarded traditionally as fulfilling a **maintenance-actualization** role, representing a way in which the adolescent can be happy and yet challenged. They have also served a **training-acculturation** role, teaching the particular behaviours and values of the surrounding culture. While schools are a place to develop optimal personal and interpersonal attributes and the ability to contribute to society (Dryfoos, 1994, 1995; Lerner, 1994; McCandless, 1970), they have also been used as a means to attempt to systematically destroy the cultures of Canada's indigenous peoples. (See Chapter 8 for a discussion of the impact of residential schools on Aboriginal families.)

The vast majority of students attend public schools in Canada, with about 5% attending a private institution and about 1600 students (about 0.0003%) attending special schools for the hearing and visually impaired (Statistics Canada, 2001). Citing religious, moral, or pedagogical reasons, a few parents choose to teach their youth at home (Luffman, 1988). The numbers of home-schooled children have increased since the early 1980s, but still make up only 0.4% of student enrollment (Luffman, 1988). The majority of these home-schooled children are in elementary grades, but this varies by province. For example, 52% of home-schooled children were in elementary grades in Saskatchwan, whereas 91% of home-schooled children in Ontario were in high-school grades (Luffman, 1998).

Second-language immersion programs are one way for Canadian students to become more knowledgeable about both official languages—French and English—as well as other languages. While students can be immersed in other languages, such as Cree or German, French is the most frequently offered to anglophone students. The number of students enrolled in French immersion programs in Canada has quadrupled since the 1980s, when less than 100 000 students participated in them (Department of Canadian Heritage, 1996). Success in learning French as a second language among anglophone students appears to be more likely if the students' parents speak some French at home (Mougeon & Rehner, 2001). Success is also related to students' perceptions of teacher support (Noels, Clement, & Pelletier, 1999; Ducharme & Bernard, 2001) and social support in school (MacIntyre, Baker, Clement, & Conrod, 2001).

In Quebec, students can pursue postsecondary studies at one of 50 public general or technical colleges called CEGEPs (Quebec Government, 2001), where they can get pre-university education or a technical education without being charged tuition.

In Ontario, high school education reform has led to the removal of the 13th year of secondary education. This, combined with a demographic shift in the population, means that twice the regular number of students were eligible to enter the postsecondary system in 2003 (the Double Cohort, 2003). Approximately 88 000 additional students will attend Ontario universities and colleges between 2003 and 2010 (the Double Cohort, 2003).

Schools provide a context for social interactions and relationship development (Ausubel et al., 1977; Dryfoos, 1994, 1995). They can facilitate the adolescent's emancipation from parents through giving youth an opportunity to earn their own social status. Status may be earned concurrently with school attendance by demonstrating a mastery of the curriculum, by attaining high class standing, and by nonacademic interactions with the peer group in school activities such as organized athletics or clubs (Ausubel et al., 1977; Lerner, 1994, 1995). In addition, social status may be earned in the future through the training and education attained in school (Johnston & Bachman, 1976; Lerner, 1994, 1995). The school also serves a custodial role in society, in that a system of **compulsory education**, such as that found in Canada and the United States, highly structures the time and activity of students (Villarruel & Lerner, 1994).

The structure and values of Western society figure prominently in Canadian schools that have not served Aboriginal youth well (B.C. Human

Parents and teachers may work together to support the school achievement of youth.

Rights Commission, 2001). Western values of individualism, competition, and dominance over nature are inconsistent with an emphasis on the collective, harmony, and balance in Aboriginal cultures and communities. Students following a traditional Aboriginal path are more likely to appreciate learning as a lifelong journey with multiple dimensions—physical, social, academic, and spiritual. Western education, in contrast, is time limited, sequential, and academically focused. Gotowiec and Beiser (1994) note that value differences between school and home for Canadian Aboriginal youth contribute to their academic problems.

The school climate also has an effect on student learning. For example, in their study of 1000 Grade 9 students in southwestern Ontario, the effects of an unfavourable school culture, including perceptions of low teacher and classmate support, student conflict, and unfair rules, combined with low student autonomy in decision-making in school affairs, contributed to low attachment to learning (DeWit, Offord, Sanford, Rye, Shain, & Wright, 2000). The classroom environment does play a role in students' self-confidence to achieve in school. In their sample of 951 Grade 8 and 10 students in four Canadian high schools, Ferguson and Dorman (2001) found that in classrooms where interest, application, and persistence were encouraged, students had higher academic self-efficacy.

Compulsory education System mandating that children and adolescents attend school up to a certain age.

Relations Between the School and Other Contexts

ISSUES TO CONSIDER

- How can support from the family context enhance school performance?
- What factors are associated with the achievement of refugee students?
- How can parents and peers have a negative effect on school performance?
- How does the neighbourhood or community context of the school influence the academic performance of youth?

Schools exist in relation to the other key contexts of adolescent development. The family, peer, and community contexts either enable or detract from the ability of schools to function as society intends. In a study of Ontario high school students it was found that absentee students could be distinguished from students who regularly attended on the basis of six variables, two from each of personal, family, and school categories (Corville-Smith, Ryan, Adams, & Dalicandro, 1998).

Support from the family context can enhance school performance. Among junior high school girls who had the ability and motivation to do well in mathematics, those whose grades increased had mothers who possessed positive attitudes toward the subject (Klebanou & Brooks-Gunn, 1992).

In a longitudinal study of the offspring of teenage mothers, family support was among the key factors reducing the likelihood of high school dropout (Brooks-Gunn, Gus, & Furstenberg, 1993). The decrease in the chances of discontinuing school were related to high maternal educational aspirations for the child in early life, number of years the father was present, being prepared for school, and not repeating an elementary school grade.

The culture transmitted through socialization by the family and by peers influences school performance. Positive family climate and peer group norms supporting positive behaviours for youth have been found to be associated with school achievement (Kurdek, Fine, & Sinclair, 1995). Social support by parents has been found to be related to youth feeling open to, excited by, and involved in school-related activities. A family climate that challenged the young person to succeed was related to an adolescent focusing on important goals (Rathunde, 1996). Youth who lived in families where both support and challenge were present had the best school experiences (Rathunde, 1996).

In a Canadian study of 91 refugee youths, aged 15 to 21, and 123 of their parents, Winkinson (2002) found that about half were doing well, but that about 20% were likely not going to complete their secondary education. The other third were experiencing difficulty finishing high school. The correlates of academic performance that were identified included ethnicity, refugee camp experience, appropriate grade placement upon arrival, parents' health, urban residence, and number of months in Canada (Wilkinson, 2002).

Parents and peers can also have negative effects on school performance. For example, when parents react negatively to school performance, youth show negative performance (Rosenthal & Feldman, 1991). In another study, low parental academic achievement and ineffective child-rearing practices were linked to antisocial behaviour among adolescent boys in Grade 6, to decreases in the engagement with academic course work in Grade 7, and to poor achievement in Grade 8 (Debaryshe, Patterson, & Capaldi, 1993).

In addition to family and peer influences, the neighbourhood or community context of the school influences the academic performance of youth. In a longitudinal study of almost 500 boys from ages 6 to 16 in low socioeconomic status areas of Montreal, family poverty had a negative effect on academic achievement, independent of family configuration (Pagani, Boulerice, Vitaro, & Tremblay, 1999). Indeed, in their analysis of a Canadian longitudinal data set, Ryan and Adams (1999) reported that a family's socioeconomic status played a significant role in their child's academic achievement, directly through grades and attitudes toward school, as well as indirectly through increased social support.

In their review of the literature on early school leaving in Canada, Audas and Willms (2000) report on the epidemic theory of early leaving, based on a nonlinear relationship between neighbourhood quality and dropout rates, with the hypothesis that there are very strong neighbourhood effects near the bottom of the distribution of neighbourhood quality. They cite a study by Crane (1991) in which early leaving rates increase dramatically when the proportion of individuals holding high status jobs in the neighbourhood falls below 5%.

Studies support the link between the type of occupations present in a community and early school leaving. In their study, Stallmann and Johnson (1996) found that a higher percentage of service occupations in a community was associated with increased rates of early school leaving. A higher

MEET THE RESEARCHER · Box 11.1 · George J. Sefa Dei

George J. Sefa Dei is a professor and the Chair of Sociology and Equity Studies at the Ontario Institute for Studies in Education, University of Toronto.

Exemplary Practices of Inclusive Schooling

In a recent piece on alternative schooling, Ernst and Statzner (1994) speak about the "imperative need for redirecting social science research from the often hopeless and stereotypical study of educational failure to the heartening exploration of new and creative ways of meeting the needs of minority teachers, students, and their families" (p. 205). Our Sciences and Humanities Research Council of Canada–funded research project focused on identifying innovative and inclusive school practices that foster successful academic and social outcomes for *all* students, and particularly for racial and ethnic minorities. I conducted my study with the assistance of graduate students in the Ontario Institute for Studies of Education (OISE) of the University of Toronto.

The first year of study involved examining "best/exemplary practices" of schooling that improve the learning outcomes of black/African Canadian (i.e., students of African descent and students who self-identify as such) and other racial, linguistic, cultural, and religious minority youth, and tapping into the cultural resource base of local communities. The focus in the second year was the examination of Nighana Alternative School, highlighting the issue of reintegration for black/African Canadian youth. An important related objective was to apply the findings of best/exemplary practices in order to inform the establishment of new "demonstration schools" and enhance the academic and school success of black youth. In the third year, faculties of education were examined for ways in which best/exemplary practices of inclusive education are conceptualized and addressed. A comparative analysis of the best/exemplary practices identified in mainstream schools and community-based schools was used to interpret the implications of these best/exemplary practices for pre- and in-service training. This phase of the study and the subsequent year of extension consisted of research to apply

best/exemplary practices as defined in the first two phases of the project.

Research information was analyzed both qualitatively and quantitatively for general trends about educational practices that address the question of inclusion and thereby promote educational change. Through triangulation (the comparison of data from three different sources to provide evidence of credibility), we compared individual narratives, observations, and responses between and among students and teachers at selected school sites with parents', families', and community groups' responses and located general patterns. We further consulted with some educational theorists/practitioners and other research subjects during the course of field ethnographic research for their input on analysis and data interpretations. The research information was also compared with other studies of inclusive schooling in Canadian and American contexts. Generally, data analysis focused on identifying specific themes that spoke to the issue of inclusive education. We also paid attention to specific educational strategies in the use of curricular resources/texts, teaching practices, and classroom instruction that helped develop students' sense of identification and connection to school.

Our study has developed the theoretical and practical underpinnings and implications of inclusive schooling. We present these as domains of inclusive schooling that form the basis of developing a theoretical and practical approach to rethinking Euro-Canadian/American schooling and education:

(Visual/Knowledge/Physical) Representation in Education: That is, inclusive educational practices address issues of representation in three areas: visual representation, or the inclusion of racial/ethnic and religious minorities and their cultures within the visual/physical landscape of the educational setting; knowledge representation, or the inclusion of non-European cultural knowledge,

cultures, histories, and experiences; staff equity, or the integration of teachers and educators from different racial, ethnic, and gender backgrounds.

Language Integration: In an inclusive educational practice, home language (often a vernacular) is used in instruction in conjunction with English. Language becomes a fundamental component of cultural identity. Family/home, community, and innovative school educational strategies validate students' first languages (local vernacular) and facilitate English skills development.

Equity, Accommodation, and Access in Education: That is, the adoption of an inclusive, integrative approach to learning and education. The ideas of "equity" and "culturally relevant" teaching are central to inclusive educational practice, dealing directly with issues of power and fairness. In inclusive educational practice, educational stakeholders allow learners to participate fully in their education while developing and practising home cultures and personal and collective identities.

Family, Local Community, and School Partnerships: That is, placing emphasis on the important roles of parents and community workers in youth education. In effective and inclusive schooling, parents become knowledge producers. Parents, guardians, caregivers, and adult community workers are seen as initiating, creating, and critiquing subjects. They are not simply inserted into the existing structures; rather, educators allow adults to claim an important degree of collective ownership of community schooling.

Cooperative Education: That is, placing an emphasis on cooperative education and developing a broader concept of "educational success." While inclusive schooling and education cultivate high academic expectations, the student's

>

"successes" are defined to recognize the extent of community involvement as well as nonacademic proficiencies in areas such as psychosocial development and cultural knowledge. Thus, the student is helped to improve and sustain her/his self-esteem and sense of identity.

Spirituality in Education: That is, the promotion of spiritual and intuitive learning in schools, not necessarily a credit to a high moral order, but an understanding of the self/personhood as a basis to engage learning. In inclusive schooling, education is anchored in a broader defini-tion of education that encompasses emotional and spiritual dimensions, parental and community advocacy, and youth empowerment. A personalized, subjective identification with the learning processes makes it possible for the student to be invested spiritually and emotionally in the cause of educational and social change.

Indigenous/Local Knowledges: That is, local knowledge associated with long-term occupancy of a place. A recognition of the important role of indigenous, tradi-tional, and culturally based knowledges in schooling as valuable educational resources for the learner.

Detailed findings of the study appear in the book *Removing the Margins: The Challenges and Possibilities of Inclusive Schooling* (by George J. Sefa Dei, Irma M. James, Sonia James-Wilson, Leeno Karumanchery, and Jasmin Zine). There is also an accompanying guide for teachers and educational practitioners: *Inclusive Schooling: A Teacher's Companion to Removing the Margins* (by George Sefa Dei, Sonia James-Wilson, and Jasmin Zine).

percentage of managerial/professional occupations was associated both with a lowered early leaving rate and a greater likelihood that high school grad-uates would continue their education.

Social differences interconnect with school culture, environment, and social life to influence how students engage or disengage from school life. By examining home, community, and school factors in inclusive schooling, research is pointing to innovative ways to improve learning for diverse groups of students (Dei, Holmes, Mazzuca, McIssac, & Campbell, 1995; Dei, Mazzuca, McIssac, & Zine, 1997).

Variation in the key contexts of youth is related to differential outcomes of school experiences, but individual differences among adolescents in their psychological and behavioural characteristics may moderate the potential influences of the school on youth development.

Adolescent Diversity and School Functions

ISSUES TO CONSIDER

- What factors influence academic achievement?
- How are self-handicapping behaviours linked to academic achievement?
- How does orientation to peers affect school performance?
- How are extracurricular activities associated with school-related behaviours?

Psychological characteristics of youth, such as self-regard, motivation, and identity, interrelate with contextual influences to influence development and achievement in schools. For instance, differences among youth in their academic motivation to succeed

Community involvement is a prominent part of many adolescents' school experiences.

in school have been identified as a key basis of academic achievement (e.g., Eccles, 1991).

Being motivated to master a subject and to be socially responsible, and expectations about one's success, are associated with good grades among young adolescents (Wentzel, 1993). Expectations for success were the major predictors of junior high school students' class effort and grades (Goodenow, 1993). Support from teachers enhanced this motivation, especially for girls. Positive motivational beliefs, such as success expectations, are associated with the ability of youth to regulate their learning in classrooms and to take more control over their knowledge acquisition (Pintrich, Roeser, & DeGroot, 1994).

Self-regard variables are also associated with academic achievement. Positive self-image is linked to academic achievement as measured through grades among young adolescents (Roberts & Petersen, 1992). This association varies across the school years. The relation between self-image and achievement decreases for girls and increases for boys as they move from Grade 6 to 7 (Roberts et al., 1990).

A key dimension of diversity related to school performance involves differences among students in their tendencies to do immediately and efficiently the schoolwork assigned to them. In a study of about 250 Grade 8 students (Midgley & Urdan, 1995), those who procrastinated, allowed other youth to keep them from studying, or deliberately did not try to do the work given to them were prototypic of low-achieving students. Boys, more so than girls, showed these **self-handicapping behaviours** (Midgley & Urdan, 1995). Feelings of self-consciousness, low self-worth, and associations with friends who had a negative orientation to academics were among the other variables linked to self-handicapping behaviours (Midgley & Urdan, 1995).

Being oriented to peers is not in itself an indicator of problematic school performance. Volunteering in school to help other students is associated with better self-esteem, less depression, and fewer problem behaviours, particularly among male adolescents (Switzer et al., 1995). In a longitudinal study of more than 200 youth between Grades 6 and 8, pursuit of social goals was associated with efforts to perform well in English classes (Wentzel, 1996).

Another way in which youth differ in regard to school-related behaviours is in respect to their involvement in nonschool **extracurricular activities**. Males in junior high school gain in status through participation in extracurricular activities more so than do females (Eder & Kinney, 1995). In their study of part-time employment and work-related aspirations, about half of the 756 respondents, who were students in three different urban high schools,

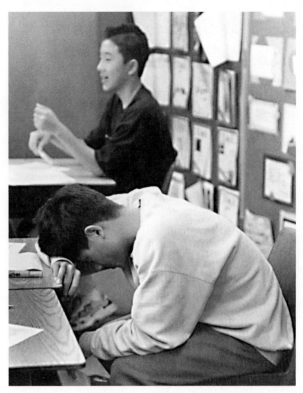

Not all young people are equally engaged in classroom activities.

from 26 Grade 10, 11, and 12 classrooms, worked part-time (Loughlin & Barling, 1998, and see Chapter 7 for a discussion of the impacts of work on adolescent development). Teachers express considerable concern about how their students' employment is related to their academic performance (Bills, Helms, & Ozcan, 1995). Nevertheless, there is little evidence that teachers adjust their classroom behaviour to accommodate the possible needs of working students (Bills et al., 1995).

The individual's behavioural, motivational, affective, and self-regulatory characteristics all play a role in academic performance during adolescence (Wentzel et al., 1990). When coupled with socially competent behaviour, significant enhancement of school achievement occurs (Wentzel, 1991).

Other individual characteristics such as spatial ability, content knowledge, knowledge about problem-solving strategies, temperamental style, and physical attractiveness are also associated with

Self-handicapping behaviours
Actions of procrastination and not studying that lead to low achievement.

Extracurricular activities
Events and activities that take place outside the academic realm of school.

academic achievement (Byrnes & Takahara, 1993; Casey et al., 1995; Guerin et al., 1994; Jovanovic & Lerner, 1994; Lerner et al., 1990). Students require not only reasoning strategies to problem-solve academic and social problems in the classroom, but the motivation to persist through challenges and relate to their peers.

Conclusions About the Functions of Schools

Together, the associations among schools, other contexts of youth development, and adolescent diversity underscore the fact that a diverse array of individual and contextual variables combine to provide the bases of the range of different outcomes for youth developing in the context of schools. Given this significance of the school context for adolescent development, it is understandable that when school problems occur they can have broad impact on the lives of young people.

School Underachievement, Failure, and Dropout

ISSUES TO CONSIDER

- What is the single most important action youth can take to improve their future economic prospects?
- What statistics support the idea that a large number of youth leave school early?

Although the school noncompletion rates for youth in Canada decreased during the 1990s by about 5% (Human Resources Development Canada, 2000a), there were still approximately one in five youth aged 15 to 19 who were neither working nor studying full-time in 1999 (Audas & Willms, 2002). The costs to society in having large numbers of youth ill prepared to contribute productively to society and the costs to youth themselves are enormous.

Remaining in school is the single most important action youth can take to improve their future economic prospects (see Figure 11.1). According to the Canadian Census in 1996, a high school leaver earned less than half of someone with a university degree (Statistics Canada, 1996). High school graduates earned, on average, about $4000 per year more than those who left school before completing Grade 12 (Statistics Canada, 1996). Based on the latest census data, it is apparent that education is still associated with higher earnings: those with the highest

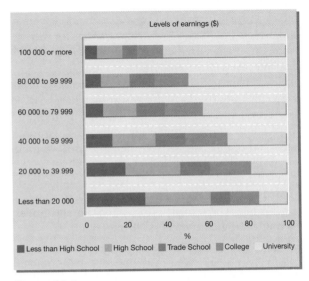

Figure 11.1
Average earnings of the population 15 years of age and over in 1995, by highest level of schooling, 1996 Census.

(*Source:* Statistics Canada, 2003, 2001 Census. Retrieved from website June 14, 2003: www12.statcan.ca/english/census01/products/analytic/companion/earn/canada.cfm.)

incomes were most likely to have a university degree and those with the lowest incomes, high school or elementary diplomas (Statistics Canada, 2003).

Despite the advantages to a youth's life chances and to the quality of life of his or her more close (e.g., family) and more distant (e.g., community) context, youth continue to drop out of school. Even for those who remain in school, growing evidence indicates that many young people do not achieve at levels expected of them.

There are numerous indicators of the seriousness of the problems of school failure and dropout among today's youth. As illustration consider the following results from the School Leaver's Survey (Human Resources Development Canada, 1995), a national study of 18- to 20-year-olds in Canada with results from 9460 participants. These are some highlights from the report:

- Almost one in five participants surveyed (18%) had not completed high school.
- More men than women had not completed high school (22% and 14%, respectively).
- Family structure, marital status and family responsibilities, parents' education, and geographical location were found to associate with higher rates of early school leaving.
- Youth who had dependent children (7% of men and 27% of women) were more likely to

be leavers than those without dependent children (1% of men and 4% of women).

- The school leaving rate was particularly high among Aboriginal youth (40%), which is associated with high occurrences of other characteristics of early school leaving (50% living with one or no parent, 16% with dependent children).

- Immigrant youth (11%) were less likely to be school leavers than the rest of the population (17%).

- For males, the most important reason for leaving school early, cited by more than one-third (36%), was work, followed by personal or family reasons (10%).

- For females, the most important reason for leaving school early, cited by one-quarter (26%), was personal or family, followed by work (16%).

- Amount of employment during school does seem to be related to early leaving. Male youth who left high school early were more likely than completers to work more than 20 hours per week (49% and 34%, respectively).

It was also noted in the report that school experiences played a role in the decision youth made to leave. Youth who left early reported more often than those who graduated that they did not enjoy school (41% and 9%, respectively), found their classes uninteresting (41% and 21%, respectively), did not participate in extracurricular activities (45% and 26%, respectively), and had friends who did not think that completing high school was important (90% and 45%, respectively) (Human Resources Development Canada, 1995).

Academic performance was also associated with early school leaving. Of those who left early, relatively few had grades in the A to B range compared to those who graduated (37% and 77%, respectively). However, more than three out of four youth who left (77%) had passing grades (Human Resources Development Canada, 1995).

Despite indications that both groups aspire to complete additional education or training (see Figure 11.2), more leavers than completers received no additional training (83% and 26%, respectively), encountered unemployment (34% and 23%, respectively), and received unemployment insurance (28% and 23%, respectively) or social assistance (18% and 8%,

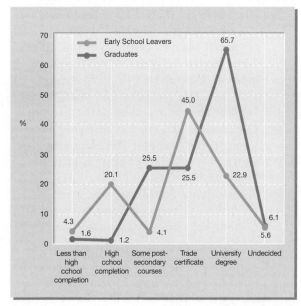

Figure 11.2
Educational aspirations of graduates and early school leavers.

Source: Adapted from Statistics Canada. (2002). *At a Crossroads: First Reults for the 18- to 20-Year-Old Cohort of the Youth in Transition Survey,* Catalogue no. RH64-12/2002E-IN, p. 41. Reproduced by permission of Statistics Canada.

respectively) (Human Resources Development Canada, 1995).

Bases and Implications of School Problems: Diversity and Context

ISSUES TO CONSIDER

- What are the individual and contextual variables linked to school problems and other risks related to youth development?
- What approach do effective dropout prevention programs take?

The problems of school underachievement, failure, and dropout are linked to other key problems and risks associated with youth development, including unsafe sex, teenage pregnancy and teenage parenting, delinquency and often violent crime, and substance use and abuse (Dryfoos, 1990; Lerner, 1995; Lerner & Galambos, 1998). School problems as well as the other problems and risks related to youth development are associated with both individual and contextual variables. These include the following:

- *Individual variables*, relating to cognitive abilities, motivation, personality, and self.

- *Peer variables*, pertaining to peer reputation or status, and to the nature of the social or antisocial behaviours shown by one's peers.
- *Family variables*, pertaining to the nature of parental child-rearing style, socialization practices, and types of behavioural interactions between the youth and his or her parents.
- *Community variables*, relating to poverty level, social support for learning, and programs providing wholesome activities to youth during nonschool hours.
- *School setting*, pertaining to the structure and curriculum of the school and to the sorts of peers and teachers one encounters and to the interactions experienced with them.

As is the case in regard to other problem behaviours of adolescence, the entire system of individual-through-contextual relations needs to be engaged to understand the source of adolescents' school problems. This same system needs attention in attempts to design programs that will be effective in keeping youth in schools and in promoting the positive developments schools can provide. These positive developments include knowledge, abilities and skills, self-esteem, social relationships, and the opportunity to contribute productively to self, family, community, and society.

Effective dropout prevention programs take a **systems approach**. They deal simultaneously with the set of risks facing youth, including poverty, substance use, unsafe sex, and delinquency. They engage all levels of the context, including the school, businesses, governmental bodies, religious institutions, and youth-serving organizations, in building a setting that not only prevents dropout but through such a collaborative setting promotes the positive development of youth.

Applications Box 11.1 describes several Canadian initiatives that demonstrate how adequate understanding of youth academic problems involves an integrated focus on individual and contextual influences on adolescent school behaviours. Although many researchers and educators may focus initially on either individual or institutional factors, most end up appreciating the interrelation of these levels. This integration is illustrated in the following sections that discuss individual and institutional bases of school problems.

Systems approach Approach to programs that deals with multiple problems simultaneously and engages all levels of the context to prevent problems and to promote the positive development of youth.

Individual Bases of School Problems in Adolescence

ISSUES TO CONSIDER
- What are some of the individual bases of school problems in adolescence?
- How does being a teenage mother affect school completion?

Among 2495 Edmonton secondary school students (Nakhaie, Silverman, & LaGrange, 2001), lack of self-control was found to be the strongest predictor of resistance to school. In their study of 4537 Grade 9 and 10 French-Canadian youth in seven Montreal public high schools, Vallerand and colleagues (Vallerand, Fortier, & Guay, 1997) found that motivational level predicted school leaving. They reported that students' self-determined school motivation was related to their likelihood to leave. The major contributors to self-determined school motivation were the behaviours of teachers, parents, and administrators in supporting students' perceptions of competence and autonomy. If autonomy and competence were low, so was self-determined school motivation.

Janosz et al. (Janosz, LeBlanc, Boulerice & Tremblay, 2000) used longitudinal data from two independent samples of over 1600 youth in Quebec to develop a typology of early leavers, suggesting that there is considerable variation among members of this group and in their personal and social risk factors. They identified four types of early leavers: quiet, disengaged, low-achiever, and maladjusted.

In their longitudinal study of 751 low socioeconomic status boys, Vitaro and colleagues (Vitaro, Larocque, Janosz, & Tremblay, 2001) found that early school behaviour problems and low academic performance triggered a trajectory that included association with deviant/early-leaving friends at the time they left. In another study of youth living in Montreal, Ellenbogen and Chamberland (1997) reported that among 14- to 16-year-old students, those at risk for early leaving had more friends who had left early, more friends who were working, and fewer friends at school.

In a study of the characteristics of about 550 high school students from a working-class community in South Africa (Flisher & Chalton, 1995), engagement in risk behaviours was associated with early school leaving. Substance abuse, and, for girls, sexual intercourse, were linked to early leaving (Flisher & Chalton, 1995).

Based on her review of the literature, Mary Bissell (2000) reports that women who become teen mothers

Preventing Youth from Leaving School Early

School dropout results in the loss of a great part of a young person's chances for a productive and healthy life. Dropout is a loss for society too—of the human and social capital it needs to prosper and grow, and thus to continue to offer a quality life to all of its citizens. Given the enormous potential costs of early school leaving and, in turn, of the several other risks associated with it, a broad community approach is warranted. All portions of the community with a stake in keeping youth in schools—and this constitutes virtually everyone in a community—and all people with expertise in helping youth with the diverse problems they face must be brought together.

This comprehensive integration is a key feature of one of the most successful dropout prevention programs. The following is a description of types of initiatives that have been developed in Canada to keep more youth in school.

Northwest Territories

The Baffin Student Support Training Program, based in Iqaluit, helps teachers develop programs that support the development of positive peer relationships in the school and community.

British Columbia

The New Westminster School District No. 40 Stay-In-School Programs use mentoring with community role models in a workplace environment, peer counselling for youth to help other youth with personal and school-related problems, and links with community businesses that can help youth see a connection between their education and the kinds of jobs they want.

Alberta

The Calgary Bridge Foundation for Youth holds afterschool homework clubs, mentorship, home study groups, and parent meetings to help immigrant and refugee students and their parents gain confidence in their academic abilities.

Saskatchewan

The Swift Current Comprehensive Board of Management provides an alternate school for youth in a downtown mall, to encourage and provide structure as well as connections to local community services for youth working through a series of high school correspondence courses.

Manitoba

In Winnipeg, the Job Education Training (JET) for Youth program provides educational counselling, goal setting, study skills training, and career counselling components for youth aged 14 to 17 who are at risk of early school leaving, or have left and are re-entering.

Ontario

In Brock, the Youth Resource Centre, Simcoe County Board of Education, and the YMCA have an alternative school for young parents aged 14 to 21, which provides academic assistance as well as parenting information, childcare, and children's items.

Quebec

In Montreal, the St Jean sur Richelieu school board held a conference for teachers and parents, as well as educational, community, and business representatives to talk to students about the problem of early school leaving.

New Brunswick

The Woodstock District School Board No. 12 conducted a local study of the issues facing Aboriginal students in the school system, and from that information started a review of the entire K-12 curriculum and established a support group for parents.

Nova Scotia

In Dartmouth, the Eastern Shore and Valley Community Education Council held public meetings to learn about the different perspectives on the issues contributing to early school leaving, and from those meetings three areas were identified: communications between parents, transportation, and future career development.

Prince Edward Island

In Charlottetown, the University of Prince Edward Island Athletic Department and the PEI Senators of the American Hockey League use hockey, soccer, and basketball team members to present clinics to high school students with the stay-in-school message.

Newfoundland

In Clarenville, the Bonavista-Trinity-Placentia Integrated School Board gave students with special needs the opportunity to participate in the workforce, to improve self-esteem, and to promote good attitudes about work, people, and money.

Source: Adapted from Human Resources Development Canada, 1996.

---

are less likely to complete high school and more likely to work at low-income jobs, experience longer periods of unemployment, receive social assistance, and experience single parenthood. However, she notes that when racial and economic variables are included, those who come from socioeconomically disadvantaged backgrounds suffer many of these consequences as a function of their prepregnancy life situation. For women from disadvantaged backgrounds, avoiding teen birth does not always improve education or employment opportunities, so there may be little perceived incentive to delay childbearing.

Institutional Bases of School Problems in Adolescence

ISSUES TO CONSIDER

- What are the goals of schools?
- Why are schools being charged with providing services that were previously supplied by other social institutions?
- Why are schools failing to provide a goodness of fit with the social, health, and cognitive needs of adolescents?
- How are some schools responding positively to address the issue of violence?

Given that the entire developmental system is involved in both the bases of school problems and in the solution to them, it is crucial to understand how any component of the system is involved in positive or negative outcomes. Individual, peer group, and family variables may influence positive or negative developments in school (Janosz, LeBlanc, Boulerice, & Tremblay, 1997), and schools in their structure and function may contribute to the problems experienced by adolescent students (Dryfoos, 1994, 1995). North American schools are intended to promote the intellectual and social development of students. Schools are also supposed to be contexts for the socialization of cultural values and for the development of citizens competent to pursue healthy individual and family lives and to contribute productively to our society. Simply, the goals of schools are the development of intellectually reflective, healthy, caring, and ethical people who are good citizens on the path to lifetimes of meaningful work (Carnegie Council on Adolescent Development, 1989).

Because of changes in the nature of the Canadian family across this century and the growth of youth poverty and of violent crime and other risk behaviours among adolescents (Dryfoos, 1990; Huston, 1991; Lerner, 1995, Schorr, 1988), schools are increasingly charged with providing services that were previously the responsibility of other social institutions (Dryfoos, 1994). That is, "Until recently and for centuries, young generations were integrated

Safety issues have become a prominent part of the school experience of many youth.

into society via their families. During this century, school experiences became the essential element—to participate in the benefits of social life in most places in the world" (Alvarez, 1992, p. 1).

All too often, schools are not fulfilling these functions. School programs and school structures frequently fail to provide a **goodness of fit** with the complex health, social, and cognitive needs of youth (Ames & Ames, 1989; Dryfoos, 1994; Eccles & Midgley, 1989). This failure is derived in part from at least three interrelated problems (Dryfoos, 1994; Lerner, 1994).

First, schools are not adequately addressing the problems presented by the large proportions of youth engaging in one, and often several, of the other major high-risk behaviours of adolescence. The risk of school failure is interrelated with the three other types of major risk behaviours in adolescence: unsafe sex, drug and alcohol use and abuse, and delinquency (Dryfoos, 1990). Other community-based organizations may have to help address these problems and "today, thousands of youth programs are complementing, and in some cases supplementing, the role of families and schools" (Alvarez, 1992, p. 1).

Second, the increasing prevalence of youth poverty is challenging the resources of schools and diminishing the relevance and utility of current portfolios of school-based programs (e.g., Pungello et al., 1996). Youth poverty exacerbates the risk behaviours of adolescents. Poverty is associated with early school failure as well as with unemployability, violent crime, and feelings of hopelessness and despair (McLoyd & Wilson, 1992; Schorr, 1988). Accordingly, "Schools cannot educate children who are too 'stressed-out' to concentrate. Teachers are not trained as social work-

Goodness of fit Degree to which two individuals and/or groups match in goals or styles.

ers, and cannot possibly attend to their jobs if they must spend all of their time trying to remedy problems" (Dryfoos, 1995, p. 149).

3 Last and perhaps most important, failure is occurring because of the absence of a thorough integration of the school into the community, an integration involving the services of other youth-serving institutions, parents, and youth themselves.

For example, the issue of school violence is becoming increasingly contentious, given the disparate views portrayed by media and the experiences of educators and those of parents (MacDonald, 1997). Some Canadian studies representing the perspectives of youth are helpful in understanding their experiences of violence in school. Many youth in MacDonald's study of 231 Grade 7 to 9 students in Edmonton did not report violence in school because they feared consequences, either peer or school-based, or saw the violent behaviours as normal (MacDonald, 1997). Among 962 junior and senior high school students in Calgary, those in the study who described the highest levels of delinquency also reported high levels of victimization (Paetsch & Bertrand, 1999).

In her ethnographic study of violent, white suburban girls, Artz (1998) noted that her participants believed that their victims caused attacks; their use of violence was justifiable because females in society are devalued and oppressed. Carter (1998) reported that the psychopathology (see Chapter 14) among boys participating in violence at school was high, and that appropriate intervention should target attitude change and skill development (Carter & Stewin, 1999). Evaluations of Canadian antiviolence programs delivered in schools, some led by youth themselves (Carroll, Hebert, & Roy, 1999), have been successful at achieving increased knowledge about violence (Hilton Harris, Rice, Krans, & Lavigne, 1998) and improved confidence in performing social skills (Schoiack-Edstrom, Frey, & Beland, 2002).

Bullying is repeated aggressive behaviour—physical, social, verbal, and indirect—toward another person. It has received media attention, which has been implicated in copycat incidents of bully-related violence in schools in the United States and Canada (e.g., school shootings in Columbine, Colorado, and Taber, Alberta). In Edmonton, Alberta, a bylaw was passed on March 11, 2003, that prohibited people from bullying anyone under the age of 18 in a public place (CBC.CA News, 2003). Recent research from Ma (2001) on a New Brunswick sample of 13 751 Grade

6 and 8 students indicates that bullies are also bullied; these two groups are not mutually exclusive. In a study of the behaviours of bullying students in a Toronto school, it was noted that the frequency of bullying was the same for girls and boys, and that in 85% of the incidents of in-class bullying, peers were involved (Atlas & Pepler, 1998). As mentioned in Chapter 10, bullies appear to be at risk for unhealthy dating relationships: they date earlier, but have less positive views of their partners, and report being physically and socially aggressive with their boyfriends or girlfriends (Connolly, Pepler, Craig, & Taradash, 2000).

Addressing School Failures: Understanding the Influence of Schools on Adolescents

Considerable evidence indicates the need to restructure schools innovatively in a manner that involves the inclusion of comprehensive, integrative services. Nevertheless, in the midst of this challenge, youth still attend schools and are affected by their structure and function. Therefore, we must understand the influence of schools on youth development. Two general approaches have been taken to understand these influences on adolescents. First, researchers study how the school as an institution influences youth behaviour and development through its organization or curriculum. Second, researchers examine the nature and bases of adolescent behaviour and development within the school context. We consider both of these approaches.

Reorganizing and Reforming Schools

ISSUES TO CONSIDER

- Through what procedures can schools better address the problems of youth in schools?
- What kind of classroom and school organizations are there, and what effects do they have?
- What are full-service schools and how do they deal with the multiple problems facing adolescent students?

One way to address the problems of the youth enrolled in schools is **school restructuring**. Schools may be

School restructuring Altering the organization of a school.

organized differently and the functions of schools may be altered. These latter changes may be termed **school reforms**. Reorganization and reform are related in the actual practice of trying to change schools to serve youth better. These links are illustrated in the following discussion of some ways in which reorganization and reform have been approached.

Schools may group students on the basis of their academic ability. Both positive and negative effects on development occur in relation to **ability grouping**. For students with low mathematics ability, grouping at the beginning of junior high school has some negative and no positive effects on Grade 10 math achievement (Fuligni, Eccles, & Barber, 1995). For students with medium and high levels of ability, grouping at the beginning of junior high has a positive influence on Grade 10 performance.

Given these differential effects of groupings on youth, it is vital to have as much information about a student as possible when deciding if and how to group him or her. Parents' input would seem valuable here. Although in most school districts parents do have some influence over the process by which their children are ability grouped and/or placed in particular courses, the degree to which such parent participation is welcomed, restricted, or even thwarted varies across school systems (Useem, 1991).

One innovation is based on Aboriginal philosophies and teaching. In such settings Aboriginal youth receive a holistic program designed specifically for them. The offerings at a school for Aboriginal students might include traditional teachings and ceremony as well as first language instruction. It is important that the school have Aboriginal staff: youth with Aboriginal teachers perceive themselves as more academically competent than Aboriginal youth enrolled within a typical school structure (Beiser, Lancee, Gotowiec, Sack, & Redshirt, 1993).

Other variations in classroom organization also influence youth, with a diversity of outcomes associated with these differences. Classrooms can be organized in regard to the formats of teacher-student interactions that take place within them. Lectures, question and answer sessions, provision of discussion

Teachers may create a classroom climate that effectively engages students in academic work.

activities, and encouraging student participation in shaping the content of the course are examples of different formats that can be used. All these formats have been found to enhance Grade 8 students' achievement in both English and social studies classes (Gamoran & Nystrand, 1991).

However, schools by themselves are unable to deal adequately with the multiple problems facing many of their adolescent students. One tactic addresses the problem that schools are not part of community-wide, multiagency, collaborative efforts to stem the tide of adolescent educational failure coupled with other risk behaviours. The leading spokesperson for the creation of schools involved collaboratively with the community in this manner in the United States is Joy G. Dryfoos. She terms schools that are collaborative with the community **full-service schools** (Dryfoos, 1994, 1995). Applications Box 11.2 describes the vision Dryfoos has developed for such schools.

Dryfoos's (1994) call for the creation of full-service schools constitutes an appeal to reorganize and reform the structure and function of these institutions. Research, although still in its initial stages, suggests that such revisions have positive influences on youth. When junior high schools in the United States undertook reforms that included building school-community partnerships, enabling teachers of different subject areas to work together on interdisciplinary teams, and bringing community volunteers into the school to help the students discuss connections

---

School reform Altering the functions of a school.

Ability grouping Placing students in a classroom based on their academic ability.

Full-service schools Schools that are part of a community-wide, multiagency, collaborative effort to prevent adolescent educational failure coupled with other risk behaviours.

The Potential Role of Full-Service Schools

Joy Dryfoos (1990, 1994, 1995) believes that enhancing the role of schools in child and adolescent development rests on the creation of full-service schools. "Full Service Schools provide the types of prevention, treatment, and support services children and families need to succeed . . . services that are high quality and comprehensive and are built on interagency partnerships . . . among state and local and public and private entities . . . [including] education, health care, transportation, job training, child care, housing, employment, and social services" (Dryfoos, 1994, p. 142).

Such schools involve, then, in a fully integrated manner: (1) community-wide, multiagency collaborations, and (2) a full range of social services (e.g., health centres, vocational guidance and career development programs, and counselling services) that are (3) embedded within schools but are administered by the collaborating nonschool agencies and use (4) citizen input and volunteerism.

These components of the full-service school concept are congruent with Dryfoos's (1995) vision for these schools. In her view, the full-service school "integrates the best of school reform with all other services that children, youth, and their families need, most of which can be located in a school building" (p. 152).

Given the comprehensive and integrative character of full-service schools, it is clear that such institutions engage children, adolescents, and their families across the life span. Emphasizing a preventive and capacity-building orientation to address the co-occurrence of child and adolescent problems, such schools provide integrated services for both, through the point that the person is launched successfully on a path involving a productive and healthy adult life.

Dryfoos (1994, 1995) finds that, to accomplish these ends, full-service schools typically incorporate several components of service (as distinguished from components pertinent to educational restructuring). These service components include the following:

A Planning Process

This process begins with assessing the capacities and needs of the community, a step aimed at ensuring that the structure and function of the full-service school use the resources and meet the specific needs of the children and families of the community (cf. Kretzmann & McKnight, 1993). Here it is critical that the school and community agencies overcome "turf" issues and create a vision of a new type of joint institution. Thus this planning process must yield "an efficient design, utilizing the contributions of each party to building strong and durable full service schools" (Dryfoos, 1995, p. 42).

A Service Design Process

This process integrates new services with those health, social, and counselling services already present in the school. Thus, rather than replace existing programs, services are designed in the supplementary manner (Alvarez, 1992).

A Collaborative Governance Structure

This governance structure often takes the form of an advisory board, one that involves personnel from the school and from service agencies and parents, community leaders, and children and adolescents as well. This governance structure is based on an agreement among all collaborators to "pursue a shared vision and have common goals,

expect to share resources, participate in joint decision-making, and use their personal and institutional power to change systems" (Dryfoos, 1995, pp. 26–27).

A System to Use Space for Primary Health Care and/or Other Services

If primary health care is provided in the local area, then an area in or near the school building is used. As noted by Dryfoos (1994, 1995), this space should be used for examination rooms, a laboratory, confidential counselling rooms, and an office for referrals and files. When primary health care is not provided in or near the school, school space should nevertheless be dedicated for individual and group counselling, parent education, and case management and referrals. Furthermore, space should be allocated for career information, play, clothing and food distribution, and food preparation. In addition to providing the space for these functions, the school provides maintenance and security. Moreover, classrooms, gyms, and computer facilities remain open for use by the community, and the doors of the school remain open before and after school, on weekends, and during the summer (Dryfoos, 1994, 1995).

Opportunities for Building Leadership

The building principal is instrumental in implementing the programs of the full-service school and in maintaining the programs' effective operation. A program director is responsible for the conduct of the services provided in the school and functions collaboratively with the governance structure.

---

between social studies and art, students' awareness of art increased, they developed attitudes and preferences of particular styles of art, and their movement from concrete to abstract thinking was enhanced (Epstein & Dauber, 1995). Changing a school's organization in the direction of the reforms described by Dryfoos (1995) can be beneficial to youth.

The School as a Context for Development

ISSUES TO CONSIDER

- What facets of adolescent development need to be understood in relation to school transitions?
- How do school transitions affect adolescents?
- How does the change from a focus on mastery to a focus on performance influence adolescents?
- How are pubertal changes and school transitions related?

The second general approach to understanding the influence of schools on adolescent behaviour involves studying the school as a developmental setting. Here the focus is on the experiences that occur within school. These experiences involve stresses on adjustment that may occur when youth make a transition from one school level or setting (e.g., elementary school) to another (e.g., junior high school), problems that may exist when school changes are linked to other developmental changes experienced by the adolescent, or how achievement may be facilitated when there is a goodness of fit (Lerner & Lerner, 1989) between the adolescent's characteristics of individuality and the demands placed on the adolescent in the classroom.

Instances of all these facets of adolescent development within the school context have been studied in relation to the transitions youth make into and out of junior high school and into and out of high school.

School Transitions in Adolescence

For adolescents, perhaps the key school organizational influence on their development is encountered when they make the transition from elementary school to junior high school. Many youth look forward to the transition.

For example, students' perceptions of junior high school tend to be positive (Berndt & Mekos, 1995), perhaps because the transition to this more advanced school is associated with their feeling more mature. For instance, in a longitudinal study of about 100 adolescents from the spring of their Grade 6 school year to the end of their Grade 7 year, youth reported more positive than negative reactions to junior high school (Berndt & Mekos, 1995). However, although misbehaving Grade 6 students showed little concern about moving to junior high school, after the transition they perceived the junior high school less positively than did

other students; in turn, high-achieving Grade 6 students expressed a lot of concern about moving to junior high school, but, after a year there, they felt more positive about it than the other students (Berndt & Mekos, 1995).

However, when the transition to junior high school entails moving from a small school to a large one, initial optimism, prior to the transition, is often transformed into anxiety about it after the move (Cotterell, 1992). Any effects of the transition on students' academic performance or on their academic feelings and motivation may be due in part to the organization and curriculum of the junior high school. In fact, the transition from elementary school to junior high school *is* linked to negative changes in academic motivation and academic performance (Eccles & Midgley, 1989; Midgley, Anderman, & Hicks, 1995; Simmons & Blyth, 1987; Wigfield et al., 1991).

The transition to junior high school is hard for youth for many reasons (Urdan, Midgley, & Wood, 1995). Changes in the adolescent's travel schedule to and from school, alterations in sleep and waking cycles to accommodate the junior high school class schedule, altered parental expectations about independence in completing homework, homework load, and a new set of youth comprising the "crowd" (see Chapter 9) of youth in the school can all be difficult for adolescents. Adjusting to any of these changes could impact the motivation and achievement of a young person. However, one key basis for the change in motivation and achievement across the transition to junior high school may be the different goals for students stressed in elementary school versus junior high school (Midgley et al., 1995).

Junior high schools place more stress on a student's relative ability (to other students), and less stress on how the student masters a given task, than

School can be a stressful context for many adolescents.

is the case in elementary school (Midgley et al., 1995). In other words, junior high schools emphasize the goal of performing well *on* a task, and not the goal of learning how *to do* a task (independent of how well one performs on the task). Both junior high school teachers and students perceive (correctly) that this stress is present in the junior high school classroom (Midgley et al., 1995).

This change in emphasis from elementary school (where learning how to do a task is important) to junior high school (where performing well on that task is important) is associated with lessened motivation in mathematics (Mac Iver & Reuman, 1988; Midgley et al., 1995; Midgley, Feldlaufer, & Eccles, 1989a, 1989b). In turn, when there continues to be a stress on task goals in junior high school, both students and teachers show self-efficacy. However, when stress on performance is present there is no connection to self-efficacy in either group (Midgley et al., 1995).

Other research has confirmed these relations between task goals and feelings of academic efficacy (Roeser, Midgley, & Urdan, 1996). Moreover, this research has been extended by demonstrating an association between perceived self-efficacy and the actual grades earned by junior high school students.

The change in the junior high school culture to a focus on performance, as opposed to one on learning activities or tasks, may contribute to students' perception that the junior high school is a context that does not match, or fit with, their preferred style of making decisions about their learning. For instance, in a study of junior high school mathematics classrooms, students saw fewer student decision-making opportunities in junior high school compared to elementary school (Midgley & Feldlaufer, 1987); teachers agree that this difference exists. More important, perhaps, students have a preference for more decision-making opportunities, whereas junior high school teachers believe they should have *fewer* opportunities. This lack of agreement between students and teachers may be one source for why junior high school influences the academic performance of youth.

Moreover, school transitions can have other effects on adolescent development. Simmons and Blyth (e.g., Simmons & Blyth, 1987; Simmons, Carlton-Ford, & Blyth, 1987) find that a decrease in self-esteem is most likely when a young adolescent female is experiencing simultaneously the changes associated with menarche and the contextual alter-

ations associated with the transition from elementary school to junior high school. Thus the work of Simmons, Blyth, and their colleagues illustrates that changes in both the adolescent and her school context contribute to developments in school.

In her study of 651 Canadian students in junior and senior high schools, Coutre (2002) found that junior high students (Grades 7 to 9) and senior high school students (Grades 10 to 12) reported different needs. The junior high students reported higher needs for clear and consistent expectations, academic skill development, sexuality, physical health, and self-esteem, whereas the high school students were more future-oriented in their needs for career information and self-management. In their study of high school students in Cape Breton, Chisolm and Edmunds (2001) found that students living in communities with recent closures of major industries who had no definite career plans also had lower career decision-making self-efficacy.

In sum, the school as an institution—its organization, "culture," and curriculum—influences youths' academic and personal development in several ways. Some of these links result in positive outcomes for youth, whereas others result in problematic ones. It is precisely because of this diversity of developmental outcomes that the school context is a key setting for youth development.

Conclusions About the Role of School in Adolescence

Today, schools are in a state of crisis. They are charged by society with doing more than just educating youth but faced with diminishing resources and challenged by the complex and serious problems shown by the young people they encounter. Important school reforms are being initiated to increase schools' capacities to fulfill their mission, and effective youth-serving programs are available to assist the efforts of schools to enhance the life chances of all youth, but schools must continue on a day-to-day basis to serve youth.

Schools, through their organization and curriculum, and by virtue of providing a key context for youth development, have an ongoing influence on youth. Some of these contributions result in positive outcomes for adolescents and others are linked to negative ones.

In both cases, this diversity of influence occurs because of the interconnections among the school, family, and peer contexts and, in turn, through the contribution made by characteristics of the developing person to the social relationships encountered in the school, the peer group, and the family.

Accordingly, to address the problems faced by schools and, in a more positive view, to enhance the contributions schools can make to healthy youth development, schools must seek more integration with the community, and thus must build bridges to the other key contexts affecting the developing adolescent.

Such innovation will require school *policy changes*, will require the school to make *revisions* in its *programs*, and will necessitate that the school take steps to *assess* how well it is doing in implementing these altered approaches to its role in youth development. Table 11.1 presents the key policy, programmatic, and assessment issues faced by schools. Implementing the changes outlined in Table 11.1 will enable schools—and families and the broader community as well—to play a new and needed role in addressing the problems not just of schools but, more significantly, of the youth they serve.

Table 11-1 Reforming Schools to Address the Problems of Youth Development: Policy, Programmatic, and Assessment Issues

Policy Issues

- *Full-service schools should be created.* Schools should become centres for the coordinated delivery of medical, mental health, and social service programs. These school-based centres should be (a) administered collaboratively by community agencies and youth-serving organizations; (b) focused on prevention and on enhancement; and (c) evaluated in both formative and summative terms that are reflective of community values and goals and engage the community in both the evaluation process and in the centres themselves.

- *The services provided by schools should be integrated.* Comprehensiveness by itself is not sufficient to support the adolescent, his or her family, and the community.

- *School structures and programs should be reorganized to better meet the developmental needs of youth.* Use of "team" or "house" organizations (i.e., of "schools within schools") can ease the junior high school transition; students should be allowed to share control of assignments and of the evaluation of these tasks.

- *The focus of teacher education should be revised.* Teaching should move from a subject matter emphasis to a holistic focus on the adolescent, and thus on his or her relations with peers, family members, and the community.

Programmatic Issues

- *Schools should offer a full range of integrated programs—those spanning the educational, medical, mental health, developmental, and social service needs of adolescents.*

- *The design and administration of these integrated school programs must involve collaborations with the community, parents, and youths themselves.* A focus on capacity building and on prevention should be maintained.

- *School policies, organization, and programs must be culturally competent (i.e., attuned to the values and traditions of the community within which the school exists).* They also must be designed in light of the developmental and social needs of youth.

- *Teacher education and professional development programs should focus teachers' efforts primarily on building competent citizens and not on building subject matter competence per se.* The latter focus is only a vehicle to produce the former, and thus greater emphasis on competency for life is warranted.

Assessment Issues

- *Schools must assess whether policies, structures, and programs are meeting the holistic needs of adolescents.*

- *Barriers to the development and implementation of full-service schools must be identified and culturally competent means used to put such schools in place.*

- *The active involvement of students, parents, school personnel, and the community must be ascertained.* Means to enhance their collaborative involvement in the policies and programs of the school must be devised.

Source: Adapted from Lerner, R. M. (1994). Schools and adolescents. In P. C. McKenry & S. M. Gavazzi (Eds.), *Visions 2010: Families and adolescents*, 2(1), (pp. 14–15, 42–43). Minneapolis: National Council on Family Relations.

Summary

- Schools are training institutions, agents of cultural transmission, and a means to instill knowledge and values. Schools fulfill a maintenance-actualization role and are a place to develop optimal personal and interpersonal attributes and the ability to contribute to society.

- Schools provide a context for social interactions and relationship development and can facilitate an adolescent's independence from his or her parents. Schools also provide the adolescent with an opportunity to gain social status. Status can be earned at school through demonstrating a mastery over the curriculum, attaining high class standing, and by nonacademic interactions with peers. Future status can be earned through the training and education attained in school.

- Perceptions by adolescents that their teachers care about them can be associated with enhanced motivation to achieve positive academic and social outcomes.

- Social support from the family is associated with students' grades, scores on a standardized achievement test, teacher ratings, and enhanced self-esteem.

- The factors associated with student achievement include having parents and peers who hold high standards, holding a belief that one succeeds through effort, having positive attitudes about achievement, studying diligently, and being less apt to distract youth from studying.

- When parents react negatively to school performance, youth show negative performance.

- Students' awareness of discrimination toward people of their race is associated with their perception that academic achievement is not important. A positive ethnic identity, however, is associated with school engagement and achievement.

- A higher percentage of service occupations in a community is associated with increased dropout; an increased percentage of managerial/professional occupations is associated with lowered dropout and a greater likelihood that high school graduates will continue their education.

- Self-handicapping behaviours such as procrastination, allowing other youth to keep one from studying, or deliberately not trying to do work are associated with low-achieving students.

- Volunteering in school to help other students is linked to better self-esteem, less depression, and fewer problem behaviours, particularly for male adolescents.

- Males in junior high school gain status through participation in extracurricular activities more so than females do.

- Work is a significant extracurricular activity for adolescents, but there is little evidence that teachers adjust their classroom behaviours to accommodate the possible needs of working students.

- About one-fifth of Canadian youth leave high school before completion.

- Remaining in school is the single most important thing a youth can do to improve his or her future economic prospects. The costs of dropping out of school are significant for society and for the quality of life of the young person.

- School problems, as well as other problems of adolescence, are associated with individual variables related to cognitive abilities, motivation, personality, and self; peer variables related to reputation and to the nature of behaviours shown by peers; family variables, relating to parental practices and parent-child interactions; community variables, relating to poverty level, social support, and the availability of programs; and school variables pertaining to structure and curriculum and to peer and teacher interactions.

- Effective dropout prevention programs take a systems approach that deals simultaneously with the set of risks facing youth and engages all levels of their contexts.

- Engagement in adolescent risk behaviours has been related to school dropout.

- Returning to school is associated with fewer life stressful events, more family support, fewer depressive symptoms, and greater commitment to a career.

- Schools are a context for the socialization of cultural values and for the development of citizens competent to pursue goals and to contribute productively to and maintain civil society.
- The risk of school failure is interrelated with three other major risk behaviours: unsafe sex, drug and alcohol use and abuse, and delinquency. Schools are not adequately addressing the multiple problems facing a large proportion of youth engaged in high-risk behaviours.
- School restructuring involves organizing the school differently; school reform involves changing the functions of the school.
- Schools' use of ability grouping has positive effects for students with medium and high mathematics ability but not for students with low ability.
- Classrooms can be organized in regard to the formats of teacher-student interactions that take place, including lectures, question and answer sessions, provision of discussion topics, and encouragement of student participation in shaping curricular content.
- Full-service schools are involved collaboratively with the community to deal with the multiple problems facing adolescent students; they have been shown to have positive benefits for youth.
- The transition to junior high school is linked to negative changes in academic motivation and performance. It alters adolescents' perceptions of future life successes. There is lower optimism and higher pessimism after the transition.
- Both junior high school teachers and students perceive a stress on performing well on a task rather than just learning how to do the task, which is associated with lessened motivation in mathematics.
- A decrease in self-esteem is most likely when an adolescent female is experiencing school transition and the changes associated with menarche at the same time.

Discussion Topics

1. How well did the structure of your high school support your development? Many school systems are questioning the schedules they employ. Did the early start of the day, timing of the lunch hour, time allowed for extracurricular activities, and number of days spent in school during the year impact your learning and/or your attitude about school in general? If so, in what ways?

2. Who were your favourite teachers in high school? What about them attracted you? Were they better able to interact socially with the students than other teachers? Alternatively, was it the depth of their knowledge about certain topics that drew you to them? Or was it both? Did they show their admiration and respect in ways that other teachers did not? In what ways were they involved in the school? How did they make their presence known?

3. Did your ethnicity, race, socioeconomic status, and/or gender determine the general expectations for school success placed *on* you *by* others? How well did you meet those expectations? Did your ability to meet those expectations impact your eventual school success and your attitude about school? Do you think it will impact the career path you choose? Why or why not?

4. Did you have a job while in high school? If so, how did it impact your ability to meet the day-to-day expectations of your teachers and the social expectations of your peers? How did your experiences at your job positively impact your development? How might schools be more supportive of those students who need to work after school in order to support their families and/or begin to save money for university or college?

5. Do you know anyone who dropped out of high school? What became of him or her? What are

some of the main factors that cause an adolescent to drop out of school? What can be done to decrease the dropout rate in Canada? Would this strategy work in other nations? If not, why not? How effective are the intervention programs and multifaceted approaches that we now employ to keep students interested and motivated to learn?

6. Do you think that schools and teachers have too much responsibility in raising today's youth? Why or why not? Do you think it is a necessary responsibility for them to take on? How well do schools live up to this responsibility?

7. What effect does grouping by ability have on student motivation, self-esteem, and school success?

8. Look over Applications Box 11.2. What do you think of Dryfoos's idea? How feasible is the idea of implementing full-service schools in your community? What needs would be met that are lacking now?

9. Think back on your transition from elementary school to high school. How well prepared were you for this transition? If you experienced any anxiety, what was the major focus of this anxiety? How well did the school you transitioned into address the anxieties of its new students? What could the school administration have done to make the students feel more at ease?

Key Terms

ability grouping, p. 264
compulsory education, p. 253
extracurricular activities, p. 257
full-service schools, p. 264
goodness of fit, p. 262

maintenance-actualization, p. 252
school reform, p. 264
school restructuring, p. 263

self-handicapping behaviours, p. 257
systems approach, p. 260
training-acculturation, p. 252

The World of Contemporary Adolescents

Mr. Spence turned the handle of the door, pushed it open, and shoved his briefcase and suitcase quickly in ahead of him. "I'm home," he shouted. There was no answer. It had been a long business trip—five cities in six days—and he had eagerly anticipated coming home to his family.

He shouted again, "Hey, everyone. I'm here." But again there was no answer. He hung up his overcoat in the hall closet. Undoing his tie, he walked slowly into the kitchen. There was a note from his wife on the counter. "Hi, Hon," it read, "I had to drive Karen to the mall for some clothes she needs for her dance class. There is a salad in the fridge. Max is home and you can call out for pizza. See you right after the mall closes."

"Welcome home, Steve," Mr. Spence thought to himself. Well, at least his son was home, he reasoned. He was glad that 12-year-old boys didn't like to go clothes shopping with their older sisters. "The poor kid," Mr. Spence observed. "Home alone with nothing to do." At least he and Max could now spend a few hours together, eating dinner and just hanging out.

He walked to the bottom of the stairs. "Max," he called. Still no answer. "Perhaps he's fallen asleep," Mr. Spence thought. He bounded up the stairs. At the end of the hall, he saw a light coming from behind Max's door. As he came closer he heard music playing. He knocked on his son's door. There was again no answer and so he opened it.

There was Max, seated at his desk in front of his computer, with his hand on the mouse. Mr. Spence saw that Max was talking online with his friends. However, at the same time his phone was cradled on his shoulder and he was immersed in a conversation with someone. Max's voice was raised because a CD player was playing on his stereo system and his TV was on and tuned to a rock video station.

Max saw his father enter the room. He nodded in recognition. "Hey, Max, how are you doing?" Mr. Spence asked. "Mom thought we should order some pizza. What would you like?"

"Nothing now, Dad. I'm busy now. I'll speak to you later . . . and please close the door when you go out."

Learning Objectives

1. To understand how the world changed in regard to media during the 20th century.
2. To recognize how a youth's use of media changes across adolescence.
3. To learn the effects of media, such as television, on youth.
4. To understand how the organization and function of the school are designed to provide youth with a context for social life.
5. To recognize how an exclusive focus on school activities puts a youth in a dilemma when applying to university or college.
6. To understand the key elements of what is developed among youth by virtue of their participation in a community-based organization.
7. To understand why it is important for young people to interact with caring adults and how such interactions can be promoted.
8. To learn how the positive experiences and developmental outcomes of youth in community sports activities can be maximized.
9. To understand how the niches selected by youth change across the adolescent years.
10. To understand how and why the different environments adolescents live in must cooperate to enable them to develop in a positive manner.

Max is not an unusual adolescent. Today, the world of adolescents is a world of **media**. As discussed in earlier chapters, family members, peers, teachers, and schools also populate the world of adolescents. These parts of the world of adolescents are perennial ones. They are influences on adolescent behaviour and development that exist across historical eras.

There are also influences on adolescent behaviour and development that are products of the contemporary historical moment. People, events, and inventions make a particular time in history different from others. To understand adolescence, we must appreciate both types of historical influences (Baltes et al., 1998, 1999).

One of the most striking features of the contemporary world of adolescents is the proliferation and ubiquitous presence of different forms of media. It is useful in a discussion of the world of contemporary adolescents to focus first on this facet of the world of today's youth.

The Media and Adolescent Behaviour and Development

ISSUE TO CONSIDER
• How did the world change in regard to media during the 20th century?

Although Max and his peers perhaps cannot imagine a world without television, radio, the movies, magazines, computers, pagers, and cell phones, the invention and spread of these media were largely phenomena of the 20th century. As Huston and Wright (1998) comment,

> It was this period that witnessed a radical transformation of the media environment. In less than 100 years, radio, movies, comic books, television, video games, CD-ROM, and audiotapes and videotapes have become a routine part of most children's environments. Digital television, the Internet, and virtual reality are spreading rapidly. (p. 999)

Media Means through which information or entertainment is passed, such as television, radio, movies, magazines, computers, pagers, cell phones, and video games.

Technology has become a prominent means through which adolescents interact.

In a compilation of indicators of electronic media use in Canadian families, Moscovitch (1998) noted that almost all households have television sets (99%) and over half (59%) have two (Statistics Canada, 1997). Approximately 80% of Canadian homes with televisions have cable and slightly more (84%) own videocassette recorders (Statistics Canada, 1997). Almost 20% of households own a cellular telephone (Statistics Canada, 1997).

In terms of Internet use, the rates vary considerably across family types. In 2001 single-family households with children under 18 were the most likely (at 80%) to use the Net; this is about double the 1997 level of 38% (Statistics Canada, 2001). There is some indication that the use of the Internet does replace time previously spent on other activities: more than one-quarter of Net users in a 2000 survey (Statistics Canada, 2000) reported that they spent less time watching television, about 15% spent less time reading books, magazines, and newspapers, and 10% spent less time sleeping, enjoying leisure activities, and doing household chores. In a Statistics Canada study, between 1999 and 2001 Canadian teenagers' television watching dropped by 2 hours per week, from 15 to 13 hours (Anderssen, 2002).

In a study of 6000 youth aged 9 to 17 from 77 schools across Canada (Shade, 2002; Taylor, 2002), it was found that 99% of those surveyed had used the Internet and 79% had used it from home. Nearly half used it at home for at least an hour per day. About half reported that they download music, surf for fun, or play games online. About two-fifths used the Internet for information, instant messaging, chat rooms, and doing homework.

Age Changes in Media Use

ISSUE TO CONSIDER

• How does the use of media change across adolescence?

Youth do not use different media with the same frequency. At some points in their lives one instance of media is used more than others. The total amount of time children or adolescents spend watching television increases from infancy to early adolescence (Huston & Wright, 1998), and then declines throughout the rest of adolescence. At the high point in this series of age changes (i.e., in early adolescence), youth average three to four hours a day of television watching (Huston & Wright, 1998). Young male German adolescents watch television about two hours a day, viewing mostly entertainment and action programs (Myrtek et al., 1996). As television viewing decreases during the middle to late years of adolescence, radio listening, primarily to music, increases (Huston & Wright, 1998). Among youth in Canada, significant television and video watching (more than four hours per day) was more prevalent among males, but for both genders decreased over Grades 6, 8, and 10 (Health Canada, 1999).

In contrast, significant computer game playing (more than four hours per week) remained low for girls, but increased for boys between Grades 6 and 10 (Health Canada, 1999). An international survey of 12- to 17-year-olds in 16 countries found that nearly twice as many boys (63%) as girls (34%) had tried online games. Canada (53%) ranked third behind China (59%) and South Korea (58%) in the proportion of Internet users who had tried online games (Ipsos-Reid, 2001). In 1998, 41% of Canadian 13-year-old males played computer games for four or more hours per week compared to only 11% of females. About the same proportion of girls in the U.S. played for four hours per week; with only 27% of American 13-year-old boys playing computer

Online computer games have become popular activities for many youth.

games for more than four hours per week (Health Canada, 1999).

Effects of Media Use

ISSUES TO CONSIDER

• What are the effects of media on the vast majority of youth?
• What effects can high levels of television viewing have on adolescent development?

Although the influence of media on youth behaviour and development continues to be a topic attracting social and political debate, the data indicate that for most forms of media that have been studied there are no major, enduring negative effects on the vast majority of youth. Current information indicates that only some youth, under specific circumstances, are negatively influenced by exposure to the media.

Across all North American youth there are, at most, only small influences of television viewing on adolescents' leisure reading, completion of homework assignments, school achievement, or physical and social activities (Huston & Wright, 1998; Katzmarzyk, Malina, Song, & Bouchard, 1998). However, high levels of viewing can have some dramatic influences on these activities. For example, extensive television viewing is associated with obesity (Huston & Wright, 1998). Although findings from about two dozen studies of the association between television watching and school achievement indicate virtually no overall relation between these two domains of youth behaviour, lowered achievement does occur when adolescents spend 30 hours a week or more watching television (Huston & Wright, 1998). This frequency of television watching approaches the time devoted to many full-time jobs. In a longitudinal study of youth, first in childhood and then in adolescence, early-life television viewing was linked in adolescence to increased obesity (Dietz & Gortmaker, 1985). Between Grades 6 and 8, high levels of television viewing are related to lower participation in organized school and community groups. Among German youth, boys who watched a lot of television read fewer books, showed diminished activities outside the home, did less homework, and had less interest in hobbies (Myrtek et al., 1996).

Higher levels of media use may be associated with other problematic features of adolescent behaviour. Among male and female 12- to 19-year-old Australian adolescents, engagement in **passive leisure activities** (e.g., watching television) is greater than participation in **active leisure activities** (e.g., playing a sport) (Gordon & Caltabiano, 1996). Among these youth, boredom in regard to their leisure time activities (in other words, being bored by watching television) is associated with drug use and delinquency (Gordon & Caltabiano, 1996). In a U.S. study, watching rock music videos was related to permissive sexual attitudes and behaviours, especially among girls and in particular among girls with problematic family relationships (Strouse, Buerkel-Rothfus, & Long, 1995).

Lacourse and colleagues (Lacourse, Claes, & Villeneuve, 2001) report that adolescents' musical preferences have been a concern to parents and mental health professionals since rock and roll began in the 1950s; in the 1970s punk and heavy metal became popular, in the '80s it was industrial and gothic music, and in the '90s death and black metal, combined with sensational images in the media (e.g., school shootings in Taber, Alberta), reinforced the perception that a causal relationship between music and violence exists. Though it appears that preference for "light" or "heavy" music is associated with different personality characteristics among Canadian youth (Schwartz & Fouts, 2003), in Lacourse's study (Lacourse, Claes, & Villeneuve, 2001) of 14- to 18-year-old high school students in Montreal, preference for heavy metal music was not associated with suicidal risk. In fact, preference for heavy metal music had an inverse relationship with suicide risk (those with a preference for

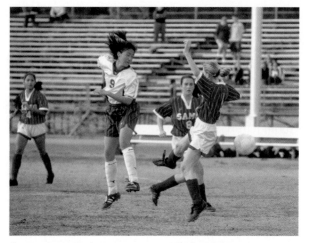

Sports events offer important opportunities for adolescents to participate in the social world of their schools.

heavy metal music had the lowest suicidal risk) (Lacourse, Claes, & Villeneuve, 2001).

In several content analyses of prime time television situation comedies, Fouts and colleagues (Fouts, Burggraf, 1999; Fouts, Burggraf, 2000; Fouts & Vaughn, 2002) found that characters with below average weight were overrepresented, and characters with above average weight were underrepresented. They found that the heavier the character, the more negative comments were made; for females, these comments were more often made by others, and for males, these comments were made by the character himself. The effects of watching television on adolescent females' eating disorder symptomatology appear to be greatest for those who see the causes of their behaviour to be outside of themselves (Fouts & Vaughan, 2002). Dr. Fouts's research is featured in Meet the Researcher Box 12.1.

Conclusions About Media and Adolescent Development

Media are a major part of the life of most youth. Although high levels of media use can be associated with problems in adolescent behaviour and development, for the vast majority of youth there are no pervasive or long-term detrimental influences of media. It will be important, however, to revisit this conclusion as more research is conducted about the possible influences of new and emerging media, such as interactive television, on youth development.

Research about the influence of contemporary features of the adolescent's world on behaviour and

Passive leisure activities Free time events that require little expenditure of energy on the part of the participant.

Active leisure activities Free time events that require a large expenditure of energy by the participant.

MEET THE RESEARCHER — Box 12.1 — Gregory T. Fouts

Effects of Media on Adolescent Development

Gregory Fouts is a professor of psychology in the Department of Psychology at the University of Calgary. He is also adjunct professor in counselling psychology in the Faculty of Education. Dr. Fouts has won several awards for excellence in teaching and in his collaboration in community research.

Children and adolescents grow and develop within a culture, and a major aspect of culture is media. My career has been devoted to studying how youth use media (e.g., television, magazines, music), what contents they are exposed to, and the possible effects of exposure to media. Although by training I am a child psychologist, my research and teaching is clearly interdisciplinary; most of our projects cut across such disciplines as child development, social psychology, education, and media/communications. Here at the Interdisciplinary Research Laboratory in Human Development, students from a variety of disciplines work together trying to discern the many threads and colours that create the media fabric to which adolescents are exposed on a daily basis. We believe that understanding adolescents requires appreciating the cultural and social contexts in which they develop. Thus, our research involves two basic approaches—analyzing the contents of media and assessing the effects of media. That is, we believe that we have to know *what is in the media* before we can understand the *effects of media exposure*.

Analyses of content. In recent years, we have examined television situation comedies (e.g., *Friends*, *Frasier*) that adolescents watch in large numbers. For example, we have found that such programs present an overrepresentation of thin women, with male characters making positive comments about thin

women and negative comments about heavier women; often these comments are followed by audience laughter. Thus, television situation comedies not only model thinness as a value for adolescent viewers, but also reinforce this value through the comments of characters and audience laughter. Our research examining the content of magazines that girls read reveals that 87% of the women in the magazines are below average in weight. The combination of exposure to television and magazines puts adolescent girls at greater risk for becoming dissatisfied with their bodies, and for a small proportion, developing an eating disorder.

Uses and effects. This research has spanned three decades and has examined several media. For example, we have shown that the personality of adolescents, as well as their developmental issues (e.g., independence, relationships), often determine the kinds of music they prefer listening to (e.g., heavy metal, Top 40, folk). Some of our other research has found that girls who increase their magazine reading during early adolescence are more at risk for developing eating problems; but if they have positive self-esteem or are happy with the way their bodies look, the effect of this increased magazine exposure is minimal. Also, if girls actually decrease their magazine reading due to being involved in other activities, they reduce their risk of eating problems. And finally,

we have recently found that many girls exposed to thin models on television are not affected at all; that is, if they have their own set of values and do not seek the attention and approval of others.

Our research for the next few years will expand on these areas. For example, what can we do to (a) help adolescents benefit from the positive content in the media (e.g., role models), and (b) prevent them from being unduly influenced by negative content (e.g., distortions, stereotypes)? Are males being subjected to unrealistic and distorted body images and are they being influenced? Does exposure to overly romantic television, magazine, and music content influence adolescents' expectations about love and relationships? Asking these questions and being able to do the research is exciting. I believe that the next three decades will offer students many opportunities to develop meaningful careers in adolescent psychology, for example, as practitioners, researchers, or even professors!

---

development will also have to focus on topics other than the media. Adolescents do more than spend time in their rooms chatting online, watching television, or listening to music. Formal and informal areas of activities texture the world of adolescents. These contexts, or niches, within the ecology of youth are places populated by other adolescents, locations where young people pursue hobbies, engage in sports, see or are seen by friends, or merely hang out.

The Community Niches of Adolescents

Portions of the world of adolescents are shaped by youth themselves. Selecting an area of town in which to hang out, such as a shopping mall or a street corner, are instances of such adolescent-shaped contexts or niches. There are also portions of the world of adolescents influenced by adults. A prime instance of such a niche is the school, where in addition to academic experiences, a range of social interaction opportunities and extracurricular activities are offered to youth. Adult-influenced settings also take the form of youth clubs, organizations, or programs (see Chapter 14). Let's first consider the two types of adult-shaped niches for youth—school and community-based youth organizations—and then look at youth-selected niches.

The Social Life of the School

ISSUES TO CONSIDER

- How is the organization and function of the school designed to provide youth with a context for social life?
- How does an exclusive focus on school activities put a youth in a dilemma when applying to a postsecondary institution?
- What evidence exists that traditional differences in school careers are changing?

Although media and electronic technology are ubiquitous parts of the world of contemporary adolescents, they are not the only features of it. For many youth, the school constitutes their social world as well as their academic one. In many ways, the organization and function of the school is designed to provide for youth a context for social life. A culture is developed within schools that in the extreme channels young people into focusing their social life within the calendar of events that occur each year within the school. These events can include sports events and rallies, homecoming weekends, and social events such as dances, class trips, proms, class plays, and awards ceremonies. In other words,

> The school year is built around a relatively unchanging sequence of activities designed to enhance the social atmosphere of the school and the school's competitiveness with other schools.... Students are expected to be motivated by loyalty to their own school and by competition with other schools. Loyalty dictates confining one's network and activities to the school at the expense of involvement in the local community and in other communities or organizations that would take time away from school activities. (Eckert, 1995, p. 180)

Community-based learning
Students learn by doing in collaboration with a community-based agency for their mutual benefit.

Such exclusive focus on building one's social life by participation in the sets of activities available within the school (e.g., student government, the school newspaper or yearbook, varsity teams, cheerleading, and academic interest clubs), to the exclusion of any form of community involvement, may put youth in a dilemma when they begin to apply to colleges and universities. Today, many higher educational institutions want applicants who have broad and varied profiles of credentials that include good grades and standardized test scores, participation in school extracurricular activities, and community service. Youth may need to find a balance between a social life that involves investing time exclusively in the school and one that involves investing time in the community, to gain entrance into a desirable college or university.

Some Canadian schools make a connection to and form relationships within their local communities for the mutual benefit of the students and community. A teaching approach used to describe a very deliberate and active connection between school and its local community has been called **community-based learning**. According to De Schiffart (2000), the

Many adolescents participate in extracurricular activities such as drama clubs, student government, or sport teams.

basic approach is to learn by doing, to "engage young people in their own learning by giving them the opportunity to perform services that directly benefit their community . . . to build lifelong connections between youth, their communities, and the rapidly changing world of work" (p. 186). Youth are assisted to make connections in their community and engage in community-based learning activities with local community groups in a collaborative process; the students gain experience and the community gains some additional person power for projects that it may not have the short-term resources to take on or complete. The value for students can be significant; they learn about trust and respect as core values for working with others and understand that there are also excellent teachers in the community, not just in the classroom.

Many youth opt to invest in both the social world of the school and in the life of the community. Although significant proportions of youth choose to live almost exclusively in the school or the community, many young people intentionally select an **in-between existence**. In a study of several suburban high schools in the United States, Eckert (1995) found that many students built their lives exclusively through participating in the social roles available in schools. These roles amounted to **social careers**, for instance, election as a member or officer of student council, selection as a varsity cheerleader or varsity team athlete, or selection as a captain of such a squad. Students who based their lives and identities in the school's extracurricular arena were labelled in the high schools as **jocks** (Eckert, 1995). Other students, labelled **burnouts**, rejected the school as a centre for social life (Eckert, 1995). These youth focused their lives and pursued identities within their neighbourhood or the local community. They stayed at the fringe of school activities. However, the majority of the students in these schools did not fall into either of these two categories. Most youth saw themselves in the in-between category (Eckert, 1995).

Youth from different socioeconomic levels were differentially distributed in the three categories. As shown in Table 12.1, the social category that youth from working-class backgrounds were most likely to be in was burnouts, whereas lower middle-class youth and upper middle-class youth were most likely

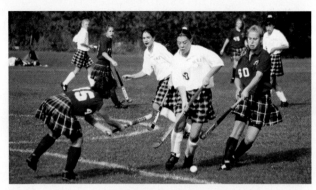
Team sports are a prominent part of the school experiences of many youth.

to be in the social categories of in-betweens and jocks, respectively (Eckert, 1995).

Given that less than half of Canadian 13-year-old students (46%), and only about one-third of their American counterparts (38%), feel that others in their school are often or always kind and helpful, compared to about 80% of Danes and Swedes (Health Canada, 1999), there is ample reason for many students to reject the school as a centre for social life because they have given up on trying to be accepted in a school culture that simply reinforces income distinctions and pigeonholes those youth in the lower socioeconomic class present in the broader society. Valaitis (2002) reported in her Canadian study of female inner-city youth that they felt unheard and disempowered by the larger community. Feeling accepted and having a sense of community is highly correlated with perceptions of well-being among Canadian youth (Pretty, Conroy, Dugay, Fowler, & Williams, 1996).

Not only do most youth merge the school-focused and the nonschool-focused worlds of the jocks and the burnouts into their personal array of interests and activities, but some evidence suggests that traditional gender differences in school life are changing. Girls are increasingly seeking prestige in school through sports and are placing decreased emphasis on activities such as cheerleading (Suitor & Reavis, 1995). Nevertheless, remnants of traditional divisions between boys and girls in the routes to school success persist. Boys continue to seek prestige through sports and achievement, and girls attempt to acquire status through physical appearance, sociability, and achievement (Suitor & Reavis, 1995).

In-between existence Balance between investing time in the social world of the school and life in the community.

Social careers Life built exclusively around participating in a particular social role.

Jocks Students who use the school's extracurricular arena as a centre for their social life.

Burnouts Students who reject the school as a centre for their social life.

Table 12-1 **Distribution of Adolescents from Different Socioeconomic Backgrounds into Types of Students: Jocks, In-Betweens, and Burnouts**

Socioeconomic Category	Percentage of Youth in the Social Category		
	Jocks	In-Betweens	Burnouts
Working class	16	16	50
Lower middle class	34	42	22
Upper middle class	50	42	23

Source: Eckert, 1995, p. 180.

Schools, at least in part by adult design, are centres of youth social development. Most youth take advantage of the opportunities for honing their academic, athletic, and social interests and skills provided by schools. The majority of youth combine their school-centred lives with activities in their communities. Schools that are active participants in the local community can facilitate the collaboration between school-based and community-based activities for the betterment of the school and community.

Community-Based Youth Organizations

ISSUES TO CONSIDER
• How can different meanings of citizenship lead to quite different developmental outcomes for youth?
• What key elements do youth develop by virtue of their participation in a community-based organization?

Just as much as the world of media that exists for contemporary adolescents is a product of inventions of the 20th century, many features of the community context provided for youth arose during this period:

> In the late 19th century social reformers invented a new set of contexts intended specifically to foster adolescents' development. These reformers initiated and promoted hobbies, youth organizations, and sports as valuable and healthful parts of adolescents' lives. . . . Boy and Girl Scouts, 4-H, the YMCA and the YWCA, Little League, and numerous recreational centers, hobby clubs, and eventually in school extracurricular activities were launched by community activists who wanted to improve the lot of developing youth. These activists believed that, with proper adult guidance, such organized activities could promote initiative, build character, discourage delinquency, and provide "laboratories for training in citizenship." (Larson, 1994, p. 46)

The clear intent of the founders of many of the community-based youth organizations was to develop a means to instill in the future generations of adult leaders a commitment to civil society (see Chapter 5), and to provide youth with the moral foundation to be engaged and productive citizens. Not only do Canadian youths benefit from community-based programming, they are also contributors to its success (Pancer & Pratt, 1999). Nearly one-quarter (23%) of Canadian youths aged 15 to 19 volunteer in their communities and contribute more hours per year to organizations on average (116 hours per year) than do older volunteers; females volunteer slightly more hours per week on average (3.9) than males (2.8). One-third of male and female volunteer time is spent in education and youth development programs.

Citizenship can mean different things in different societies. In North America, Little League is intended to teach fair play and teamwork, and in Scotland, jazz bands for girls are used to provide a stabilizing influence in their lives (Larson, 1994). However, the goal of the Soviet Pioneer youth groups in the former USSR was to make good communists and the Hitler Youth groups in Germany in the 1930s and 1940s was to create good Nazis (Larson, 1994) in order to support the goals of the government at the time.

Thus it is possible to subvert the energy and potential commitment of youth to community engagement and create citizens who embrace ideas antithetical to civil society. This danger was explained by Erik Erikson (1950) more than a half century ago, when he described how the Hitler Youth movement capitalized on the striving of German adolescents for an identity (see Chapter 6) and on the orientation of all youth to show fidelity toward an ideology associated with their identity. Hitler offered German youth an identity as a Nazi and an ideology that was antidemocratic and linked to dehumanizing, subjugating, and even murdering other people (Lerner, 1992).

Hitler was responsible for the murder of millions of Jewish people during World War II.

It is not automatic that a community organization for youth will build citizens promoting civil society (Damon, 1997; Larson, 1994). The moral values of the community are key elements of what is developed among youth by virtue of their participation in a community-based youth organization. Within those countries such as Canada, in which good citizenship is linked to democratic ideas, the value of civil society, and the promotion of social justice, it is important to know whether the vision of the founders of community organizations for youth is being actualized. Does participation in such organizations enhance the positive development of youth?

Benefits of Community-Based Youth
Organizations Participation in community-based youth organizations can be effective in promoting values and positive developments and in preventing undesirable values and development among adolescents. For instance, 4-H participation is associated with increased understanding and communication in families (Larson, 1994). In a longitudinal study of extracurricular participation, delinquency and sports participation were found to exist together in the junior high school grades (Larson, 1994). By Grades 11 and 12, however, there was an inverse relation with higher levels of sports participation associated with lower levels of delinquency (Larson, 1994).

However, while adolescents' engagement in arts or hobbies (e.g., coin or stamp collecting, model airplane construction) and their participation in youth organizations (e.g., 4-H, YMCA; see Chapter 14) are also not inversely related to delinquency, participation in these activities does appear to decrease delinquency in the high school years (Larson, 1994). These beneficial influences of organizational membership and engagement in the arts or in hobbies continue to play a role in the positive development of people into their adult years (Larson, 1994). Among Australian high school students, being involved in organizations that enable them to perform at exceptional or elite levels in such activities as dance, music, and drama is associated with a self-concept as an artist and with positive self-esteem (Marsh & Roche, 1996).

Because of the benefits for positive youth development of involving youth in leisure activities that engage their interests in the arts and in hobbies, numerous programs have been developed to offer

young people a range of such experiences. Applications Box 12.1 presents examples of programs from around the world.

A key feature of the programs described in Applications Box 12.1, and in community-based youth organizations in general, is the opportunity provided for young people to interact in positive ways with caring adults who model the sorts of citizenship behaviours that community organizations seek to instill in young people. Contemporary adolescents have relatively few opportunities to interact with adults other than family members or teachers (Larson, 1994). Extracurricular activities offer a chance to get to know and learn from other adults (e.g., coaches and leaders of community organizations) (Larson, 1994).

Youth sports organizations represent an important instance of such an opportunity for beneficial youth-adult interactions. Young people engage in formal, organized, community-based athletic activities involving sports such as baseball, football, basketball, soccer, ice hockey, field hockey, track and field, swimming, diving, bicycling, and gymnastics. When we consider the additional millions of youth who participate in informal but adult-supervised athletic activities as well, it is clear that in North America there is enormous potential for sports to provide a route to positive adult-youth relations and healthy adolescent development.

Unfortunately, the potential benefits of sports participation are not being fully realized. As explained by William Damon in his book *The Youth Charter: How Communities Can Work Together to Raise Standards for All Our Children* (1997) (see Chapter 5), many coaches and parents have lost sight of the founding purpose of such athletic activities, which is to build moral character and promote citizenship (Larson, 1994). Very few of the youth involved in the sports activities expect to go on to have careers as professional athletes. For example, among a sample of 138 Canadian male and female gymnasts aged 8 to 15 years, the top five reasons for participating in sport were to have fun, for the challenge, to improve skills, to be fit, and to learn new things (Kolt, Kirkby, Bar-Eli, Blumenstein, Chadha, & Kerr, 1999). In a group of 1387 Canadian Grade 10 students, almost all (94%) had withdrawn from at least one sport; the top five reasons for withdrawing were because they did not enjoy it, wanted more time for nonsport activities, other sports took too much time, they were not good enough, and were

Using Leisure Activities, Culture, Media, and the Theatre Arts to Promote Positive Youth Development

Vicaria Zona Norte (The North Zone Vicarship)
Santiago, Chile

In Chile, many children are forced by circumstance to work at an early age. Others may be left at home with little developmental stimulation. Established in 1981 by an outreach office of the Catholic Church, Vicaria Zona Norte (The North Zone Vicarship) unites communities to improve the quality of life for such children through recreational and cultural activities. Community organizations known as "Urban Colonies" (Colonias Urbanas) train youth as monitors to work with children. The program annually coordinates activities of community groups in over 30 neighbourhoods in northern Santiago. During the school year, at each Urban Colony between 10 to 50 youth monitors, aged 14 to 20 years, work with 100 to 200 children between 3 and 12 years old. The older youth address social problems and prevent risky behaviours among children, and organize weekly meetings for cultural, urban camps, where children receive meals, basic assistance, and recreation. To date, the program has served over 65 000 children and trained more than 700 youth monitors. Studies of adults who were formerly youth counsellors reveal that they have enhanced leadership skills, increased awareness of children's rights, and a heightened sense of civic responsibility.

The Mirror Art Group (MAG)
Manila, Philippines

Established in 1989 by the Philippine Educational Theatre Association, the Theatre in Education Program (TIE) develops the creative and analytical skills of young people through theatre. TIE has two components: the Children's Theatre Collective and the Metropolitan Teen Theatre League. Together they organize children and youth collectives in schools and organizations, providing a curriculum and assistance in theatre training. In addition to students, TIE works with street children, refugees, and dropouts. Indeed, it has succeeded in joining children from disparate backgrounds in theatre training and productions. Children view, plan, and participate in plays and evaluate their activities at the end of performances. Some teen members have even gone on to assume positions in the organization as program directors, project coordinators, music directors, and playwrights. In its first five years, TIE reached more than 60 000 children as audiences of its mobile theatre performances and trained more than 5000 in newly formed theatre collectives. Impressively, the TIE program has given birth to more than 350 theatre guilds throughout the Philippines.

Source: International Youth Foundation, 2001. www.iyfnet.org

under too much pressure to perform well (Butcher, Lindner, & Johns, 2002).

However, all young people will be expected, and needed, to contribute to the future of a just and civil society. Damon (1997) explains how a youth charter can be developed to maximize the positive experiences and long-term desired developmental outcomes of youth in community sports activities (see Applications Box 12.2).

Conclusions About the Role of Adult-Organized Youth Niches Adults care about, and have an investment in, the healthy development of young people. The niches provided by adults to foster such development have met with considerable successes; but significant challenges remain in order to maximize the life chances of all young people. Community-based initiatives such as those envisioned by Damon (1997) through the youth charter constitute a potentially productive means to enhance the contributions of adults to the positive development of youth.

Enhancement through such endeavours as a communitywide charter for the welfare of youth has the added benefit of helping create a seamless safety net for young people no matter where they may go in their communities. Such a safety net is important in that not all the niches within which contemporary youth interact are ones organized by adults. Youth select and shape their own niches, and some of these contexts may not be ones linked to positive development. These niches are a product of the lifestyles of contemporary youth.

Youth-Selected Niches and Lifestyles

ISSUES TO CONSIDER

- How do the niches selected by youth change across the adolescent years?
- What is the pattern of change in lifestyle that occurs with developmental change for adolescents?
- How and why must the contexts of adolescents cooperate to enable them to develop in a positive manner?

Sports: A "Youth Charter" to Promote Positive Adolescent Development

Participation in sports is a significant part of the lives of many contemporary adolescents. Damon (1997) points out the many important benefits of such participation. Young people enhance their physical fitness, learn athletic and physical skills, and, through sports, they experience lessons pertinent to the development of their character (for example, they learn about the importance of diligence, motivation, teamwork, balancing cooperation versus competition, balancing winning and losing, and the importance of fair play) (Damon, 1997). Sports can be a context for positive parent-child relations, and such interactions can further the adolescent's successful involvement in sports. For instance, parental support of their male and female adolescents' participation in tennis is associated with the enjoyment of the sport by the youth and with an objective measure of their performance (Hoyle & Leff, 1997).

Damon (1997) notes that organized and even informal opportunities for sports participation for youth, such as baseball, soccer, or pickup games in school yards, often fall short of providing these benefits for young people. He points out that in modern North American society, sports participation is often imbued with a "win at any cost" orientation among coaches and their young players. Parents may also have this attitude. Together, a value is conveyed that winning is not only the main goal of competition, it is the *only* important thing (Damon, 1997, p. 210).

Damon believes that this orientation corrupts the purposes of youth participation in sports. Parents and coaches often forget that most of the young people on these teams will not become professional athletes. Even if they were to make sports a career, they, as well as the majority of young people involved in sports, need moral modelling and guidance about sportsmanship (Damon, 1997).

In order to enable youth sports to make these contributions to positive adolescent development, Damon (1997) proposes a youth charter (see also Chapter 5) that constitutes a set of guidelines for the design and conduct of youth sports programs. Adherence to the principles of the charter will enable communities to realize the several assets for young people provided by youth participation in sports. Components of the charter include the following commitments:

1. Make youth sports a priority for public funding and other forms of community support (space, facilities, volunteer coaches);

2. Emphasize standards of conduct as a primary goal of youth sports;

3. Provide young people with opportunities to participate in individual as well as team sports;

4. Encourage broad participation by ordinary players as well as stars; and

5. Carefully coordinate sports programs for youth with other community events for young people. (Damon, 1997, pp. 123–125)

Adolescents have their own ideas about what they want to do, about how and where they spend their time, and about the sorts of people with whom they interact (e.g., Bibby, 2001; Larson, Gillman, & Richards, 1997). These preferences and the behaviours associated with them constitute the **lifestyle** of adolescents. At any one point in adolescence, youth differ in regard to their lifestyles and thus in respect to the niches they choose to frequent. For instance, in early adolescence, some youth may elect to spend their leisure time in shopping malls, others may elect to stay at home, and still others may opt to just hang out on the street. Across the adolescent years, the lifestyles and the niches selected by adolescents may alter (Hendry et al., 1994). A shopping mall may be replaced by a dance club or, although youth may not be of legal drinking age, by a bar. Similarly, whereas younger adolescents may have their choices of niches and activities constrained because of not being licensed to drive, a broader set of possibilities is available to older adolescents who can drive a car.

Developmental changes in the lifestyles of youth create a pattern of change that appears to move the person from a youth-centred world, where hanging out and recreation are central, to a lifestyle marked by concern with the imminent entry into the world of young adulthood (see Chapter 15) (Hendry et al., 1994). Developmental changes in lifestyles were assessed in a longitudinal study of about 300 British male and female adolescents between the times when they were 15 to 16 years old and when they were 17 to 18 years of age (Hendry et al., 1994). When they were between 15 and 16 years, the lifestyles of girls were characterized by visiting friends or being visited by them, spending a lot of time with their best friend,

Lifestyle Preferences and behaviours of adolescents regarding what they want to do, how and where they will spend their time, and with whom they want to interact.

Many older adolescents spend time at dance clubs.

or hanging out on the street with friends; by going dancing and to clubs; by working at a job; and by engaging in sports. When they were between 17 and 18 years of age, these girls' lifestyles were characterized first by being involved full time in pursuing their education, but going to bars and clubs with friends was also a key focus of their lives (Hendry et al., 1994).

The focus on education seen among the 17- and 18-year-old girls was present among boys at a younger age. When they were between 15 and 16 years of age, educational goals were most important for the boys. In addition, the lifestyles of the boys were characterized by having hobbies, by staying away from drugs and tobacco, and by sports participation (Hendry et al., 1994). However, although the boys' focus on educational goals continued to characterize their lifestyles when they were between 17 and 18 years of age, their world was also characterized by going to bars and clubs with friends and by using tobacco (Hendry et al., 1994).

In a longitudinal study comparing adolescents from Berlin, Germany, with adolescents from Warsaw, Poland (Silbereisen, Noack, & Schönpflug, 1994), the most frequent leisure contexts among 12- through 15-year-olds from both nations were home, sports areas, streets, cultural settings (e.g., museums), nightclubs, youth clubs, and nature (e.g., woods, lakes, mountains) (Silbereisen et al., 1994). Adolescents used these settings to promote their social contacts with same-sex peers and with romantic friends (Silbereisen et al., 1994).

Among older German adolescents, and akin to the British youth studied by Hendry et al. (1994), a niche preference that differed from the ones of younger adolescents was found (Todt, Drewes, & Heils, 1994). As with the British youth, this difference involved an emphasis on education. Specifically, these youth said that the most significant feature of

their lives was an emphasis on specialization in school and the selection of a life path involving either vocational training or a university education (Todt et al., 1994). Other significant features of their lives were identified as involving an interest in having satisfying free time and friendships, by working to develop their identities and especially their gender identities (see Chapters 6 and 7), and by striving to enhance further their cognitive competencies (see Chapter 4) (Todt et al., 1994).

To live in a world marked by such activities, the environments adolescents live in must cooperate (Todt et al., 1994). To enable adolescents to develop in a healthy manner, families, peers, schools, and the residential and recreational areas of communities need to provide structures and values supporting the competent development of youth in regard to the significant features of their world (Todt et al., 1994). As we discussed in Chapter 5, creating a healthy world for adolescent development involves providing them with ecological resources or assets (Benson, 1997; Scales & Leffert, 1999; Scales et al., 2000).

Conclusions: Issues and Assets of the World of Modern Youth

Contemporary youth occupy a world that is in some respects just like the one their parents experienced when they were adolescents. As was true for their parents, family, peers, schools, and community play a significant part in their lives. They share with their parents an adolescence marked by the availability of technological achievements in communication and entertainment. Movies, television, radio, books and magazines, and even VCRs, were present during the adolescence of the parents of many of today's youth.

However, parts of the modern adolescents' world (e.g., fax machines in the office and home, cell phones, and electronic mailing to friends through home or laptop computers) were not part of their parents' adolescent world; yet they are an ordinary part of the world of contemporary youth.

In addition, modern adolescents live in a world that in still other respects is totally unlike the one of their parents. Today, shopping for almost anything in any part of the world can be done through a home computer. Almost all of the world's knowledge is readily accessible through the same technology. Breakthroughs in the speed of travel, in medicine, and in use of machines to conduct many of the routine tasks of life (from banking to residential climate control) have given contemporary youth more options for pursuing their interests and for realizing their aspirations.

For most youth living in contemporary society the innovations and opportunities available to them are not diminishing the likelihood of their healthy development. In many cases the interaction of youth with modern media and with the community niches of their world is enhancing their chances for positive development.

Nevertheless, the modern world also presents unique challenges to youth. The parents of today's youth grew up in a world that was not beset by the AIDS epidemic (see Chapter 10). Youth of past eras were not faced with an increase in problems of adolescent health and behaviour such as burgeoning crises of drug and alcohol use and abuse, and of youth violence, or with a growing tendency for such problems to occur together in the lives of young people.

The special challenges of modern youth find both their sources and their solutions in the perennial components of the world of adolescents—family, peers, schools, and communities. As we turn to key dilemmas of youth development (Chapter 13) and to the policies and programs that may effectively address these issues (Chapter 14), we acknowledge the individual strengths of youth, when coupled with the assets of the traditionally key contexts of their lives, as the link to overcoming the unique set of problems besetting modern youth.

Summary

- The invention and spread of television, radio, movies, magazines, computers, pagers, cell phones, and video games are largely 20th-century phenomena.

- Almost all Canadian youth use the Internet, and the majority use it daily.

- At certain points in the life span, the use of certain types of media is different from that of other points in the life span. For example, television viewing increases from infancy to early adolescence, and then decreases throughout the rest of adolescence.

- Data indicate that most forms of media have no major, enduring effects on adolescents. Only certain youth, under specific circumstances, are influenced by exposure to media.

- A culture of loyalty and competitiveness is developed within schools that channels young people into focusing their social life around events that occur within the school during the school year.

- Community-based learning offers students the opportunity to learn about their community and make a contribution to it at the same time.

- Today, universities and colleges want students with good academic credentials who also demonstrate participation in school extracurricular activities and community service.

- Girls are increasingly seeking social status through sports and placing a decreased emphasis on activities such as cheerleading. However, boys continue to seek prestige through sports and achievement and girls through physical appearance, sociability, and achievement.

- The moral values of a community are the key elements of what is developed in youth by virtue of their participation in community-based youth organizations.

- Canadian youth actively contribute to the success of community-based organizations through voluntarism.

- Caring adults can model positive citizenship behaviours for young people, and extracurricular activities offer young people a chance to get to know and learn from other adults.

- A youth charter containing commitments for the design and conduct of sports programs can be developed to maximize the positive experiences and the long-term developmental outcomes of participation in sports activities.

- In early adolescence, youth may spend leisure time at the mall, at home, or hanging out on the street. By late adolescence, the niches may change so that a dance club or, illegally, a bar replaces the mall. Older adolescents have a broader set of possibilities for finding niches by virtue of having a driver's licence.

- The family, peer, school, and community contexts of adolescents must provide structures and values supporting the competent development of youth in regard to civil society and the promotion of assets.

Discussion Topics

1. How much television did you watch as a high school student? Were there specific shows you tried not to miss? What about these shows attracted you? What purposes did these shows serve? Were there specific lessons/morals/experiences you were able to apply to your life? Were you more attracted to real-life dramas or fantastical story lines?

2. Has any media experience (i.e., television show, movie, newspaper) made such an impression on you that you changed your way of thinking about or approaching some topic or situation? Describe that experience and explain what made it so powerful.

3. What do you think about the associations made between certain rock videos and lyrics and high-risk behaviour among adolescents? Why are some youth so much more drawn to media that promotes negative behaviour? What about the messages they hear in the lyrics and see on the videos is so powerful? Should adults and peers be concerned about teens who are attracted to these powerful negative images and the behaviours they espouse?

4. How has the Internet affected your life? What role do parents play in terms of monitoring the use of the Internet by their adolescents? What role do the Internet providers play? Do you feel that adolescents are mature enough to make their own decisions about appropriate and healthy use of the Internet? Why or why not?

5. Where did you and your friends hang out in high school? When you visit your hometown now, are teens still frequenting this spot? Why or why not? What characteristics define a healthy and supportive environment for adolescents to hang out in? How much adult interaction/involvement needs to be included in these environments? Does your response depend on the group of adolescents in question and their specific character traits?

6. How knowledgeable were you and your friends about available community resources in which you could spend your free time? Did you make use of these resources? Why or why not?

7. How involved were you with student activities at school? Were you involved in extracurricular activities? If so, how did your involvement support your development? Was there a specific club you were interested in but never joined? What about that club and its members attracted you? How proactive were the teachers and administration in your school at involving all students in extracurricular activities? Why do some youth choose not to become involved in any extracurricular activities? What are they missing out on? If you were involved in such activities, did your involvement require you to manage your time more effectively? In terms of prioritizing, how important was watching your favourite television shows or spending time surfing the Web? What, if anything, did you sacrifice/give up, because there just was not enough time in the day?

8. What, if any, were the different expectations of teachers, parents, and peers for males and females in terms of the route to school success? Do you feel these expectations impacted the decisions you made or the goals you set for yourself? In what ways?

9. Think back on the various adult role models you encountered in school and in the extracurricular activities you were involved in both in and out of school. What did you learn from these people that you might not have learned from your parents?

10. How well did your immediate community support your changing interests in terms of where and how you chose to spend your time? When your interests and needs were not met, did you ever search for entertainment outside of your environment? Did you ever have to partake in risky behaviour to satisfy these interests? Was part of the attraction stepping outside of environments that were familiar? How could your community better meet its adolescents' interests?

Key Terms

active leisure activities, p. 276
burnouts, p. 279
community-based learning, p. 278

in-between existence, p. 279
jocks, p. 279
lifestyle, p. 283

media, p. 274
passive leisure activities, p. 276
social careers, p. 279

Problem Behaviours in Adolescence

I had just graduated from university that spring. Armed with undergraduate degrees in psychology and social work, I figured that I knew about youth and their problems as well as how to help them. After all, I had been through teen years myself, managed to make it through unscathed, and learned a bit more about myself in the process.

I started my first human services job in a program helping youth who had juvenile records get into the workforce, and it was there that I met James, an 18-year-old who taught me more than any textbook or professor ever had. James was a survivor of a violent home life and a street lifestyle that was equally violent. As I got to know him better, I learned that he was also a poet, a caring father, and a talented musician.

He had been through a lot in his short life. James could remember moving with his mother, who was leaving a violent relationship. Their moves took him to four different cities in two provinces before he turned 12. It was hard for him to keep up in school and he had a lot of trouble keeping friends. His mother could barely afford to keep a roof over their heads and feed him. He said that he felt stupid and awkward at school, but at least he felt safe. When his stepfather was laid off, there was more drinking and violence at home. He decided that he couldn't help his mother, but he could help himself.

After leaving home at the age of 13, he stayed with his grandmother, stepbrother, an aunt and uncle, and some friends before spending his first night, two years later, on the street. Another three years later, having completed the cycle again, he was also a veteran of foster homes and group homes, as well as the young offender centre. No longer a child, he could not stay with the youth at the shelter and, as a young adult, did not want to stay at an adult shelter with men twice his age. He had been involved in the sex trade for money to survive and used drugs to cope with anger over the abuse he endured. His anger also got him into fights, and once he was stabbed. When he awoke in hospital he was told that he was lucky to be alive.

When I met James, he was living in a tent. He was hopeful that a new job would help him get back on his feet. I was intrigued, horrified, and touched by his words. I was impressed by his courage and resourcefulness, intensely angry with his victimizers, and felt privileged to hear his story. He taught me that there was much more I needed to learn.

Learning Objectives

1. To learn some of the major categories of adolescent risk behaviour and the dangers of engaging in them.
2. To define the two general dimensions of problem behaviours: internalizing and externalizing; to understand the attributes of adolescents and the contexts associated with these behaviours.
3. To understand the nature of poverty among youth and its relation to the behavioural risks of adolescence.
4. To understand the individual and social bases of delinquency, and the relationship between violence toward the self and others.
5. To understand adolescent substance abuse in terms of the adolescent's individual characteristics and relationships with parents and peers.
6. To appreciate gender differences in internalizing problem behaviours.
7. To understand the development of adolescent internalizing behaviours in terms of multiple individual characteristics, including gender and social contexts, such as family life.
8. To recognize that understanding the relation between developing adolescents and their social contexts may help design policies and programs to address adolescent problem behaviours.

Across North America and indeed across the world, adolescents are dying every day. They are dying from violence, drug and alcohol use and abuse, unsafe sex, poor nutrition, and the consequences of persistent and pervasive poverty (Annie E. Casey Foundation, 1999; Children's Defense Fund, 1996; Dryfoos, 1990, 1998; Hamburg, 1992; Huston, 1991; Lerner, 1995; Lerner & Galambos, 1998; Little, 1993; McKinney et al., 1994; Schorr, 1988, 1997; World Health Organization, 1993).

Even if our youth are not dying, their life chances are being squandered. They experience academic problems, underachievement, and early school leaving, crime, teenage pregnancy and parenting, lack of job preparedness, and health risks such as lack of immunizations and inadequate screening for disabilities. The infants of teenage mothers often suffer from insufficient prenatal care and insufficient infant and childhood medical services. Youth often experience despair and hopelessness as they see their parents struggle with poverty and realize they have little opportunity for a life marked by societal respect, achievement, and opportunity (Annie E. Casey Foundation, 1999; Carnegie Corporation of New York, 1995; Children's Defense Fund, 1996; di Mauro, 1995; Dryfoos, 1990, 1998; Huston, 1991; Huston, McLoyd, & Garcia Coll, 1994; Johnston, Bachman, & O'Malley, 1999; Statistics Canada, 2002).

Dimensions of Youth Problem Behaviours

ISSUES TO CONSIDER

- Despite improving trends in several categories relating to quality of life in Canada, why are statistics still alarming?
- What are some of the major categories of adolescent risk behaviours?
- What are the dangers of risk behaviours and, in particular, comorbidity of risk behaviours?

- Youth aged 15 to 19 make up about 7% of the total population of Canada (Statistics Canada, 2002), but have declined in the proportion they make up since the mid 1970s when they accounted for 10% of the total. This trend is expected to continue; Statistics Canada (2002) estimates that by 2051, youth will make up only 5% of the total population.
- Aboriginal youth aged 15 to 19 make up 9% of the total Aboriginal population of Canada,

and are projected to maintain this proportion into 2016 (Statistics Canada, 2002).

- While four out of every five Canadian youth report their health as excellent or very good, only two of five youth rate their self-esteem as high (Statistics Canada, 2002).
- Despite the relatively low mortality rate (50.8/100 000) for youth aged 15 to 19 and an apparent decline during the 1990s (from 96.8/100 000 to 69.4/100 000 for males, and 38.5/100 000 to 31.1/100 000 for females), males are at greater risk than females of being involved in motor vehicle accidents (20.7/100 000 and 10.8/100 000), other accidents (11.2/100 000 and 2.7/100 000) and of taking their own lives (18.2/100 000 and 6.4/100 000) (Statistics Canada, 2002).
- The frequency of sexually transmitted infections (STIs) remains especially high among female youth but appears to be on the decline. In particular, chlamydia infection rates are the highest for youth aged 15 to 19 (1138.9/100 000 for females and 186.7/100 000 for males in 1999), representing a decrease of 26% for females and 21% for males since 1991 (Statistics Canada, 2002).
- In contrast to the high rates of STIs among youth, AIDS cases are very low. Up to June 2000, only 58 cases had been reported in Canada for youth aged 15 to 19 (Statistics Canada, 2002). This may be because of the long incubation period for AIDS; youth who contract HIV may not show symptoms until their 20s.
- Over one-quarter of Canadian youth smoke cigarettes, and more smokers are female (32%) than male (23%) (Statistics Canada, 2002). Almost half of youth drink alcohol at least once per month; more often drinkers are male (51%) than female (44%) (Statistics Canada, 2002).
- Though early school leaving appears to be declining among youth, about 1 in 10 Canadian youth does not graduate from high school. Males (22% in 1991 to 15% in 1999) are more likely to leave early than females (14% in 1991 to 9% in 1999) (Statistics Canada, 2002).
- Overall, crime committed by youth appears to be on the decline. Charges for all criminal

code violations by 15- to 19-year-olds in Canada between 1995 and 2000 decreased from 49.3/1000 to 38.4/1000 (Statistics Canada, 2002). During this time charges for property offences decreased from 33.1/1000 to 21.4/1000, while charges for violent offences increased slightly from 7.3/1000 to 8.7/1000 (Statistics Canada, 2002).

- More than 1 in 10 (13%) of Canadian youth aged 16 to 19 live in poverty (income below Statistics Canada's low income cut-off, or LICO) (Statistics Canada, 2002). Among Aboriginal youth and immigrant youth, this proportion is doubled (Statistics Canada, 2002).
- In families where the primary income earner is 16 to 19 years old, over half (54%) live in poverty (Statistics Canada, 2002). Four of every five youth (85%) who live on their own, or with nonrelatives, live in poverty (Statistics Canada, 2002).

Despite some positive trends, the levels of these indicators of well-being suggest that Canadian youth in their late teens may be in particular peril. To illustrate, consider four major categories of risk behaviours in late childhood and adolescence: (1) drug and alcohol use and abuse; (2) unsafe sex, teenage pregnancy, and teenage parenting; (3) school underachievement and early leaving; and (4) involvement in crime and violence (Dryfoos, 1990). Participation in any one of these behaviours could diminish a youth's life chances. Involvement in some of these behaviours could eliminate the young person's chances of even having a life.

Approximately 50% of adolescents engage in *two or more* of the categories of risk behaviours just noted, and approximately 10% of North American youth engage in *all* of the four categories of risk behaviours (Dryfoos, 1990). These data suggest that risk behaviours are highly interrelated among adolescents. Dryfoos (1990, p. 3) describes this situation:

> Many children are growing up . . . today without a hope of enjoying the benefits that come with adulthood. They are not learning the skills necessary to participate in the educational system or to make the transition into the labor force. They cannot become responsible parents because they have limited experience in family life and lack the resources to raise their own children. The gap between achievers and nonachievers is expanding. A new class of "untouchables" is emerging . . . on the social fringes of suburbia, and in some rural areas: young people who are functionally illiterate, disconnected from school, depressed, prone to drug abuse and early criminal activity, and eventually parents of unplanned and unwanted babies. These are the children who are at high risk of never becoming responsible adults.

Table 13.1 summarizes recent information about the **comorbidity** of risk behaviours among youth. Comorbidity refers to the simultaneous occurrence of problem behaviours among adolescents. The level of comorbidity among adolescent risk behaviours suggests that risk is a typical, or normally occurring, feature of the lives of many, if not most, adolescents. Meet the Researcher Box 13.1, which focuses on the work of Lisa J. Crockett, discusses the nature of risk in normal adolescent development.

To grasp the full magnitude of the problems facing North America's youth and the challenges we as a society face in addressing these problems, let's examine more closely some of the risks besetting them and discuss their diverse individual and contextual bases.

Individual and Contextual Bases of Adolescent Problem Behaviours

ISSUES TO CONSIDER
- What are the two general dimensions of problem behaviours? How do they differ? How do they overlap?
- Which attributes of adolescents are associated with the occurrence of problem behaviours?

Problem behaviours may be associated with several attributes of the individual young person, for example, cognitive, personality, and behavioural characteristics. They are also associated with numerous features of the individual's context, for example culture, community, family, school, and peers. The diversity of individual and contextual influences on problem behaviours is associated with both externalizing problems and internalizing problems. **Externalizing problems** are directed to other people or, more generally, to the social context (e.g., aggression, arson, disruptive behaviours

Comorbidity Simultaneous occurrence of two or more problems or risk behaviours or symptoms (e.g., violence and substance abuse often occur together).

Externalizing problems Problems directed to other people or, more generally, to the social context, for example, aggression, arson, disruptive or conflictual behaviour in the school or in the home.

Table 13-1 **Examples of the Co-Occurrence of Sex-Related and Nonsex-Related Problem Behaviours in Adolescence**

Sex-Related Problem of the Adolescent	Nonsex-Related Problem	References
Unsafe sexual practices	Peer relations and alcohol use	Feldman et al., 1995
	Sexually active peers and siblings	East, Felice, & Morgan, 1993
	Friends with low educational expectations	Scott, Jones, & White, 1990
	Parenting style and parental marital status	Whitbeck, Simons, & Kao, 1994
	Substance abuse, conduct problems, and emotional distress	Borus et al., 1995
	Living in poverty settings	East & Felice, 1996; Sullivan, 1993
Initiation of sexual behaviour	Attitudes that reject social norms, nonconforming behaviour	Costa et al., 1995
	Poor psychological adjustment	Bingham & Crockett, 1996
	Pubertal maturation	Savin-Williams, 1995; Stattin & Magnusson, 1990
Teenage parenting	Use of income support	Carnegie Corporation of New York, 1995; di Mauro, 1995
	Ambivalent attitudes about childbearing, contraception, and abortion	Zabin, Astone, & Emerson, 1996
Sex-related crimes (abuse, rape)	Parent characteristics, peer relations	Blaske et al., 1989; Small & Kerns, 1993
	Personality problems	Henry et al., 1996

Source: Lerner, 1998.

in school, or inordinate family conflict). **Internalizing problems** are directed to the person himself or herself and affect his or her mental, cognitive, and emotional functioning (e.g., **depression** or **anxiety**).

Some problem behaviours involve both externalizing problems and internalizing problems. For example, substance use and abuse or unsafe sex can have features that involve both externalizing behaviours such as engaging in drug trafficking or in unprotected sex. These behaviours can also involve internalizing features such as becoming addicted to drugs or contracting a sexually transmitted disease. In such cases, both diverse individual and contextual characteristics are associated with these behaviours.

Certain components of the context of human development affect the incidence and development of internalizing and externalizing behaviours. Across

history, culture is always such an ecological influence (Shweder et al., 1998). In the contemporary world of adolescents, poverty is another key ecological basis of problem behaviours (Abernathy, Webster, & Vermeulen, 2002). To help frame the discussion of the two domains of problem behaviours in adolescence, we discuss these two key features of the human development system next.

Culture and Problem Behaviours

ISSUE TO CONSIDER
• What are some of the effects of cultural context on problem behaviours and on attitudes about their presence?

Culture provides a frame for the definition of behaviour problems. Youth have distinct ideas about the nature of adolescent problem behaviours, and these

Internalizing problems Problems directed inward to the individual and that affect his or her mental, cognitive, or emotional functioning, such as depression or anxiety.

Depression Emotional problem characterized by listlessness, lethargy, a blunting of affect, and disengagement from social activity.

Anxiety Unpleasant feeling state associated with such reactions as dread, fear, general uneasiness, or panic.

Normal Risky Behaviour and Adolescent Development

Lisa J. Crockett is professor of psychology and associate dean of arts and sciences at the University of Nebraska-Lincoln. She is associate editor of the *Journal of Research on Adolescence* and serves on the editorial board of the *Journal of Early Adolescence* and the *Journal of Adolescent Research*.

Most adolescents in North America engage in some amount of risky behaviour during their teenage years. For example, they experiment with sex, drinking, and other forms of drug use; they may drink and drive, or ride with others who have been drinking. Clearly, these behaviours can increase the risk of such problems as sexually transmitted infections, pregnancy, substance abuse, and serious accidents. However, some adolescents seem to be able to experiment with risk behaviours without experiencing lasting negative consequences, whereas others may not be so lucky. Which adolescents experience negative consequences and why? Also, are there certain characteristics of adolescents or their experiences that help us predict who will continue risky behaviours in adulthood?

I am studying a group of American adolescents that my colleagues and I have followed since they were in junior high school. They are now adults in their mid to late 20s. These adolescents all grew up in the same rural community. In adolescence, we surveyed them every year about their feelings, relationships with family and friends, and activities, including participation in risky behaviours. We have also surveyed them twice since they left high school. The goal of this research is to understand the role that risk behaviours play in adolescents' lives, both during adolescence and later as they move into adulthood.

With funding from the U.S. Office of Adolescent Pregnancy Programs and the National Institute on Alcohol Abuse and Alcoholism, my collaborator, Judith Vicary, and I have examined the changes in risk behaviours these young people exhibit as they move through adolescence. For example, as they get older, more teenagers report some experience with having sex, getting drunk, and getting high. Moreover, the frequency of these behaviours tends to increase with age, although the frequency of drug use declines in adulthood and heavy drinking levels off. Focusing on drinking specifically, we find that heavy drinking decreases in early adulthood for some youth but not others. Youth who reported high levels of misconduct as adolescents and those who delay marriage and parenthood continue to drink more heavily and are also more likely to initiate heavy drinking in adulthood if they did not do so in adolescence. On a related note, we have asked whether the age at which adolescents begin to experiment matters for their future psychological adjustment. What we find is sometimes surprising. For example, although adolescents who start to have sex at young ages also engage in other risky behaviours and show poorer adjustment in other ways, having sex early does not appear to cause these outcomes. Rather, adolescents who initiate sex early are already on a path that involves greater risk. Finally, we have asked what family characteristics and adolescent behaviours predict early versus late initiation of intercourse. Family background (for example, having a sister who became pregnant as a teenager or not living with both parents), academic investment, and involvement in other risky behaviours all appear to predict early initiation of intercourse.

What puts children on a path to engage in risky behaviour as adolescents? Are some young people attracted to risk? Are they unable to resist the lure of risky behaviour because they lack self-control? In a research project, funded by the National Institute of Mental Health, Marcela Raffaelli and I explored these questions. Using data from a national sample, the National Longitudinal Survey of Youth, we studied the development of self-regulation (the regulation of attention, affect, and behaviour) in middle childhood to learn whether young people's capacity to self-regulate helps them refrain from early intercourse and unprotected sex when they reach adolescence. We also identified individual characteristics, such as temperament, and contextual variables, such as maternal characteristics and parenting practices, that play a role in the development of self-regulation and risky sexual behaviour.

conceptions vary in relation to cultural context. One study of high school students from North America, China, and Japan assessed the perceptions of the behaviours and personality characteristics associated with a "bad kid" (Crystal & Stevenson, 1995). Among youth from North America, the behaviour most frequently associated with a "bad kid" was lack of self-control. In China, the key problem behaviours defining a "bad kid" were acts against society, and in Japan the most significant behaviours of a "bad kid" were disruptions of interpersonal harmony. In addition, the perception that substance abuse is a mark of a "bad kid" was more prevalent among North American youth than among the Chinese or Japanese adolescents (Crystal & Stevenson, 1995).

Other studies support the conclusion that the presence of behavioural problems among youth is linked to culture and cognition, for example, perceptions or ideas about problem behaviours. Among about 2800 15- and 16-year-olds from the Netherlands, youth with behavioural problems had negative perceptions of their families, school, and peers (Garnefski & Okma, 1996). Among boys, problems in school were the most important predictors of behavioural problems. For girls, problems at home were most associated with problem behaviours.

In a longitudinal study of about 100 Canadian youth, beginning when they were between 11 and 12 years of age and continuing for 3.5 years, disobedience to parents, school misconduct, and substance use increased with age (Maggs, Almeida, & Galambos, 1995). These increases in problem behaviours were associated with decreases in positive self-images and increases in peer acceptance and involvement and were linked to beliefs among the youth that engaging in risk behaviours was fun (Maggs et al., 1995). Similarly, among 650 Australian male and female adolescents, both peer approval and ideas about pleasure and risk were associated with perceptions about risk behaviours (Smith & Rosenthal, 1995).

In short, culture constitutes a key contextual influence on youth problem behaviour. Another factor, poverty, also exerts a strong influence. Poverty is a part of the contemporary context of over one-tenth of youth living in Canada.

Poverty and Youth Development

ISSUES TO CONSIDER

- What is the level and depth of poverty among children and youth in Canada?
- What are some of the "rotten outcomes" of poverty?
- What issues should be considered when designing interventions against youth poverty and the associated "rotten outcomes"?

Poverty is a key structural issue in Canadian society that impacts all behavioural risks engaged in by youth (e.g., Abernathy, Webster, & Vermeulen, 2002). The LICO can be used as an indicator of poverty; it represents the income level at which a family or individual spends 20% more than average on basic necessities of life (food, clothing, and shelter). The LICO for a family of four in a large urban centre (2000) was $34 572, and for a family of two, $22 964 (Statistics Canada, 2003). In families where a youth aged 16 to 19 is the main income earner, the average family income (1999) is $26 890 (well below the average family income in Canada of $63 800); if the major income earner is a female youth, the aver-

About two-fifths of Canadian children live in poverty.

age family income is $16 012 (Statistics Canada, 2002). The average Canadian female single parent aged 16 to 19 needs about $10 000 per year of additional income just to reach the poverty line!

The latest Canadian population data indicate that the poorest families in Canada made no gains in income through the 1990s, but that the richest made considerable gains; in 2000, the income of the top 10% families accounted for 28% of all family income, and the bottom 10% of families accounted for 2% of all family income (Campaign 2000, 2003). In Canada, almost two of every five children and youth under the age of 18 live in poverty (Campaign 2000, 2003).

"Rotten Outcomes" of Poverty The trends involving youth poverty are associated with problems of youth development. Schorr (1988) has described these relations as the **"rotten outcomes"** of poverty. They include early school leaving, employment problems, use of income supports, crime, and feelings of hopelessness and despair (Schorr, 1991; Simons et al., 1991). Poor youth are also at high risk for low self-confidence, conduct problems, depression, and peer conflict, and for encountering severe health problems (e.g., infant mortality, lack of immunization against common childhood diseases), physical or mental disabilities, and physical abuse, neglect, and unintended injury (Klerman, 1991; McLoyd & Wilson, 1991; Simons et al., 1991). Female adolescents from the most disadvantaged backgrounds are the most likely to leave

"Rotten outcomes" Problems of youth development associated with poverty.

school early and/or become teenage mothers (Upchurch, 1993).

Societal and cultural conditions have created and maintained poverty in Canada. The breadth and impact of youth poverty represents a formidable challenge for intervention programs. Ideally, efforts should be designed to be sensitive to the diverse conditions of poverty. Many poor youth are homeless or live in diverse families or family-type settings such as foster care homes, institutions, shelters, and other types of placements (Allison, 1993; Huston, 1991). Lack of attention to this contextual variation may lead to an inadequate appreciation of the diverse role of "the family" in poor children's development. Inattention to this contextual variation may lead to insufficiently differentiated policies and programs related to the family life of poor children. Programs that are successful in addressing the several risks and "rotten outcomes" linked to youth poverty adopt diverse strategies and approaches. One example is described in Applications Box 13.1.

In sum, individual-psychological variables associated with cognition, personality, and health are linked to cultural context and to poverty in the development of adolescent problem behaviours. The diversity of individual and contextual influences is involved in both externalizing and internalizing problem behaviours. To illustrate the links among diverse individual and contextual characteristics and problem behaviours, we first discuss associations with externalizing behaviours.

Externalizing Problems in Adolescence

The role of diverse individual and contextual characteristics in the development of externalizing problems among youth may be discussed in relation to problem behaviours generally and in respect to those problem behaviours that result in a youth being labelled as delinquent.

Delinquency, Crime, and Violence

ISSUES TO CONSIDER
- How might different psychological and behavioural attributes of adolescents and varied social contexts influence the development of problem behaviours?
- In what way might the values and goals of an adolescent and his or her culture be linked to delinquent behaviour?

Of all the problems confronting contemporary youth, no set of issues has attracted as much public concern *and* public alarm as youth delinquency and violent

---

APPLICATIONS Box 13.1

Designing Programs to Reduce or Prevent the "Rotten Outcomes" of Youth Poverty

Youth poverty is the single most important predictor of problems in youth development (Huston, 1991). The "rotten outcomes" (Schorr, 1988) linked to poverty include early school and employment problems, reliance on income support, involvement in crime, and feelings of hopelessness and despair.

Given the many negative impacts of poverty, effective programs must address the whole child and his or her community in both integrative and innovative ways. One outstanding and effective program has had an impact in different Canadian cities. It is summarized here.

Developing Literacy Skills with Street-Experienced Youth: "Beat the Street" Program of Toronto

Beat the Street (BTS) was founded in 1985 to provide youth with a more positive alternative to the streets of Toronto. The program is based on a literacy model developed by Frontier College. Youth are matched, based on their interests, with peer tutors who assist them in reading, writing, math, and computers, and also prepare them for high school equivalency testing. The program also provides

counselling and referrals to other service providers.

Approximately 350 youth are involved each year. Many of the participants are males aged 16 to 24. They set their own goals and work toward them. Internal evaluations show that 70% of the youth who participated reached some or all of their goals. Based on its success, this program model has been replicated in five other Canadian cities.

Source: International Youth Foundation, YouthNet International, 2003. www.iyfnet.org

crimes. People point in fear to the growth of **youth gangs** (Mathews, 1993) and to territorial battles, drug trafficking violence, random street violence, and the seemingly younger and younger ages of violent criminals.

Adolescents are the perpetrators of and also the victims of a disproportionately large share of the crime in Canada. In recent years, the crime rate among youth has been declining. Between 1995 and 2000, for example, charges for nontraffic-related offences decreased from 49/1000 to 38/1000 for 15- to 19-year-olds nationally (Statistics Canada, 2002). While crimes against property have decreased considerably in this same period (35/1000 to 21/1000), crimes against people, called violent offences, have increased slightly (7/1000 to 9/1000) (Statistics Canada, 2002).

Youth still account for about a quarter of all nontraffic-related charges in Canada, which is disproportionate to their 7% makeup in the total population (Statistics Canada, 2002). They also account for about 17% of all charges for violence and 28% of all charges for property offences (Statistics Canada, 2002). Males are charged more frequently than females; in 2000, males were charged at a rate of 62/1000, and females at a rate of 13/1000 (Statistics Canada, 2002).

Youth are more likely to be victims of crime than adults. In 1999, the rate for victimization by crime across Canada was 157/1000, and there were 434 victims reported for every 1000 youth aged 15 to 19 (Statistics Canada, 2002). Youth have the highest criminal victimization rate in Canada (the next closest age group are 20- to 29-year-olds at 281/1000), and are more likely to be victims of violent crime (248/1000) than property crime (187/1000) (Statistics Canada, 2002). Female youth (450/1000) are more likely to be victims of crime than males (419/1000) (Statistics Canada, 2002).

Some recent research has explored the link between adolescent delinquency and victimization. In their study of 962 junior and senior high school students in Alberta, Paetsch and Bertrand (1999) found that students who reported moderate to high levels of illegal behaviour also reported moderate to high levels of victimization. However, in her study of homicide data from 1985 to 1995 across Canada, Regoeczi (2000) found weak support for the hypothesis that youth who are violent are more likely to be victims of violence; youth aged 12 to 17 who were murdered in Canada had little involvement in illegal behaviour themselves.

Delinquency and Youth Gangs The term **juvenile delinquency** refers to the violation of a law by a person who is not yet an adult. It does not speak to the context or longevity of behaviour, so it should not be considered unalterable or stable. For example, gangs are an outgrowth of the importance of peer groups in the social behaviour of adolescence. These groups of youth probably come into existence because they meet certain needs of the individuals who participate in them. They may create security, status, and belonging, provide a way to pass idle time, and offer members a way to gain new experiences (Mathews, 1993), and not necessarily to become involved in illegal behaviour, although gangs, by definition, involve antisocial or illegal activities. Some younger youth may only be temporarily involved in a gang. In their study of 10- to 14-year-old youth in Quebec, Craig and colleagues (2002) found that boys with more consistent involvement in a gang were rated more aggressive, active, inattentive, and oppositional by their teachers, self-reported more delinquent activities, and had peers who rated them as more aggressive than boys who were not involved in a gang.

Some of the problems of adolescence classified as delinquent really signify more an issue of poor social relationships than of criminality. Running away from home technically is considered a delinquent act,

During adolescence, delinquency often occurs in gangs.

Youth gangs Groups of youth potentially involved in criminal activity.

Juvenile delinquency Violation of a law committed by a person prior to his or her 18th birthday, a violation that would have been a crime if committed by an adult.

but it is really more than that. Whatever its classification, running away represents a large and significant problem in adolescence (Adams, 1991).

Other problematic behaviours also skirt the borderlines between social relationship issues and actual illegality. It is important to appreciate not only the incidence of problems of delinquency but the bases of their development. Such understanding is crucial for the design of intervention programs and public policies to prevent these problems and promote positive alternatives among youth.

Developmental and Contextual Bases of Delinquency

The development of problem behaviours among youth has been associated with several different psychological and behavioural attributes of youth and numerous levels of the context. It is not surprising to learn that aggressive conduct is strongly associated with aggressive youth (Cairns & Cairns, 1994; Pakiz, Reinherz, & Frost, 1992) beginning in childhood (Brame, Nagin, & Tremblay, 2001), feelings of anger among incarcerated male adolescents are associated with both verbal and physical aggression (Cornell, Peterson, & Richards, 1999), and, among youth offenders, violent and nonviolent offences are associated with alcohol use more strongly and consistently than with either marijuana or heroin use (Dawkins, 1997).

It may be surprising to learn that certain styles of thought are associated with delinquency. Delinquent youth appear to use particular cognitive strategies to solve social problems (Kuperminc, Allen, & Arthur, 1996; Seguin, Arsenault, Boulerice, Harden, & Tremblay, 2002). In a study of 80 youth aged 11 through 18 at high risk for delinquency, acts of delinquency were more frequent among youth whose problem-solving strategies were not based on trying to form relations with others (Kuperminc et al., 1996). Among about 300 American male 14- to 18-year-olds who were committed to a state training school for hard-core youth offenders, treatment to decrease externalizing behaviours such as aggression was successful if youth conceptualized treatment success as due to their own behaviour and when they perceived themselves as worried or anxious (Swenson & Kennedy, 1995). When youth with these problems perceived themselves as happy, treatment tended not to be successful. Treatment was also not successful among these youth if they perceived themselves as highly physically competent or if they saw problems as being of their own making (Swenson & Kennedy, 1995). It is useful

to note that some of these youth in this study had internalizing problems as well, for example, anxiety or depression.

Poor judgment may also be associated with aggression by delinquent youth (Graham, Hudley, & Williams, 1992). In situations where negative outcomes of a social interaction are unintentional, aggressive male adolescents make more extreme judgments of the other person and of the situation than comparable groups of nonaggressive youth (Graham & Hudley, 1994). Other beliefs about aggression may influence youth violence. Some adolescents believe that their parents would disapprove more if they retaliated against their siblings than against peers (Herzberger & Hall, 1993).

Values and goals are other psychological attributes that have been linked to delinquency. In a study comparing Caucasian and Asian high school students living in Hong Kong (Stewart et al., 1998), valuing tradition and conformity was associated with fewer disciplinary violations in both groups. In a study of 80 delinquent youth, 90 youth at risk for delinquency, and 90 not-at-risk youth (Carroll et al., 1997), members of the first two groups placed more importance on goals associated with developing a social image linked to both delinquency and to freedom/autonomy than youth in the latter group. The goals of youth not at risk were associated with developing an academic image (Carroll et al., 1997).

Bullying behaviour also seems to be prototypic of delinquents. In a study of young male offenders incarcerated in Ontario, 70% reported being involved in bullying at least several times a week, either as perpetrators (45%) or as victims (25%) (Connell & Farrington, 1996).

In addition to the psychological and behavioural attributes of delinquent youth, several components of their social context are linked to their problem behaviours. The type of peer group a youth is in influences the probability of his or her behaving in a delinquent manner (Brendgen, Vitaro, & Burkowski, 2000a, 2000b). In a study of 315 Chinese Canadian youth in Winnipeg, Wong reported that their adherence to Chinese culture was associated with lower delinquency (1999), but that the association with delinquent friends increased delinquent involvement (1998). In another Canadian study of more than 860 young adolescent males, moderately disruptive 11- and 12-year-old youth who had peers who were aggressively disturbing to others showed higher levels of delinquency at age 13 years than did mildly disruptive youth with other types of friends (Vitaro et al., 1997). Vitaro and colleagues (Vitaro, Bredgen, & Tremblay, 2000) found that, among a group of boys from Montreal, parental attachment moderated the connection between the illegal behaviour of the boys' best friends and their own behaviour. The youth were followed from kindergarten to 11 to 12 years of age.

There were few differences in the peer relationships described by Canadian teens in high school and those in a correctional setting sample. However, female youth in the correctional setting reported that the greater peer pressure they experienced was an important contributor to their delinquent behaviour (Pleydon & Schner, 2001).

Early maturing girls are at greater risk for delinquency when they are involved in mixed-sex social settings (Caspi et al., 1993). In a longitudinal study of Swedish youth, girls' early maturation was related to norm breaking and delinquent behaviour when the girls were part of a peer group of older girls (Stattin & Magnusson, 1990). When early maturing girls had a same-age peer group, no association was found between delinquency and maturational status. Their reasons for verbal and physical fights are many and varied, but in a sample of 70 Canadian girls aged 12 to 19 living in a group or custody home in Ontario (Cummings & Leschied, 2001), researchers found that they felt more negative feelings about verbal than physical fights and more took responsibility for starting fights with parents than peers.

Peer context acts in conjunction with family variables to influence delinquency. Male delinquents who have committed assault offences have family relations characterized by rigidity and low cohesion and peers who are highly aggressive (Blaske, Borduin, Henggelen, & Mann, 1989). In the face of the youth offences, the offenders and their mothers show little anxiety or interpersonal discomfort. Male delinquents who have committed sexual offences have high levels of neurotic symptoms. Their mothers show such problems as well (Blaske et al., 1989). Sexually offending youth also have low-level emotional bonds with their peers.

Multiple family factors are associated with conviction by age 18 for both violent and nonviolent criminal offences. These factors include authoritarian parenting, deviant mother-child interactions, number of parent changes experienced by a child, having a single-parent family, quality of family relationships, mother's reading level, and socioeconomic level (Henry et al., 1996). In a study of 15- and 16-year-olds from

London, England, the youth who had been repeatedly arrested by the police showed high levels of family disruption (Hagell & Newburn, 1996). Although these youth reported good relationships with their mothers and strong ties to their friends, they also frequently said they lacked social support. In addition, they reported that they had few constructive daily activities and used a lot of drugs and alcohol. These patterns may emerge as early as kindergarten; in a study of 1037 boys from Montreal followed from 6 to 15 years of age, those who displayed the highest hyperactivity and oppositional behaviour, and whose mothers had the lowest educational level and had given birth as teenagers, were the most likely to persist in the highest levels of aggressive behaviour at age 15 (Nagin & Tremblay, 2001).

It is possible, however, that the community setting within which a youth lives can counteract negative influences from parents or peers. In one intriguing study (Sampson, 1997), 80 different neighbourhoods were assessed in regard to the presence of informal social control provided by the citizens living in the community. When such control was high, the incidence of adolescent delinquency in the neighbourhood was lessened.

A diversity of individual and contextual variables is linked to the incidence of a range of delinquent behaviours. Such influence by both individual and ecological components of the developmental system is also evident when we consider specific instances of delinquency, such as running away and violence.

Runaways and Homeless Youth Running away from home is an act of delinquency for adolescents. It is often a sign of the youth's inability to tolerate the social setting in which he or she resides. Leaving home may be a way to tell parents that the home situation has become seriously negative, and/or it may be a way to indicate that the individual needs and wants help.

Exact numbers of youth who run away are difficult to obtain for several reasons (Kufeldt & Burrows, 1994), including definitional inconsistencies both within and between cities, inconsistencies in the way that data are kept and reported, as well as age and geographical boundary inconsistencies. Estimates of youth who have left home from the National Missing Children's Registry are among the best indicators of the size of this problem in Canada. In 2001, 53 434 cases of runaway children under 18 years who had left home or substitute home care were reported to police agencies, and the majority

majority

of those cases (60%) were females (National Missing Children Services, 2001).

Youth who run away generally have more problems at home, school, and socially than other youth (English & English, 1999). They run away for a variety of personal and family reasons (Adams, 1991). Youth at a temporary shelter in Edmonton left home because of their own or others' involvement in crime, or a desire for independence; some youth who ran away were pushed out of the family home or experienced high levels of conflict or violence at home (Brown, 1996).

It is not uncommon for homeless youth to run between family, friends, shelters, foster and group homes, institutions, and the street. Major challenges include procuring shelter and food. The options for income among youth who are too young to work, do not want to be found, or have no connection to school or a job include the drug and sex trade (Adams, 1991) as well as panhandling or stealing (Brown, 1996).

Canadian researchers have reported that the precursors to homelessness for many youth (e.g., abuse) and the nature of street lifestyle are such that there is a heavy reliance among youth who are street-involved on the use of aggression to settle disputes (Baron, Forde, & Kennedy, 2001), following rules about honour, protection, and retribution (Baron & Hartnegel, 1998). In contrast, the problem-solving styles of nonrunaway youth are less aggressive, and they tend to cope with their relatively lower levels of stress and depression without resorting to acts of self-harm and substance use (Ayerst, 1999).

Health problems among street-involved youth are more common than among other Canadian youth. The frequency of mental health problems varies according to the degree of involvement they have in a street lifestyle (Adlaf & Zdanowicz, 1999). HIV prevalence among 13- to 25-year-olds in Montreal who were street-involved was 1.9% (Roy et al, 2000). High-risk sexual practices (Dematteo, et al., 1999; Hayley, et al, 2002) and substance abuse (Baron, 1999), including high-risk injection practices (Roy et al., 2002), have been cited as reasons for the higher prevalence of HIV among street youth.

The problems of runaway and/or homeless youth are not limited to one geographic area, either within or among countries. Rather, they are global problems. Applications Box 13.2 describes two programs used in different nations to address the problems faced by runaway and homeless youth.

Violence Delinquent youth are often violent, although violence is a major problem for all adolescents whether

Many runaway adolescents are homeless and live on the streets.

or not they are delinquent. Youth are often the targets of violent delinquent acts. This tragic circumstance has been illustrated by the occurrences of youth shooting their classmates and teachers.

Violence breeds violence as well as other risk behaviours. Growing up in a neighbourhood replete with violence is associated with enactment of risk behaviours linked to substance use and abuse. Youth living in violent communities often become involved with illicit drug use (Taylor, 1990, 1993), they are more likely to smoke than other adolescents (Fick & Thomas, 1995), and they are more likely to behave in ways that may make violence more likely, for example, carrying a weapon.

In a study of more than 200 American youth 11 to 19 years old, living in an urban high-poverty, high-violent crime community (DuRant et al., 1995), certain behaviours were associated with previous exposure to violence and with having been a victim of violent crime. These behaviours included carrying a weapon during the previous 30 days and carrying a hidden weapon during the last year. Weapon carrying was related as well to other contextual and individual characteristics, such as family conflict and depression (DuRant et al., 1995).

Although most youth exposed to violence do not become murderers, exposure to violence can result in the commission of violent acts. For example, homicidal youth from Great Britain were likely to have witnessed serious violence and to have experienced neglect and deprivation (Hardwick & Rowton-Lee, 1996). These youth also showed signs of poor impulse control and had learning difficulties. Living in an environment where one is exposed to violence and may even often be the target of violence can have profoundly negative effects (Garbarino, 1995, 1999).

Enhancing the Life Chances of Street Children

Youth run away from home and/or are forced to live on the streets for many reasons. Homelessness and street life in general can affect the immediate health and safety of youth and have long-term negative influences on their development. Street children exist throughout both the industrialized and the developing world. Programs have arisen around the globe to address the problems faced by these youth. Two exemplary ones from around the world are described here.

Movimento Nacional de Meninos e Meninas de Rua
Brasilia, Brazil

Brazil has the largest population of street-based and working children in the world, with one in every 8 children under the age of 15 spending the majority of his or her time on the streets. Most of such children have either no schooling or dropped out of school after Grade 1. Many work in low-paying jobs, ranging from selling candies and lottery tickets to washing cars, shining shoes, and running errands.

In response to growing violence and abuse against street-based children and youth, Movimento Nacional de Meninos e Meninas de Rua (MNMMR) was founded in 1985. Today, MNMMR, a national movement of street children and adult educators, coordinates the activities of 40 organizations reaching out to 900 000 youth nationwide.

MNMMR is a multifaceted program offering youth and youth service providers training, education, research, materials development, and public policy advocacy. Through regularly scheduled workshops, courses, and conferences, MNMMR provides educators with professional training in child psychology and family counselling and allows them to share ideas and approaches with others in the field. One of its main priorities is to detect, document, and denounce the widespread and often fatal violence committed against street children.

Since its inception, MNMMR has had a tremendous impact on the way Brazilian society views street-based children. In the past, such children were viewed with suspicion, fear, and were often abused. Society traditionally labelled them as "delinquent," putting them away in jails or juvenile institutions. As a result of MNMMR's public education campaigns the needs of such children and their reasons for being on the street are now far better understood. MNMMR was instrumental in introducing advanced laws on family welfare and children's rights into the Brazilian constitution. Both the Philippines and India have used its model to lobby their own governments for the more humane treatment of street-based children.

Bosconia/La Florida
Bogota, Colombia

Rapid urbanization in Colombia and widespread poverty have contributed to a dramatic increase in the number of street-based youth. At any one time there are between 7000 and 10 000 street-based youth, or "gamines," in Bogota alone.

In response to the growing numbers of young people living and working on the streets, Bosconia/La Florida was established in 1971. Its aim is to enable Bogota's street children to become responsible, productive members of society. Over the past 20 years, Bosconia has expanded from a small, experimental program to a complex system of classrooms, group homes, farms, vocational training, and productive activities. Currently, it serves approximately 5400 boys and girls, ages 8 through 22.

Program participants move through its various phases at their own pace. Most are first introduced to the program through its outreach activities known as Operation Friendship. Two nights each week, dedicated educators visit the "gamines" where they live on the streets. Through direct contact on the street or by word of mouth, "gamines" find their way to one of the six program-operated "patios" around the city. The patios are drop-in centres where young people may come to take a shower, wash their clothes, get a meal, receive medical attention, and play games.

Those young people who choose to leave the streets participate in a 30-day motivation and detoxification program. Following, both boys and girls are given the opportunity to enter group homes, providing them with a more structured learning and living environment.

To date, more than 17 000 young people have graduated from the program. The majority of graduates become successfully integrated into society as productive adults. A substantial number continue on with the program as educators, or work in other youth programs. Fifty graduates have received fellowships for study abroad.

As a result of the success of Bosconia/La Florida, the Colombian government has reduced the number of juvenile detention homes and opted for alternative education programs. The program has served as a model to many nongovernmental groups working to reduce the number of street-based youth in their communities. Bosconia/La Florida's approach has been successfully adapted to other Colombian cities as well as in Ecuador, Paraguay, the Dominican Republic, Mexico, Brazil, and Venezuela.

Source: International Youth Foundation, 2001. www.ifynet.org

Such an environment is known as a **"socially toxic"** environment. James Garbarino's continuing research about these contexts is presented in Meet the Researcher Box 13.2.

"Socially toxic" environment
Environment in which one is exposed to multiple high-risk factors.

Understanding Violent Youth

For more than 25 years I have been searching for answers to three questions: "Why do human beings hurt each other?" "What effect does this hurt have on the development of children and adolescents?" and "How can we transform our lives to heal the hurt?" This work has taken me to war zones around the world to understand the impact of political violence. It has taken me all over the world, from Yugoslavia to Mozambique, from Cambodia to Nicaragua, from Israel and Palestine to Northern Ireland. For example, in the wake of the Gulf War, I was sent to Kuwait and Iraq on behalf of UNICEF to assess the impact of the violence on children there.

In my work here at home as a psychologist and a researcher, I go to neighbourhoods, schools, courtrooms, and prisons all over North America, where I try to understand how violence at home compares with violence abroad and what lessons we can learn from the one to help us deal with the other. I have been focusing my work on the problem of lethal youth violence in America: kids who kill. This means that I sit down hour after hour with violent boys and young men to hear their stories. I have learned a great deal from these hours spent listening. I have learned to see beyond the outside toughness so many violent youth project to glimpse their inner sadness and pain. And I have come to see the central importance of spiritual

development in understanding and dealing with the issue of youth violence—preventing it and curing it. This is what my book *Lost Boys* is all about.

I think it has something to offer to every adult who cares about kids—as the parent, grandparent, aunt, uncle, friend, or neighbour of a particular boy or in some general way as a teacher, a counsellor, a coach, a police officer, a lawyer, or a therapist. I hope readers will come away from *Lost Boys* with a renewed sense of hope and sympathy for the difficulties many boys face in growing up in our society and the devastating costs to all of us when boys grow up hurt and sad, costs that take the form of violence directed at self or others. Remember that about the same number of boys kill themselves as kill other people in our society.

In many ways *Lost Boys* is a work of love. It reflects my love for the boys in my life—my son, my stepson, and my nephews. Learning how to love them has taught me a great deal. And it reflects my love for the girls in my life—my daughter and my niece—because the quality of the lives "my girls" will live depends to a great extent on the relationships they will have with the boys of today who will become the men of tomorrow.

Lost Boys is also a work of love in that it reflects the love I have found in my own spiritual life. This recognition of the central importance of spirituality runs

James Garbarino is the Elizabeth Lee Vincent Professor of Human Development and co-director of the Family Life Development Center at Cornell University. He is the author of 17 books, most recently *Lost Boys: Why Our Sons Turn Violent and How We Can Save Them* (New York: Free Press, 1999; paperback: Anchor Books, 2000).

through the book as a complement to all the psychology, sociology, biology, and anthropology I use to make sense of violence in the lives of boys.

A research project we call "The Secret Lives of Teenagers" grew out of my understanding of the families of the two boys in Littleton, Colorado, who attacked their school on April 20, 1999. They killed 13 before killing themselves. In the wake of this terrible event many people assumed the two boys' parents must have been negligent. I have set out to explore how common and how "normal" it is for "good" parents to be unaware of the secret lives of their teenage offspring. This research sets the stage for further explorations of the difficulties parents face when raising temperamentally vulnerable children in today's socially toxic society. My colleague Claire Bedard and I are working on a new book based on these explorations entitled *Parents Under Siege*.

Unfortunately, evidence shows that such a harmful context is becoming widespread and these negative effects are growing in prevalence. In a sample of 10- to 16-year-old youth, one-third reported having been the victims of an assault (Boney-McCoy & Finkelhor, 1995b). Compared to nonvictimized youth, these youth victims showed more problem behaviours and emotions, such as **post-traumatic stress disorders,** feelings of sadness, and school difficulties (Boney-McCoy & Finkelhor, 1995b).

Self-Injury and Suicide Many adolescents think about hurting themselves, and a large number act on such thoughts. In their sample of Quebec youth, Choquet and Kovess (1993) reported that the proportion of 15- to 19-year-olds who thought about suicide at least once in the week preceding the survey was 10% for males and 12% for females. The prevalence found by Breton et al. (2002) of Quebec

Post-traumatic stress disorder
Set of emotional and behavioural problems that occurs after experiencing a severe stress, for example an assault.

adolescents aged 12 to 14 for suicidal thoughts was 7.2%, and in their study of concordance between parent and child reports, they found that parents identified 6 of 59 adolescents in their sample who reported suicidal thoughts, and 2 of the 36 adolescents who reported a suicide attempt.

Johnson, Krug, and Potter (2000) compared the suicide rates for adolescents and young adults in 34 high- and upper-middle-income countries. Canada's 15- to 24-year-olds had the eighth highest rate at 16.1/100 000. Rates for males were significantly higher, at 25.2/100 000, than for females at 6.3/100 000. Canadian youth had a higher rate of suicide than youth in the United States, which had the 12th highest rate at 13.8/100 000. As in Canada, the suicide rate for males was much higher (23.4/100 000) than for females (3.7/100 000) in the United States. Among the 34 countries with rates included in Johnson et al.'s analysis, firearm-related suicides accounted for about one-third of the total, and correlated with firearm availability in some countries.

Feelings of hopelessness and depression are associated with self-harm in adolescence (Enns et al., 1997). Such behaviours may involve cutting, burning, or self-mutilation (Solomon & Farrand, 1996). Problems with social relationships are also associated with both self-harm and suicide (e.g., Adam, Sheldon-Keller, & West, 1996). In American youth, lack of cohesion in the family is associated with thinking about suicide (Zhang & Jin, 1996). Among Canadian youth, suicide is linked to family disruption, for example, parental divorce (Leenaars & Lester, 1995).

Whether inflicted on the self or others, violence is not an isolated problem. Rather, violence occurs

Adolescents may inflict injuries upon themselves, such as lacerations or burns.

often in relation to other adolescent problem behaviours such as substance use and abuse.

Substance Use and Abuse

ISSUE TO CONSIDER
● How might different psychological attributes and varied social contexts influence adolescent substance use and abuse?

Overall, cigarette smoking and alcohol use has been decreasing among youth (Johnston, Bachman, & O'Malley, 1998). Since 1970, the overall proportion of Canadian youth aged 15 to 19 who smoke has decreased from about 50% to 28% (Statistics Canada, 2002). However, this general downward trend masks some important differences in smoking behaviour. For example, the largest drop in smoking occurred during the 1970s and 1980s, and fell to a low of 20% in 1990. Since then, however, the rates have been climbing, and women aged 18 to 19 currently have the highest smoking rate in Canada at 44% (Statistics Canada, 2002).

Based on the Ontario Student Drug Abuse Survey, it appears that the rates of lifetime alcohol use have decreased in the past 20 years from about 75% to 59% among students in Grades 7 to 13 (Adlaf, 1995). In another survey of 1236 Grade 9 to 13 students in Ontario, Feldman et al. (1999) found that about 22% had tasted alcohol but did not currently drink, 39% were current moderate drinkers, and 11% were heavy drinkers (defined as having five drinks or more during one occasion at least once per month). Those who did not drink said most often that they abstained for health reasons or reasons related to their upbringing, and those who did drink said they did it because they enjoyed it and it got them into the party mood (Feldman et al., 1999). Among Ontario students who reported serious alcohol-related problems, 2.7% had been in a treatment program, 5.4% felt they needed treatment, and 31% wished they could drink less alcohol (Smart & Stoduto, 1997). It appears that the overall rate of illicit drug use and abuse is increasing.

After tobacco and alcohol, the third most frequently used substance among youth is marijuana (Paglia & Room, 1999). Though there was an upward trend in the use of pot in the early to mid-1990s, it appears to have levelled off. In 1997 the rate of lifetime use among Ontario students in Grades 9 to 13 was 30% and use in the year prior to being surveyed was 25%. About 1 in 10 students had used a hallucinogenic drug in the previous year (Paglia & Room, 1999). In a study of problematic drug use among 1808 Quebec youth aged 14 to 17 years, among those who had used illicit drugs more than five times, over two-thirds had gone to school high, and many played sports while high or had used drugs in the morning (Zoccolillo et al., 1999).

One class of substances that is becoming more popular among some youth is "rave drugs" or "designer drugs" (Rintoul & MacKillican, 2001). A drug called MDMA, after its chemical name 3,4-methylendioxymethamphetamine—more commonly known as "Ecstasy"—is an amphetamine derivative that has become popular among participants in raves (all-night dance parties) because of its effects on energy, endurance, sociability, and sex drive (Kalant, 2001). Rave attendance increased from 13% to 18% between 1995 and 2001 among Ontario youth in Grades 7, 9, and 11 (Centre for Addiction and Mental Health, 2002). Those who attend raves are more likely than nonattenders to use drugs (Gross et al., 2002).

The breadth of the use and abuse of tobacco, alcohol, and illicit drugs is substantial among contemporary youth. As with the behaviours associated with delinquency and violence, there exists a diverse range of individual and contextual influences on substance use and abuse.

Developmental and Contextual Bases of Substance Use and Abuse

The use and abuse of substances among adolescents is associated with the individual's personality as well as with relationships with parents and peers. In a study of more than 2000 high school students, alcohol use was associated with depression and antisocial behaviour (Mitchell et al., 1996). Among adolescents hospitalized for psychiatric problems, those youth who abused drugs had personality characteristics different from other hospitalized youth (Hart, 1995). They had negative attitudes toward their family and toward authority figures in general, and they showed personalities marked by aggression, low conscientiousness, lack of academic confidence, and impulsiveness. In a longitudinal study of about 750 boys between the ages of 6 and 13, substance abuse was associated with individual characteristics linked to aggression, hyperactivity, and oppositional behaviour (Dobkin et al., 1995).

Sensation-seeking Canadian youth are more likely to use substances than those with lower scores on measures of sensation seeking (Baker & Yardley, 2002). In an interesting study of young adults in Ontario (1998) by DeWit, frequent moves before the age of 16 predicted earlier timing of first drug use. This result *in one study*

may relate to the finding that school adjustment problems, not uncommon among youth experiencing frequent moves, are associated with substance use. In a study of about 1000 Grade 6 and 7 youth, poor adjustment to the school context was associated with substance use (Flannery, Vazsonyi, & Rowe, 1996).

Adolescent substance abuse is associated with maternal substance use (Stephenson, Henry, & Robinson, 1996) and the perception that parents approve of using substances (McMaster & Wintre, 1996). In a study of young adolescents and their mothers and fathers, maternal smoking was highly associated with smoking among youth, especially daughters (Kandel & Wu, 1995).

Parenting style has been found to correlate with adolescent substance use. In a study of more than 1000 12- to 16-year-old youth, males who perceived their families as "authoritarian" or "neglecting" (see Chapter 8) used more alcohol, cigarettes, stimulants, or sedatives (Foxcroft & Lowe, 1995). In contrast, females who saw their families as warm and directive used less alcohol, but were more likely to use sedatives or stimulants and to report they would use cigarettes to cope with a problem.

Parental supervision and support are also linked to adolescent substance use (Bogenschneider et al., 1998a). In a study assessing the association between single-mother households and heavy drinking and illicit drug use, rates of substance use among 600 youth were associated with the role of the nonresident father (Thomas, Farrell, & Barnes, 1996). When the father provided no support to the youth, male adolescents showed higher rates of substance problems. However, when the father did support the adolescent, the rate of substance problems was comparatively lower. Parental religiosity is also associated with adolescent substance use. In a longitudinal study of about 1550 12- through 14-year-olds, higher maternal religiosity was linked to lower levels of adolescent alcohol use (Foshee & Hollinger, 1996).

The impact of peers on adolescent substance use and abuse may be significant. In a study of about 5200 Grade 8 and 4700 Grade 11 students from South Korea, perceived peer smoking was the major influence on smoking among both boys and girls (Juon, Shin, & Nam, 1995). In a study of approximately 500 German adolescents, intensity of peer relations was related to substance use (Maggs & Hurrelmann, 1998). In a sample of 1942 junior and senior high school students in Alberta, males who drank reported greater peer pressure to drink, and females who drank

There are several different illicit substances that are used or abused by some adolescents.

reported greater intrapersonal problems (Barber et al., 1998). In a study of 2200 randomly selected Grade 8, 10, and 12 students, the strongest correlate of drug use was affiliation with drug-using friends (Jenkins, 1996). Among about 1000 Grade 6 through 10 adolescents studied longitudinally, use of cigarettes by one's group of friends was associated with transition into smoking, and use of alcohol by close friends was associated with the start of drinking (Urberg, Degirmencioglu, & Pilgrim, 1998). Changes in adolescent drug use seem to occur in relation to increases in peer drug use as well (Curran, Stice, & Chassin, 1997).

In addition, the quality of peer relations may differ between substance-abusing and nonsubstance-abusing youth. For instance, among Icelandic youth, frequent drug and alcohol use was linked to lower social ability (Sigurdsson & Gudjonsson, 1996).

Substance use is associated with other risk behaviours such as unplanned sexual intercourse and inconsistent condom use among Canadian high school students (Poulin & Graham, 2001). Alcohol use by adolescents is also associated with self-destructive thoughts and behaviours—thinking about suicide, attempting suicide, and engaging more frequently in risky behaviours such as taking someone else's medication (Windle, Miller-Tutzauer, & Domenico, 1992). The use of alcohol, marijuana, cocaine, and amphetamines has been linked to violent delinquency among Ontario junior and senior high school students (Harrison et al., 2001; Smart, Mann, & Tyson, 1997).

Canadian research on substance-abusing youth suggests that they are also more likely than nonsubstance-abusing youth to have problems with gambling (Vitaro, Ladouceur, & Bujold, 1996). Youth who abuse substances and have gambling problems were more impulsive than either group separately (Vitaro

et al., 1998). Among male youth followed from age 13 to 17 years, those who were most impulsive in early adolescence were the most likely to have gambling problems in mid-adolescence (Vitaro, Arsenault, & Tremblay, 1997).

There are also individual psychological characteristics and contextual resources related to a lessened probability of substance use and abuse. In general, such protective factors involve personal and social controls against the occurrence of problem behaviours. Personal controls include religious beliefs and good self-concepts. Social controls include social support and authoritative parenting (Jessor et al., 1995). As suggested earlier by the findings pertinent to the role of family (maternal) religiosity in protecting youth from alcohol use, religious commitments and beliefs protect some adolescents against the use of alcohol (Barnes, Farrell, & Banerjee, 1994).

Conclusions About Externalizing Behaviour Problems in Adolescence

The externalizing problems common in adolescence may influence the context, for example, in regard to violence toward peers. These problems also may be influenced by the context, for example, in regard to parental effects on substance use (Bogenschneider et al., 1998a). In addition, any one externalizing problem can and often does occur together with other such problems—for instance, violence and substance use occur together, that is, they are *comorbid*. Externalizing problems are also comorbid with internalizing problems that express themselves primarily in regard to the adolescent's psychological or behavioural functioning.

Internalizing Problems in Adolescence

ISSUES TO CONSIDER
• What influences the expression of internalizing behaviours in adolescence?
• How are the internalizing problems differently expressed in male and female adolescents?

Just as adolescents exhibit several instances of externalizing problems, they also exhibit numerous types of internalizing problems. These problems can be somewhat benign, for example, negative self-esteem, which can often be bolstered with assistance from

Box 13.3 **David R. (Dan) Offord**

Epidemiology of Adolescent Psychiatric Disorders

David R. (Dan) Offord, CM, MD, is director of the Offord Centre for Child Studies, McMaster University and Hamilton Health Sciences, Hamilton, Ontario.

Descriptive epidemiology is concerned about the frequency and distribution of a disorder or condition in a population. Experimental epidemiology centres on identifying causal risk and protective factors for disorders, and then determining what interventions can reduce the effects of risk factors or increase the benefits of protective factors, and thus lessen the occurrence of the disorder.

The Ontario Child Health Study (OCHS) (a descriptive epidemiology study) was a large community survey of over 3200 children and adolescents, 4 to 16 years of age (and their families), carried out in 1983, which gathered data on the prevalence of selected psychiatric disorders, correlates and risk factors for disorders, and rates of service utilization.

Important results included the high prevalence rates of clinically important psychiatric disorders among a community sample of children and adolescents. For example, the prevalence of one or more of conduct disorder, hyperactivity, emotional disorder, and somatization (physical health problems caused by emotional problems) in boys 12 to 16 years of age was 18.8%; the corresponding rate in girls was 21.8%. Comorbidity (the presence of more than one disorder in an adolescent) was high, with

the majority of youth with one disorder having at least one additional disorder. Emotional disorders were much higher in teenage girls than boys (13.6% versus 4.9%), and conduct disorder showed the reverse pattern, with the rates higher in boys than girls (10.4% versus 4.1%). Another important finding was the extent of the unmet need in learning of specialized mental health/social services. For instance, only 16.2% of the boys, 12 to 16 years of age, and 9.4% of the girls in that age group with a disorder had received specialized care from mental health/social services in the six months prior to the study.

There have been two follow-ups of the 1983 cohort of the OCHS, which were carried out in 1987 and 2000. The original survey and follow-ups have contributed helpful data in a number of areas in descriptive epidemiology of adolescent psychiatric disorders, including definition of disorder, patterns of comorbidity, importance of informant or source of diagnostic information (e.g., parent, teacher, adolescent), markers, correlates, and risk factors for disorders, outcome, prognosis and risk of specific disorders, and the identification of different developmental pathways of specific groups of children and adolescents.

The mismatch between prevalence rate of disorders and the availability of specialized mental health/social services highlights the need for effective interventions other than clinical services if the immense burden of suffering from adolescent psychiatric disorders is to be reduced to an important degree. I and my colleagues have argued that an effective strategy to bring about this reduction should consist of a combination of effective universal, targeted, and clinical programs carried out in the context of a civic community where all adolescents have the right of full participation in community life, and community members assume a collective responsibility for the well-being of teenagers in their neighbourhood. Much of our work centres on finding ways to help communities mobilize themselves effectively to raise the life quality and improve the life chances of their children and adolescents, and to monitor the success of their efforts at a community level.

---

parents, teachers, or friends or may improve over the course of typical developmental changes. The problems can also be more serious, involving the individual's mental health. All mental health problems require professional intervention. These include sustained and pervasive feelings of depression or anxiety or the

occurrence of a **psychotic** disorder—all examples of common adolescent **psychopathology.**

David Offord has spent his career studying the mental health of Canadian youth. His research is featured in Meet the Researcher Box 13.3.

Frequency of Internalizing Problems

Psychopathology can occur in any youth. In a large sample of 1201 14- to 17-year-olds in Quebec, the rate of psychiatric disorders was between 1 and 2 out of every 10 youth. Rates of internalizing disorders among females were found to be significantly higher

Psychosis Severe mental disorder, characterized by problematic behaviours and thoughts that reflect a disengagement from reality.

Psychopathology Serious problems of mental health that require professional treatment, for example, sustained and pervasive feelings of depression, anxiety, or the occurrence of a psychotic disorder.

than for males, and the rates of externalizing disorders were significantly higher for males than females (Romano et al., 2001). In their study of 2400 Quebec youth, aged 6 to 14 years, Breton et al. (1999) found the prevalence of depression to range between 1.1% and 3.5%; adolescent girls reported a higher rate than adolescent boys and preadolescent girls. Marcotte (1996) reported opposing trends by gender between 11- and 18-year-olds in relation to depressive symptomatology; symptoms in females increased during this period, and for males, there was a decrease.

In their study of 339 high school students in Quebec, Lapointe and Marciotte (2000) reported that depressed adolescents used fewer positive reappraisal strategies and more avoidance coping strategies than their nondepressed peers. Aube and colleagues (2000) found that Canadian youth who felt more responsible for the welfare of others and less assertive in their relationships were more likely to report symptoms of depression. In their study of 306 14- to 17-year-old francophone youth in Quebec, Marcotte et al. (1999) found that female youth were more expressive in their coping style and males were more active. In their interviews with depressed women between the ages of 14 and 17 years, Hetherington and Stoppard (2002) reported the theme of disconnection from relationships as salient.

Contextual Influences

As with externalizing behaviours, internalizing problems are associated with variation in both contextual and individual characteristics. In regard to the family, maternal acceptance decreases the likelihood of depression among young adolescents (Garber, Robinson, & Valentiner, 1997). However, maternal psychological control is associated with increases in depression. Such control includes attempting to govern the behaviour of the child through techniques such as inducing guilt (Garber et al., 1997). In a study of about 450 adolescents, depression was associated with less intimate relations with parents and with less social support (Lasko et al., 1996).

In a longitudinal study of Albanian youth beginning when they were 12 years old, depression and antisocial behaviour among girls was associated with parental economic problems and value differences, low marital happiness, low nurturance by parents, and parental hostility toward and value differences with the daughter (Kloep, 1995). Male and female adolescents hospitalized for psychopathological problems report

Depression is a serious internalizing problem that may affect adolescents.

less marital satisfaction between parents than nonhospitalized youth (King et al., 1995). Marital conflict over child rearing and a weak father-adolescent relationship were associated with severe behaviour problems in school and in spare time (King et al., 1995).

The nature of the involvement with or attachment to the parent can affect the presence of internalizing problems in adolescents. In a longitudinal study of youth between the ages of 14 and 25 years, those who had been hospitalized for severe psychopathology had insecure attachments with their parents (Allen, Hauser, & Borman-Spurrell, 1996). Similarly, adolescents hospitalized for psychiatric reasons who have problems of attachment are also likely to suffer from conduct or substance abuse disorders, antisocial problems, and paranoid personality characteristics (Rosenstein & Horowitz, 1996). For Grade 6 to 8 adolescents, problems of attachment to the father were highly associated with the presence of antisocial behaviour among both boys and girls (Marcus & Betzer, 1996).

Individual-Psychological Influences

Contextual influences on internalizing problems exist along with influences associated with psychological and behavioural characteristics of the adolescent. Boys who are depressed also possess feelings of antagonism toward other people, and girls who are depressed also show an overly introspective concern with the self and an overly high concern with the rules of socialization (Gjerde, 1995). In a longitudinal study of 330 young adolescents, feelings of depression were associated with feelings of anxiety

(Cole et al., 1998). The more anxious the youth became over time, the higher the resulting level of depression (Cole et al., 1998). Moreover, covariation between anxiety and depression is associated with delinquent behaviours (Hinden et al., 1997).

Other psychological characteristics are involved in the occurrence of internalizing problems. In a study comparing junior high students from North America and Japan (King, Akiyama, & Elling, 1996), feelings of depression among North American youth were associated with problematic self-perceptions regarding physical attractiveness and social acceptance and with problematic behavioural conduct. Among the Japanese adolescents, feelings of depression were related to problematic self-perceptions involving interpersonal connectedness, peer social acceptance, and physical attractiveness and to problems of behavioural conduct (King et al., 1996).

A longitudinal study of 800 youth between the ages of 3 and 18 found that youth who had problems controlling their behaviour were also highly impulsive, danger seeking, and aggressive, and they felt alienated from others (Caspi & Silva, 1995). However, youth who were inhibited had low levels of impulsivity, danger seeking, aggression, and social ability (Caspi & Silva, 1995). Perhaps not surprisingly, youth who lacked control had more externalizing problems than other adolescents (Caspi et al., 1995).

Conclusions About Internalizing Behaviour Problems in Adolescence

As with adolescent externalizing problems, several contextual and individual variables create diversity in the development of internalizing problems in adolescence. Although girls show a higher incidence of internalizing problems than boys, the development of psychopathology in adolescence for both males and females is significantly influenced by social relationships, particularly with parents. There are also high degrees of comorbidity between internalizing and externalizing problems, and the individual and contextual variables associated with one domain of problems are linked to the other domain as well.

Thus the domains of externalizing and internalizing problems are related to the diversity of the individual and contextual variables comprising the ecology of human development. To address these problems, it is important to capitalize on this person-context developmental system.

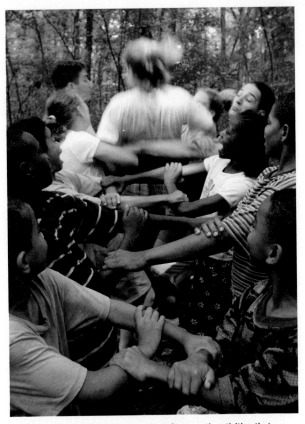

Positive youth development may result from youth activities that involve the support from and trust of peers: A young girl falls into the arms of fellow campers and counsellors from a 1.2 metre high perch, an exercise in building trust and group conclusion.

From Problem Behaviours to Prevention and the Promotion of Positive Development in Adolescence

ISSUES TO CONSIDER

• What explains the failure of so many policies and programs designed to support adolescents with problems?
• What are leading factors that contribute to the success of some intervention programs designed to support adolescents?

To rephrase an old metaphor, the glass of adolescence is both half full and half empty. About 50% of youth are at moderate or greater levels of risk for engaging in unhealthy, unproductive, and even life-threatening behaviours. These behaviours arise because of the unfortunate confluence of sets of individual and contextual factors. Given the diversity of behaviours that a youth can exhibit over the course of adolescence, parents can hope for the best but should be ready to deal with problematic and/or risky behaviour. Implications for Parenting Box 13.1 may provide some assistance.

Many people have argued that the solution to the problems of adolescence, and perhaps especially those that involve delinquency, is to build more and/or different sorts of institutions (more psychiatric hospitals or special types of youth prisons, e.g., "boot camps"; Taylor, 1996). These policy prescriptions are often made with little understanding of, and almost no research evidence about, the influence of youth institutionalization or incarceration on youth development (Schwartz, 1999; Taylor, 1996). These policy ideas are often predicated on the belief that delinquent youth, and troubled adolescents more generally, cannot be helped, nor can their problems be diminished or prevented. With such a perspective, there is little, if any, consideration that positive development could be promoted among these adolescents (Schwartz, 1999).

Rather than pursue policies and programs untested by systematic research, a more useful approach to the problems of youth is one that reflects the developmental contextual/developmental systems perspective. This approach deals with all facets of the developing person and his or her context and is committed to integrating these facets in treatment. In this manner, all the people with a stake in the youth's positive development, including the youth themselves, can pool their resources to protect the adolescents and to promote positive outcomes in their lives.

Current thinking about public policy and youth-serving programs supports pursuing paths of application that emphasize the potential of young people for positive development and healthy lives. The presentation in Chapter 14 is framed by stressing the importance of reducing or eliminating youth problems through a systematic integration of individual and contextual characteristics of adolescents. Chapter 14 also addresses how this system may be used to devise intervention programs and public policies aimed at both preventing the development of problems in adolescence and in promoting healthy and positive lives among them.

IMPLICATIONS FOR PARENTING   Box 13.1

Why Smart Kids Do Risky Things

Despite the fact that they are more sophisticated thinkers than they were a few years earlier, one of the paradoxes of child development is that teenagers do thoughtless and dangerous things. They are not quite thinking with the sophistication and insight of an adult. Understanding differences in levels of thinking, and the other developmental issues facing teenagers, can be helpful in keeping them out of trouble.

Adolescents see themselves as the centre of the universe. They're not as simplistic in their egocentric view as toddlers, although the similarities can at times be striking. At some level many adolescents believe that other people are as interested in them as they are in themselves. They believe they are special and that the ordinary rules and consequences that adults (rightfully) worry about need not apply to them.

This egocentric, invulnerable attitude can lead them into risky situations.

A true story: A police officer pulls over a car late at night for speeding. The driver is a 17-year-old boy who is wearing sunglasses. Several other teens are in the car with him, giggling. From the smell of the driver's breath and the stagger in his gait, it is clear he has been drinking heavily. The officer tells him he is lucky—people get killed when they drink and drive. The teenager replies, "Hey, you can't kill The Kid!"

Because adolescents see themselves as invulnerable, they often cannot conceive of the world existing without them living. Although they will tell you in one breath that drinking and driving is dangerous, they still may brag about doing it. Probate judges say that over 90% of the traffic violations involving teenagers are alcohol related.

Another factor that can lead to risky behaviour is your teenager's need to forge an independent self. A major task of adolescence is coming up with a new and separate identity. Your teenager is going through the physical changes of puberty, changes in thinking abilities, social changes in school, and often the new experience of part-time employment. When everything about an adolescent is changing inside and outside, he or she wonders, Who am I?

To deal with all the changes in their lives, adolescents turn to their peer group. In trying their best to differentiate themselves from their parents, they put significant efforts into assimilating into a peer group. To get peer approval, young people will often do things that intellectually they know are risky (e.g., playing "chicken" with speeding cars, chugging beers until they are sick).

It is unrealistic for any of us to say, "It won't happen to my child!" It's not that you should not trust your teenager, but you need to understand that there is often an intense pressure to get acceptance from peers.

>

This does not mean parents should give up trying and hope simply for the best. One thing you can do is pay more attention to how your teenagers spend their time—not in a punitive or suspicious way, just monitoring what they're up to. Even as teenagers push for more independence, they want and need clear and consistent supervision.

Rules work best when the adolescents' perspective is brought in and when they try to develop their own point of view of why they should behave in a particular way. Although only one of you is the parent, when you supply reasons for rules beyond "Because I say so!" it shows respect for your teenagers' new thinking skills. Encourage them to participate in generating household rules. If teenagers take part in discussing and setting rules, those rules will more likely become part of their own set of standards and, therefore, be adhered to. Supportive and open communication increases the likelihood that your child will end up having values consistent with your own and will choose friends with similar values.

Remember, your teenager will spend more time with peers than with you. Try to get a sense of what your child's friends are like. Chat with them and build trust over time. Strive for a home atmosphere where your child's friends feel welcome. (An extra few dollars per week for pretzels and frozen pizza may be a good investment.) Take care not to be too intrusive and not to embarrass your teenagers, or they will not bring their friends home to meet you.

Such home-based socializing also provides opportunities to know the friends' parents, as you coordinate schedules. Try to find out their standards for acceptable teenage behaviour and agree to help each other monitor activities. Many risky activities, such as sexual intercourse, happen most often not in motels or cars, but in the homes of adolescents' friends or relatives. If you and other parents can present a united front to the peer group, it helps your children understand that widely agreed-on standards exist, and it is not just you who are "impossible." Peers' parents can also reinforce common values by befriending your child. As teenagers strive to be different from their own parents, they may find it easier to talk over some concerns with other adults.

If you know that some of your child's peers engage in potentially high-risk behaviours, share your concerns with him or her. Try to provide alternative less risky experiences. Perhaps your teenager would enjoy ice-skating, horseback riding, computer workshops, or a youth club. Additional activities are likely to expose teenagers to more potential friends. Look into ways your adolescents can volunteer to work with younger kids. For example, they can teach younger kids about the consequences of high-risk behaviours. This benefits both sides: Teenagers tend to have great credibility with younger children, and the exposure to the naïveté and misinformation others have about risky behaviours reduces teenagers' own egocentric feelings of invulnerability.

Finally, even though your child pretends to "know it all," and probably does know a great deal about life's dangers, keep talking. Your child is more likely to listen to you if you do not preach and if you focus on the short-term risks (e.g., smoking gives you bad breath and hurts your athletic performance).

Ideas About Talking to Your Teenager About Risk

Most parents feel uncomfortable talking about issues such as drinking and driving or sexual behaviour. Unfortunately, these topics can literally be matters of life and death. Here are several things parents might need to do to be helpful to their adolescents:

■ Try to be as direct and open with your adolescent as possible, even about your own discomfort.

■ As you listen to your teenager's perceptions and ideas, resist the urge to say, "I went through exactly the same thing!" That works against your child's need to establish a separate identity from you. Instead, you might say you've heard from other teens' parents that their children feel the same.

■ Go from general to specific. You might start a conversation by saying, "I want to talk about drinking and driving. I've been hearing from other parents (or at the PTA meeting) that there's a lot of drinking and driving among kids at your school. What kinds of things would you say go on at your school?" By keeping the subject distant from your teenager and his friends, at least at first, you are not seen as accusing him or her. Next, you might ask, "How do your friends deal with it?" Or, "You must confront this all the time. How do you handle it?"

■ Talk about alternatives. Research has shown time and again that knowledge is not enough to change behaviour. Adolescents need skills and resources to get out of risky situations without losing face. For example, you might say, "The person who drives you to a party may not be the person you want to go back with. I'll give you a quarter to call me, and $20 for a cab. Keep it in a separate part of your wallet, and use it only for that. If I'm out, and you're out, I'll give you the number where I am." This lets your child know that even if you are going out, you are still the parent, and you are there if he or she needs you.

■ Try rehearsing possible scenarios and realistic responses, and generate ideas together. Ask your child, "What else can I do to help you deal with this kind of situation?"

■ Share your values. Make sure your child is clear on what your values are and why you believe those values are appropriate and useful. For example, "Even if nothing happens, I'd be very upset if you rode in a car with a driver who'd been drinking. That's like giving your okay to behaviour that could get you or someone else seriously hurt."

The issue of sex can be particularly uncomfortable and confusing. For example, although you may feel strongly that your 15-year-old should abstain from sex, do you mean from intercourse or any sort of sensual touching? Try to offer your teenager realistic alternatives to engaging in unsafe or too-early sex, ones that are compatible with your values.

Source: Adapted from Lerner & Olson, 1996.

Summary

- Despite improvements in some indicators, the overall rate of quality of life for adolescents remains poor in comparison to other industrialized countries.

- Four major categories of risk behaviours in adolescence are drug and alcohol use and abuse; unsafe sex and teenage pregnancy and parenting; school underachievement, failure and early school leaving; and delinquency, crime, and violence.

- Engagement in risk behaviours diminishes life chances, and evidence indicates that risk behaviours are highly interrelated; that is, adolescents often participate in more than one risk behaviour.

- There are two general dimensions of problem behaviours among youth. Internalizing problems are directed inward to the individual and affect cognitive, mental, and emotional functioning. Externalizing problems are directed outward toward other people or the social context. Some problem behaviours involve both internalizing and externalizing features.

- Poverty is a pervasive problem in Canada and it impacts all behavioural risks engaged in by youth.

- Poverty is associated with "rotten outcomes," or problems with youth development, in all domains of individual and social behaviour and development.

- Effective interventions for poverty and the associated "rotten outcomes" must take into account the diverse contextual conditions of youth, for example, family, peers, neighbourhood, and culture.

- Problem behaviours of adolescence occur in clusters; for example, runaways are at a high risk for substance abuse.

- Adolescent girls show more internalizing problems and fewer externalizing problems compared to adolescent boys.

- There is a high degree of comorbidity between internalizing and externalizing problems.

- Many policies and programs fail to support adolescents. In order to deal successfully with the multiple problems of adolescence, policies and programs should focus on the relations between the individual's development and the specifics of his or her social context.

Discussion Topics

1. Are all teenagers equally at risk for engaging in a single risk behaviour? Why or why not? Are all teenagers equally at risk for engaging in multiple risk behaviours? Why or why not?

2. Name some problem behaviours common in adolescence and decide whether they are internalizing, externalizing, or both. How do you know?

3. Why does culture influence attitudes about problem behaviours?

4. Recognizing the pervasiveness and implications of poverty in Canada, what are the first issues to consider when designing a program to promote positive youth development?

5. How do the individual and social contexts influence adolescent development? What are potential risk factors that may lead to delinquency in teen youth? How might a limited view of contextual influences contribute to social prejudices?

6. Why is there such a high level of concern over violence in Canadian high schools? How might you lead a youth group discussion about how to prevent violence in high schools?

7. Understanding the influence of social context, how might the media meaningfully support and encourage teens to avoid peer pressure to use and/or abuse substances?

8. Why do adolescent girls tend to have more internalizing problems than adolescent boys?

9. What are some characteristics of a program that would successfully promote positive adolescent development?

Key Terms

anxiety, p. 291
comorbidity, p. 290
depression, p. 291
externalizing problems, p. 290
internalizing problems, p. 291

juvenile delinquency, p. 295
posttraumatic stress disorder,
 p. 300
psychopathology, p. 304
psychosis, p. 304

"rotten outcomes", p. 293
"socially toxic" environment,
 p. 299
youth gangs, p. 295

14

Potentials of Adolescents: Community Programs and Public Policy

Kent was so nervous. But he was not as worried as his teacher, Ms. Reiser, who was arguing the case for a different type of graduation celebration for students in the southern Manitoba high school to a group of representatives from the administration, parents' association, and school board.

It was difficult for Kent to attend this meeting, but he felt very strongly about it. After all, the events that led up to it were very personal to him. It was four years ago, almost to the day, that he and his friend, both in Grade 8 at the time, were riding their bikes on a warm spring evening. The two were crossing a busy street when his friend was struck by a car that sped through the crosswalk. His friend was killed instantly, and Kent was only a split second away from being struck himself. The car was driven by a Grade 12 student who had been drinking and was rushing to catch up with a carload of others who were heading out of the city where they would have an unofficial high school graduation party.

That year the school administration, in response to parents' concerns that the school was condoning alcohol use at graduation parties for students, had made the decision to stop supporting "safe grad." The idea for a safe graduation party was to prevent some of the most serious negative outcomes of alcohol use by students during their graduation celebrations. Students were bused out to an undisclosed location for a supervised party where there were trained security and medical staff and no enforcement of alcohol laws.

In the four years since the accident, graduating students had been invited to attend a "super grad" party sponsored by the high school. However, at these events there was a zero tolerance policy in effect, banning the use of any substances, including alcohol. The students who attended "super grad" did not drink or use drugs, and those who did, planned and went to their own unofficial parties. The unofficial graduation parties were held in different locations, purposely kept secret because the students did not want them to be shut down by police. The level of coordination was not good, so there were several parties going on at the same time, and travel was necessary to get from one party to another.

The recent accidental death of another student who had been partying at an unofficial grad celebration was another tragic reminder of the decision to discontinue "safe grad" parties. The young man was driving his motorcycle to a different party when he was struck by a passing vehicle as he crossed a road without looking. Kent knew that young man too.

It made Kent angry, really angry, that the school would cater to the voice of the abstainers. It was also hypocritical, he thought, that these same parents could go out and have a drink or two as part of their social activities before driving home. He also knew that some of those parents who so strongly opposed the "safe grad" idea had teenagers that, unbeknownst to them, also drank. However, Kent decided to keep his cool and listen to his teacher, Ms. Reiser.

Ms. Reiser cited some statistics about the use of alcohol and drugs among teenagers in their school. She said that many youth who experiment do so under risky circumstances, and that most do not go on to develop serious substance use problems. The risks of experimentation, as she saw them, concerned unsafe use and situation mismanagement. These were the very risks that the "safe grad" was set up to manage and that "super grad" exacerbated. She argued that the change from "safe" to "super" had caused the deaths of two students in four years.

The group of representatives took their comments into consideration, and the school administration, in consultation with the parents' association and school board, made the statement two weeks later that they had decided not to support or endorse any high school graduation parties.

Learning Objectives

1. To define youth programs and what they attempt to do.

2. To learn Stephen Hamilton's definition of positive youth development.

3. To learn about the three key issues of youth programs.

4. To gain knowledge of the need for evaluations, the different types of evaluations, and their goals.

5. To learn what needs to be done to determine the appropriate scale for a program.

6. To understand why many youth programs are not sustainable.

7. To understand the difference between efficacy research and outreach research.

8. To understand how universities and communities can collaborate effectively in support of positive youth development.

9. To understand what "prevention does not equal provision" means for the future of youth programs.

10. To learn what must be done to develop effective youth programs and what influences must be engaged.

11. To gain knowledge of the features of a positive youth development program that are needed for best practice.

12. To define public policies and to understand the need for a national youth policy.

13. To understand how assets can be promoted through existing community youth-serving organizations.

14. To understand the importance of mentoring programs and how they are most effective.

In Chapter 13 we discussed the problems faced by contemporary adolescents. The breadth, severity, and interrelationship among these externalizing and internalizing problems and the added challenges of poverty make it clear that our communities need to have greater access to existing, effective family- and youth-serving programs (e.g., Dryfoos, 1998; Hamburg, 1992; Lerner, 1995; Pickett et al., 2002; Schorr, 1997). New programs must also be devised, evaluated, and, if effective, sustained (Lerner, 1995; Lerner & Galambos, 1998).

All youth-serving organizations are involved in sets of actions aimed at addressing the significant challenges affecting contemporary adolescents. However, what precisely is being provided to youth in such programs? Are such programs actually helping youth lead better lives? To address these questions we need to both define youth programs and understand how their effectiveness may be ascertained.

Defining and Evaluating Youth Programs

ISSUES TO CONSIDER

- What are youth programs? What do they attempt to do?
- What is Stephen Hamilton's three-part definition of positive youth development?
- What is an intervention program?

Programs are planned and systematic initiatives designed to: (1) reduce the presence of an emotional, behavioural, or social problem, (2) prevent such problems from occurring, or (3) promote positive, healthy behaviours among people. The terms "reduction," "prevention," and "promotion" have been associated respectively with these three different approaches. As we discussed in Chapter 5, key attributes of positive youth development are competence, confidence, character, connection, and caring/compassion (Lerner, Fisher, & Weinberg, 2000b; Lerner, Sparks, & McCubbin, 1999; Little, 1993).

Programs that seek to develop these attributes of positive development in young people constitute attempts to optimize the lives of individuals by building up their strengths. Such programs reflect an abiding concern for youth well-being, employ principles of effective youth programs, and are committed to going beyond traditional preventive or remedial interventions, instead stressing skill and competency development (Roth et al., 1997). Jodie L. Roth and her colleagues have studied how youth programs may contribute to positive development (see Meet the Researcher Box 14.1).

Stephen F. Hamilton (1999) has provided a comprehensive definition of positive youth development programs that reflects three interrelated facets of such programs: (1) the conception of the process of youth development used by proponents of such programs, (2) the approach to programming associated with this conception, and (3) the characteristics of programs or organizations that use such an approach. Hamilton's (1999) three-part definition of positive youth development programs is presented in Table 14.1.

In programs of problem reduction, problem prevention, and positive development promotion, the work undertaken constitutes attempts to *intervene* into the course of a person's development by changing the

Helping Create Positive Spaces for Positive Development

Jodie L. Roth is a research scientist at the Center for Children and Families, a research centre at Teachers College, Columbia University. She studies how different settings, such as after-school programs, contribute to how adolescents think and act.

Drive through different communities at 3:00 p.m., when school is over for the day, and you are likely to see dissimilar scenes. In one, athletic fields are teeming with youth practising soccer, football, and field hockey. Inside a school building or community centre, other youth are gathered for meetings of a variety of after-school activities—from drama to model airplane building. In another, the streets are empty. Youth are at home, by themselves, watching television, playing video games, or online. In still another, adolescents are hanging out on the streets or in the malls with their friends, looking for something to do.

What adolescents do after school offers another avenue for understanding adolescent development. That is, it represents one more environment affecting their lives. Unlike school or family, this environment has not been the focus of much research. In my research, my colleague Jeanne Brooks-Gunn and I look at how the choices adolescents have, and the choices they make, for what to do during this time contributes to their development. In doing so, we hope to identify common positive elements from seemingly diverse after-school experiences. These elements can then serve as the basis for developing new programs or strengthening existing ones, particularly in communities with few after-school opportunities for youth.

We are reviewing evaluations of community-based and school-based after-school programs to identify common program elements that foster positive development in youth. Unfortunately, most of the thousands of programs that aim to promote positive outcomes for their adolescent participants do not get evaluated using rigorous methods.

From our review of those that have been evaluated thus far, we have identified three common elements. First, positive youth development programs promote positive behaviours and competencies. They strive to prepare youth for their futures by building their competence in academic, social, and vocational areas and fostering positive traits such as caring, compassion, confidence, and character. Second, these programs have a positive atmosphere. Youth are viewed as resources to be developed rather than as problems to be managed. Often this is done through the relationship between the youth and staff. The staff creates an atmosphere in which youth feel safe, supported, and challenged. Third, positive youth development programs offer challenging, authentic activities, with an emphasis on active participation. Numerous types of activities—athletic, academic, or artistic—can be offered in such a way.

Programs that share these elements go a long way in helping promote positive development for youth. Of course, one program is not going to be right for all youth in a community. We still need to better understand how youth use the array of opportunities in their community to best meet their needs for positive spaces. Furthermore, after-school activities are just one of the many environments influencing adolescents' development. A next step in our research is to better understand how the after-school program environment interacts and influences the other spheres of adolescents' worlds. In doing so, we hope we can help families and communities provide more positive spaces for their youth.

---

person's life for the better. **Intervention programs** may be conducted by professionals trained to use particular methods (e.g., psychotherapy, group interactions) or they may be presented to youth through community-based clubs or organizations (e.g., YMCA, 4-H, Boys and Girls Clubs, or Big Brother/Big Sister programs).

Intervention program Program conducted by professionals or through community-based organizations that attempts to change a person's life for the better.

Representative Focal Issues of Youth Programs

ISSUES TO CONSIDER
- What are examples of the target behaviours of youth programs?
- What are the three key issues of youth programs?

The target behaviours of youth programs vary. Interventions may be aimed at externalizing and/or internalizing problems and may focus primarily on the individual or on the developmental system within which the youth is embedded; that is, in addition to the individual adolescent the program may involve his

Table 14-1 Positive Youth Development: Hamilton's Three-Part Definition

Hamilton (1999) envisions positive youth development as a process, as a philosophy of or an approach to youth programming, and as a specific type of organization or program.

1. **A natural process: The growing capacity of a young person to understand and act on the environment.**
   Youth development is the natural unfolding of the potential inherent in the human organism in relation to the challenges and supports of the physical and social environment. People can actively shape their own development through their choices and interpretations. Development lasts as long as life, but youth development enables individuals to lead a healthy, satisfying, and productive life, as youth and later as adults, because they gain the competence to earn a living, to engage in civic activities, to nurture others, and to participate in social relations and cultural activities. The five C's are a useful summary of the goals of youth development: caring/compassion, competence, character, connection, and confidence. The process of development may be divided into age-related stages (infancy, childhood, adolescence, and smaller divisions of these stages) and into domains (notably physical, cognitive, social, emotional, and moral).

2. **A philosophy of or an approach to programming: Active support for the growing capacity of young people by individuals, organizations, and institutions, especially at the community level.**
   The youth development approach is rooted in a commitment to enabling all young people to achieve their potential. It is characterized by a positive, asset-building orientation, building on strengths rather than categorizing youth according to their deficits. However, it also recognizes the need to identify and respond to specific problems faced by some youth (e.g., substance abuse, involvement in violence, premature parenthood). The most important manifestation of youth development as a philosophy or approach is the goal of making communities better places for young people to grow up. Youth participation is essential to the achievement of that goal.

3. **Programs and organizations: A planned set of activities that foster young people's growing capacity.**
   Youth development programs are inclusive. Participation is not limited to those identified as at risk or in need. They give young people the chance to make decisions about their own participation and about the program's operation, and to assume responsible roles. They engage young people in constructive and challenging activities that build their competence and foster supportive relationships with peers and with adults. They are developmentally appropriate and endure over time, which requires them to be adaptable enough to change as participants' needs change. Youth development is done with and by youth. Something done to or for youth is not youth development, even though it may be necessary and valuable. Youth development organizations exist specifically for the purpose of promoting youth development. Some other organizations operate youth development programs but have other functions as well. Programs to prevent or treat specific problems stand in contrast to youth development programs. However, problem-oriented programs may incorporate youth development principles by acknowledging participants' strengths and the wider range of issues they must cope with and by giving participants a strong voice in the choice to participate and in the operation of the program.

Source: Hamilton, 1999.

or her peer group, family, school, or community. For example, for externalizing behaviours, interventions focus primarily on the individual in regard to problems of alcohol use and abuse (e.g., Marlatt et al., 1998), smoking (e.g., Prince, 1995), conduct disorders (e.g., Foster & Webster, 1998; Walsh, Pepler, & Levine, 2002), social skills (e.g., Royer et al., 1999), and delinquency (e.g., Richards & Sullivan, 1996). Interventions that involve the developmental system exist in regard to such problems as juvenile delinquency (e.g., Battistich et al., 1996; Chamberlain & Reid, 1998; Henggeler et al., 1997), alcohol use and abuse (e.g., Hohlman & LeCroy, 1996; Johnson et al., 1996; Richards-Colocino, McKenzie, & Newton, 1996), smoking (Health Canada, 1999), violence (e.g., Corvo, 1997; Henggeler et al., 1996), and drug use (e.g., Battistich et al., 1996; Gottfredson, Gottfredson, & Skroban, 1996; Johnson et al., 1996; LoSciuto et al., 1996; Richards-Colocino et al., 1996).

In regard to internalizing behaviours, interventions focus primarily on the individual for such problems as depression (e.g., Field et al., 1996), anger (e.g., Kellner & Tutin, 1995), eating disorders (Tonkin, 1997) and suicide (e.g., Kirmayer, Boothroyd, & Hodgins, 1998). Interventions that involve the developmental system focus on such problems as anxiety (e.g., Copping et al., 1999; Kendall & Southam-Gerow, 1996), conduct disorders (e.g., Mann-Feder, 1996), or multiple "emotional problems" (e.g., Pazaratz et al., 1999). Some systems-level efforts focus on multiple internalizing and externalizing problems such as several health needs (Gullotta & Noyes, 1995) or emotional and behavioural problems (e.g., Dolan, 1995; Wassef et al., 1995a).

Moreover, in programs that seek to promote positive development there may be efforts that focus either on the individual level (for instance, attempts to enhance cognitive and ego development may adopt

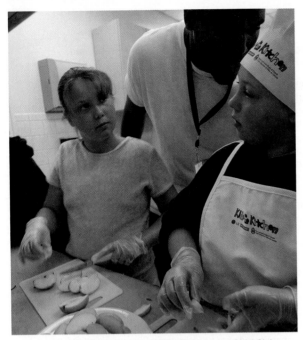

Many Canadian young people participate in Boys' and Girls' Clubs.

another caring adult, as in the case of Big Brother/Big Sister programs) (Thompson, 1997), parents' ability to support their children (Alaggia, Michalski, & Vine, 1999), body image (e.g. McVey & Davis, 2002), or general health (e.g., Brack, Brack, & Orr, 1996; Emshoff et al., 1996). Programs that emphasize relationship building with youth have shown positive results (Moore, Moretti, & Holland, 1998). Youth with experience in child welfare, corrections, and mental health systems indicate that collaboration between service partners is helpful only if service providers engage them in the development of a health-enhancing identity and not a problem-saturated one (Ungar, 2001).

Whatever the focus of an intervention program might be—whether it is an individual adolescent or includes features of his or her developmental system, or whether the interest is on reducing or preventing one or more internalizing and/or externalizing behaviours or in promoting one or several facets of positive development—every program must in some way consider three key issues: effectiveness, scale, and sustainability (Little, 1993). To understand these issues, let's focus first on the issue of effectiveness.

Program Effectiveness and the Role of Program Evaluation

ISSUES TO CONSIDER

- Why is program effectiveness difficult to determine?
- What can be done to determine if a program is effective?
- What are some types of evaluations, and what are their purposes?

Does a program accomplish its aims? For example, does it reduce youth violence? Does it prevent unsafe sexual behaviours? Does it enhance self-esteem among adolescents? If a program achieves what it is intended to achieve it is effective. It is a program that is valid for its intended purpose.

But **program effectiveness** is often difficult to determine (Jacobs, 1988; Jacobs & Kapuscik, 2000). Young people are not randomly assigned to programs; rather they enter a program for particular reasons based on their past and/or current life experiences. For instance, adolescents are in a drug reduction program because they use drugs, in a violence prevention program because there is a risk they will engage in violence, or in a positive youth development program because they live in a community that has the resources to provide a potentially beneficial experience to its young people. Because of the reasons youth enter into a program, it may not be possible to determine if any changes that occur during their

such an orientation; e.g., Faubert et al., 1996) or on the developmental system. Ontario researchers Prilleltensky, Peirson, Gould, and Nelson (1997) contend that organizations should be clear about the values that underlie their intervention programs, such as self-determination, collaboration, and democratic participation.

The need for collaborative program coordination or development has been stressed by Gordon (2002) and other Canadian authors, who emphasize the need for involvement of various stakeholders in planning (Collins, 2002) and recognize that there is no single model that can be applied to all successful collaborations (Nicholson, Artz, Armitage, & Fagan, 2000). Successful collaborative school-based interventions (Graham-Migel, 2002) involve youth, parents, teachers, and administrators (Bond, Glover, Godfrey, Butler, & Patton, 2001; DeWit, Offord, Sanford, Rye, Shain, & Wright, 2000; Stirtzinger, Campbell, Green, deSouza, & Dawe, 2001).

Examples include programs that seek to enhance social skills (Halas, 2002), emotional functioning (Mishna, Michalski, & Cummings, 2001), relationship skills (in the development of a relationship with

Program effectiveness Concept indicating whether a program is accomplishing its goals by achieving what it intended to achieve.

Evaluations Procedures used to ascertain if changes in program participants are due to the program.

participation are due to who they were when they started the program or to the program itself.

Procedures—termed **evaluations**—are used to ascertain if changes in participants are due to the program, if programs are effective, and if programs attain their goals (Connell et al., 1995; Fetterman, Kaftarian, & Wadersman, 1996; Jacobs, 1988; Millett, 1996; Lerner, Ostrom, & Freel, 1995; Ostrom, Lerner, & Freel, 1995). Evaluations try to *prove* that any changes youth experience over the course of their participation in a program are due to the program itself and not due to the factors that involved them in drugs, that led them to be at risk for violence, or that gave them the opportunity to live in a community that provides programs promoting positive development. In an evaluation of a Montreal YMCA drop-in centre, researchers used information from scholarly literature, interviews with staff, and interviews with youth as data for their study. The agreement between these three different sources of information, a process called **triangulation**, gives confidence to others that findings are accurate (Mercier, Piat, Peladeau, & Dagenais, 2000). Evaluations aimed at proving that a program is effective are often termed **outcome** or **summative evaluations.**

Evaluations also try to *improve* the quality of a program as it is being conducted. Here, the evaluator tries to ascertain if the program can be improved, if midcourse corrections can be made to the program so better efforts at promoting self-esteem or preventing violence can be made. For instance, in their process evaluation of a program in Ontario to support students at risk for externalizing problems during the transition from elementary to junior high school, the researchers sought the feedback of participants in order to make the program more responsive to their needs (Rye, Humpartzoomian, & Steep, 2001). So before any outcomes are seen, efforts should be made to improve the work involved in the delivery of the program. Evaluations that seek to improve programs are often called **formative evaluations.** Because they seek to enhance the process through which a program provides its services, such evaluations may also be termed **process evaluations.**

Evaluations try to *empower* the people who are delivering the program and the young people and/or

In attempts to reduce or prevent problems such as drug and alcohol use and abuse, some community-based programs engage the peer group.

families who are participating in it. A key goal of evaluators of contemporary youth programs—especially those programs located in communities and begun and continued through the efforts of members of the community (as compared to trained professionals, such as psychologists, social workers, nurses, or physicians)—is to increase capacity among community members to both provide evidence of program effectiveness and improve the program (Connell et al., 1995; Fetterman et al., 1996; Jacobs, 1988; Jacobs & Kapuscik, 2000; Millett, 1996; Ostrom et al., 1995). These **empowerment evaluations** (Fetterman et al., 1996) are seen as critical to enact if the community is to use evidence of program effectiveness to bring the program to all youth who need it and to maintain the program over time. Such goals for a program pertain to the issues of scale and sustainability, respectively.

Program Scale

ISSUES TO CONSIDER

- Why is determining appropriate program scale important?
- What factors might contribute to a youth program not reaching all eligible youth?

As we discuss further on, we know a good deal about the characteristics of effective youth programs. We know how to provide evidence that programs are effective and how to improve their quality while they are in process. In addition, researchers are studying how to empower communities through evaluation (Connell et al., 1995; Fetterman et al., 1996; Jacobs,

Triangulation The comparison of information about a particular issue from three different sources, where consistency between them adds strength to the conclusion.

Outcome or summative evaluation Procedures used to determine if a program is effective.
Formative evaluation Procedures that seek to improve programs.

Process evaluation Procedures that seek to improve programs through enhancing the process through which the program provides its services.

Empowerment evaluation Procedures used to increase the ability of community members to prove the effectiveness of the program and to improve it.

1988; Millett, 1996; Ostrom et al., 1995). However, even if programs are known to be effective, they may not be reaching all the youth for whom they are appropriate, and for whom they could have positive benefits. This is a problem of **program scale**. Often the number of youth that would be appropriate for a given program is not known. For instance, if a Boys' and Girls' Club after-school basketball program involves a dozen youth, it may not be known if greater skill attainment could be developed in the participants if the maximum number of youth in the program were 8 or if equivalent skill attainment could be achieved among youth if the program size were increased to 20 youth.

In turn, we may have information that more people could benefit from a program; for instance, we might know that a program that sends visitors to the homes of adolescent mothers to help improve their skills as parents is effective, but that only 50% of the youth eligible for the program participate in it. We might not know, however, why we cannot involve all eligible youth in the program. What are the psychological, social, economic, and political reasons that keep youth from participating in the program? Alternatively, we might understand the economic reasons that keep adolescent mothers out of home visiting programs (e.g., they have to work and are not available when the program is offered), but we may not know how to change the social system (e.g., by developing labour law policies regarding flexible working hours or time off from work for program participation) in a manner that would enable the program to be brought to scale.

Program Sustainability

ISSUES TO CONSIDER

• Why are many youth programs not sustained?
• What is Francine Jacobs's five-tier model of evaluation?

If there is a lot of scholarship to conduct about program scale, there is even more to learn about **program sustainability**. A sustained program is one maintained over time. Most programs, especially community-based ones, are not sustained over long periods of time. Many programs are initiated through start-up grants made by government agencies or private, philanthropic foundations or by university faculty who have obtained a grant to demonstrate that a particular intervention they have created is effective. In either case, after the start-up funds have run out or the demonstration project is completed, the project usually ends either immediately or after a relatively short period (e.g., Dryfoos, 1998; Hamburg, 1992; Lerner, Sparks, & McCubbin, 1999; Little, 1993; Schorr, 1988, 1997). This lack of sustainability occurs even for programs that have been shown through evaluations to be effective (Little, 1993).

Typically, after start-up funds end or the expertise possessed by university faculty has left the community, members of the community may not have the capacity to identify new resources to sustain the program. They may not have the skills to conduct the program, especially in ways that will enable them both to improve the program and provide evidence to potential funders that they are effectively changing youth for the better (Jacobs, 1988; Jacobs & Kapuscik, 2000; Lerner, Ostrom, & Freel, 1995, 1997; Ostrom et al., 1995; Weiss & Greene, 1992).

Because of the need to assist community program leaders to develop such capacities, increasingly greater attention has been paid in recent years to the empowerment approach to evaluation (Fetterman et al., 1996). Arguably, the most useful of these approaches has been developed by Francine Jacobs (Jacobs, 1988; Jacobs & Kapuscik, 2000). In her five-tier model of evaluation, Jacobs provides means for a community to develop a stronger program in regard to both the impact and improvement dimensions of evaluation. Applications Box 14.1 summarizes Jacobs's five-tier model.

Toward a New Research Model for Youth Programs

ISSUES TO CONSIDER

• What is the difference between efficacy research and outreach research?
• Why should more effort be focused on outreach research than before?
• How can universities and communities collaborate to support positive youth development?

Some researchers have suggested that the predominant research model used to conduct program evaluations may be flawed and that its use may be the reason effective youth programs have not been sustained (Jensen, Hoagwood, & Trickett, 1999).

Program scale Concept indicating whether a program is reaching the appropriate number of people for whom it could have positive benefits.

Program sustainability Concept indicating whether a program is maintained over time.

Francine Jacobs's Five-Tier Model of Program Evaluation

Level/Title	Purposes of Evaluation	Audiences	Tasks	Kinds of Data to Collect/Analyze
TIER ONE Needs assessment	1. To document the size and nature of a public problem 2. To determine unmet need for services in a community 3. To propose program and policy options to meet needs 4. To set a data base-line from which later progress can be measured 5. To broaden the base of support for a proposed program	1. Policymakers 2. Funders 3. Community stake-holders	1. Review existing community, county, and state/provincial data 2. Determine additional data needed to describe problem and potential service users 3. Conduct "environ-mental scan" of avail-able resources 4. Identify resource gaps and unmet need 5. Set goals and objec-tives for interventions 6. Recommend one program model from range of options.	1. Extant data on target population; services currently available 2. Interviews with community leaders 3. Interviews or survey data from prospective participants 4. Information about similar programs in other locations
TIER TWO Monitoring and Accountability	1. To monitor program performance 2. To meet demands for accountability 3. To build a constituency 4. To aid in program planning and decision making 5. To provide a ground-work for later evalua-tion activities	1. Program staff and administrators 2. Policymakers 3. Funders 4. Community stake-holders 5. Media	1. Determine needs and capacities for data collection and management 2. Develop clear and consistent proce-dures for collecting essential data elements 3. Gather and analyze data to describe program along dimen-sions of *clients, serv-ices, staff,* and *costs*	1. MIS (management information system) data: collected at program, county, and/or state/ provincial level 2. Case material; obtained through record reviews, program contact forms, etc.
TIER THREE Quality Review and Program Clarification	1. To develop a more detailed picture of the program as it is being implemented 2. To assess the quality and consistency of the intervention 3. To provide informa-tion to staff for program improvement	1. Program staff and administrators 2. Policymakers 3. Community stake-holders	1. Review monitoring data 2. Expand on program descriptions using information about participants' views 3. Compare program with standards and expectations 4. Examine participants' perceptions about effects of program 5. Clarify program goals and design	1. MIS monitoring data 2. Case material 3. Other qualitative and quantitative data on program operations, customer satisfac-tion, and perceived effects; obtained using questionnaires, interviews, observa-tions, and focus groups

>

TIER FOUR Achieving Outcomes	1. To determine what changes, if any, have occurred among beneficiaries 2. To attribute changes to the program 3. To provide information to staff for program improvement	1. Program staff and administrators 2. Policymakers 3. Community stakeholders 4. Funders 5. Other programs	1. Choose short-term objectives to be examined 2. Choose appropriate research design, given constraints and capacities 3. Determine measurable indicators of success for outcome objectives 4. Collect and analyze information about effects on beneficiaries	1. Client-specific data; obtained using questionnaires, interviews, goal attainment scaling, observations, and functional indicators 2. Client and community social indicators 3. MIS data
TIER FIVE Establishing Impact	1. To contribute to knowledge development in the field 2. To produce evidence of differential effectiveness of treatments 3. To identify models worthy of replication	1. Academic and research communities 2. Policymakers 3. Funders 4. General public	1. Decide on impact objectives based on results of Tier Four evaluation efforts 2. Choose appropriately rigorous research design and comparison group 3. Identify techniques and tools to measure effects in treatment and comparison groups 4. Analyze information to identify program impacts	1. Client-specific data; obtained using questionnaires, interviews, goal attainment scaling, observations, and functional indicators. 2. Client and community social indicators 3. MIS data 4. Comparable data for control group

Source: Jacobs, 1988; Jacobs & Kapuscik, 2000.

Jensen et al. (1999) describe two distinct models of research pertinent to the promotion of positive youth development. The first model has been predominant in social and behavioural science and is termed by Jensen et al. (1999) the **"efficacy research"** model. Research conducted within the frame of this model addresses this key question: "What works under optimal, university-based research conditions?"

Studies using this model try to determine what is maximally effective under "optimal," that is, university-designed as opposed to real-world conditions, in regard to preventing the onset of behavioural or emotional problems, ameliorating the course of problems after their onset, and treating problems that have reached clinical severity. Jensen et al. (1999) note that the results of the studies conducted within this model indicate that effective preventive interventions for several high-risk behaviours and/or outcomes are possible.

However, a second model of research exists, although it has not received the financial support given to efficacy research. Indeed, this second model has been rarely used and poorly funded. It is one of **outreach research**; it is research conducted in real-world community settings.

This model addresses this key question: "What works that is also (1) palatable; (2) feasible; (3) durable; (4) affordable; and (5) sustainable in real-world settings?" Jensen et al. (1999) conclude that when this question is asked, the answer in regard to prevention or to positive youth development programs is "Very few (if any)."

"Efficacy research" Model of research conducted under optimal, university-based research conditions.

Outreach research Model of research conducted in real-world, community-based settings.

Jensen et al. (1999) argue that governments must move to support outreach research, to change the answer to the last-noted question to "Many, if not most." To create this sea change in the way scholars conduct their research, Jensen et al. (1999) recognize that universities and communities must create new, more effective partnerships. Jensen et al. (1999) believe there must be a qualitative change in the way universities interact with communities in regard to identifying ways to promote positive youth development (see, too, Eccles, 1996; McHale & Lerner, 1996). Table 14.2 presents the ideas suggested by Jensen et al. (1999) and others (e.g., Chibucos & Lerner, 1999; Eccles, 1996; McHale & Lerner, 1996) about how universities and communities can collaborate in sustaining effective youth-serving programs.

Conclusions About Defining and Evaluating Youth Programs

Youth programs vary in numerous ways. They differ in their emphasis on problem reduction or prevention or in their attempts to promote positive development. They also differ in their emphasis on changing the individual versus changing the developmental system, or changing both the individual and some portion of his or her developmental system. Finally, they differ in regard to their approach to the issues of evaluation, effectiveness, scale, and sustainability. Together, these variations make the picture of contemporary youth programs quite complex.

Themes of Contemporary Youth Programs

There are some themes that characterize contemporary discussions of youth programs. Focus on these themes allows the complexity involved in understanding youth programs to be reduced to a few key concepts. First, most scholars and practitioners want to prevent problems before they occur. Offord (2000) reports that there are trade-offs inherent in any decisions about universal versus targeted prevention programs, and that, overall, a mix is desirable. Although the plasticity of human development (see Chapter 2) means there is always optimism about finding some intervention to reduce problem behaviours, it is both more humane and more cost effective

Table 14-2 Sustaining Effective Youth-Serving Programs: Ideas for Building University-Community Collaborations

Jensen et al. (1999) point out that effective university-community collaborations in support of positive youth development should be based on several specific principles:

1. An enhanced focus on the relevance of research to the actual ecology of youth (Bronfenbrenner, 1979; Bronfenbrenner & Morris, 1998; Hultsch & Hickey, 1978). The experiences of youth must be understood in the actual settings in which they live (Banister & Schreiber, 2001).
2. Incorporating the values and needs of community collaborators within research activities (Richardson, 1996; Spanier, 1997, 1999).
3. Understanding and measuring both the intended and the unintended outcomes of an intervention program for youth and their context (Carroll, Hebert, & Roy, 1999).
4. Flexibility to fit local needs and circumstances and an orientation to adjust the design or procedures of the research to unexpected changes in the community within which the work is enacted (Jacobs, 1988; Jacobs & Kapuscik, 2000).
5. Accordingly, a willingness to make modifications to research methods in order to fit the circumstances of the local community.
6. Embracing long-term perspectives and the commitment of the university to remain in the community for a time period sufficient to see the realization of community-valued developmental goals for its youth.

Chibucos and Lerner (1999), Ebata (1996), Eccles (1996), Fitzgerald et al. (1996), Lerner and Simon (1998), McHale et al. (1996), McHale and Lerner (1996), Peterson (1995), Small (1996), Weinberg and Erikson (1996), Zeldin (1995), and Zeldin & Price (1995) proposed ideas that allow several other principles to be forwarded, including:

7. A commitment by both the university and the community to learn from each other (to co-learn) what is required to enhance the lives of particular youth (Higgitt, Wingert, Ristock, Brown, Ballantyne, Caett, Coy, Quoquat, & Operation Go Home, 2003).
8. Humility on the part of the university and its faculty, so that (a) true co-learning and collaboration among equals can occur; and (b) cultural integration is achieved and, through this, the university and the community recognize and appreciate each other's perspective.

to prevent problems from occurring than to wait for them to develop.

Second, although steps need to be taken to ensure effective preventive programs are being developed, the focus should shift to promoting positive development rather than preventing negative outcomes (e.g., Furstenberg & Hughes, 1995; Lerner, 1993, 1995; Moore & Glei, 1995; Oden, 1995). Several scholars (e.g., Benson, 1997; Lerner et al., 1999; Pittman, 1996) have emphasized that prevention is not the same as provision. *Preventing a problem from occurring does not guarantee that youth are being provided with the assets they need for positive development.*

As we noted in Chapter 5, in the discussion of the individual and ecological assets for positive development identified by the Search Institute (Benson, 1997; Benson et al., 1998; Blyth & Leffert, 1995; Leffert et al., 1998; Scales et al., 2000; Scales & Leffert, 1999), communities need to provide resources proactively to youth to ensure that they develop the "five C's" of positive youth development and thus thrive across their lives.

Preventing problems does not provide these assets, but effective programs do. Researchers from the Search Institute report the following:

> Time spent in youth programs appeared to have the most pervasive positive influence [predicting] thriving outcomes. . . . [G]ood youth programs provide young people with access to caring adults and responsible peers, as well as skill-building activities that can reinforce the values and skills that are associated with doing well in school and maintaining good physical health. (Scales et al., 2000, p. 43)

Developing Effective Programs for Youth

ISSUES TO CONSIDER
- What must be done to develop effective youth programs?
- Why is it important to engage both individual and contextual influences?
- What are protective factors, and what is their role in positive youth development?

If programs are to succeed in addressing the combined individual and contextual influences on youth prob-

lems and if they are to be associated with positive youth development, programs must engage both of these levels (individual and contextual) (Benson, 1997; Lerner, 1995; Pittman, 1996; Pittman & Irby, 1995; Pittman, Irby, & Cahill, 1995; Trickett, Barone, & Buchanan, 1996; Wassef et al., 1995b; Whalen & Wynn, 1995). Whether aimed at drug use (e.g., Rohrback et al., 1994), alcohol use (e.g., Maguin, Zucker, & Fitzgerald, 1994; Wagenaar & Peery, 1994), aggression and delinquency (Guerra & Slaby, 1990), school problems (Switzer et al., 1995), or socioeconomic disadvantage (Furstenberg & Hughes, 1995), effective programs engage the system of individual and contextual variables affecting youth development.

By involving multiple characteristics of the young person—for instance, his or her developmental level, knowledge of risk taking, intrapersonal resources (e.g., self-esteem, self-competence, beliefs, and values), interpersonal management skills (e.g., being able to engage useful social support and prosocial behaviours from peers)—successful risk prevention programs may be developed (Dickson, Derevensky, & Gupta, 2002). However, the programs described here are more than ones focusing on diminishing risk. They "recognize their [the youth's] ability to adapt, develop and function in the face of severe stress and/or disadvantage, and the ability of the stressed person to rebound to pre-stress level of adaptation," which, according to Canadian psychiatrist Paul Steinhauer (2001, p. 53), is the definition of **resilience**. These programs also emphasize the assets of young people and their capacities for positive development. These capacities are their possession of attributes, or **protective factors**, that keep them moving forward in a positive developmental path. Protective factors are individual attributes (such as self-esteem, spiritual values, and knowledge, skills, and motivation to do well) and contextual attributes (such as the experience of having authoritative parents and a socially supportive, prosocial peer group) that researchers have identified as integral in the healthy development of young people (e.g., Browne & Rife, 1991; Feldman, 1995; Jessor et al., 1995; Stiffman, Church, & Earls, 1992).

A Vision for Youth Development Programs

ISSUES TO CONSIDER
- From a community development perspective, what are some of the basic needs of youth?
- How can these needs be met?

Resilience The strength to succeed despite adversity.

Protective factors Strengths and assets of young people that keep them on a positive developmental path.

In keeping with an emphasis on factors that are associated with successful development of youth, it is crucial to ask the youth themselves what they need and how others can support them in their construction of the life they want for themselves. The use of a top-down approach to understanding youth development (telling them what is best for them) is quite different from a community development perspective (Health Canada, 1997). "Community development is the process which involves reaching out into the community, identifying key groups and leaders, working with them on problems of mutual concern, helping to empower the community and thus strengthening its own inherent organization and its support systems, and taking the initiative in coping with its own concerns" (City of Toronto Health Department, 1991, cited in Health Canada, 1997, p. 5).

Community development can also be seen as a process in which youth are actively involved in decisions affecting their lives, and not passive recipients of programming directed by others for their consumption. From this perspective, youth need the opportunity to develop skills to be equal contributors in decisions about how their community, the social world in which they live, can support them, and how they can support others for change. It is also crucial for adults to recognize the legitimacy of youth in this process of community development (Health Canada, 1997). In a review of Canadian research and consultation documents, Caputo (1999) reported several themes and common concerns of youth. The concerns were associated with self-esteem, family and school-related issues, substance use, violence, and sexuality. The youth also were concerned about their futures in communities they saw as being challenging due to effects of racism and discrimination, and increasing globalization.

The same review (Caputo, 1999) included recommendations about how to respond more effectively to youth. It was suggested that adults recognize youth's strengths and abilities, provide opportunities for inclusion, educate others to value them, respect their right to be treated fairly and to be portrayed accurately in media, and recognize the importance of school in their lives. There were also several barriers for youth to achieve greater inclusion in communities: negative stereotypes, different goals and values from adults, discontinuity of interests over time, and unequal ability to participate in decisions affecting their lives due to less experience and opportunity.

In her research with street-experienced youth in Winnipeg, Nancy Higgitt and co-researchers (Higgitt, Wingert, Ristiock, Brown, Ballantyne, Caett, Coy, Quoquat, & Operation Go Home, 2003) employed a participatory approach to understanding the experiences of this group of youth. Her research is featured in Meet the Researcher Box 14.2.

Key Features of Effective Youth Programs

ISSUES TO CONSIDER
- What are the features of a positive youth development program that are needed for "best practice"?
- What are some examples of community-based positive youth development programs?

Numerous scholars, practitioners, advocates for youth, and policymakers have studied and discussed effective youth programs (e.g., Benson, 1997; Damon, 1997; Dryfoos, 1990, 1998; Hamilton & Hamilton, 1999; Lerner, 1993, 1995; Lerner & Galambos, 1998; Little, 1993; Pittman, 1996; Roth et al., 1997; Schorr, 1988, 1997). Although all contributors to this discussion may have their own ways of phrasing their conclusions, it is possible to provide an overview of the **best practices** that should be integrated into effective positive youth development programs. These features of best practice involve coordinated attention to the youth's characteristics of individuality and to the specifics of his or her social context. Programs that are effective in promoting positive youth development incorporate the following ideas:

1. They are predicated on a vision of positive youth development (for example, the "Five C's" of positive youth development; Hamilton, 1999; Lerner et al., 1999) and have clear aims (goals), developed in partnership with youth, for the program.
2. They focus on the assets of youth and on the importance of their participation in every facet of the program—including its design, conduct, and evaluation.
3. They pay attention to the diversity of youth and family, community, and cultural context. Both the special strengths and the particular needs of youth and their contexts are of central concern.

Best practice Set of procedures or program attributes believed to be most effective in constituting a good program.

Voices from the Street: Understanding the Experiences of Street-Involved Youth

Nancy Higgitt is an associate professor in the Department of Family Studies at the University of Manitoba. As a sociologist, she studies housing and community issues that affect individuals and families living in the inner city.

Have you ever wondered about curb kids, panhandlers, or squatters: who they are, why they are there, how they survive, or why they don't do something to get off the street? Lacking answers to these questions motivated me to learn more about kids on the street. What I learned was eye opening.

As a researcher, I sought answers to these questions by developing a participatory research study with Dr. Janice Ristock (Women's Studies, University of Manitoba), Susan Wingert (graduate student, University of Manitoba), Operation Go Home (a national organization that assists youth who are not living in a safe and stable environment), and four street-experienced youth who served as research interns (Melvina Ballantyne, Sammy Caett, Kristin Coy, and Rachel Quoquat). We interviewed 12 young people who had been involved with the street. Although their situations varied, all their stories highlighted personal struggles to survive and to transcend the harsh realities of their lives. The data for this study come from their narratives about their experiences.

For many of our participants, life before the street involved breaking curfews, using drugs or alcohol, or skipping school. Most reported stress, conflict, or violence at home. Several indicated being abandoned by one or both parents or not fitting into parents' new lives. In many families, there was a

history of street involvement among siblings. Many reported being let down by the child protection system. For a variety of reasons, the kids in our study felt they had nowhere to go but the street.

Once on the street, meeting basic needs was a struggle. Their focus was solely on the present—make money, get food, find shelter, and stay safe. Panning, flagging, and "squeegeeing" were common sources of income. Food for the day was often a hot dog, a drink, and chips. When not couch surfing with friends or extended family, most young people slept outside, stayed in squats, or sometimes in a cheap hotel. Using drugs or alcohol made the time pass and helped to ease the pain. Staying safe involved looking tough, hanging with friends, and avoiding adults.

The longer young people remain on the street, the harder it is for them to leave, since the street has a strong gravitational pull. Yet, the youth in our study all wanted to reach the milestones of adulthood that are sanctioned by society. They dreamed of having meaningful employment, education, homes, cars, and families. It was evident, however, that no progress toward larger goals was possible while they were locked in a daily battle for survival on the street. Most youth in our study wanted to get off the street but were afraid that they couldn't survive away from it.

Overall, what we learned from our interviews with street youth is consistent with the findings of other researchers who have

examined the issue of youth homelessness. Living on the street is not a choice that young people make easily. Many perceive that they have no other alternative to leaving home. Youth become homeless because of the failures of many systems, including family, school, community, child protection agencies, and youth correction systems. They become alienated from the systems that normally keep youth anchored in mainstream society.

At the heart of youth homelessness lie the larger issues of poverty, unemployment, family violence, social isolation, and myriad other social problems. Concrete suggestions for assisting street youth include intervention on the street, support for getting off the street, and assistance in staying off the street. The best strategy of all would be prevention. However, that requires answers to a number of questions, such as: What makes some youth more resilient than others? How can problems with families be better addressed? How can schools and communities support at-risk youth? What are the gaps in the social safety net for youth at risk?

---

4. They ensure that the program represents a safe space and is accessible to them. Such a setting should also provide a context within which youth can use their time constructively.

5. In recognition of the interrelated challenges facing youth, they integrate the assets for positive youth development that exist within the community. Such integration involves collaborations (partnerships) among all youth-serving organizations and contributions by families, peers, and schools.

6. Through the presence of safety, accessibility, and collaboration, they provide broad, sustained, and integrated services to youth and a seamless social support system across the community.

7. In recognition of the importance of caring adult-youth relations in healthy adolescent development, they provide training to adult leaders. Useful training may involve enhancing sensitivity to diversity and providing information about the principles of positive youth development.

8. They act to develop life skills, competency, caring, civic responsibility, and community service, or the "Five C's" of positive youth development.

9. They are committed to program evaluation and to strengthening the use of research in the design, delivery, and evaluation of the program. The role of university-community partnerships is important here.

10. They advocate for youth. Although programs are not (and should not) be partisan, they should provide a clear voice to policymakers across the political spectrum about the importance of investing in positive youth development.

Multiple features of person and context must be combined to design and deliver a program that effectively promotes positive youth development. Building on the general developmental characteristics of the period—involving identity and family, peer, and institutional (e.g., school and workplace) contextual levels—these programs, when attuned to the specific characteristics and needs of the youth and his or her setting, will help the adolescent not just avoid the development of risk behaviours, but will also promote positive youth development.

There are numerous examples of how the elements of effective positive youth development programs have been successfully combined in a community-based effort. In Applications Box 14.2 the results of a study of program characteristics among youth and family agencies in Quebec are presented.

Conclusions About Effective Youth Programs

We should be optimistic about the likely success of prevention efforts if they are designed and delivered while keeping in mind that no single or isolated effort is apt to succeed, given the multiple interrelated challenges facing youth (Dryfoos, 1990; Roth et al., 1997). A coordinated set of community-based programs, aimed at both individuals and their contexts, is required for success. These programs should begin early and be maintained for as many of the adolescent years as possible. No one effort, even a comprehensive one, can continue to prevent the appearance of risk across all of adolescence.

Clearly, then, means may be found to capitalize on the potentials and strengths of all youth, their families, and communities. By meeting their developmental needs, their positive development is promoted. However, if the hope is to reach the maximum number

Faith-based programs may make important contributions to positive youth development.

of youth possible in a sustained manner, the resources of society need to be organized. To attain this end, scholars of youth development must engage policymakers in the support of effective programs (Lerner, 1995; Lipsitz, 1991; Ralston et al., 1999; Takanishi & Hamburg, 1996).

Public Policy for Youth Development Programs

ISSUE TO CONSIDER
• What are public policies, and what do they mean for society?

Public policies represent standards, or rules, for the conduct of individuals, organizations, and institutions (Lerner, 1995; Lerner et al., 1999). As such, policies structure our actions; they let others know how they may expect us to function in regard to particular substantive issues. In addition, policies reflect what we value, what we believe, and what we think is in our best interests. Simply, policies indicate the things we are invested in and care about.

If we value our youth, we will promote public policies that enable effective programs to be designed and sustained for all youth that need them. We know how to design effective programs. Our task now is to formulate a set of social rules—policies—that will enable our values about youth to be translated into effective actions. But why, specifically, do we need a

Public policy Standards or values for the conduct of individuals, organizations, and institutions that structure actions and indicate appropriate investment of resources.

Community Programs That Promote the Positive Development of Youth

In their review of 307 prevention and promotion projects for children, youth, and families across Quebec, Chamberland and colleagues (2000) present a profile of the problems addressed, activities engaged in, change strategies used, organizational links, and funding types. In addition to having objectives that were consistent with prevention or promotion programs to serve children, youth, and families at individual, family, or community levels, these programs had to have been in operation for two years and viewed as successful by their stakeholders.

Seven main categories or problems were addressed by these programs: prenatal care, children and youth, families, social support, living conditions, social values, and the promotion of well-being. The institutional sector focused on more specific problems faced by youth and their families. Problems specific to youth included school-related problems, such as early leaving and substance abuse. Problems specific to the families included child abuse, child neglect, and parenting issues. Projects based in the community targeted a diverse range of problems, but placed the greatest emphasis on programs addressing social support and difficult living conditions. Projects that specifically targeted living

conditions addressed a variety of concerns such as hunger, family poverty, and inadequate housing, as well as issues of social support.

The following differences were noted between institutional programs, community-based ones, and programs targeting living conditions:

- While there was variation in the targets for change among all of the programs reviewed, the institutional programs were most likely to emphasize changes to the population served, while the community-based projects and those focusing on living conditions were more likely to target living environments and decision makers.
- The types of activities engaged in also varied among the programs reviewed. However, the institutional projects favoured group education and screening of program participants, and the community-based projects favoured training, education, recreation, and concrete support (e.g., food). Projects targeting living conditions favoured education, concrete support, and tactics for social change such as petitions and demonstrations.
- Institutional projects had by far the most stable sources of income, while

the community-based projects and those focusing on living conditions had the least stable sources of income.
- Institutional projects had fewer links with other organizations than the community-based and living conditions projects.
- Projects targeting living conditions formally recognized structural inequities (defined by the authors as "either in terms of economic or political disparity or in terms of processes which result in the exclusion or marginalization of certain social groups," p. 119) more often than community-based projects, and far more often than institutional projects.

The results suggest that although there is common interest in the prevention of negative outcomes for youth and their families in Quebec and promotion of positive outcomes, the ways in which problems and targets for change are defined vary considerably depending on whether the project is run by an institution or is based in the community, and if in the community, whether it is oriented toward changing population characteristics or living conditions.

Source: Chamberland et al., 2000.

---

youth policy? What will happen if we continue to be without such a policy?

Why Is a Youth Development Policy Needed?

Youth constitute 100% of the future human and social capital on which our society depends. The

Youth policy Set of social policies that will enable the values of positive youth development to be translated into effective actions.

healthy rearing of children has often been identified as the essential function of the family (Bowman & Spanier, 1978; Lerner & Spanier, 1980). As such, although family policy is not the same as child or youth policy (e.g., family policies may involve aged adults living in retirement and without children or grandchildren), it is arguably the case that no policy issues are of greater concern to Canada's families than those that pertain to the health and welfare of their children.

Indeed, in Chapter 8 we stressed the view that society has charged the family with the primary responsibility for rearing children; we maintained that the family was "invented" as the institution that could best raise children in a safe, healthy, and effective manner (Johanson & Edey, 1981; Lerner, 1984; Lerner & Spanier, 1978, 1980) and as the setting best able to produce citizens committed to maintaining and perpetuating society. Thus, as we noted in the discussion of civil society in Chapter 5, the family is the key institution contributing to civil society (Lerner, 1984; Lerner & Spanier, 1978, 1980; Lerner, Sparks, & McCubbin, 1999), and—in this sense—*family policies represent societal principles or strategies for furthering civil society through the nurturance and socialization of children by families*. If families are effective institutions, children will become productive and committed members of society.

Despite the crucial connection between families, children, and civil society, all too many Canadians today still do not see the need for a comprehensive and integrated national policy pertinent to all of the nation's children. To the contrary, many associate youth problems with other people's children. Their stereotyped image of the at-risk or poor child is of a youth living in the inner city. Yet the probability that a Canadian child or adolescent will be poor—and thus experience the several "rotten outcomes" (Schorr, 1988) of poverty—is the same whether that youth lives in an urban or a rural setting (Statistics Canada, 2002), and the reality is that any person is only one misfortunate event away from living with low or no income. Poverty, then, is a major issue that needs to be addressed in the discussions of programs and policies pertinent to children and youth in Canada. Hertzman and colleagues (2003), at the University of British Columbia, University of Victoria, Simon Fraser University, and University of Northern British Columbia, use community mapping to examine the relationship between child development, community assets, and socioeconomic characteristics. Chandler and Lalande (1998) have described cultural continuity—community efforts to rehabilitate and vouchsafe their cultural continuity—in First Nations communities in British Columbia as a protective factor against youth suicide.

However, complicating the problems of poverty is the high incidence of risk behaviours among youth (Dryfoos, 1990, 1994). The breadth of these risks extends the problems of Canada's children and adolescents far beyond the bounds associated with the numbers of the nation's poor children.

These reasons alone make the development of a national youth policy pertinent to all of Canada's children and adolescents. However, there are additional

reasons. Just as we may be concerned with developing better policies for sustaining and/or enhancing agricultural, industrial, manufacturing, and business interests, we must not lose sight of the need to sustain the communities—and the people—involved in the production, distribution, *and* the consumption of the products of our economy.

Still, we often neglect the fact that problems of youth—problems that are similarly structured, similarly debilitating, and similarly destructive of Canada's human capital—diminish significantly the nation's present and future ability to sustain and enhance economic productivity. Clearly, then, both from the standpoint of the problems of children and adolescents and from the perspective of enlightened self-interest within Canada's industrial, agricultural, business, and consumer communities, policies need to be directed to enhancing youth development, to preventing the loss of human capital associated with the breadth and depth of the problems confronting children and youth.

Problems Resulting from the Absence of a National Youth Policy

Despite the magnitude of problems among Canada's youth, and of the contextual conditions that exacerbate these problems (e.g., changes in family structure and function and, most alarming, the growth of child poverty rates—described in Chapters 8 and 13, respectively), few major policy initiatives have been taken to seriously address these increasingly dire circumstances. Indeed, as Kitchen (1997, quoted in Armitage, 2003, p. 76) noted,

> Child poverty has become a mainstream issue. It has been put on the political agenda. Everybody is against child poverty. The idea of national (and provincial) child benefits has political appeal. It allows them (governments) to appear to be doing something to help poor children, to reform their welfare programs and receive federal money. To actually improve the material circumstances of poor children, the federal government would have to spend billions of dollars more than it is currently doing. It would require the same type of serious fiscal commitment that was given to fighting the deficit . . . The amount that the federal government actually has allocated is not nearly enough, even as a down payment to seriously begin the fight against child poverty.

Social and economic policies are clearly inter-related. Canada's economy is based on a capitalist system, with relatively few controls on the market. In this system, income distribution is by definition inequitable. Poverty is an inevitable outcome of this system. It is a chronic and increasing social problem linked to multiple negative outcomes for youth. Canadian income redistribution programs since World War II have been based on addressing threats to "family" income in capitalist industrial society (Armitage, 2003). As such, they have tended to focus on unemployment, family allowance, old age or disability, illness, and industrial injury (Armitage, 2003).

Although it is debatable whether these programs have had a positive influence on the financial status of some families, they clearly fail to emphasize and may not readily impact on youth development. That is, these policies do not focus on the enhancement of the capacities and the potential of Canada's children and adolescents. For instance, a policy or program that provides a job for an unemployed single mother, but results in the placement of her child in an inadequate after-school care environment for extended periods of time, may enhance the financial resources of the family. However, it may do so at the cost of placing the child in an unstimulating and possibly detrimental environment (Lerner et al., 1999).

If the current waste of human potential caused by the problems confronting contemporary Canadian youth is to be substantially reduced, we must pursue new policy options that focus on children and adolescents and that emphasize positive youth development and not just amelioration, remediation, and/or deterrence of problems. As argued by Pittman and Zeldin (1994, p. 53), "The reduction of problem behaviours among young people is a necessary policy goal. But it is not enough. We must be equally committed to articulating and nurturing those attributes that we wish adolescents to develop and demonstrate."

Possible Features of a National Youth Policy

ISSUES TO CONSIDER

• What are key features of a national youth policy?
• How can the media be involved in promoting the message of a national youth policy?

The Carnegie Council (1995, pp. 13–14) has elucidated key features of a national youth policy in the United States. In the *Great Transitions* report they offer five policy directions that will marshal the resources needed to enhance the lives of youth if followed. These are the recommendations: "(1) Reengage families with their adolescent children; (2) Create developmentally appropriate schools for adolescents; (3) Develop health promotion strategies for young adolescents; (4) Strengthen communities with young adolescents; and (5) Promote the constructive potential of the media."

This last recommendation is crucial. A chapter in a textbook may broaden understanding of the nature of youth problems and of effective means that exist to address them. But other ways of disseminating this information must also be found. Most people in Canada do not study adolescent development. Most get their information about youth development not from science or scholarship, but from their personal experience and the media. Canadians must be convinced that resources will not be wasted if invested in youth-serving programs. The media can help convey this story of hope and potential to all segments of society.

As described by Benson (1997), and reviewed in Chapter 5, assets must be marshalled to promote the competencies and potentials of youth and to develop and evaluate programs designed to promote these positive attributes. Policy must go beyond the two necessary but not sufficient goals of "meeting basic human needs [through ensuring] economic security, food, shelter, good and useful work, and safety" (Benson, 1997, p. xiii) and reducing or even eliminating "the risks and deficits that diminish or thwart the healthy development of children and adolescents. Guns, unsafe streets, predatory adults, abuse, family violence, exclusion, alcohol and other drugs, racism, and sexism are among the threats" (Benson, 1997, pp. xiii–xiv). Policy must add a third component—of assets—that is crucial for building a strong young person supported through positive relationships with his or her family and community. As Benson et al. (1998, p. 156) note,

> Ultimately, the most critical question is how communities can be supported to integrate and simultaneously pursue strength-building in three community infrastructures—economic, service delivery, and development. The goal of this integration is to develop a combination of policy, resources, and actions which will meet basic human needs, reduce threats to human development, provide humane and effective access to services, and promote healthy development.

Implementing Policy: The Potential of Community-Collaborative Programs

How might a system be developed to implement the policy objective of delivering these assets to youth in their communities? There are numerous answers to this question, but an obvious principle is to build on existing assets, such as the youth-serving organizations and programs that exist in virtually all communities in Canada.

Whether programs in a particular community are associated with national organizations or with the thousands of existing community-specific grassroots organizations, many scholars and advocates for youth stress the important role of these organizations in building a system to deliver assets that enhance the life chances of youth (cf. Dryfoos, 1990; National Research Council, 1993; Schorr, 1988). Advocates for the support and sustainability of youth-serving programs argue that policies must promote the financial health and broad acceptance of community-based youth organizations (Pittman & Zeldin, 1994). In so doing, policies support the socialization experiences and youth services provided by these organizations.

All across Canada there are multiple youth-serving organizations and agencies. Caputo (2000) attempted to determine what was happening in 30 Canadian communities regarding youth participation in order to find out about the most important concerns, how communities identify concerns of youth, how inclusive is the participation of youth from marginal or high-risk situations, and how best to involve youth in communities.

Through a series of telephone interviews and focus groups with key participants, municipal officials, representatives of youth-serving agencies, and police officers, Caputo (2000) found that youth were concerned about their futures and finding a job, society's negative image of them, and that they had nothing to do and nowhere to go. In many communities, youth did not feel their voices were heard and found that few systematic opportunities existed for identifying their concerns other than occasional surveys or forums. The term "participation" has different meanings to different people, but mainstream youth who want adults to listen to them do find a way. Reaching out-of-the-mainstream youth was more challenging. To involve out-of-the-mainstream youth in the community, participants reported that an approach needs to be community-based, deal with "real" issues, have agency support, and involve politicians. "Youth friendly" adults can make a positive contribution by mentoring youth to become community leaders.

How University Students May Collaborate with Youth Development Organizations

Organizations serving the interests of youth are open to being contacted in regard to accessing their resources. Akin to organizations like those that participated in Caputo's (2000) study, they are collaborative agencies.

Youth and their families can work with these organizations in numerous ways. One way is to contact local grassroots neighbourhood organizations or civic, provincial, or national groups. For instance, many cities have Boys' and Girls' Clubs as well as Big Brother/Big Sister and Planned Parenthood organizations. For example, one could direct inquiries about possible routes to collaboration with the Planned Parenthood Federation of Canada in Ottawa.

In addition, potential resources exist in university departments of family social sciences, psychology, sociology, social work, nursing, and education in institutions across the country. Exploring your campus may result in both new academic understanding and new resources for the youth of your community. You may become involved, for instance, in opportunities to integrate the information you are learning in classes (e.g., about adolescent development) with opportunities for **community-based learning** organized by your university (Kenny & Gallagher, 2000).

Community-based learning may take many forms. You may serve at various community-based youth-serving organizations, by volunteering at community hot lines that provide services to youth through telephone referrals (e.g., Dolan, 1995; Schondel et al., 1995), or by working at your local Boys' and Girls' Club offices. As a university student you may also be a mentor to a younger person (e.g., Grossman & Rhodes, 1999; Rhodes & Davis, 1996; Turner & Scherman, 1996). Mentoring is a significant way to promote positive youth development.

Promoting Positive Youth Development Through Mentoring **Mentoring** programs for youth involve a structured, one-to-one relationship or partnership that focuses on the needs of the mentored participant. A responsible mentoring program fosters caring and supportive relationships, encourages individuals to develop to their fullest potential, helps an individual develop his or her own vision for the future, and represents a strategy to develop active community partnerships.

The scholarship of Jean E. Rhodes and her colleagues provides considerable evidence that mentoring programs having these characteristics can effectively promote the positive development of youth. Among pregnant and parenting adolescents, the support of a natural mentor lowers depression and increases optimism, career activities, and beliefs about opportunity (Klaw & Rhodes, 1995; Rhodes, Ebert, & Fischer, 1992). Adolescent mothers with natural mentors have lower levels of depression and anxiety, are more satisfied with their support resources, and are more able to cope effectively with relationship problems (Rhodes, Contreras, & Mangelsdorf, 1994). Only 20% of urban adolescent girls with mentors continue to show sexual- and school-related risk behaviours (Rhodes & Davis, 1996). Urban youth involved in Big Brother/Big Sister mentor relationships for a year or longer show the largest number of improvements.

Mentoring appears to work best when it is extended for specific lengths of time, and some people profit more from mentoring than others. Among youth who are in mentoring relationships that terminate earlier, progressively fewer positive effects occur. Adolescents in relationships that terminate after a very short period of time show decrements in behaviour. Older adolescents, adolescents referred for having experienced sustained emotional, sexual, or physical abuse, married volunteers aged 26 to 30 years, and volunteers with low incomes are most likely to be in early terminating relationships (Grossman & Rhodes, 1999).

Mentoring One-on-one relationship that is structured and focuses on the needs of the person being mentored.

College and university students can make important contributions to the positive development of younger people.

Particular levels of mentoring seem most effective. Among 10- to 16-year-old youth involved in Big Brother/Big Sister programs, mentoring relationships that involve moderate levels of both support and structure are associated with improvements in parent and peer relationships, in personal development, and in academic performance (Langhout et al., 1999). The positive effects of mentoring relationships on academic performance are mediated primarily through improvements in the parent-child relationships and associated with reductions in unexcused absences and improvements in academic perceived competence (Rhodes, Grossman, & Resch, 1999).

Evidence indicates that mentoring programs can also be effective with youth in difficult family circumstances. Among foster care youth involved in Big Brother/Big Sister programs, mentoring relationships are associated with improved social skills, greater trust and comfort in social interactions, stable peer relationships, prosocial behaviour, and self-esteem (Rhodes, Haight, & Briggs, 1999). Jean Rhodes continues to study youth mentoring programs, and her ideas about her scholarship are presented in Meet the Researcher Box 14.3.

Conclusions

Given the evidence about the outcomes of positive youth development programs, it is reasonable to conclude that public policy must move from a focus on just building

MEET THE RESEARCHER   Box 14.3   Jean E. Rhodes

Risks and Rewards in Youth Mentoring

Jean E. Rhodes is director of Gender Studies in the Harvard University Graduate School of Education. She has written a book and over 20 chapters and articles on the topic of youth mentoring and served as a guest editor of the *American Journal of Community Psychology* special issue on mentoring.

Adolescents who develop into competent adults, despite the profound stress associated with urban poverty, often demonstrate an ability to locate a positive, nonparent role model. Anecdotal reports of mentors' protective qualities are corroborated by a growing body of literature that has underscored the positive influence of nonparent adults in the lives of adolescents. Despite the promising results of mentoring, as well as the recent growth in volunteer programs, many questions remain concerning the nature and influence of mentor relationships.

My research is designed to uncover the processes by which mentors promote resilience, the extent to which protective relationships can be arranged through mentoring interventions, and the conditions under which such interventions are most effective. In a series of investigations—supported by the William T. Grant Foundation, the U.S. National Institute of Child Health and Human Development, and the Spencer Foundation—my students and I have examined the role of both natural and assigned mentors in the lives of minority adolescent mothers. We have found, for example, that adolescents with natural mentors exhibit better vocational and educational outcomes and lower levels of alcohol consumption during pregnancy.

Unfortunately, families, schools, and communities have changed in ways that have dramatically reduced the availability of caring adults. To address the needs of adolescents who lack close attention from prosocial adults, volunteer mentoring programs have been increasingly advocated in such diverse areas as welfare reform, education, violence prevention, school-to-work transition, and national service. For the past several years, I have been working with colleagues to analyze longitudinal data collected from over 1000 urban American adolescents who participated in a national study of Big Brothers, Big Sisters. We have explored the predictors and effects of relationship duration and the mediators of the interventions' effects on adolescents' academic, emotional, and behavioural outcomes. In addition, we have empirically distinguished a range of mentor relationships and evaluated their influence on youth outcomes, tested the differential benefits of mentor relationships on foster versus nonfoster youth, and examined the role of youth characteristics on outcomes.

The findings that have emerged from these other studies have provided ample evidence of the extraordinary potential that exists within mentoring relationships. They have also exposed the rarely acknowledged risk for harm that unsuccessful relationships can render. It is true that one good relationship can transform a life, becoming the means by which youth connect with themselves, others, their schools, and their futures. Yet because a close relationship is at the heart of this intervention, a careless approach can do tremendous damage to a child's sense of self and faith in others. My strong contention—which is clearly supported by data—is that vulnerable children would be better left alone than paired with mentors who do not fully recognize and, in a sense, honour the responsibility they have been given. It is my hope that a deeper understanding of these important relationships will lead to interventions and policies that better address the needs of youth.

effective programs to also building cohesive and effective communities (Pittman & Zeldin, 1994). Hamburg (1992) suggests three policy initiatives that together would enhance the capacity of communities to (1) provide comprehensive and integrated services that (2) promote positive youth development through (3) the provision of effective programs delivered by a well-trained staff. Thus Hamburg (1992, p. 166) would:

First, use government mechanisms to provide funding to local communities in ways that encourage the provision of coherent, comprehensive services. This funding should provide incentives to encourage collaboration and should be adaptable to local circumstances.

Second, provide training programs to equip professional staff and managers with the necessary skills. Such programs would include training for collaboration among professionals in health, mental health, education, and social services, and would instill a respectful, sensitive attitude toward working with clients, patients, parents, and students from different backgrounds. Third, use widespread evaluation to determine what intervention is useful for whom, how funds are being spent, and whether the services are altogether useful.

A report by the U.S. National Research Council (1993) makes a similar argument, noting that building supportive communities for youth faced with the destruction of their life chances "will require a major commitment from governments and the private sector, including support for housing, transportation, economic development, and the social services required by poor and low-income residents" (p. 239).

Furthermore, Pittman and Zeldin (1994) emphasize that for youth development programs to attain
sustained successes—across the span of individual
lives and across multiple generations—issues of individual and economic diversity must be clearly and
directly confronted. Specifically, poverty and racism
must be a continued, core focus of social policy. We
must continue to be vigilant about the vicious cycle
of poverty among children and adolescents, about the
vast overrepresentation of minority youth among the
ranks of the poor, and about the greater probability
that minority youth will be involved in the several
problem behaviours affecting their generation.

The policy recommendations forwarded by
Pittman and Zeldin (1994), Hamburg (1992), Benson
(1997), and Lerner et al. (1999) stress the importance
of comprehensive and integrative actions linking youth,
families, programs, evaluation research, and policymakers. These actions involve both proximal community participation and the contributions of broader
segments of the public and private sectors, community-
based evaluations, diversity, and the promotion of positive development across the life span (Damon, 1997).

Adolescence is a double-edged sword. It is a period
in which myriad individual and social problems may
exist; yet the scientific evidence indicates that individual differences are prominent throughout adolescence,
and conditions exist or can be created to allow most
youth to pass through this period with few, if any, problems. Youth are very resilient (Wener & Smith, 1982),
and for most adolescents the period is or can be one
of quite favourable physical and mental health.

Most youth can successfully meet the challenges
of this transition period. They integrate the biological, cognitive, emotional, and social changes they
experience and can form a useful self-definition. A
sense of self allows most youth to make decisions and
commitments that result in adopting social roles that
keep society moving forward effectively into the
future. Parents, educators, and other caregivers can
be confident that if the social context is attuned to
the individuality and developmental changes of youth,
healthy and successful people will emerge from the
adolescent period. Policies and programs focused on
positive youth development can make this happen.

Summary

- Youth-serving programs are involved in *reducing* the presence of an emotional, behavioural,
or social problem, *preventing* such problems
from occurring, and/or *promoting* positive,
healthy behaviours among people.

- Three interrelated facets define the programs
aimed at the *promotion* of the key positive attributes of youth: (1) the conception that the
programs hold about the process of youth development, (2) the approach to programming associated with this conception, and (3) the specific
characteristics of the approach these programs
use. Programs that seek to promote positive
development tend to focus on the individual
and/or on the developmental system.

- Every program must in some way consider issues
of *effectiveness, scale,* and *sustainability.*

- Effectiveness exists if a program achieves what
it is intended to achieve; an effective program
produces the effects it is designed to create.

- Program evaluations are used to ascertain if
changes in participants are due to the program,
if programs are effective, and if programs attain

their goals. Evaluations try to *demonstrate* that
any changes youth experience are due to the
program itself. Evaluations also try to *improve*
the quality of the program as it is being
conducted. Evaluations also try to *empower* the
people participating in a program.

- Even if programs are known to be effective, they
may not be reaching all the youth for whom they
are appropriate, a problem of program *scale.*
Research needs to examine why some programs
fail to involve all eligible youth and how the
social system might be changed to enable the
program to be brought to scale.

- A sustained program is maintained over time. For
reasons typically related to funding, most programs
are not sustained over long periods of time.

- Studies using the "efficacy research" model try
to determine what is maximally effective under
"optimal" conditions, in regard to (1) preventing the onset of behavioural or emotional problems; (2) ameliorating the course of problems
after their onset; and (3) treating problems that
have reached clinical severity.

- Studies using the "outreach" model address this question: "What works that is also (1) palatable, (2) feasible, (3) durable, (4) affordable, and (5) sustainable in real-world settings?"
- To assist communities in developing effective community-university collaborations, greater attention has been paid to empowerment approaches to evaluation. Jacobs's five-tier model of evaluation provides a means for communities to develop stronger programs in regard to both the proving and improving dimensions of evaluation and to empowering program participants.
- Although it is both more humane and cost effective to prevent problems before they occur, the primary focus of programs should be on promoting positive development. Preventing a problem from occurring does not guarantee that youth are being provided with the assets needed for positive development.
- Youth policies must be created that enable the values about positive youth development to be translated into effective actions.

- Existing assets such as the youth-serving organizations and programs that exist in virtually all Canadian communities are good building blocks for positive youth development programs.
- Community-based learning involves combining classroom work and information with opportunities for participation in community programs.
- A responsible mentoring program fosters caring and supportive relationships, encourages individuals to develop to their fullest potential, helps an individual to develop his or her own vision for the future, and represents a strategy to develop active community partnerships. Mentoring appears to work best when it is extended for specific lengths of time, and some people get more benefits from mentoring than do others.
- Hamburg suggested policy initiatives that can enhance the capacity of communities to provide comprehensive and integrated services, which promote positive youth development.

Discussion Topics

1. Were you ever involved in a youth-serving organization and/or are there such programs in your community you are familiar with? What do you believe is the mission or goal of the organization(s) in terms of serving youth? Is the mission focused more on internalizing problems, externalizing problems, equally focused on both, or focused mainly on promoting positive attributes?
2. If you were to conduct your own outcome evaluation on the program discussed in number 1, how effective would you say it is in meeting its mission? If you were to conduct your own formative evaluation, how might you improve on the efforts of this organization in how it strives to promote the 5 C's of positive youth development?
3. What steps would you take in your evaluations to determine if a program is operating at an appropriate scale? For example, if you were evaluating a program, run by only two staff members, designed to offer parenting skills to teen mothers, what would be an appropriate number of teens to work with to promote their parenting skills effectively? What issues must you consider in determining this scale?

4. Look back at Francine Jacobs's five-tier model. Why is such an empowerment evaluation necessary for the long-term sustainability of programs?
5. What might be some arguments for approaching youth problems from a prevention perspective or from a promotion perspective? In some cases, it is difficult to know whether financial support should be directed toward immediate concerns or if the money would be better spent on long-term asset promotion. What would you do if you were in a position to decide where to direct funding in countries that have extremely high rates of disease such as AIDS and whose children are infected and dying at alarming rates?
6. Knowing that time spent in a youth-serving program is the asset that has the most positive influence on youth behaviour, what are some ways your community could attract youth to participate in such programs?
7. Youth face multiple and interrelated challenges. To be successful in their attempts to promote positive youth development, community-based programs must work together, coordinating their aims to meet both the individual and contextual needs of youth.

Brainstorm some ideas about how different service organizations within your community could volunteer time and support to take responsibility for developing assets in its youth.

8. Why is a national youth policy needed? Why has it been so difficult to get such a policy accepted? How have children been viewed historically in Canada? Does society see them as assets to support and nurture? Do you believe that the country has begun the 21st century ready and willing to make changes in public policy that are more supportive of Canada's children and their future? Why or why not?

9. How might racism and/or classism affect the development of community-based service organizations, specifically the funding of these organizations? What steps can be taken to combat such destructive mindsets?

10. What organizations are available to the students at your school and how do they support the promotion of assets? What other services are needed? How might departments collaborate to ensure that the needs of all students are addressed?

11. How might mentoring a student from a nearby community affect your life? What do you think you might be able to offer this young person?

Key Terms

best practice, p. 323
"efficacy research," p. 320
empowerment evaluation, p. 317
evaluations, p. 316
formative evaluation, p. 317
intervention program, p. 314
mentoring, p. 330

outcome or summative
    evaluation, p. 317
outreach research, p. 320
process evaluation, p. 317
program effectiveness, p. 316
program scale, p. 318
program sustainability, p. 318

protective factors, p. 322
public policy, p. 325
resilience, p. 322
triangulation, p. 317
youth policy, p. 326

Beyond Adolescence: Launching the Young Adult Years

It seemed to have all happened too quickly. Mrs. Ismail felt like it had been just a short while ago that she and her husband had taken the 150-kilometre trip from their home to Andrea's university dorm. They had unpacked the car, gone to an orientation for parents of new students, had a terrific dinner together, and then made the 90-minute trip back home.

The tears that filled Mrs. Ismail's eyes that evening, as Andrea waved goodbye from the front steps of her dormitory, were diminished then by the recognition that in a few weeks she and her husband would return for Parents' Weekend and then, only a few weeks later, Andrea would be home for Thanksgiving, and maybe Remembrance Day. And after these holidays the long Christmas break would quickly follow. "It's as if she is going to summer camp," Mrs. Ismail recalled thinking.

But now, as she and her husband sat in the warm May sun, listened to the recessional music, and watched her daughter and the other graduates file out of convocation hall, she knew that things would be different.

"Mom, I've got the job! I've got the job!" Andrea had exclaimed as she had hung up the phone a week ago. "They want me to start right after graduation. I can't believe it. I'm so excited!"

Mrs. Ismail was proud of her daughter. And happy for her. But this job was 1200 kilometres away. This would change everything. No more quick trips to campus or home. No more weekends and term breaks spent together. Now, with her daughter beginning her career, Mrs. Ismail knew that their time together would be measured in days per year, not weeks or months.

Mr. and Mrs. Ismail came out of convocation hall onto the sidewalk. After a moment they saw Andrea standing among several friends. Her graduation gown was folded and draped over her arm; her cap was in her hand. It seemed symbolic to Mrs. Ismail. Andrea had taken off the mantle of being a student. She was now a young adult with her own career and an independent life about to begin. Mrs. Ismail rushed through the crowd to congratulate the young woman who stood before her and also to kiss goodbye the little girl she loved so much.

Learning Objectives

1. To understand why choice and commitment constitute the key developmental tasks of young adulthood.
2. To understand the theoretical models of Erik Erikson and of Daniel Levinson about young adult development.
3. To understand the concept of being "off time" in achieving the tasks of young adulthood.
4. To understand why young adulthood may be a safe haven for testing out possible adult roles and an opportunity to get back on a positive developmental track.
5. To understand the childhood and adolescent antecedents and the consequences for adulthood of getting back on track during young adulthood.
6. To understand the ways in which the family influences the young person's development during and after the transition to young adulthood.
7. To recognize the strong connection between school and work.
8. To learn why, in Stephen F. Hamilton's studies of the transition from school to work, the concepts of transparency and permeability describe the link between school and work.
9. To recognize why a national apprenticeship system is needed in Canada to promote positive transitions from school to work.
10. To understand the essential characteristics of a youth apprenticeship system.
11. To recognize the importance for civil society of enhancing the school-to-work transition for all youth within a nation.

Often, as we recount our lives to ourselves and others, meaningful events or entire periods may seem to have moved by quite fast. Perhaps, metaphorically, we can view the life course as a train moving rapidly across the tracks of time and space. If so, then each period of life, each stop along the tracks, may be regarded as a "life station" (Cohler & Musick, 1996, p. 204). In the stop labelled "Young Adulthood" we may ask what is present when we get off at this station. What fills the world of the young adult?

Lerner and Hultsch (1983) described young adulthood as a time of serious choice and relatively permanent commitment. Individuals make their first major (that is, potentially enduring) selections related to marriage, children, occupation, and lifestyle.

Other scientists agree with these descriptions. They see young adulthood as a time when "many individuals try out their first adult life structures by committing to their first careers. Educational and occupational decisions, at this juncture, represent major developmental tasks" (Bell et al., 1996, p. 346). Indeed, pursuing postsecondary education and initiating a career are key challenges for the young adult. Canadian research suggests that young adults who have the most detailed expectations (Pancer, Hunsberger, Pratt, & Alisat, 2000), and who have higher success motivation (Côté & Levine, 2000) and willingness to enter into reciprocal relationships with people in their learning environment (Côté & Levine, 1997), are the most successful in making the transition to postsecondary studies. Another challenge is attaining autonomy from one's family while, at the same time, retaining sufficient connection with parents so as to maintain their continued support (Bell et al., 1996). In a recent release of data from the National Longitudinal Survey of Children and Youth, it was reported that 95% of Canadian 16- and 17-year-olds feel optimistic about their future (Statistics Canada, 2003a). Canadian university students (Bu & McKeen, 2000) are also optimistic about their ability to successfully navigate this transition both globally as well as specifically in terms of work and family life.

Although they agree that the transition from the end of adolescence to the beginning of adulthood is a time of choice and commitment, several scholars have presented theories of development that emphasize that the commitments of young adults serve both individual and societal ends.

Theories of the Young Adult Period

ISSUES TO CONSIDER
- Why is young adulthood a period of choice and commitment?
- What are the tasks of young adulthood envisioned by Erikson?
- What are the tasks of young adulthood envisioned by Levinson?

Several theorists supplement the descriptions of the young adult period by stressing that the choices made by individuals at this time of life contribute to both the quality of the individual life span and to the maintenance and perpetuation of society. For instance, Erik H. Erikson (1959, 1968; see also Chapter 6) believed that young adulthood is a period within which the individual must make commitments that ensure the institutions of society (e.g., the family, the economy, the structure of civil society) will continue into the future. For example, Erikson (1968) discusses the importance for youth within this portion of life to form an intimate relationship with another person so a stable family may be formed and so that, as a consequence, the next generation of children—of society's citizens—will be reared in an institutional context reflecting and conveying the values and mores of the culture.

The Canadian sociologist James Côté (2002) argues that the amount of investment youth have in their adult identities affects how successfully they make the transition to adulthood. This identity capital affects timing and satisfaction of different paths to adulthood.

Other theories of young adulthood exist as well. A key one has been proposed by Levinson (1978).

Levinson's Theory of the Tasks of Young Adulthood

An interesting theory of young adulthood was proposed a quarter century ago by Daniel Levinson (1978). Although Levinson's theory and the research he conducted in relation to it were focused on the nature of young adulthood among men, to the extent the theory is useful it can also apply to women. Nevertheless, in the years since Levinson (1978) proposed his theory, no definitive research pertinent to the relation of his ideas to young adult women has been presented.

Levinson believed that males must accomplish four tasks during young adulthood: (1) forming a dream, (2) finding an occupation, (3) establishing a relationship with a mentor, and (4) establishing love relationships, marriage, and a family. To Levinson, the dream is a vague sense of the self in an adult world. The dream can take on a dramatic form, for example, the great scientist, the world-acclaimed artist, or the record-setting professional athlete. In turn, the dream can be more modest, for example, the skilled craftsman, the effective father, or the respected community member (Lerner & Hultsch, 1983).

The task of the young man is to define the dream and to find ways to live it out. In many cases, the realization of the dream involves identifying an occupation. This occupation will define the set of activities the young adult will pursue to attain the dream.

Levinson (1978) argues that forming a relationship with a mentor is critical in actualizing the dream and, perhaps especially, to attaining it in the context of an occupational choice. The **mentor** serves as a teacher, guide, or counsellor to the young adult. The mentor is usually several years older than the young adult and often in the work setting (e.g., a senior colleague). However, neighbours, friends, or relatives may play this role. The mentor enables the young adult to see how all the tasks of this period can be woven together to realize the life dream and to do so in a manner that allows integration with others (through love, marriage, and family).

The transition to the world of work involves such tasks as preparing a résumé, completing applications for employment, and going to job interviews.

Mentor Teacher, guide, or counsellor to another person. The mentor is usually several years older than the person he or she mentors.

The Timing of the Tasks of Young Adulthood

ISSUE TO CONSIDER

● What are the implications of being "off time" in accomplishing the tasks of young adulthood?

Whether one embraces the theory of Levinson (1978) or of Erikson (1968), or the general descriptions of the period provided by Lerner and Hultsch (1983), Cohler and Musick (1996), or Bell et al. (1996), specific socially defined tasks involving choice and commitment clearly define the life station of young adulthood. But the time allotted in life for the completion of these tasks is not infinite (Cohler & Musick, 1996). Spending one's 20s looking for an occupation may be accepted by modern, industrialized society. However, if one is still not committed during one's 30s or, certainly, during one's 40s, not only will there be a lack of societal acceptance, but social approbation will almost certainly follow.

Thus the train leaves the life station after some period of time or, at the least, it is expected to move on (Cohler & Musick, 1996). In other words, young adulthood is a socially defined life period. Although this definition takes into account biology (e.g., young adulthood and, for women, especially the 20s to 30s, which is associated with the task of reproduction), society maintains conceptions of how much time is appropriate to devote to accomplishing the tasks associated with the young adult period (Cohler & Musick, 1996; Hagestad & Neugarten, 1985; Neugarten & Moore, 1968).

Ideas about what is appropriate change over time. Two changes that are significant in relation to the transition to adulthood are pregnancy and leaving home. Birth rates among 15- to 19-year-olds have steadily decreased from the 1960s into the 1990s (58.2/1000 in 1961 to 20/1000 in 1998) (Statistics Canada, 2002). Abortion rates in the late 1980s to 1990s have increased significantly (15.7/1000 in 1987 to 20.9/1000 in 1998) (Statistics Canada, 2002). The abortion rate is now slightly higher than the birth rate for young women in Canada.

It is no longer unusual for young adults to live with their parents. In 2001, about 40% of young Canadian adults between the ages of 20 and 29 lived with their parents, representing an increase from the 27% of those in the same age group living with their parents in 1981 (Statistics Canada, 2003b). This increase in the number of Canadians in their 20s

Many youth gain knowledge of the adult world through receiving mentoring from an older adult.

Challenges During the Transition of Young Adulthood: Contemporary Dimensions

ISSUES TO CONSIDER

- In contemporary society, what is the relation between attaining physical maturity and adultlike independence?
- In what ways is college or university a safe haven for young adult development?

living with parents has been associated with education (increasing enrollment in postsecondary studies), labour markets (poor job prospects during recessions in the 1980s and 1990s), and marriage status (young adults are remaining unmarried longer) (Boyd & Norris, 1999). Quebec youth who leave home during their 20s and early 30s do so, most often, to lead their own life (49%), further their studies (34%), or for work (11%); the other 6% leave as a result of relationship or financial problems with their parents (Molgat, 2002).

It appears that the source of normative prescriptions about the appropriate age to "leave the nest" lies outside of the family (Veevers, Gee, & Wister, 1996). Life changes taking place too early—or too late for that matter (e.g., leaving a parent's home for the first time at the age of 40)—are regarded as problems by society. Indeed, events taking place too early (e.g., becoming a widow in young adulthood) have greater negative impacts than those taking place too late (Cohler & Musick, 1996). This is perhaps because being early off time is not only unexpected, but there is typically no preparation for this occurrence and, by definition, few people of one's age share this situation (Cohler & Musick, 1996).

In any case, not only is being off time in regard to the life tasks of young adulthood a problem as seen by society, but in addition, the person experiences it as a problem. Being off time diminishes feelings of psychological well-being and morale (Cohler & Musick, 1996).

As evidenced by the ideas just described regarding young adulthood, this period of life is a significant one for the individual and for society, which requires competent and committed young people to maintain and perpetuate its institutions. The challenges for the person, then, are to make choices about aspirations, careers, and relationships that serve both individual and societal needs, and to do so within the temporal boundaries imposed by his or her culture. Vondracek and Skorikov (1997) found that youth in their sample of 642 Grade 7 to 12 students showed consistency between their leisure, school, and work activities.

However, the transition from late adolescence to young adulthood may be especially problematic for contemporary young people. In modern society, there is an "increasing delay between the acquisition of physical maturity and the assumption of adult responsibilities" (Sherrod, Haggerty, & Featherman, 1993, p. 218). This gap creates a change in the period of dependency of youth on adults. Moreover, modern society is marked by a diversity of developmental paths (e.g., involving different career possibilities, some of which—such as software designer, e-commerce specialist, or manufacturer of digital television equipment—did not exist in earlier historical periods), and this variation makes achieving adult independence more complicated. Evidence of the varied paths chosen by Canadian young adults is apparent in recent studies about the career decision making of rural adolescent girls facing the conflicting values relating to work and family (Shepard & Marshall, 2000), experiences of adolescent females in science, engineering, and technology career paths (Ciccocioppo, Stewin, Madill, Montgomerie, Tovell, Armour, & Fitzimmons, 2002), and culturally appropriate career counselling approaches with First Nations youth (Neumann, McCormick, Amundson, & McLean, 2000).

Different adult responsibilities (completion of career training, establishing an intimate adult relationship, establishing a home, paying off educational loans) are increasingly segmented and separated across chronological periods (Sherrod, Haggerty, & Featherman, 1993). Further complicating the transition to young adulthood is the relative lack of funding, public support, or public policies and programs facilitating the transition to adulthood for the half of the adolescent population that moves directly from secondary school to full-time work, that is, the half of the population of youth that does not go on to university or college from high school (Sherrod et al., 1993). University gives youth a slower transition to adulthood; that is, it provides a

"safe haven to experiment with a variety of adult behaviors, values, and life styles; the developmental opportunities provided by this privilege are not well explored, but half of the population not attending university may be missing more than continued academic achievement" (Sherrod et al., 1993, p. 219). This luxury of a slow transition is limited to Western cultures.

Julian Tanner's work at the University of Toronto is concerned with understanding the transition to adulthood for youth who were at risk for negative developmental outcomes (see Meet the Researcher Box 15.1).

MEET THE RESEARCHER   Box 15.1   Julian Tanner

Researching Transitions

Inspired by musings about my own early life experiences, I have been involved with several projects on adolescent issues at various times in my research career. Most of these deal with school to work transitions and the factors and experiences that make them more or less difficult and problematic.

One question that parents often worry about is the effect of rebellion and misbehaviour in adolescence upon adult work prospects. Is getting into trouble at school or with the law when young something that is only going to make it harder to find work once students have left school? Or, instead, do employers pay no attention to these incidents, writing them off as youthful indiscretion, or as the "sowing of wild oats"? I also had a more personal reason for posing these questions. More and more, I began ruminating about the boys I was at school with in England during the 1960s: What happened to them? Did the classroom rebels become antisocial or low-achieving adults; or did they instead become solid and respectable citizens?

The availability of longitudinal data from a large, ongoing U.S.-based survey permitted a systematic examination of these and related questions. With collaborators Scot Davies and Bill O'Grady, I was able to explore the long-term effects of deviance in adolescence upon occupational outcomes in early adulthood. We found that those who reported deviant activity (of any kind) in their youth (when they were between ages 14 and 17) were, 12 years later when they were between ages 25 and 30, more likely

to attain poorer paying, lower status jobs than their peers who had refrained from delinquent activity or contact with the police when they were younger. We were thus able to confirm that for both males and females, there is a long-term negative dividend attached to teenage deviance.

One particular segment of the adolescent population who routinely encounter problematic transitions are high school dropouts. They are commonly perceived as being especially prone to crime and delinquency, and face particularly stringent difficulties in the labour market. In the absence of Canadian research on this topic, I, along with Tim Hartnagel and Harvey Krahn, undertook a case study of the dropout problem in Edmonton, Alberta. We found, on the basis of our interviews with 168 male and female dropouts, that many of our young respondents did not always conform very easily to prevailing stereotypes: While many of them had not liked school very much, and while finding work without a high school diploma was difficult, they had not given up on either the educational system or the labour market. In particular, many of them regretted their decision to quit school and had plans to rectify their mistake. We called them reluctant rebels.

Another issue relating to adolescent development, particularly school-work transitions, that I have researched is the impact of part-time jobs. In terms of adolescent well-being, part-time jobs have been viewed in very different ways. On the one hand, some people regard them as offering an important preparation for adult work life,

Julian Tanner is a professor of sociology at the University of Toronto. He received his undergraduate education in England at what is now called the University of East London, and the University of Leicester School of Education. After a short stint as a teacher in a comprehensive school near Birmingham, he came to Canada, where he did his graduate training at the University of Alberta. He has been at the University of Toronto since 1985.

providing young people with important job skills, instilling a respect for the work ethic, and teaching them "the value of a buck." On the other hand, part-time jobs have been linked to less positive outcomes, such as lower levels of academic achievement and increased incidents of crime and deviance. Focusing on the latter issue, Harvey Krahn and I, using survey information collected from high school students in Edmonton, Toronto, and Sudbury, found that those students who held part-time jobs were more likely to drink alcohol and use other drugs than were their peers who did not work. However, we found no relationship between jobs and other, more serious, kinds of deviant activity.

Finally, I am currently involved in a large project on crime and victimization among both high school students and street youth in Toronto, looking at the role that encounters with crime play in adolescent development.

The Transition to Young Adulthood as a Means to Reestablish a Healthy Developmental Path

ISSUES TO CONSIDER

- How may young adulthood offer opportunities for young people to get back on track after high school?
- What problems may emerge for the young adult as he or she explores life options?

The presence of a safe haven may be quite useful for adolescents making the transition to young adulthood. If there were problems of personal adjustment and/or of social relationships in high school, the transition to adulthood might provide an opportunity to get back on track (Sherrod et al., 1993).

For example, in a study of 920 students randomly selected from three public schools in the Boston, Massachusetts, area, relations with parents improved across the transition to adulthood, and these enhanced relations were associated with lower depressed mood and less delinquency among the youth (Aseltine & Gore, 1993). In addition, and also suggestive of using the transition to adulthood to get back on a healthy developmental track, among high school graduates prior mental health and behaviour problems were not substantially related to posttransition mental and behaviour functioning. This finding suggests that graduation from high school may have given youth the chance to break away from the troubles of their past (Aseltine & Gore, 1993). However, not all explorations of possible life tracks during the transition to young adulthood might be beneficial to youth. For instance, the nature of personal and social exploration of the world was investigated among 198 youth making the transition to young adulthood. Youth who were in the foreclosure identity status category (see Chapter 6) were not open to new experiences (Clancy & Dollinger, 1993). Youth who were in the moratorium identity status category spent more of their time experimenting with negative identities than exploring positive identities (Clancy & Dollinger, 1993). In a study by Vondracek and colleagues (Vondracek, Schulenberg, Skorikov, & Gillespie, et al., 1995), it was found among 407 Grade 7 to 12 students that identity achievers were different from all their peers in their relative lack of career indecision.

But the presence of developmental problems, even chronic ones, need not preclude achieving a successful transition to young adulthood. A study using a nationally representative sample of 10 485

Canadian individuals who participated in the National Longitudinal Study of Youth (NLSY) provides a dramatic illustration of this point (Gortmaker et al., 1993). Of these youth, 1.9% were identified as having a chronic physical health condition between the ages of 14 and 21 years. These conditions involved such disorders as asthma, anomalies of the spine, diabetes mellitus, rheumatoid arthritis, epilepsy, cerebral palsy, scoliosis, congenital heart anomalies, eye, lower limb, or foot anomalies, muscular dystrophy, and sickle cell anemia. Although youth who had very severe chronic health conditions had substantial limitations in their transitions to adulthood, such severely debilitating conditions were rare (Gortmaker et al., 1993). The great majority of chronically physically challenged youth made successful transitions to adulthood (Gortmaker et al., 1993). Canadian researchers Magill-Evans, Darrah, Pain, Adkins, and Kratochvill (2001) have noted that similarities in the overall levels of family functioning, life satisfaction, and perceived social support between families with adolescents or young adults who have disabilities and those who do not may explain why these youth are functioning well; a supportive family environment for youth with and without disabilities promotes a successful transition to adulthood.

Developmental Antecedents and Consequences of Behaviour During the Transition to Young Adulthood

ISSUES TO CONSIDER

- What features of childhood and adolescent development may influence young adult development?
- How may young adult development influence later life?

Getting back on track during the transition to young adulthood may be influenced by events in earlier developmental periods, that is, by *antecedents* of the transition. In turn, the degree to which the person functions well during the transition to young adulthood has consequences for behaviour and development in later life.

In regard to the antecedents of behaviour during the transition to young adulthood, in a 20-year follow-up of the children of about 250 teenage mothers, the bases of success in completing high school and in pursuing education beyond high school were explored (Brooks-Gunn, Gus, & Furstenberg, 1993). Among the participants in the study, 37% had dropped out of high school, 46% had completed high

Youth with diverse abilities and backgrounds can make a successful transition to the world of work and young adulthood.

school, and 17% had gone on to postsecondary education (Brooks-Gunn et al., 1993). Completion of high school was associated with the number of years the father was present in the life of the girl, high maternal educational aspirations in the child's first year of life, being prepared for school, and not repeating a grade in elementary school (Brooks-Gunn et al., 1993). In turn, continuing education beyond high school was related to fewer years on government assistance, high cognitive ability in preschool, attending a preschool, and no grade failures in elementary school (Brooks-Gunn et al., 1993).

In turn, in regard to the consequences of behaviour during the transition of young adulthood on functioning in later life, in a study of about 4700 men and women from their adolescence through their young adulthood, failure to complete high school was associated with psychological dysfunction in young adulthood (Kaplan, Damphousse, & Kaplan, 1996). Similarly, in a longitudinal study of about 2000 young adults in Norway (Hammer, 1996), unemployment during the transition to adulthood was related to a greater tendency to pursue gender-typical adult roles (see Chapter 7). For instance, young women who were unemployed during the transition had a higher probability than other women of staying at home with children (Hammer, 1996).

In addition to behaviours associated with high school completion and employment during the transition, behaviours associated with interpersonal relationships during this period can have later-life influences. For example, in Canada, cohabitation before marriage appears to delay the timing of first marriage by about 26% for women and 19% for men (Zheng, 1999). It may also be linked to some later-life outcomes, which may or may not be related: divorce and problems with alcohol. Canadian couples who cohabitate before marriage have a higher divorce rate than couples who do not (Wu & Balakrishnan, 1995). In a longitudinal study, unmarried young adults were assessed when they were 18, 21, or 24 years of age and then retested 7 years later, when they were 25, 28, or 31 years old, respectively (Horwitz & White, 1998). It was found that cohabitation during the first assessment period was not related to depression at the time of the second assessment (Horwitz & White, 1998). However, men who had cohabited during the first assessment reported more alcohol problems than men who were single or married at the time; similarly, women who had cohabited reported more alcohol problems than women who were married during the first assessment (Horwitz & White, 1998).

Having more complex expectations of parenthood before the birth of a first child seems to be associated with better adjustment to life with a newborn (e.g., as found in a sample of women in the Waterloo region of Ontario; Pancer, Pratt, Hunsberger, & Gallant, 2000). However, having children at all during the transition to adulthood is associated with having family-related goals (Salmela-Aro & Nurmi, 1997). The presence of these goals is related to both additional transitions in the family (e.g., having additional children) and feelings of well-being (Salmela-Aro & Nurmi, 1997).

Family Influences on the Success of the Transition to Young Adulthood

ISSUES TO CONSIDER

- How may the family promote positive development during young adulthood?
- How may the family have a detrimental influence?

As is true for other facets of youth development, the definition and function of their families matter to youth (Marshall, 2001) and have a major influence on the nature of the transition to young adulthood and, as well, on behaviour later in adult life. In their comparative study of family relationships described by a total of 2587 university students in 16 different countries, Georgas and colleagues (2001) found that family structure, that is, who one lives with, is less relevant than function, or the connection young adults have to others in their families. They also found that compared to their peers in other countries, Canadian young adults were in the middle of the pack on emotional distance to different relatives, but that they lived farther away from and had less contact with their grandparents, uncles/aunts, and cousins than young adults in other countries (Georgas et al., 2001).

In a longitudinal study of the bases of the pursuit of gender-atypical careers among 235 Finnish women, a nonagricultural vocational background of grandparents was related to a higher educational level among parents, which, in turn, was associated with both greater high school academic success and the attainment of gender-atypical careers (Nummenmaa & Nummenmaa, 1997).

Similarly, in a longitudinal study of about 80 two-parent families, educational attainment and healthy ego development in young adulthood were related to mothers and fathers behaving in ways that both promoted autonomy in their adolescents and maintained their relatedness to the family (Best, Hauser, & Allen, 1997). Moreover, youth who come from relatively small, intact, middle-class families, in which parents maintain the expectation for success of their children, attain more education and higher prestige jobs in young adulthood than do peers from other types of families (Bell et al., 1996). In addition, parents who encourage their children to pursue education beyond high school, and who encourage both the autonomy of their young adult children and their continuing relationship with them, are more likely to have youth who complete high school and who have better educational attainment and higher occupational prestige in young adulthood (Bell et al., 1996).

Other studies confirm that individuals who, as adolescents, had parents who granted autonomy to them are, as young adults, more psychologically healthy, for example, in regard to feelings of control and adjustment (Mayseless & Hai, 1998). Moreover, in such families, relationships between young adults and their parents tend to become more positive over time (Mayseless & Hai, 1998). Indeed, as young adults make transitions to marriage, to full-time employment, and even to cohabitation (but not to parenthood), relationships with parents become closer, more supportive, and less conflicted (Aquilino, 1997).

In turn, family conflict or poor parenting practices during the late adolescent period are often related to both problematic parent-child relations and to negative behavioural or emotional outcomes in young adulthood. For example, in a study of about 2600 men and about 4100 women from 39 countries on 6 continents, feelings of well-being among young adults were lower in families that had been characterized by marital conflict (Gohm et al., 1998).

Moreover, young adults do not generally receive help from parents involved in low-quality marriages (Amato, Rezac, & Booth, 1995); in addition, divorce lowers help between fathers and young adults but not between mothers and young adults. Similarly, low maternal communication and problem-solving ability, and high maternal depression, in adolescence are linked to delinquency during the transition to young adulthood (Klein et al., 1997). In turn, high levels of maternal problem-solving skill and the absence of maternal depression were linked to lower rates of delinquency during this transition (Klein et al., 1997).

Conclusions About the Challenges of the Young Adult Transition

The young adult transition challenges the young person to keep his or her train—the course of his development—on a healthy path or, if it is off course, the period represents an opportunity to find a healthy track. The person leaving the period of adolescence and entering young adulthood must, then, find a way to exit the world of adolescence—a world defined in large measure by the culture of high school (see Chapter 12)—and enter the realm of adults—a context defined in the main by commitment to work and career. In short, the transition to young adulthood is, in essence, a transition from school to work.

Accordingly, in trying to understand young adult life, and to take actions to enhance behaviour and development during this period, it is crucial to focus attention on the nature of the connections between school and work. Applications Box 15.1 presents several programs that have been developed around the world to improve the chance that diverse youth will have positive and productive school-to-work connections across the young adult transitional period. In turn, in the next section of this chapter we discuss scholarship that has been central in helping researchers and practitioners conceptualize, study, and improve the school-to-work connection.

Enhancing the School-to-Work Connection Across the Transition of Young Adulthood

The Serowe Brigades
Serowe, Botswana

When the Serowe Brigades began in 1965, only 65% of Botswana's children attended primary school, with less than 10% receiving a secondary education. Now expanded throughout Botswana, the Brigades were created to provide the country's youth with practical education based on self-reliance. Although Botswana has experienced numerous political and economic changes since the 1960s, the Brigades continue to provide youth, ages 12 and older, with hands-on training as apprentices in more than 20 technical trades. As a result of their training, Brigade members attain marketable skills that are critical for acquiring jobs. The work of the Brigades benefits not only young people but the community as well, providing essential services such as construction and production of household goods. The Brigades are a highly effective and socially relevant alternative to formal education in Botswana. Indeed, participants are more likely to find work after graduation than graduates of formal schooling. As of 1999, 39 registered Brigades were training more than 3000 youth annually.

Industrial Technician Program (ITP)
Cebu City, Philippines

The Industrial Technician Program (ITP) uniquely integrates technical training and human development. It not only addresses the Philippines's need for unemployment reduction and more competent technicians, but it also provides future workers with a spiritual education that imbues them with professionalism and a social-oriented spirit. ITP was established by the Center for Industrial Technology and Enterprise for poor young men, ages 16 to 25, living in Cebu City. Although they have the ability to attain advanced education, these youth cannot afford it. Through a scholarship fund, they are able to complete a three-year program that integrates technical training in electrical, electronic, and mechanical technologies with cultural education. In addition to traditional classroom lectures, students participate in laboratory sessions, workshops, and an internship. Ultimately, the program produces middle level employees who are well trained and committed to their families, society, and exemplary work performance. In 1995, 83 of the first 97 participants graduated; all obtained jobs in well-established companies.

Programa Formación Professional (Professional Training Program)
Montevideo, Uruguay

All children in Uruguay have the advantage of a free elementary education, but one-third of them drop out before completing Grade 6. Also, the quality of education varies based on the economic strength of the community. Thus most young people find themselves ill equipped to enter the work world. The Programa Formación Professional (Professional Training Program) was founded to better train youth for the work force. Established in 1989, the program works with a wide range of related public and private institutions and serves about 500 youth annually, most of whom are early school leavers between the ages of 14 and 20. Participants attend classes and workshops to develop their skills in a chosen trade such as cooking, gardening, textile machinery, or electrical work. Complementing this training are sessions that strengthen students' personal development in areas such as drug prevention, sex education, and family relations. After they complete the program, students are assisted in their search for work and follow-up occurs for six months thereafter. Success, when measured by the number of youth employed, varies from year to year depending on the job market. In 1997, 40% of graduates found jobs. Additional studies show that youth have a better understanding of the society in which they live and a greater ability to face the challenges of daily life.

Jobs for America's Graduates (JAG)
Alexandria, Virginia

In the United States, 25% of all students are expected to drop out before completing high school; in some urban areas, this figure soars as high as 50%. Since its inception in 1980, Jobs for America's Graduates (JAG) has achieved extraordinary success in keeping at-risk and disadvantaged youth in school through graduation (or receipt of a General Educational Development diploma) and assisting them with their transition into the workplace and/or to a postsecondary education. The program seeks to help young people secure work that will lead to a career with or without a postsecondary education. JAG uses a comprehensive approach combining early school leaving prevention and recovery activities with school-to-career transition activities. Trained job specialists work one on one with students, serving as mentors and helping youth overcome personal, academic, and economic barriers to success. JAG is the largest, most consistently applied model of school-to-career transition for at-risk youth in the United States. It has graduated over 90% of program participants from high school and successfully placed over 80% in jobs, the military, postsecondary training, or a combination of all three. The program annually serves more than 65 000 young people in 1100 high schools in 27 states. JAG's National Data Management System captures data regarding students served, services delivered, and outcomes achieved. JAG has also been replicated in the United Kingdom.

Canada World Youth
Montreal, Quebec

The goal of Canada World Youth (CWY) is to provide young people from Canada and

>

around the world with the opportunity to participate in international educational programs. Participants develop their language and intercultural skills, and learn about community as well as international development. Canada World Youth was created in 1971 and has more than 25 years of experience in coordinating

international programs and exchanges for youth. Young adults from Canada and around the world have participated in programs located in 56 countries in Africa, Asia, Latin America, the Caribbean, and Eastern and Central Europe. Teams of participants from Canada and from an exchange country, in counterpart pairs,

integrate into their new communities by living with a host family and working with local organizations on a volunteer basis. This presence has considerable impact on the families and residents in the host communities and provides the youth with work experience in the field of community development.

Source: International Youth Foundation, 2001. www.iyfnet.org

Understanding the School-to-Work Connection: The Theory and Research of Hamilton

ISSUES TO CONSIDER

- What is the nature of the transition from school to work in Canada?
- What does Hamilton envision as the motivation for youth to work hard in high school to forge a connection between school and work?
- How do the concepts of transparency and permeability enhance understanding of the transitions between school and work in different nations?

Almost all youth in Canada make a transition from school to work. The majority of these youth (about 75%; see Chapter 11) graduate from high school and then either try to enter the work force or, in turn, first pursue postsecondary education before beginning to look for full-time employment. More than three in five Canadians, between 25 and 34 years of age, have qualifications beyond a high school diploma (28% have a university degree, 21% a college diploma, and 12% trade credentials; Statistics Canada, 2003c). The growth in post–high school credentials from 49% in 1991 to 61% in 2001 is associated with the increase in university and college degrees and diplomas, because the proportion of youth with a trade credential has remained stable (Statistics Canada, 2003c). In a study of 127 young adults in Ontario, it was noted that postsecondary education partially protects against negative psychological consequences of unemployment when there are few employment opportunities (Jackson, 1999). However, the experience of unemployment or job

instability, among high school graduates in four Canadian cities who directly entered the job market after graduation, did not lead to criminal behaviour four years later (Hartnagel, 1998).

How do people make this transition from school to work? How do they learn what they need to do to get a job in general or, more specifically, to obtain a particular type of job? How easy is it for them to enter the job of their choice? And what if they want to change jobs? How does one go about moving from one line of work to another? Are the answers to these questions the same for all young people? Or is there one set of answers for people who move directly from high school to work and another set for youth who first get a postsecondary education before entering the world of work?

Clearly, the answers to these questions are critical for young people undergoing the transition to young adulthood. In addition, answers are central to society, given the importance of maximizing productivity and of citizens maintaining and perpetuating its institutions.

Vocational education facilitates youth in making a successful transition from school to work.

Stephen F. Hamilton (1994) has conducted the most important scholarship to date pertinent to understanding the connections between school to work that occur across the late adolescence to early adulthood transition. His scholarship provides theory and research that helps frame our understanding of the issues faced by youth trying to connect school and work. In addition, Hamilton offers ideas for policies and programs useful for enhancing the school-to-work connection for all youth and, in particular, for those adolescents who seek full-time employment immediately after completion of high school.

Hamilton's (1994; Hamilton & Hamilton, 1999; Hamilton & Lempert, 1996) scholarship has involved the study of adolescents and young adults from seven different nations: the United States, Germany, Japan, Austria, Switzerland, Denmark, and Sweden. He (1994) observes that adolescents' expectations about the "payoff" in the labour market for achievement in secondary school motivates them to work hard in high school and forges a connection between the educational and work contexts of life. He points out that "Adolescents who believe their current efforts will bring them closer to a desirable future are far more likely to work hard in school and avoid self-destructive behaviour than those who are either unable to think about the future or who believe their prospects are beyond their control" (Hamilton, 1994, pp. 267–268).

Hamilton (1994) explains that to attain the link they desire between their adolescent school context and their young adult work context, youth must consider two key facets of the worlds of education and work/career: transparency and permeability. Hamilton (1994) explains that **transparency** refers to the extent to which young people can "see through" the intricacies of the stated and the unstated rules of the educational system and the labour market and, using this understanding, plan a course of action that will lead them from where they are in the present (e.g., last year of high school) to a goal they have for the future (e.g., employment as an electrical engineer, as

an accountant, or as a beautician). How easy is it to understand what one must do and what one must achieve to prepare in high school for a career as an engineer or as a beautician? The education-work/career system is transparent, to the extent that these pathways are clear and may be learned by any student interested in knowing them.

In turn, **permeability**, Hamilton notes, refers to the ease of movement from one part of the education-work/career market system to another. For example, permeability involves the amount of effort needed to move from, say, a plan involving becoming an electrical engineer to a plan involving becoming an orthodontist. A completely permeable system would be one where, after years of planning to be a beautician following high school, and working within the educational-work/career system to reach this goal, there would be no problems encountered and it would be equally easy to now switch one's goal to electrical engineering, brain surgery, rocket science, or forestry.

Hamilton (1994) explains that formal credentials, or qualifications, are important in understanding both the transparency and the permeability of the education-work/career system. He finds an *inverse* relation between transparency and permeability (Hamilton, 1994). That is, the more there are particular and clearly specified qualifications for a given type of employment (e.g., four years of university, followed by four years of medical school, a one-year internship, a three-year residency in surgery, and a three-year subspecialty residency in brain surgery for employment as a brain surgeon), the greater the transparency of the system. However, to the extent that the qualifications are difficult to obtain, the system, although transparent, is not permeable (Hamilton, 1994).

Hamilton (1994) notes that the North American education-career/work system is, overall, not very transparent; it is, instead, opaque. For instance, what precise pathways can be specified for becoming a rock or a movie star, the CEO of a Fortune 500 company, the goalie of a winning hockey team, a successful lawyer and spouse/mother or father, or the proprietor of a successful e-commerce business? The education-work/career system in North America is quite permeable, however (Hamilton, 1994). For example, Hamilton notes that it is possible to switch between the career of auto mechanic to the career of chef. Similarly, lawyers become entrepreneurs, teachers become store owners, and athletes become actors.

In turn, in other countries studied by Hamilton (1994) there are different connections between

---

Transparency Extent to which young people can see through the intricacies of the rules of the education system and the world of work and then plan a course of action to lead them successfully from school to work.

Permeability Ease of movement from one part of the education-work/career system to another; permeability involves the amount of effort (e.g., additional education or training) needed to move from one occupation or career to another.

transparency and permeability. For example, in Germany the relation between credentials and employment are completely transparent. Youth are directed into particular educational paths that will lead either to a particular vocation (e.g., a machinist, a printer, or an electrician) or to university training and subsequent professional activity (e.g., as a physician, scientist, lawyer, or professor).

However, in all the countries Hamilton (1994) studied, professional life paths were quite similar. He noted that the connections between subsequent employment and preparation within universities for professional life were characterized in all countries by high transparency and low permeability. Becoming a surgeon, a contract lawyer, an aeronautical engineer, or a professor of human development requires, in all countries, attaining a quite formidable set of credentials. Although it is clear to anyone interested in these professional careers what these credentials are, the arduous tasks associated with meeting these qualifications make their attainment quite difficult. This difficulty acts as a disincentive for moving out of the career and into another one, once one has finally obtained the requisite qualifications.

Implications of the School-to-Work System for Diverse Youth

ISSUE TO CONSIDER

• How do youth employment programs facilitate school-to-work transitions in Canada?

Of course, not all youth, even in highly industrialized nations such as Canada, enter into professional career paths. For example, as we noted previously, after high school half of the youth in Canada do not go on to university or college, and thus the nature of the transparency and permeability of professional career trajectories is, in effect, largely irrelevant to them. As we discussed, Sherrod et al. (1993) pointed to the need for public policies aimed at enhancing the success of the school-to-work transitions of this half of the youth population.

Canada's Youth Employment Strategy (Human Resources Development Canada, 2003) is an attempt to address the transitional needs of youth looking for work, whether or not they are postsecondary graduates. Two different funding initiatives will: (1) support community agencies to assist youth facing multiple barriers to employment, to develop employment skills, knowledge, and experience, and

(2) support employers to help postsecondary graduates get career-related work experience. However, there is no specific public policy in Canada to address the gap between the completion of full-time schooling and entry into "adult" careers by young people who do not graduate from colleges or universities.

Apprenticeships have been common in some nations, most notably Germany. However, they have not been typical in Canada. Although it is an option, there is a need for greater concerted efforts to involve business, labour, educators, governments, and other labour market partners (Canadian Apprenticeship Forum, 2003). Hamilton and Lempert (1996) believe that apprenticeships may be a key means to enhance the school-to-work connections for youth who do not attend colleges or universities.

A Vision for a Canadian Apprenticeship System

ISSUE TO CONSIDER

• What are the key features of a useful apprenticeship system?

Based on what has been learned from the apprenticeship system in Germany, Hamilton and Lempert (1996) make several recommendations for building a developmental system to enhance the school-to-work transition of youth who seek adult employment after the completion of high school. As described by Hamilton and Lempert (1996), in the German system,

> Apprenticeships typically last for 3 years. Participants usually spend a day or a day-and-a-half each week attending a part-time vocational school (*Berufsschule*), where they receive instruction in German and social studies; in math, science, and other academic knowledge related to their occupation; and in the essential skills of their occupation, such as drafting or accounting. During their working time apprentices perform productive tasks and are paid, but they also receive instruction and the opportunity to gain proficiency in a range of new skills, which are specified for each occupation, as are the experiences and training they receive at work. Employers absorb the costs of training apprentices at work; state (*Land*) governments pay for schooling. Joint committees, with membership drawn from employers, workers, and government, design and monitor the system. The committees are convened by "chambers," nonvoluntary but self-governing associations of employers in related fields. Apprentices who pass the qualifying examination administered by the chamber at the completion of their training are certified as skilled workers and are thereby entitled to the compensation established for their occupation by collective bargaining agreements. They are privileged

by law in applying for positions related to their career area; because they have received the training specified for their occupation, they have priority even if other applicants have more years of schooling. (pp. 430–431)

Accordingly, with the German system as a model, Hamilton and Lempert (1996) make some recommendations for the development of an American apprenticeship system, which also apply to the development of such a system in Canada:

1. An apprenticeship system should be implemented with breadth being a key design principle. Youth should be trained in diverse and challenging tasks. "Occupations in which simple, highly repetitive tasks predominate should not be apprenticeable" (Hamilton & Lempert, 1996, p. 447).
2. Academic rigour must accompany occupational breadth. The courses taken by apprentices should focus on the theoretical components of their occupations (e.g., the principles of electronics or of accounting). In addition, apprentices should take academic courses (for instance, in math or science) that are at the level of college preparatory courses (Hamilton & Lempert, 1996).
3. Inclusion of diverse groups should be a hallmark of apprenticeship programs. Aboriginal and ethnocultural groups, youth, women, and those living in poverty must be afforded equal access to desirable occupations and to training with good firms or businesses (Hamilton & Lempert, 1996).
4. Only high-quality firms or businesses should be allowed to participate in the apprenticeship system. "Apprenticeship training should be restricted to firms that are competent to teach 'all aspects of the industry,' to provide caring supervision, and to provide pedagogically sound training" (Hamilton & Lempert, 1996, p. 449).

Hamilton and Hamilton (1999) reviewed the successes of five different contexts within which the system they suggest has been implemented: single schools, school districts, regional collaborations among school districts, states, and corporate initiatives. They found that for school-to-work programs to function effectively, all these levels must work in harmony.

Indeed, Hamilton and Hamilton (1999) note that strong partnerships will be crucial to maintain the school-to-work system. All levels of the system must make not only youth employment a priority but, as well, they must have youth participation in family and civic life as a central component of their efforts and an essential outcome of their programs. The ongoing research of Stephen F. Hamilton on education, employment, and the transition to young adulthood is presented in Meet the Researcher Box 15.2.

Conclusions: Integrating All Youth Into Civil Society

ISSUE TO CONSIDER

- How may the enhancement of the transition from school to work promote civil society?

As illustrated by the approach to research, policy, and programs pertinent to enhancing the school-to-work component of the transition to young adulthood, scholars and practitioners working with youth agree on a core set of ideas about promoting positive youth development. All components of the developmental system involved in adolescent life—including the active participation of young people themselves—need to be integrated to enhance the life chances of youth.

The developmental system of youth can—if engaged with a vision of civil society and with the values of social justice, and if coupled with the active application of the individual and ecological assets for healthy youth development—be a powerful basis for life success among the diverse youth of the nations of the world. It is our hope that you, as a reader of this book, can better appreciate this system. It is our hope as well that you, in your role as citizen, will actively and positively contribute to the developmental system in order to enhance the opportunities for positive lives for all young people and the chances that all of us will, together, live in a healthier, more just world.

Education and Employment in the Transition to Adulthood

Stephen F. Hamilton is professor of human development in the College of Human Ecology at Cornell University. As a Fulbright senior research fellow he studied the German apprenticeship system and wrote *Apprenticeship for Adulthood: Preparing Youth for the Future,* urging the adaptation of elements of that system in the United States.

Electronic technology and global competition have changed the work people do, increasing the demand for technical competence but also for personal and social competencies such as communication, teamwork, problem solving, and lifelong learning. A growing gap in earnings between those who have a college or university diploma and those without one demonstrates that employers are willing to pay a premium for these competencies, but also reveals a limitation in the North American educational system. We have invested heavily in higher education but neglected other pathways to learning and to productive employment. When high school graduates, even dropouts, could get well-paid factory jobs, that neglect did not have such serious consequences as it has today when jobs that pay enough to support a family nearly all require academic and technical competence beyond the high school level.

German-style apprenticeship (variants are also found in Denmark, Austria, and Switzerland) combines part-time schooling with work experience that is carefully designed to teach competencies needed in specific occupations and more general competencies that can be used in other occupations and in other realms of adult life, especially civic activity. It bridges school and work, adolescence and adulthood. Many young people who do not learn well in school are diligent and adept learners in the workplace. In contrast to teenagers whose days are spent predominantly in the company of their peers, apprentices are surrounded by adults throughout the day, and some of those

adults are charged with helping them succeed as workers. This gives apprentices access to adult mentors and role models who are neither their parents nor their classroom teachers, a decided advantage at the time in their life when they are faced with decisions about what kinds of adults they want to become.

The German system is embedded in German history, culture, law, and economic institutions; it cannot be transplanted intact to other countries. It serves rather as a point of comparison and source of ideas about how we might make the transition to adulthood smoother for those who do not graduate from university. Working with my wife, Mary Agnes Hamilton, I designed and directed a demonstration project to test how elements of German apprenticeship might be adapted in the United States. We created apprenticeships for high school students in three broad occupational areas: manufacturing and engineering technology, health care, and administration and office technology. The occupational areas were defined much more broadly than in Germany because of the fluid nature of the labour market and the need for people to be able to change occupations. Another critical adaptation was to tie youth apprenticeship closely to postsecondary education, ensuring that enrollment in university remained an option and avoiding career paths leading to dead ends.

Youth apprentices quickly learned to do work that is far more challenging than typical youth jobs. Many adults proved to be caring and competent mentors. Compared to their classmates in matriculation

courses, apprentices were as likely to enroll in university, and when they did they were more likely to pursue a subject related to their career interests. When they worked full time after high school graduation, apprentices earned more money, held higher-level positions, and were more likely to be in jobs related to their career plans than their classmates. Without random assignment of youth to either apprenticeship or no apprenticeship, which was not feasible in this project, these differences cannot be attributed with certainty to participation in the program; but they are encouraging indicators.

Making apprenticeships like these available to large numbers of adolescents will require employers to invest in training youth and schools to work closely with employers to coordinate school-based with work-based learning. Even if we do not create a fully developed apprenticeship system, the example of the German system and its adaptation in other countries suggests smaller scale improvements, notably more work-based learning (e.g., cooperative education, internships) and more opportunities for adolescents to work with adults toward common goals (e.g., in joint community service projects).

Summary

- At the end of adolescence, people make a transition to young adulthood, a time of serious choices about life roles and relatively permanent commitments, for instance, involving marriage, children, occupation, and lifestyle.
- Erik Erikson believed that young adulthood is a period characterized by the crisis of intimacy versus isolation.
- Daniel Levinson proposed a model of young adult development for males involving four tasks: forming a dream, finding an occupation, establishing a relationship with a mentor, and establishing love relationships, marriage, and a family.
- Young adulthood is a period of choice and commitment, and a person does not have an indefinitely long period within the life span to achieve these tasks.
- Extending the time taken to meet these tasks well into the adult years means the person is "off time," a situation experienced by the person and regarded by society as a problem.
- In contemporary society there is an increasing separation in time between reaching physical maturity and assuming adult roles.
- Transitions to young adulthood may involve moving from high school to university or to the workplace. However, relatively few programs or policies exist in contemporary society to facilitate adolescents' transitions to young adulthood.
- Young adulthood may constitute a period in which youth have a safe haven for testing out possible adult roles. The period may afford an opportunity to get back on a positive developmental track if the young person has had personal or social problems in adolescence. However, some explorations of life paths and experiences in young adulthood may not be beneficial to youth (e.g., having a baby out of wedlock).
- Development in young adulthood can influence development in later adult life.
- The family is a major influence on the young person's development during and after the transition to young adulthood.

- In Canada there is a strong connection between school and work. Almost all youth make a transition from school to work.
- Stephen F. Hamilton has studied the transition from school to work in several nations (the United States, Germany, Japan, Austria, Switzerland, Denmark, and Sweden). He has found that adolescents' expectations about the "payoff" in the labour market for achievement in secondary school, and their beliefs that their future prospects are within their control, motivate them to work hard in high school and to avoid self-destructive behaviours.
- Hamilton indicates that for youth to attain a positive link between school and work they must consider two issues summarized by the concepts of transparency and permeability.
- Transparency refers to the extent to which the young person can see through the intricacies of the rules of the education system and the world of work and then plan a course of action to lead him or her successfully from school to work.
- Permeability refers to the ease of movement from one part of the education-work/career system to another.
- There is typically an inverse relation between transparency and permeability.
- The education-work/career system is not very transparent in Canada; it is opaque (e.g., it is not clear what qualifications are needed to be a movie star or a real estate agent). However, the system is very permeable.
- In the other countries that Hamilton studied, the relation between transparency and permeability varies, but the paths to professional careers (e.g., becoming a physician, lawyer, or physicist) were similar.
- There is a great need for a public policy to enhance the school-to-work transition for all youth in Canada
- Enhancing the school-to-work transition for all youth within a nation is an essential ingredient in expanding and sustaining civil society across generations.

Discussion Topics

1. What important choices have you made since graduating from high school? Have they changed at all since you have been in university? Has university made it more or less difficult for you to make significant commitments to people and to careers?

2. In what ways do you feel the experiences you have had since high school have made you a different person? Do you believe most people change significantly when they become young adults? In what ways do they change? Are these changes for the better?

3. Do the tasks of young adulthood described by theorists such as Erikson and Levinson correspond to your own experience? Do you and other people of your age feel pressure to form an enduring intimate relationship, to form a vision for life, to find a mentor, and to make a commitment to a career?

4. Do you feel time is running out for you to make important life commitments? When might you think the right time to make decisions such as these has passed?

5. How has your family influenced your transition to young adulthood? Who has been the major influence on the choices and commitments you have made during your young adulthood? Would your friends have analogous answers to this question?

6. How easy has it been for you to develop a plan to use your education to move you successfully into a career or occupation? What would have enhanced your ability to develop a plan? How might society (educational institutions, businesses, government) improve the opportunity for all youth—whether or not they are college or university bound—to make a successful transition from school to work?

Key Terms

mentor, p. 338   permeability, p. 346   transparency, p. 346

Appendix

Studying Adolescent
Development: Methods and Designs

Will Gandalf loved teaching high school psychology. It was a great break from the required Canadian history courses he usually taught. Students in psychology elected to be there and they were eager to hear what he had to say.

Yes, he loved teaching the class, except of course when he got a question like the one he just received from Tina Frodo, one of the more oppositional students in the class.

"Where," she had asked, "does all this information come from? Who says that kids and their parents behave that way?"

"Well, Tina," he began, "scientists, psychologists, or sociologists, for example, find these things out. They do research. Like the research I am sure you learned about in biology, chemistry, or other science courses."

"But people are not like chemicals," Tina protested. "You can't put them in test tubes or dissect them like we did to frogs in biology."

"Well, of course not, Tina. But psychologists and sociologists have scientific methods for studying people, just like biologists have their methods for studying frogs."

"But Mr. Gandalf, that's just the point I'm making. People are different from frogs. You don't need scientific methods to study them. You can just ask them what they think about things."

"Yes." Mr. Gandalf smiled. He sensed a teachable moment coming his way. "You're right, Tina. Scientists can ask people what they think. And in fact this is something they often do! This is one method for doing research."

"Well," Tina proclaimed triumphantly, "if you can just ask somebody, why in the world do you need to do research?"

Learning Objectives

1. To understand the approach to knowledge embodied in the scientific method.
2. To learn the basic characteristics of the scientific method and why all sciences rest on empiricism (observation).
3. To learn the characteristics, assets, and limitations of the five major types of observational methods used to study human development (naturalistic, controlled, experimental, questionnaires/interviews, and qualitative).
4. To understand how research designs provide a plan through which scientists make their observations.
5. To recognize that to study development a design must involve two or more times of observation.
6. To understand how variation associated with age, birth cohort, and time of measurement may influence developmental change.
7. To learn the characteristics of the three designs that have been used traditionally to study human development (longitudinal, cross-sectional, and time-lag) designs.
8. To understand the concept of confounded observations and to learn the assets and limitations associated with each of these designs.
9. To understand the characteristics of sequential designs, and why they represent improvements over traditional designs but also have limitations.
10. To understand the need for and the characteristics of ethical standards for research in human development.

Many people do not understand what scientists do and why what they do is deemed "scientific." We accept the fact that physicists, chemists, and astronomers are scientists and do not raise questions about whether their work reflects the appropriate practice of science. But when it comes to the social and behavioural sciences—the subject matter of psychology, sociology, anthropology, or human development, for instance—scepticism is often expressed about whether the work of researchers in these areas actually reflects science.

Typically, we think of a scientist as a person in a white lab coat, toiling over test tubes and charts and experimenting. Certainly, some scientists do these things; and some of them study human development. Yet a scientist—and science—is not defined by a uniform or a workplace. Rather it is defined by whether the person adheres to the scientific method.

Characteristics of the Scientific Method

ISSUES TO CONSIDER

- What is the approach to knowledge termed the *scientific method?*
- What are the key characteristics of the scientific method?

All scientists—whether they are physicists, chemists, biologists, sociologists, or psychologists—are scientists because they work in accordance with the scientific method. However, when scholars speak of the scientific method, they are not referring per se to a particular way of doing research (e.g., using test tubes in a laboratory to assess the combination of chemicals, studying the speed of particles in a nuclear accelerator, or observing infants as they interact with their mothers in the natural setting of the home). Rather, the **scientific method** refers to a series of steps taken by a scholar to ensure that what he or she observes (no matter how it is observed) is accurate and able to be verified by other researchers. In other words, the scientist adheres to certain principles to be certain that what he or she learns from research—his or her knowledge—is information that anyone else, following the same procedures, would have observed.

Of course, science is not the only route to knowledge. For instance, one may know certain things because of one's faith or religion. However, to know something scientifically means that one follows a series of steps to obtain and verify knowledge. These steps are the components of the scientific method (Kaufmann, 1968).

First, all science rests on *observations*. This foundational basis of science is termed *empiricism*. When something is **empirical**, it is capable of observation. In science, anything that enters into the knowledge of a scientist must, in some way, be observable; it must, in some manner, be empirical. Although scientists cannot directly observe all **constructs** (a particular phenomenon of interest), they collect empirical evidence of the existence of a construct by observing characteristics of it. For example, miners used to send canaries into mines before they entered in order to determine if the air was safe to breathe. The death of a canary lowered into a mineshaft provided evidence to the miners that the air was unsafe. The survival of a canary lowered into the mineshaft provided evidence that the air was safe. Although they could not directly observe the air, the miners could observe the behaviour of the canary, which provided information about air quality in the shaft.

In addition, scientists do not just observe anything. Rather there is a *purpose* to their observations. For example, they may want to see if observations about parent-child relations are consistent with the idea of storm and stress during adolescence (see Chapter 1), or the purpose of their observations may be to learn if certain types of parenting (e.g., authoritative ones) are associated with healthy development among youth, as predicted by scholarship in the field of adolescent development (see Chapter 8).

To fulfill the purposes of their observations, scientists do not observe behaviour haphazardly. Rather, scientists arrange an order or sequence for their observations. They observe *systematically*.

If scientists' systematic and purposeful observations are accurate, then if other scientists follow their procedures, they should be able to make the same observations. In other words, scientific observations must be **replicable**. Moreover, scientists cannot keep their observations secret. If scientists do not *communicate* their observations to other scientists (e.g., through publications in journals or books, or through presentations at scientific conferences), there cannot be any hope of independent and objective replication (and thus verification of the accuracy of the scientist's observations).

When a scientist's observations are communicated, the scientific community (other scientists working in the same area of research) can then work to verify

---

Scientific method Series of steps taken by a researcher to ensure that what is observed is accurate and able to be verified by other researchers.

Empirical Capable of being observed.

Construct An abstract concept of interest to researchers.

Replicable Capable of being repeatedly observed.

Observation—empiricism—is the most basic characteristic of the scientific method.

and/or correct the work of the scientist. In other words, through communication within the scientific community, science has the characteristic of *self-correction*. Finally, then, when an observation has been subjected to communication, replication, and correction it may enter the knowledge base of an area of science. In this way, science is a *cumulative* endeavour, a community process whereby knowledge is shared, verified, and integrated by the group of scholars working on a particular problem of concern to them.

In sum, the seven characteristics of the scientific method (Kaufmann, 1968) are observation (empiricism), purposefulness, systematicity, replicability, communication, self-correction (by the scientific community), and cumulativeness. All areas of science share these characteristics.

However, the manner—the specific empirical procedures—through which a scientist makes observations depends on the subject matter of his or her investigation. How we observe the molecules of a particular gas under a specific temperature differs from the way we observe 15-year-old adolescents interacting at a shopping mall. Accordingly, it is important to discuss the ways in which scientists interested in the study of adolescent development make their observations.

Methods of Observation

ISSUE TO CONSIDER

• What are the methods of observation available to researchers interested in studying adolescent development?

The scientific procedures (the particular observational methods) a scientist uses, even when he or she is working within the confines of one area of science (e.g., psychology or sociology), may be quite diverse. Indeed, because of their varied interests, scholars of adolescent development study youth in many ways. Nevertheless, each method allows systematic, purposeful observations to be made in a useful manner.

Scholars use different methods of scientific observation to pursue their interests because there are many different ways in which development occurs and can be best studied. In fact, five major types of scientific method of observation are used in the study of development: naturalistic observation, controlled observation, experimental observation, observation through the use of questionnaires and/or interviews, and observation using qualitative procedures. We consider the characteristics, advantages, and disadvantages of each of these methods next.

Naturalistic Observation

ISSUES TO CONSIDER
- What are the characteristics of naturalistic observation?
- What are its assets and limitations?
- What is ecological validity?

In naturalistic observation, the researcher attempts to see things as they exist naturally; that is, the researcher tries to observe things uninterrupted and as they are actually happening in a real-life setting. For example, suppose a scientist was interested in the aggressive behaviour shown by 12-year-olds during a recess period at school. Such behaviour might be defined as hitting, pushing, and throwing things at others. The researcher might want to know if such behaviour is shown by 12-year-olds, and if so, how often and in what manner. Naturalistic observation might be chosen as a way of making the observations necessary to find out these things.

Naturalistic observation may be used to study people's behaviour in the actual settings of life.

The researcher would find a group of 12-year-old children during recess. After the youth got used to the researcher's presence (or through the use of unobtrusive film or videotape techniques), he or she would simply observe and record the behaviour of the children. The researcher would in no way interfere with the children's behaviour. Rather, their behaviour, as it naturally occurred in the real-play situation, would be observed and recorded.

Such naturalistic observation has real-world, or **ecological validity**, because it is *actually* an observation of behaviour as it exists in its true ecology. If we want to see how aggressive behaviour exists among 12-year-olds when they are playing, a good way to find this out is to observe 12-year-olds at play!

But naturalistic observation also has its disadvantages. Although we see behaviour as it actually occurs in the real world, all we can do is describe how the behaviour looks and when we saw it appear. We cannot be certain *why* the behaviour happened as it did. *no cause & effect*

Because the researcher neither controls the situation nor **manipulates** (i.e., attempts to influence) the behaviour, it is not known what caused or affected it. There are many reasons for the inability to know causes. One is that many things may be happening at once. The scientist, even with the help of cameras, may be unable to observe everything. And even if many things are observed, the researcher does not know that what has been chosen for observation is really important or relevant to the reason for the behaviour's occurrence. Thus incomplete or biased observations may be obtained.

It may also be difficult to see the behaviour of interest. In other words, there is no way to *ensure* that the behaviour of interest (e.g., aggression) will be seen often enough to ensure systematic observations of it. The behaviour of interest may be so infrequent that no systematic or repeatable observations can be communicated, and naturalistic observations of infrequent behaviours can produce misleading conclusions. Because of these disadvantages, other methods of observation are also used to study development.

Controlled Observation

ISSUES TO CONSIDER   *Controlling situation*
- What are the characteristics of controlled observations?
- What are its uses and limitations?

Rather than studying behaviour based on observations of its occurrence in the real world, the methods of

Ecological validity Observation of behaviour as it exists in its true ("real-world") context.

Manipulation Attempts by a researcher to influence behaviour and/or the situation within which behaviour is studied.

controlled observation can be employed to increase the likelihood of observing the behaviour of interest. This goal is sought by controlling the situation in which the behaviour will take place. If a researcher believes that aggression in 12-year-olds does not occur very frequently and yet wants to study this behaviour, he or she might see the advantage of controlled observation. Suppose that two 12-year-olds are placed in a room with a very attractive video game that can be used by only one youth at a time. After putting the adolescents in this situation for a very short time we might expect to see some aggression as we defined it.

Controlled observation allows the scientist to influence the observations because he or she controls and manipulates the situation. Situations are chosen on the basis of their likelihood of producing the behaviour of interest. Yet this technique also has a disadvantage: by itself it allows the scientist directly to manipulate the situation alone, not the behaviour of the people in the study. The researcher knows that a certain type of behaviour may be expected to occur in this standard, controlled situation with some certain degree of regularity, but may not know what in the situation influenced the behaviour to take the form it took.

A **norm** is behaviour we may typically expect from certain people in specific situations. Controlled observation can provide *normative* information; that is, by having people respond in standard, controlled situations, we learn what behaviour to expect in such situations. In fact, when scientists use a special type of controlled observation technique—known as a **psychological test**—important normative information about such aspects of functioning as intelligence and personality may be discovered.

The Controlled Experiment

ISSUES TO CONSIDER *Controlling situation & person's*

- What are the characteristics of a controlled experiment? *beh.*
- What are its limitations?
- What are independent and dependent variables?
- What are controls?

The controlled experiment is the observational technique that gives the researcher the best understanding of the basis of people's behaviour *in a particular situation.* In a controlled experiment the scientist actually attempts to manipulate events that he or she believes will influence the person's behaviour. That is, besides controlling a situation, the researcher also controls exactly what happens to the person in the situation. Such **controls** are used to see what will result when people are exposed to certain specific events. The goal is to establish a cause-effect relationship, and the researcher hopes to find evidence that "a change in X will cause (have the effect of) a change in Y." In an experiment the researcher tries to control the important influencing factors that act on the participants of the study; of course, what the participants do *depends* on these factors.

To illustrate, a researcher might conduct an experiment to determine whether high school students learn better when their environment is quiet versus when music is playing. The researcher might ask: How will different students learn if one half are stimulated with (or distracted by) contemporary music while trying to study, and the other half are not stimulated (or distracted) by sound at all? The researcher would then randomly assign students to the two groups and expose them to the different events—either the "music" or the "quiet" stimulation. The researcher would be interested in observing if differences in learning resulted between students exposed to one condition as opposed to the other. In an experiment, then, the researcher tries to see if the person's behaviour can be affected, or changed, as a consequence of the different conditions the researcher manipulates.

The Independent Variable Anything that can change or vary is a **variable**. Noise (or sound level), number of people in the room, teaching method, and speed of video games are all variables. Anything that can change (or vary) in terms of how much of it exists is a variable. The condition that the researcher chooses to vary, that is, the various events with which the researcher stimulates the participants, is called the **independent variable**. An independent variable is something the researcher chooses to vary through intentional manipulation in an experimental study

---

Norm Behaviour typical of certain people at certain points in development and/or in specific situations.

Psychological test Standardized, or controlled, device used to elicit behaviour from or information about a person.

Controls Variables that a researcher holds constant in a research study because of their presumed potential to influence the dependent variable.

Variable Anything that can change or vary.
Independent variable Condition that a researcher chooses to vary in a research study and present to research participants.

of development. This variable is independent of the participant's behaviour. It is what the researcher chooses to manipulate. Variables such as age, height, intelligence, amount of tenseness, and years in university or college can change (or vary), but are not under the researcher's control, so are called *quasi-independent variables*. Definite conclusions about cause cannot be made with quasi-independent variables.

The Dependent Variable Although the independent variables, or the stimulus conditions, are chosen by the researcher for manipulation and are thus independent of the participants, their effects on the participants' behaviours are not independent of the participants. How the participants behave in response to the different stimulations they receive *depends* on them, and in an experiment the behaviour shown in response to an independent variable's stimulation is termed the **dependent variable.**

In an experiment the scientist alters a specific stimulus—the independent variable—to see its effect on the dependent variable (i.e., the participants' *responses* to the various stimuli). As in our example, the researcher manipulates the background sound stimulus (sound or quiet) to see what effect this change will have on the students' learning. In this illustrative experiment, then, the level of background sound is the independent variable, and the resulting degree of participant learning constitutes the dependent variable.

Controls Controlling the independent variable to which participants are exposed is important, but the researcher also has to control many other variables. In fact, in an ideal experiment the only thing that can be different between the two groups of students is that one studies with music playing while the other studies in a quiet environment. Any other stimulus that, if varied, could have some effect on the students' responses (on the dependent variable) must not be allowed to vary. Only through control will the researcher be sure that any changes in the participants' learning are due *only* to the changes in the independent (stimulus) variable.

Thus the scientist would want to make sure that such factors as age, intelligence, and educational background of the two groups were not different before the study was conducted. If the scientist found differences

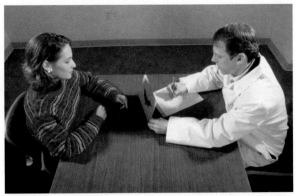

The behaviour of adolescents may be assessed in standardized testing situations.

in how well students learned when stimulated with music versus quiet, he or she would want to be sure that such differences were due to this different stimulation between the two groups and did not arise because one group was composed of, say, 12-year-olds while the other group was composed of, say, 20-year-olds, or because one group consisted of very bright students while the other group contained students of average intelligence. If such differences existed between the two groups, the researcher could not be sure the differences found in the dependent variable were, after all, really due only to the variations introduced by the independent variable.

Unless an experiment is properly controlled, the differences could just as easily have been due to age, intelligence, or educational differences. When an experiment is properly controlled, the researcher can make sound conclusions of what caused the variations in the dependent variable. Controlled experimental observations have an advantage not found with either naturalistic observation or controlled observation. When the scientist observes how changes in the independent variable affect the students' behaviours, he or she may state that the difference in the participants' behaviours was caused by the different conditions to which they were exposed. In other words, experimental observation allows the researcher to discover a cause of a particular behaviour within the specific situation used for study.

Suppose the group that studied with a quiet environment learned better than the group that studied with music. Given all the proper controls, the researcher examining this difference could now say that the reason for the different levels of learning seen in the situation used in the experiment was the different sound stimulation given the two groups.

Dependent variable Behaviour shown in response to the presentation of the independent variable.

Hence experimental observations allow the researcher to discover causes for studied behaviour within a controlled experimental setting.

The controlled experiment also has disadvantages, however. The results of an experiment tell us only the effect of a specific stimulus on a certain behaviour in one specific situation. We cannot necessarily apply these results to a different situation, where perhaps other stimuli may be used and/or other things may or may not be controlled. Thus we cannot easily apply results of one experiment to other experimental situations *unless* everything about the two situations is identical. Moreover, in the real world everything is not as controlled as it is in an experiment. Things vary naturally, and because many variables stimulate a person at the same time (instead of one at a time), each of these variables may affect behaviour singularly or in combination. Experimental observations give us important information about a cause of behaviour in a specific situation, but that situation is rarely identical to events in the real world. Hence we must apply or "generalize" the results of controlled experimental observations cautiously to the real world.

A disadvantage of experimental observation—that it may not have real-world validity—is an advantage of naturalistic observation. The disadvantage of naturalistic observation—that it cannot easily discover a cause for a behaviour—is an advantage of the controlled experiment. Ideally, a researcher interested in discovering the most accurate information about behaviour should try to move back and forth between these two methods of scientific observation, observing reality in the natural world but testing hypotheses carefully under controlled conditions. Actually, researchers tend to use one or the other of the foregoing types of observation; or, because of the disadvantages associated with each technique, they may choose yet another type of method of observation.

In experimental research, there is always a trade-off between **internal validity** (confidence that the changes in the dependent variable are solely due to the independent variable) and **external validity** (confidence that the observed effects on the dependent variable apply to more cases than were studied). The more isolated the variables of interest are, the less relevant their relationship may be to real-world settings. For example, if the 12-year-olds in our study of the effect of classroom music on learning were bright, Caucasian, middle-class children from suburban Toronto, listening to Celine Dion in their new private school classroom with 10 of their peers, we would know that with these students, under these conditions, listening to Celine Dion helps them score higher on a spelling test than not listening to any music. This study would have good internal validity because the researcher ensured that the only difference between conditions (Celine Dion versus a quiet environment) was the music. However, these results would be difficult to apply to most regular school classrooms (i.e., would have low external validity) due to differences in geographical location and physical condition of schools, socioeconomic status of the neighbourhood served by the school, classroom size, as well as intellectual and cultural diversity of the students.

Questionnaires and Interviews

ISSUES TO CONSIDER
- What are the characteristics of questionnaires and interviews?
- What are their uses and limitations?

Rather than try to observe all the possible variables that may influence behaviour in all possible naturalistic situations, and/or try to study each variable separately in one experiment after another, many researchers choose merely to ask people about themselves. That is, researchers often ask people they are interested in studying a series of questions about behaviour. The questions may pertain to just about anything—for example, beliefs about politics, religion, sex, or drug use; typical reactions to events; what experiences the respondents recall from childhood; and many, many more. How the questions are both asked and answered can also take many forms. A printed series of questions may be given to participants, or the same questions may be asked in an oral interview. Participants may respond to such questions through writing, speaking, or both.

Such techniques have obvious disadvantages. People may lie; they may try to answer in a way they think is favourable to them, and/or they may respond with answers they think the researcher wants to hear. For example, when asked whether they have ever "engaged in illegal drug use," people may respond "no" because they think this makes them look better

Internal validity Confidence that the changes in the dependent variable are solely due to the independent variable.

External validity Confidence that the observed effects on the dependent variable apply to more cases than were studied.

rather than because "no" is the truth. Similarly, when asked if they think people of one religion are inferior to people of another religion, participants may also respond "no" because they think that is the "politically correct" response or because they think researchers want to discover a lack of prejudice in people.

Another potential disadvantage is that what people say about their behaviour may differ from how they actually behave. We may not be intentionally lying when we say we behave in certain ways; yet we may be too involved with ourselves to describe our behaviour accurately. Hence we may unintentionally be distorting the facts of our behaviour, or we may be forgetting and/or not remembering certain things accurately. For instance, we may report that we *always* obey traffic laws, and yet, a bit later, we may speed home to dinner.

Finally, researchers may include questions that make certain answers more likely than others, or their behaviour may bias the participants' answers to questions. For instance, a researcher who establishes a warm rapport with an adolescent may elicit answers that differ from those elicited by a cold and/or hostile interviewer.

Despite these disadvantages, questionnaires and interviews do have important advantages. They allow scientists to obtain considerable information about behaviour quickly. If a questionnaire has both written questions and answers, for instance, one scientist may obtain information from several hundred people at the same time. Moreover, some aspects of behaviour may not be ethical or easy to investigate except through questionnaires or interviews. For instance, whereas few people would allow their sexual behaviour to be observed daily, more people might provide anonymous information on a questionnaire about their sexuality.

Scientists have long favoured questionnaires and interviews and have sought to overcome the disadvantages of such techniques (Cattell, 1973). For instance, techniques have been developed to measure people's tendency to lie on questionnaires, and scientists have attempted to devise ways to screen the actual purpose of the questions from the participant, or at least make it hard to guess.

Qualitative Research

ISSUES TO CONSIDER

- How does qualitative research differ from quantitative research?
- When should qualitative research be used?

More and more frequently, social and behavioural scientists are using qualitative research to explore answers to research questions. This involves research that does not use statistical procedures or quantification. The method takes the approach that "truth" is relative, situational, contextual, and changeable (Smith & Davis, 1997). Thus, it focuses on description rather than analysis. The aim is to understand how participants construct their world views, and their own words are often used to portray their perceptions. Qualitative research enabled Bazylak (2002) to learn how five female Aboriginal high school graduates achieved their academic success, given that only 37% of First Nations adolescents completed high school in 2000. By using a qualitative approach to his study of nine Canadian university athletes, Poglog (2002) discovered that success and failure in their sport involved much more than winning or losing. It also involved meeting their own and the team's expectations, doing their best, feeling good about their achievements, and not giving up on a goal until they had tried their hardest to meet it. Qualitative research allowed Ellis to discover how junior high school students in Alberta felt teachers could help students with behavioural difficulties (Ellis, Hart, & Small-McGinley, 1998). This is a small sample of the ways in which qualitative research has been used.

Conclusions About Methods of Observation

A scientist may observe behaviours associated with human development in several different ways. However, a special observational task is presented to a scientist concerned with studying development.

Interviews are a frequently used means to study adolescents' attitudes, values, or ideas.

As explained in Chapter 1, development involves change. Change—an alteration over time in some characteristic of the person—cannot be observed by studying a person only once. To observe change, at least two points in time must be involved.

Accordingly, in order to study human development, researchers must plan—or design—their observations to encompass two or more occasions. In other words, measures related to development must be taken on at least two occasions in order to determine if a change has in fact occurred.

Designs of Developmental Research

ISSUES TO CONSIDER

- What are the ways in which researchers interested in studying development may design their observations?
- Why is variation associated with age, cohort, and time of measurement important to assess?
- How may these variables be confounded in designs of developmental research?

Many people who attempt to understand the basis of an individual's development do so by specifying age-related changes. An example is attributing storm and stress to the adolescent "stage of life." Although such age-related changes may be one source of a person's development, they are not the only processes that provide a basis for change. For example, if a prominent event occurs, as for instance a school shooting, behaviours of people might be affected despite what stage or age of development they are in. As such, it is possible that time of measurement, as well as age-related phenomena, can influence development.

In addition, not only may age and a particular historical event influence behaviour, but people may change as a consequence of being exposed to a particular series of historical events. For example, the availability of the Internet, which was 20 years old in Canada on January 1, 2003, has changed the way that youth interact with one another. Imagine a study of out-of-school social interaction patterns conducted by researchers interested in adults' memories of their hobbies and time spent with friends during their teen years. If participants in their 50s and 30s were interviewed and compared, it might be expected that people who were members of the 1950s birth cohort (or group) and thus went through adolescence without access to the Internet might have developed differently than people born in the 1970s.

So we may see at least three components of developmental change: birth cohort–related events, time of measurement, and age-related phenomena. Recognizing that reference is always made to phenomena that change in relation to these components, we may label these components cohort, time, and age, for convenience. Thus when we see change in a person from one point in the life span to another, we must be able to determine how processes associated with each of these three components may influence change.

Until the 1960s (Baltes, 1968; Schaie, 1965), the three commonly used designs for developmental research—termed longitudinal, cross sectional, and time-lag—did not allow for an adequate determination of the contributions of age, time, and cohort. Developmental research typically involves a confounding of two of the three components of change, and as a consequence, the design's utility is severely limited. When a variable is confounded, its influence on behaviour cannot be separated from that of another variable which could be simultaneously influencing behaviour.

For instance, if we wanted to know whether males or females could score higher on a test of reading comprehension, we would not want all the males to be university educated and all the females grade school educated. If we did not equate the two sex groups on education level (if we did not "control" for the contributions of education), then we would not know if differences between the groups were influenced by their sex or by their educational disparities (or some combination of the two). Thus sex would be confounded with education. In other words, we could not separate the effects of the two variables. When the separate influence of two variables cannot be determined, these variables may be confounded, and any study that involves such a confounding has a potential methodological flaw.

Table A.1 presents the particular confounding factors in each of the three commonly used developmental designs. Refer to this table as our discussion

---

Design Plan for the observation of behaviour.
Cohort Group of people experiencing an event in common.

Birth cohort Group of people who were born in the same year.

Confounding Situation in research in which the influence of one variable on behaviour cannot be separated from the influence of another variable on behaviour.

Table A-1 **Some Characteristics of Longitudinal, Cross-Sectional, and Time-Lag Designs of Developmental Research**

Design	Study Involves:	Confounded Components of Developmental Change
Longitudinal	One birth cohort	Age with time
Cross sectional	One time of measurement	Age with birth cohort
Time-lag	One age at different times in history	Time with birth cohort

Adolescents' preferred styles of dress and grooming have changed across history.

turns to an examination of the characteristics of each of these designs and an explanation of why they confound what they do.

The Longitudinal Design

ISSUES TO CONSIDER
- What are the characteristics of a longitudinal design?
- What are its assets and its limitations?

The **longitudinal design** (also known as a **panel design**) involves observing the same group of people at more than one point in time. The main asset of this approach is that because the same people are studied over time, the similarities or changes in behaviour across their development can be directly ascertained. If we did not repeatedly observe the same people through the use of longitudinal observations, we would not be able to know if and how a given behaviour seen in a person early in life may be

Longitudinal design Design in which the same group of people is studied repeatedly.

Panel design Another term used to label a longitudinal design.

expressed by that same person later in life. Without longitudinal measurement, we would not know whether behaviour stays the same or changes in a person. Lorrie Sippola's research on peer relationships utilizes a longitudinal design. Her research is detailed in Meet the Researcher Box A.1.

However, there are some limitations to longitudinal studies. It obviously takes a relatively long time to do some studies. If researchers wanted, for instance, to do a longitudinal study of personality development from birth through late adolescence, they would have to devote about 20 years of their

---

MEET THE RESEARCHER · Box A.1 · Lorrie K. Sippola

Peer Relationships During Adolescence

Lorrie K Sippola, Ph.D., is an associate professor in culture and human development in the Psychology Department of the University of Saskatchewan.

Relationships are a fundamental aspect of human life. Like the air we breathe, the water we drink, or the food we eat, relationships help to keep us healthy and happy. The primary goal of my program of research, conducted in collaboration with Dr. W. M. Bukowski from Concordia University in Montreal, is to understand the changing nature of peer relationships during the transition into adolescence. Two main issues form the foundation for this program of research.

The first issue that we are exploring is how adolescents negotiate the transition into relationships involving other-sex peers. Prior to adolescence, children generally prefer to spend their time in the company of same-sex peers. If you asked a child to name his or her best friend, he or she would probably name a same-sex peer first. If you watched a child on the playground, you would notice that most of his or her time would be spent engaged in activities with same-sex peers. However, this trend begins to change in early adolescence. Negative attitudes toward other-sex peers begin to decline and we see that cross-sex interactions become more frequent and more meaningful during this period of development (Bukowski, Sippola, & Newcomb, 2000). In spite of the public awareness that cross-sex relationships become more observable in adolescence, we know very little about the development and maintenance of these relationships (Sippola, 1999). Nor do we know much about how these relationships contribute to individual development. Much of the early work in this area has focused exclusively on the sexual aspects of cross-sex relationships. More recently, researchers have begun to examine the emotional aspects of romantic relationships. However, the

goal of our longitudinal research is to explore the diversity of relationships that emerge between boys and girls in adolescence. Using self-report survey methods, we are examining the features and functions of cross-sex friendships and how these relationships uniquely contribute to social development and emotional well-being in adolescence (Bukowski, Sippola, & Hoza, 1999).

The second issue that we are examining in our research concerns the link between aggressive behaviour and adaptation to developmental changes in social networks during adolescence. Initially, we were interested in understanding the nature and prevalence of peer victimization in rural schools. However, our preliminary results are directing us to more closely examine the potential link between popularity and relational aggression among girls as they make the transition into high school. Popularity is generally viewed by researchers, parents, and teachers as a positive indicator of adjustment to the transition to high school. However, we have observed that, for some girls, the pursuit of popularity and the maintenance of one's status in the social hierarchy may be related to the use of coercive dominant strategies, including gossiping about others, interfering with others' relationships, and social exclusion. A longitudinal research design is pivotal to understanding the link between these types of behaviours and developmental goals in adolescence.

For many students, learning about developmental research generally involves learning about practical issues such as methodology, design, and statistics. My own research training emphasized these aspects of research. However, working within the public school system in

Saskatoon and the surrounding area has taught me the importance of the relationship between researcher, participants, and community. It is important to recognize that research frequently takes place within the context of a community that is concerned about the educational, personal, and social development of youth. Although my research examines questions from a basic developmental perspective, my interests correspond with numerous issues facing teachers, parents, and school administrators. Each of us has the desire to make a contribution to the well-being of youth in our community, and we each bring unique skills to this task. Thus, when I approach a community organization to conduct research or when its members approach me, I acknowledge that my expertise in the area of adolescent development is limited and that each of my research partners has his or her own expertise and perspective. Working from this underlying premise, we collaborate to find a way to meet the needs of all involved. Activism takes many forms—mine involves using the skills and knowledge that I have been fortunate to acquire to help others examine their own research questions. Being a member of a smaller urban community has taught me that research, even basic developmental research, is a form of helping others and has the potential to contribute significantly to change within that community.

own lives to such an endeavour. Such a commitment would be expensive, as well as time consuming, and thus relatively few long-term longitudinal studies have been done (e.g., see Jones, 1958; Kagan & Moss, 1962; Livson & Peskin, 1980; Thomas & Chess, 1977). However, in 1994 Statistics Canada began a longitudinal study of 22 500 children from birth to age 11. New infants were added in 1996, 1998, and 2000. All of these children will be studied every two years until they reach adulthood. This study, called the National Longitudinal Survey of Children and Youth, has provided information on a variety of issues including biological, social, and environmental correlates of preschool development (To, Cadarette, & Liu, 2001), parents' involvement at school (Lipps & Frank, 1997), prediction of conduct disorder (Bennett & Offord, 2001), and aggression among girls (Pepler & Sedighdeilami, 1998).

Other limitations of longitudinal studies pertain to the nature of the people studied and to problems with the measurements that may be used. Not everyone would be willing to be a participant in a study that required their continual observation over the course of many months or years of their lives. Hence samples tend to be small in such studies. Those people who are willing to take part may not be representative of most people. Thus longitudinal studies often involve unrepresentative, or "biased," samples of people. Results of such studies may not be easily applied, or "generalized," to a broader population; that is, such studies may not be externally valid. In addition, longitudinal samples typically become increasingly biased as the study continues. Some people drop out of the group, and we cannot assume the remaining people are identical to the former group. After all, the people who stay may be different just by virtue of the fact that they continue to participate.

Another problem with longitudinal studies is that after some time people may become accustomed to the tests of their behaviour. They may learn "how to respond," or they may respond differently than they would if they had never been exposed to the test. Hence the meaning of a particular test to the participants may be altered over time through the repeated use of the instrument with the same sample. Such an occurrence would make it difficult to say that the

same variable was actually being measured at different times in the participants' lives.

Often the purpose of using a longitudinal design is to ascertain the developmental time course for a particular type of behaviour or psychological function. Researchers also want information that they may apply to understanding development about future generations of people. Yet a longitudinal study is only studying people who are born in one historical era and who are measured at certain points in time. It is unclear whether findings about this one cohort can be generalized to people in other cohorts.

Thus a confounding of age and time occurs during such a study. Because a longitudinal design involves assessing one particular cohort of people (e.g., a group of males and females born in 1975), such people can be age 15 at only one time of measurement (1990 in this case). Thus their behaviour at age 15 may be due to age-related phenomena or to phenomena present at the time of measurement (or to both). Similarly, members of one birth cohort can only be age 20 at one time of measurement. Thus, as noted in Table A.1, age and time are confounded in a longitudinal study. One does not know if results of a longitudinal study can be applied to other 15- or 20-year-olds who are measured at other times.

Hence the findings about development gained from a longitudinal study may reflect age-related changes, *or*, alternatively, they may reflect only characteristics of people born and studied at particular points in time. One does not know in a longitudinal study whether the findings are due to universal rules, or "laws," of development (i.e., rules that describe a person's development no matter when it occurs), *or* to particular times the participants are measured, *or* to some combination of all these influences. Because of such problems, alternatives to the longitudinal method are often used.

The Cross-Sectional Design

ISSUES TO CONSIDER
● What are the characteristics of a cross-sectional design?
● What are its assets and its limitations?

The most widely used developmental research design is the **cross-sectional design**. Here different groups of people are studied at one point in time, and hence all observations can be completed relatively quickly. The design is less expensive than longitudinal research and requires less time. Because of these characteristics, some have argued that the method allows

Cross-sectional design Design in which people of different ages are studied at one time of measurement.

for a more efficiently derived description of development. However, cross-sectional research has important limitations.

If we wanted to study the development of aggression in individuals who range in age from 2 to 20 years, we could use the cross-sectional method. Instead of observing one group of people every year, for example, for 18 years, we could observe groups of individuals at each age between 2 and 20 at one point in time. The first group of people would be 2-year-olds, a second group would be 3-year-olds, and so on, through the last group, which would be 20-year-olds.

However, it is difficult to fully and adequately control for all variables that may affect behaviour differences. We may not be certain whether differences between the various age groups are reflections of real age changes or merely reflections of the groups not being really identical to begin with.

Sometimes the researcher attempts to match the individuals on a number of important variables other than age (e.g., ethnicity, father's or mother's educational background, income level, or type of housing) to ensure some degree of comparability. However, such comparability is difficult to achieve. Moreover, although it is possible to get less biased, more representative samples for cross-sectional research than for longitudinal studies (people cooperate more readily because they are only committed to being observed or interviewed once), such better sampling may still not lead to a useful description of the components of developmental change. This failure occurs because of a flaw in the rationale for the use of a cross-sectional method instead of a longitudinal one.

The expectation in some cross-sectional studies is that they yield results comparable to those obtained from studying the same group of people over time, and do so more efficiently, as long as the only differences among cross-sectional groups are their ages. However, despite how adequately participants are matched, it is rarely the case that the results of cross-sectional and longitudinal studies are consistent (Schaie & Strother, 1968).

For example, when studying intellectual development with a cross-sectional design, most researchers report that highest performance occurs in the early 20s or 30s and considerable decreases in performance levels occur after this period (e.g., Horn & Cattell, 1966). With longitudinal studies of these same variables, however, often no decrease in performance is seen at all. In fact, some studies (e.g., Bayley & Olden, 1955) have found some increase in performance levels

into the 50s. As has been pointed out, the characteristics of the participants typically used in the longitudinal design may be considerably different from those of the participants used in the cross-sectional study.

Longitudinal studies, as we have noted, may be composed of a select sample to begin with, and as the study proceeds, some people will drop out of the research. Such attrition may not be random. Rather, it may be due to the fact that the participants of lower intellectual ability, for example, leave the study. Hence, in the example of research on intellectual development, this bias could account for lack of decreases in level of performance. In addition, as Schaie and Strother (1968) point out, these longitudinal studies have not assessed intellectual development in the 60s and 70s, the age periods during which the greatest performance decreases have been seen in the cross-sectional studies (e.g., Jones, 1959). Thus comparisons of the age-associated changes found with the two methods are not appropriate.

Cross-sectional samples have not escaped criticism, however. Schaie (1959) has argued that such samples do not give the researcher a good indication of age-associated changes because it is difficult to control for extraneous variables in the samples used to represent people of widely different age ranges.

Although these arguments may be appropriately used to reconcile the discrepancies (or perhaps to explain them away), Schaie (1965) suggests that these arguments miss an essential point: They do not show a recognition of an essential *methodological* problem involved in the consideration of longitudinal and cross-sectional designs. Just as longitudinal studies are confounded (between age and time), cross-sectional studies also are confounded. As seen in Table A.1, the confounding is between age and cohort. Because the two types of studies involve different confounding, it is unlikely they will reveal the same results.

The confounding of age and cohort that exists in cross-sectional studies occurs because at any one time of measurement (e.g., 1990) people who are of different ages can only be so because they were born in different years. To be 20 in 1990, one has to have been born in 1970; to be 25 at this time of measurement, one has to be a member of the 1965 birth cohort. Consequently, because cross-sectional studies focus only on one time of measurement, there is no way of telling whether differences between age groups are due to age-related changes or to differences associated with being born in historically different eras.

The Time-Lag Design

ISSUES TO CONSIDER
• What are the characteristics of a time-lag design?
• What are its assets and its limitations?

Although not as frequently used in research as the cross-sectional or longitudinal designs, the **time-lag design** allows a researcher to see differences in behaviour associated with particular ages at various times in history. In contrast to focusing on one cohort or one time of measurement, the time-lag design considers only one age level and looks at characteristics associated with being a particular age at different times in history. For example, when the focus of research is to discern the characteristics associated with being a particular age (e.g., 15 years old) at different times of measurement (e.g., 1960, 1970, 1980, and 1990), a time-lag design is implied. The study described in Chapter 7, presented in Table 7.1 by Broverman et al. (1972) and Nesbitt and Penn (2000), is an example of a time-lag design. They looked at university students' attitudes about gender stereotypes in 1972 and in 2000. They were able to discover whether characteristics (in this case, views of gender stereotypes) are associated with being a university student, or whether these characteristics are associated with a particular time in history. Given that students' views of gender stereotypes were quite different in 1972 and 2000, the researchers could conclude that gender stereotypes are not likely a characteristic of university students. Instead, gender stereotypes probably changed due to different historical time points.

Of course, such a design involves cross sections of people and has all the problems of control, matching, and sampling associated with such designs. But there are also additional problems. As indicated in Table A.1, because only one age is studied at different times, the different groups are members of different birth cohorts. Thus, in a time-lag design, time and birth cohort are confounded, and we do not know, for example, whether the behaviours of 12-year-olds studied at two points in time are associated with events acting on all people—no matter what their age—at a particular test time *or* are due to

historical events associated with membership in a specific cohort.

In sum, the three types of conventional designs of developmental research do not allow for the unconfounded assessment of the contributions of the three components of developmental change. Because of these shortcomings, it is difficult to decide which method gives the most useful depiction of developmental changes. Each method may potentially introduce serious, but different, distortions into measures of developmental changes. This is perhaps the major reason why information about developmental changes derived from the three techniques often is not consistent (Schaie & Strother, 1968). Although each design has some advantages, the problem of each places limitations on the ability of developmental researchers to describe adequately how individual, sociocultural, or historical influences can influence change.

This point might lead some to conclude that a bleak picture exists for the study of human development because the three conventional designs of developmental research have some methodological problems. But, of course, *no research method is without its limitation*. As such, our view is that *all* the conventional methods of developmental research may be used to enhance understanding *if* they are employed with a recognition of their limitations. These limitations, however, can be transcended, as we describe in the following section. Although these other methods also have their limitations (e.g., they typically require large samples of people and are quite expensive to implement), they offer a useful alternative to traditional approaches.

Sequential Strategies of Design

ISSUES TO CONSIDER
• What are the sequential designs?
• What are their strengths and limitations?

Due to the influence of K. Warner Schaie (1965), Paul B. Baltes (1968), and John R. Nesselroade (Nesselroade & Baltes, 1974), the problems of confounding involved in cross-sectional, longitudinal, and time-lag designs may be resolved. Some of John Nesselroade's recent work in regard to the methods used to study development is presented in Meet the Researcher Box A.2.

Schaie (1965) demonstrated how the conventional methods were part of a more **general developmental model**. Presentation of this model allowed

Time-lag design Design in which people of the same age are studied at different times in history.
General developmental model Concept guiding the design of developmental research that involves the idea that designs must unconfound variation associated with age, time of measurement, and cohort.

MEET THE RESEARCHER   Box A.2   John R. Nesselroade

Modelling Developmental Process and Change

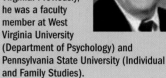

John R. Nesselroade is Hugh Scott Hamilton Professor of Psychology at the University of Virginia. Previously, he was a faculty member at West Virginia University (Department of Psychology) and Pennsylvania State University (Individual and Family Studies).

As developmental researchers have become more and more sophisticated in the way they ask their questions regarding change at both the individual and the context levels, the methods by which the answers are sought have also undergone remarkable transformation. Mathematical and statistical modelling are general mainstays of quantitative, rational science. In each disciplinary context, however, specialized applications of quantitative methods that usefully reflect the current levels of theory, concept definition, measurement, and so on, need to be evaluated and disseminated. In the past 30 years or so, for instance, we have witnessed a striking rise in the application of multivariate "thinking" and methods to the study of development. Much of my own career has been devoted to the creation and elaboration of rigorous methods of multivariate analysis by which the study of development could be better carried out.

Nearly three decades ago, my colleagues and I (Baltes, Reese, & Nesselroade, 1977) opined that the business of developmental psychology was to study intra-individual change patterns and inter-individual differences (and similarities) in those patterns of intra-individual change. In part, our arguments reflected the fact that not all of the interesting developmental questions could be answered by the methods of experimental psychology in which some important variables can be manipulated and others controlled by the researcher. The void created by the need to answer developmental questions that do not lend themselves to experimental manipulation has been increasingly filled by multivariate methodologies (e.g., structural equation modelling, latent growth curve modelling). These classes of models feature testing the goodness of fit between empirical data and theory-derived propositions regarding relationships among concepts and variables.

Even as the relatively sophisticated multivariate methods have settled into place among seasoned researchers and are being taught to new generations of graduate students, the attentive methodologist is hearing a new summons from several quarters. It is the call for rigorous methods of representing *dynamic* relationships in the patterning of changes in individual and in context. A major focus of my work, which involves collaborations with Steve Boker (University of Notre Dame), Michael Browne (Ohio State University), Jack McArdle (University of Virginia), and Peter Molenaar (University of Amsterdam), is the development and testing of multivariate models that explicitly recognize the dynamic character of change and process. This is the future of developmental research methodology, but, more importantly, it is the future of developmental science in general.

him to offer a new type of approach to designing developmental research: sequential methods.

Sequential methods combine features of longitudinal, cross-sectional, and time-lag designs and allow the researcher to assess the relative contributions of age, cohort, and time in one study, and to know what differences (or portion of the differences) between groups are due to age differences, to cohort (historical) differences, or to time of testing differences. In addition, a sequential design allows these sources of differences to be ascertained in a relatively short period of time.

Research based on sequential designs is complex, due in part to the usual involvement of **multivariate** (many variable) statistical analyses and the numerous measurements that have to be taken of different groups. But a simplified example of such a design may be offered. It will suggest how use of such a design allows the developmental researcher to avoid the potential confounding involved with traditional cross-sectional and longitudinal approaches.

Basically, a **sequential design** involves the remeasurement of a cross-sectional sample of people after a given, fixed interval of time has passed. A researcher selects a cross-sectional sample composed of various cohorts and measures each cohort longitudinally (with the provision that each set of measurements occurs at about the same point in time for each cohort). In other words, this design calls for obtaining repeated measures from each of the different

Multivariate Many variables.
Sequential designs Designs in which cross-sectional samples are studied longitudinally.

Student protests were ubiquitous during the Vietnam War and have been common more recently on a global level as well.

cohort groups included in a given cross-sectional sample. Data can be also obtained from new control groups to assess effects of being tested multiple times (and becoming accustomed to the tests). For example, if three times of testing are included as the longitudinal component of the design, then control cohort groups (for instance, assessed only at the third testing time) may be used to control for any effects of repeated testing. If there are no differences in results between the new control cohort group and the original cohort group, one can conclude that there are no effects of being retested. (This is illustrated by the last two columns of Table A-2.) The researcher is now in a position to make statements about the relative influences of age, cohort, and times of measurement on any observed developmental changes in the results.

Cross-sectional and longitudinal sequences consist of sequences of either simple cross-sectional or longitudinal designs. The successive application of these strategies in sequential designs permits us to describe the extent to which behaviour change is associated with age-related or history-related influences. Figure A.1 provides a contrast between the simple and sequential strategies. The top portion of the figure shows the simple cross-sectional and longitudinal designs described previously; the bottom portion of the figure shows the two sequential strategies. Cross-sectional sequences involve a series of two or more cross-sectional studies completed at different times of measurement. Longitudinal sequences involve successions of longitudinal studies begun at different times of measurement. The strategies differ in that cross-sectional sequences involve independent measures on different individuals, and longitudinal sequences

involve repeated measures of the same individuals. In practice, one can apply both strategies simultaneously. In any event, the application of sequential strategies permits the discrimination of within- and between-cohort sources of change.

To see how this works, consider a sample design of a sequential study (presented in Table A.2 and recast in the form of a matrix in Figure A.2). Different cohort levels are composed of different groups of people born at different historical periods (1954, 1955, 1956, or 1957). Thus, at the time of the first testing (1970 for this design), the study has the attributes of a cross-sectional study.

Indeed, there are three such cross-sectional studies in this particular design, one for each time of measurement (see Figure A.2). However, the sequential feature is introduced when these same participants are again measured in 1971 and 1972. Thus for each cohort there is now a longitudinal study. As seen in Figure A.2, each cohort in a sequential design of this

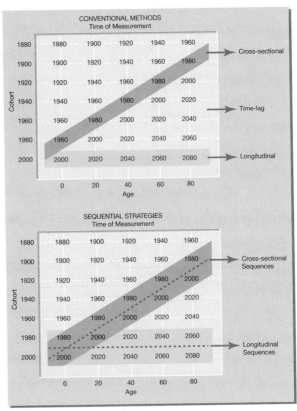

Figure A.1

Illustration of simple cross-sectional, longitudinal, and time-lag designs (top) and cross-sectional and longitudinal sequences (bottom).

(*Source:* Baltes, Reese, & Nesselrode, 1977.)

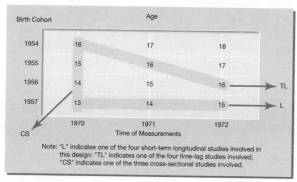

Figure A.2
The design of a sequential study put into the form of a matrix.

sort is involved in its own short-term longitudinal study (there are four of these in the design shown in Figure A.2; one of these is highlighted in pink). In addition, note that the diagonals of the design matrix of Figure A.2 represent time-lag studies; people of the same age are studied at different times (one example of this is highlighted in purple). Thus a sequential study involves all combinations of observations of other designs in one integrated matrix of observations.

With such a matrix, the researcher can answer a number of questions involving the potentially interrelated influences of cohort, age, and time. Referring to Table A.2 and Figure A.2, if, for example, the cohort composed of people born in 1957 underwent changes between times of measurement 2 and 3 and were found to be different at age 15 from the people in the 1956 cohort group when they were 15, then there must be some historical difference between these two cohort levels. (Perhaps a historical event in 1972 such as Canada winning an important hockey game against Russia in the final minutes affected adolescents so much

that 15-year-olds tested differently in 1972 than did 15-year-olds tested in 1971.) If differences were due simply to age-related changes, one should see the same performance for every cohort group, no matter when measured. If only age-related changes matter, then people of the same age should perform the same no matter what cohort they are from or when they are measured. A younger cohort group should perform similarly to that of an older cohort group as members of each group age *if* there were no historical differences between cohorts and if time of testing did not matter. Again from Table A.2 and Figure A.2, the 1957 cohort should show a level of performance on its second measurement comparable to that of the first measurement for the 1956 cohort *if* there were no historical differences between the generations.

In turn, if time of testing were a source of change, then people should respond the same despite their age or cohort. If events in 1972 were the strongest influence on behaviour, then one should see that people of all cohorts represented in Table A.2 and Figure A.2 respond the same way when tested in 1972.

Finally, of course, if birth cohort was of most importance, then people of a particular cohort should respond in a given way no matter what age they are and no matter at what time they are measured. As illustrated by the example of adults' memories of friendships during adolescence before and after the arrival of the Internet in Canada, membership in a particular cohort would override influences due to age or time of measurement.

In addition, note that by including groups of participants to be tested for the first time at the end of the study, in this example in 1972 (see Table A.2), sequential research allows assessment of effects of repeated use of the measuring instruments, noted

Birth Cohort	Time of Measurement 1	Age at Time 1	Time of Measurement 2	Age at Time 2	Time of Measurement 3	Age at Time 3	Time of Measurement of Retest Control Group	Age of "Retest" Control Group
1957	1970	13	1971	14	1972	15	1972	15
1956	1970	14	1971	15	1972	16	1972	16
1955	1970	15	1971	16	1972	17	1972	17
1954	1970	16	1971	17	1972	18	1972	18

Table A-2 **The Design of a Sequential Study**

earlier. If participants in the core sample did not respond differently as a consequence of their having been repeatedly measured (e.g., by the same tests of personality or IQ), then their behaviour at the end of the study should be comparable to a group of participants matched in every way with them except for the fact that no repeated testing was given. If there are differences, however, between the core sample and these "retest" controls, then statistical techniques are available to researchers to measure the effects of retesting (Nesselroade & Baltes, 1974).

Despite the complexity of data analysis, and the more complex research design and reasoning process associated with it, sequential methodology has desirable attributes not associated with other techniques. It allows for the unconfounding of the components of developmental change functions in one research effort. As such, it allows the contributions of variables associated with multiple levels of influence to be evaluated adequately.

In fact, although sequential research studies are relatively few in number, the design illustrated in Table A.2 and Figure A.2 was used because it corresponds to the one employed by Nesselroade and Baltes (1974) in their classic sequential study of adolescent personality development (see Applications Box A.1).

Don McCreary, Stan Sadava, and Nancy DeCourville from Brock University in Ontario have been conducting a modified cohort-sequential study called the Niagara Young Adult Health Study (NYAHS; McCreary & Sadava, 2000). This began in 1990–91 with more than 800 randomly selected 20- to 29-year-olds. In 1995 this group was contacted again, along with a new cohort of randomly selected 20- to 24-year-olds. The NYAHS assesses whether life stressors (e.g., unemployment) have an effect on participants' health and health behaviours (e.g., alcohol use).

Conclusions

ISSUES TO CONSIDER
- Why must all research about development be ethical and humane?
- What are important standards for ethical research in human development?

Ethical standards Principles for the humane, caring, and responsible treatment of participants in research.

Scientists interested in the study of adolescent development have available to them a wide array of procedures for making systematic and purposeful observations. Moreover, there are several different designs of developmental research, and these observational plans afford the scientist several choices about how to make his or her observations of adolescent behaviour and/or development systematic.

However, across all procedures used by developmental scientists, care must be taken to treat the participants of their research—youth, their parents and other family members, and all people involved in the lives of adolescents—in a humane, caring, and responsible manner. In other words, researchers must follow ethical principles when they work with youth and the other people in their social world (Fisher, 1993, 1994, 1997; Fisher & Brennan, 1992; Fisher & Fyrberg, 1994; Fisher et al., 1996a, 1996b; Fisher, Hoagwood, & Jensen, 1996; Fisher & Tryon, 1990). Applications Box A.2 presents the **ethical standards** for research with children followed by the Society for Research in Child Development (1999). The Canadian Psychological Society's Code of Ethics (1991) has been adopted by most provinces and territories (Adair, Paivio, & Richie, 1995). It is based on four principles: respect for the dignity of persons, responsible caring, integrity in relationships, and responsibility to society.

In summary, throughout this textbook we have discussed how adolescents living in today's complex society experience a world where opportunities are more abundant than ever before in history and yet, at the same time, where risks are rampant, poverty pervasive, and routes to positive life outcomes not equally available to all youth. To understand and enhance the life chances of all youth requires that scientists use their research (methodological) abilities to devise means to apply developmental science in the service of promoting civil society (Fisher et al. 1993; Fisher & Lerner, 1994; Lerner, Sparks, & McCubbin, 1999).

With such an applied developmental science, scholarship in adolescence may do more than support the wise observation made by the famous psychologist Kurt Lewin (1943), more than a half century ago, that nothing is as practical as a good theory. Such scholarship may also demonstrate that nothing is of greater value to society than a science devoted to using its expertise to improve the life chances of all young people.

The Nesselroade and Baltes (1974) Sequential Study of Adolescent Personality Development

Noting that most conceptions of adolescent personality development suggest that age-related progressions are influential in this period of life, Nesselroade and Baltes (1974) argued that historical (cohort) and specific sociocultural (time) influences may also be involved. As such, they applied a sequential design to see how these three components contributed to changes in personality in the period from 1970 to 1972.

About 1800 West Virginian male and female adolescents were measured in 1970, 1971, and 1972. These adolescents were from birth cohorts 1954 to 1957, and thus, as in Table A.2 and Figure A.2, ranged in age at the time of first measurement from 13 to 16. Personality questionnaires and measures of intelligence were administered to these participants.

Contrary to what is stressed by those theorists who focus on organismic components of adolescent development (e.g., Erik Erikson, 1968, and Anna Freud, 1969; see Chapter 2),

Nesselroade and Baltes (1974) found that change at this time of life was quite responsive to sociocultural-historical influences. In fact, age per se was not found to be a very influential contributor to change. Rather, for these groups of adolescents developmental change was influenced more by a two-year historical period than by age-related sequences.

For instance, adolescents as a whole, *despite their age or birth cohort*, decreased in "superego strength," "socio-emotional anxiety," and achievement during the 1970 to 1972 period. Moreover, most adolescents, regardless of age or cohort, increased in independence during this period.

Accordingly, the Nesselroade and Baltes (1974) data show that it was the time at which all these differently aged adolescents were measured that was most influential in their changes. Perhaps due to the events in the society of that time (e.g., those associated with the Vietnam War), all adolescents performed similarly in regard to these

personality domains. Despite where they were (in regard to age) on "entering" the 1970–72 historical era, members of different cohorts changed in similar directions due to events surrounding them at the times they were tested.

Without sequential methodology, the role of the specific sociocultural setting on adolescents at that time could not have been suggested. This suggestion is supported by data derived from other sequential studies that have shown the influence of birth cohort on intellectual developments in children (Baltes, Baltes, & Reinert, 1970) and adults (Schaie, Labouvie, & Buech, 1973). These data imply that to understand developmental change, we should consider the dynamic interactions between individual and sociocultural-historical processes, a point emphasized in the developmental contextual view of human development. Indeed, sequential designs are of particular value in obtaining information pertinent to this view of development.

Ethical Standards for Research with Children

The principles listed below were published in the 1990–91 Membership Directory of the Society for Research in Child Development, except for Principles 15 and 16, first published in the Fall 1991 edition of its *Newsletter*.

Principle 1. Nonharmful procedures: The investigator should use no research operation that may harm the child either physically or psychologically. The investigator is

also obligated at all times to use the least stressful research operation whenever possible. Psychological harm in particular instances may be difficult to define; nevertheless its definition and means for reducing or eliminating it remain the responsibility of the investigator. When the investigator is in doubt about the possible harmful effects of the research operations, consultation should be sought from others. When harm seems inevitable, the investigator is obligated to find other means of obtaining the information or to abandon the research. Instances may,

nevertheless, a rise in which exposing the child to stressful conditions may be necessary if diagnostic or therapeutic benefits to the child are associated with the research. In such instances careful deliberation by an Institutional Review Board should be sought.

Principle 2. Informed consent: Before seeking consent or assent from the child, the investigator should inform the child of all features of the research that may affect his or her willingness to participate and should answer the child's questions in terms appropriate to the

>

child's comprehension. The investigator should respect the child's freedom to choose to participate in the research or not by giving the child the opportunity to give or not give assent to participation as well as to choose to discontinue participation at any time. Assent means that the child shows some form of agreement to participate without necessarily comprehending the full significance of the research necessary to give informed consent. Investigators working with infants should take special effort to explain the research procedures to the parents and be especially sensitive to any indicators of discomfort in the infant. In spite of the paramount importance of obtaining consent, instances can arise in which consent or any kind of contact with the participant would make the research impossible to carry out. Nonintrusive field research is a common example. Conceivably, such research can be carried out ethically if it is conducted in public places, participants' anonymity is totally protected, and there are no foreseeable negative consequences to the participant. However, judgments on whether such research is ethical in particular circumstances should be made in consultation with an Institutional Review Board.

Principle 3. Parental consent: The informed consent of parents, legal guardians, or those who act *in loco parentis* (e.g., teachers, superintendents of institutions) similarly should be obtained, preferably in writing. Informed consent requires that parents or other responsible adults be informed of all the features of the research that may affect their willingness to allow the child to participate. This information should include the profession and institution affiliation of the investigator. Not only should the right of the responsible adults to refuse consent be respected, but they should be informed that they may refuse to participate without incurring any penalty to them or to the child.

Principle 4. Additional consent: The informed consent of any persons, such as school teachers, for example, whose interaction with the child is the subject of the study should also be obtained. As with the child and parents or guardians, informed consent requires that the persons interacting with the child during the study be informed of all features of the research which may affect their willingness to participate. All questions posed by such persons should be answered and the persons should be free to choose to participate or not, and to discontinue participation at any time.

Principle 5. Incentives: Incentives to participate in a research project must be fair and must not unduly exceed the range of incentives that the child normally experiences. Whatever incentives are used, the investigator should always keep in mind that the greater the possible effects of the investigation on the child, the greater is the obligation to protect the child's welfare and freedom.

Principle 6. Deception: Although full disclosure of information during the procedure of obtaining consent is the ethical ideal, a particular study may necessitate withholding certain information or deception. Whenever withholding information or deception is judged to be essential to the conduct of the study, the investigator should satisfy research colleagues that such judgment is correct. If withholding information or deception is practised, and there is reason to believe that the research participants will be negatively affected by it, adequate measures should be taken after the study to ensure the participant's understanding of the reasons for the deception. Investigators whose research is dependent upon deception should make an effort to employ deception methods that have no known negative effects on the child or the child's family.

Principle 7. Anonymity: To gain access to institutional records, the investigator should obtain permission from responsible authorities in charge of records. Anonymity of the information should be preserved and no information used other than that for which permission was obtained. It is the investigator's responsibility to ensure that responsible authorities do, in fact, have the confidence of the participant and that they bear some degree of responsibility in giving such permission.

Principle 8. Mutual responsibilities: From the beginning of each research investigation, there should be clear agreement between the investigator and the parents, guardians or those who act *in loco parentis,* and the child, when appropriate, that defines the responsibilities of each. The investigator has the obligation to honour all promises and commitments of the agreement.

Principle 9. Jeopardy: When, in the course of research, information comes to the investigator's attention that may jeopardize the child's well-being, the investigator has a responsibility to discuss the information with the parents or guardians and with those expert in the field in order that they may arrange the necessary assistance for the child.

Principle 10. Unforeseen consequences: When research procedures result in undesirable consequences for the participant that were previously unforeseen, the investigator should immediately employ appropriate measures to correct these consequences, and should redesign the procedures if they are to be included in subsequent studies.

Principle 11. Confidentiality: The investigator should keep in confidence all information obtained about research participants. The participants' identity should be concealed in written and verbal reports of the results, as well as in informal discussion with students and colleagues. When a possibility exists that others may gain access to such information, this possibility, together with the plans for protecting confidentiality, should be explained to the participants as part of the procedure of obtaining informed consent.

Principle 12. Informing participants: Immediately after the data are collected, the investigator should clarify for the research participant any misconceptions that may have arisen. The investigator also recognizes a duty to report general findings to participants in terms appropriate to their understanding. Where scientific or humane values justify withholding information, every effort should be made so that withholding the information has no damaging consequences for the participant.

Principle 13. Reporting results: Because the investigator's words may carry unintended weight with parents and children, caution should be exercised in reporting results, making evaluative statements, or giving advice.

Principle 14. Implications of findings: Investigators should be mindful of the social, political, and human implications of their research and should be especially careful in the presentation of findings from the research. This principle, however, in no way denies investigators the right to pursue any area of research or the right to observe proper standards of scientific reporting.

Principle 15. Scientific misconduct: Misconduct is defined as the fabrication or falsification of data, plagiarism, misrepresentation, or other practices that seriously deviate from those that are commonly accepted within the scientific community for proposing, conducting,

analyzing, or reporting research. It does not include unintentional errors or honest differences in interpretation of data.

The Society shall provide vigorous leadership in the pursuit of scientific investigation which is based on the integrity of the investigator and the honesty of research and will not tolerate the presence of scientific misconduct among its members. It shall be the responsibility of the voting members of Governing Council to reach a decision about the possible expulsion of members found guilty of scientific misconduct.

Principle 16. Personal misconduct: Personal misconduct that results in a criminal conviction of a felony may be sufficient grounds for a member's expulsion from the Society. The relevance of the crime to the purposes of the Society should be considered by the Governing Council in reaching a decision about the matter. It shall be the responsibility of the voting members of Governing Council to reach a decision about the possible expulsion of members found guilty of personal misconduct.

Source: Society for Research in Child Development, 1999.

Summary

- The scientific method refers to procedures used by researchers to ensure that their observations are accurate and able to be verified by other researchers.

- Science is only one route to knowledge. However, scientific knowledge involves the use of the scientific method to obtain and verify knowledge.

- The most basic characteristic of the scientific method is empiricism. All science rests on making observations about the topic (the subject matter) one wants to know about (e.g., chemicals, planets, or adolescent behaviour).

- Other characteristics of the scientific method are having a purpose for one's observations and making observations systematically (according to a specific plan).

- If scientists' systematic and purposeful observations are accurate, then other scientists should be able to replicate their observations.

- To enable replication scientists must communicate their observations, which enables science to be a self-correcting means of obtaining knowledge.

- After information is communicated and replicated or corrected, it can be added to the body of knowledge in an area of science. Such addition means science is a cumulative endeavour.

- Five major types of observational methods are used to study human development: naturalistic observation, controlled observation, experimental observation, observation through the use of questionnaires and interviews, and observation using qualitative methods.

- When using naturalistic observation a researcher attempts to view behaviour as it exists in its actual real-life setting. Such observations are therefore ecologically valid.

- Controlled observations can be used to increase the likelihood of viewing the behaviour of interest. In controlled observation, the researcher controls and manipulates the situation within which the person is observed. However, the people in the situation are not directly influenced or manipulated.

- In a controlled experiment the researcher selects the observational setting and the quantity or quality of the events presented to research participants.

- The condition that the researcher selects to vary in an experiment is termed the *independent variable*. The behaviour that is studied in the experiment is termed the *dependent variable*.

- Although enabling statements to be made about the influence of particular variables on particular behaviours among specific people studied in a specific situation, the results of controlled experiments may not necessarily be applied to other situations. They have weak ecological validity.

- Questionnaires and interviews use written and/or oral reports about behaviour; these techniques do not directly observe the behaviour of interest.

- Advantages of such techniques include the ability to collect a lot of information about one or several behaviours, from one or from large groups of people, in relatively efficient ways. Another advantage is the opportunity to collect information about behaviours (e.g., ones regarding sexual intimacy or voting behaviour) that may not be easily or ethically available to a researcher.

- Disadvantages of such techniques include a possible lack of correspondence between reports about behaviour and actual behaviour, and tendencies by participants to give researchers the answers they believe are being sought in the study.

- Techniques exist to assess if people are lying on questionnaires or in interviews.

- Qualitative research focuses on description rather than analysis, with the aim of understanding how participants construct their world views.

- Because change can only be assessed across time, to study developmental changes researchers must develop a plan, or a design, for their observations that involves two or more times of observation.

- Developmental changes may be associated with variation in the age or stage of life of a person. These sorts of changes may be labelled *age variation*.

- Variation may be associated also with the period in history when the person was born: People born at different historical times are in different birth cohorts, and there may be variation in the experiences of such groups. These sorts of changes may be labelled *cohort variation*.

- Events occurring in the lives of people at the time that they are observed may also affect changes in their development. These sorts of changes may be labelled *time* (of measurement) *variation*.

- Three designs of observation have been used traditionally to study human development: longitudinal, cross-sectional, and time-lag designs. A

fourth type of design, described by K. Warner Schaie, is sequential design.

- A confound in a research design occurs when the influence of one variable cannot be separated from the influence of another variable. Each of the three traditional designs of developmental research involves a confounding among two of the three sources of variation (age, cohort, and time) in development.

- A longitudinal (or panel) design involves repeatedly observing the same group of people. This design allows changes within people (intra-individual change) to be studied.

- In a cross-sectional design, people of different ages are studied at the same point in time.

- In a time-lag design, people of the same age are observed at different times of measurement. As in cross-sectional designs, only differences between groups can be measured.

- Sequential designs combine features of longitudinal, cross-sectional, and time-lag designs. Cross-sectional groups of people are studied longitudinally. A longitudinal sequential design involves observing the same group of people from each cross-sectional group and therefore enables intra-individual change to be measured. Cross-sectional sequential designs involve observing different samples of people from the same birth cohort at each measurement time, and therefore enable only inter-individual differences to be measured. In addition, designs often include control groups to ascertain the effects of repeated testing.

- In all research, developmental scientists must be certain that they treat participants ethically and humanely. The Society for Research in Child Development offers a set of ethical standards for research with children that all people conducting human development research should follow. The Canadian Psychological Association also has a code of ethics for all professional psychologists to follow.

Discussion Topics

1. Reflect on what you know and believe to be true. How much of your knowledge and beliefs rests on empirical observation? How much of what you believe do you accept on faith?
2. Does information from a research study have to correspond to what can be seen in the real world to be true? Would you believe the results of a study of adolescent development if the findings could only be demonstrated in a controlled experimental situation?
3. Would you volunteer to participate in a controlled observational study? What about an experiment or study using a questionnaire or interview? Do you think people from all walks of life would be willing to participate as much, less, or more than you? How might such willingness to participate in developmental research affect what we know about adolescence?
4. Why might cross-sectional, time-lag, and longitudinal studies attract different sorts of people as volunteers? What sorts of motivation might be required to remain in a longitudinal study for 20 or 30 years? Would all people who participate in a cross-sectional study be likely to have this motivation? Does it make a difference if they do not?
5. Much developmental research is supported by governmental grants, that is, from taxpayers' money. Are the results of longitudinal or sequential research worth their greater cost (as compared to cross-sectional research)?
6. Have you participated in a research study? If so, do you believe you were treated ethically and humanely? How do your experiences correspond to the experiences of others you know? What might be done to improve the ethical treatment of research participants? Does the age of the participant affect your answer? How so? Why?

Key Terms

birth cohort, p. 361
cohort, p. 361
confounding, p. 361
construct, p. 354
controls, p. 357
cross-sectional design, p. 364
dependent variable, p. 357
design, p. 361
ecological validity, p. 356

empirical, p. 354
ethical standards, p. 370
external validity, p. 359
general developmental model, p. 366
independent variable, p. 357
internal validity, p. 359
longitudinal design, p. 362
manipulation, p. 356

multivariate, p. 367
norm, p. 357
panel design, p. 362
psychological test, p. 357
replicable, p. 354
scientific method, p. 354
sequential designs, p. 367
time-lag design, p. 366
variable, p. 357

GLOSSARY

Ability grouping Placing students in a classroom based on their academic ability. 264

Accommodation Piagetian term used to define process of changing already existing knowledge to fit external stimulation. With assimilation, part of the equilibration process. 47

Accommodation Process during which a person (the subject) modifies his or her cognitive schemas (structure) to conform with new information (the object) in the external world. 89

Acculturation Process of cultural change during which a member/group of one culture gives up his or her/their own values and customs and adopts those from a different culture. 194

Active leisure activities Free time events that require a large expenditure of energy by the participant. 276

Adaptive functioning Development that responds to biological, psychological, and social influences in ways that are healthy, positive, and successful. 12

Adolescence Period of transition spanning the second decade of life during which a person's biological, psychological, and social characteristics undergo change in an interrelated manner and the person goes from being childlike to adultlike. 3

Adolescent egocentrism Term introduced by Elkind in 1967 to label problems in adolescents' thoughts; the belief that others are preoccupied with them and that they are unique individuals. 96

Adulthood Stage 7 of Erikson's psychosocial theory. Involves a crisis between developing a sense of generativity versus stagnation. 45

Advantage index Index formed by scoring children on the basis of the absence of risk factors (such as factors pertinent to poverty) and the presence of more favourable circumstances in the children's lives. 121

AIDS (Acquired Immune Deficiency Syndrome) Condition of acquired deficiency of the immune system caused by the presence of a retrovirus. 232

Amenorrhea Failure to menstruate. 74

Anabolic steroids Synthetic derivatives of testosterone, the primary natural androgen that is responsible for androgenic (masculinizing) and anabolic effects. 76

Anal musculature stage Stage 2 of Erikson's psychosocial theory. Involves a crisis between developing toward a sense of autonomy versus a sense of shame and doubt. 44

Anal stage Second psychosexual stage as defined by Freud. Occurs during second and third years of life, when the libido centres in the anal area. Gratification is obtained through exercising anal muscles, expelling or holding bowel movements. 41

Androgens Male sex hormones associated with the development of secondary sexual characteristics in boys. 60

Anorexia nervosa Eating disorder characterized by low body weight due to a person's misperception of his or her body image and by the mistaken belief that he or she is overweight. 74

Anxiety Unpleasant feeling state associated with such reactions as dread, fear, general uneasiness, or panic. 291

Applied developmental science Approach that uses research about human development to promote positive changes in individuals, families, and communities. 22

Applied developmental science Field of science that focuses on development, diversity, and context to interrelate basic and applied knowledge. Knowledge is applied to promote policies and programs to enhance the life chances of youth. 31

Assets (Developmental assets) Resources of a person (e.g., commitment to learning), a family (e.g., caring attitudes toward children), and a community (e.g., social support) that are needed for positive youth development. 118

Assimilation Piagetian term to define process of changing external stimulation to fit already existing knowledge. With accommodation, part of the equilibration process. 47

Assimilation Process during which a person modifies his or her external world to fit into the already existing cognitive schemas (structures) of the person (the subject). 89

Attitudes Mental structures that have both an emotional and a cognitive component. 242

Authoritarian parenting Parenting marked by lack of warmth and rigid adherence to the rules set by parents. Authoritarian parents emphasize their power in the family and tend to use physical punishment. 191

Authoritative parenting Parenting marked by parental warmth and the use of rules and reasoning to promote obedience and keep discipline. Authoritative parents use nonphysical punishment and maintain consistency between their statements and actions across time. 191

Average status Peer reputation characterized by not showing extreme numbers of either positive or negative nominations. 206

Best practice Set of procedures or program attributes believed to be most effective in constituting a good program. 323

Birth cohort Group of people who were born in the same year. 361

Bulimia Eating disorder characterized by self-induced binge eating and purging behaviour. 74

Bullying A way of attaining power through aggression. 212

Burnouts Students who reject the school as a centre for their social life. 279

Castration anxiety Boy's fear that father will punish him for his affections for his mother by performing castration. Fear leads boy to alter affection and turn to identify with father. 42

Centration In Piaget's theory, a focus on one's own point of view, which involves therefore a lack of balance between assimilation and accommodation. 95

Civil society Society in which cultural and political values, as well as all nongovernmental and governmental institutions, both provide rights to people and require responsibilities of individuals. 105

Clique Subdivision of a crowd in which a set of three or more people with a key common identity or interest form a tightly knit and often exclusive group. 208

Cognitive reorganization Changes in the way a person thinks or reasons. 17

Cohort Group of people experiencing an event in common. 361

Colonization Subjugation of another group's culture. 132

Community-based learning Students learn by doing in collaboration with a community-based agency for their mutual benefit. 278

Comorbidity Simultaneous occurrence of two or more problems or risk behaviours or symptoms (e.g., violence and substance abuse often occur together). 290

Compensation Investing additional resources, or substituting or applying additional means, geared toward the maintenance of functioning when the pathways youth follow to reach their goals fail. 50

Compulsory education System mandating that children and adolescents attend school up to a certain age. 253

Concrete operational stage Third stage of cognitive development as defined by Piaget. The child is capable of internalized, reversible actions. 47

Conditional reasoning Type of deductive reasoning, characterized by "if p, then q" statements. 92

Confounding Situation in research in which the influence of one variable on behaviour cannot be separated from the influence of another variable on behaviour. 361

Conscience Component of the superego that represents the internalization of society's standards, ethics, and morals. 42

Conspecifics Organisms that are members of the same species. 191

Construct An abstract concept of interest to researchers. 354

Context Environments in which an individual exists, such as family, school, work, and culture. 4

Continuous growth Developmental path through adolescence characterized by smooth, nonabrupt change. 18

Controls Variables that a researcher holds constant in a research study because of their presumed potential to influence the dependent variable. 357

Controversial status Peer reputation characterized by receiving a lot of positive nominations and a lot of negative nominations. 206

Conventional morality Second level of moral development as defined by Kohlberg. The individual is bound by issues of the good-person orientation and is concerned with upholding social order and the institutional maintenance of morality. 48

Correlative transformation Process of thinking of all aspects of a problem by relating them to other problems. 92

Critical period Time in life when particular developments must occur if development is to proceed normally. 44

Cross-cultural variation Differences in values, beliefs, attitudes, and actions that occur between societies. 19

Cross-sectional design Design in which people of different ages are studied at one time of measurement. 364

Cross-sectional study Study that assesses a particular variable (e.g., youth-parent relations) at one point in time (e.g., during the year 2000). Often, different age groups are studied at this point in time. 178

Crowd (liaison) Collective group of similarly stereotyped individuals who may or may not spend time together. 00

Culturally conditioned Ideas, views, beliefs, attitudes, or values engendered by the social, cultural, and historical environment in which we live. 15

Deductive reasoning Type of reasoning that begins with a set of statements (premises) used to infer if another statement (conclusion) is valid. 93

Defence mechanisms Developed by the ego to take the pressures imposed by the id and place them into the unconscious part of the mind. 45

Delayed puberty Being behind schedule, for a given age group, in reaching puberty. 74

Dependent variable Behaviour shown in response to the presentation of the independent variable. 358

Depression Emotional problem characterized by listlessness, lethargy, a blunting of affect, and disengagement from social activity. 00

Design Plan for the observation of behaviour. 361

Developmental systems theories Theories which stress that development occurs as a consequence of organized and mutually influential relations among different levels of organization (e.g., biology, society, culture, history). 29

Developmental task Challenge to healthy or positive development that exists at a particular point in life; a challenge that must be met for development to proceed optimally. 130

Developmental tasks Behaviour that must be achieved at a particular age or stage in order for adaptive development to occur. 11

Developmental trajectories Individual's path through life as influenced by combinations of biology, psychology, and context unique to each person. 4

Disequilibration Cognitive process that occurs when our cognitive schemas (structures) are not in an agreement with one another, when there is an imbalance between assimilation and accommodation. 90

Display behaviours Actions designed to enhance one's attractiveness to others. 211

Diversity In development, systematic differences among individuals, groups, or institutions of society. 30

Down syndrome Genetic anomaly characterized by extra chromosome in the 21st pair of chromosomes. 36

Drive state Energizer of behavior that exists within the individual. 40

Dynamic interaction Interaction characterized by two different variables simultaneously influencing one another. For example, biological variables influence and are influenced by contextual variables. 33

Dysmenorrhea Difficult or painful menstruation. 74

Early maturers Adolescents who attain the physical maturation characteristics of puberty earlier than the rest of their same-age peers. 62

Ecological milieu Particular environmental settings of a species/individual. 39

Ecological validity A theory or an observation that reflects accurately real-life situations. 38

Ecological validity Observation of behaviour as it exists in its true ("real-world") context. 356

Ecology Levels of a person's social context that influences individual development. 5

Ecology Real-world setting(s) of the individual and/or species.

"Efficacy research" Model of research conducted under optimal, university-based research conditions. 320

Ego One of three structures of the mind in psychoanalytic theory. Enables person to adapt to reality. 43

Ego ideal Component of the superego that represents the perfect, or ideal, person. 42

Egocentrism Cognitive focus on the self. Egocentrism changes as the child moves throughout Piagetian stages. 47

Egocentrism When the person is centred on his or her own cognitive structure/s and unable to differentiate between one's own point of view and the views of others; when there is more concern with the perspective of the subject than with the actual details of the object (i.e., the world surrounding the subject). 90

Electra complex For girls, the purported emotional crisis that occurs within the phallic stage of development in Freud's theory. 42

Empirical Capable of being observed. 354

Empowerment evaluation Procedures used to increase the ability of community members to prove the effectiveness of the program and to improve it. 317

Endocrine glands Ductless glands, such as the pituitary gland, that secrete their content into the bloodstream. 59

Equilibration Individual's attempt to maintain cognitive balance between existing cognitive structures and what is encountered in the environment. Maintained through continuous process of assimilation and accommodation. 47

Equilibration Process of reaching a balanced relationship between assimilation and accommodation. 89

Estrogens Female sex hormones associated with the development of secondary sexual characteristics in girls. 60

Ethical standards Principles for the humane, caring, and responsible treatment of participants in research. 370

Evaluations Procedures used to ascertain if changes in program participants are due to the program. 316

Exosystem As defined by Bronfenbrenner, the third of several interrelated systems whose composition defines the ecology of human development. The formal and informal social structures that do not themselves contain the developing person but impinge on the setting within which the person exists. 49

External validity Confidence that the observed effects on the dependent variable apply to more cases than were studied. 359

Externalizing problems Behaviour problems expressed through actions toward one's environment and, thereby, easily visible to others (e.g., aggression). 186

Externalizing problems Problems directed to other people or, more generally, to the social context, for example, aggression, arson, disruptive or conflictual behaviour in the school or in the home. 290

Extracurricular activities Events and activities that take place outside the academic realm of school. 257

Falsification strategies Proving one's ideas by trying to identify information that would disconfirm these ideas. 93

Fidelity Emotional orientation toward showing commitment to a role and ideology. 134

Five Cs Five attributes (Competence, Connection, Character, Confidence, and Caring) representing positive developmental outcomes in youth. 124

Fixation Freudian term to describe an arrest of the development of the libido; the person attempts to obtain missed gratification of a previous stage. 41

Foreclosure Adopting a socially approved, easily available role and thereby avoiding the identity crisis. 132

Formal operational stage Fourth stage of cognitive development as defined by Piaget. Most representative of adolescents and adults in modern Western society. The person is capable of thinking counterfactually and hypothetically. Can think of all possible combinations of elements of a problem to find a solution. 47

Formal operational thought Fourth stage of Piaget's theory of cognitive development, when a person attains the ability to see that reality and his or her thoughts about reality are different, and when the person can generate and recognize hypotheses about reality. 90

Formative evaluation Procedures that seek to improve programs. 317

Friendship Voluntary and reciprocal relationship between individuals acknowledged by the people in it, with reciprocal affection and existing within a network of other relationships. 206

Full-service schools Schools that are part of a community-wide, multi-agency, collaborative effort to prevent adolescent educational failure coupled with other risk behaviours. 264

Gender intensification hypothesis Adolescents' socialization by institutions of society, such as the family, aimed at making the youth more gender stereotyped in their personal behaviour. The hypothesis rests on the idea that adolescents experience quite different socialization by virtue of being either male or female. 169

Gender role behaviour Behavioural functioning in accordance with the prescriptions set by the society one lives in. 164

Gender role stereotypes Generalized beliefs that particular behaviours are more characteristic of one sex group than the other. 164

Gender roles Socially and culturally defined set of behaviours linked to being a male or a female in a given society. 156

General developmental model Concept guiding the design of developmental research that involves the idea that designs must unconfound variation associated with age, time of measurement, and cohort. 366

Genital locomotor stage Stage 3 of Erikson's psychosocial theory. Involves a crisis between developing toward a sense of initiative versus guilt. 44

Genital stage Fifth psychosexual stage as defined by Freud. Occurs during puberty as the libido reemerges in the genital area, in an adult form. 42

Genotype Complement of genes transmitted to people at conception by the union of the sperm and ovum. 36

Goodness of fit Degree to which two individuals and/or groups match in goals or styles. 262

Group Collection of interacting individuals who have influence over one another and who have relationships based on common interests or circumstances. 00

Heteronomous morality Form of moral reasoning in which the person does not consider the interests of others or recognize that the interests of others differ from his or her own. 107

Heterosexism Ideology that excludes reference to gay people, effectively making them invisible. 228

HIV Type of retrovirus (human immunodeficiency virus) responsible for AIDS. 232

Homonegativity Expressing negative attitudes toward homosexuals. 231

Homosexuality Sexual orientation to people of the same gender as oneself. Propensity to fall in love with a person of the same sex. 231

Hormones Chemicals released into the bloodstream that have specific regulatory effects on the activity of certain organs. 59

Id One of the three structures of the mind in psychoanalytic theory. The initial source of the libido. 43

Identity Set of thoughts, feeling, values, attitudes, and behaviours that defines a person's self. 131

Identity conflict Crisis in which the person is uncertain of how to define self and is not sure about the role he or she wants to play in society. 140

Identity crisis Crisis between identity and role confusion elicited by the emotional upheaval provoked by the personal and social mandate to adopt a role in adolescence. 130

Identity deficit Identity crisis in which the person fails to resolve the identity crisis because of an inability to make decisions. 140

Identity diffusion Feeling an adolescent gets if he or she cannot resolve the identity crisis. The defining characteristic is a lack of commitment,

about which the adolescent is not concerned. 132

Identity transformation Process of approaching a problem by recognizing the problem in terms of its singular attributes. 92

Ideology Set of attitudes, beliefs, and values that serves to define a role. 132

Imaginary audience Adolescents' belief that others are as preoccupied with the object of their own thoughts as they are. 47

Imaginary audience When adolescents become preoccupied with self, they come to believe that others are as preoccupied with their appearance and behaviour as they are. 96

In-between existence Balance between investing time in the social world of the school and life in the community. 00

Independent variable Condition that a researcher chooses to vary in a research study and present to research participants. 357

Inductive reasoning When reasoning inductively we use our observations and experiences to draw conclusions about the general truth of a particular statement. 93

Indulgent parenting Parenting marked by overly permissive and condoning behaviour toward one's child (e.g., "If my child wants something, I give it to him"). 00

INRC grouping Cognitive structure that characterizes formal operations and implies that all solutions to a problem may be obtained through the application of four components: identity, negation, reciprocity, and correlation. 91

Intellectualization Ego defence mechanism of highly abstract, intellectual reasoning used to justify behaviour. 46

Inter-individual differences Variability between people that leads to different developmental outcomes.

Interactions Integration of the behaviours of two individuals into a social exchange of some duration.

Internal validity Confidence that the changes in the dependent variable are solely due to the independent variable. 00

Internalizing problems Behaviour problems not expressed toward one's environment but rather directed to one's mental or emoting

functioning (e.g., depression or anxiety. 00

Internalizing problems Problems directed inward to the individual and that affect his or her mental, cognitive, or emotional functioning, such as depression or anxiety. 00

Intervention program Program conducted by professionals or through community-based organizations that attempts to change a person's life for the better. 314

Intervention studies Research designed to understand how changing aspects of the social world or an individual's behaviour can lead to improvements in a person's life. 6

Interventions Actions planned to reduce or to prevent problems or to promote positive development. 00

Intra-individual changes Alterations within a person that occur with development. 13

IQ The intelligence quotient. A numerical scale measuring level of intelligence. For example, to compute an IQ score, mental age (i.e., how much you know) is divided by chronological age (i.e., how much is known on average by others of your age) and multiplied by 100 (to eliminate fractions). 83

Jocks Students who use the school's extracurricular arena as a centre for their social life. 00

Juvenile delinquency Violation of a law committed by a person prior to his or her 18th birthday, a violation that would have been a crime if committed by an adult. 295

Late maturers Adolescents who attain the physical maturation characteristics of puberty later than the rest of their same-age peers. 62

Latency Stage 4 of Erikson's psychosocial theory. Involves a crisis between developing toward a sense of industry versus inferiority. 44

Latency period Incubation period of a disease (period between the time an infection takes place and the time first symptoms of the infection appear). 237

Latency stage Fourth psychosexual stage as defined by Freud. Occurs around the fifth year of life until puberty. The libido is said to be latent in this stage. 42

Libido Freudian term that defines the finite amount of energy that each human is born with which governs human mental life. Localization of the libido within the body changes over the course of development. Placement of the libido within the body determines what stimulation is appropriate and what stimulation is inappropriate to the developing individual. 41

Life-span perspective Approach that characterizes individual development as occurring across a lifetime through the combination of internal and external influences; the approach stresses differences within and between people and attempts to optimize lifetime development. 7

Lifestyle Preferences and behaviours of adolescents regarding what they want to do, how and where they will spend their time, and with whom they want to interact. 283

Longitudinal design Design in which the same group of people is studied repeatedly. 362

Longitudinal research/studies Research composed of repeated observations. 30

Longitudinal study Study that assesses a particular variable (e.g., sibling relationships) repeatedly over time. 178

Loss-based selection When compensatory efforts fail or their costs outweigh their gains, individuals restructure their goal hierarchy, lower their standards, or look for new goals. 52

Macrosystem As defined by Bronfenbrenner, the fourth of several interrelated systems whose composition defines the ecology of human development. Composed of cultural values and beliefs and historical events that affect the other ecological systems. 49

Maintenance-actualization Function of schools in which students are both made happy about their current status and yet challenged to do better. 252

Manipulation Attempts by a researcher to influence behaviour and/or the situation within which behaviour is studied. 356

Maturity Stage 8 of Erikson's psychosocial theory. Involves a crisis between developing toward a sense of ego integrity versus despair. 45

Media Means through which information or entertainment is passed such as television, radio, movies, magazines, computers, pagers, cell phones, and video games. 274

Meiosis Process of division resulting in formation of sex cells, sperm, and ova. 36

Menarche Beginning of the first menstrual cycle. 63

Mentor Teacher, guide, or counsellor to another person. The mentor is usually several years older than the person he or she mentors. 338

Mentoring One-on-one relationship that is structured and focuses on the needs of the person being mentored. 330

Mesosystem As defined by Bronfenbrenner, the second of several interrelated systems whose composition defines the ecology of human development. Composed of interrelations among the major settings containing the individual, the developing person at a particular point in his or her life. 49

Microsystem As defined by Bronfenbrenner, the first of several interrelated systems whose composition defines the ecology of human development. Composed of relations between the developing person and the environment in the immediate setting within which the person exists. 49

Moderate interaction theory Places equal stress on the influence of both nature and nurture but sees the two sources as independent of each other. 41

Monozygotic (MZ) twins Twins developed from one fertilized egg that splits after conception. In contrast, dizygotic (DZ) twins develop from separate fertilized eggs. 35

Moratorium Period in which an adolescent avoids commitment. 132

Multidisciplinary Research and knowledge from diverse fields. 9

Multilevel research/studies Research focusing on biological, psychological, and social facets of a phenomenon. 30

Multiple levels of organization Idea that development occurs as a consequence of relations among biology, person, social groups, culture, history, and other levels in the ecology of human development. 29

Multivariate Many variables.

Multivariate research/studies Research involving several variables. 30

Nature-nurture controversy Debate about whether or how biology and/or environment provide the basis of human behaviour and development. 29

Negation operation Process of approaching a problem by cancelling the existence of the problem. 92

Negative identity formation Resolving the identity crisis by adopting an available but socially disapproved role or ideology. 132

Neglected status Peer reputation characterized by receiving very few nominations, either positive or negative. 206

Neglectful parenting Parenting marked by inattentive, careless behaviour toward one's child (e.g., "I really don't know what my child is up to. I don't really keep close tabs on her"). 192

Norm Behaviour typical of certain people at certain points in development and/or in specific situations. 357

Nuclear family Family characterized by the presence of both biological parents and one or more children. 177

Obesity Condition chararcterized by an excessive accumulation of fat in the body. 77

Oedipus complex Boy's emotional reaction to his mother at the time when the libido has moved to the boy's genital area and when he obtains gratification through stimulation of the genitals. When the boy realizes his father is his rival for his mother's affection, the boy comes to fear his father will punish him by performing castration. The boy is so moved by his anxiety that he gives up desires for his mother and identifies with his father.

On-time maturers Adolescents who attain the physical maturation characteristics of puberty at the same time as most of their same-age peers. 62

Ontogeny Development, or life course, of an individual organism. 38

Operation Piagetian term referring to the internalized actions that are mentally reversible. 47

Optimization How youth acquire and refine the means to reach their goals. Describes process geared toward achieving higher levels of functioning. 50

Oral sensory stage Stage 1 of Erikson's psychosocial theory. Involves a crisis between developing a sense of basic trust versus mistrust toward one's world. 44

Oral stage First psychosexual stage defined by Freud. Occurs during the first year of life when the libido is said to be located in the region of the mouth. Gratification is obtained through stimulation of this region through sucking and biting. 41

Outcome or summative evaluation Procedures used to determine if a program is effective. 317

Outreach research Model of research conducted in real-world, community-based settings. 320

Panel design Another term used to label a longitudinal design. 362

Passive leisure activities Free time events that require little expenditure of energy on the part of the participant. 276

Penis envy Girl realizes she does not have a penis but, rather, an inferior (to Freud) organ, the clitoris. The girl experiences envy of the penis and this envy impels her to relinquish her incestuous love for her father and identify with her mother. 42

Permeability Ease of movement from one part of the education-work/career system to another; permeability involves the amount of effort (e.g., additional education or training) needed to move from one occupation or career to another. 346

Permissive parenting Parenting marked by lack of consistency in parents' use of rules. Permissive parents tend to have a laissez-faire attitude toward their child(ren)'s behaviours. The parents often overindulge their child(ren)'s requests and act more as a peer or an independent observer. 191

Personal fable Belief that one is a unique, one-of-a-kind individual; the idea that one is a singular person having singular feelings and thoughts. 96

Personal fable Due to attention of the imaginary audience, adolescents come to believe that they are special and/or unique. 47

Phallic stage Third psychosexual stage as defined by Freud. Spans the period from about the third through fifth years when the libido moves to the genital area. Males and females experience this stage differently because their genitalia differ. See Oedipal complex and Electra complex. 41

Phenylketonuria (PKU) Illness characterized by body's inability to metabolize fatty substances due to lack of a particular digestive enzyme. 37

Phylogeny Evolutionary history of a species. 40

Plasticity Potential for systematic change across life. 35

Policies Actions (e.g., the enactment of laws) taken by social institutions, such as governments, to ensure or increase desired behaviours (e.g., better school performance) or to decrease unwanted behaviours (e.g., drunk driving). 6

Popular status Peer reputation characterized by receiving many positive nominations and few negative ones. 206

Post-traumatic stress disorder Set of emotional and behavioural problems that occurs after experiencing a severe stress, for example an assault. 300

Post-traumatic stress disorder (PTSD) Psychological disorder experienced by individuals who have gone through some major traumatic experiences, such as a serious accident or war. 113

Postconventional morality Third level of moral development as defined by Kohlberg. The individual is concerned with legalistic reasoning oriented around principles and conscience. 48

Postpubescence Stage in pubertal maturation during which the bodily changes associated with adolescence are completed. 61

Precocious puberty Early or premature puberty. 74

Preconventional morality First level of moral development as defined by Kohlberg. The individual is bound by issues of punishment and obedience and naive and egoistic reasoning. 48

Preoperational stage Second stage of cognitive development as defined by Piaget. The child can represent mentally absent objects and can use symbols to represent objects. 47

Prepubescence Stage in pubertal maturation during which some of the bodily changes associated with adolescence (e.g., changes in height, weight, fat and muscle distribution, glandular secretions, or sexual characteristics) have begun. 60

Primary sexual characteristics Physical attributes present at birth that involve internal and external genitalia (e.g., the penis in males and the vagina in females). 60

Process evaluation Procedures that seek to improve programs through enhancing the process through which the program provides its services. 317

Program effectiveness Concept indicating whether a program is accomplishing its goals by achieving what it intended to achieve. 316

Program scale Concept indicating whether a program is reaching the appropriate number of people for whom it could have positive benefits. 318

Program sustainability Concept indicating whether a program is maintained over time. 318

Programs Standardized procedures followed to enable a person or group to increase desired behaviours (e.g., the enhancement of literacy through instruction in reading) or to decrease unwanted ones (e.g., school dropout). 14

Projection Process of attributing one's own feelings to other objects or people. 45

Prosocial behaviour Behaviour that allows society to create a just and equitable system; individuals act in a way that contributes to a just social order. 105

Protective factors Strengths and assets of young people that keep them on a positive developmental path. 322

Psychological test Standardized, or controlled, device used to elicit behaviour from or information about a person. 357

Psychopathology Serious problems of mental health that require professional treatment, for example, sustained and pervasive feelings of depression, anxiety, or the occurrence of a psychotic disorder. 304

Psychosis Severe mental disorder, characterized by problematic behaviours and thoughts that reflect a disengagement from reality. 304

Psychosocial development Emphasizes the role of the ego and, specifically, the role of society in determining what the ego must do to fulfill its function of adapting to the demands of reality. 44

Pubertal maturation Process through which the primary sexual characteristics develop into adult form and the secondary sexual characteristics associated with puberty emerge and develop. 58

Puberty Period during which the primary sexual characteristics develop into adult form and the secondary sexual characteristics are emerging and developing and the capability to reproduce is attained. 59

Puberty and adolescence Stage 5 of Erikson's psychosocial theory. Involves a crisis between developing toward a sense of identity versus role confusion. 44

Pubescence Stage in pubertal maturation during which most of the bodily changes associated with adolescence have been initiated. 61

Public policy Standards or values for the conduct of individuals, organizations, and institutions that structure actions and indicate appropriate investment of resources. 325

Public policy Standards, or rules, for the conduct of individuals, organizations, and institutions. 124

Qualitative differences (in cognition) Differences in "kind" or "type" of thought shown by a person. 88

Rationalization Ego defence mechanism of applying plausible but untrue reasoning for behaviour. 45

Reality principle Ego develops only to deal with reality, to allow the person to adjust to demands of real world and hence survive. 43

Recapitulation Developmental changes within the human life cycle that are the hypothetical repetition of the sequence of changes the species followed during evolution. 39

Reciprocal transformation Process of approaching a problem by considering and taking its opposite. 92

Rejected status Peer reputation characterized by receiving few positive nominations and many negative nominations. 206

Relationships Succession of interactions between two individuals known and committed to each other, which is influenced by the past interactions between the two individuals and by their expectations for the future. 00

Replicable Capable of being repeatedly observed. 354

Repression Ego defence mechanism by which unwanted desires and/or pressures are placed in the unconscious. 45

Reproductive assimilation When a person initially tries to deal with new information by treating it as something he or she already knows. 89

Resilience The strength to succeed despite adversity. 322

Resiliency Presence of considerable physical and physiological ability to overcome adversities. 73

Retrospection Constructing the past through memories. A technique used by Freud. 43

Reversibility Ability to know that by reversing one's actions on an object one can return the object to its original state. 47

Role Socially prescribed set of behaviours to which the person can show commitment. 131

Role Socially prescribed set of behaviours. 156

Role confusion Feeling an adolescent gets if he or she cannot find a role that fits his or her biological, psychological, and social characteristics. 132

Role strain Often associated with maternal employment, the difficulty of balancing the demands of one's role as a worker and the demands of being a parent. 189

"Rotten outcomes" Problems of youth development associated with poverty. 293

School reform Altering the functions of a school. 264

School restructuring Altering the organization of a school. 263

Scientific method Series of steps taken by a researcher to ensure that what is observed is accurate and able to be verified by other researchers. 354

Secondary process Functions (e.g., perception, reasoning) that enable ego to adjust to and deal with reality. 43

Secondary sexual characteristics Physical attributes that develop during puberty (e.g., breast development in females and pigmented facial hair in males). 60

Secular trend Variation of adolescent bodily changes across history. 66

Selection How youth develop, structure, and commit to their goals. Gives direction to development by directing and focusing resources on certain domains of functioning and preventing diffusion of resources. 50

Self-definition Understanding of who you are as a person based on how you view yourself physically, psychologically, and socially. 11

Self-esteem Degree of positive or negative feelings one holds about the self. 134

Self-handicapping behaviours Actions of procrastination and not studying that lead to low achievement. 257

Self-regulation Feature of adolescent psychological and social functioning that allows the individual to select goals, find the means to attain those goals, and cope with failures or losses to reach these goals. 135

Sensorimotor stage First stage of cognitive development as defined by Piaget. The child develops the knowledge that external stimulation continues to exist even when not sensed by the person. 47

Sequential designs Designs in which cross-sectional samples are studied longitudinally. 367

Sex steroids Sex hormones (androgens in males and estrogens in females) that control development of physical and physiological changes associated with pubertal maturation. 60

Social careers Life built exclusively around participating in a particular social role. 00

Social cognition Thinking about interpersonal relationships and the social world. 96

Social constructionism A school of thought now dominant in women's studies and gay studies that holds that categories of gender and sexuality like masculine/feminine and heterosexuality/homosexuality derive from cultural influences, not from essential features of an individual's biology or psychology. 230

Social networks Distinct groups of relationships such as best friends, close friends, cliques, crowds, and romantic relationships. 205

Social role Socially prescribed set of behaviours that society believes is important for its maintenance and perpetuation. 6

Socialization Process by which one generation (the parental one) influences another (the adolescent one) to adopt the values, beliefs, and desired behaviours of society. 176

"Socially toxic" environment Environment in which one is exposed to multiple high-risk factors. 299

Statistical significance Statistical significance is reached when the results could not have been caused by random chance alone. 69

STD (sexually transmitted disease) or **STI (sexually transmitted infection)** Disease, such as HIV or gonorrhea, that is transmitted by sexual contact. 236

Stereotype Exceptionless generalization or commonly held belief about a group (e.g., adolescents) or social institution (e.g., fraternities or sororities). 14

Stereotype Overgeneralized belief. 207

Storm and stress Phrase often used to stereotype general and universal turmoil throughout the adolescent years. 3

Strong interaction theory Sees nature and nurture as reciprocally related and inextricably fused in all development. 41

Substitution Process of replacing one goal for another. 45

Superego Freudian personality structure made up of two components: the ego ideal and the conscience. Formed as a result of the resolution of the Oedipal complex. 42

Surgent growth Developmental path through adolescence characterized by abrupt spurts or changes in behaviour, but not necessarily with turmoil, storm, or stress. 18

Systems approach Approach to programs that deals with multiple problems simultaneously and engages all levels of the context to prevent problems and to promote the positive development of youth. 260

Thriving Concept defined and measured by Scales et al. Thriving is defined as involving the following seven attributes: school success, leadership, valuing diversity, physical health, helping others, delay of gratification, and overcoming adversity. 120

Time-lag design Design in which people of the same age are studied at different times in history. 366

Training-acculturation Function of schools in which students are taught particular behaviours and values of the surrounding culture. 252

Transparency Extent to which young people can see through the intricacies of the rules of the education system and the world of work and then plan a course of action to lead them successfully from school to work. 346

Triangulation The comparison of information about a particular issue from three different sources, where consistency between them adds strength to the conclusion. 317

Tumultuous growth Developmental path through adolescence experienced by a minority of adolescents, characterized by turmoil, storm, and stress. 18

Variable Anything that can change or vary. 357

Weak interaction theory Places primary stress on one source (usually nature) as the determinant of the sequence and character of development. 40

Young adulthood Stage 6 of Erikson's psychosocial theory. Involves a crisis between developing toward a sense of intimacy versus isolation. 45

Youth gangs Groups of youth potentially involved in criminal activity. 295

Youth policy Set of social policies that will enable the values of positive youth development to be translated into effective actions. 326

Zygote Fertilized egg. 35

REFERENCES

A

Abernathy, T. J., Massad, L., & Romano-Dwyer, L. (1995). The relationship between smoking and self-esteem. *Adolescence, 30*(120), 899–907.

Abernathy, T. J., Webster, G., & Vermeulen, M. (2002). Relationship between poverty and health among adolescents. *Adolescence, 37*(145), 55–68.

Adair, J. G., Paivio, A., & Ritchie, P. (1996). Psychology in Canada. *Annual Review of Psychology, 47,* 341.

Adam, K. S., Sheldon-Keller, A. E., & West, M. (1996). Attachment organization and history of suicidal behavior in clinical adolescents. *Journal of Consulting and Clinical Psychology, 64*(2), 264–272.

Adams, G. R. (1977). Physical attractiveness research: Toward a developmental social psychology of beauty. *Human Development, 20,* 217–239.

Adams, G. R. (1991). Runaways, negative consequences for. In R. M. Lerner, A. C. Petersen, & J. Brooks-Gunn (Eds.), *Encyclopedia of adolescence* (Vol. 2, pp. 947–950). New York: Garland.

Adams, G. R. (1997). Identity: A brief critique of a cybernetic model. *Journal of Adolescent Research, 12*(3), 358–362.

Adams, G. R., & Jones, R. M. (1983). Female adolescents' identity development: Age comparisons and perceived child-rearing experiences. *Developmental Psychology, 19,* 249–256.

Adams, G. R., & Marshall, S. K. (1996). A developmental social psychology of identity: Understanding the person-in-context. *Journal of Adolescence, 19,* 429–442.

Adams, G. R., & Côté, J. E. (2002). *Parent/Adolescent Relationships and Identity Development: Literature Review and Policy Statement.* Division of Childhood and Adolescence Health Canada, Ottawa, Ontario. Cat. No. H39-614/2002E.

Adams, G. R., Munro, B., Doherty-Poirer, M., Munro, G., Petersen, A-M, & Edwards, J. (2001). Diffuse-avoidance, normative, and informational identity styles: Using identity theory to predict maladjustment. *Identity: An International Journal of Theory and Research, 1*(4), 307–320.

Adelson, J. (1970, January 18). What generation gap? *New York Times Magazine* (Sec. 6), pp. 10–45.

Adlaf, E. (1995). *Student drug and alcohol use 1977–1995.* Toronto: Addiction Research Foundation.

Adlaf, E. M., & Zdanowicz, Y. M. (1999). A cluster-analytic study of substance problems and mental health among street youths. *American Journal of Drug and Alcohol Abuse, 25*(4), 639–660.

Adler, N. J. (1999). Global leaders: Women of influence. In G. N. Powell (Ed.), *Handbook of gender and work.* Thousand Oaks: Sage.

Ahlburg, D. A., & De Vita, C. J. (1992). New realities of the American families. *Population Bulletin, 47*(2), 1–44.

Alaggia, R., Michalski, J. H., & Vine, C. (1999). The use of peer support for parents and youth living with the trauma of child sexual abuse: An innovative approach. *Journal of Child Sexual Abuse, 8*(2), 57–75.

Alan Guttmacher Institute. (1994). *Sex and America's teenagers.* New York: Author.

Alberta Alcohol and Drug Abuse Commission (2000). Position on performance and appearance enhancing drugs. Retrieved from: http://corp.aadac.com/whoweare/positions/pdf/PerfEnhancDrugs.pdf

Alderson, K. (2002). Reflecting on shattered glass: Some thoughts about gay youth in schools. *The Alberta Counsellor, 27*(2), 3–11.

Alderson, K. G. (2000). *Beyond coming out: Experiences of positive gay identity.* Toronto: Insomniac Press.

Allen, J. P., Hauser, S. T., & Borman-Spurrell, E. (1996). Attachment theory as a framework for understanding sequelae of severe adolescent psychopathology: An 11-year follow-up study. *Journal of Consulting and Clinical Psychology, 64*(2), 254–263.

Allen, J. P., Hauser, S. T., Bell, K. L., & O'Connor, T. G. (1994). Longitudinal assessment of autonomy and relatedness in adolescent family interactions as predictors of adolescent ego development and self-esteem. *Child Development, 65,* 179–194.

Allen, J. P., Hauser, S., Eickholt, C., Bell, K., & O'Connor, T. (1994). Autonomy and relatedness in family interactions as predictors of expressions of negative adolescent affect. *Journal of Research on Adolescence, 4*(4), 535–552.

Allen, J. P., Moore, C., Kuperminc, G., & Bell, K. (1998). Attachment and adolescent psychosocial functioning. *Child Development, 69*(5), 1406–1419.

Allen, J. P., Philliber, S., Herrling, S., & Kuperminc, G. P. (1997). Preventing teen pregnancy and academic failure: Experimental evaluation of a developmentally based approach. *Child Development, 64*(4), 729–742.

Allison, K. W. (1993). Adolescents living in "non-family" and alternative settings. In R. M. Lerner (Ed.), *Early adolescence: Perspectives on research, policy, and intervention* (pp. 37–50). Hillsdale, NJ: Erlbaum.

Allport, G. W. (1954). *The nature of prejudice.* Reading, MA: Addison-Wesley.

Almeida, D. M., & Galambos, N. L. (1991). Examining father involvement and the quality of father-adolescent relations. *Journal of Research on Adolescence, 1*(2), 155–172.

Alnajjar, A. A. (1996). Adolescents' perceptions of family functioning in the United Arab Emirates. *Adolescence, 31*(122), 433–442.

Alsaker, F. D. (1992). Pubertal timing, overweight, and psychological adjustment. *Journal of Early Adolescence, 12,* 396–419.

Alsaker, F. D. (1995). Is puberty a critical period for socialization? *Journal of Adolescence, 18,* 427–444.

Alsaker, F., & Olweus, D. (1986). Assessment of global self-evaluations and perceived stability of self in Norwegian preadolescents and adolescents. *Journal of Early Adolescence, 6,* 269–278.

Alsaker, F., & Olweus, D. (1992). Is this right? Stability of global self-evaluations in early adolescence: A cohort longitudinal study. *Journal of Research on Adolescence, 2,* 123–145.

Alva, S., & Jones, M. (1994). Psychosocial adjustment and self-reported patterns of alcohol use among Hispanic adolescents. *Journal of Early Adolescence, 14,* 432–448.

Alvarez, R. (1992). *Assessing youth programs: An international perspective.* Unpublished manuscript. Battle Creek, MI: International Youth Foundation.

Amato, P. R., Rezac, S. J., & Booth, A. (1995). Helping between parents and young adult offspring: The role of parental marital quality, divorce, and remarriage. *Journal of Marriage and the Family, 57,* 363–374.

Ambert, A.-M. (1998). Contemporary family trends. Divorce: Facts, figures, and consequences. The Vanier Institute of the Family. Retrieved from the World Wide Web, http://www.vifamily.ca/cft/divorce/divorce.htm.

Ames, C., & Ames, R. (Eds.). (1989). *Research in motivation in educations: Vol. 3. Goals and cognitions.* New York: Academic Press.

Anastasi, A. (1958). Heredity, environment, and the question "how?" *Psychological Review, 65,* 197–208.

Anderman, E. M., Griesinger, T., & Westerfield, G. (1998). Motivation and cheating during early adolescence. *Journal of Educational Psychology, 90*(1), 84–93.

Anderson, L. E., & Walsh, J. A. (1998). Prediction of adult criminal status from juvenile psychological assessment. *Criminal Justice and Behavior, 25*(2), 226–239.

Anderson, T., & Dixon, W. E., Jr. (1995). Confirmatory factor analysis of the Wechsler Intelligence Scale for children—revised with normal and psychiatric adolescents. *Journal of Research on Adolescence, 5*(3), 319–332.

Anderssen, E. (2002, December 2). Children abandon remote, grab mouse. *Globe and Mail,* p. A1.

Anisef, P., & Kilbride, K. (2000). The needs of newcomer youth and emerging "best practices" to meet those needs. Toronto, ON: Joint Centre of Excellence for Research on Immigration and Settlement.

Andrews, J. A., Hops, H., Ary, D. V., & Tildesley, E. (1993). Parental influence on early adolescent substance use: Specific and nonspecific effects. *Journal of Early Adolescence, 13*(3), 285–310.

Annie E. Casey Foundation. (1996). *Kids Count Data Book 1996: State profiles of child well-being.* Baltimore: Author.

Annie E. Casey Foundation. (1997). *Kids Count Data Book 1997: State profiles of child well-being.* Baltimore: Author.

Annie E. Casey Foundation. (1998). *Kids Count Data Book 1998: State profiles of child well-being.* Baltimore: Author.

Annie E. Casey Foundation. (1999). *Kids Count Data Book 1999: State profiles of child well-being.* Baltimore: Author.

Annie E. Casey Foundation. (2000). *Kids Count Data Book: State profiles of child well-being.* Baltimore: Author.

Anonymous (December, 2000). The time parents spend with their kids. *Canada and the World Backgrounder,* 14–15.

Ansari, A. A., Gouthro, S., Ahmad, K., & Steele, C. (1996). Hospital-based behavior modification program for adolescents: Evaluation and predictors of outcome. *Adolescence, 31*(122), 469–476.

Ansuini, C. G., Fiddler-Woite, J., & Woite, R. S. (1996). The source, accuracy, and impact of initial sexuality information on lifetime wellness. *Adolescence, 31*(122), 283–289.

Anthony, J. (1969). The reaction of adults to adolescents and their behavior. In G. Caplan & S. Lebovici (Eds.), *Adolescence* (pp. 54–78). New York: Basic.

Aquilino, W. S. (1997). From adolescent to young adult: A prospective study of parent-child relations during the transition to adulthood. *Journal of Marriage and the Family, 59,* 670–686.

Araoye, M. O., & Adegoke, A. (1996). AIDS-related knowledge, attitude and behaviour among selected adolescents in Nigeria. *Journal of Adolescence, 19,* 179–181.

Archer, S. L. (1984, March). Rudiments of identity formation among early and mid-adolescents: An examination of process and content. In C. Cooper (Chair), *An assessment of adolescent identity research: An update with commentary on implications for future research.* Symposium conducted at the meetings of the Second Biennial Conference on Adolescent Research, Tucson, AZ.

Archer, S. L. (1985). Identity and the choice of social rules. *New Directions for Child Development, 30,* 79–99.

Archer, S. L. (1989). Adolescent identity: An appraisal of health and intervention. *Journal of Adolescence, 12,* 341–343.

Archer, S. L. (1991). Identity development, gender differences in. In R. M. Lerner, A. C. Petersen, & J. Brooks-Gunn (Eds.), *Encyclopedia of adolescence* (pp. 522–524). New York: Garland.

Archer, S. L. (1992). A feminist's approach to identity research. In G. R. Adams, T. P. Gullotta, & R. Montemayor (Eds.), *Adolescent identity formation* (pp. 25–49). Newbury Park, CA: Sage.

Archer, S. L., & Waterman, A. S. (1991). Ego development. In R. M. Lerner, A. C. Petersen, & J. Brooks-Gunn (Eds.), *Encyclopedia of adolescence* (Vol. 1, pp. 295–300). New York: Garland.

Armistead, L., Wierson, M., & Forehand, R. (1990). Adolescents and maternal employment: Is it harmful for a young adolescent to have an employed mother? Parent work and early adolescent development. [Special issue]. *Journal of Early Adolescence, 10*(3), 260–278.

Armitage, A. (2003). *Social Welfare in Canada* (4th ed.). Don Mills, ON: Oxford University Press.

Artz, S. (1998). Where have all the school girls gone? Violent girls in the school yard. *Child and Youth Care Forum, 27*(2), 77–109.

Aseltine, R. H., & Gore, S. (1993). Mental health and social adaptation following the transition from high school. *Journal of Research on Adolescence, 3,* 247–270.

Atlas, R. S., & Pepler, D. J. (1998). Observations of bullying in the classroom. *Journal of Educational Research, 92*(2), 86–99.

Atwood, M. (1970). *The Journals of Suzanna Moodie: Poems.* Toronto: Oxford University Press.

Aube, J., Fichman, L., Saltaris, C., & Koestner, R. (2000). Gender differences in adolescent depressive symptomatology: Towards an integrated social-developmental model. *Journal of Social and Clinical Psychology, 19*(3), 297–313.

Audas, R., & Willms, J. D. (2001). *Engagement and dropping out of school: A life-course perspective.* Hull: Human Resources Development Canada.

Ausubel, D. P., Montemayor, R., & Svajian, P. (1977). *Theory and problems of adolescent development* (2nd ed.). New York: Grune & Stratton.

Ayatollahi, S. A. R. (2002). Age at menarche in Iran. *Annals of Human Biology, 29*(4), 355–362.

Ayerst, S. L. (1999). Depression and stress in street youth. *Adolescence, 34*(135), 567–575.

B

Bäckman, L., & Dixon, R. A. (1992). Psychological compensation: A theoretical framework. *Psychological Bulletin, 112*, 259–283.

Baer, D., Grabb, E., & Johnston, W. A. (1993). National character, regional culture, and the values of Canadians and Americans. *Canadian Review of Sociology and Anthropology, 30*(1), 13–36.

Bagley, C., Bolitho, F., & Bertrand, L. (1997). Sexual assault in school, mental health and suicidal behaviors in adolescent women in Canada. *Adolescence, 32*(126), 341–366.

Bagley, C., Wood, M., & Young, L. (1994). Victim to abuser: Mental health and behavioral sequels of child sexual abuse in a community survey of young adult males. *Child Abuse and Neglect, 18*(8), 683–697.

Bagley, C. R. (1999). Adolescent prostitution in Canada and the Philippines: Statistical comparisons, an ethnographic account and policy options. *International Social Work 42*(4), 445–454.

Bagwell, C. L., Newcomb, A. F., & Bukowski, W. M. (1998). Preadolescent friendship and peer rejection as predictors of adult adjustment. *Child Development, 69*(1), 140–153.

Bahr, S. J., Maughan, S. L., Marcos, A. C., & Li, B. (1998). Family, religiosity, and the risk of adolescent drug use. *Journal of Marriage and the Family, 60*, 979–992.

Bakan, D. (1966). *The duality of human existence.* Chicago: Rand McNally.

Baker, J. R., & Yardley, J. K. (2002). Moderating effect of gender on the relationship between sensation seeking-impulsivity and substance use in adolescents. *Journal of Child and Adolescent Substance Abuse, 12*(1), 27–43.

Bala, M., & Bala, N. (1996). A Canadian perspective on adolescent sexuality and public policy: requiring parental involvement is bad law and bad medicine. *Politics and the Life Sciences, 15*, 285–287.

Baltes, M. M., & Carstensen, L. L. (1996). The process of successful aging. *Aging and Society, 16*, 397–422.

Baltes, M. M., & Carstensen, L. L. (1998). Social-psychological theories and their applications to aging: From individual to collective. In V. L. Bengtson & K. W. Schaie (Eds.), *Handbook of theories of aging* (pp. 209–226). New York: Springer.

Baltes, P. B. (1968). Longitudinal and cross-sectional sequences in the study of age and generation effects. *Human Development, 11*, 145–171.

Baltes, P. B. (1987). Theoretical propositions of life-span developmental psychology: On the dynamics between growth and decline. *Developmental Psychology, 23*, 611–626.

Baltes, P. B. (1997). On the incomplete architecture of human ontology: Selection, optimization, and compensation as foundation of developmental theory. *American Psychologist, 52*, 366–380.

Baltes, P. B., & Baltes, M. M. (1990). Psychological perspectives on successful aging: The model of selective optimization with compensation. In P. B. Baltes & M. M. Baltes (Eds.), *Successful aging: Perspectives from the behavioral sciences* (pp. 1–34). New York: Cambridge University Press.

Baltes, P. B., Baltes, M. M., and Reinert, G. (1970). The relationship between time of measurement and age in cognitive development of children: An applicant of cross-sectional sequences. *Human Development, 13*, 258–268.

Baltes, P. B., Lindenberger, U., & Staudinger, U. M. (1998). Life-span theory in developmental psychology. In W. Damon (Series Ed.) & R. M. Lerner (Vol. Ed.), *Handbook of child psychology: Vol. 1. Theoretical models of human development* (5th ed., pp. 1029–1144). New York: Wiley.

Baltes, P. B., Reese, H. W., & Nesselroade, J. R. (1977). *Life-span developmental psychology: Introduction to research methods.* Monterey, CA: Brooks/Cole.

Baltes, P. B., Reese, H. W., & Nesselroade, J. R. (1988). *Life-span developmental psychology: An introduction to research methods.* Hillsdale, NJ: Erlbaum.

Baltes, P. B., Staudinger, U. M., & Lindenberger, U. (1999). Lifespan psychology: Theory and application to intellectual functioning. In J. T. Spence, J. M. Darley, & D. J. Foss (Eds.), *Annual review of psychology* (Vol. 50, 471–507). Palo Alto, CA: Annual Reviews.

Bandura, A. (1964). The stormy decade: Fact or fiction? *Psychology in the School, 1*, 224–231.

Banister, E., & Schreiber, R. (2001). Young women's health concerns: Revealing paradox. *Health Care for Women International, 22*(7), 633–647.

Barbara, A. M., Quandt, S. A., & Anderson, R. T. (2001). Experiences of lesbians in the health care environment. *Women and Health, 34*(1), 45–61.

Barber, B. K. (1994). Cultural, family, and person contexts of parent-adolescent conflict. *Journal of Marriage and the Family, 56*, 375–386.

Barber, B. K., & Olsen, J. A. (1997). Socialization in context: Connection, regulation, and autonomy in the family, school, and neighborhood, and with peers. *Journal of Adolescent Research, 12*(2), 287–315.

Barber, J. G., Bolitho, F., & Bertrand, L. (2001). Parent-child synchrony and adolescent adjustment. *Child and Adolescent Social Work Journal, 18*, 51–64.

Barber, J. G., Bolitho, F., & Bertrand, L. D. (1998). Age and gender differences in the predictors of adolescent drinking. *Social Work Research, 22*(3), 164–172.

Barling, J., & Mendelson, M. B. (1999). Parents' job insecurity affects children's grade performance through the indirect effects of beliefs in an unjust world and negative mood. *Journal of Occupational Health Psychology, 4*(4), 347–355.

Barling, J., Rogers, K.-A., & Kelloway, E. K. (1995). Some effects of teenagers' part-time employment: The quantity and quality of work make the difference. *Journal of Organizational Behaviour, 16*, 143–154.

Barnes, G. M. (1984). Adolescent alcohol abuse and other problem behaviors: Their relationships and common parental influences. *Journal of Youth & Adolescence, 13*, 329–348.

Barnes, G. M., & Farrell, M. P. (1992). Parental support and control as predictors of adolescent drinking, delinquency, and related problem behaviors. *Journal of Marriage and the Family, 54*, 763–776.

Barnes, G. M., Farrell, M. P., & Banerjee, S. (1994). Family influences on alcohol abuse and other problem behaviors among black and white adolescents in a general population sample. *Journal of Research on Adolescence, 4*, 183–202.

Barnes, H. L., & Olson, D. H. (1985). Parent-adolescent communication and the Circumplex model. *Child Development, 56*(2), 438–447.

Baron, S. W., & Hartnagel, T. F. (1998). Street youth and criminal violence. *Journal of Research in Crime and Delinquency, 35*(2), 166–192.

Baron, S. W., Forde, D. R., & Kennedy, L. W. (2001). Rough justice: Street youth and violence. *Journal of Interpersonal Violence, 16*(7), 662–678.

Barrera, M., Li, S. A., & Chassin, L. (1995). Effects of parental alcoholism and life stress on Hispanic and non-Hispanic Caucasian adolescents: A prospective study. *American Journal of Psychology, 23*(4), 479–507.

Barrouillet, P., Fayol, M., & Lathulière, E. (1997). Selecting between competitors in multiplication tasks: An explanation of the errors produced by adolescents with learning disabilities. *International Journal of Behavioral Development, 21*(2), 253–275.

Barwick, M. A., & Siegel, L. S. (1996). Learning difficulties in adolescent clients of a shelter for runaway and homeless street youths. *Journal of Research on Adolescence, 6*(4), 649–670.

Basen-Engquist, K., Edmundson, E. W., & Parcel, G. S. (1996). Structure of health risk behavior among high school students. *Journal of Consulting and Clinical Psychology, 64*(4), 764–775.

Basinger, K. S., Gibbs, J. C., & Fuller, D. (1995). Context and the measurement of moral judgement. *International Journal of Behavioral Development, 18*(3), 537–556.

Battistich, V., Schaps, E., Watson, M., & Solomon, D. (1996). Prevention effects of the Child Development Project: Early findings from an ongoing multisite demonstration trial. *Journal of Adolescent Research, 11*(1), 12–35.

Baumeister, R. F. (1986). *Identity: Cultural change and the struggle for self*. New York: Oxford University Press.

Baumeister, R. F. (1991). Identity crisis. In R. M. Lerner, A. C. Petersen, & J. Brooks-Gunn (Eds.), *Encyclopedia of adolescence* (Vol. 1, pp. 518–521). New York: Garland.

Baumeister, R. F., & Muraven, M. (1996). Identity as adaptation to social, cultural, and historical context. *Journal of Adolescence, 19*, 405–416.

Baumeister, R. F., Shapiro, J. P., & Tice, D. M. (1985). Two kinds of identity crisis. *Journal of Personality, 53*(3), 407–424.

Baumrind, D. (1967). Child care practices anteceding three patterns of preschool behavior. *Genetic Psychology Monographs, 75*, 43–88.

Baumrind, D. (1971). Current patterns of parental authority. *Developmental Psychology Monographs, 4*(1, Pt. 2).

Baumrind, D. (1991). The influence of parenting style on adolescent competence and substance use. *Journal of Early Adolescence, 11*(1), 56–95.

Baydar, N., Brooks-Gunn, J., & Furstenberg, F. F. (1993). Early warning signs of functional illiteracy: Predictors in childhood and adolescence. *Child Development, 64*, 815–829.

Bayley, N., & Olden, M. H. (1955). The maintenance of intellectual ability in gifted adults. *Journal of Gerontology, 10*, 91–107.

Bazylak, D. (2002). Journeys to success: Perceptions of five female aboriginal high school graduates. *Canadian Journal of Native Education, 26*(2), 134.

Beal, A. L., Dumont, R., Branche, A. E. H., & Cruse, C. L. (1996). Practical implications of differences between the American and Canadian norms for WISC-III and a short form for children with learning disabilities. *Canadian Journal of School Psychology, 12*(1), 7–14.

Bear, G., & Stewart, M. (1990). Early adolescents' acceptability of interventions: Influence of problem severity, gender, and moral development. *Journal of Early Adolescence, 10*, 191–208.

Beaty, L. A. (1995). Effects of paternal absence on male adolescents' peer relations and self-image. *Adolescence, 30*, 873–900.

Beaumont, S. L. (1996). Adolescent girls' perceptions of conversations with mothers and friends. *Journal of Adolescent Research, 11*(3), 325–346.

Bedwell, P. D. (1999). Compensation for Residential School Survivors. *Wabanaki Legal News*. Retrieved from: www.ptla.org/wabanaki/Webshu.htm

Beiser, M. & Gotowiec, A. (2000). Accounting for Native/non-Native differences in IQ scores. *Psychology in the Schools, 37*(3), 237–252.

Beiser, M., Lancee, W., Gotowiec, A., Sack, W., & Redshirt, R. (1993). Measuring self-perceived role competence among First Nations and non-Native children. *Canadian Journal of Psychiatry, 38*, 412–419.

Bell, K. L., Allen, J. P., Hauser, S. T., & O'Connor, T. G. (1996). Family factors and young adult transitions: Educational attainment and occupational prestige. In J. A. Graber & J. Brooks-Gunn (Eds.), *Transitions through adolescence: Interpersonal domains and context* (pp. 345–366). Mahwah, NJ: Erlbaum.

Belsky, J., Lerner, R. M., & Spanier, G. B. (1984). *The child in the family*. Reading, MA: Addison-Wesley.

Bengtson, V. L., & Troll, L. (1978). Youth and their parents: Feedback and intergenerational influence in socialization. In R. M. Lerner & G. B. Spanier (Eds.), *Child influences on marital and family interaction: A life-span perspective*. New York: Academic Press.

Bennett, K. J. & Offord, D. R. (2001). Screening for conduct problems: Does the predictive accuracy of conduct disorder symptoms improve with age? *Journal of the American Academy of Child and Adolescent Psychiatry, 40*(12), 1418–1425.

Benson, M. J., Harris, P. B., & Rogers, C. S. (1992). Identity consequences of attachment to mothers and fathers among late adolescents. *Journal of Research on Adolescence, 2*(3), 187–204.

Benson, P. (1997). *All kids are our kids: What communities must do to raise caring and responsible children and adolescents*. San Francisco: Jossey-Bass.

Benson, P. L., Leffert, N., Scales, P. C., & Blyth, D. A. (1998). Beyond the "village" rhetoric: Creating healthy communities for children and adolescents.

Applied Developmental Science, 2(3), 138–159.

Berman, H., McKenna, K., Arnold, C. T., Taylor, G., & MacQuarrie, B. (2000). Sexual harassment: Everyday violence in the lives of girls and women. *Advances in Nursing Science, 22*(4), 32–46

Berndt, T. J., & Keefe, K. (1995). Friends' influence on adolescents' adjustment to school. *Child Development, 66*, 1312–1329.

Berndt, T. J., & Mekos, D. (1995). Adolescents' perceptions of the stressful and desirable aspects of the transition to junior high school. *Journal of Research on Adolescence, 5*(1), 123–142.

Berndt, T. J., Miller, K. E., & Park, K. (1989). Adolescents' perceptions of friends' and parents' influence on aspects of their school adjustment. *Journal of Early Adolescence, 9*(4), 419–435.

Berzonsky, M. D. (1993). A constructivist view of identity development: People as postpositivist self-theorists. In J. Kroger (Ed.), *Discussions on ego identity* (pp. 169–203). Hillsdale, NJ: Erlbaum.

Berzonsky, M. D. (1997). Identity development, control theory, and self-regulation: An individual differences perspective. *Journal of Adolescent Research, 12*(3), 347–353.

Berzonsky, M. D., & Neimeyer, G. J. (1994). Ego identity status and identity processing orientation: The moderating role of commitment. *Journal of Research in Personality, 28*(4), 425–435.

Berzonsky, M.D. (1989). Identity style: Conceptualization and measurement. *Journal of Adolescent Research, 4*, 268–282.

Best, K. M., Hauser, S. T., & Allen, J. P. (1997). Predicting young adult competencies: Adolescent era parent and individual influences. *Journal of Adolescent Research, 12*(1), 90–112.

Bibby, R. (2001). *Canada's teens: Today, yesterday, and tomorrow.* Toronto: Stoddart.

Bigelow, B. J. (2001). Relational scaffolding of school motivation: Developmental continuities in students' and parents' ratings of the importance of school goals. *Journal of Genetic Psychology, 162*(1), 75–92.

Bills, D. B., Helms, L. B., & Ozcan, M. (1995). The impact of student employment on teachers' attitudes and behaviors toward working students. *Youth & Society, 27*(2), 169–193.

Bingham, C. R., & Crockett, L. J. (1996). Longitudinal adjustment patterns of boys and girls experiencing early, middle, and late sexual intercourse. *Developmental Psychology, 32*(4), 647–658.

Bishop, J. A., & Inderbitzen, H. M. (1995). Peer acceptance and friendship: An investigation of their relations to self-esteem. *Journal of Early Adolescence, 15*(4), 476–489.

Bissell, M. (2000). Socio-economic outcomes of teen pregnancy and parenthood: A review of the literature. *Canadian Journal of Human Sexuality, 9*(3), 191–204.

Bittle, S. (2002). *Youth involvement in prostitution: A literature review and annotated bibliography.* Research and Statistics Division. Department of Justice Canada. rr2001–13e. Retrieved from: http://canada.justice.gc.ca/en/ps/rs/rep/rr01-13.pdf.

Black, M. M., Ricardo, I. B., & Stanton, B. (1997). Social and psychological factors associated with AIDS risk behaviors among low-income, urban, African American adolescents. *Journal of Research on Adolescence, 7*(2), 173–195.

Blaske, D. M., Borduin, C. M., Henggeler, S. W., & Barton, M. J. (1989). Individual, family, and peer characteristics of adolescent sex offenders and assaultive offenders. *Developmental Psychology, 25*, 846–855.

Block, J. H. (1971). *Living through time.* Berkeley: Bancroft.

Block, J. H. (1973). Conceptions of sex roles: Some cross-cultural and longitudinal perspectives. *American Psychologist, 28*, 283–308.

Block, J. H., & Robins, R. W. (1993). A longitudinal study of consistency and change in self-esteem from early adolescence to early adulthood. *Child Development, 64*, 909–923.

Bloom, B. S. (1964). *Stability and change in human characteristics.* New York: Wiley.

Blyth, D. A., & Leffert, N. (1995). Communities as contexts for adolescent development: An empirical analysis. *Journal of Adolescent Research, 10*(1), 64–87.

Blyth, D. A., Hill, J., & Thiel, K. (1982).

Early adolescents' significant others: Grade and gender differences in perceived relationships with familial and nonfamilial adults and young people. *Journal of Youth and Adolescence, 11*, 425–450.

Bogenschneider, K. (1997). Parental involvement in adolescent schooling: A proximal process with transcontextual validity. *Journal of Marriage and the Family, 59*, 718–733.

Bogenschneider, K., Small, S. A., & Tsay, J. C. (1997). Child, parent, and contextual influences on perceived parenting competence among parents of adolescents. *Journal of Marriage and the Family, 59*, 345–362.

Bogenschneider, K., Wu, M., Raffaelli, M., & Tsay, J. C. (1998a). Parent influences on adolescent peer orientation and substance use: The interface of parenting practicing and values. *Child Development, 69*, 1672–1688.

Bogenschneider, K., Wu, M.-Y., Raffaelli, M., & Tsay, J. C. (1998b). "Other teens drink, but not my kid": Does parental awareness of adolescent alcohol use protect adolescents from risky consequences? *Journal of Marriage and the Family, 60*, 356–373.

Boivin, M., Hymel, S., & Hodges, E. V. E. (2001). Toward a process view of peer rejection and harassment. In J. Juivonen & S. Graham (Eds.) *Peer harassment in school: The plight of the vulnerable and victimized* (pp. 265–289). New York: Guilford Press.

Bolgar, R., Zweig-Frank, H., Paris, J. (1995). Childhood antecedents of interpersonal problems in young adult children of divorce. *Journal of the American Academy of Child and Adolescent Psychiatry, 34*(2), 143.

Bolognini, M., Plancherel, B., Bettschart, W., & Halfon, O. (1996). Self-esteem and mental health in early adolescence: Development and gender differences. *Journal of Adolescence, 19*, 233–245.

Bond, L., Glover, S., Godfrey, C., Butler, H., & Patton, G. C. (2001). Building capacity for system-level change in schools: Lessons from the Gatehouse project. *Health Education and Behavior, 28*(3), 368–383.

Bond, L., Glover, S., Godfrey, C., Butler, H., & Patton, G. C. (2001). Building capacity for system-level change in schools: Lessons from the Gatehouse project. *Health Education and Behavior, 28*(3), 368–383.

Boney-McCoy, S., & Finkelhor, D. (1995a). Prior victimization: A risk factor for child sexual abuse and for PTSD-related symptomatology among sexually abused youth. *Child Abuse and Neglect, 19,* 1401–1421.

Boney-McCoy, S., & Finkelhor, D. (1995b). Special populations: Psychosocial sequelae of violent victimization in a national youth sample. *Journal of Consulting and Clinical Psychology, 63*(5), 726–736.

Boon, S.D. and Brussoni, M.J. (1996). Young adults' relationships with their "closest" grandparents: Examining emotional closeness. *Journal of Social Behavior and Personality, 11,* 439–458.

Bornstein, M. H. (Ed.). (1995). *Handbook of parenting: Vol. 3. Status and social conditions of parenting.* Mahwah, NJ: Erlbaum.

Borus, M., Rosario, M., Van Rossem, R., & Reid, H. (1995). Prevalence, course, and predictors of multiple problem behaviors among gay and bisexual male adolescents. *Developmental Psychology, 1,* 75–85.

Bosacki, S., Innerd, W., & Towson, S. (1997). Field independence—dependence and self-esteem in preadolescents: Does gender make a difference? *Journal of Youth and Adolescence, 26*(6), 691–703.

Bouffard, T., Boileau, L., & Vezeau, C. (2001). Students' transition from elementary to high school and changes of the relationship between motivation and academic performance. *European Journal of Psychology of Education, 16*(4), 589–604.

Bowman, H. A., & Spanier, G. B. (1978). *Modern marriage* (8th ed.). New York: McGraw-Hill.

Boyd, G. M., Howard, J., & Zucker, R. A. (1994). Preventing alcohol abuse among adolescents: Preintervention and intervention research. *Journal of Research on Adolescence, 4,* 175–181.

Boyd, M., & Norris, D. (1999). The crowded nest: Young adults at home. *Canadian Social Trends* (Spring), 2–5.

Boyer, C. B., & Hein, K. (1991). AIDS and the HIV infection in adolescents: The role of education and antibody testing. In R. M. Lerner, A. C. Petersen, & J. Brooks-Gunn (Eds.), *Encyclopedia of Adolescence* (Vol. 2, pp. 1028–1041). New York: Garland.

Boyer, C. B., Shafer, M., & Tschann, J. M. (1997). Evaluation of a knowledge- and cognitive-behavioral skills-building intervention to prevent STDs and HIV infection in high school students. *Adolescence, 32*(125), 25–42.

Boyes, M. & Allen, S. (1993). Styles of parent-child interaction and moral reasoning in adolescence. *Merrill-Palmer Quarterly, 39,* 551–570.

Boyes, M. C., & Chandler, M. (1992). Cognitive development, epistemic doubt, and identity formation in adolescence. *Journal of Youth and Adolescence, 21*(3), 277–304.

Brabeck, M. (1983). Moral judgment: Theory and research on differences between males and females. *Developmental Review, 3,* 274–291.

Brack, C., Brack, G., & Orr, D. P. (1996). Adolescent health promotion: Testing a model using multidimensional scaling. *Journal of Research on Adolescence, 6*(2), 139–149.

Brame, B., Nagin, D. S., & Tremblay, R. E. (2001). Developmental trajectories of physical aggression from school entry to late adolescence. *Journal of Child Psychology and Psychiatry and Allied Disciplines, 42*(4), 503–512.

Brandtstädter, J. (1998). Action perspectives on human development. In W. Damon (Series Ed.) & R. M. Lerner (Vol. Ed.), *Handbook of child psychology: Vol. 1. Theoretical models of human development* (5th ed., pp. 807–863). New York: Wiley.

Brandtstädter, J. (1999). The self in action and development: Cultural, biosocial, and ontogenetic bases of intentional self-development. In J. Brandtstädter & R. M. Lerner (Eds.), *Action and self-development: Theory and research through the life span.* Thousand Oaks, CA: Sage.

Brandtstädter, J., & Wentura, D. (1995). Adjustment to shifting possibility frontiers in later life: Complementary adaptive modes. In R. A. Dixon & L. Bäckman (Eds.), *Psychological compensation: Managing losses and promoting gains* (pp. 83–106). Hillsdale, NJ: Erlbaum.

Bray, N., Hersh, R. E., & Turner, L. A. (1985). Selective remembering during adolescence. *Developmental Psychology, 21*(2), 290–294.

Breen, D. T., & Crosbie-Burnette, M. (1993). Moral dilemmas of early adolescents of divorced and intact families: A qualitative and quantitative analysis. *Journal of Early Adolescence, 13,* 168–182.

Brendgen M., Vitaro, F., and Bukowski, W. M. (2000). Stability and variability of adolescents' affiliation with delinquent friends: Predictors and consequences. *Social Development, 9*(2), 205–225.

Brendgen, M., Vitaro, F., & Bukowski, W. M. (2000a). Deviant friends and early adolescents' emotional and behavioural adjustment. *Journal of Research on Adolescence, 10*(2), 173–189.

Brendgen, M., Vitaro, F., & Bukowski, W. M. (2000b). Stability and variability of adolescents' affiliation with delinquent friends: Predictors and consequences. *Social Development, 9*(2), 205–225.

Breton, J. J., Bergeron, L., Valla, J. P., Berthiaume, C., Gaudet, N., Lambert, J., et al. (1999). Quebec Child Mental Health Survey: Prevalence of DSM-III—R mental health disorders. *Journal of Child Psychology and Psychiatry and Allied Disciplines, 40*(3), 375–384.

Breton, J. J., Tousignant, M., Bergeron, L., & Berthiaume, C. (2002). Informant-specific correlates of suicidal behavior in a community survey of 12- to 14-year-olds. *Journal of the American Academy of Child and Adolescent Psychiatry, 41*(6), 723–730.

Brewster, K. L., Cooksey, E. C., Guilkey, D. K., & Rindfuss, R. R. (1998). The changing impact of religion on the sexual and contraceptive behavior of adolescent women in the United States. *Journal of Marriage and the Family, 60,* 493–504.

British Columbia Ministry of Children and Family Development (2002). *The health and well-being of Aboriginal children and youth in British Columbia.*

Brittain, C. V. (1963). Adolescent choices and parent-peer cross pressures. *American Sociological Review, 28,* 385–391.

Brody, F., & Forehand, R. (1990). Interparental conflict, relationship with the noncustodial father, and adolescent post-divorce adjustment. *Journal of Applied Developmental Psychology, 32*(4), 696–706.

Brody, G. H., Stoneman, Z., & Flor, D. (1995). Linking family processes and academic competence among rural

African American youths. *Journal of Marriage and the Family, 57,* 567–579.

Brody, G. H., Stoneman, Z., & Flor, D. (1996). Parental religiosity, family processes, and youth competence in rural, two-parent African American families. *Developmental Psychology, 32*(4), 696–706.

Broman, S. (1979). Seven-year outcome of 4,000 children born to teenagers in the U.S. In K. G. Scott, T. Field, & E. Robertson (Eds.), *Teenage parents and their offspring* (pp. 195–226). New York: Grune & Stratton.

Bronfenbrenner, U. (1960). Freudian theories of identification and their derivatives. *Child Development, 31,* 15–40.

Bronfenbrenner, U. (1977). Toward an experimental ecology of human development. *American Psychologist, 32,* 513–531.

Bronfenbrenner, U. (1979). *The ecology of human development: Experiments by nature and design.* Cambridge: Harvard University Press.

Bronfenbrenner, U., & Morris, P. A. (1998). The ecology of developmental process. In W. Damon (Series Ed.) & R. M. Lerner (Vol. Ed.), *Handbook of child psychology: Vol. 1. Theoretical models of human development* (5th ed., pp. 993–1028). New York: Wiley.

Bronstein, P., Fitzgerald, M., Briones, M., & Pieniadz, J. (1993). Family emotional expressiveness as a predictor of early adolescent social and psychological adjustment. *Journal of Early Adolescence, 13,* 448–471.

Brook, J. S., Whiteman, M., Gordon, A. S., & Cohen, P. (1986). Some models and mechanisms for explaining the impact of maternal and adolescent characteristics on adolescent stages of drug use. *Developmental Psychology, 22,* 460–467.

Brookins, G. K. (1991). Socialization of African American adolescents. In R. M. Lerner, A. C. Petersen, & J. Brooks-Gunn (Eds.), *Encyclopedia of adolescence* (Vol. 2, pp. 1072–1076). New York: Garland.

Brooks-Gunn, J. (1987). Pubertal processes in girls' psychological adaptation. In R. M. Lerner & T. T. Foch (Eds.), *Biological-psychosocial interactions in early adolescence: A life-span perspective* (pp. 123–153). Hillsdale, NJ: Erlbaum.

Brooks-Gunn, J. (1989). Pubertal processes and the early adolescent transition. In W. Damon (Ed.), *Child development today and tomorrow. The Jossey-Bass social and behavioral science series* (pp. 155–176). San Francisco: Jossey-Bass.

Brooks-Gunn, J., & Chase-Lansdale, P. L. (1995). Adolescent parenthood. In M. H. Bornstein (Ed.), *Handbook of parenting: Vol. 3. Status and social conditions of parenting* (pp. 113–149). Mahwah, NJ: Erlbaum.

Brooks-Gunn, J., & Furstenberg, F. F. (1986). The children of adolescent mothers: Physical, academic, and psychological outcomes. *Developmental Review, 6*(3), 224–251.

Brooks-Gunn, J., & Furstenberg, F. F., Jr. (1987). Continuity and change in the context of poverty: Adolescent mothers and their children. In J. J. Gallagher & C. T. Ramey (Eds.), *The malleability of children* (pp. 171–188). Baltimore: Brooks.

Brooks-Gunn, J., & Petersen, A. C. (1983). *Girls at puberty: Biological and psychosocial perspectives.* New York: Plenum.

Brooks-Gunn, J., Gus, G., & Furstenberg, F. F. (1993). Who drops out of and continues beyond high school? A 20-year follow-up of black urban youth. *Journal of Research on Adolescence, 3*(3), 271–294.

Brooks-Gunn, J., Petersen, A. C., & Eichorn, D. (1985). The study of maturational timing effects in adolescence. *Journal of Youth & Adolescence, 14*(3), 149–161.

Broverman, I. K., Vogel, S. R., Broverman, D. M., Clarkson, F. E., & Rosenkrantz, P. S. (1972). Sex-role stereotypes: A current appraisal. *Journal of Social Issues, 28,* 59–78.

Brown, B. B. (1990). Peer groups and peer cultures. In S. S. Feldman & G. R. Elliott (Eds.), *At the threshold: The developing adolescent* (pp. 171–196). Cambridge: Harvard University Press.

Brown, B. B. (1996). Visibility, vulnerability, development, and context: Ingredients for a fuller understanding of peer rejection in adolescence. *Journal of Early Adolescence, 16*(1), 27–36.

Brown, B. B., Clasen, D. R., & Neiss, J. D. (1987, April). *Smoke in the looking glass: Adolescents' perceptions of peer group status.* Paper presented at the biennial meetings of the Society for Research in Child Development, Baltimore.

Brown, B. B., Mory, M. S., & Kinney, D. (1994). Casting adolescent crowds in a relational perspective: Caricature, channel, and context. In R. Montemayor, G. R. Adams, & T. P. Gullotta (Eds.), *Personal relationships during adolescence. Advances in adolescent development: An annual book series* (Vol. 6, pp. 123–167). Thousand Oaks, CA: Sage.

Brown, B. B., Mounts, N., Lamborn, S. D., & Steinberg, L. (1993). Parenting practices and peer group affiliation in adolescence. *Child Development, 62,* 1008–1029.

Brown, J. (1996). *Homeless adolescents in Edmonton: A descriptive study.* University of Alberta, Edmonton.

Browne, C. S., & Rife, J. C. (1991). Social, personality, and gender differences in at-risk and not-at-risk sixth-grade students. *Journal of Early Adolescence, 11,* 482–495.

Brussoni, M. J. and Boon, S. D. (1998). Grandparental impact in young adults' relationships with their closest grandparents: The role of relationship strength and emotional closeness. *International Journal of Aging and Human Development, 45,* 267–286.

Bu, N., & McKeen, C. A. (2000). Work and family expectations of the future managers and professionals of Canada and China. *Journal of Managerial Psychology, 15*(7–8), 77–190.

Bubolz, M. M., & Sontag, M. S. (1993). Human ecology theory. In P. G. Boss, W. J. Doherty, R. LaRossa, W. R. Schumm, & S. K. Steinmetz (Eds.), *Sourcebook of family theories and methods: A contextual approach* (pp. 419–448). New York: Plenum.

Buchanan, C. M. (1991). Assessment of pubertal development. In R. M. Lerner, A. C. Petersen, and J. Brooks-Gunn (Eds.), *Encyclopedia of adolescence* (Vol. 2, pp. 875–883). New York: Garland.

Buchanan, C. M., Maccoby, E. E., & Dornbusch, S. M. (1992). Adolescents and their families after divorce: Three residential arrangements compared. *Journal of Research on Adolescence, 2*(3), 261–291.

Buchanan, C. M., Maccoby, E., & Dornbusch, S. M. (1991). Caught between parents: Adolescents' experience in divorced homes. *Child Development, 62,* 1008–1029.

Buehler, C., Krishnakumar, A., Stone, G., Anthony, C., Pemberton, S., Gerard,

J., & Barber, B. K. (1998). Interparental conflict styles and youth problem behaviors: A two-sample replication study. *Journal of Marriage and the Family, 60*, 119–132.

Buhrmester, D. (1988, March). *Interpersonal competence and friuendship in early adolescence.* Paper presented at the Second Biennial Meeting of the Society for Research on Adolescence, Alexandria, VA.

Bukowski, W. M., & Kramer, T. L. (1986). Judgments of the features of friendship among early adolescent boys and girls. *Journal of Early Adolescence, 6*(4), 331–338.

Bukowski, W. M., & Newcomb, A. F. (1987, April). *Friendship quality and the "self" during early adolescence.* Paper presented at the Biennial Meeting of the Society for Research in Child Development, Baltimore.

Bukowski, W. M., Hoza, B., & Boivin, M. (1993). Popularity, friendship, and emotional adjustment during early adolescence. *New Directions for Child Development, 60*, 23–37.

Bulcroft, R. A., Carmody, D. C., & Bulcroft, K. A. (1996). Patterns of parental independence giving to adolescents: Variations by race, age, and gender of child. *Journal of Marriage and the Family, 58*, 866–883.

Bull, L. (1991). Indian residential schooling: The Native perspective. *Canadian Journal of Native Education, 18* (supplement), 1–64.

Bumpass, L., & Sweet, J. (1989). National estimates of cohabitation. *Demography, 26*(4), 615–625.

Burke, M.A. (1986). Families: Diversity the new norm. *Canadian Social Trends.* Ottawa: Statistics Canada.

Butcher, J., Lindner, K. J., & Johns, D. P. (2002). Withdrawal from competitive youth sport: A retrospective ten-year study. *Journal of Sport Behavior, 25*(2), 145–163.

Buzwell, S., & Rosenthal, D. (1996). Constructing a sexual self: Adolescents' sexual self-perceptions and sexual risk-taking. *Journal of Research on Adolescence, 6*(4), 489–513.

Byrnes, J. P., & Takahira, S. (1993). Explaining gender differences in SAT-math items. *Developmental Psychology, 29*, 805–810.

C

Cairns, E., & Dawes, A. (1996). Children: Ethnic and political violence—a commentary. *Child Development, 67*, 129–139.

Cairns, R. B., & Cairns, B. D. (1994). *Lifelines and risks: Pathways of youth in our time.* New York: Cambridge University Press.

Cairns, R. B., Leung, M., Buchanan, L., & Cairns, B. D. (1995). Friendships and social networks in childhood and adolescence: Fluidity, reliability, and interrelations. *Child Development, 66*, 1330–1345.

Call, K. T., Mortimer, J. T., & Shanahan, M. J. (1995). Helpfulness and the development of competence in adolescence. *Child Development, 66*, 129–138.

Camarena, P. M., Stemmler, M., & Petersen, A. C. (1994). The gender-differential significance of work and family: An exploration of adolescent experience and expectation. In R. K. Silbereisen & E. Todt (Eds.), *Adolescence in context: The interplay of family, school, peers, and work in adjustment* (pp. 201–221). New York: Springer-Verlag.

Camino, L. A. (1995). Understanding intolerance and multiculturalism: A challenge for practitioners, but also for researchers. *Journal of Adolescent Research, 10*(1), 155–172.

Campaign 2000 (2003). *No gains in child poverty over the past decade, shows 2001 census.* Ottawa: Campaign 2000.

Canadian Council on Social Development (1998). *The progress of Canada's children 1998: Focus on youth.*

Canadian Council on Social Development (2002). *The progress of Canada's children: 2002 highlights.* Retrieved from: www.ccsd.ca/pubs/2002/pcc02/hl.pdf.

Canadian Policy Research Networks (CPRN; 2000). *Backgrounder: Youth and work in troubled times: A report on Canada in the 1990s.* Changing patterns of school-to-work transition. Retrieved from www.cprn.com/Release/Back/bywt_e.htm#text_2.

Canadian Policy Research Networks Inc. (CPRN; February, 2001). *CPRN Backgrounder: Youth Recreation: A Pathway to Citizenship.* A Family Network Research Initiative. Retrieved from: www.cprn.org.

Canadian Race Relations Foundation (2000) *Unequal access: A Canadian profile of racial differences in education, employment and income: Report Highlights.* Retrieved from: www.crr.ca/en/Publications/Research Reports/doc/ePub_UneqlAcc_highlights.pdf.

Canals, J., Carbajo, G., Fernandez, J., Marti-Henneberg, C., & Domenech, E. (1996). Biopsychopathologic risk profile of adolescents with eating disorder symptoms. *Adolescence, 31*(122), 443–450.

Cannetti, L., Bachar, E., Galili-Weisstub, E., De-Nour, A. K., & Shalev, Arieh Y. (1997). Parental bonding and mental health in adolescence. *Adolescence, 32*(126), 381–394.

Capaldi, D. M. (1996). The reliability of retrospective report timing first sexual intercourse for adolescent males. *Journal of Adolescent Research, 11*(3), 375–387.

Capaldi, D. M., Crosby, L., & Stoolmiller, M. (1996). Predicting the timing of first sexual intercourse for at-risk adolescent males. *Child Development, 67*, 344–359.

Caputo, T. (1999). *Hearing the Voices of Youth: A review of Research and Consultation Documents.* Ottawa, ON: Health Canada.

Caputo, T. (2000). *Hearing the Voices of Youth: Youth participation in Selected Canadian Municipalities.* Ottawa, ON: Health Canada.

Carlo, G., Eisenberg, N., & Knight, G. (1992). An objective measure of adolescents' prosocial moral reasoning. *Journal of Research on Adolescence, 2*(4), 331–349.

Carnegie Corporation of New York. (1992). *A matter of time: Risk and opportunity in the nonschool hours.* New York: Author.

Carnegie Corporation of New York. (1994). *Starting points: Meeting the needs of our youngest children.* New York: Author.

Carnegie Corporation of New York. (1995). *Great transitions: Preparing adolescents for a new century.* New York: Author.

Carnegie Council on Adolescent Development. (1989). *Turning points: Preparing American youth for the twenty-first century.* Washington, DC: Author.

Carroll, A., Durkin, K., Hattie, J., & Houghton, S. (1997). Goal setting among adolescents: A comparison of delinquent, at risk, and not-at-risk youth. *Journal of Educational Psychology, 89*(3), 441–450.

Carroll, G. B., Hebert, D. M. C., & Roy, J. M. (1999). Youth action strategies in violence prevention. *Journal of Adolescent Health, 25*(1), 7–13.

Carroll, G.B., Hebert, D.M.C., & Roy, J.M. (1999). Youth action strategies in violence prevention. *Journal of Adolescent Health, 25*(1), 7–13.

Carskadon, M.A. (1999). Sleepy students fight the school clock. *Education Digest, 64*(9), 12–14.

Carson, A., Madison, T., & Santrock, J. (1987). Relationships between possible selves and self-reported problems of divorced and intact family adolescents. *Journal of Early Adolescence, 7*(20), 191–204.

Carstensen, L. L., Hanson, K. A., & Freund, A. (1995). Selection and compensation in adulthood. In R. A. Dixon & L. Bäckman (Eds.), *Compensating for psychological deficits and declines: Managing losses and promoting gains* (pp. 107–126). Hillsdale, NJ: Erlbaum.

Casey, M. B., Nuttall, R., Pezaris, E., & Benbow, C. P. (1995). The influence of spatial ability on gender differences in mathematics college entrance test scores across diverse samples. *Developmental Psychology, 31*(4), 697–705.

Caspi, A., & Silva, P. A. (1995). Temperamental qualities at age three predict personality traits in young adulthood: Longitudinal evidence from a birth cohort. *Child Development, 66*, 486–498.

Caspi, A., Henry, B., McGee, R. O., Moffitt, T. E., & Silva, P. A. (1995). Temperamental origins of child and adolescent behavior problems: From age three to age fifteen. *Child Development, 66*, 55–68.

Caspi, A., Lynam, D., Moffitt, T. E., & Silva, P. A. (1993). Unraveling girls' delinquency: Biological, dispositional, and contextual contributions to adolescent misbehavior. *Developmental Psychology, 29*, 19–30.

Cassidy, L., & Hurrell, R. M. (1995). The influence of the victim's attire on adolescents' judgements of date rape. *Adolescence, 30*(118), 319–323.

Castellino, D. R., & Lerner, R. M. (1999, May). *Youth and vocational development: A developmental contextual perspective.* Paper presented at the Fourth

National Conference of the Society for Vocational Psychology, a section of the Counseling Psychology Division of the American Psychological Association, on "Examining the interaction of person in environment: Role of context factors in vocational development," Milwaukee, WI.

Catell, R. B. (1963). Theory of fluid and crystallized intelligence: A critical experiment. *Journal of Educational Psychology, 54*, 1–22.

Cattell, R. B. (1973). *Personality and mood by questionnaire.* San Francisco: Jossey-Bass.

Cauffman, E., & Steinberg, L. (1996). Interactive effects of menarcheal status and dating on dieting and disordered eating among adolescent girls. *Developmental Psychology, 32*(4), 631–635.

CBC.ca News (2003). Edmonton police can ticket bullies under new bylaw. Published by the Canadian Broadcasting Corporation. Retrieved on June 26, 2003, from: www.cbc.ca/stories/2003/03/12/edm_bullying030312.

Ceci, S. J., & Bronfenbrenner, U. (1985). "Don't forget to take the cupcakes out of the oven": Prospective memory, strategic time-monitoring, and context. *Child Development, 56*(1), 152–164.

Center for the Study of Social Policy. (1992). *1992 Kids Count Data Book: State profiles of child well-being.* Washington, DC: Author.

Center for the Study of Social Policy. (1993). *1993 Kids Count Data Book.* Washington, DC: Author.

Center for the Study of Social Policy. (1995). *Kids count data book.* Washington, DC: Author.

Centers for Disease Control and Prevention. (1998). Youth risk behavior surveillance—United States, 1997. *Morbidity and Mortality Weekly Report, 47*, (33–3).

Centre for Addiction and Mental Health (2002). Rave attendance stabilizes among Ontario students. *CAMH Population Studies eBulletin, 13.*

Chamberlain, P., & Reid, J. B. (1998). Comparison of two community alternatives to incarceration for chronic juvenile offenders. *Journal of Consulting and Clinical Psychology, 66*(4), 624–633.

Chamberland, C., Dallaire, N., Hebert, J., Frechette, L., Lindsay, J., &

Cameron, S. (2000). Are ecological and social models influencing prevention practices? An overview of the state of affairs in Quebec for child, youth and family intervention. *Journal of Primary Prevention, 21*(1), 101–125.

Chandler, M. & Lalonde, C. (1998). Cultural continuity as a hedge against suicide in Canada's First Nations. *Transcultural Psychiatry, 35*(2), 191–219.

Chase-Lansdale, P. L., Cherlin, A. J., & Kiernan, K. E. (1995). The long-term effects of parental divorce on the mental health of young adults: A developmental perspective. *Child Development, 66*, 1614–1634.

Chase-Lansdale, P. L., Wakschlag, L. S., & Brooks-Gunn, J. (1995). A psychological perspective on the development of caring in children and youth: The role of the family. *Journal of Adolescence, 18*, 515–556.

Chassin, L. A., Presson, C. C., Sherman, S. J., Montello, D., & McGrew, J. (1986). Changes in peer and parent influence during adolescence: Longitudinal versus cross-sectional perspectives on smoking initiation. *Developmental Psychology, 22*(3), 327–334.

Che, J. (2002). Underweight Canadians. *Canadian Social Trends.* Catalogue No. 11-008. Ottawa: Statistics Canada.

Che-Alford, J., & Hamm, B. (1999). Under one roof: Three generations living together. *Canadian Social Trends.* Catalogue No. 11-008. Ottawa: Statistics Canada.

Cheesbrough, S., Ingham, R., & Massey, D. (2002) Reducing the rate of teenage conception: A review of the international evidence on preventing and reducing teenage conceptions: the United States, Canada, Australia and New Zealand. London, UK: Health Development Agency. Retrieved from www.hda-online.org.uk/downloads/pdfs/teenconcep_revise_v3.pdf.

Chen, C., & Stevenson, H. W. (1995). Motivation and mathematics achievement: A comparative study of Asian-American, Caucasian-American, and East Asian high school students. *Child Development, 66*, 1215–1234.

Chen, C., Lee, S.-Y., & Stevenson, H. W. (1996). Long-term prediction of academic achievement of American, Chinese, and Japanese adolescents.

Journal of Educational Psychology, 18(4), 750–759.

Chess, S., & Thomas, A. (1984). *The origins and evolution of behavior disorders: Infancy to early adult life.* New York: Brunner/Mazel.

Chibucos, T., & Lerner, R. M. (1999). *Serving children and families through community-university partnerships: Success stories.* Norwell, MA: Kluwer.

Children's Defense Fund. (1992). *Child poverty data from 1990 census.* Washington, DC: Author.

Children's Defense Fund. (1995). *The state of America's children yearbook.* Washington, DC: Author.

Children's Defense Fund. (2001). *The state of America's children yearbook.* Washington, DC: Author.

Chisholm, J., & Edmunds, A. (2001). Career decision making in the shadow of economic downturn: A study of Cape Breton high school students. *Canadian Journal of Counselling, 35*(4), 277–287.

Chiu, M. L., Feldman, S. S., & Rosenthal, D. A. (1992). The influence of immigration on parental behavior and adolescent distress in Chinese families residing in two Western nations. *Journal of Research on Adolescence, 2,* 205–239.

Choi, P. Y. L., Pope, H. G., Jr., Olivardia, R., & Cash, T. F. (2002). Muscle dysmorphia: A new syndrome in weightlifters. *British Journal of Sports Medicine, 36*(5), 375–377.

Choquet, M., Kovess, V., & Poutignat, N. (1993). Suicidal thoughts among adolescents: An intercultural approach. *Adolescence, 28*(111), 649–659.

Chow, H. P. H. (2001a). English-language use among Chinese adolescent immigrants. *Alberta Journal of Educational Research, 47*(2), 191–195.

Chow, H. P. H. (2001b). Learning the Chinese language in a multicultural milieu: Factors affecting Chinese-Canadian adolescents' ethnic language school experience. *Alberta Journal of Educational Research, 47*(4), 369–374.

Chowdhury, S., Shahabuddin, A. K. M., Seal, A. J., Talukder, K. K., Hassan, Q., Begum, R. A., Rahman, Q., Tomkins, A. Costello, A. and Talukder, M. Q. K. (2000). Nutritional status and age at menarche in a rural area of Bangladesh. *Annals of Human Biology, 27*(3), 249–256.

Chubb, N. H., Fertman, C. I., & Ross, J. L. (1997). Adolescent self-esteem and locus of control: A longitudinal study of gender and age differences. *Adolescence, 32*(125), 113–129.

Ciccocioppo, A., Stewin, L., Madill, H., Montgomerie, T., Tovell, D., Armour, M., et al. (2002). Transitional patterns of adolescent females in non-traditional career paths. *Canadian Journal of Counselling, 36*(1), 25–37.

Claes, M. (1998). Adolescents' closeness with parents, siblings, and friends in three countries: Canada, Belgium, and Italy. *Journal of Youth and Adolescence, 27*(2), 165–184.

Clancy, S. M., & Dollinger, S. J. (1993). Identity, self, and personality: I. Identity status and the five-factor model of personality. *Journal of Research on Adolescence, 3*(3), 227–245.

Clark, J., & Barber, B. L. (1994). Adolescents in postdivorce and always-married families: Self-esteem and perceptions of fathers' interest. *Journal of Marriage and the Family, 56,* 608–614.

Clark, W. (2000). Education. *Canadian Social Trends* (Winter), 3–7.

Clark, W. (2000). Patterns of religious attendance. *Canadian Social Trends, 59,* 23–27.

Clark-Lempers, D., Lempers, J., & Netusil, A. (1990). Family financial stress, parental support, and young adolescents' academic achievement and depressive symptoms. *Journal of Early Adolescence, 10*(1), 21–36.

Clausen, J. A. (1975). The social meaning of differential physical and sexual maturation. In S. E. Dragastin & G. H. Elder, Jr. (Eds.), *Adolescence in the life cycle* (pp. 25–97). New York: Wiley.

Clingempeel, W. G., Colyar, J. J., Brand, E., & Hetherington, E. M. (1992). Children's relationships with maternal grandparents: A longitudinal study of family structure and pubertal status effects. *Child Development, 63*(6), 1404–1422.

Cnattingius, S., Hultman, C. M., Dahl, M., & Sparen, P. (1999). Very preterm birth, birth trauma, and the risk of anorexia among girls. *Archives of General Psychiatry, 56*(7), 634.

Coates, D. L. (1991). Social networks in adolescence. In R. M. Lerner, A. C. Petersen, & J. Brooks-Gunn (Eds.), *Encyclopedia of adolescence* (Vol. 2, pp. 1077–1085). New York: Garland.

Coates, D. L., & Van Widenfelt, B. (1991). Pregnancy in adolescence. In R. M. Lerner, A. C. Petersen, & J. Brooks-Gunn (Eds.), *Encyclopedia of adolescence* (Vol. 1, pp. 794–802). New York: Garland.

Cohen, M. (1997). Cracking the glass ceiling. *Canadian Medical Association Journal, 157*(12), 1713–1714.

Cohler, B. J., & Musick, J. S. (1996). Adolescent parenthood and the transition to adulthood. In J. Graber, J. Brooks-Gunn, & A. C. Petersen (Eds.), *Transitions through adolescence: Interpersonal domains and context* (pp. 201–231). Mahwah, NJ: Erlbaum.

Colby, A. (1978). Evolution of a moral-development theory. *New Directions for Child Development, 2,* 89–104.

Colby, A., & Damon, W. (1992). *Some do care: Contemporary lives of moral commitment.* New York: Free Press.

Colby, A., Kohlberg, L., Gibbs, J., & Lieberman, M. (1983). A longitudinal study of moral judgment. *Monographs of the Society for Research in Child Development, 48*(200).

Cole, D. A., Peeke, L. G., Martin, J. M., Truglio, R., & Seroczynski, A. D. (1998). A longitudinal look at the relation between depression and anxiety in children and adolescents. *Journal of Consulting and Clinical Psychology, 66*(3), 451–460.

Collins, S. (2002). Building collaboration and balancing stakeholder needs in Comprehensive Health and Guidance programming. *Canadian Journal of Counselling, 36*(1), 63–72.

Collins, W. A. (1997). Relationships and development during adolescence: Interpersonal adaptation to individual change. *Personal Relationships, 4,* 1–14.

Collins, W. A., Laursen, B., Mortensen, N., Luebker, C., & Ferreira, M. (1997). Conflict processes and transitions in parent and peer relationships: Implications for autonomy and regulation. *Journal of Adolescent Research, 12,* 178–198.

Comer, J. (1989). Educating poor minority children. *Scientific American, 259*(5), 42–48.

Comite, F., Pescovitz, O., Sonis, W., Hench, K., McNemar, A., Klein, R. P., Loriaux, D., & Cutler, G. (1987). Premature adolescence: Neuroendocrine and psychosocial studies. In R. M. Lerner & T. T. Foch (Eds.), *Biological-psychosocial interactions in early adolescence* (pp. 155–171). Hillsdale, NJ: Erlbaum.

Compas, B. E., Howell, D. C., Phares, V., Williams, R. A., & Giunta, C. (1989). Risk factors for emotional/behavioral problems in young adolescents: A prospective analysis of adolescent and parental stress and symptoms. *Journal of Consulting & Clinical Psychology, 57,* 732–740.

Compas, B. E., Oppedisano, G., Connor, J. K., Gerhardt, C. A., Hinden, B. R., Achenbach, T. M., & Hammen, C. (1997). Gender differences in depressive symptoms in adolescence: Comparison of national samples of clinically referred and nonreferred youths. *Journal of Consulting and Clinical Psychology, 65*(4), 617–626.

Condon, R., & Stern, P. R. (1993). Gender-role preference, gender identity, & gender socialization among contemporary Inuit youth. *Ethos, 21*(4), 384–416.

Conger, K. J., Conger, R. D., & Scaramella, L. V. (1997). Parents, siblings, psychological control, and adolescent adjustment. *Journal of Adolescent Research, 12*(1), 113–138.

Conger, R. D., & Elder, G. H., Jr. (1994). *Families in troubled times: Adapting to change in rural America. Social institutions and social change.* New York: Aldine de Gruyter.

Conger, R. D., Conger, K. J., Elder, G. H., Jr., Lorenz, F. O., Simons, R. L., & Whitbeck, L. B. (1992). A family process model of economic hardship and adjustment of early adolescent boys. *Child Development, 63,* 526–541.

Conger, R. D., Lorenz, F. O., Elder, G. H., Jr., Melby, J. N., Simons, R. L., & Conger, K. J. (1991). A process model of family economic pressure and early adolescent alcohol use. *Journal of Early Adolescence, 11,* 430–499.

Conger, R. D., Patterson, G. R., & Ge, X. (1995). It takes two to replicate: A mediational model for the impact of parents' stress on adolescent adjustment. *Child Development, 66,* 80–97.

Connell, A., & Farrington, D. P. (1996). Bullying among incarcerated young offenders: Developing an interview

schedule and some preliminary results. *Journal of Adolescence, 19,* 75–93.

Connell, J. P., Halpern-Felsher, B. L., Clifford, E., Crichlow, W., & Usinger, P. (1995). Hanging in there: Behavioral, psychological, and contextual factors affecting whether African American adolescents stay in high school. *Journal of Adolescence Research, 10*(1), 41–63.

Connell, J. P., Kubisch, A. C., Schorr, L. B., & Weiss, C. H. (1995). *New approaches to evaluating community initiatives: Concepts, methods, and contexts.* Washington, DC: The Aspen Institute.

Connolly, J., Pepler, D., Craig, W., & Taradash, A. (2000). Dating experiences of bullies in early adolescence. *Child Maltreatment, 5*(4), 299–310.

Constantinople, A. (1969). An Eriksonian measure of personality development in college students. *Developmental Psychology, 1,* 357–372.

Coontz, S. (1992). *The way we never were.* NY: Basic Books.

Cooper, C. R. (1994a). Cultural perspectives on continuity and change in adolescents' relationships. In R. Montemayor, G. R. Adams, & T. P. Gulotta (Eds.), *Advances in adolescent development: Vol. 6. Personal relationships during adolescence* (pp. 78–100). Thousand Oaks, CA: Sage.

Cooper, C. R. (1994b). Cultural perspectives on individuality and connectedness in adolescent development. In C. Nelson & A. Masten (Eds.), *Minnesota symposium on child psychology: Cultural processes in child development.* Hillsdale, NJ: Erlbaum.

Cooper, C. R., Grotevant, H. D., & Condon, S. M. (1983). Individuality and connectedness in the family as a context for adolescent identity formation and role-taking skill. *New Directions for Child Development, 22,* 43–59.

Cooper, C. R., Jackson, J. F., Azmitia, M., & Lopez, E. M. (1998). Multiple selves, multiple worlds: Ethnically sensitive research on identity, relationships, and opportunity structures in adolescence. In V. McLoyd & L. Steinberg (Eds.), *Conceptual and methodological issues in the study of minority adolescents and their families.* Hillsdale, NJ: Erlbaum.

Copping, V. E., Warling, D. L., Benner, D. G., & Woodside, D. W. (2001). A child trauma treatment pilot study.

Journal of Child and Family Studies, 10(4), 467–475.

Corbett, T. (1995). Changing the culture of welfare. *Focus, 16,* 12–22.

Cornell, D. G., Peterson, C. S., & Richards, H. (1999). Anger as a predictor of aggression among incarcerated adolescents. *Journal of Consulting and Clinical Psychology, 67*(1), 108–115.

Cornwell, G. T., Eggebeen, D. J., & Meschke, L. L. (1996). The changing family context of early adolescence. *Journal of Early Adolescence, 16*(2), 141–156.

Corville Smith, J., Ryan, B.A., Adams, G.R., & Dalicandro, T. (1998). Distinguishing absentee students from regular attenders: The combined influence of personal, family, and school factors. *Journal of Youth and Adolescence, 27*(5), 629–640.

Corvo, K. N. (1997). Community-based youth violence prevention: A framework for planners and funders. *Youth & Society, 28*(3), 291–316.

Costa, F. M., Jessor, R., Donovan, J. E., & Fortenberry, J. D. (1995). Early initiation of sexual intercourse: The influence of psychosocial unconventionality. *Journal of Research on Adolescence, 5*(1), 93–121.

Côté, J. (2003). College as a transition to adulthood. In G. R. Adams and M. D. Berzonsky (Eds.) *Blackwell handbook of adolescence* (pp. 149–172). Malden, MA: Blackwell.

Côté, J. E. (1996). Sociological perspectives on identity formation: The culture-identity link and identity capital. *Journal of Adolescence, 19,* 417–428.

Côté, J. E. & Levine, C. G. (1997). Student motivations, learning environments, and human capital acquisition: Toward an integrated paradigm of student development. *Journal of College Student Development, 38*(3), 229–243.

Côté, J. E. & Levine, C. G. (2000). Attitude versus aptitude: Is intelligence or motivation more important for positive higher-educational outcomes? *Journal of Adolescent Research, 15*(1), 58–80.

Côté, J. E. (2000a). The Mead-Freeman controversy in review. *Journal of Youth and Adolescence, 29*(5), 525–538.

Côté, J. E. (2000b). The implausibility of Freeman's hoaxing theory: An update. *Journal of Youth and Adolescence, 29*(5), 575–585.

Côté, J. E. (2002). The role of identity capital in the transition to adulthood: The individualization thesis examined. *Journal of Youth Studies, 5*(2), 117–134.

Côté, J. E., & Allahar, A. L. (1994). *Generation on hold: Coming of age in the late twentieth century.* Toronto: Stoddart.

Cotgrove, A., Zirinsky, L., Black, D., & Weston, D. (1995). Secondary prevention of attempted suicide in adolescence. *Journal of Adolescence, 18*, 569–577.

Cotterell, J. L. (1992). School size as a factor in adolescents' adjustment to the transition to secondary school. *Journal of Early Adolescence, 12*(1), 28–45.

Couture, S. (2002). Addressing student needs throughout development. *Canadian Journal of Counselling, 36*(1), 38–48.

Covell, K. (1996). National and gender differences in adolescents' war attitudes. *International Journal of Behavioral Development, 19*(4), 871–883.

Covell, K., & Howe, B. (1999). Working adolescents in economically depressed areas of Canada. *Canadian Journal of Behavioural Science, 31*(4), 229–239.

Covell, K., & Howe, R. B. (2001). Moral Education through the 3 Rs: Rights, respect and responsibility. *Journal of Moral Education, 30*(1), 29–41.

Craig, W. M., Vitaro, F., Gagnon, C., & Tremblay, R. E. (2002). The road to gang membership: Characteristics of male gang and nongang members from ages 10 to 14. *Social Development, 11*(1), 53–68.

Craig, W., Pepler, D., & Connolly, J. (1997). Bullying and victimization: The problems and solutions for school-aged children. National Crime Prevention Council of Canada. Retrieved from the World Wide Web: www.prevention.gc.ca/en/library/publications/children/violence/index.html.

Craig, W., Pepler, D., Connolly, J., & Henderson, K. (2001). Developmental context of peer harassment in early adolescence: The role of puberty and the peer group. In J. Juivonen & S. Graham (Eds.) *Peer harassment in school: The plight of the vulnerable and victimized* (pp. 242–261). N.Y: Guilford Press.

Crockett, L., & Petersen, A. (1987). Pubertal status and psychosocial development: Findings from the Early Adolescence Study. In R. M. Lerner & T. Foch (Eds.), *Biological-psychosocial interactions in early adolescence* (pp. 173–188). Hillsdale, NJ: Erlbaum.

Crockett, L., Losoff, M., & Petersen, A. C. (1984). Perceptions of the peer group and friendship in early adolescence. *Journal of Early Adolescence, 4*(2), 155–181.

Crognier, E., Elizondo, S. M., Caratini, A. L., Zubieta, N. I., Niborsky, R., Carnese, F. R. (1996). LOS Comportamientos Reproductivos De La Poblacion Mapuche De La Provincia De Rio Negro. *Argentina Magazine of Antropologia Biologica. Rev. Arg. Antrop. Biol. 1*(1), 86–97.

Crouter, A. C., Manke, B. A., & McHale, S. M. (1995). The family context of gender intensification in early adolescence. *Child Development, 66*, 317–329.

Crystal, D. S., & Stevenson, H. W. (1995). What is a bad kid? Answers of adolescents and their mothers in three cultures. *Journal of Research on Adolescence, 5*(1), 71–91.

Csapó, B. (1997). The development of inductive reasoning: Cross-sectional assessments in an educational context. *International Journal of Behavioral Development, 20*(4), 609–626.

Csikszentmihalyi, M., & Larson, R. (1987). Validity and reliability of the experience-sampling method. *Journal of Nervous & Mental Disease, 175*(9), 526–536.

Culp, A. M., Clyman, M. M., & Culp, R. E. (1995). Adolescent depressed mood, reports of suicide attempts, and asking for help. *Adolescence, 30*(120), 827–837.

Cummings, A. L., & Leschied, A. W. (2001). Understanding aggression with adolescent girls: Implications for policy and practice. *Canadian Journal of Community Mental Health, 20*(2), 43–57.

Cunningham, M., & Spencer, M. B. (1996). The black male experiences measure. In R. L. Jones (Ed.), *Handbook of tests and measurements for black populations* (pp. 301–307). Hampton, VA: Cobb & Henry.

Curran, P. J., Stice, E., & Chassin, L. (1997). The relation between adolescent alcohol use and peer alcohol use: A longitudinal random coefficients model. *Journal of Consulting and Clinical Psychology, 65*(1), 130–140.

Cutler, G. B. (1991). Adrenarche. In R. M. Lerner, A. C. Petersen, & J. Brooks-Gunn (Eds.), *Encyclopedia of adolescence.* (Vol. 1). New York: Garland.

D

D'Angelo, L. L., Weinberger, D. A., & Feldman, S. S. (1995). Like father, like son? Predicting male adolescents' adjustment from parents' distress and self-restraint. *Developmental Psychology, 31*(6), 883–896.

D'Augelli, A. R., & Patterson, C. J. (Eds.). (1995). *Lesbian, gay, and bisexual identities over the lifespan: Psychological perspectives.* New York: Oxford University Press.

Daly, M. P., & Sobol, K. J. (1994). Canadian adoption statistics: 1981–1990. *Journal of Marriage and the Family, 56*(2), 493.

Damon, W. (1991). Problems of direction in socially shared cognition. In L. B. Resnick, J. M. Levine, & S. D. Teasley (Eds.), *Perspectives on socially shared cognition* (pp. 384–397). Washington, DC: American Psychological Association.

Damon, W. (1997). *The youth charter: How communities can work together to raise standards for all our children.* New York: Free Press.

Damon, W., & Gregory, A. (1997). The youth charter: Towards the formation of adolescent moral identity. *Journal of Moral Education, 26*, 117–131.

Damon, W., & Hart, D. (1988). *Self-understanding in childhood and adolescence.* New York: Cambridge University Press.

Darroch, J. E., Singh, S., & Frost, J. J. (2001). Differences in teenage pregnancy rates among five developed countries: The roles of sexual activity and contraceptive use. *Family Planning Perspectives, 33*(6), 244–250, 281.

Davis, A. A., Rhodes, J. E., & Hamilton-Leaks, J. (1997). When both parents may be a source of support and problems: An analysis of pregnant and parenting female African-American adolescents' relationships with their mothers and fathers. *Journal of Research on Adolescence, 7*(3), 331–348.

Dawkins, M. P. (1997). Drug use and violent crime among adolescents. *Adolescence, 32*(126), 395–405.

Day, K. M., & Devlin, R. A. (1998). The payoff to work without pay: Volunteer work as an investment in human capital. *Canadian Journal of Economics*, 31(5), 1179–1191.

De Gaston, J. F., Weed, S., & Jensen, L. (1996). Understanding gender differences in adolescent sexuality. *Adolescence*, 31(121), 217–231.

De Schiffart, C. (2000). Community Service Learning with unemployed young Nova Scotians. *Canadian Journal of Counselling*, 34(3), 186–192.

De Wit, M. L., Embree, B. G., & De Wit, D. (1999). Determinants of the risk and timing of alcohol and illicit drug use onset among natives and non-natives: Similarities and differences in family attachment processes. *Social Biology*, 46, 100–121.

DeBaryshe, B. D., Patterson, G. R., & Capaldi, D. M. (1993). A performance model for academic achievement in early adolescent boys. *Developmental Psychology*, 29, 795–804.

Degirmencioglu, S. M., Urberg, K. A., Tolson, J. M., & Richard, P. (1998). Adolescent friendship networks: Continuity and change over the school year. *Merrill-Palmer Quarterly*, 44(3), 313–337.

Dei, G. J. S., & James, I. M. (2002). Beyond the rhetoric: Moving from exclusion, reaching for inclusion in Canadian schools. *Alberta Journal of Educational Research*, 48(1), 61–87.

Delaney, M. E. (1996). Across the transition to adolescence: Qualities of parent/adolescent relationships and adjustment. *Journal of Early Adolescence*, 16(3), 274–300.

DeMatteo, D., Major, C., Block, B., Coates, R., Fearon, M., Goldberg, E., et al. (1999). Toronto street youth and HIV/AIDS: Prevalence, demographics and risks. *Journal of Adolescent Health*, 25(5), 358–366.

Demetriou, A., Pachaury, A., Metallidou, Y., & Kazi, S. (1996). Universals and specificities in the structure and development of quantitative-relational thought: A cross-cultural study in Greece and India. *International Journal of Behavioral Development*, 19(2), 255–290.

Demo, D. H., & Acock, A. C. (1988). The impact of divorce on children. *Journal of Marriage and the Family*, 50, 619–648.

Demo, D. H., & Acock, A. C. (1996). Family structure, family process, and adolescent well-being. *Journal of Research on Adolescence*, 6(4), 457–488.

Demos, D. H., Allen, K., & Fine, M. (2000). *Handbook of family diversity*. New York: Oxford University Press.

Demos, V. (1986). Crying in early infancy: An illustration of the motivational function of affect. In T. B. Brazelton & M. W. Yogman (Eds.), *Affective development in infancy* (pp. 39–73). Norwood, NJ: Ablex.

Department of Canadian Heritage (1996). French immersion in Canada. Published by the Government of Canada. Retrieved from: www.pch.gc.ca/progs/lo-ol/publications/trousse-kit/EF02c.htm.

Department of Indian & Northern Affairs. (2000). *Royal Commission on Aboriginal Peoples*. Retrieved from: www.ainc-inac.gc.ca/ch/rcap/rpt/lk_e.html.

Deslandes, R., Bouchard, P., & St Amant, J. C. (1998). Family variables as predictors of school achievement: Sex differences in Quebec adolescents. *Canadian Journal of Education*, 23, 390–404.

Deslandes, R., Royer, E., Potvin, P., & Leclerc, D. (1999). Patterns of home and school partnership for general and special education students at the secondary level. *Exceptional Children*, 65(4), 496–506.

DeWit, D. J. (1998). Frequent childhood geographic relocation: Its impact on drug use initiation and the development of alcohol and other drug-related problems among adolescents and young adults. *Addictive Behaviors*, 23(5), 623–634.

DeWit, D. J., Offord, D. R., Sanford, M., Rye, B. J., Shain, M., & Wright, R. (2000). The effect of school culture on adolescent behavioural problems: Self-esteem, attachment to learning, and peer approval of deviance as mediating mechanisms. *Canadian Journal of School Psychology*, 16(1), 15–38.

di Mauro, D. (1995). *Sexuality research in the United States: An assessment of social and behavioral sciences*. New York: Social Science Research Council.

Dickson, L. M., Derevensky, J. L., & Gupta, R. (2002). The prevention of gambling problems in youth: A conceptual framework. *Journal of Gambling Studies*, 18(2), 97–159.

Dietz, W. H., Jr., & Gortmaker, S. L. (1985). Do we fatten our children at the television set? Obesity and television viewing in children and adolescents. *Pediatrics*, 75, 807–812.

Dimant, R. J., & Bearison, D. J. (1991). Development of formal reasoning during successive peer interactions. *Developmental Psychology*, 27, 277–284.

Dishion, T. J., Andrews, D. W., & Crosby, L. (1995). Antisocial boys and their friends in early adolescence: Relationship characteristics, quality, and interactional process. *Child Development*, 66(1), 139–151.

Dishion, T. J., Patterson, G. R., Stoolmiller, M., & Skinner, M. L. (1991). Family, school, and behavioral antecedents to early adolescent involvement with antisocial peers. *Developmental Psychology*, 27(1), 172–180.

Dixon, R. A., & Lerner, R. M. (1999). History and systems in developmental psychology. In M. Bornstein & M. Lamb (Eds.), *Developmental psychology: An advanced textbook* (4th ed., pp. 3–45). Mahwah, NJ: Erlbaum.

Dobkin, P. L., Tremblay, R. E., & Sacchitelle, C. (1997). Predicting boys' early-onset substance abuse from father's alcoholism, son's disruptiveness, and mother's parenting behavior. *Journal of Consulting and Clinical Psychology*, 65, 86–92.

Dobkin, P. L., Tremblay, R. E., Masse, L. C., & Vitaro, F. (1995). Individual and peer characteristics in predicting boys' early onset of substance abuse: A seven-year longitudinal study. *Child Development*, 66, 1198–1214.

Doherty, W. J., & Needle, R. H. (1991). Psychological adjustment and substance use among adolescents before and after a parental divorce. *Child Development*, 62, 328–337.

Dolan, B. (1995). A Teen hot line. *Adolescence*, 30(117), 195–200.

Dolcini, M. M., Cohn, L. D., Adler, N. E., Millstein, S. G., Irwin, C. E., Kegeles, S. M., & Stone, G. C. (1989). Adolescent egocentrism and feelings of invulnerability: Are they related? *Journal of Early Adolescence*, 9, 409–418.

Donnelly, M. (1995). Depressions among adolescents in Northern Ireland. *Adolescence*, 30(118), 339–350.

Dornbusch, S. M., Carlsmith, J. M., Bushwall, S. J., Ritter, P. L., Leiderman, H., Hastorf, A. H., & Gross, R. T. (1985). Single parents' extended households and the control of adolescents. *Child Development, 56,* 326–341.

Dornbusch, S. M., Carlsmith, J. M., Gross, R. T., Martin, J. A., Jennings, D., Rosenberg, A., & Duke, P. (1981). Sexual development, age, and dating: A comparison of biological and social influences upon one set of behaviors. *Child Development, 52,* 179–185.

Douglas, J. D., & Wong, A. C. (1977). Formal operations: Age and sex differences in Chinese and American children. *Child Development, 48,* 689–692.

Douvan, J. D., & Adelson, J. (1966). *The adolescent experience.* New York: Wiley.

Doyle, A. B., Markiewicz, D., Brendgen, M., Lieberman, M., & Voss, K. (2000). Child attachment security and self-concept: Associations with mother and father attachment style and marital quality. *Merrill Palmer Quarterly, 46,* 514–539.

Doyle, A-B. (2000). Cultural competence: A Canadian perspective. In H.P. Edwards (Ed.), *Trilateral forum on professional psychology working notes of the year 2000 meeting.* Ottawa. Retrieved from: www.cpa.ca/trilat2000.PDF.

Dreessen, E. A. J. (2000). *What do we know about the voluntary sector? An overview.* Ottawa: Statistics Canada.

Drumm, P., & Jackson, D. W. (1996). Developmental changes in questioning strategies during adolescence. *Journal of Adolescent Research, 11*(3), 285–305.

Dryfoos, J. G. (1990). *Adolescents at risk: Prevalence and prevention.* New York: Oxford University Press.

Dryfoos, J. G. (1994). *Full service schools: A revolution in health and social services for children, youth, and families.* San Francisco: Jossey-Bass.

Dryfoos, J. G. (1995). Full service schools: A revolution or fad? *Journal of Research on Adolescence, 5,* 149–150.

Dryfoos, J. G. (1998). *Safe passage: Making it through adolescence in a risky society.* New York: Oxford University Press.

Dubois, D. L., & Hirsch, B. J. (1993). School/nonschool friendship patterns in early adolescence. *Journal of Early Adolescence, 13*(1), 102–122.

Dubois, D. L., Eitel, S. K., & Felner, R. D. (1994). Effects of family environment and parent-child relationships on school adjustment during the transition to early adolescence. *Journal of Marriage and the Family, 56,* 405–414.

DuBois, D. L., Felner, R. D., Brand, S., Phillips, R. S. C., & Lease, A. M. (1996). Early adolescent self-esteem: A developmental-ecological framework and assessment strategy. *Journal of Research on Adolescence, 6*(4), 543–579.

Ducharme, D., & Bernard, R. (2001). Communication breakdowns: An exploration of contextualization in native and non-native speakers of French. *Journal of Pragmatics, 33*(6), 825–847.

Ducharme, J., Doyle, A. B., & Markiewicz, D. (2002). Attachment security with mother and father: Associations with adolescents' reports of interpersonal behaviour with parents and peers. *Journal of Social and Personal Relationships, 19,* 203–231.

Duncan, G. J. (1991). The economic environment of childhood. In A. C. Huston (Ed.), *Children in poverty: Child development and public policy* (pp. 23–50). Cambridge: Cambridge University Press.

Dunlop, R., & Burns, A. (1995). The sleeper effect—myth or reality? *Journal of Marriage and the Family, 57,* 375–386.

Dunn, L., Ross, B., Caines, T., & Howorth, P. (1998). A school-based HIV/AIDS prevention education program: Outcomes of peer-led versus community health nurse-led interventions. *Canadian Journal of Human Sexuality, 7*(4), 339–344.

Dunn, M. E., & Goldman, M. S. (1998). Age and drinking-related differences in the memory organization of alcohol expectancies in 3rd-, 6th-, 9th-, and 12th-grade children. *Journal of Consulting and Clinical Psychology, 66*(3), 579–585.

Duplisea, B. (2001). The real dope on beef hormones. *Alive: Canadian Journal of Health & Nutrition, 221,* 102–104.

DuRant, R. H., Getts, A. G., Cadenhead, C., & Woods, E. R. (1995). The association between weapon-carrying and the use of violence among adolescents living in or around public housing. *Journal of Adolescence, 18*(5), 579–592.

Durbin, D. L., Darling, N., Steinberg, L., & Brown, B. B. (1993). Parenting style and peer group membership among European-American adolescents. *Journal of Research on Adolescence, 3*(1), 87–100.

Dyck, N. (1997). Tutelage, resistance, and co-optation in Canadian Indian administration. *The Canadian Review of Sociology and Anthropology, 34,* 333–348.

Dyl, J., & Wapner, S. (1996). Age and gender differences in the nature, meaning, and function of cherished possessions for children and adolescents. *Journal of Experimental Child Psychology, 62,* 340–377.

Dylan, B. (1964). My back pages. *Another side of Bob Dylan.* New York: Columbia Records.

E

East, P. L. (1989). Early adolescents' perceived interpersonal risks and benefits: Relations to social support and psychological functioning. *Journal of Early Adolescence, 2*(4), 374–395.

East, P. L. (1991). The parent-child relationships of withdrawn, aggressive, and sociable children: Child and parent perspectives. *Merrill-Palmer Quarterly, 37*(3), 425–443.

East, P. L. (1996). The younger sisters of childbearing adolescents: Their attitude, expectations, and behaviors. *Child Development, 67,* 267–282.

East, P. L., & Felice, M. E. (1996). *Adolescent pregnancy and parenting: Findings from a racially diverse sample.* Mahwah, NJ: Erlbaum.

East, P. L., Felice, M. E., & Morgan, M. C. (1993). Sisters' and girlfriends' sexual and childbearing behavior: Effects on early adolescent girls' sexual outcomes. *Journal of Marriage and the Family, 55,* 953–963.

East, P. L., Hess, L. E., & Lerner, R. M. (1987). Peer social support and adjustment of early adolescent peer groups. *Journal of Early Adolescence, 7*(2), 153–163.

East, P., Lerner, R. M., Lerner, J. V., Soni, R. T., Ohannessian, C. M., & Jacobson, L. P. (1992). Early adolescent-peer group fit, peer relations, and psychosocial competence: A short-term longitudinal study. *Journal of Early Adolescence, 12*(2), 132–152.

Ebata, A. T. (1996). Making university-community collaborations work:

Challenges for institutions and individuals. *Journal of Research on Adolescence, 6*(1), 71–79.

Eccles, J. S. (1991). Academic achievement. In R. M. Lerner, A. C. Petersen, & J. Brooks-Gunn (Eds.), *Encyclopedia of adolescence* (Vol. 1, pp. 1–9). New York: Garland.

Eccles, J. S. (1996). The power and difficulty of university-community collaboration. *Journal of Research on Adolescence, 6*(1), 81–86.

Eccles, J. S., & Midgley, C. (1989). Stage-environment fit: Developmentally appropriate classroms for young adolescents. In C. Ames & R. Ames (Eds.), *Research on motivation in education. Goals and cognitions* (Vol. 3, pp. 139–186). New York: Academic Press.

Eccles, J. S., Early, D., Frasier, K., Belansky, E., & McCarthy, K. (1997). The relation of connection, regulation, and support for autonomy to adolescents' functioning. *Journal of Adolescent Research, 12*(2), 263–286.

Eckert, P. (1995). Trajectory and forms of institutional participation. In L. J. Crockertt & A. C. Crouter (Eds.), *Pathways though adolescence: Individual development in relation to social contexts* (pp. 175–195). Mahway, NJ: Erlbaum.

Eder, D., & Kinney, D. A. (1995). The effect of middle school extracurricular activities on adolescents' popularity and peer status. *Youth & Society, 26*(3), 298–324.

Edwards, W. J. (1996). A sociological analysis of an invisible minority group. *Youth & Society, 27*(3), 334–355.

Eisenberg, N. (1986). *Altruistic emotion, cognition, and behavior.* Hillsdale, NJ: Erlbaum.

Eisenberg, N. (1991). Values, sympathy, and individual differences: Toward a pluralism of factors influencing altruism and empathy. *Psychological Inquiry, 2*(2), 128–131.

Eisenberg, N., & Fabes, R. A. (1998). Prosocial development. In N. Eisenberg (Ed.) & W. Damon (Ed. in chief), *Handbook of child psychology: Vol. 3. Social, emotional, and personality development* (5th ed., pp. 1097–1149). New York: Wiley.

Eisenberg, N., & McNally, S. (1993). Socialization and mothers' and adolescents' empathy-related characteristics. *Journal of Research on Adolescence, 3*(2), 171–191.

Eisenberg, N., & Mussen, P. (1989). *The roots of prosocial behavior in children.* Cambridge, England: Cambridge University Press.

Eisenberg, N., Carlo, G., Murphy, B., & Van Court, P. (1995). Prosocial development in late adolescence: A longitudinal study. *Child Development, 66,* 1179–1197.

Eisenberg-Berg, N. (1979). The development of children's prosocial moral judgment. *Developmental Psychology, 15,* 128–137.

Eisenberg-Berg, N., & Geisheker, E. (1979). Content of preachings and power of the model-preacher: Effect on children's generosity. *Developmental Psychology, 15*(2), 168–175.

Eiser, C., Havermans, T., & Eiser, J. R. (1995). The emergence during adolescence of gender differences in symptom reporting. *Journal of Adolescence, 18,* 307–316.

Elder, G. H., Jr. (1974). *Children of the Great Depression: Social change in life experiences.* Chicago: University of Chicago Press.

Elder, G. H., Jr. (1980). Adolescence in historical perspective. In J. Adelson (Ed.), *Handbook of adolescent psychology* (pp. 3–46). New York: Wiley.

Elder, G. H., Jr. (1998). The life course and human development. In W. Damon (Series Ed.) & R. M. Lerner (Vol. Ed.), *Handbook of child psychology: Vol. 1. Theoretical models of human development* (5th ed., pp. 939–991). New York: Wiley.

Elder, G. H., Jr. (1999). *Children of the Great Depression: Social change in life experience* (25th anniversary ed.). Boulder, CO: Westview Press.

Elder, G. H., Jr., & Conger, R. D. (2000). *Children of the land: Adversity and success in rural America.* Chicago: University of Chicago Press.

Elder, G. H., Jr., Modell, J., & Parke, R. D. (Eds.). (1993). Children in time and place: Developmental and historical insights. New York: Cambridge University Press.

Elkind, D. (1967). Egocentrism in adolescents. *Child Development, 38,* 1025–1034.

Elkind, D. (1968). Combinatorial thinking in adolescents from graded to ungraded classrooms. *Perceptual and Motor Skills, 27,* 1015–1018.

Elkind, D. (1980). The role of play in religious education. *Religious Education, 75,* 282–293.

Elkind, D., & Bowen, R. (1979). Imaginary audience behavior in children and adolescents. *Developmental Psychology, 15*(1), 38–44.

Ellenbogen, S., & Chamberland, C. (1997). The peer relations of dropouts: A comparative study of at-risk and not at-risk youths. *Journal of Adolescence, 20*(4), 355–367.

Ellis, Hart, S., & Small-McGinley, J. (1998). The perspectives of "difficult" students on belonging and inclusion in the classroom. *Reclaiming Children and Youth, 7*(3), 142.

Elster, J. (1991). Local justice and interpersonal comparisons. In J. Elster & J. E. Roemer (Eds.), *Interpersonal comparisons of well-being. Studies in rationality and social change* (pp. 98–126). Cambridge: Cambridge University Press.

Emmons, L. (1996). The relationship of dieting to weight in adolescents. *Adolescence, 31*(121), 167–178.

Emshoff, J., Avery, E., Raduka, G., Anderson, D. J., & Calvert, C. (1996). Findings from SUPER STARS: A health promotion program for families to enhance multiple protective factors. *Journal of Adolescent Research, 11*(1), 68–96.

Enarson, H. L. (1989). *Revitalizing the landgrant mission.* Blacksburg: Virginia Polytechnic Institute and State University.

England, E. M., & Petro, K. D. (1998). Middle school students' perceptions of peer groups: Relative judgments about group characteristics. *Journal of Early Adolescence, 18*(4), 349–373.

English, N. D., & English, L. M. (1999). A proactive approach to youth who run. *Child Abuse and Neglect, 23*(7), 683–698.

Ennett, S. T., & Bauman, K. E. (1993). Peer group structure and adolescent cigarette smoking: A social network analysis. *Journal of Health & Social Behavior, 34*(3), 226–236.

Ennett, S. T., & Bauman, K. E. (1996). Adolescent social networks: School, demographic, and longitudinal considerations. *Journal of Adolescent Research, 11*(2), 194–215.

Enns, M. W., Inayatulla, M., Cox, B., & Cheyne, L. (1997). Prediction of suicide intent in Aboriginal and non-Aboriginal adolescent inpatients: A research note. *Suicide and Life Threatening Behavior, 27*(2), 218–224.

Enright, R. D., Lapsley, D. K., & Shukla, D. G. (1979). Adolescent egocentrism in early and late adolescence. *Adolescence, 14*(56), 687–695.

Enright, R. D., Shukla, D. G., & Lapsley, D. K. (1980). Adolescent egocentrism-sociocentrism and self-consciousness. *Journal of Youth and Adolescence, 9*(2), 101–116.

Ensminger, M. E., Lamkin, R. P., & Jacobson, N. (1996). School leaving: A longitudinal perspective including neighborhood effects. *Child Development, 67*, 2400–2416.

Epstein, J. L. (1983). Selection of friends in differently organized schools and classrooms. In J. L. Epstein & N. Karweit (Eds.), *Friends in school: Patterns of selection and influence in secondary schools* (pp. 73–92). New York: Wiley.

Epstein, J. L., & Dauber, S. L. (1995). Effects on students of an interdisciplinary program linking social studies, arts, and family volunteers in the middle grades. *Journal of Early Adolescence, 15*(1), 114–144.

Erikson, E. (1963). *Childhood and society* (2nd ed.). New York: Norton.

Erikson, E. (1964). Inner and outer space: Reflections on womanhood. In R. J. Lifton (Ed.), *The woman in America* (pp. 1–26). Boston: Beacon Press.

Erikson, E. H. (1950). *Childhood and society.* New York: Norton.

Erikson, E. H. (1959). Identity and the life-cycle. *Psychological Issues, 1,* 18–164.

Erikson, E. H. (1968). *Identity, youth and crisis.* New York: Norton.

Estrada, P. (1995). Adolescents' self-reports of prosocial responses to friends and acquaintances: The role of sympathy-related cognitive, affective, and motivational processes. *Journal of Research on Adolescence, 5*(2), 173–200.

Etaugh, C., & Liss, M. B. (1992). Home, school, and playroom: Training grounds for adult gender roles. *Sex Roles, 26*(3-4), 129–147.

F

Fabes, R. A., & Eisenberg, N. (1996). [An examination of age and sex differences in prosocial behavior and empathy.] Unpublished data. Arizona State University.

Falkner, F. (1972). Physical growth. In H. L. Bennett & A. H. Einhorn (Eds.), *Pediatrics.* New York: Appleton-Century-Crofts.

Farran, D. C., & Margolis, L. H. (1987). The family economic environment as a context for children's development. *New Directions for Child Development, 35,* 69–87.

Farrell, A. D., & White, K. S. (1998). Peer influence and drug use among urban adolescents: Family structure and parent–adolescent relationship as protective factors. *Journal of Consulting and Clinical Psychology, 66*(2), 248–258.

Faubert, M., Locke, D. C., Sprinthall, N. A., & Howland, W. H. (1996). Promoting cognitive and ego development of African-American rural youth: A program of deliberate psychological education. *Journal of Adolescence, 19,* 533–543.

Feather, N. T. (1998). Attitudes toward high achievers, self-esteem, and value priorities for Australian, American, and Canadian students. *Journal of Cross-Cultural Psychology, 29*(6), 749–759.

Featherman, D. L., & Lerner, R. M. (1985). Ontogenesis and sociogenesis: Problematic for theory about development across the lifespan. *American Sociological Review, 50,* 659–676.

Featherman, D. L., Spenner, K. I., & Tsunematsu, N. (1988). Class and the socialization of children: Constancy, change, or irrelevance? In R. M. Lerner, E. M. Hetherington, & M. Perlmutter (Eds.), *Child development in life-span perspective* (pp. 67–90). Hillsdale, NJ: Erlbaum.

Feiring, C. (1996). Concepts of romance in 15-year-old adolescents. *Journal of Research on Adolescence, 6*(2), 181–200.

Feldman, B. (1995). The search for identity in late adolescence. In M. Sidoli & G. Bovensiepen (Eds.), *Incest fantasies and self-destructive acts: Jungian and post-Jungian psychotherapy in adolescence* (pp. 153–166). New Brunswick, NJ: Transaction.

Feldman, D. H. (2000). *Piaget's stages: The unfinished symphony.* Unpublished manuscript, Eliot-Pearson Department of Child Development, Tufts University.

Feldman, L., Harvey, B., Holowaty, P., & Shortt, L. (1999). Alcohol use beliefs and behaviors among high school students. *Journal of Adolescent Health, 24*(1), 48–58.

Feldman, S. S., & Elliott, G. E. (1990). *At the threshold: The developing adolescent.* Cambridge: Harvard University Press.

Feldman, S. S., & Weinberger, D. A. (1994). Self-restraint as a mediator of family influences on boys' delinquent behavior: A longitudinal study. *Child Development, 65,* 195–211.

Feldman, S. S., & Wentzel, K. R. (1995). Relations of marital satisfaction to peer outcomes in adolescent boys: A longitudinal study. *Journal of Early Adolescence, 15*(2), 220–237.

Feldman, S. S., & Wood, D. N. (1994). Parents' expectations for preadolescent sons' behavioral autonomy: A longitudinal study of correlates and outcomes. *Journal of Research on Adolescence, 4*(1), 45–70.

Feldman, S. S., Fisher, L., & Seitel, L. (1997). The effect of parents' marital satisfaction on young adults' adaptation: A longitudinal study. *Journal of Research on Adolescence, 7,* 55–80.

Feldman, S. S., Fisher, L., Ransom, D. C., & Dimiceli, S. (1995). "Is what is good for the goose good for the gander?" Sex differences in relations between adolescent coping and adult adaptation. *Journal of Research on Adolescence, 5*(3), 333–359.

Feldman, S. S., Mont-Reynaud, R., & Rosenthal, D. A. (1992). When East moves West: The acculturations of values of Chinese adolescents in the U.S. and Australia. *Journal of Research on Adolescence, 2*(2), 147–173.

Feldman, S. S., Rosenthal, D. R., Brown, N. L., & Canning, R. D. (1995). Predicting sexual experience in adolescent boys from peer rejection and acceptance during childhood. *Journal of Research on Adolescence, 5*(4), 387–411.

Felner, R. D., Brand, S., DuBois, D. L., & Adan, A. (1995). Socioeconomic disadvantage, proximal environmental experiences, and socioemotional and academic adjustment in early adolescence: Investigation of a mediated effects model. *Child Development, 66,* 774–792.

Felner, R. D., Brand, S., DuBois, D. L., Adan, A. M., Mulhall, P. F., & Evans, E. G. (1995). Socioeconomic disadvantage, proximal environmental experiences, and socioemotional and academic adjustment in early adolescence: Investigation of a mediated effects model. *Child Development, 66,* 774–792.

Fenzel, L. M. (1992). The effect of relative age on self-esteem, role strain, GPA, and anxiety. *Journal of Early Adolescence, 12,* 253–266.

Ferguson, J. M., & Dorman, J. P. (2001). Psychosocial classroom environment and academic efficacy in Canadian high school mathematics classes. *Alberta Journal of Educational Research, 47*(3), 276–279.

Ferry, J. (1999). How will the health of the Inuit fare in their new land? *The Lancet, 354*(9175), 312.

Fetterman, D. M., Kaftarian, S. J., & Wandersman, A. (Eds.). (1996). *Empowerment evaluation: Knowledge and tools for self-assessment and accountability.* Thousand Oaks, CA: Sage.

Fick, A. C., & Thomas, S. M. (1995). Growing up in a violent environment: Relationship to health-related beliefs and behaviors. *Youth & Society, 27*(2), 136–147.

Field, T. (1991). Mothers, adolescent and their young children. In R. M. Lerner, A. C. Petersen, & J. Brooks-Gunn (Eds.), *Encyclopedia of adolescence* (Vol. 2, pp. 669–674). New York: Garland.

Field, T., Grizzle, N., Scafidi, F., & Schanberg, S. (1996). Massage and relaxation therapies' effects on depressed adolescent mothers. *Adolescence, 31*(124), 903–911.

Field, T., Lang, C., Yando, R., & Bendell, D. (1995). Adolescents' intimacy with parents and friends. *Adolescence, 30*(117), 133–140.

Fine, M. A., & Kurdek, L. A. (1992). The adjustment of adolescents in stepfather and stepmother families. *Journal of Marriage and the Family, 54,* 725–736.

Finkelhor, D. (1994). Current information on the scope and nature of child sexual abuse. *Future of Children, 4*(2), 31–53.

Finkelstein, J. W. (1993). Familial influences on adolescent health. In R. M. Lerner (Ed.), *Early adolescence: Perspectives on research, policy, and intervention* (pp. 111–126). Hillsdale, NJ: Erlbaum.

Finken, L. L., & Jacobs, J. E. (1996). Consultant choice across decision contexts: Are abortion decisions

different? *Journal of Early Adolescence, 11*(2), 235–260.

Fisher, C. B. (1993). Integrating science and ethics in research with high risk children and youth. *SRCD Social Policy Report, 7,* 1–27.

Fisher, C. B. (1994). Reporting and referring research participants: Ethical challenges for investigators studying children and youth. *Ethics and Behavior, 4,* 87–95.

Fisher, C. B. (1997). A relational perspective on ethics-in-science decision making for research with vulnerable populations. *IRB: A Review of Human Subjects Research, 19,* 1–4.

Fisher, C. B., & Brennan, M. (1992). Application and ethics in developmental psychology. In D. L. Featherman, R. M. Lerner, & M. Perlmutter (Eds.), *Life-span development and behavior* (Vol. 11, pp. 189–219). Hillsdale, NJ: Erlbaum.

Fisher, C. B., & Fyrberg, D. (1994). Participant partners: College students weigh the costs and benefits of deceptive research. *American Psychologist, 49*(5), 417–427.

Fisher, C. B., & Johnson, B. L. (1990). Getting mad at mom and dad: Children's changing views of family conflict. *International Journal of Behavioral Development, 13,* 31–48.

Fisher, C. B., & Lerner, R. M. (1994b). Foundations of applied developmental psychology. In C. B. Fisher & R. M. Lerner (Eds.), *Applied developmental psychology* (pp. 3–20). New York: McGraw-Hill.

Fisher, C. B., & Lerner, R. M. (Eds.). (1994a). *Applied developmental psychology.* New York: McGraw-Hill.

Fisher, C. B., & Tryon, W. W. (1990). Emerging ethical issues in an emerging field. In C. B. Fisher & W. W. Tryon (Eds.), *Ethics in applied developmental psychology: Emerging issues in an emerging field* (pp. 1–15). Norwood, NJ: Ablex.

Fisher, C. B., Higgins, A., Rau, J. M., Kuther, T. L., & Belanger, S. (1996). Reporting and referring research participants at risk: Views from urban adolescents. *Child Development, 67,* 2086–2100.

Fisher, C. B., Higgins-D'Alessandro, A., Rau, J. B., Kuther, T. L., & Belanger, S. (1996). Referring and reporting research participants at risk: Views from urban adolescents. *Child Development, 67,* 2086–2100.

Fisher, C. B., Hoagwood, K., & Jensen, P. S. (1996). Casebook on ethical issues in research with children and adolescents with mental disorders. In K. Hoagwood & P. S. Jensen (Eds.), *Ethical issues in mental health research with children and adolescents* (pp. 135–266). Mahwah, NJ: Erlbaum.

Fisher, C. B., Murray, J. P., Dill, J. R., Hagen, J. W., Hogan, M. J., Lerner, R. M., Rebok, G. W., Sigel, I., Sostek, A. M., Smyer, M. A., Spencer, M. B., & Wilcox, B. (1993). The national conference on graduate education in the applications of developmental science across the life span. *Journal of Applied Developmental Psychology, 14,* 1–10.

Fisher, S. (1995). The amusement arcade as a social space for adolescents: An empirical study. *Journal of Adolescence, 18,* 71–86.

Fisher, W. A. & Boroditsky, R. (2000). Sexual activity, contraceptive choice, and sexual and reproductive health indicators among single Canadian women aged 15–29: Additional findings from the Canadian Contraception Study. *Canadian Journal of Human Sexuality, 9*(2), 79–93.

Fitzgerald, H. E., Abrams, A., Church, R. L., Votruba, J. C., & Imig, G. L. (1996). Applied developmental science at Michigan State University: Connecting university and community via programs for children, youth, and families. *Journal of Research on Adolescence, 6*(1), 55–69.

Fitzgerald, J. M., Nesselroade, J. R., & Baltes, P. B. (1973). Emergence of adult intellectual structure. *Developmental Psychology, 9,* 114–119.

Flanagan, C. A., & Eccles, J. S. (1993). Changes in parents' work status and adolescents' adjustment at school. *Child Development, 64,* 246–257.

Flannery, D. J., Vazsonyi, A. T., & Rowe, D. C. (1996). Caucasian and Hispanic early adolescent substance use: Parenting, personality, and school adjustment. *Journal of Early Adolescence, 16*(1), 71–89.

Fletcher, A. C., Darling, N. E., Steinberg, L., & Dornbusch, S. (1995). The company they keep: Relation of adolescents' adjustment and behavior to their friends' perceptions of authoritative parenting in the social network. *Developmental Psychology, 31*(2), 300–310.

Flisher, A. J., & Chalton, D. O. (1995). High-school dropouts in a working-class South African community: Selected characteristics and risk-taking behavior. *Journal of Adolescence, 18*, 105–121.

Foltz, C., Overton, W. F., & Ricco, R. B. (1995). Proof construction: Adolescent development from inductive to deductive problem-solving strategies. *Journal of Experimental Child Psychology, 59*, 179–195.

Ford, D. L., & Lerner, R. M. (1992). *Developmental systems theory: An integrative approach*. Newbury Park, CA: Sage.

Forehand, R., Miller, K. S., Dutra, R., & Chance, M. W. (1997). Role of parenting in adolescent deviant behavior: Replication across and within two ethnic groups. *Journal of Consulting and Clinical Psychology, 65*(6), 1036–1041.

Fortenberry, J. D., Costa, F. M., Jessor, R., & Donovan, J. E. (1997). Contraceptive behavior and adolescent lifestyles: A structural modeling approach. *Journal of Research on Adolescence, 7*(3), 307–329.

Foshee, V. A., & Hollinger, B. R. (1996). Maternal religiosity, adolescent social bonding, and adolescent alcohol use. *Journal of Early Adolescence, 16*(4), 451–468.

Foster, L., & Webster, A. (1998). The Natural Personality Enhancement Model: A program for the management of conduct disordered children. *Residential Treatment for Children and Youth, 16*(1), 11–20.

Foster-Clark, F. S., & Blyth, D. A. (1991). Peer relations and influences. In R. M. Lerner, A. C. Petersen, & J. Brooks-Gunn (Eds.), *Encyclopedia of adolescence* (Vol. 2, pp. 767–771). New York: Garland.

Fouts, G. & Burggraf, K. (1999). Television situation comedies: Female body images and verbal reinforcements. *Sex Roles, 40*(5/6), 473–481.

Fouts, G. & Burggraf, K. (2000). Television situation comedies: Female weight, male negative comments, and audience reactions. *Sex Roles, 42*(9/10), 925–932.

Fouts, G. & Vaughan, K. (2002). Locus of control, television viewing, and eating disorder symptomatology in young females, *Journal of Adolescence, 25*, 307–311.

Fouts, G. & Vaughan, K. (2002). Television situation comedies: Male weight, negative references, and audience reactions. *Sex Roles, 46*(11/12), 439–442.

Foxcroft, D. R., & Lowe, G. (1995). Adolescent drinking, smoking and other substance use involvement: Links with perceived family life. *Journal of Adolescence, 18*, 159–177.

Freedland, J., & Dwyer, J. (1991). Nutrition in adolescent girls. In R. M. Lerner, A. C. Petersen, & J. Brooks-Gunn (Eds.), *Encyclopedia of Adolescence* (Vol. 2, pp. 714–723). New York: Garland.

Freedman-Doan, C. R., Arbreton, A. J., Harold, R. D., & Eccles, J. S. (1993). Looking forward to adolescence: Mothers' and fathers' expectations for affective and behavioral change. *Journal of Early Adolescence, 13*(4), 472–502.

Freud, A. (1969). Adolescence as a developmental disturbance. In G. Caplan & S. Lebovier (Eds.), *Adolescence* (pp. 5–10). New York: Basic.

Freund, A. M., & Baltes, P. B. (1998). Selection, optimization, and compensation as strategies of life-management: Correlation with subjective indicators of successful aging. *Psychology and Aging, 13*, 513–543.

Freund, A. M., & Baltes, P. B. (2000). The orchestration of selection, opitimization, and compensation: An action-theoretical conceptualization of a theory of developmental regulation. In W. J. Perrig & A. Grob (Eds.), *Control of human behavior, mental processes, and consciousness: Essays in honor of the 60th birthday of August Flammer* (pp. 35–58). New York: Erlbaum.

Freund, A. M., Li, K. Z. H., & Baltes, P. B. (1999). The role of selection, opitimization, and compensation in successful aging. In J. Brandtstädter & R. M. Lerner (Eds.), *Action and self-development: Theory and research through the life-span* (pp. 401–434). Thousand Oaks, CA: Sage.

Fuhrman, T., & Holmbeck, G. N. (1995). A contextual-moderator analysis of emotional autonomy and adjustment in adolescence. *Child Development, 66*, 793–811.

Fuligni, A. J. (1997). The academic achievement of adolescents from immigrant families: The roles of family background, attitudes, and behavior. *Child Development, 68*(2), 351–363.

Fuligni, A. J., & Eccles, J. S. (1993). Perceived parent-child relationships and early adolescents' orientation toward peers. *Developmental Psychology, 29*(4), 622–632.

Fuligni, A. J., & Stevenson, H. W. (1995). Time use and mathematics achievement among American, Chinese, and Japanese high school students. *Child Development, 66*, 830–842.

Fuligni, A. J., Eccles, J. S., & Barber, B. L. (1995). The long-term effects of seventh-grade ability grouping in mathematics. *Journal of Early Adolescence, 15*(1), 58–89.

Furman, D., & Buhrmester, D. (1992). Age and sex differences in perceptions of networks of person relationships. *Child Development, 63*, 103–115.

Furman, W. (1993). Theory is not a four-letter word: Needed directions in the study of adolescent friendships. *New Directions for Child Development, 60*, 89–103.

Furman, W., & Brown, B. B. (Eds.). (1999). *The development of romantic relationships in adolescence. Cambridge studies in social and emotional development*. New York: Cambridge University Press.

Furstenberg, F. F., & Cherlin, A. J. (1991). *Divided families: What happens to children when parents part*. Cambridge: Harvard University Press.

Furstenberg, F. F., Jr., & Hughes, M. E. (1995). Social capital and successful development among at-risk youth. *Journal of Marriage and the Family, 57*, 580–592.

Furstenberg, F. F., Jr., Brooks-Gunn, J., and Morgan, P. (1987). *Adolescent mothers in later life*. New York: Cambridge University Press.

G

Galambos, N. & Almeida, D. M. (1992). Does parent-adolescent conflict increase in early adolescence? *Journal of Marriage and the Family, 54*, 737–747.

Galambos, N. & Ehrenberg, M. F. (1997). The family as health risk and opportunity: A focus on divorce and working families. In J. Schulenberg, J. L. Maggs, & K. Hurrelmann (Eds.) *Health risks and developmental transitions during adolescence*. Cambridge: Cambridge University Press.

Galambos, N. L., & Maggs, J. L. (1990). Putting mothers' work-related stress in perspective: Mothers and adolescents in dual-earner families. *Journal* of Early Adolescence, 10(3), 313–328.

Galambos, N. L., & Maggs, J. L. (1991). Out-of-school care of young adolescents and self-reported behavior. Developmental Psychology, 27(4), 644–655.

Galambos, N. L., Almeida, D. M., & Petersen, A. C. (1990). Masculinity, femininity, and sex role attitudes in early adolescence: Exploring gender intensification. Child Development, 61, 1905–1914.

Galambos, N. L., Sears, H. A., Almeida, D. M., Kolaric, G. C. (1995). Parents' work overload and problem behavior in young adolescents. Journal of Research on Adolescence, 5(2), 201–223.

Gallatin, J. E. (1975). Adolescence and individuality. New York: Harper & Row.

Gallimore, M., & Kurdek, L. A. (1992). Parent depression and parent authoritative discipline as correlates of young adolescents' depression. Journal of Early Adolescence, 12(2), 187–196.

Gamoran, A., & Nystrand, M. (1991). Background and instructional effects on achievement in eighth-grade English and social studies. Journal of Research on Adolescence, 1(3), 277–300.

Garbarino, J. (1995). Growing up in a socially toxic environment: Life for children and families in the 1990s. In G. B. Melton (Ed.), The individual, the family, and social good: Personal fulfillment in times of change. Nebraska Symposium on Motivation (Vol. 42, pp. 1–20). Lincoln: University of Nebraska Press.

Garbarino, J. (1999). The effects of community violence on children. In L. Balter, C. S. Tamis-LeMonda (Eds.), Child psychology: A handbook of contemporary issues (pp. 412–425). Philadelphia: Psychology Press/Taylor & Francis.

Garbarino, J., & Kostelny, K. (1996). The effects of political violence on Palestinian children's behavior problems: A risk accumulation model. Child Development, 67, 33–45.

Garber, J., Robinson, N. S., & Valentiner, D. (1997). The relation between parenting and adolescent depression: Self-worth as a mediator. Journal of Adolescent Research, 12(1), 12–33.

Garn, S. M. (1980). Continuities and change in maturational timing. In O.

G. Brim, Jr., & J. Kagan (Eds.), Constancy and change in human development (pp. 113–162). Cambridge: Harvard University Press.

Garnefski, N., & Okma, S. (1996). Addiction-risk and aggressive/criminal behaviour in adolescence: Influence of family, school and peers. Journal of Early Adolescence, 19, 503–512.

Garton, A. F., & Pratt, C. (1995). Stress and self-concept in 10- to 15-year-old school students. Journal of Adolescence, 18, 625–640.

Gauze, C., Bukowski, W. M., Aquan-Assee, J., & Sippola, L. K. (1996). Interactions between family environment and friendship and associations with self-perceived well-being during early adolescence. Child Development, 67, 2201–2216.

Gavazzi, S. M. (1995). The Growing Up FAST: Families and adolescents Surviving and Thriving program. Journal of Adolescence, 18, 31–47.

Gavin, L. A., & Furman, W. (1989). Age differences in adolescents' perceptions of their peer groups. Developmental Psychology, 25(5), 827–834.

Gavin, L. A., & Furman, W. (1996). Adolescent girls' relationships with mothers and best friends. Child Development, 67, 375–386.

Ge, X., Best, K. M., Conger, R. D., & Simons, R. L. (1996). Parenting behaviors and the occurence and co-occurence of adolescent depressive symptoms and conduct problems. Developmental Psychology, 32(4), 717–731.

Ge, X., Conger, R. D., & Elder, G. H., Jr. (1996). Coming of age too early: Pubertal influences on girls' vulnerability to psychological distress. Child Development, 67, 3386–3400.

Ge, X., Conger, R. D., Lorenz, F. O., Elder, G. H., Jr., Montague, R. B., & Simons, R. L. (1992). Linking family economic hardship to adolescent distress. Journal of Research on Adolescence, 2, 351–378.

Gfellner, B. M., & Hundleby, J. D. (1991). Family and peer predictors of substance use among aboriginal and non-aboriginal adolescents. The Canadian Journal of Native Studies, 11(2), 267–294.

Gilligan, C. (1982). New maps of development: New visions of maturity. American Journal of Orthopsychiatry, 52(2), 199–212.

Gillmore, M. A., Hawkins, J. D., Day, L. E., & Catalano, R. F. (1992). Friendship and deviance: New evidence on an old controversy. Journal of Early Adolescence, 12(1), 80–95.

Gillmore, M. R., Lewis, S. M., Lohr, M. J., Spencer, M. S., & White, R. D. (1997). Repeat pregnancies among adolescent mothers. Journal of Marriage and the Family, 59, 536–550.

Gjerde, P. F. (1986). The interpersonal structure of family interaction settings: Parent-adolescent relations in dyads and triads. Developmental Psychology, 22(3), 297–304.

Gjerde, P. F. (1995). Alternative pathways to chronic depressive symptoms in young adults: Gender differences in developmental trajectories. Child Development, 66, 1277–1300.

Gjerde, P. F., & Shimizu, H. (1995). Family relationships and adolescent development in Japan: A family-systems perspective on the Japanese family. Journal of Research on Adolescence, 5(3), 281–318.

Glasgow, K. L., Dornbusch, S. M., Troyer, L., Steinberg, L., & Ritter, P. L. (1997). Parenting styles, adolescents' attributions, and educational outcomes in nine heterogeneous high schools. Child Development, 68(3), 507–529.

Gohm, C. L., Oishi, S., Darlington, J., & Diener, E. (1998). Culture, parental conflict, parental marital status, and the subjective well-being of young adults. Journal of Marriage and the Family, 60, 319–334.

Goodenow, C. (1993). Classroom belonging among early adolescent students: Relationships to motivation and achievement. Journal of Early Adolescence, 13(1), 21–43.

Goodnow, J. J. (1962). A test of milieu differences with some of Piaget's tasks. Psychological Monographs, 76(36), 555.

Goodnow, J. J., & Bethon, G. (1996). Piaget's tasks: The effects of schooling and intelligence. Child Development, 57, 573–582.

Goossens, L., & Phinney, J. S. (1996). Commentary: Identity, context, and development. Journal of Adolescence, 19, 491–496.

Gordon, T. R. (2002). Comprehensive school health and comprehensive guidance and counselling programs: A call for collaboration. Canadian Journal of Counselling, 36(1), 49–62.

Gordon, W. R., & Caltabiano, M. L. (1996). Urban-rural differences in adolescent self-esteem, leisure boredom, and sensation-seeking as predictors of leisure-time usage and satisfaction. *Adolescence, 31*(124), 883–901.

Gore, S., Aseltine, R. H., & Colten, M. E. (1993). Gender, social-relational involvement, and depression. *Journal of Research on Adolescence, 3*(2), 101–125.

Gortmaker, S. L., Perrin, J. M., Weitzman, M., Homer, C. J., & Sobol, A. M. (1993). An unexpected success story: Transition to adulthood in youth with chronic physical health conditions. *Journal of Research on Adolescence, 3*, 317–336.

Gotowiec, A., & Beiser, M. (1993). Aboriginal children's mental health: Unique challenges. *Canada's Mental Health, 41*(4), 7–11.

Gottfredson, D. C., Gottfredson, G. D., & Skroban, S. (1996). A multimodel school-based prevention demonstration. *Journal of Adolescent Research, 11*(1), 97–115.

Gottlieb, G. (1991). The experiential canalization of behavioral development: Theory. *Developmental Psychology, 27*, 4–13.

Gottlieb, G. (1992). *Individual development and evolution: The genesis of novel behavior.* New York: Oxford University Press.

Gottlieb, G. (1997). *Synthesizing nature-nurture: Prenatal roots of instinctive behavior.* Mahwah, NJ: Erlbaum.

Gottlieb, G., Wahlsten, D., & Lickliter, R. (1998). The significance of biology for human development: A developmental psychobiological systems view. In W. Damon (Series Ed.) & R. M. Lerner (Vol. Ed.), *Handbook of child psychology: Vol. 1. Theoretical models of human development* (5th ed., pp. 233–273). New York: Wiley.

Gould, S. J. (1981). *The mismeasure of man.* New York: Norton.

Gouvernement du Quebec (2001). *Education in Quebec: An overview.* Montreal: Author.

Graafsma, T. L., Bosma, H. A., Grotevant, H. D., & de Levita, D. J. (1994). Identity and development: An interdisciplinary approach. In H. A. Bosma, T. L. G. Graafsma, H. D. Grotevant, & D. J. deLevita (Eds.), *Identity and development: An interdisciplinary approach.* Thousand Oaks, CA: Sage.

Grabb, E., Baer, E., & Curtis. J. (1999). Origins of American individualism: reconsidering the historical evidence. *Canadian Journal of Sociology, 24*(4), 511–533.

Graber, J. A., & Petersen, A. C. (1991). Cognitive changes at adolescence: Biological perspectives. In K. R. Gibson & A. C. Petersen (Eds.), *Brain maturation and cognitive development: Comparative and cross-cultural perspectives* (pp. 253–279). New York: Aldine de Gruyter.

Graber, J. A., Brooks-Gunn, J., & Warren, M. P. (1995). The antecedents of menarcheal age: Heredity, family environment, and stressful life events. *Child Development, 66*, 346–359.

Graham, S. (1992). "Most of the subjects were white and middle class": Trends in published research on African Americans in selected APA journals, 1970–1989. *American Psychologist, 47*, 629–639.

Graham, S., & Hudley, C. (1994). Attributions of aggressive and non-aggressive African American male early adolescents: A study of construct accessibility. *Developmental Psychology, 30*(3), 365–373.

Graham, S., Hudley, C., & Williams, E. (1992). Attributional and emotional determinants of aggression among African-American and Latino young adolescents. *Developmental Psychology, 28*(4), 731–740.

Graham, S., Taylor, A. Z., & Hudley, C. (1998). Exploring achievement values among ethnic minority early adolescents. *Journal of Educational Psychology, 90*(4), 606–620.

Graham-Migel, J. (2002). Comprehensive Guidance and Counselling Programs: The Beechville-Lakeside-Timberlea experience. *Canadian Journal of Counselling, 36*(1), 6–13.

Grams, N. (2003). PM: tune in to Ottawa Hills 70125. Public Service Alliance of Canada asks prime minister to intervene. *Horizons, 16*(4), 13.

Gray, M. R., & Steinberg, L. (1999). Adolescent romance and the parent-child relationship: A contextual perspective. In W. Furman & B. B. Brown (Eds.), *The development of romantic relationships in adolescence. Cambridge studies in social and emotional development* (pp. 235–262). New York: Cambridge University Press.

Gray-Little, B., & Carels, R. A. (1997). The effect of racial dissonance on academic self-esteem and achievement in elementary, junior high, and high school students. *Journal of Research on Adolescence, 7*(2), 109–131.

Greaven, S. H., Santor, D. A., Thompson, R., & Zuroff, D. C. (2000). Adolescent self-handicapping, depressive affect, and maternal parenting style. *Journal of Youth and Adolescence, 29*, 631–646.

Greenberger, E. (1984). Defining psychosocial maturity in adolescence. *Advances in Child Behavioral Analysis & Therapy, 3*, 1–37.

Greenberger, E., & Chen, C. (1996). Perceived family relationships and depressed mood in early and late adolescence: A comparison of European and Asian Americans. *Developmental Psychology, 32*(4), 707–716.

Greenberger, E., & Steinberg, L. D. (1986). *When teenagers work: The psychological and social costs of adolescent employment.* New York: Basic.

Greenfield, P. M. (1994). Video games as cultural artifacts. *Journal of Applied Developmental Psychology, 15*, 2–11.

Grindstaff, C. F. (1995). Canadian fertility: 1951–1993. *Canadian Social Trends.* Catalogue No. 11-008E. Ottawa: Statistics Canada.

Grindstaff, C. F. (1988). Adolescent marriage and childbearing: The long-term economic outcome, Canada in the 1980s. *Adolescence, 23*(89), 45–58.

Grob, A., Flammer, A., & Wearing, A. J. (1995). Adolescents' perceived control: Domain specificity, expectations, and appraisal. *Journal of Adolescence, 18*, 403–425.

Gross, R.M. (2003). What went wrong? Feminism and freedom from the prison of gender roles. *Crosscurrents, 53*(1), 8–20.

Gross, S. R., Barrett, S. P., Shestowsky, J. S., & O Pihl, R. (2002). Ecstacy and drug consumption patterns: A Canadian rave population study. *The Canadian Journal of Psychiatry, 47*(7), 546–551.

Grossman, J. B., & Rhodes, J. E. (1999). The test of time: Predictors and effects of duration in youth mentoring relationships. Philadelphia: Public/Private Ventures.

Grotevant, H. (1998). Adolescent development in family contexts. In W. Damon & N. Eisenberg (Eds.). *Handbook of child psychology: Vol. 3. Social, emotional, and personality development* (pp. 1097–1149). New York: Wiley.

Grotevant, H. D. (1987). Toward a process model of identity formation. *Journal of Adolescent Research, 2*(3), 203–222.

Grotevant, H. D. (1994). Assessment of parent-adolescent relationships. In C. B. Fisher & R. M. Lerner (Eds.), *Applied developmental psychology* (pp. 315–338). New York: McGraw-Hill.

Grotevant, H. D. (1997a). Family processes, identity development, and behavioral outcomes for adopted adolescents. *Journal of Adolescent Research, 12*(1), 139–161.

Grotevant, H. D. (1997b). Identity processes: Integrating social psychological and developmental approaches. *Journal of Adolescent Research, 12*(3), 354–357.

Grotevant, H. D., & Bosma, H. A. (1994). History and literature. In H. A. Bosma, T. L.G. Graafsma, H. D. Grotevant, & D. J. deLevita (Eds.), *Identity and development: An interdisciplinary approach* (pp. 119–122). Thousand Oaks, CA: Sage.

Grotevant, H. D., & Cooper, C. R. (1985). Patterns of interaction in family relationships and the development of identity exploration in adolescence. *Child Development, 56*(2), 415–428.

Grotevant, H. D., & Cooper, C. R. (1986). Individuation in family relationships and the development of identity exploration. *Child Development, 56*, 415–428.

Grotevant, H. D., & Cooper, C. R. (1998). Individuality and connectedness in adolescent development: Review and prospects for research on identity, relationships, and context. In E. E.A. Skoe & A. L. von der Lippe (Eds.), *Adolescence and society* (pp. 3–37). New York: Routledge.

Grotevant, H., & Cooper, C. R. (1983). *Adolescent development in the family.* San Francisco: Jossey-Bass.

Grotpeter, J. K., & Crick, N. R. (1996). Relational aggression, overt aggression, and friendship. *Child Development, 67*, 2328–2338.

Grunseit, A., Kippax, S., Aggleton, P., Baldo, M., & Slutkin, G. (1997). Sexuality education and young people's sexual behavior: A review of studies. *Journal of Adolescent Research, 12*(4), 421–453.

Guerin, D. W., Gottfried, A. W., Oliver, P. H., & Thomas, C. W. (1994). Temperament and school functioning during early adolescence. *Journal of Early Adolescence, 14*(2), 200–225.

Guerney, L., & Arthur, J. (1984). Adolescent social relationships. In R. M. Lerner & N. L. Galambos (Eds.), *Experiencing adolescence: A sourcebook for parents, teachers, and teens* (pp. 87–118). New York: Garland.

Guerra, N. G., & Slaby, R. G. (1990). Cognitive mediators of aggression in adolescent offenders: Intervention. *Developmental Psychology, 26*(2), 269–277.

Guilford, J. P. (1967). *The nature of human intelligence.* New York: McGraw-Hill.

Gullotta, T. P., & Noyes, L. (1995). The changing of community health: The role of school-based health centers. *Adolescence, 30*, 107–115.

H

Habekothe, H. T, & Van Den Wittenboer, G. L. H. (2000). Time in bed, quality of sleep and school functioning of children. *Journal of Sleep Research, 9*, 145–153.

Hagell, A., & Newburn, T. (1996). Family and social contexts of adolescent re-offenders. *Journal of Adolescence, 19*, 5–18.

Hagen, J. W., Paul, B., Gibb, S., & Wolters, C. (1990). *Trends in research as reflected by publications in child development: 1930–1989.* Paper presented at the Biennial Meeting of the Society for Research on Adolescence, Atlanta, GA.

Hagestad, G. O., & Neugarten, B. L. (1985). Age and the life course. In R. H. Binstock & E. Shanas (Eds.), *Handbook of aging and the social sciences* (pp. 35–61). New York: Van Nostrand Reinhold.

Hagstrom, T., & Gamberale, F. (1995). Young people's work motivation and value orientation. *Journal of Adolescence, 18*, 475–490.

Hahn, A. B. (1994). Toward a national youth development policy for young African-American males: The choices policy makers face. In R. B. Mincy (Ed.), *Nurturing young black males* (pp. 165–186). Washington, DC: The Urban Institute Press.

Halas, J. (2002). Engaging alienated youth in physical education: An alternative program with lessons for the tradi-

tional class. *Journal of Teaching in Physical Education, 21*(3), 267–286.

Haldimond-Norfolk Health Unit (2002). Haldimond-Norfolk youth unhappy with body image! Survey highlights. Retrieved from: www.haldimand-norfolk.org/health/pdfs/HNYouthUnhappyBI.pdf.

Haley, N., Roy, E., Leclerc, P., Lanbert, G., Boivin, J. F., Cedras, L., et al. (2002). Risk behaviours and prevalence of Chlamydia trachomatis and Neisseria gonorrhoeae genital infections among Montreal street youth. *International Journal of STD and AIDS, 13*(4), 238–245.

Hall, G. S. (1904). *Adolescence* (Vols. 1 & 2). New York: Appleton.

Hall, G. S. (1922). *Senescence: The last half of life.* New York: Appleton.

Hall, M., McKeown, L., & Roberts, K. (2001). *Caring Canadians, involved Canadians: Highlights from the 2000 National Survey of Giving, Volunteering and Participating.* Statistics Canada. Catalogue no. 71-542-XPE.

Hamburg, D. A. (1992). *Today's children: Creating a future for a generation in crisis.* New York: Time.

Hamilton, S. F. (1994). Employment prospected as motivation for school achievement: Links and gaps between school and work in seven countries. In R. K. Silbereisen & E. Todt (Eds.), *Adolescence in context: The interplay of family, school, peers, and work in adjustment* (pp. 267–303). New York: Springer.

Hamilton, S. F. (1999). *A three-part definition of positive youth development.* Unpublished manuscript, College of Human Ecology, Cornell University.

Hamilton, S. F., & Hamilton, M. (1999). Creating new pathways to adulthood by adapting German apprenticeship in the United States. In W. R. Heinz (Ed.), *From education to work: Cross-national perspectives* (pp. 194–213). New York: Cambridge University Press.

Hamilton, S. F., & Lempert, W. (1996). The impact of apprenticeship on youth: A prospective analysis. *Journal of Research on Adolescence, 6*(4), 427–455.

Hammer, T. (1996). Consequences of unemployment in the transition from youth to adulthood in a life course perspective. *Youth & Society, 27*(4), 450–468.

Hampton, M. R., Jeffery, B., Smith, P., McWatters, B. (2001). Sexual experience, contraception, and STI prevention among high school students: Results from a Canadian urban centre. *Canadian Journal of Human Sexuality, 10*(3/4), 111–126.

Hanna, N. A., & Berndt, T. J. (1995). Relations between friendship, group acceptance, and evaluations of summer camp. *Journal of Early Adolescence, 15*(4), 456–475.

Hannah, T. E., & Morrisey, C. (2001). Correlates of psychological hardiness in Canadian adolescents. *The Journal of Social Psychology, 1271*(4), 339–344.

Hardesty, C., Wenk, D., & Morgan, C. S. (1995). Paternal involvement and the development of gender expectations in sons and daughters. *Youth & Society, 26*(3), 283–297.

Hardwick, P. J., & Rowton-Lee, M. A. (1996). Adolescent homicide: Towards assessment of risk. *Journal of Adolescence, 19,* 263–276.

Harold, G. T., & Conger, R. D. (1997). Marital conflict and adolescent distress: The role of adolescent awareness. *Child Development, 68*(2), 333–350.

Harrison, A. O., Stewart, R., Myambo, K., & Clarkston, T. (1997). Social networks among early adolescent Zimbabweans in extended families. *Journal of Research on Adolescence, 7*(2), 153–172.

Harrison, L. D., Erickson, P. G., Adlaf, E., & Freeman, C. (2001). The drugs-violence nexus among American and Canadian youth. *Substance Use and Misuse, 36*(14), 2065–2086.

Hart, B. I., & Thompson, J. M. (1996). Gender role characteristics and depressive symptomatology among adolescents. *Journal of Early Adolescence, 16*(4), 407–426.

Hart, D., & Fegley, S. (1995). Prosocial behavior and caring in adolescence: Relations to self-understanding and social judgement. *Child Development, 66,* 1346–1359.

Hart, L. R. (1995). MAPI personality correlates of comorbid substance abuse among adolescent psychiatric inpatients. *Journal of Adolescence, 18,* 657–667.

Harter, S. (1986). Processes underlying the construction, maintenance, and enhancement of the self-concept in children. In J. Suls & A. Greenwald (Eds.), *Psychological perspectives on the self* (pp. 136–181). Hillsdale, NJ: Erlbaum.

Harter, S. (1988). Cause, correlates, and the functional role of global self-worth: A life-span perspective. In J. Kolligan & R. J. Sternberg (Eds.), *Perceptions of competence and incompetence across the life-span.* New Haven, CT: Yale University Press.

Harter, S. (1998). The development of self-representations. In W. Damon (editor-in-chief) & N. Eisenberg (Ed.), *Handbook of child psychology: Vol. 3. Social, emotional, and personality development* (5th ed., pp. 1097–1149). New York: Wiley.

Harter, S., & Jackson, B. K. (1993). Young adolescents' perceptions of the link between low self-worth and depressed affect. *Journal of Early Adolescence, 13,* 383–407.

Harter, S., Stocker, C., & Robinson, N. S. (1996). The perceived directionality of the link between approval and self-worth: The liabilities of a looking glass self-orientation among young adolescents. *Journal of Research on Adolescence, 6*(3), 285–308.

Harter, S., Waters, P., & Whitesell, N. R. (1998). Relational self-worth: Differences in perceived worth as a person across interpersonal contexts among adolescents. *Child Development, 69*(3), 756–766.

Hartnagel, T. F. (1998). Labour-market problems and crime in the transition from school to work. *Canadian Review of Sociology and Anthropology 35*(4), 435–459.

Harton, H. C., & Latané, B. (1997). Social influence and adolescent lifestyle attitudes. *Journal of Research on Adolescence, 7*(2), 197–220.

Hartup, W. W. (1983). Peer relations. In P. H. Mussen (Ed.), *Handbook of child psychology* (Vol. 4, pp. 103–196). New York: Wiley.

Hartup, W. W. (1993). Adolescents and their friends. *New Directions for Child Development, 60,* 3–22.

Hartup, W. W. (1996). The company they keep: Friendships and their developmental significance. *Child Development, 67,* 1–13.

Hartup, W. W., & Overhauser, S. M. (1991). Friendships. In R. M. Lerner, A. C. Petersen, & J. Brooks-Gunn (Eds.), *Encyclopedia of adolescence* (Vol. 1, pp. 378–384). New York: Garland.

Harvey, S. M., & Spigner, C. (1995). Factors associated with sexual behavior among adolescents: A multivariate analysis. *Adolescence, 30*(118), 253–264.

Hatzichristou, C., & Hopf, D. (1996). A multiperspective comparison of peer sociometric status groups in childhood and adolescence. *Child Development, 67,* 1085–1102.

Hauser, S. T., & Safyer, A. W. (1994). Ego development and adolescent emotions. *Journal of Research on Adolescence, 4*(4), 487–502.

Hauser, S. T., Powers, S. I., & Noam, G. G. (1991). *Adolescents and their families: Paths of ego development.* New York: Free Press.

Hauser, S. T., Powers, S. I., Noam, G. G., Jacobson, A. M., Weiss, B., & Fallansbee, D. J. (1984). Familial contexts of adolescent ego development. *Child Development, 55,* 195–213.

Hauser, S., Houlihan, J., Powers, S., Jacobson, A., Noam, G., Weiss-Perry, B., Follansbee, D., & Book, B. (1991). Adolescent ego development within the family: Family styles and family sequences. *International Journal of Behavioral Development, 14*(2), 165–193.

Health Canada (1998). Trends in the Health of Canadian Youth. Strategic Policy and Systems Coordination Section. Childhood and Youth Division. Ottawa, Ontario. Retrieved from: http://www.hc-sc.gc.ca/hppb/childhood-youth/spsc/e_trends.html.

Health Canada (1999). Aboriginal peoples and the AIDS epidemic Canada: An update: Report from Health Canada Laboratory Centre for Disease Control. Retrieved from: http://www.caan.ca/Epi/Dev/Design/eindex.html.

Health Canada (1999). Trends in the Health of Canadian Youth. Strategic Policy and Systems Coordination Section. Childhood and Youth Division. Ottawa, Ontario Retrieved from: http://www.hcsc.gc.ca/hppb/childhood-youth/spsc.html.

Health Canada (2002). HIV and AIDS in Canada. Surveillance Report to June 30, 2002. Division of HIV/AIDS Epidemiology and Surveillance, Centre for Infectious Disease Prevention and Control, Health Canada.

Health Canada (2003). HIV/AIDS Epi update. Centre for Infectious Disease Prevention and Control, Health Canada.

Health Canada. (1997). *Meeting the Needs of Youth-At-Risk in Canada: Learnings from a National Community Development Project.* Ottawa, ON: Health Canada.

Health Canada. (1999). *Youth and Tobacco.* Ottawa: Health Canada.

Health Canada. (1999).*Trends in the health of Canadian youth.* Ottawa: Health Canada.

Hebert, Y. & Page, M. (2000). Research initiatives in citizenship education. *Education Canada, 40*(3), 24–27.

Heilman, M. E. (2001). Description and prescription: How gender stereotypes prevent women's ascent up the organizational ladder. *Journal of Social Issues, 57*(4), 657–674.

Helwig, C. C. (1995). Adolescents' and young adults' conceptions of civil liberties: Freedom of speech and religion. *Child Development, 66,* 152–166.

Helwig, C. C. (1998). Children's conceptions of fair government and freedom of speech. *Child Development, 69*(2), 518–531.

Hendry, L. B., Glendinning, A., Shucksmith, J., Love, J., & Scott, J. (1994). The developmental context of adolescent life-styles. In R. K. Silbereisen & E. Todt (Eds.), *Adolescence in context: The interplay of family, school, peers, and work in adjustment* (pp. 66–81). New York: Springer.

Henggeler, S. W., Brondino, M. J., Melton, G. B., Scherer, D. G., & Hanley, J. H. (1997). Multisystemic therapy with violent and chronic juvenile offenders and their families: The role of treatment fidelity in successful dissemination. *Journal of Consulting and Clinical Psychology, 65*(5), 821–833.

Henggeler, S. W., Cunningham, P. B., Pickrel, S. G., Schoenwald, S. K., & Brondino, M. J. (1996). Multisystemic therapy: An effective violence prevention approach for serious juvenile offenders. *Journal of Adolescence, 19,* 47–61.

Henrich, C. C., Kuperminc, G. P., Sack, A., Blatt, S. J., & Leadbeater, B. J. (2000). Characteristics and homogeneity of early adolescent friendship groups: A comparison of male and female clique and nonclique members. *Applied Developmental Science, 4*(1), 15–26.

Henry, B., Caspi, A., Moffitt, T. E., & Silva, P. A. (1996). Temperamental and familial predictors of violent and nonviolent criminal convictions: Age 3 to age 18. *Developmental Psychology, 32,* 614–623.

Herdt, G. (Ed.). (1989). *Gay and lesbian youth.* New York: Haworth Press.

Herman, M. R., Dornbusch, S. M., Herron, M. C., & Herting, J. R. (1997). The influence of family regulation, connection and psychological autonomy on six measures of adolescent functioning. *Journal of Adolescent Research, 12*(1), 34–67.

Hernandez, D. J. (1993). *America's children: Resources for family, government, and the economy.* New York: Russell Sage Foundation.

Hernandez-Guzman, L., & Sanchez-Sosa, J. J. (1996). Parent-child interactions predict anxiety in Mexican adolescents. *Adolescence, 31*(124), 955–963.

Hershberger, S. L., Pilkington, N. W., & D'Augelli, A. R. (1997). Predictors of suicide attempts among gay, lesbian, and bisexual youth. *Journal of Adolescent Research, 12*(4), 477–497.

Hertzman, C. (2003). Helping children thrive, Vancouver: HELP.

Herzberger, S. D., & Hall, J. A. (1993). Children's evaluations of retaliatory aggression against siblings and friends. *Journal of Interpersonal Violence, 8*(1), 77–89.

Hetherington, E. M. (1989). Coping with family transitions: Winners, losers, and survivors. *Child Development, 60,* 1–14.

Hetherington, E. M. (1991). Presidential address: Families, lies, and videotapes. *Journal of Research on Adolescence, 1*(4), 323–348.

Hetherington, E. M., & Clingempeel, W. G. (1988, March). *Coping with remarriage: The first two years.* Symposium presented at the Conference on Human Development, Charleston, SC.

Hetherington, E. M., Anderson, E. R., & Hagan, M. S. (1991). Divorce: Effects on adolescents. In R. M. Lerner, A. C. Petersen, & J. Brooks-Gunn (Eds.), *Encyclopedia of adolescence* (Vol. 1, pp. 237–243). New York: Garland.

Hetherington, E. M., Cox, M., & Cox, R. (1985). Long-term effects of divorce and remarriage on the adjustment of children. *Journal of the American Academy of Child Psychiatry, 24*(5), 518–530.

Hetherington, J. A., & Stoppard, J. M. (2002). The theme of disconnection in adolescent girls' understanding of depression. *Journal of Adolescence, 25*(6), 619–629.

Higgitt, N., Wingert, S., Ristock, J., Brown, M., Ballantyne, M., Caett, S., et al. (2003). *Voices from the Margins: Experiences of street-involved youth in Winnipeg.* Winnipeg: University of Manitoba, Department of Family Studies.

Hill, J. P., & Holmbeck, G. (1987). Familial adaptation to biological change during adolescence. In R. M. Lerner & T. Foch (Eds.), *Biological-psychosocial interactions in early adolescence* (pp. 207–223). Hillsdale, NJ: Erlbaum.

Hill, J. P., & Lynch, M. E. (1983). The intensification of gender-related role expectations during early adolescence. In J. Brooks-Gunn & A. C. Petersen (Eds.), *Girls at puberty* (pp. 201–228). New York: Plenum.

Hill, J. P., Holmbeck, G. N., Marlow, L., Green, T. M., & Lynch, M. E. (1985a). Menarcheal status and parent-child relations in families of seventh-grade girls. *Journal of Youth and Adolescence, 14,* 301–316.

Hill, J. P., Holmbeck, G. N., Marlow, L., Green, T. M., & Lynch, M. E. (1985b). Pubertal status and parent-child relations in families of seventh-grade boys. *Journal of Early Adolescence, 5,* 31–44.

Hilton, N. Z., Harris, G. T., Rice, M. E., Krans, T. S., & Lavigne, S.E. (1998). Antiviolence education in high schools: Implementation and evaluation. *Journal of Interpersonal Violence, 13*(6), 726–742.

Hinden, B. R., Compas, B. E., Howell, D. C., & Achenbach, T. M. (1997). Covariation of the anxious–depressed syndrome during adolescence: Separating fact from artifact. *Journal of Consulting and Clinical Psychology, 65*(1), 6–14.

Hines, A. M. (1997). Divorce-related transitions, adolescent development, and the role of the parent-child relationship: A review of the literature. *Journal of Marriage and the Family, 59,* 375–388.

Hockenberry-Eaton, M., Richman, M. J., DiIorio, C., Rivero, T., & Maibach, E. (1996). Mother and adolescent knowledge of sexual development: The effects of gender, age, and sexual experience. *Adolescence, 31*(121), 35–47.

Hodos, W., & Campbell, C. B. G. (1969). Scala naturae: Why there is no theory in comparative psychology. *Psychological Review, 76,* 337–350.

Hoffmann, J. P., & Johnson, R. A. (1998). A national portrait of family structure and adolescent drug use. *Journal of Marriage and the Family, 60,* 633–645.

Hogue, A., & Steinberg, L. (1995). Homophily of internalized distress in adolescent peer groups. *Developmental Psychology, 31*(6), 897–906.

Hohman, M., & LeCroy, C. W. (1996). Predictors of adolescent A.A. affiliation. *Adolescence, 31*(122), 339–352.

Hoksbergen, R. A. C. (1997). Turmoil for adoptees during their adolescence? *International Journal of Behavioral Development, 20*(1), 33–46.

Holmbeck, G. N., & Hill, J. P. (1991). Conflictive engagement, positive affect, and menarche in families with seventh-grade girls. *Child Development, 62,* 1030–1048.

Holmbeck, G., & Hill, J. P. (1988). Storm and stress beliefs about adolescence: Prevalence, self-reported antecedents, and effects of an undergraduate course. *Journal of Youth & Adolescence, 17*(4), 285–306.

Horn, J. L., & Cattell, R. B. (1966). Age differences in primary mental ability factors. *Journal of Gerontology, 21,* 210–220.

Horwitz, A. V., & White, H. R. (1998). The relationship of cohabitation and mental health: A study of a young adult cohort. *Journal of Marriage and the Family, 60,* 505–514.

Hoshi, H., & Kouchi, M. (1981). Secular trend of the age at menarche of Japanese girls with special regard to the secular acceleration of the age at peak height velocity. *Human Biology, 53*(4), 593–598.

Hoyle, R. H., & Leff, S. S. (1997). The role of parental involvement in youth sport participation and performance. *Adolescence, 32*(125), 233–243.

Hudley, C. A. (1995). Assessing the impact of separate schooling for African American male adolescents. *Journal of Early Adolescence, 15*(1), 38–57.

Huen, K. F., Leung, S. S. F., Lau, J. T. F., Cheung, A. U. K., Leung, N. K., & Chiu, M. C. (1997). Secular trend in the sexual maturation of southern Chinese girls. *Acta Paediatr, 86,* 1121–1124.

Huerta-Franco, R., Diaz de Leon, J., & Malacara, J. M. (1996). Knowledge and attitudes toward sexuality in adolescents and their associations with the family and other factors. *Adolescence, 31,* 179–191.

Hughes, K. D., & Lowe, G. S. (1993). Unequal returns: Gender differences in initial employment among university graduates. *The Canadian Journal of Higher Education, 23*(1), 37–55.

Hulanicka, B., & Waliszko, A. (1991). Deceleration of age at menarche in Poland. Annals of *Human Biology, 18*(6), 507–513.

Hultsch, D. F., & Hickey, T. (1978). External validity in the study of human development: Theoretical and methodological issues. *Human Development, 21,* 76–91.

Human Resources Development Canada (1996). Youth Employment: Some Explanations and Future Prospects. *Applied Research Bulletin, 2*(2). Retrieved from: www.hrdcdrhc.gc.ca/sp-ps/arb-dgra/publications/bulletin/vol2n2/e/v2n2_02e.shtml.

Human Resources Development Canada (2000a). *Profile of Canadian youth in the labour market.* Catalogue No. RH61-1/2000E. Hull: Applied Research Branch, Strategic Policy, Human Resources Development Canada.

Human Resources Development Canada (2000b). *Dropping out of high school: Definitions and costs.* Hull: Applied Research Branch, Strategic Policy, Human Resources Development Canada.

Human Resources Development Canada. (1995). *High school may not be enough: An analysis of results from the school leavers follow-up survey.* Hull: Human Resources Development Canada.

Human Resources Development Canada. (2000). *Profile of Canadian youth in the labour market.* Hull: Human Resources Development Canada.

Hunt, E., Streissguth, A. P., Kerr, B., & Olson, H. C. (1995). Mothers' alcohol consumption during pregnancy: Effects on spatial-visual reasoning in 14-year-old children. *Psychological Society, 6,* 339–342.

Hunt, N. (1967). *The world of Nigel Hunt: The diary of a Mongoloid youth.* New York: Garrett.

Hunter, S. M., Vizelberg, I. A., & Berenson, G. S. (1991). Identifying mechanisms of adoption of tobacco and alcohol use among youth: The Bogalusa heart study. *Social Networks, 13,* 91–104.

Huston, A. C. (Ed.). (1991). *Children in poverty: Child development and public policy.* Cambridge: Cambridge University Press.

Huston, A. C., & Wright, J. C. (1998). Mass media and children's development. In W. Damon (Ed. in chief) & I. E. Sigel & K. A. Renninger (Eds.), *Handbook of child psychology: Vol. 4. Child psychology in practice* (5th ed., pp. 999–1058). New York: Wiley.

Huston, A. C., McLoyd, V. C., & Garcia Coll, C. (1994). Children and poverty: Issues in contemporary research. *Child Development, 65,* 275–282.

Hyman, I., Vu, N., & Beiser, M. (2000). Post-migration stresses among Southeast Asian refugee youth in Canada: A research note. *Journal of Comparative Family Studies, 31,* 281–293.

I

Ing, N.R. (1991). The effects of residential schools on Native child-rearing practices. *Canadian Journal of Native Education, 18,* 65–118.

Inhelder, B., & Piaget, J. (1958). *The growth of logical thinking from childhood to adolescence.* New York: Basic.

Ivis, F. J. & Adlaf, E. M. (1999). A comparison of trends in drug use among students in the USA and Ontario, Canada: 1975–1997. *Drugs: education, prevention and policy, 6*(1), 17–27.

J

Jaccard, J., Dittus, P. J., & Gordon, V. V. (1998). Parent-adolescent congruency in reports of adolescent sexual behavior and in communications about sexual behavior. *Child Development, 69,* 247–261.

Jackson, A. (2002). Canada beats USA—but loses gold to Sweden. Canadian Council on Social Development. Retrieved from: http://www.ccsd.ca/pubs/2002/olympic/indicators.htm.

Jacobs, F. (1988). The five-tiered approach to evaluation: Context and implementation. In H. B. Weiss & F. Jacobs (Eds.), *Evaluating family programs* (pp. 37–68). Hawthorne, NY: Aldine de Gruyter.

Jacobs, F. H., & Kapuscik, J. L. (2000). *Making it count: Evaluating family preservation services.* Medford, MA: Eliot-Pearson Department of Child Development, Tufts University.

Jacobs, J., Bennett, M., & Flanagan, C. (1993). A longitudinal study of the relation between representations of attachment in childhood and cognitive functioning in childhood and adolescence. *Journal of Early Adolescence, 13*(3), 245–266.

Jacobsen, T., Edelstein, W., & Hofmann, V. (1994). A longitudinal study of the relation between representations of attachment in childhood and cognitive functioning in childhood and adolescence. *Developmental Psychology, 30,* 112–124.

Jacobvitz, D. B., & Bush, N. F. (1996). Reconstructions of family relationships: Parent-child alliances, personal distress, and self-esteem. *Developmental Psychology, 32*(4), 732–743.

Jadack, R. A., Hyde, J. S., Moore, C. F., & Keller, M. L. (1995). Moral reasoning about sexually transmitted diseases. *Child Development,* 66, 167–177.

Jagers, R. J. (1996). Culture and problem behaviors among inner-city African-American youth: Further explorations. *Journal of Adolescence,* 19, 371–381.

Jakobsen, R. (1997). Stages of progression in noncoital sexual interactions among young adolescents: An application of the Mokken Scale analysis. *International Journal of Behavioral Development, 21*(3), 537–553.

Janosz, M., Le Blanc, M., Boulerice, B., & Tremblay, R. E. (2000). Predicting different types of school dropouts: A typological approach with two longitudinal samples. *Journal of Educational Psychology, 92*(1), 171–190.

Janosz, M., LeBlanc, M., Boulerice, B., & Tremblay, R. E. (1997). Disentangling the weight of school dropout predictors: A test on two longitudinal samples. *Journal of Youth and Adolescence, 26*(6), 733–762.

Jeary, J. (2001). *Character Education Report.* Report compiled by Joan Jeary for the Calgary Board of Education, November 2001. Retrieved from: www.cbe.ab.ca/ch_supt/bulletin/Dec4b.PDF.

Jenkins, J. E. (1996). The influence of peer affiliation and student activities on adolescent drug involvement. *Adolescence, 31*(122), 297–306.

Jenkins, P. (1998). *School enrolment and the declining youth participation rate.* Hull: Applied Research Branch, Strategic Policy. Human Resources Development Canada.

Jensen, L. (1988). Rural-urban differences in the utilization of ameliorative effects on welfare programs. *Policy Studies Review, 7,* 782–794.

Jensen, P., Hoagwood, K., & Trickett, E. (1999). Ivory towers or earthen trenches?: Community collaborations to foster "real world" research. *Applied Developmental Science, 3*(4), 206–212.

Jenson, J. (2001). Shifting the paradigm: Knowledge and learning for Canada's future. *CPRN Discussion Paper No. F/18.* Ottawa: Canada Policy Research Networks.

Jessor, R. (1987). Problem-behavior theory, psychosocial development, and adolescent problem drinking. *British Journal of Addiction, 82,* 331–342.

Jessor, R. (1992). Risk behavior in adolescence: A psychosocial framework for understanding and action. *Developmental Review, 12,* 374–390.

Jessor, R., & Jessor, S. L. (1977). *Problem behavior and psychosocial development: A longitudinal study of the young.* New York: Academic Press.

Jessor, R., Donovan, J. E., & Costa, F. M. (1991). *Beyond adolescence: Problem behavior and young adult development.* Cambridge, England: Cambridge University Press.

Jessor, R., Van Den Bos, J., Vanderryn, J., & Costa, F. M. (1995). Protective factors in adolescent problem behavior: Moderator effects and developmental change. *Developmental Psychology, 31*(6), 923–933.

Joebgen, A. M., & Richards, M. H. (1990). Maternal education and employment: Mediating maternal and adolescent emotional adjustment. *Journal of Early Adolescence, 10*(3), 329–343.

Johanson, D. C., & Edey, M. A. (1981). *Lucy: The beginnings of humankind.* New York: Simon & Schuster.

Johnson, E. A., Vincent, N., & Ross, L. (1997). Self-deception versus self-esteem in buffering the negative effects of failure. *Journal of Research in Personality, 31*(3), 385–405.

Johnson, G. R., Krug, E. G., & Potter, L. B. (2000). Suicide among adolescents and young adults: A cross-national comparison of 34 countries. *Suicide and Life-Threatening Behavior, 30*(1), 74–82.

Johnson, K., Strader, T., Berbaum, M., Bryant, D., Bucholtz, G., Collins, D., & Noe, T. (1996). Reducing alcohol and other drug use by strengthening community, family, and youth resiliency: An evaluation of the Creating Lasting Connections program. *Journal of Adolescent Research, 11*(1), 36–67.

Johnston, L. D., & Bachman, J. G. (1976). Educational institutions. In J. F. Adams (Ed.), *Understanding adolescence* (3rd ed., pp. 299–315). Boston: Allyn & Bacon.

Johnston, L. D., Bachman, J. G., & O'Malley, P. M. (1991). *Monitoring the future: Questionnaire responses from the nation's high school seniors.* Ann Arbor: Survey Research Center.

Johnston, L. D., Bachman, J. G., & O'Malley, P. M. (1998). *Monitoring the future.* Ann Arbor: Survey Research Center.

Johnston, L. D., Bachman, J. G., & O'Malley, P. M. (1999). *Monitoring the Future.* Ann Arbor: Survey Research Center.

Jones, H. E. (1958). Problems of method in longitudinal research. *Vita Humana, 1,* 93–99.

Jones, H. E. (1959). Intelligence and problem solving. In J. E. Birren (Ed.), *Handbook of aging and the individual.* Chicago: University of Chicago Press.

Jones, J., Bennett, S., Olmsted, M. P., Lawson, M. L., & Rodin, G. (2001). Disordered eating attitudes and behaviours in teenaged girls: A school-based study. *Canadian Medical Association Journal, 165*(5), 547–552.

Jordan, W. J., Lara, J., & McPartland, J. M. (1996). Exploring the causes of early dropout among race-ethnic and gender groups. *Youth & Society, 28*(1), 62–94.

Jory, B., Rainbolt, E., Karns, J. T., Freeborn, A., & Greer, C. V. (1996). Communication patterns and alliances between parents and adolescents during a structured problem-solving task. *Journal of Adolescence,* 19, 339–346.

Jourmaine, R. (1994). *Baby think it over.* Eau Claire, WI: Baby Think It Over.

Jovanovic, J., & Lerner, R. M. (1994). Individual-contextual relationships and mathematics performance:

Comparing American and Serbian young adolescents. *Journal of Early Adolescence, 14*(4), 449–470.

Juon, H.-S., Shin, Y., & Nam, J. J. (1995). Cigarette smoking among Korean adolescents: Prevalence and correlates. *Adolescence, 30*(119), 631–642.

Jurich, A. P., & Collins, O. P. (1996). 4-H Night at the Movies: A program for adolescents and their families. *Adolescence, 31*(124), 863–874.

Juvonen, J. (1991). Deviance, perceived responsibility, and negative peer reactions. *Developmental Psychology, 27*(4), 672–681.

Juvonen, J., & Murdock, T. B. (1995). Grade-level differences in the social value of effort: Implications for self-presentation tactics of early adolescents. *Child Development, 66,* 1694–1705.

K

Kac, G., Auxiliadora de Santa Cruz Coelho, M., and Velasquez-Melendez, G. (2000). Secular trend in age at menarche for women born between 1920 and 1979 in Rio de Janeiro, Brazil. *Annals of Human Biology, 27*(4), 423–428.

Kagan, J., & Moss, H. A. (1962). *Birth to maturity: A study in psychological development.* New York: Wiley.

Kahlbaugh, P., & Haviland, J. M. (1991). Formal operational thinking and identity. In R. M. Lerner, A. C. Petersen, & J. Brooks-Gunn (Eds.), *Encyclopedia of adolescence* (Vol. 1, pp. 369–372). New York: Garland.

Kalant, H. (2001). The pharmacology and toxicology of "ecstacy" (MDMA) and related drugs. *Canadian Medical Association Journal, 165*(7), 917–928.

Kalil, A., & Eccles, J. S. (1998). Does welfare affect family processes and adolescent adjustment? *Child Development, 69*(6), 1597–1613.

Kandel, D. B. (1974). Inter- and intra-generational influences on adolescent marijuana use. *Journal of Social Issues, 30,* 107–135.

Kandel, D. B. (1986). Processes of peer influences in adolescence. In R. K. Silbereisen, K. Eyferth, & G. Rudinger (Eds.), *Development as action in context: Problem behavior and normal youth development* (pp. 203–227). New York: Springer.

Kandel, D. B., & Andrews, K. (1987). Processes of adolescent socialization by parents and peers. *International Journal of the Addictions, 22*(4), 319–344.

Kandel, D. B., & Lesser, G. S. (1969). Paternal and peer influences on educational plans of adolescents. *American Sociological Review, 34,* 213–223.

Kandel, D. B., & Lesser, G. S. (1972). *Youth in two worlds.* San Francisco: Jossey-Bass.

Kandel, D. B., & Wu, P. (1995). The contributions of mothers and fathers to the intergenerational transmission of cigarette smoking and adolescence. *Journal of Research on Adolescence, 5*(2), 225–252.

Kandel, D. B., Rosenbaum, E., & Chen, K. (1994). Impact of maternal drug use and life experiences on preadolescent children born to teenage mothers. *Journal of Marriage and the Family, 56,* 325–340.

Kaplan, D. S., Damphousse, K. R., & Kaplan, H. B. (1996). Moderating effects of gender on the relationship between not graduating from high school and psychological dysfunction in young adulthood. *Journal of Educational Psychology, 88*(4), 760–774.

Katchadourian, H. (1977). *The biology of adolescence.* San Francisco: Freeman.

Katz, P. A., & Ksansnak, K. R. (1994). Developmental aspects of gender role flexibility and traditionality in middle childhood and adolescence. *Developmental Psychology, 30,* 272–282.

Katzmarzyk, P.T., Malina, R.M., Song, T.M.K., & Bouchard, C. (1998). Television viewing, physical activity, and health-related fitness of youth in the Quebec Family Study. *Journal of Adolescent Health, 23*(5), 318–325.

Kaufmann, H. (1968). *Introduction to the study of human behavior.* Philadelphia: Saunders.

Kavsek, M. J., & Seiffge-Krenke, I. (1996). The differentiation of coping traits in adolescence. *International Journal of Behavioral Development, 19*(3), 651–668.

Keating, D. P. (1991). Cognition, adolescent. In R. M. Lerner, A. C. Petersen, & J. Brooks-Gunn (Eds.), *Encyclopedia of adolescence* (Vol. 1, pp. 119–129). New York: Garland.

Keefe, K., & Berndt, T. J. (1996). Relations of friendship quality to self-esteem in early adolescence. *Journal of Early Adolescence, 16*(1), 110–129.

Keith, J. G., Nelson, C. S., Schlabach, J. H., & Thompson, C. J. (1990). The relationship between parental employment and three measures of early adolescent responsibility: Family-related, personal, and social. *Journal of Early Adolescence, 10*(3), 399–415.

Kellner, M. H., & Tutin, J. (1995). A school-based anger management program for developmentally and emotionally disabled high school students. *Adolescence, 30*(120), 813–825.

Kellogg Commission on the Future of State and Land-Grant Colleges. (1999). *Returning to our roots: The engaged institution.* Washington, DC: National Association of State Universities and Land-Grant Colleges.

Kendall, P. C., & Southam-Gerow, M. A. (1996). Long-term follow-up of a cognitive-behavioral therapy for anxiety-disordered youth. *Journal of Consulting and Clinical Psychology, 64*(4), 724–730.

Keniston, K. (1970). Youth: A "new" stage of life. *American Scholar, 39,* 631–641.

Kennedy, R. E. (1991). Delinquency. In R. M. Lerner, A. C. Petersen, & J. Brooks-Gunn (Eds.), *Encyclopedia of adolescence* (Vol. 1, pp. 199–206). New York: Garland.

Kenny, M. E., Moilanen, D. L., Lomax, R., & Brabeck, M. M. (1993). Contributions of parental attachments to view of self and depressive symptoms among early adolescents. *Journal of Early Adolescence, 13*(4), 408–430.

Kenny, M., & Gallagher, L. (2000). Service-learning as a vehicle in training psychologists for revised professional roles. In F. T. Sherman & W. R. Torbert (Eds.), *Transforming social inquiry, transforming social action: New paradigms for crossing the theory/practice divide in universities and communities* (pp. 189–205). Norwell, MA: Kluwer Academic.

Kenny, M., Simon, L. A. K., Brabeck, K., & Lerner, R. M. (Eds.). 2001. *Learning to serve: Promoting civil society through service learning.* Norwell, MA: Kluwer Academic.

Kenrick, D. T., Gabrielidis, C., Keefe, R. C., & Cornelius, J. S. (1996). Adolescents' age preferences for dating partners: Support for an evolutionary model of life-history strategies. *Child Development, 67,* 1499–1511.

Kerfoot, M., Harrington, R., & Dyer, E. (1995). Brief home-based intervention with young suicide attempters and their families. *Journal of Adolescence, 18,* 557–568.

Kerpelman, J. L., Pittman, J. F., & Lamke, L. K. (1997). Toward a microprocess perspective on adolescent identity development: An identity control theory approach. *Journal of Adolescent Research, 12*(3), 325–346.

Kershner, K. (1996). Adolescent attitudes about rape. *Adolescence, 31*(121), 29–33.

Ketterlinus, R. D., & Lamb, M. E. (Eds.). (1994). *Adolescent problem behaviors: Issues and research.* Hillsdale, NJ: Erlbaum.

Kidwell, J. S., Dunham, R. M., Bacho, R. A., Pastorino, E., & Portes, P. R. (1995). Adolescent identity exploration: A test of Erikson's theory of transitional crisis. *Adolescence, 30*(120), 785–793.

Kiener, R. (2000). What teens really think. *Reader's Digest, 156*(938), 50.

Kier, C. A. & Berzonsky, M. (2003). Identity processing orientation: Do students change their identity style to meet situational demands? Poster presented at the 10th annual meeting of the Society for Research on Identity Formation, Vancouver, 15–18 May.

Kieren, D. K, & Morse, J (1995). Development Factors and Pre- and Postmenarcheal Menstrual Attitudes [Part 1 of 2]. Age at menarche is an important factor on attitude towards menstruation. *Canadian Home Economics Journal, 45*(2), 61–67.

King, C. A., Akiyama, M. M., & Elling, K. A. (1996). Self-perceived competencies and depression among middle school students in Japan and the United States. *Journal of Early Adolescence, 16*(2), 192–210.

King, C. A., Radpour, L., Naylor, M. W., Segal, H. G., & Jouriles, E. N. (1995). Parents' marital functioning and adolescent psychopathology. *Journal of Consulting and Clinical Psychology, 63*(5), 749–753.

King, V., & Elder, G. (1995). American children view their grandparents: Linked lives across three rural generations. *Journal of Marriage and the Family, 57,* 165–178.

Kingsley, C., & Mark, M. (2000). *Sacred lives: Canadian Aboriginal children and youth speak out about sexual exploitation.* Vancouver: Save the Children Canada.

Kinsey, A. C., Pomeroy, W. B., & Martin, C. E. (1948). *Sexual behavior in the human male.* Philadelphia: Saunders.

Kinsey, A. C., Pomeroy, W. B., Martin, C. E., & Gebhard, P. H. (1953). *Sexual behavior in the human female.* Philadelphia: Saunders.

Kipke, M. D., Palmer, R. F., LaFrance, S., O'Connor, S. (1997). Homeless youths' descriptions of their parents' child-rearing practices. *Youth & Society, 28*(4), 415–431.

Kirchmeyer, C. (1996). Gender roles and decision-making in demographically diverse groups: a case for reviving androgyny. *Sex Roles: A Journal of Research, 34*(9–10) 649–664.

Kirmayer, L. J., Boothroyd, L. J., & Hodgins, S. (1998). Attempted suicide among Inuit youth: Psychosocial correlates and implications for prevention. *Canadian Journal of Psychiatry, 43*(8), 816–822.

Kitchener, K. S., & Wood, P. K. (1987). Development of concepts of justification in German university students. *International Journal of Behavioral Development, 10,* 171–185.

Klaczynski, P. A., & Gordon, D. H. (1996). Self-serving influences on adolescents' evaluations of belief-relevant evidence. *Journal of Experimental Child Psychology, 62,* 317–339.

Klaw, E. L., & Rhodes, J. E. (1995). Mentor relationships and the career development of pregnant and parenting African-American teenagers. *Psychology of Women Quarterly, 19*(4), 551–562.

Klebanov, P., & Brooks-Gunn, J. (1992). Impact of maternal attitudes, girls' adjustment, and cognitive skills upon academic performance in middle and high school. *Journal of Research on Adolescence, 2,* 81–102.

Klein, K., Forehand, R., Armistead, L., & Long, P. (1997). Delinquency during the transition to early adulthood: Family and parenting predictors from early adolescence. *Adolescence, 32*(125), 61–80.

Klerman, L. V. (1991). The health of poor children: Problems and programs. In A. C. Huston (Ed.), *Children in poverty: Child development and public policy* (pp. 1–22). Cambridge: Cambridge University Press.

Kloep, M. (1995). Concurrent and predictive correlates of girls' depression and antisocial behavior under conditions of economic crisis and value change: The case of Albania. *Journal of Adolescence, 18,* 445–458.

Knight, G. P., Virdin, L. M., & Roosa, M. (1994). Socialization and family correlates of mental health outcomes among Hispanic and Anglo American children: Consideration of cross-ethnic scalar equivalence. *Child Development, 65,* 212–224.

Koch, P. B., Maney, D. W., & Susman, E. J. (1993). Introduction: Health promotion for early adolescents. In R. M. Lerner (Ed.), *Early adolescence: Perspectives on research, policy, and intervention* (pp. 241–245). Hillsdale, NJ: Erlbaum.

Koff, E., & Rierdan, J. (1995). Preparing girls for menstruation: Recommendations from adolescent girls. *Adolescence, 30*(120), 795–811.

Koff, E., Rierdan, J., & Stubbs, M. L. (1990). Gender, body image, and self-concept in early adolescence. *Journal of Early Adolescence, 10,* 56–68.

Kohlberg, L. (1958). *The development of modes of moral thinking and choice in the years ten to sixteen.* Unpublished doctoral dissertation, University of Chicago.

Kohlberg, L. (1963a). The development of children's orientations toward a moral order: Sequence in the development of moral thought. *Vita Humana, 6,* 11–33.

Kohlberg, L. (1963b). Moral development and identification. In H. Stevenson (Ed.), *Child psychology. 62nd yearbook of the National Society for the Study of Education* (pp. 277–332). Chicago: University of Chicago Press.

Kohlberg, L. (1964). Development of moral character and moral ideology. In M. L. Hoffman & L. W. Hoffman (Eds.), *Review of child development research* (Vol. 1, pp. 283–432). New York: Sage.

Kohlberg, L. (1970). Education for justice: A modern statement of the platonic view. In N. F. Sizer & T. R. Sizer (Eds.), *Moral education: Five lectures* (pp. 56–83). Cambridge: Harvard University Press.

Kohlberg, L. (1971). From is to ought: How to commit the naturalistic fallacy and get away with it in the study of moral development. In T. Mischel

(Ed.), *Cognitive development and epistemology* (pp. 151–235). New York: Academic Press.

Kohlberg, L. (1976). Moral stages and moralization: The cognitive developmental approach. In T. Luckona (Ed.), *Moral development and behavior: Theory, research, and social issues.* New York: Holt.

Kohlberg, L. (1978). Revisions in the theory and practice of moral development. *New Directions for Child Development, 2,* 83–88.

Koizumi, R. (1995). Feelings of optimism and pessimism in Japanese students' transition to junior high school. *Journal of Early Adolescence, 15*(4), 412–428.

Kolaric, G. C., & Galambos, N. L. (1995). Face-to-face interactions in unacquainted female-male adolescent dyads: How do girls and boys behave? *Journal of Early Adolescence, 15*(3), 363–382.

Kolt, G. S., Kirkby, R. J., Bar Eli, M., Blumenstein, B., Chadha, N. K., Liu, J., et al. (1999). A cross-cultural investigation of reasons for participation in gymnastics. *International Journal of Sport Psychology, 30*(3), 381–398.

Krahn, H., Lowe, G. S., & Lehmann, W. (2002). Acquisition of employability skills by high school students. *Canadian Public Policy, 28*(2), 275–296.

Kramer, L. R. (1991). The social construction of ability perceptions: An ethnographic study of gifted adolescent girls. *Journal of Early Adolescence, 11,* 340–362.

Krampen, G. (1989). Perceived childrearing practices and the development of locus of control in early adolescence. *International Journal of Behavioral Development, 12,* 177–193.

Kretzmann, J. P., & McKnight, J. L. (1993). *Building communities from the inside out: A path toward finding and mobilizing a community's assets.* Chicago: ACTA.

Kroger, J. (1995). The differentiation of "firm" and "developmental" foreclosure identity statuses: A longitudinal study. *Journal of Adolescent Research, 10*(3), 317–337.

Kufeldt, K., & Burrows, B. A. (1994). *Issues affecting public policies and services for homeless youth: Final report.* Calgary: University of Calgary

& Memorial University of Newfoundland.

Kuhn, D. (1976). Short-term longitudinal evidence for the sequentiality of Kohlberg's early stages of moral development. *Developmental Psychology, 12,* 162–166.

Kuhn, D. (1991). *The skills of argument.* New York: Cambridge University Press.

Kuhn, D., Amsel, E., & O'Loughlin, M. (1988). *The development of scientific thinking skills.* San Diego: Academic Press.

Kuntz, J. L., & Hanvey, L. (2000). *Immigrant Youth in Canada.* Ottawa, ON: Canadian Council on Social Development.

Kuntz, J. L., & Schellenberg, G. (1998). *Youth at work in Canada: a research report.* Ottawa, ON: Canadian Council on Social Development.

Kuperminc, G. P., Allen, J. P., & Arthur, M. W. (1996). Autonomy, relatedness, and male adolescent delinquency: Toward a multidimensional view of social competence. *Journal of Adolescent Research, 11*(4), 397–420.

Kurdek, L. A., Fine, M. A., & Sinclair, R. J. (1995). School adjustment in sixth graders: Parenting transitions, family climate, and peer norm effects. *Child Development, 66,* 430–445.

Kurtines, W., & Greif, E. B. (1974). The development of moral thought: Review and evaluation of Kohlberg's approach. *Psychological Bulletin, 81,* 453–469.

Kvernmo, S., & Heyerdahl, S. (1996). Ethnic identity in aboriginal Sami adolescents: The impact of the family and the ethnic community context. *Journal of Adolescence, 19,* 453–463.

L

La Novara, P. (1993). *A portrait of families in Canada. Target Groups Project.* Catalogue 89-523E-Occasional. Ottawa: Statistics Canada.

Labouvie-Vief, G. (1981). Proactive and reactive aspects of constructivism: Growth and aging in life-span perspective. In R. M. Lerner & N. A. Busch-Rossnagel (Eds.), *Individuals as producers of their development: A life-span perspective* (pp. 197–230). New York: Academic Press.

Lackie, L., & de Man, A. F. (1997). Correlates of sexual aggression

among male university students. *Sex Roles, 37*(5/6), 451–457.

Lacourse, E., Claes, & Villeneuve, M. (2001). Heavy metal music and adolescent suicidal risk. *Journal of Youth and Adolescence, 30*(3), 321–332.

Lalonde, C., Chandler, M. J., Hallett, & Paul, D. (2001). A longitudinal study of identity formation processes in Native North American youth. Poster presented at the biennial meeting of the Society for Research in Child Development, April 18–22, 2001, Minneapolis, MN.

Lamborn, S. D., Dornbusch, S. M., & Steinberg, L. (1996). Ethnicity and community context as moderators of the relations between family decision making and adolescent adjustment. *Child Development, 67,* 283–301.

Lamborn, S. D., Mounts, N. S., Steinberg, L., & Dornbusch, S. M. (1991). Patterns of competence and adjustment among adolescents from authoritative, authoritarian, indulgent, and neglectful families. *Child Development, 62,* 1049–1065.

Langer, L. M., Zimmerman, R. S., & Katz, J. A. (1995). Virgins' expectations and nonvirgins' reports: How adolescents feel about themselves. *Journal of Adolescent Research, 10*(2), 291–306.

Langhout, R. D., Osborne, L. N., Grossman, J. B., & Rhodes, J. E. (1999). An exploratory study of volunteer mentoring: Toward a typology of relationships. Unpublished manuscript. Cambridge, MA: Harvard University Graduate School of Education.

Lapointe, V., & Marcotte, D. (2000). Gender-typed characteristics and coping strategies of depressed adolescents. *European Review of Applied Psychology/Revue Europeenne de Psychologie Appliquee, 50*(4), 451–460.

Lapsley, D. K. (1991). Egocentrism theory and the "new look" at the imaginary audience and personal fable in adolescence. In R. M. Lerner, A. C. Petersen, & J. Brooks-Gunn (Eds.), *Encyclopedia of adolescence* (Vol. 1, pp. 281–286). New York: Garland.

Larose, S., & Boivin, M. (1998). Attachment to parents, social support expectations, and socioemotional adjustment during the high school-college transition. *Journal of Research on Adolescence, 8,* 1–27.

Larson, R. W. (1994). Youth organization, hobbies, and sports as developmental contexts. In R. K. Silbereisen & E. Todt (Eds.), *Adolescence in context: The interplay of family, school, peers, and work in adjustment.* (pp. 46–65). New York: Springer.

Larson, R. W. (1997). The emergence of solitude as a constructive domain of experience in early adolescence. *Child Development, 68*(1), 80–93.

Larson, R. W. (2000). Toward a psychology of positive youth development. *American Psychologist, 55*(1), 170–183.

Larson, R. W., & Richards, M. H. (1994). Family emotions: Do young adolescents and their parents experience the same states? *Journal of Research on Adolescence, 4*(4), 567–583.

Larson, R. W., Clore, G. L., & Wood, G. A. (1999). The emotions of romantic relationships: Do they wreak havoc on adolescents? In W. Furman & B. B. Brown (Eds.), *The development of romantic relationships in adolescence. Cambridge studies in social and emotional development* (pp. 19–49). New York: Cambridge University Press.

Larson, R. W., Gillman, S. A., & Richards, M. H. (1997). Divergent experiences of family leisure: Fathers, mothers, and young adolescents. *Journal of Leisure Research, 29*(1), 78–97.

Larson, R. W., Richards, M. H., Moneta, G., & Holmbeck, G. (1996). Changes in adolescents' daily interactions with their families from ages 10 to 18: Disengagement and transformation. *Developmental Psychology, 32*(4), 744–754.

Larson, R., & Richards, M. H. (1991). Daily companionship in late childhood and early adolescence: Changing developmental contexts. *Child Development, 62*, 284–300.

Lasko, D. S., Field, T. M., Gonzalez, K. P., Harding, J., Yando, R., & Bendell, D. (1996). Adolescent depressed mood and parental unhappiness. *Adolescence, 31*(121), 49–57.

Lau, S., & Lau, W. (1996). Outlook on life: How adolescents and children view the life-style of parents, adults and self. *Journal of Adolescence, 19*, 293–296.

Laursen, B. (1993). Conflict management among close peers. *New Directions for Child Development, 60*, 39–54.

Laursen, B. (1995a). Conflict and social interaction in adolescent relationships. *Journal of Research on Adolescence, 5*(1), 55–70.

Laursen, B. (1995b). Variations in adolescent conflict and social interaction associated with maternal employment and family structure. *International Journal of Behavioral Development, 18*(1), 151–164.

Laursen, B., Coy, K. C., & Collins, W. A. (1998). Reconsidering changes in parent-child conflict across adolescence: A meta-analysis. *Child Development, 69*(3), 817–832.

Law, C., & Peixoto Labre, M. (2002). Cultural standards of attractiveness: A thirty-year look at changes in male images in magazines. *Journalism and Mass Communication Quarterly, 79*(3), 697–711.

Lay, C., & Verkuyten, M. (1999). Ethnic identity and its relation to personal self-esteem: A comparison of Canadian-born and foreign-born Chinese adolescents. *Journal of Social Psychology, 139*(3), 288–299.

Le Bourdais, C., & Marcil-Gratton, N. (1996). Family transformations across the Canadian/American border: When the laggard becomes the leader. *Journal of Comparative Family Studies, 27*, 415–436.

Leadbeater, B. J. (1991). Relativistic thinking in adolescence. In R. M. Lerner, A. C. Petersen, & J. Brooks-Gunn (Eds.), *Encyclopedia of adolescence* (Vol. 2, pp. 921–925). New York: Garland.

Leadbeater, B. J. (1996). School outcomes for minority-group adolescent mothers at 28 to 36 months postpartum: A longitudinal follow-up. *Journal of Research on Adolescence, 6*(4), 629–648.

Leadbeater, B. J., & Dionne, J. (1981). The adolescent's use of formal operational thinking in solving problems related to identity resolution. *Adolescence, 16*, 111–121.

Leadbeater, B. J., Blatt, S. J., & Quinlan, D. M. (1995). Gender-linked vulnerabilities to depressive symptoms, stress, and problem behaviors in adolescents. *Journal of Research on Adolescence, 5*(1), 1–29.

Lee, M., & Larson, R. (1996). Effectiveness of coping in adolescence: The case of Korean examination stress. *International Journal of Behavioral Development, 19*(4), 851–869.

Lee, V. E., Burkam, D. T., Zimiles, H., & Ladewski, B. (1994). Family structure and its effect on behavioral and emotional problems in young adolescents. *Journal of Research on Adolescence, 4*(3), 405–437.

Leenaars, A. A., & Lester, D. (1995). The changing suicide pattern in Canadian adolescents and youth, compared to their American counterparts. *Adolescence, 30*(119), 539–547.

Leffert, N., Benson, P., Scales, P., Sharma, A., Drake, D., & Blyth, D. (1998). Developmental assets: Measurement and prediction of risk behaviors among adolescents. *Applied Developmental Science, 2*, 209–230.

Lenerz, K., Kucher, J., East, P., Lerner, J. V., & Lerner, R. M. (1987). Early adolescents' physical organismic characteristics and psychosocial functioning: Findings from the Pennsylvania Early Adolescent Transitions Study (PEATS). In R. M. Lerner & T. Foch (Eds.), *Biological-psychosocial interactions in early adolescence. Child Psychology* (pp. 225–247). Hillsdale, NJ: Erlbaum.

Leon, G. R. (1991). Bulimia nervosa in adolescence. In R. M. Lerner, A. C. Petersen, & J. Brooks-Gunn (Eds.), *Encyclopedia of adolescence* (Vol. 1). New York: Garland.

Lerman, R. I. (1985). *Who are the young absent fathers?* Paper prepared for the Department of Health and Human Services, Assistant Secretary for Policy and Evaluation. Waltham, MA: Brandeis University, Heller Graduate School.

Lerner, J. S. (1995). Foreword. In R. M. Lerner (Ed.), *America's youth in crisis: Challenges and options for programs and policies* (pp. xi–xii). Thousand Oaks, CA: Sage.

Lerner, J. V. (1994). *Working women and their families.* Thousand Oaks, CA: Sage.

Lerner, J. V., & Galambos, N. L. (1985). Mother role satisfaction, mother-child interaction, and child temperament: A process model. *Developmental Psychology, 21*(6), 1157–1164.

Lerner, J. V., & Galambos, N. L. (1991). *Employed mothers and their children.* New York: Garland.

Lerner, R. M, Castellino, D. R., Terry, P. A., Villarruel, F. A., & McKinney, M. H. (1995). A developmental contextual perspective on parenting. In M.

H. Bornstein (Ed.), *Handbook of parenting: Biology and ecology of parenting* (Vol. 2, pp. 285–309). Mahwah, NJ: Erlbaum.

Lerner, R. M. (1976). *Concepts and theories of human development.* Reading, MA: Addison-Wesley.

Lerner, R. M. (1982). Children and adolescents as producers of their own development. *Developmental Review, 2,* 342–370.

Lerner, R. M. (1984). *On the nature of human plasticity.* New York: Cambridge University Press.

Lerner, R. M. (1985). Individual and context in developmental psychology: Conceptual and theoretical issues. In J. R. Nesselroade & A. von Eye (Eds.), *Individual development and social change: Explanatory analysis* (pp. 155–187). New York: Academic Press.

Lerner, R. M. (1986). *Concepts and theories of human development* (2nd ed.). New York: Random House.

Lerner, R. M. (1987). A life-span perspective for early adolescence. In R. M. Lerner & T. T. Foch (Eds.), *Biological-psychosocial interactions in early adolescence* (pp. 9–34). Hillsdale, NJ: Erlbaum.

Lerner, R. M. (1988). Early adolescent transitions: The lore and the laws of adolescence. In M. D. Levine & E. R. McArarney (Eds.), *Early adolescent transitions* (pp. 1–40). Lexington, MA: D.C. Heath.

Lerner, R. M. (1991a). Changing organism-context relations as the basic process of development: A developmental contextual perspective. *Developmental Psychology, 27,* 27–32.

Lerner, R. M. (1991b). Editorial: Continuities and changes in the scientific study of adolescence. *Journal of Research on Adolescence, 1,* 1–5.

Lerner, R. M. (1992a). Dialectics, developmental contextualism, and the further enhancement of theory about puberty and psychosocial development. *Journal of Early Adolescence, 12,* 366–388.

Lerner, R. M. (1992b). *Final solutions: Biology, prejudice, and genocide.* University Park: Penn State Press.

Lerner, R. M. (1993a). Early adolescence: Toward an agenda for the integration of research, policy, and intervention. In R. M. Lerner (Ed.), *Early adolescence: Perspectives on research, policy, and intervention,* pp. 1–13.

Lerner, R. M. (1993b). Investment in youth: The role of home economics in enhancing the life chances of America's children. *AHEA Monograph Series, 1,* 5–34.

Lerner, R. M. (1994). Schools and adolescents. In P. C. McKenry & S. M. Gavazzi (Eds.), *Visions 2010: Families and adolescents, 2*(1), pp. 14–15, 42–43. Minneapolis: National Council on Family Relations.

Lerner, R. M. (1995). *America's youth in crisis: Challenges and options for programs and policies.* Thousand Oaks, CA: Sage.

Lerner, R. M. (1998b). Theories of human development: Contemporary perspectives. In W. Damon (Series Ed.) & R. M. Lerner (Vol. Ed.), *Handbook of child psychology: Vol. 1. Theoretical models of human development* (pp. 1–24). New York: Wiley.

Lerner, R. M. (Ed). (1998a). Theoretical models of human development. In W. Damon (Ed.), *Handbook of Child Psychology* (5th ed., Vol. 1). New York: Wiley.

Lerner, R. M. (2001). *Concepts and theories of human development* (3rd ed.). Mahwah, NJ: Erlbaum.

Lerner, R. M., & Castellino, D. R. (1999). Adolescents and their families: A view of the issues. In R. M. Lerner & D. R. Castellino (Eds.), *Adolescents and their families: Structure, function, and parent-youth relations* (pp. ix–xiii). New York: Garland.

Lerner, R. M., & Castellino, D. R. (2002). Contemporary developmental theory and adolescence: Developmental systems and applied developmental science. *Journal of Adolescent Health, 31*(6): 122–135.

Lerner, R. M., & Fisher, C. B. (1994). From applied developmental psychology to applied developmental science: Community coalitions and collaborative careers. In C. B. Fisher & R. M. Lerner (Eds.), *Applied developmental psychology* (pp. 502–522). New York: McGraw-Hill.

Lerner, R. M., & Foch, T. T. (Eds.). (1987). *Biological-psychosocial interactions in early adolescence.* Hillsdale, NJ: Erlbaum.

Lerner, R. M., & Galambos, N. L. (1998). Adolescent development: Challenges and opportunities for research, programs, and policies. In J. T. Spence (Ed.), *Annual Review of Psychology* (Vol. 49, pp. 413–446). Palo Alto, CA: Annual Reviews.

Lerner, R. M., & Hoopfer, L. C. (1993, October 12). The family answer book: Teens and tweens. *Family Circle,* p. 43.

Lerner, R. M., & Hultsch, D. F. (1983). *Human development: A life-span perspective.* New York: McGraw-Hill.

Lerner, R. M., & Kauffman, M. B. (1985). The concept of development in contextualism. *Developmental Review, 5,* 309–333.

Lerner, R. M., & Knapp, J. R. (1975). Actual and perceived intrafamilial attitudes of late adolescents and their parents. *Journal of Youth and Adolescence, 4,* 17–36.

Lerner, R. M., & Lerner, J. V. (1983). Temperament-intelligence reciprocities in early childhood: A contextual model. In M. Lewis (Ed.), *Origins of intelligence: Infancy and early childhood* (pp. 399–421). New York: Plenum.

Lerner, R. M., & Lerner, J. V. (1987). Children in their contexts: A goodness-of-fit model. In J. B. Lancaster & J. Altmann (Eds.), *Parenting across the life span: Biosocial dimensions* (pp. 377–404). Hawthorne, NY: Aldine.

Lerner, R. M., & Lerner, J. V. (1989). Organismic and social contextual bases of development: The sample case of early adolescence. In W. Damon (Ed.), *Child development today and tomorrow* (pp. 69–85). San Francisco: Jossey-Bass.

Lerner, R. M., & Miller, J. R. (1993). Integrating human development research and intervention for America's children: The Michigan State University Model. *Journal of Applied Developmental Psychology, 14,* 347–364.

Lerner, R. M., & Olson, C. K. (1994, December). "Don't talk back!" *Parents,* pp. 97–98.

Lerner, R. M., & Olson, C. K. (1994, February). The imaginary audience. *Parents,* pp. 133–134.

Lerner, R. M., & Olson, C. K. (1995, February). My body is so ugly! *Parents,* pp. 87–88.

Lerner, R. M., & Olson, C. K. (1995, September). Teen idols. *Parents,* pp. 91–92.

Lerner, R. M., & Olson, C. K. (1996, September). Keeping tabs . . . without being a nag. *Parents,* pp. 111–112.

Lerner, R. M., & Simon, L. A. K. (1998). The new American outreach university:

Challenges and options. In R. M. Lerner & L. A. K. Simon (Eds.), *University-community collaborations for the twenty-first century: Outreach scholarship for youth and families* (pp. 3–23). New York: Garland.

Lerner, R. M., & Spanier, G. B. (Eds.). (1978a). *Child influences on marital and family interaction: A life span perspective.* New York: Academic Press.

Lerner, R. M., & Spanier, G. B. (1978b). A dynamic interactional view of child and family development. In R. M. Lerner & G. B. Spanier (Eds.), *Child influences on marital and family interaction: A life-span perspective* (pp. 1–22). New York: Academic Press.

Lerner, R. M., & Spanier, G. B. (1980). A dynamic interactional view of child and family development. In R. M. Lerner & G. B. Spanier (Eds.), *Child influences on marital and family interaction: A life-span perspective* (pp. 1–20). New York: Academic Press.

Lerner, R. M., & Villarruel, F. A. (1994). Adolescence. In T. Husen & N. Postlethwaite (Eds.), *International encyclopedia of education* (2nd ed., Vol. 1, pp. 83–89). Oxford: Pergamon.

Lerner, R. M., Castellino, D. R., Terry, P. A., Villarruel, F. A., & McKinney, M. H. (1995). A developmental contextual perspective on parenting. In M. H. Bornstein (Ed.), *Handbook of parenting: Biology and ecology of parenting* (Vol. 2, pp. 285–309). Hillsdale, NJ: Erlbaum.

Lerner, R. M., Delaney, M., Hess, L. E., Jovanovic, J., & von Eye, A. (1990). Early adolescent physical attractiveness and academic competence. *Journal of Early Adolescence, 10,* 4–20.

Lerner, R. M., Fisher, C. B., & Weinberg, R. A. (2000a). Toward a science for and of the people: Promoting civil society through the application of developmental science. *Child Development, 71,* 11–20.

Lerner, R. M., Fisher, C. B., & Weinberg, R. A. (2000b). Applying developmental science in the twenty-first century: International scholarship for our times. *International Journal of Behavioral Development, 24,* 24–29.

Lerner, R. M., Fisher, C. B., & Weinberg, R. A. (1997). Editorial: Applied developmental science: Scholarship for our times. *Applied Developmental Science, 1,* 2–3.

Lerner, R. M., Freund, A. M., DeStefanis, I., & Habermas, T. (2001). Understanding developmental regulation in adolescence: The use of the selection, optimization, and compensation model. *Human Development, 44,* 29–50.

Lerner, R. M., Karson, M., Meisels, M., & Knapp, J. R. (1975). Actual and perceived attitudes of late adolescents and their parents: The phenomenon of the generation gaps. *Journal of Genetic Psychology, 126,* 195–207.

Lerner, R. M., Lerner, J. V., Hess, L. E., Schwab, J., et al. (1991). Physical attractiveness and psychosocial functioning among early adolescents. *Journal of Early Adolescence, 11,* 300–320.

Lerner, R. M., Ostrom, C. W., & Freel, M. A. (1995). Promoting positive youth and community development through outreach scholarship: Comments on Zeldin and Peterson. *Journal of Adolescent Research, 10,* 486–502.

Lerner, R. M., Ostrom, C. W., & Freel, M. A. (1997). Preventing health compromising behaviors among youth and promoting their positive development: A developmental contextual perspective. In J. Schulenberg, J. L. Maggs, & K. Hurrelmann (Eds.), *Health risks and developmental transitions during adolescence* (pp. 498–521). New York: Cambridge University Press.

Lerner, R. M., Sparks, E., & McCubbin, L. (1999). *Family diversity and family policy: Strengthening families for America's children.* Norwell, MA: Kluwer.

Lerner, R. M., Sparks, E., & McCubbin, L. (2000). Family diversity and family policy. In D. Demo, K. R. Allen, & M. A. Fine (Eds.), *Handbook of family diversity* (pp. 380–401). New York: Oxford University Press.

LeRoux, J. (1996). Street children in South Africa: Findings from interviews on the background of street children in Pretoria, South Africa. *Adolescence, 31*(122), 423–431.

Leung, C. (2001). The sociocultural and psychological adaptation of Chinese migrant adolescents in Australia and Canada. *International Journal of Psychology, 36,* 8–19.

Levinson, D. J. (1978). Mid-life transition period in adult psychosocial development. *Psychiatry, 129,* 173–174.

Levitt, C. (1996). Illusion of difference: realities of ethnicity in Canada and the United States. Jeffrey G. Reitz; Raymond Breton. *Canadian Journal of Sociology, 21*(4), 582–583.

Levitt, M. J., Guacci-Franco, N., & Levitt, J. L. (1993). Convoys of social support in childhood and early adolescence: Structure and function. *Developmental Psychology, 29,* 811–818.

Levitt, M. J., Guacci-Franco, N., & Levitt, J. L. (1994). Social support and achievement in childhood and early adolescence: A multicultural study. *Journal of Applied Developmental Psychology, 15*(2), 207–222.

Levitt, M. Z., Selman, R. L., & Richmond, J. B. (1991). The psychosocial foundations of early adolescents' high-risk behavior: Implications for research and practice. *Journal of Research on Adolescence, 1*(4), 349–378.

Levy, G. D., Taylor, M. G., & Gelman, S. A. (1995). Traditional and evaluative aspects of flexibility in gender roles, social conventions, moral rules, and physical laws. *Child Development, 66,* 515–531.

Lewin, K. (1943). Psychology and the process of group living. *Journal of Social Psychology, 17,* 113–131.

Lewis, C. (1987). Early sex-role socialization. In D.J. Hargreaves & A.M. Colley (Eds.), *The psychology of sex roles.* London: Harper & Row.

Li, X., Sano, H., & Merwin, J. C. (1996). Perception and reasoning abilities among American, Japanese, and Chinese adolescents. *Journal of Adolescent Research, 11*(2), 173–193.

Lieberman, M., Doyle, A. B., & Markiewicz, D. (1999). Developmental patterns in security of attachment to mother and father in late childhood and early adolescence: Associations with peer relations. *Child Development, 70,* 202–213.

Lindsay, C., Devereux, M. S., & Bergob, M. (1994). *Youth in Canada* (2nd ed.). Target groups project. Catalogue No. 89-511E. Ottawa: Statistics Canada.

Linn, M. C. (1991). Scientific reasoning, adolescent. In R. M. Lerner, A. C. Petersen, & J. Brooks-Gunn (Eds.), *Encyclopedia of adolescence* (Vol. 2, pp. 981–986). New York: Garland.

Linn, M., & Petersen, A. (1985). Emergence and characterization of sex differences in spatial ability: A meta-analysis. *Child Development, 56*(6), 1479–1498.

Lintunen, T., Leskinen, E., Oinonen, M., Salinto, M., & Rahkila, P. (1995). Change, reliability, and stability in self-perceptions in early adolescence: A four-year follow-up study. *International Journal of Behavioral Development, 18*(2), 351–364.

Lipps, G., & Frank, J. (1997). The social ♣ context of school for young children. Catalogue Number 11-008-XPE. *Canadian Social Trends.* Ottawa: Statistics Canada.

Lipset, S. M. (1986.) Historical traditions and national characteristics: A comparative analysis of Canada and the United States. *Canadian Journal of Sociology 11*(2): 113–155.

Lipsitz, J. (1977). *Growing up forgotten.* Lexington, MA: Lexington.

Lipsitz, J. (1991). Public policy and young adolescents: A 1990s context for researchers. *Journal of Early Adolescence, 11*, 20–37.

Litchfield, A. W., Thomas, D. L., & Li, B. D. (1997). Dimensions of religiosity as mediators of the relations between parenting and adolescent deviant behavior. *Journal of Adolescent Research, 12*(2), 199–226.

Litt, I. F. (1991). Eating disorders, medical complications of. In R. M. Lerner, A. C. Petersen, & J. Brooks-Gunn (Eds.), *Encyclopedia of Adolescence* (Vol. 1, pp. 278–280). New York: Garland.

Little, R. R. (1993). *What's working for today's youth: The issues, the programs, and the learnings.* Paper presented at the ICYF Fellows Colloquium, Michigan State University.

Livson, N., & Peskin, H. (1980). Perspectives on adolescence from longitudinal research. In J. Adelson (Ed.), *Handbook of adolescent psychology* (pp. 47–98). New York: Wiley.

Looker, E. D. (2000). Gender and work: ♣ The occupational expectations of young women and men in the 1990s. *Gender Issues, 18*(2), 74–89.

Looker, E. D., & Thiessen, V. (1999). ♣ Images of work: Women's work, men's work, housework. *Canadian Journal of Sociology, 24*(2), 225–254.

Lord, S. E., Eccles, J. S., & McCarthy, K. A. (1994). Surviving the junior high school transition: Family processes and self-perceptions as protective and

risk factors. *Journal of Early Adolescence, 14*, 162–199.

LoSciuto, L., Rajala, A. K., Townsend, T. N., & Taylor, A. S. (1996). An outcome evaluation of Across Ages: An intergenerational mentoring approach to drug prevention. *Journal of Adolescent Research, 11*(1), 116–129.

Loughlin, C. A., & Barling, J. (1998). Teenagers' part-time employment and their work-related attitudes and aspirations. *Journal of Organizational Behavior, 19*(2), 197–207.

Loukid, M., Baali A., & Hilali, M. K. (1996). Secular trend in age at menarche in Marrakesh (Morocco). *Annals of Human Biology, 23*(4), 333–335.

Lourenço, O. M. (1990). From cost-perception to gain-construction: Toward a Piagetian explanation of the development of altruism in children. *International Journal of Behavioral Development, 13*, 119–132.

Luffman, J. L. (1998). When parents ♣ replace teachers: The home schooling option. *Canadian Social Trends, 50*, 8–10.

Luster, T., & McAdoo, H. (1996). Family and child influences on educational attainment: A secondary analysis of the High/Scope Perry Preschool data. *Developmental Psychology, 32*(1), 26–39.

Luster, T., & McAdoo, H. P. (1994). Factors related to the achievement and adjustment of young African American children. *Child Development, 65*, 1080–1094.

Luster, T., & McAdoo, H. P. (1995). Factors related to self-esteem among African-American youths: A secondary analysis of the High/Scope Perry Preschool data. *Journal of Research on Adolescence, 5*(4), 451–467.

Luster, T., & Small, S. A. (1997). Sexual abuse history and problems in adolescence: Exploring the effects of moderating variables. *Journal of Marriage and the Family, 59*, 131–142.

Luthar, S. S. (1995). Social competence in the school setting: Prospective cross-domain associations among inner-city teens. *Child Development, 66*, 416–429.

Luthar, S. S., & McMahon, T. J. (1996). Peer reputation among inner-city adolescents: Structure and correlates. *Journal of Research on Adolescence, 6*(4), 581–603.

Lynch, M. E. (1991). Gender intensification. In R. M. Lerner, A. C. Petersen, & J. Brooks-Gunn (Eds.), *Encyclopedia of adolescence* (Vol. 1, pp. 389–391). New York: Garland.

Lyon, M., Chatoor, I., Atkins, D., Silber, T., Mosimann, J., & Gray, J. (1997). Testing the hypothesis of the multidimensional model of anorexia nervosa in adolescents. *Adolescence, 32*(125), 101–111.

Lysne, M., & Levy, G. D. (1997). Differences in ethnic identity in Native American adolescents as a function of school context. *Journal of Adolescent Research, 12*(3), 372–388.

M

Ma, X. (2001). Bullying and being bul- ♣ lied: To what extent are bullies also victims? *American Educational Research Journal, 38*(2), 351–370.

Ma, X., & Klinger, D.A. (2000). ♣ Hierarchical linear modelling of student and school effects on academic achievement. *Canadian Journal of Education, 25*(1), 41–55.

Mac Iver, D. J., & Reuman, D. A. (1988, April). *Decision-making in the classroom and early adolescents' valuing of mathematics.* Paper presented at the annual meeting of the American Educational Research Association, New Orleans.

Maccoby, E., & Martin, J. (1983). Socialization in the context of the family: Parent-child interaction. In E. M. Hetherington (Ed.), *Handbook of child psychology: Socialization, personality, and social development* (Vol. 4, pp. 1–101). New York: Wiley.

MacDonald, I. M. (1997). Violence in ♣ schools: Multiple realities. *Alberta Journal of Educational Research, 43*(2-3), 142–156.

Macdonald, S. M. (1999). Obesity: Worldwide Prevalence and Trends. *Healthy Weight Journal, 13*(6), 84–87.

MacIntyre, P. D., Baker, S. C., Clement, R., & Conrod, S. (2001). Willingness to communicate, social support, and language-learning orientations of immersion students. *Studies in Second Language Acquisition, 23*(3), 369–388.

Mackey, K., Arnold, M. L., & Pratt, M. ♣ W. (2001). Adolescents' stories of decision making in more and less authoritative families: Representing the voices of parents in narrative.

Journal of Adolescent Research, 16, 243–268.

Macksoud, M. S., & Aber, J. L. (1996). The war experiences and psychosocial development of children in Lebanon. *Child Development*, 67, 70–88.

Magarey, A. M., Boulton, T. J. C., Chatterton, B. E., Schultz, C, Nordin, B. E. C., & Cockington, R. A. (1999). Bone growth from 11 to 17 years: relationship to growth, gender and changes with pubertal status including timing of menarche. *Acta Podiatr*, 88, 139–146.

Maggs, J. L., & Galambos, N. L. (1993). Alternative structural models for understanding adolescent problem behavior in two-earner families. *Journal of Early Adolescence*, 13(1), 79–101.

Maggs, J. L., & Hurrelmann, K. (1998). Do substance use and delinquency have differential associations with adolescents' peer relations? *International Journal of Behavioral Development*, 22(2), 367–388.

Maggs, J. L., Almeida, D. M., & Galambos, N. L. (1995). Risky business: The paradoxical meaning of problem behavior for young adolescents. *Journal of Early Adolescence*, 15(3), 344–362.

Magnusson, D. (1988). Individual development from an interactional perspective. In D. Magnusson (Ed.), *Paths through life* (Vol. 1, pp. 3–31). Hillsdale, NJ: Erlbaum.

Magnusson, D., & Stattin, H. (1998). Person-context interaction theories. In W. Damon (Series Ed.) & R. M. Lerner (Vol. Ed.), *Handbook of child psychology: Vol. 1. Theoretical models of human development* (5th ed., pp. 685–759). New York: Wiley.

Magnusson, D., Stattin, H., & Allen, V. L. (1986). Differential maturation among girls and its relations to social adjustment: A longitudinal perspective. In P. B. Baltes, D. L. Featherman, & R. M. Lerner (Eds.), *Life-span development and behavior* (pp. 135–172). Hillsdale, NJ: Erlbaum.

Maguin, E., Zucker, R. A., & Fitzgerald, H. E. (1994). The path to alcohol problems through conduct problems: A family-based approach to very early intervention with risk. *Journal of Research on Adolescence*, 4, 249–269.

Mann-Feder, V. R. (1996). Adolescents in therapeutic communities. *Adolescence*, 31(121), 17–28.

Marcia, J. (1966). Development and validations of ego-identity status. *Journal of Personality and Social Psychology*, 5, 551–558.

Marcia, J. (1991). Identity and self-development. In R. M. Lerner, A. C. Petersen, & J. Brooks-Gunn (Eds.), *Encyclopedia of adolescence* (Vol. 1, pp. 529–533). New York: Garland.

Marcia, J. E. (1964). *Determination and construct validity of ego identity status*. Unpublished doctoral dissertation. Ohio State University.

Marcia, J. E. (1980). Identity in adolescence. In J. Adelson (Ed.), *Handbook of adolescent psychology* (pp. 159–187). New York: Wiley.

Marcia, J. E., Waterman, A. S., Matteson, D. R., Archer, S., & Orlofsky, J. (1992). *Ego identity: A handbook for psychosocial research*. Vancouver: Simon Fraser University. (Original work published 1985.)

Marcotte, D. (1996). Irrational beliefs and depression in adolescence. *Adolescence*, 31(124), 935–954.

Marcotte, D., Alain, M., & Gosselin, M. J. (1999). Gender differences in adolescent depression: Gender-typed characteristics or problem-solving skills deficits? *Sex Roles*, 41(1-2), 31–48.

Marcotte, D., Fortin, L., Potvin, P., & Papillon, M. (2002). Gender differences in depressive symptoms during adolescence: Role of gender-typed characteristics, self-esteem, body image, stressful life events, and pubertal status. *Journal of Emotional and Behavioral Disorders*, 10(1), 29–42.

Marcus, R. F. (1996). The friendships of delinquents. *Adolescence*, 31(121), 145–158.

Marcus, R. F., & Betzer, P. D. S. (1996). Attachment and antisocial behavior in early adolescence. *Journal of Early Adolescence*, 16(2), 229–248.

Marini, Z., & Case, R. (1994). The development of abstract reasoning about the physical and social world. *Child Development*, 65, 147–159.

Markstrom, C., Berman, R. C., & Brusch, G. (1998). An exploratory examination of identity formation among Jewish adolescents according to context. *Journal of Adolescent Research*, 13(2), 202–222.

Markstrom-Adams, C., & Smith, M. (1996). Identity formation and religious orientation among high school students from the United States and Canada. *Journal of Adolescence*, 19, 247–261.

Marlatt, G. A., Baer, J. S., Kivlahan, D. R., Dimeff, L. A., Larimer, M. E., Quigley, L. A., Somers, J. M., & Williams, E. (1998). Screening and brief intervention for high-risk college student drinkers: Results from a 2-year follow-up assessment. *Journal of Consulting and Clinical Psychology*, 66(4), 604–615.

Marrodain, M. D., Mesa, M. S., Areichiga, J., and Peireiz-Magdaleno, A. (2000). Trend in menarcheal age in Spain: rural and urban comparison during a recent period. *Annals of Human Biology*, 27(3), 313–319.

Marsh, H. W., & Roche, L. A. (1996). Structure of artistic self-concepts for performing arts and non-performing arts students in a performing arts high school: "Setting the stage" with multigroup confirmatory factor analysis. *Journal of Educational Psychology*, 88(3), 461–477.

Marshall, S. K. (2001). Do I matter? Construct validation of adolescents' perceived mattering to parents and friends. *Journal of Adolescence*, 24(4), 473–490.

Marshall, W. A., & Tanner, J. M. (1986). Puberty. In F. Falkner & J. M. Tanner (Eds.), *Human growth* (2nd ed., Vol. 2, pp. 171–209). New York: Plenum.

Marsiglio, W. (1987). Male teenage fertility: An analysis of fatherhood commitment and its association with educational outcomes and aspirations. *Dissertation Abstracts International*, 48(2-A), 358.

Marsiske, M., Lang, F. R., Baltes, P. B., & Baltes, M. M. (1995). Selective optimization with compensation: Life-span perspectives on successful human development. In R. A. Dixon & L. Bäckman (Eds.), *Compensating for psychological deficits and declines: Managing losses and promoting gains* (pp. 35–79). Mahwah, NJ: Erlbaum.

Martin, K., & Zheng, W. (2000). Contraceptive use in Canada: 1984–1995. *Family Planning Perspectives*, 32(2), 65–73.

Mason, C. A., Cauce, A. M., Gonzales, N., & Hiraga, Y. (1996). Neither too sweet nor too sour: Problem peers, maternal control, and problem behavior in African American adolescents. *Child Development*, 67, 2115–2130.

Masten, A. S., Coatsworth, J. D., Neeman, J., Gest, S. D., Tellegen, A., & Garmezy, N. (1995). The structure and coherence of competence from childhood through adolescence. *Child Development, 66,* 1635–1659.

Mathews, F. (1993). *Youth gangs on youth gangs.* Ottawa: Solicitor General of Canada.

Maticka-Tyndale, E. (2000). Adolescent sexual and reproductive health in Canada: A review of national data sources and their limitations. *Canadian Journal of Human Sexuality, 9*(1), 41–67.

Maticka-Tyndale, E. (2001). Sexual health and Canadian youth: How do we measure up? *Canadian Journal of Human Sexuality, 10*(1/2), 1–17.

Maticka-Tyndale, E., Barrett, M., & McKay, A. (2000). Adolescent sexual and reproductive health in Canada: A review of national data sources and their limitations. *Canadian Journal of Human Sexuality, 9*(1), 41–65.

Matthews, D. J., & Keating, D. P. (1995). Domain specificity and habits of mind: An investigation of patterns of high-level development. *Journal of Early Adolescence, 15*(3), 319–343.

Mattson, L., & Caffrey, L. (2001). *Barriers to equal education for Aboriginal learners.* Vancouver: British Columbia Human Rights Commission.

Mayseless, O., & Hai, I. (1998). Leaving home transition in Israel: Changes in parent-adolescent relationships and adolescents' adaptation to military service. *International Journal of Behavioral Development, 22*(3), 589–609.

Mboya, M. M. (1995). Variations in parenting practices: Gender and age-related differences in African adolescents. *Adolescence, 30*(120), 955–962.

McAdoo, H. P. (1995). Stress levels, family help patterns, and religiosity in middle- and working-class African American single mothers. *Journal of Black Psychology, 21,* 424–449.

McAdoo, H. P. (1998). African American families: Strength and realities. In H. C. McCubbin, E. Thompson, & J. Futrell (Eds.), *Resiliency in ethnic minority families: African American families* (pp. 17–30). Thousand Oaks, CA: Sage.

McAdoo, H. P. (1999). Diverse children of color. In H. E. Fitzgerald, B. M. Lester, & B. S. Zuckerman (Eds.), *Children of color: Research, health, and policy issues* (pp. 205–218). New York: Garland.

McCandless, B. R. (1970). *Adolescents.* Hinsdale, IL: Dryden Press.

McCandless, B. R. (1967). *Children.* New York: Holt, Rinehart and Winston.

McClearn, G. E. (1981). Evolution and genetic variability. In E. S. Gollin (Ed.), *Developmental plasticity: Behavioral and biological aspects of variations in development* (pp. 3–31). New York: Academic Press.

McCreary Centre (1999). Healthy connections: Connectedness and B.C. youth. *Adolescent Health Survey Fact Sheet II.* Burnaby, BC: McCreary Centre Society. Retrieved from: www.mcs.bc.ca/pdfstuff/connections.pdf.

McCreary Centre (1999a). Keeping fit: Physical activity among BC youth. *Adolescent Health Survey Fact Sheet II.* Burnaby, BC: McCreary Centre Society. http://www.mcs.bc.ca/pdfstuff/fitness.pdf.

McCreary Centre (1999b). Mirror image: Weight issues among BC youth. *Adolescent Health Survey Fact Sheet II.* Burnaby, BC: McCreary Centre Society. http://www.mcs.bc.ca/pdfstuff/weight.pdf.

McCreary Centre (2000). *Silk road: Health of Chinese youth in BC.* Burnaby, BC: McCreary Centre Society.

McCreary, D. & Sadava, S. W. (2000). Stress, alcohol use and alcohol-related problems: the influence of negative and positive affect in two cohorts of young adults. *Journal of Studies on Alcohol, 61*(3), 466–474.

McCreary, D. R., & Sasse, D. K. (2000). An exploration of the drive for muscularity in adolescent boys and girls. *Journal of American College Health, 48*(6), 297–304.

McCreary, M. L., Slavin, L. A., & Berry, E. J. (1996). Predicting problem behavior and self-esteem among African American adolescents. *Journal of Adolescent Research, 11*(2), 216–234.

McCullum, C., & Achterberg, C. L. (1997). Food shopping and label use behavior among high school-aged adolescents. *Adolescence, 32*(125), 181–197.

McDermott, P. A., & Spencer, M. B. (1997). Racial and social class prevalence of psychopathology among school-age youth in the United States. *Youth & Society, 28*(4), 387–414.

McFarlane, T., McCabe, R. E., Jarry, J., Olmsted, M. P., & Polivy, J. (2001). Weight-related and shape-related self-evaluation in eating-disordered and non-eating-disordered women. *International Journal of Eating Disorders, 29,* 328–335.

McHale, S. M., & Lerner, R. M. (1996). University-community collaborations on behalf of youth. *Journal of Research on Adolescence, 6*(1), 1–7.

McHale, S. M., Crouter, A. C., Fennelly, K., Tomascik, C. A., Updegraff, K. A., Graham, J. E., Baker, A. E., Dreisbach, L., Ferry, N., Manlove, E. E., McGroder, S. M., Mulkeen, P., & Obeidallah, D. A. (1996). Community-based interventions for young adolescents: The Penn State PRIDE Project. *Journal of Research on Adolescence, 6*(1), 23–36.

McInerney, D. M., Roche, L. A., McInerney, V., & Marsh, H. W. (1997). Cultural perspectives on school motivation: The relevance and application of goal theory. *American Educational Research Journal, 34*(1), 207–236.

McKay, A. (1999). Review of Healthy Connections: Listening to BC Youth, Highlights from the Adolescent Health Survey II. *Canadian Journal of Human Sexuality, 8*(3), 224.

McKay, A. (2000). Common questions about sexual health education. *Canadian Journal of Human Sexuality. 9*(2), 129–138.

McKechnie, J., Lindsay, S., Hobbs, S., & Lavalette, M. (1996). Adolescents' perceptions of the role of part-time work. *Adolescence, 31*(121), 193–204.

McKeown, R. E., Garrison, C. Z., Jackson, K. L., Cuffe, S. P., Addy, C. L., & Waller, J. L. (1997). Family structure and cohesion, and depressive symptoms in adolescents. *Journal of Research on Adolescence, 7,* 267–281.

McKinney, M., Abrams, L. A., Terry, P. A., & Lerner, R. M. (1994). Child development research and the poor children of America: A call for a developmental contextual approach to research and outreach. *Family and Consumer Sciences Research Journal, 23,* 26–42.

McLaren, A.T. (1996). Coercive invitations: How young women in school make sense of mothering and waged labour. *British Journal of Sociology of Education, 17*(3), 79–99.

McLaughlin, C. S., Chen, C., Greenberger, E., & Biermeier, C. (1997). Family, peer, and individual correlates of sexual experience among Caucasian and Asian American late adolescents. *Journal of Research on Adolescence*, 7(1), 33–53.

McLaughlin, J.-A., Miller, P., & Warwick, H. (1996). Deliberate self-harm in adolescents: Hopelessness, depression, problems and problem-solving. *Journal of Adolescence*, 19, 523–532.

McLean, P. E. (1995). Sexual behaviors and attitudes of high school students in the kingdom of Swaziland. *Journal of Adolescent Research*, 10(3), 400–420.

McLean, R. (1997). Selected attitudinal factors related to students' success in high school. *Alberta Journal of Educational Research*, 43(2–3), 165–168.

McLernon, F., Ferguson, N., & Cairns, E. (1997). Comparison of Northern Irish children's attitudes to war and peace before and after the paramilitary cease-fires. *International Journal of Behavioral Development*, 20(4), 715–730.

McLoyd, V. C. (1994). Research in the service of poor and ethnic/racial minority children: A moral imperative. *Family and Consumer Sciences Research Journal*, 23, 56–66.

McLoyd, V. C., & Wilson, L. (1991). The strain of living poor: Parenting, social support, and child mental health. In A. C. Huston (Ed.), *Children in poverty: Child development and public policy*. Cambridge: Cambridge University Press.

McLoyd, V. C., & Wilson, L. (1992). Telling them like it is: The role of economic and environmental factors in single mothers' discussions with their children. *American Journal of Community Psychology*, 20(4), 419–444.

McMaster, L. E., & Wintre, M. G. (1996). The relations between perceived parental reciprocity, perceived parental approval, and adolescent substance use. *Journal of Adolescent Research*, 11(4), 440–460.

McNelles, L. R., & Connolly, J. A. (1999). Intimacy between adolescent friends: Age and gender differences in intimate affect and intimate behaviours. *Journal of Research on Adolescence*, 9(2), 143–160.

McVey, G., & Davis, R. (2002). A program to promote positive body image: A 1-year follow-up evaluation. *Journal of Early Adolescence*, 22(1), 96–108.

McVey, Jr., W. W., & Kalbach, W. E. (1995). Chapter 8: Nuptiality and the Family. *Canadian population*. Toronto: Nelson.

Mead, M. (1928). *Coming of age in Samoa: A psychological study of primitive youth for Western civilization*. New York: Morrow.

Mead, M. (1930). *Growing up in New Guinea*. New York: Morrow.

Mead, M. (1935). *Sex and temperament in three primitive societies*. New York: Morrow.

Meeus, W., & Dekovic, M. (1995). Identity development, parental and peer support in adolescence: Results of a national Dutch survey. *Adolescence*, 30(120), 931–944.

Melby, J. N., & Conger, R. D. (1996). Parental behaviors and adolescent academic performance: A longitudinal analysis. *Journal of Research on Adolescence*, 6(1), 113–137.

Melia, P., Pipe, A., & Greenberg, L. (1996). The use of anabolic-androgenic steroids by Canadian students. *Clinical Journal of Sport Medicine*. 6(1), 9–14.

Mercier, C., Piat, M., Peladeau, N., & Dagenais, C. (2000). An application of theory-driven evaluation to a drop-in youth center. *Evaluation Review*, 24(1), 73–91.

Merten, D. E. (1996). Visibility and vulnerability: Responses to rejection by nonaggressive junior high school boys. *Journal of Early Adolescence*, 16(1), 5–26.

Meyer, J. W. (1988). The social construction of the psychology of childhood: Some contemporary processes. In E. M. Hetherington, R. M. Lerner, & M. Perlmutter (Eds.), *Child development in life-span perspective* (pp. 47–65). Hillsdale, NJ: Erlbaum.

Midgley, C., & Feldlaufer, H. (1987). Students' and teachers' decision-making fit before and after the transition to junior high school. *Journal of Early Adolescence*, 7(2), 225–241.

Midgley, C., & Urdan, T. (1995). Predictors of middle school students' use of self-handicapping strategies. *Journal of Early Adolescence*, 15(4), 389–411.

Midgley, C., Anderman, E., & Hicks, L. (1995). Differences between elementary and middle school teachers and students: A goal theory approach. *Journal of Early Adolescence*, 15(1), 90–113.

Midgley, C., Arunkumar, R., & Urdan, T. C. (1996). "If I don't do well tomorrow, there's a reason": Predictors of adolescents' use of academic self-handicapping strategies. *Journal of Educational Psychology*, 88(3), 423–434.

Midgley, C., Feldlaufer, H., & Eccles, J. S. (1989a). Changes in teacher efficacy and student self- and task-related beliefs in mathematics during the transition to junior high school. *Journal of Educational Psychology*, 81, 247–258.

Midgley, C., Feldlaufer, H., & Eccles, J. S. (1989b). Student/teacher relations and attitudes toward mathematics before and after the transition to junior high school. *Child Development*, 60, 981–992.

Mihalic, S. W., & Elliot, D. (1997). Short- and long-term consequences of doing work. *Youth & Society*, 28(4), 464–498.

Milan, A. (2000). One hundred years of families. *Canadian Social Trends*. Catalogue No. 11-008. Ottawa: Statistics Canada.

Miller, K. E. (1996). The effects of state terrorism and exile on indigenous Guatemalan refugee children: A mental health assessment and an analysis of children's narratives. *Child Development*, 67, 89–106.

Millett, R. A. (1996). Empowerment evaluation and the W. K. Kellogg Foundation. In D. M. Fetterman, S. J. Kaftarian, & A. Wandersman (Eds.), *Empowerment evaluation: Knowledge and tools for self-assessment & accountability* (pp. 65–76). Thousand Oaks, CA: Sage.

Mills, R., & Mills, R. (1996). Adolescents' attitudes toward female gender roles: Implications for education. *Adolescence*, 31(123), 741–745.

Millstein, S. G. (1989). Adolescent health: Challenges for behavioral scientists. *American Psychologist*, 44(5), 837–842.

Mincy, R. B. (1994). *Nurturing young black males: Challenges to agencies, programs, and social policy*. Washington, DC: Urban Institute Press.

Miron, L. F., & Lauria, M. (1995). Identity politics and student resistance to inner-city public schooling. *Youth & Society*, 27(1), 29–54.

Mishna, F., Michalski, J., & Cummings, R. (2001). Camps as social work interventions: Returning to our roots. *Social Work with Groups, 24*(3-4), 153–171.

Mishna, F., Michalski, J., & Cummings, R. (2001). Camps as social work interventions: Returning to our roots. *Social Work with Groups, 24*(3-4), 153–171.

Misiak, H., & Sexton, V. S. (1966). *History of psychology in overview.* New York: Grune & Stratton.

Mitchell, C. M., O'Nell, T. D., Beals, J., Dick, R. W., Keane, E., & Manson, S. M. (1996). Dimensionality of alcohol use among American Indian adolescents: Latent structure, construct validity, and implications for developmental research. *Journal of Research on Adolescence, 6*(2), 151–180.

Mitchell, J. J. (1996). *Adolescent Vulnerability.* Calgary: Detselig.

Mitchell, J. J. (2001). *The Mental and Emotional Life of Teenagers.* Calgary: Detselig.

Modell, J. (1985). *A social history of American adolescents 1945–1985.* Unpublished manuscript. Pittsburgh: Department of History, Carnegie-Mellon University.

Molina, B. S. G., & Chassin, L. (1996). The parent-adolescent relationship at puberty: Hispanic ethnicity and parent alcoholism as moderators. *Developmental Psychology, 32,* 675–686.

Molgat, M. (2002). Leaving home in Quebec: Theoretical and social implications of (im)mobility among youth. *Journal of Youth Studies, 5*(2), 135–152.

Montemayor, R. (1986). Family variation in parent-adolescent storm and stress. *Journal of Adolescent Research, 1,* 15–31.

Montemayor, R., & Flannery, D. J. (1991). Parent-adolescent relations in middle and late adolescence. In R. M. Lerner, A. C. Petersen, & J. Brooks-Gunn (Eds.), *Encyclopedia of adolescence* (Vol. 2, pp. 729–738). New York: Garland.

Montemayor, R., Eberly, M., & Flannery, D. (1993). Effects of pubertal status and conversation topic on parent and adolescent affective expression. *Journal of Early Adolescence, 13*(4), 431–447.

Moore, K. A., & Glei, D. (1995). Taking the plunge: An examination of positive youth development. *Journal of Adolescent Research, 10*(1), 15–40.

Moore, K., Moretti, M. M., & Holland, R. (1998). A new perspective on youth care programs: Using attachment theory to guide interventions for troubled youth. *Residential Treatment for Children and Youth, 15*(3), 1–24.

Moore, M. (1989). Dual-earner families: The new norm. *Canadian Social Trends,* 24–26.

Moore, S. M. (1995). Girls' understanding and social constructions of menarche. *Journal of Adolescence, 18,* 87–104.

Moore, S. M., Laflin, M. T., & Weis, D. L. (1996). The role of cultural norms in the self-esteem and drug use relationship. *Adolescence, 31*(123), 523–542.

Morelli, G. A., & Verhoef, H. (1999). Who should help me raise my child? A Cultural approach to understanding non-maternal child care decisions. In C. Le Monda & L. Balter (Eds.), *Child psychology: A handbook of contemporary issues* (pp. 491–509). Philadelphia: Psychology Press/Taylor & Francis.

Moreno, A. B., & Thelen, M. H. (1995). Eating behavior in junior high school females. *Adolescence, 30*(117), 171–174.

Morgan, T., & Ness, D. (2003). Career decision-making difficulties of first-year students. *Canadian Journal of Career Development, 2*(1), 33–39.

Morison, P., & Masten, A. S. (1991). Peer reputation in middle childhood as a predictor of adaptation in adolescence: A seven-year follow-up. *Child Development, 62,* 991–1007.

Morrison, T. G., McLeod, L. D., Morrison, M. A., Anderson, D., & O'Connor, W. E. (1997). Gender stereotyping, homonegativity, and misconceptions about sexually coercive behavior among adolescents. *Youth & Society, 28*(3), 351–382.

Morrissette, P. J. (1994). The holocaust of First Nation people: Residual effects on parenting and treatment implications. *Contemporary Family Therapy, 16*(5), 381–392.

Mortimer, J. T. (1991). Employment. In R. M. Lerner, A. C. Petersen, & J. Brooks-Gunn (Eds.), *Encyclopedia of adolescence* (Vol. 1, pp. 311–318). New York: Garland.

Mortimer, J. T., Finch, M. D., Ryu, S., Shanahan, M. J., & Call, K. T. (1996). The effects of work intensity on adolescent mental health, achievement, and behavioral adjustment: New evidence from a prospective study. *Child Development, 67,* 1243–1261.

Mortimer, J. T., Shanahan, M., & Ryu, S. (1994). The effects of adolescent employment on school-related orientation and behavior. In R. K. Silbereisen & E. Todt (Eds.), *Adolescence in context: The interplay of family, school, peers, and work in adjustment* (pp. 304–326). New York: Springer-Verlag.

Moscovitch, A. (1998). *Electronic media and the family.* Ottawa: Vanier Institute of the Family.

Moshman, D., & Franks, B. A. (1986). Development of the concept of inferential validity. *Child Development, 57*(1), 153–165.

Mougeon, R. & Rehner, K. (2001). Acquisition of sociolinguistic variants by French immersion students: The case of restrictive expressions, and more. *Modern Language Journal, 85*(3), 398–415.

Mounts, N. S., & Steinberg, L. (1995). An ecological analysis of peer influence on adolescent grade point average and drug use. *Developmental Psychology, 31*(6), 915–922.

Mukai, T. (1996). Mothers, peers, and perceived pressure to diet among Japanese adolescent girls. *Journal of Research on Adolescence, 6*(3), 309–324.

Muller, C. (1995). Maternal employment, parent involvement, and mathematics achievement among adolescents. *Journal of Marriage and the Family, 57,* 85–100.

Munsch, J., & Kinchen, K. M. (1995). Adolescent sociometric status and social support. *Journal of Early Adolescence, 15*(2), 181–202.

Murray, J., & Henjum, R. (1993). Analysis of sexual abuse in dating. *Guidance & Counseling, 8*(4), 56–68.

Murray, V. M. (1996). An ecological analysis of coital timing among middle-class African American adolescent females. *Journal of Adolescent Research, 11*(2), 261–279.

Musaiger, A.O. (1991). Height, weight and menarchal age of adolescent girls in Oman. *Annals of Human Biology, 18*(1), 71–74.

Mussen, P. H., Harris, S., Rutherford, E., & Keasey, C. B. (1970). Honesty and altruism among preadolescents. *Developmental Psychology, 3,* 169–194.

Mutz, D. C., Roberts, D. F., & van Vuuren, D. P. (1993). Reconsidering the displacement hypothesis: Television's influence on children's time use. *Communication Research, 20*(1), 51–75.

Muuss, R. E. (1996). *Theories of adolescence* (6th ed.). New York: McGraw-Hill.

Myrtek, M., Scharff, C., Brugner, G., & Muller, W. (1996). Physiological, behavioral, and psychological effects associated with television viewing in schoolboys: An exploratory study. *Journal of Early Adolescence, 16*(3), 301–323.

N

Nadon, S. M., Koverola, C., & Schludermann, E. H. (1998). Antecendents to prostitution: Childhood victimization. *Journal of Interpersonal Violence, 13*(2), 206–221.

Nagin, D. S., & Tremblay, R. E. (2001). Parental and early childhood predictors of persistent physical aggression in boys from kindergarten to high school. *Archives of General Psychiatry, 58*(4), 389–394.

Nakhaie, M. R., Silverman, R. A., & LaGrange, T. C. (2000). Self-control and resistance to school. *Canadian Review of Sociology and Anthropology, 37*(4), 443–460.

National Missing Children Services (2001). *Canada's missing children: Annual report.* Ottawa: Author.

National Research Council. (1993). *Losing generations: Adolescents in high-risk settings.* Washington, DC: National Academy Press.

Neimark, E. D. (1975). Intellectual development during adolescence. In F. D. Horowitz (Ed.), *Review of child development research* (Vol. 4, pp. 541–594). Chicago: University of Chicago Press.

Neimark, E. D. (1979). Current status of formal operations research. *Human Development, 22,* 60–67.

Nelson-Le Gall, S. (1990). Academic achievement and help-seeking behavior in early adolescent girls. *Journal of Early Adolescence, 10,* 176–190.

Nesbitt, M. N., & Penn, N. E. (2000). Gender stereotypes after thirty years:

A replication of Rosenkrantz et al. (1968). *Psychological Reports, 87,* 493–511.

Nesselroade, J. R., & Baltes, P. B. (1974). Adolescent personality development and historical changes: 1970–1972. *Monographs of the Society for Research in Child Development, 39* (Whole No. 154).

Neugarten, B. L., & Moore, J. W. (1968). The changing age-status system. In B. L. Neugarten (Ed.), *Middle age and aging.* Chicago: University of Chicago Press.

Neumann, H., McCormick, R. M., Amundson, N. E., & McLean, H. B. (2000). Career counselling First Nations youth: Applying the First Nations career-life planning model. *Canadian Journal of Counselling, 34*(3), 172–185.

Neville, B., & Parke, R. D. (1991). Fathers, adolescent. In R. M. Lerner, A. C. Petersen, & J. Brooks-Gunn (Eds.), *Encyclopedia of adolescence* (Vol. 1, pp. 354–359). New York: Garland.

Newcombe, N., & Dubas, J. S. (1992). A longitudinal study of predictors of spatial ability in adolescent females. *Child Development, 63,* 37–46.

Newton-Taylor, B., DeWit, D., & Giiksman, I. (1998). Prevalence and factors associated with physical and sexual assault of female university students in Ontario. *Health Care for Women International, 19*(2), 155–165.

Nicholson, D., Artz, S., Armitage, A., & Fagan, J. (2000). Working relationships and outcomes in multidisciplinary collaborative practice settings. *Child and Youth Care Forum, 29*(1), 39–73.

Nicholson, D., Artz, S., Armitage, A., & Fagan, J. (2000). Working relationships and outcomes in multidisciplinary collaborative practice settings. *Child and Youth Care Forum, 29*(1), 39–73.

Noels, K. A., Clement, R., & Pelletier, L. G. (1999). Perceptions of teachers' communicative style and students' intrinsic and extrinsic motivation. *Modern Language Journal, 83*(1), 23–34.

Norris, J. M., & Wylie, A. M, (1995). Gender stereotyping of the managerial role among students in Canada and the United States. *Group and Organization Management, 20*(2), 167–182.

Nottlemann, E. D., Susman, E. J., Blue, J. H., Inoff-Germain, G., Dorn, L. D., Loriaux, D. L., Cutler, G. B., Jr., & Chrousos, G. P. (1987). Gonadal and adrenal hormone correlates of adjustment in early adolescence. In R. M. Lerner & T. T. Foch (Eds.), *Biological-psychosocial interactions in early adolescence* (pp. 303–323). Hillsdale, NJ: Erlbaum.

Nucci, L., & Turiel, E. (1993). God's word, religious rules, and their relation to Christian and Jewish children's concepts of morality. *Child Development, 64,* 1475–1491.

Nummenmaa, A. R., & Nummenmaa, T. (1997). Intergenerational roots of Finnish women's sex-atypical careers. *International Journal of Behavioral Development, 21*(1), 1–14.

Nurmi, J.-E., Berzonsky, M. D., Tammi, K., & Kinney, A. (1997). Identity processing orientation, cognitive and behavioural strategies and well-being. *International Journal of Behavioral Development, 21*(3), 555–570.

Nurmi, J.-E., Poole, M. E., & Kalakoski, V. (1996). Age differences in adolescent identity exploration and commitment in urban and rural environments. *Journal of Adolescence, 19,* 443–452.

O

O'Connell, B. (1999). *Civil society: The underpinnings of American democracy.* Hanover, NH: University Press of New England.

O'Koon, J. (1997). Attachment to parents and peers in late adolescence and their relationship with self-image. *Adolescence, 32*(126), 471–482.

Oden, S. (1995). Studying youth programs to assess influences on youth development: New roles for researchers. *Journal of Adolescent Research, 10*(1), 173–186.

Oderkirk, J., Silver, C., & Prud'homme, M. (1994). Traditional-earner families. *Canadian Social Trends.* Catalogue No. 11-008E. Ottawa: Statistics Canada.

Oettingen, G. (1999). Free fantasies about the future and the emergence of developmental goals. In J. Bandtstädter, & R. M. Lerner (Eds.), *Action and self-development: Theory and research through the life-span* (pp. 315–342). Thousand Oaks, CA: Sage.

Offer, D. (1969). *The psychological world of the teen-ager.* New York: Basic.

Offord, D.R. (2000). Selection levels of prevention. *Addictive Behaviors, 25*(6), 833–842.

Ohannessian, C. M., Lerner, R. M., Lerner, J. V., & von Eye, A. (1995). Discrepancies in adolescents' and parents' perceptions of family functioning and adolescent emotional adjustment. *Journal of Early Adolescence, 15*(4), 490–516.

Okagaki, L., & Frensch, P. A. (1994). Effects of video game playing on measures of spatial performance: Gender effects in late adolescence. *Journal of Applied Developmental Psychology, 15*, 33–58.

Okasha, M., Mccarron, P., Mcewen, J., and Davey Smith, G. (2001). Age at menarche: Secular trends and association with adult anthropometric measures. *Annals of Human Biology, 28*(1), 68–78.

Okonofua, F. E., Coplan, P., Collins, S., Oronsaye, F., Ogunsakin, D., Ogonor, J. T., Kaufman, J. A., & Heggenhougen, K. (2003). Impact of an intervention to improve treatment-seeking behavior and prevent sexually transmitted diseases among Nigerian youths. *International Journal of Infectious Diseases*; 7(1), 61–73.

Oláh, A. (1995). Coping strategies among adolescents: A cross-cultural study. *Journal of Adolescence, 18*, 491–512.

Olivardia, R., Pope, H. G., Jr., Mangweth, B., & Hudson, J. I. (1995). Eating disorders in college men. *The American Journal of Psychiatry, 152*(9), 1279.

Ondercin-Bourne, G. (2003). The myth of the traditional family: Diversity in Canadian Families. In P.U. Angelini (Ed.) *Our society: Human diversity in Canada.* Scarborough, ON: Thomson/Nelson.

Ontario Ministry of Education (2000). *Update: New high school curriculum.* Retrieved from: www.edu.gov.on.ca/eng/document/brochure/update/highsch/highcu.html

Osofsky, J. D., & Eberhart-Wright, A. (1988). Affective exchanges between high risk mothers and infants. *International Journal of Psycho-Analysis, 69*(2), 221–231.

Ostrom, C. W., Lerner, R. M., & Freel, M. A. (1995). Building the capacity of youth and families through university-community collaborations: The development-in-context evaluation (DICE) model. *Journal of Adolescent Research, 10*(4) 427–448.

Oswald, M. A. (1994). Perceptions of autonomy, perfectionism, and social ineffectiveness in women with disordered eating patterns. *Dissertation Abstracts International Section A: Humanities & Social Sciences, 55*(3-A), 472.

Ouimet, M. (2002). Explaining the American and Canadian crime "drop" in the 1990s. *Canadian Journal of Criminology, 44*(1), 33–50.

Out, J. W. (2001). Baby Think It Over: Using role-play to prevent teen pregnancy. *Adolescence, 36*(143), 571–582.

Overton, W. (1998). Developmental psychology: Philosophy, concepts, and methodology. In W. Damon (Series Ed.) & R. M. Lerner (Ed.), *Handbook of child psychology: Vol. 1. Theoretical models of human development* (5th ed., pp. 107–187). New York: Wiley.

Overton, W. F. (1990). *Reasoning, necessity, and logic: Developmental perspectives.* Hillsdale, NJ: Erlbaum.

Overton, W. F. (1991). The structure of developmental theory. In H. W. Reese & W. Hayne (Eds.), *Advances in child development and behavior* (Vol. 23, pp. 1–37). San Diego, CA: Academic Press.

Overton, W. F., & Byrnes, J. P. (1991). Cognitive development. In R. M. Lerner, A. C. Petersen, & J. Brooks-Gunn (Eds.), *Encyclopedia of adolescence* (Vol. 1, pp. 151–156). New York: Garland.

Overton, W., Byrnes, J., & O'Brien, D. (1985). Developmental and individual differences in conditional reasoning: The role of contradiction training and cognitive style. *Developmental Psychology, 21*(4), 692–701.

Oyserman, D., Radin, N., & Benn, R. (1993). Dynamics in a three-generational family: Teens, grandparents, and babies. *Developmental Psychology, 29*(3), 564–572.

P

Paetsch, J. J., & Bertrand, L. D. (1999). Victimization and delinquency among Canadian youth. *Adolescence, 34*(134), 351–367.

Pagani, L., Boulerice, B., Vitaro, F., & Tremblay, R.E. (1999). Effects of poverty on academic failure and delinquency in boys: A change and process model approach. *Journal of Child Psychology and Psychiatry and Allied Disciplines, 40*(8), 1209–1219.

Paglia, A., & Room, R. (1999). Preventing substance use problems among youth: A literature review and recommendations. *Journal of Primary Prevention, 20*(1), 3–50.

Pakiz, B., Reinherz, H. Z., & Frost, A. K. (1992). Antisocial behavior in adolescence: A community study. *Journal of Early Adolescence, 12*(3), 300–313.

Pancer, S. M., & Pratt, M. W. (1999). Social and family determinants of community service involvement in Canadian youth. In M. Yates & J. Youniss (Eds.), *Roots of civic identity: International perspectives on community service and activism in youth* (pp. 32–55). New York, NY: Cambridge University Press.

Pancer, S. M., Pratt, M., Hunsberger, B., & Gallant, M. (2000). Thinking ahead: Complexity of expectations and the transition to parenthood. *Journal of Personality, 68*(2), 253–280.

Panchaud, C., Singh, S., Feivelson, D., & Darroch, J. E. (2000). Sexually Transmitted Diseases among adolescents in developed countries. *Family Planning Perspectives, 32*(1), 24.

Papadimitriou, A., Gousia, E. Pitaouli, E., Tapaki, G., and Philippidis, P. (1999). Age at menarche in Greek girls. *Annals of Human Biology, 26*(2), 175–177.

Papini, D. R., & Roggman, L. A. (1992). Adolescent perceived attachment to parents in relation to competence, depression, and anxiety: A longitudinal study. *Journal of Early Adolescence, 12*(4), 420–440.

Papini, D. R., Roggman, L. A., & Anderson, J. (1991). Early-adolescent perceptions of attachment to mother and father: A test of the emotional-distancing and buffering hypotheses. *Journal of Early Adolescence, 11*(2), 258–275.

Papini, D., & Datan, N. (1983, April). *Transition into adolescence: An interactionist perspective.* Paper presented at the Biennial Meetings of the Society for Research in Child Development, Detroit, MI.

Park, E. K. (1995). Voices of Korean-American students. *Adolescence, 30*(120), 945–953.

Parke, R. D., Burks, V., Carson, J., Neville, B., & Boyum, L. (1994). Family-peer relationships: A tripartite model. In R. D. Parke & S. Kellam (Eds.), *Advances in family research: Vol. 4. Family relationships with other social systems* (pp. 115–145). Hillsdale, NJ: Erlbaum.

Parker, J. G., & Asher, S. R. (1987). Peer relations and later personal adjustment: Are low-accepted children at risk? *Psychological Bulletin, 102*(3), 357–389.

Paschall, M. J., & Hubbard, M. L. (1998). Effects of neighborhood and family stressors on African American male adolescents' self-worth and propensity for violent behavior. *Journal of Consulting and Clinical Psychology, 66*(5), 825–831.

Pasquet, P., Manguelle-Dicoum Biyong, A., Rikong-Adie, H., Befidi-Mengue, R., Garba, M.-T., and Froment, A. (1999). Age at menarche and urbanization in Cameroon: current status and secular trends. *Annals of Human Biology, 26*(1), 89–97.

Patrikakou, E. N. (1996). Investigating the academic achievement of adolescents with learning disabilities: A structural modeling approach. *Journal of Educational Psychology, 88*(3), 435–450.

Pattishall, E. (1984). Health issues in adolescence. In R. M. Lerner & N. L. Galambos (Eds.), *Experiencing adolescents: A sourcebook for parents, teachers, and teens. Guidance and counseling series* (pp. 191–230). New York: Teachers College Press.

Paulson, S. E. (1994). Relations of parenting style and parental involvement with ninth-grade students' achievement. *Journal of Early Adolescence, 14*, 250–267.

Paulson, S. E., Hill, J. P., & Holmbeck, G. N. (1991). Distinguishing between perceived closeness and parental warmth in families with seventh-grade boys and girls. *Journal of Early Adolescence, 11*, 276–293.

Pazaratz, D., Randall, D., Spekkens, J. F., Lazor, A., & Morton, W. (1999). The four phase system: A multi-agency coordinated service for very disturbed adolescents. *Residential Treatment for Children and Youth, 17*(1), 31–48.

Peiser, N. C., & Heaven, P. C. L. (1996). Family influences on self-reported delinquency among high school students. *Journal of Adolescence, 19*, 557–568.

Peluffo, N. (1962). The notions of conservation and causality in children of different physical and sociocultural environments. *Archives de Psychologie, 38*, 275–291.

Peluffo, N. (1967). Culture and cognitive problems. *International Journal of Psychology, 2*, 187–198.

Pendley, J. S., & Bates, J. E. (1996). Mother/daughter agreement on the eating attitudes test and the eating disorder inventory. *Journal of Early Adolescence, 16*(2), 179–191.

Pepler, D., & Sedighdeilami, F. (1998). *Aggressive girls in Canada.* Applied Research Branch Strategic Policy. Human Resources Development Canada. W-98-30E

Pepler, D., Craig, W., & Connolly, J. (1997). Bullying and Victimization: The Problems and Solutions for School-aged children. National Crime Prevention Council of Canada. Retrieved from: www.prevention.gc.ca/en/library/publications/children/violence/index.html.

Perkins, D. F., & Lerner, R. M. (1995). Single and multiple indicators of physical attractiveness and psychosocial behaviors among young adolescents. *Journal of Early Adolescence, 15*(3), 269–298.

Perkins, D. F., Luster, T., Villarruel, F. A., & Small, S. (1998). An ecological, risk-factor examination of adolescents' sexual activity in three ethnic groups. *Journal of Marriage and the Family, 60*, 660–673.

Perron, J., Vondracek, F. W., Skorikov, V., Tremblay, C., & Corbiere, M. (1998). A longitudinal study of vocational maturity and ethnic identity development. *Journal of Vocational Behavior 52*, 409–424.

Perry, C. M., & McIntire, W. G. (1995). Modes of moral judgement among early adolescents. *Adolescence, 30*(119), 707–715.

Peters, J. F. (1994). Gender socialization of adolescents in the home: Research and discussion. *Adolescence, 29*(116), 913–935.

Petersen, A. C. (1988). Adolescent development. In M. R. Rosenzweig (Ed.), *Annual review of psychology* (Vol. 39, pp. 583–607). Palo Alto, CA: Annual Reviews.

Petersen, A. C. (1985). Pubertal development as a cause of disturbance: Myths, realities, and unanswered questions. *Genetic, Social, & General Psychology Monographs, 111*(2), 205–232.

Petersen, A. C. (1987). The nature of biological psychosocial interactions: The sample case of early adolescence. In R. M. Lerner & T. T. Fochs (Eds.), *Biological-psychosocial interactions in early adolescence: A life-span perspective* (pp. 35–61). Hillsdale, NJ: Erlbaum.

Petersen, A. C., & Taylor, B. (1980). The biological approach to adolescence: Biological change and psychological adaptation. In J. Adelson (Ed.), *Handbook of adolescent psychology* (pp. 117–155). New York: Wiley.

Peterson, G. W. (1995). The need for common principles in prevention programs for children, adolescents, and families. *Journal of Adolescent Research, 10*(4), 470–485.

Peterson, P. L., Hawkins, J. D., Abbott, R. D., & Catalano, R. F. (1994). Disentangling the effects of parental drinking, family management, and parental alcohol norms on current drinking by black and white adolescents. *Journal of Research on Adolescence, 4*(2), 203–277.

Phares, V., & Renk, K. (1998). Perceptions of parents: A measure of adolescents' feelings about their parents. *Journal of Marriage and Family, 60*, 646–659.

Phillips, C. A., Rolls, S., Rouse, A., & Griffiths, M. D. (1995). Home video game playing in schoolchildren: A study of incidence and patterns of play. *Journal of Adolescence, 18*, 687–691.

Phinney, J. S., & Chavira, V. (1995). Parental ethnic socialization and adolescent coping with problems related to ethnicity. *Journal of Research on Adolescence, 5*, 31–53.

Phinney, J. S., & Cobb, N. J. (1996). Reasoning among intergroup relations among Hispanic and Euro-American adolescents. *Journal of Adolescent Research, 11*, 306–324.

Phinney, J. S., & Devich-Navarro, M. (1997). Variations in bicultural identification among African American and Mexican American adolescents. *Journal of Research on Adolescence, 7*(1), 3–32.

Phinney, J. S., Ferguson, D. L., & Tate, J. D. (1997). Intergroup attitudes among ethnic minority adolescents: A causal model. *Child Development, 68*(5), 955–969.

Piaget, J. (1950). *The psychology of intelligence*. New York: Harcourt Brace.

Piaget, J. (1965). *The moral judgment of the child*. New York: Free Press. (Original work published 1932.)

Piaget, J. (1969). The intellectual development of the adolescent. In G. Caplan & S. Lebovici (Eds.), *Adolescence: Psychosocial perspective* (pp. 22–26). New York: Basic.

Piaget, J. (1970). Piaget's theory. In P. H. Mussen (Ed.), *Carmichael's manual of child psychology* (3rd ed., Vol. 1, pp. 703–723). New York: Wiley.

Piaget, J. (1972). Intellectual evolution from adolescence to adulthood. *Human Development, 15*, 1–12.

Piaget, J., & Inhelder, B. (1969). *The psychology of the child*. New York: Basic.

Pick, S., & Palos, P. A. (1995). Impact of the family on the sex lives of adolescents. *Adolescence, 30*(119), 667–675.

Pickering, D. (2003). Youth giving and volunteering. Canadian Centre for Philanthropy. Retrieved from: www.givingandvolunteering.ca/factsheets.asp?fn=view&id=8256.

Pickett, W., Garner, M. J., Boyce, W. F., & King, M. A. (2002). Gradients in risk for youth injury associated with multiple-risk behaviours: A study of 11, 329 Canadian adolescents. *Social Science and Medicine, 55*(6), 1055–1068.

Pike, A., McGuire, S., Hetherington, E. M., Reiss, D., & Plomin, R. (1996). Family environment and adolescent depressive symptoms and antisocial behavior: A multivariate genetic analysis. *Developmental Psychology, 32*(4), 574–589.

Pintrich, P. R., Roeser, R. W., & DeGroot, E. (1994). Classroom and individual differences in early adolescents' motivation and self-regulated learning. *Journal of Early Adolescence, 14*(2), 139–161.

Pirog-Good, M. A. (1995). The family background and attitudes of teen fathers. *Youth & Society, 26*(3), 351–376.

Pirog-Good, M. A. (1996). The education and labor market outcomes of adolescent fathers. *Youth & Society, 28*(2), 236–262.

Pittman, K. J. (1996, Winter). Community, youth, development: Three goals in search of connection.

New Designs for Youth Development, pp. 4–8.

Pittman, K. J., & Irby, M. (1995, January 22–25). *Promoting investment in life skills for youth: Beyond indicators for survival and problem prevention.* Paper presented at the Monitoring and Measuring the State of Children: Beyond Survival, an interactional workshop, Jerusalem, Israel.

Pittman, K. J., & Zeldin, S. (1994). From deterrence to development: Shifting the focus of youth programs for African-American males. In R. B. Mincy (Ed.), *Nurturing young black males* (pp. 45–55). Washington, DC: Urban Institute Press.

Pittman, K. J., Irby, M., & Cahill, M. (1995). *Mixing it up: Participatory evaluation as a tool for generating parent and community empowerment.* Unpublished manuscript. Cambridge, MA: Harvard Family Research Project, Harvard University.

Pleydon, A. P., & Schner, J. G. (2001). Female adolescent friendship and delinquent behavior. *Adolescence, 36*(142), 189–205.

Poglog, L. (2002). Perceptions of success and failure among university athletes in Canada. *Journal of Sport Behaviour, 25*(4), 368–394.

Pomerleau, A. & Bolduc, D. (1990). Pink or blue: Environmental gender stereotypes in the first two years of life. *Sex Roles, 22*(5-6), 359–367.

Pong, S.-L. (1997). Family structure, school context, and eighth-grade math and reading achievement. *Journal of Marriage and the Family, 59*, 734–746.

Pope, Jr., H. G., Gruber, A. J., Mangweth, B., & Bureau, B. (2000). Body image perception among men in three countries. *The American Journal of Psychiatry, 157*(8), 1297–1301.

Poulin, C., & Graham, L. (2001). The association between substance use, unplanned sexual intercourse and other sexual behaviours among adolescent students. *Addiction, 96*(4), 607.

Powers, S. I., Hauser, S. T., Schwartz, J., Noam, G. G., & Jacobson, A. M. (1983). Adolescent ego development and family interactions: A structural-developmental perspective. In H. D. Grotevant & C. R. Cooper (Eds.), *Adolescent development in the family. New Directions for Child Development*, No. 22. San Francisco: Jossey-Bass.

Pratt, M. W., Arnold, M. L, Pratt, A. T. and Diessner, R. (1999). Predicting adolescent moral reasoning from family climate: A longitudinal study. *Journal of Early Adolescence, 19*(2), 148–175.

Pratt, M. W., Golding, G., Hunter, W., & Sampson, R. (1988). Sex differences in adult moral orientations. *Journal of Personality, 56*, 373–391.

Pretty, G. M. H., Conroy, C., Dugay, J., Fowler, K., & et al. (1996). Sense of community and its relevance to adolescents of all ages. *Journal of Community Psychology, 24*(4), 365–379.

Price, E. L., Byers, E. S. Sears, H. A., Whalen, J., & St.-Pierre, M. (2000). Dating violence amongst New Brunswick adolescents: A summary of two studies. Muriel McQueen Fergusson Centre for Family Violence Research, Research Paper Series, Number 2.

Prilleltensky, I., Peirson, L., Gould, J., & Nelson, G. (1997). Planning mental health services for children and youth: Part I—A value-based approach. *Evaluation and Program Planning, 20*(2), 163–172.

Prince, F. (1995). The relative effectiveness of a peer-led and adult-led smoking intervention program. *Adolescence, 30*(117), 187–194.

Pulos, S. (1997). Adolescents' implicit theories of physical phenomena: A matter of gravity. *International Journal of Behavioral Development, 20*(3), 493–507.

Punamäki, R.-L. (1996). Can ideological commitment protect children's psychosocial well-being in situations of political violence? *Child Development, 67*, 55–69.

Pungello, E. P., Kupersmidt, J. B., Burchinal, M. R., & Patterson, C. J. (1996). Environmental risk factors and children's achievement from middle childhood to early adolescence. *Developmental Psychology, 32*(4), 755–767.

Pychyl, T. A., Coplan, R. J., & Reid, P. A. M. (2002). Parenting and procrastination: Gender differences in the relations between procrastination, parenting style, and self-worth in early adolescence. *Personality and Individual Differences, 33*, 271–285.

R

Rabinovitch, J., & Lewis, M. (2001). Impossible, eh? The story of PEERS (Prostitutes Empowerment Education and Resource Society). Vancouver: Save the Children Canada.

Raffaelli, M., & Larson, R. (1987, April). Sibling interaction in late childhood and early adolescence. Paper presented at the Biennial Meeting of the Society for Research in Child Development, Baltimore, MD.

Ralston, P., Lerner, R. M., Mullis, A., Simerly, C., & Murray, J. (Eds.) (1999). Social change, public policy and community collaboration: Training human development professionals for the twenty-first century. Norwell, MA: Kluwer Academic Publishers.

Rathunde, K. (1996). Family context and talented adolescents' optimal experience in school-related activities. Journal of Research on Adolescence, 6(4), 605–628.

Ratti, L. A., Humphrey, L. L., & Lyons, J. S. (1996). Structural analysis of families with a polydrug-dependent, bulimic, or normal adolescent daughter. Journal of Consulting and Clinical Psychology, 64(6), 1255–1262.

Ravelli, B. (2000). Culture. In M. Kanwar & D. Swenson (Eds.) Canadian sociology, pp. 39–62. Dubuque, IA: Kendall/Hunt.

Ravert, A. A., & Martin, J. (1997). Family stress, perception of pregnancy, and age of first menarche among pregnant adolescents. Adolescence, 32(126), 261–270.

Reed, J. S., & Dubow, E. F. (1997). Cognitive and behavioral predictors of communication in clinic-referred and nonclinical mother-adolescent dyads. Journal of Marriage and Family, 59, 91–102.

Regoeczi, W. C. (2000). Adolescent violent victimization and offending: Assessing the extent of the link. Canadian Journal of Criminology, 42(4), 493–505.

Reid, P. T. (1991). Black female adolescents, socialization of. In R. M. Lerner, A. C. Petersen, & J. Brooks-Gunn (Eds.), Encyclopedia of adolescence (Vol. 1, pp. 85–87). New York: Garland.

Reimer, M. S., Overton, W. F., Steidl, J. H., Rosenstein, D. S., & Horowitz, H. (1996). Familial responsiveness and behavioral control: Influences on adolescent psychopathology, attachment, and cognition. Journal of Research on Adolescence, 6(1), 87–112.

Remafedi, G. (1991). Homosexuality, adolescent. In R. M. Lerner, A. C. Petersen, & J. Brooks-Gunn (Eds.), Encyclopedia of adolescence (Vol. 1, pp. 504–507). New York: Garland.

Remafedi, G. J. (1985). Adolescent homosexuality: Issues for pediatricians. Clinical Pediatrics, 24(9), 481–485.

Remafedi, G. J. (1988). Preventing the sexual transmission of AIDS during adolescence. Journal of Adolescent Health Care, 9(2), 139–143.

Reynolds, A. J., & Temple, J. A. (1998). Extended early childhood intervention and school achievement: Age thirteen findings from the Chicago longitudinal study. Child Development, 69(1), 231–246.

Rhodes, J. E., & Davis, A. B. (1996). Supportive ties between nonparent adults and urban adolescent girls. In B. J. Leadbeater & N. Way (Eds.), Urban girls: Resisting stereotypes, creating identities (pp. 213–225). New York: New York University Press.

Rhodes, J. E., Contreras, J. M., & Mangelsdorf, S. C. (1994). Natural mentor relationships among Latina adolescent mothers: Psychological adjustment, moderating processes, and the role of early parental acceptance. American Journal of Community Psychology, 22(2), 211–227.

Rhodes, J. E., Ebert, L., & Fischer, K. (1992). Natural mentors: An overlooked resource in the social networks of young, African American mothers. American Journal of Community Psychology, 20, 445–461.

Rhodes, J. E., Grossman, J. B., & Resch, N. L. (2000). Agents of change: Pathways through which mentoring relationships influence adolescents' academic adjustment. Child Development, 71(6), 1662–1671.

Rhodes, J. E., Haight, W. L., & Briggs, E. C. (1999). The influence of mentoring on the peer relationships of foster youth in relative and nonrelative care. Journal of Research on Adolescence, 9(2), 185–201.

Rhynard, J., & Krebs, M. (1997). Sexual assault in dating relationships. Journal of School Health, 67(3), 89–93.

Rice, K. G., & Mulkeen, P. (1995). Relationships with parents and peers: A longitudinal study of adolescent intimacy. Journal of Adolescent Research, 10(3), 338–357.

Richard, H. H., & Larson, R. W. (1993). Pubertal development and the daily subjective states of young adolescents. Journal of Research on Adolescence, 3, 145–169.

Richards, I., & Sullivan, A. (1996). Psychotherapy for delinquents? Journal of Adolescence, 19, 63–73.

Richards, M. H., & Duckett, E. (1994). The relationship of maternal employment to early adolescent daily experience with and without parents. Child Development, 65, 225–236.

Richards, M. H., Crowe, P. A., Larson, R., & Swarr, A. (1998). Developmental patterns and gender differences in the experience of peer companionship during adolescence. Child Development, 69(1), 154–163.

Richards-Colocino, N., McKenzie, P., & Newton, R. R. (1996). Project success: Comprehensive intervention services for middle school high-risk youth. Journal of Adolescent Research, 11(1), 130–163.

Richardson, R. A., Barbour, N. E., & Bubenzer, D. L. (1995). Peer relationships as a source of support for adolescent mothers. Journal of Adolescent Research, 10(2), 278–290.

Richardson, W. C. (1996). A new calling for higher education. Paper presented at the John W. Olswald Lecture, The Pennsylvania State University, University Park.

Riegel, K. F. (1976). From traits and equilibrium toward developmental dialectics. In W. J. Arnold & J. K. Cole (Eds.), Nebraska symposium on motivation (pp. 348–408). Lincoln: University of Nebraska Press.

Rigby, K., & Slee, P. (1999). Suicidal ideation among adolescent school children, involvement in bully-victim problems, and perceived social support. Suicide and Life-Threatening Behaviour, 29(2), 119–130.

Rintoul, S., & MacKillican, C. (2001). Designer drugs and raves (2nd ed.). Vancouver: Addictive Drug Information Council.

Roberts, L. R., & Petersen, A. C. (1992). The relationship between academic achievement and social self-image during early adolescence. *Journal of Early Adolescence, 12*(2), 197–219.

Roberts, L. R., Sarigiani, P. A., Petersen, A. C., & Newman, J. L. (1990). Gender differences in the relationship between achievement and self-image during early adolescence. *Journal of Early Adolescence, 10*(2), 159–175.

Roberts, W., & Strayer, J. (1996). Empathy, emotional expressiveness, and prosocial behavior. *Child Development, 67,* 449–470.

Robinson, N. S. (1995). Evaluating the nature of perceived support and its relation to perceived self-worth in adolescents. *Journal of Research on Adolescence, 5*(2), 253–280.

Roeser, R. W., Midgley, C., & Urdan, T. C. (1996). Perceptions of the school psychological environment and early adolescents' psychological and behavioral functioning in school: The mediating role of goals and belonging. *Journal of Educational Psychology, 88*(3), 408–422.

Rohner, R., & Pettengill, S. (1985). Perceived parental acceptance-rejection and parental control among Korean adolescents. *Child Development, 56,* 524–528.

Rohr, M. E. (1996). Identifying adolescent runaways: The predictive utility of the personality inventory for children. *Adolescence, 31*(123), 605–623.

Rohrbach, L. A., Hodgson, C. S., Broder, B. I., Montgomery, S. B., Flay, B. R., Hansen, W. B., & Pentz, M. A. (1994). Parental participation in drug abuse prevention: Results for the midwestern prevention project. *Journal of Research on Adolescence, 4*(2), 295–318.

Roid, G. H., & Worrall, W. (1997). Replication of the Wechsler Intelligence Scale for Children—Third edition four-factor model in the Canadian normative sample. *Psychological Assessment, 9*(4), 512–515.

Romano, E., Tremblay, R. E., Vitaro, F., Zoccolillo, M., & Pagani, L. (2001). Prevalence of psychiatric diagnoses and the role of perceived impairment: Findings from an adolescent community sample. *Journal of Child Psychology and Psychiatry and Allied Disciplines, 42*(4), 451–461.

Roosa, M. W., & Tein, J. (1997). The relationship of childhood sexual abuse to teenage pregnancy. *Journal of Marriage and the Family, 59,* 119–130.

Rosario, M., Hunter, J., & Gwadz, M. (1997). Exploration of substance use among lesbian, gay, and bisexual youth: Prevalence and correlates. *Journal of Adolescent Research, 12*(4), 454–476.

Rosenberg, M. (1991). Menarcheal age for Norwegian women born 1830–1960. *Annals of Human Biology, 18*(3), 207–219.

Rosenstein, D. S., & Horowitz, H. A. (1996). Adolescent attachment and psychopathology. *Journal of Consulting and Clinical Psychology, 64*(2), 244–253.

Rosenthal, C. J. & Gladstone, J. (2000). Grandparenthood in Canada. *Contemporary Family Trends.* Vanier Institute of the Family.

Rosenthal, D. A., & Feldman, S. S. (1991). The influence of perceived family and personal factors on self-reported school performance of Chinese and Western high school students. *Journal of Research on Adolescence, 1*(2), 135–154.

Rosenthal, D. A., & Peart, R. (1996). The rules of the game: Teenagers communicating about sex. *Journal of Adolescence, 19,* 321–332.

Rosenthal, S. L., Lewis, L. M., & Cohen, S. S. (1996). Issues related to the sexual decision-making of inner-city adolescent girls. *Adolescence, 31*(123), 731–739.

Roth, J., Brooks-Gunn, J., Galen, B., Murray, L., Silverman, P., Liu, H., Man, D., & Foster, W. (1997). *Promoting healthy adolescence: Youth development frameworks and programs.* New York: Teachers College, Columbia University.

Rotherman-Borus, M. J., & Koopman, C. (1991). AIDS and adolescents. In R. M. Lerner, A. C. Petersen, & J. Brooks-Gunn (Eds.), *Encyclopedia of adolescence* (Vol. 1, pp. 29–36). New York: Garland.

Rousseau, C., & Drapeau, A. (2000). Scholastic achievement of adolescent refugees from Cambodia and Central America. *Adolescence, 35*(138), 243–258.

Roy, E., Haley, N., Leclerc, P., Cedras, L., & Boivin, J. F. (2002). Drug injection among street youth: The first time. *Addiction, 97*(8), 1003–1009.

Roy, E., Haley, N., Leclerc, P., Lemire, N., Boivin, J. P., Frappier, J. Y., et al. (2000). Prevalence of HIV infection and risk behaviours among Montreal street youth. *International Journal of STD and AIDS, 11*(4), 241–247.

Royer, E., Desbiens, N., Bitaudeau, I., Maltais, N., & Gagnon, M. (1999). The impact of a social skills training program for adolescents with behavioural difficulties. *Emotional and Behavioural Difficulties, 4*(2), 4–10.

Royer, E., Desbiens, N., Bitaudeau, I., Maltais, N., & Gagnon, M. (1999). The impact of a social skills training program for adolescents with behavioural difficulties. *Emotional and Behavioural Difficulties, 4*(2), 4–10.

Rubenstein, J. L., & Feldman, S. S. (1993). Conflict-resolution behavior in adolescent boys: Antecedents and adaptational correlates. *Journal of Research on Adolescence, 3*(1), 41–66.

Rubin, K. H., Bukowski, W., & Parker, J. G. (1998). Peer interactions, relationships, and groups. In W. Damon & N. Eisenberg (Eds.), *Handbook of child psychology: Vol. 3. Social, emotional, and personality development* (pp. 619–700). New York: Wiley.

Ruble, D. N., & Martin, C. L. (1998). Gender development. In N. Eisenberg (Ed.), *Handbook of child psychology: Vol. 1. Theoretical models of human development* (5th ed., pp. 933–1016). New York: Wiley.

Ruck, M. D., Abramovitch, R., & Keating, D. P. (1998). Children's and adolescents' understanding of rights: Balancing nurturance and self-determination. *Child Development, 64*(2), 404–417.

Rudy, D., & Grusec, J. E. (2001). Correlates of authoritarian parenting in individualist and collectivist cultures and implications for understanding the transmission of values. *Journal of Cross Cultural Psychology, 32,* 202–212.

Rueter, M. A., & Conger, R. D. (1995a). Antecedents of parent-adolescent disagreements. *Journal of Marriage and Family, 57,* 435–448.

Rueter, M. A., & Conger, R. D. (1995b). Interaction style, problem-solving behavior, and family problem-solving effectiveness. *Child Development, 66,* 98–115.

Rutter, M., Graham, P., Chadwick, O., and Yule, W. (1976). Adolescent turmoil: fact or fiction? *Journal of Child Psychology and Psychiatry, 17,* 35–56.

Ryan, B., & Adams. G. (1999). Which family characteristics make the most difference in children's success in school? Hull: Human Resources Development Canada. Retrieved from: www.red-seal.ca/sp-ps/arbdgra/publications/bulletin/child_dev/e/chi_dev_04e.shtml.

Rye, B. J., Humpartzoomian, R., & Steep, B. (2001). Feedback from participants and leaders in an intervention program: The 1997–1998 Opening Doors process evaluation. *Journal of Drug Education, 31*(2), 185–206.

S

Sack, W. H., Clarke, G. N., & Seeley, J. (1996). Multiple forms of stress in Cambodian adolescent refugees. *Child Development, 67,* 107–116.

Sakinofsky, I., & Leenaars, A. A. (1997). Suicide in Canada with special reference to the difference between Canada and the United States. *Suicide and Life-Threatening Behaviour, 27*(1), 112–126.

Salmela-Aro, K., & Nurmi, J.-E. (1997). Goal contents, well-being, and life context during transition to university: A longitudinal study. *International Journal of Behavioral Development, 20*(3), 471–491.

Sam, D. L. (1995). Acculturation attitudes among young immigrants as a function of perceived parental attitudes toward cultural change. *Journal of Early Adolescence, 15*(2), 238–258.

Sameroff, A. (1975). Transactional models in early social relations. *Human Development, 18,* 65–79.

Sameroff, A. J. (1983). Developmental systems: Contexts and evolution. In W. Kessen (Ed.), *Handbook of child psychology: Vol. 1. History, theory, and methods* (pp. 237–294). New York: Wiley.

Sameroff, A. J., Seifer, R., Baldwin, A., & Baldwin, C. (1993). Stability of intelligence from preschool to adolescence: The influence of social and family risk factors. *Child Development, 64,* 80–97.

Sampson, R. J. (1997). Collective regulation of adolescent misbehavior: Validation results from eighty Chicago neighborhoods. *Journal of Adolescent Research, 12*(2), 227–244.

Sarigiani, P. A., Wilson, J. L., Petersen, A. C., & Vicary, J. R. (1990). Self-image and educational plans of adolescents from two contrasting communities. *Journal of Early Adolescence, 10,* 37–55.

Sarwal, S., Wong, T., Sevigny, C., & Ng, L.-K. (2003). Increasing incidence of ciprofloxacin-resistant Neisseria gonorrhoeae infection in Canada. *Canadian Medical Association Journal, 168*(7), 872–873.

Sauer, R. J. (1998). Furthering community youth development. In R. M. Lerner & L. A. K. Simon (Eds.), *University-community collaborations for the twenty-first century: Outreach scholarship for youth and families* (pp. 389–396). New York: Garland.

Sauve, R. (1994). *Borderlines: What Canadians and Americans should—but don't—know about each other: A witty, punchy and personal look.* Toronto: McGraw-Hill Ryerson.

Savin-Williams, R. C. (1990). *Gay and lesbian youth: Expressions of identity.* New York: Hemisphere.

Savin-Williams, R. C. (1991). Gay and lesbian youth. In R. M. Lerner, A. C. Petersen, & J. Brooks-Gunn (Eds.), *Encyclopedia of adolescence* (pp. 385–388). New York: Garland.

Savin-Williams, R. C. (1994). Dating those you can't love and loving those you can't date. In R. Montemayor, G. R. Adams, & T. P. Gullotta (Eds.), *Personal relationships during adolescence. Advances in adolescent development* (Vol. 6, pp. 196–215). Thousand Oaks, CA: Sage.

Savin-Williams, R. C. (1995). An exploratory study of pubertal maturation timing and self-esteem among gay and bisexual male youths. *Developmental Psychology, 31*(1), 56–64.

Savin-Williams, R. C. (1999). Matthew Shepard's death: A professional awakening. *Applied Developmental Science, 3,* 150–154.

Savin-Williams, R. C., & Small, S. A. (1986). The timing of puberty and its relationship to adolescent and parent perceptions of family interactions. *Developmental Psychology, 22,* 342–347.

Scales, P., & Leffert, N. (1999). *Developmental assets: A synthesis of the scientific research on adolescent development.* Minneapolis: Search Institute.

Scales, P., Benson, P., Leffert, N., & Blyth, D. A. (2000). The contribution of developmental assets to the prediction of thriving among adolescents. *Applied Developmental Science, 4*(1), 27–46.

Schaie, K. W. (1959). Cross-sectional methods in the study of psychological aspects of aging. *Journal of Gerontology, 14,* 208–215.

Schaie, K. W. (1965). A general model for the study of developmental problems. *Psychosocial Bulletin, 64,* 92–107.

Schaie, K. W., & Strother, C. R. (1968). A cross-sequential study of age changes in cognitive behavior. *Psychological Bulletin, 70,* 671–680.

Schaie, K. W., Labouvie, G. V., & Buech, B. V. (1973). Generational and cohort-specific differences in adult cognitive functioning: A fourteen-year study of independent samples. *Developmental Psychology, 9,* 151–166.

Schiedel, D. G., & Marcia, J. E. (1985). Ego identity, intimacy, sex role orientation, and gender. *Developmental Psychology, 21*(1), 149–160.

Schissel, B., & Fedec. K. (1999). Selling of innocence: the gestalt of danger in the lives of youth prostitutes. *Canadian Journal of Criminology, 41*(1), 33–56.

Schludermann, E. H., Schludermann, S. M. & Huynh, C.-L. (2000). Religiosity, prosocial values, and adjustment among students in Catholic high schools in Canada. *Journal of Beliefs & Values, 21*(1), 99–115.

Schneider, B. H., & Younger, A. J. (1996). Adolescent-parent attachment and adolescents' relations with their peers: A closer look. *Youth & Society, 28*(1), 95–108.

Schondel, C., Boehm, K., Rose, J., & Marlowe, A. (1995). Adolescent volunteers: An untapped resource in the delivery of adolescent preventive health care. *Youth & Society, 27*(2), 123–135.

Schonert-Reichl, K. (1999). Relations of peer acceptance, friendship adjustment, and social behaviour to moral reasoning during early adolescence, *Journal of Early Adolescence, 19*(2), 249–279.

Schonert-Reichl, K. (2001). *Promoting Historical Consciousness in Childhood and Adolescence: A Moral Developmental Perspective.* Paper presented at Canadian Historical

Consciousness in an International Context: Theoretical Frameworks. Vancouver: University of British Columbia.

Schonert-Reichl, K. A. (1994). Gender differences in depressive symptomatology and egocentrism in adolescence. *Journal of Early Adolescence, 14*, 49–65.

Schonert-Reichl, K., & Muller, Jennifer R (1996). Correlates of help-seeking in adolescence. *Journal of Youth and Adolescence, 25*(6), 705–731.

Schonfeld, W. A. (1969). The body and the body image in adolescents. In G. Caplan & S. Lebovici (Eds.), *Adolescence: Psychosocial perspectives.* New York: Basic.

Schönpflug, U., & Jansen, X. (1995). Self-concept and coping with developmental demands in German and Polish adolescents. *International Journal of Behavioral Development, 18*(3), 385–405.

Schorr, L. (1997). *Common purpose: Strengthening families and neighborhoods to rebuild America.* New York: Doubleday.

Schorr, L. B. (1988). *Within our reach: Breaking the cycle of disadvantage.* New York: Doubleday.

Schorr, L. B. (1991). Effective programs for children growing up in concentrated poverty. In A. C. Huston (Ed.), *Children in poverty: Child development and public policy* (pp. 260–281). Cambridge: Cambridge University.

Schwartz, R. (1999, October). *Super-predator or the boy next door? Policy trends in juvenile justice.* Paper presented at the Loyola Forum on the Child: Reclaiming childhood: Shaping policy for the future. Chicago: Loyola University.

Schwatrz, K., & Fouts, G. (2003). Music preferences, personality style, and developmental issues of adolescents, *Journal of Youth and Adolescence, 32*(3), 205–213.

Scott-Jones, D., & White, A. B. (1990). Correlates of sexual activity in early adolescence. *Journal of Early Adolescence, 10*(2), 221–238.

Seguin, J. R., Arseneault, L., Boulerice, B., Harden, P. W., & Tremblay, R. E. (2002). Response perseveration in adolescent boys with stable and unstable histories of physical aggression: The role of underlying processes. *Journal of Child*

Psychology and Psychiatry and Allied Disciplines, 43(4), 481–494.

Seifert, T. L., & O'Keefe, B.A. (2001). The relationship of work avoidance and learning goals to perceived competence, externality and meaning. *British Journal of Educational Psychology, 71*(1), 81–92.

Selman, R. L., & Schultz, L. H. (1990). *Making a friend in youth: Developmental theory and pair therapy.* Chicago: University of Chicago Press.

Seltzer, V. C., & Waterman, R. P. (1996). A cross-national study of adolescent peer concordance on issues of the future. *Journal of Adolescent Research, 11*(4), 461–482.

September, A. N., McCarrey, M., Baranowsky, A. Patent, C., & Schindler, D. (2001). The relation between well-being, impostor feelings, and gender role orientation among Canadian university students. *Journal of Social Psychology, 141*(2), 218–232.

Serbin, L. A., Cooperman, J. M., Peters, P. L., Lehoux, P. M., Stack, D. M., & Schwartzman, A. E. (1998). Intergenerational transfer of psychosocial risk in women with childhood histories of aggression, withdrawal, or aggression and withdrawal. *Developmental Psychology, 34*(6), 1246–1262.

Serbin, L. A., Moskowitz, D. S., Schwartzman, A. E., & Ledingham, J. E. (1991). Aggressive, withdrawn, and aggressive/withdrawn children in adolescence: Into the next generation. In D. J. Pepler & K. H. Rubin (Eds.) *The development and treatment of childhood aggression.* Hillsdale, New Jersey: Lawrence Erlbaum Associates.

Serbin, L. A., Poulin-Dubois, D., & Eichstedt, J. A. (2002). Infants' responses to gender inconsistent events. *Infancy, 3*(4), 531–542.

Sessa, F., & Steinberg, L. (1991). Family structure and the development of autonomy during adolescence. *Journal of Early Adolescence, 11*(1), 38–55.

Shade, L. R. (2002). Canadian kids online. *Transition,* Autumn, 7–12.

Shagle, S. C., & Barber, B. K. (1993). Effects of family, marital, and parent-child conflict on adolescent self-derogation and suicidal ideation. *Journal of Marriage and the Family, 55*, 964–974.

Shanahan, J. (1995). Television viewing and adolescent authoritarianism. *Journal of Adolescence, 18*, 271–288.

Shanahan, M. J., Elder, G. H., Jr., Burchinal, M., & Conger, R. D. (1996). Adolescent paid labor and relationships with parents: Early work-family linkages. *Child Development, 67*, 2183–2200.

Sharma, A. R., McGue, M. K., & Benson, P. L. (1998). The psychological adjustment of United States adopted adolescents and their non-adopted siblings. *Child Development, 69*(3), 791–802.

Sharma, K. (1990). Age at menarche in Northwest Indian females and a review of Indian data. *Annals of Human Biology, 17*(2), 159–162.

Shepard, B., & Marshall, A. (2000). Career development and planning issues for rural adolescent girls. *Canadian Journal of Counselling, 34*(3), 155–171.

Sherrod, L. R., Haggerty, R. J., & Featherman, D. L. (1993). Introduction: Late adolescence and the transition to adulthood. *Journal of Research on Adolescence, 3*, 217–226.

Shoda, Y., Mischel, W., & Peake, P. K. (1990). Predicting adolescent cognitive and self-regulatory competencies from preschool delay of gratification: Identifying diagnostic conditions. *Developmental Psychology, 26*, 978–986.

Shorter-Gooden, K., & Washington, N. C. (1996). Young, black, and female: The challenge of weaving an identity. *Journal of Adolescence, 19*, 465–475.

Shucksmith, J., Hendry, L. B., & Glendinning, A. (1995). Models of parenting: Implications for adolescent well-being within different types of family contexts. *Journal of Adolescence, 18*, 253–270.

Shulman, S., & Knafo, D. (1997). Balancing closeness and individuality in adolescent close relationships. *International Journal of Behavioral Development, 21*, 687–702.

Shweder, R. A., Goodnow, J., Hatano, G., Kessel, F., LeVine, R. A., Markus, H., Miller, P., & Worthman, C. (1998). The cultural psychology of development: One mind, many mentalities. In W. Damon & R. M. Lerner (Eds.), *Handbook of child psychology: Vol. 1. Theoretical models of human development.* (5th ed., pp.

867–937). New York: Wiley.

Siegel, J., & Shaughnessy, M. F. (1995). There's a first time for everything: Understanding adolescence. *Adolescence, 30*(117), 217–221.

Sigelman, C., Derenowski, E., Woods, T., Mukai, T., Alfred-Liro, C., Durazo, O., & Maddock, A. (1996). Mexican-American and Anglo-American children's responsiveness to a theory-centered AIDS education program. *Child Development, 67,* 253–266.

Sigurdsson, J. F., & Gudjonsson, G. H. (1996). Psychological characteristics of juvenile alcohol and drug users. *Journal of Adolescence, 19,* 41–46.

Silbereisen, R. (1995). How parenting styles and crowd contexts interact in actualizing potential for development: Commentary. In L. J. Crockett & A. C. Crouter (Eds.), *Pathways through adolescence: Individual development in relation to social contexts* (pp. 197–207). Mahwah, NJ: Erlbaum.

Silbereisen, R., Noack, P., & Schönpflug, U. (1994). Comparative analyses of beliefs, leisure contexts, and substance abuse in West Berlin and Warsaw. In R. Silbereisen & E. Todt (Eds.), *Adolescence in context: The interplay of family, school, peers, and work in adjustment* (pp. 176–198). New York: Springer.

Silverberg, S. B., Marczak, M. S., & Gondoli, D. M. (1996). Maternal depressive symptoms and achievement-related outcomes among adolescent daughters: Variations by family structure. *Journal of Early Adolescence, 16*(1), 90–109.

Simmons, R. G., & Blyth, D. A. (1987). *Moving into adolescence: The impact of pubertal change and school context.* Hawthorne, NJ: Aldine.

Simmons, R. G., Carlton-Ford, S. L., Blyth, D. A. (1987). Predicting how a child will cope with the transition to junior high school. In R. M. Lerner & T. T. Foch (Eds.), *Biological-psychosocial interactions in early adolescence. Child psychology* (pp. 325–375). Hillsdale, NJ: Erlbaum.

Simmons, R., Rosenberg, F., & Rosenberg, M. (1973). Disturbances in the self-image in adolescence. *American Sociological Review, 38,* 553–568.

Simons, J. M., Finlay, B., & Yang, A. (1991). *The adolescent and young adult fact book.* Washington, DC: Children's Defense Fund.

Simons, R. L., Johnson, C., & Conger, R. D. (1994). Harsh corporal punishment versus quality of parental involvement as an explanation of adolescent maladjustment. *Journal of Marriage and the Family, 56,* 591–607.

Simons, R. L., Whitbeck, L. B., Beaman, J., & Conger, R. D. (1994). The impact of mothers' parenting, involvement by nonresidential fathers, and parental conflict on the adjustment of adolescent children. *Journal of Marriage and the Family, 56,* 356–374.

Sims, M. W. (2000). Gay/straight alliance clubs—understanding our differences. Retrieved from: www.bchrc.gov.bc.ca/PressReleases2000.asp.

Singh, K., & Hernandez-Gantes, V. M. (1996). The relation of English language proficiency to educational aspirations of Mexican-American eighth graders. *Journal of Early Adolescence, 16*(3), 253–273.

Singh, S. & Darroch, J. E. (2000). Adolescent pregnancy and childbearing: Levels and trends in developed countries. *Family Planning Perspectives, 32*(1), 14–23.

Singh, S. Darroch, J. E., & Frost, J. J. (2001). Socioeconomic disadvantage and adolescent women's sexual and reproductive behavior: The case of five developed countries. *Family Planning Perspectives, 33*(6), 251–258 & 289.

Sissingh, F. (2002). Netting the NET: An anorexia nervosa gene is caught! Retrieved from: www.eurekalert.org/pub_releases/2002-08/mp-ntn072502.php.

Skoe, E. E., & Gooden, A. (1993). Ethic of care and real-life moral dilemma content in male and female early adolescents. *Journal of Early Adolescence, 13,* 154–167.

Skoe, E. E. A, Hansen, K. L., Morch, W-T., Bakke, I., Hoffmann, T., Larsen, B., Aasheim, M. (1999). Care-based moral reasoning in Norwegian and Canadian early adolescents: A cross-national comparison. *Journal of Early Adolescence, 19*(2), 280–291.

Slavin, R., Karweit, N., & Wasik, B. (1994). *Preventing early school failure: Research on effective strategies.* Boston: Allyn & Bacon.

Slonim-Nevo, V., Auslander, W. F., Ozawa, M. N., & Jung, K. G. (1996). The long-term impact of AIDS-preventive interventions for delinquent and abused adolescents. *Adolescence, 31*(122), 409–421.

Small, S. A. (1996). Collaborative, community-based research on adolescents: Using research for community change. *Journal of Research on Adolescence, 6*(1), 9–22.

Small, S. A., & Kerns, D. (1993). Unwanted sexual activity among peers during early and middle adolescence: Incidence and risk factors. *Journal of Marriage and the Family, 55,* 941–952.

Small, S. A., & Luster, T. (1994). An ecological risk-factor approach to adolescent sexual activity. *Journal of Marriage and the Family, 56,* 181–192.

Smart, R. G., & Stoduto, G. (1997). Treatment experiences and need for treatment among students with serious alcohol and drug problems. *Journal of Child and Adolescent Substance Abuse, 7*(1), 63–72.

Smart, R. G., Mann, R. E., & Tyson, L. A. (1997). Drugs and violence among Ontario students. *Journal of Psychoactive Drugs, 29*(4), 369–373.

Smetana, J. G. (1988). Concepts of self and social convention: Adolescents' and parents' reasoning about hypothetical and actual family conflicts. In M. R. Gunnar & W. A. Collins (Eds.), *Development during the transition to adolescence. Minnesota symposium on child psychology* (Vol. 21, pp. 79–122). Hillsdale, NJ: Erlbaum.

Smetana, J. G. (1993). Conceptions of parental authority in divorced and married mothers and their adolescents. *Journal of Research on Adolescence, 3*(1), 19–39.

Smetana, J. G. (1995). Parenting styles and conceptions of parental authority during adolescence. *Child Development, 66,* 299–316.

Smetana, J. G., & Asquith, P. (1994). Adolescents' and parents' conceptions of parental authority and personal autonomy. *Child Development, 65*(4), 1147–1162.

Smetana, J. G., Yau, J., & Hanson, S. (1991). Conflict resolution in families with adolescents. *Journal of Research on Adolescence, 1*(2), 189–206.

Smith, A. M. A., & Rosenthal, D. A. (1995). Adolescents' perceptions of their risk environment. *Journal of Adolescence, 18,* 229–245.

Smith, D. E., & Muenchen, R. A. (1995). Gender and age variations in the self-image of Jamaican adolescents. *Adolescence, 30*(119), 643–654.

Smith, P. K., & Ananiadou, K. (2003). The nature of school bullying and the effectiveness of school-based interventions. *Journal of Applied Psychoanalytic Studies, 5*(2), 189–209.

Smith, R. E., & Smoll, F. L. (1990). Self-esteem and children's reactions to youth support coaching behaviors: A field study of self-enhancement processes. *Developmental Psychology, 26,* 987–993.

Smith, R. A., & Davis, S.F. (1997). *The psychologist as detective: An introduction to conducting research in psychology.* Upper Saddle River, NJ: Prentice Hall.

Smith, T. E. (1997). Adolescent gender differences in time alone and time devoted to conversation. *Adolescence, 32*(126), 483–496.

Snider, B. A., & Miller, J. P. (1993). The land-grant system and 4-H: A mutually beneficial relationship of scholars and practitioners in youth development. In R. M. Lerner (Ed.), *Early adolescence: Perspectives on research, policy, and intervention* (pp. 481–499). Hillsdale, NJ: Erlbaum.

Society for Research in Child Development. (1999). Ethical standards for research with children. In *The SRCD directory of members, 1999–2000* (pp. 283–284). Ann Arbor, MI: Author.

Solomon, Y., & Farrand, J. (1996). "Why don't you do it properly?" Young women who self-injure. *Journal of Adolescence, 19,* 111–119.

Spanier, G. B. (1997). *Enhancing the quality of life for children, youth, and families.* Unpublished manuscript. University Park: Pennsylvania State University.

Spanier, G. B. (1999). Enhancing the qualty of life: A model for the 21st century land-grant university. *Applied Developmental Science, 3*(4), 199–205.

Spearman, C. (1927). *The abilities of man.* New York: Macmillan.

Speicher, B. (1994). Family patterns of moral judgment during adolescence and early adulthood. *Developmental Psychology, 30,* 624–632.

Spencer, M. B. (1990). Development of minority children: An introduction. *Child Development, 61,* 267–269.

Spencer, M. B. (1991). Identity, minority development of. In R. M. Lerner, A. C. Petersen, & J. Brooks-Gunn (Eds.), *Encyclopedia of adolescence* (Vol. 1, pp. 111–130). New York: Garland.

Spencer, M. B. (1995). Old issues and new theorizing about African American youth: A phenomenological variant of ecological systems theory. In R. L. Taylor (Ed.), *Black youth: Perspectives on their status in the United States* (pp. 38–69). Westport, CT: Praeger.

Spencer, M. B. (1999). Social and cultural influences on school adjustment: The application of an identity-focused cultural ecological perspective. *Educational Psychologist, 34,* 43–57.

Spencer, M. B., & Dornbusch, S. (1990). Challenges in studying minority youth. In S. Feldman & G. Elliott (Eds.), *At the threshold: The developing adolescent* (pp. 123–146). Cambridge: Harvard University Press.

Spencer, M. B., & Markstrom-Adams, C. (1990). Identity process among racial and ethnic minority children in America. *Child Development, 61,* 290–310.

Spencer, M. B., Dupree, D., & Hartmann, T. (1997). A phenomenological variant of ecological systems theory (PVEST): A self-organization perspective in context. *Development and Psychopathology, 9,* 817–833.

Spieker, S., & Bensley, L. (1994). Roles of living arrangements and grandmother social support in adolescent mothering and infant attachment. *Developmental Psychology, 30*(1), 102–111.

Spivack, G., Marcus, J., & Swift, M. (1986). Early classroom behaviors and later misconduct. *Developmental Psychology, 22*(1), 124–131.

St. Lawrence, J. S., Brasfield, T. L., Jefferson, K. W., Alleyne, E., O'Bannon, R. E., III, & Shirley, A. (1995a). Cognitive-behavioral intervention to reduce African-American adolescents' risk for HIV infection. *Journal of Consulting and Clinical Psychology, 63*(2), 221–237.

St. Lawrence, J. S., Jefferson, K. W., Alleyne, E., & Brasfield, T. L. (1995b). Comparison of education versus behavioral skills training interventions in lowering sexual HIV-risk behavior of substance-dependent adolescents. *Journal of Consulting and Clinical Psychology, 63*(1), 154–157.

Stallmann, J. I., & Johnson T. G. (1996). Community factors in secondary educational achievement in Appalachia. *Youth & Society, 27*(4), 469–484.

Statistics Canada (1999). Participation rates and unemployment rates by age and sex, Canada and selected countries. Retrieved from: www.statcan.ca/english/Pgdb/labor23a.htm.

Statistics Canada (2002). *Youth in Canada* (Catalogue No. 89-511-XPE). Ottawa: Author.

Statistics Canada (2003). *2001 census dictionary* (Catalogue No. 92-378-XIE). Ottawa: Author.

Statistics Canada (Summer, 1998). *Canadian Social Trends,* Keeping Track (p. 28). (Catalogue No. 11-008-XPE). Ottawa: Author.

Statistics Canada (1987). *Women in the Workplace: Selected data.* (Catalogue No. 71-534). Ottawa: Author.

Statistics Canada. (1996). *National Census.* Ottawa: Author.

Statistics Canada. (1997). *Household facilities and equipment.* Ottawa: Author.

Statistics Canada (2000). *General social survey.* Ottawa: Author.

Statistics Canada (2000). *Health Statistics.* (Catalogue No. 82M0009XCB). Retrieved from: www.statcan.ca/english/Pgdb/health19b.htm.

Statistics Canada. (2001). *Household internet use survey.* Ottawa: Author.

Statistics Canada (2001). The Canada E-Book (Catalogue No.11-404-XIE). Retrieved from: http://142.206.72.67/02/02c/02c_005d_e.htm.

Statistics Canada (2002). *At a crossroads: first results of the 18- to 20-year-old cohort of the youth in transition survey.* Hull: Human Resources Development Canada.

Statistics Canada. 1999. *Statistical Report on the Health of Canadians. Lifestyle behaviours.* Retrieved from: www.hc-sc.gc.ca/hppb/phdd/pdf/report/stats/eng39–52.pdf.

Statistics Canada. *The Daily* (Thursday, September 28, 2000). Divorces. Ottawa: Author.

Statistics Canada. *The Daily* (Tuesday, October 22, 2002). 2001 Census: Marital status, common-law status, families, dwellings and households. Ottawa: Author.

Stattin, H., & Magnusson, D. (1990). *Pubertal maturation in female development.* Hillsdale, NJ: Erlbaum.

Staudinger, V. M., Marsiske, M., & Baltes, P. (1995). Resilience and reserve capacity in later adulthood: Potentials and limits of development across the life-span. In D. Cicchetti & D. Cohen (Eds.), *Developmental psychopathology: Vol. 2. Risk disorder and adaptation* (pp. 801–847). New York: Wiley.

Stefanich, G. P., Wills, F. A., & Buss, R. R. (1991). The use of interdisciplinary teaming and its influence on student self-concept in middle schools. *Journal of Early Adolescence, 11*(4), 404–419.

Stein, D., & Reichert, P. (1990). Extreme dieting behaviors in early adolescence. *Journal of Early Adolescence, 10*(2), 108–121.

Steinberg, L. (1977). *A longitudinal study of physical growth, intellectual growth, and family interaction in early adolescence.* Unpublished doctoral dissertation, Cornell University, Ithaca, NY.

Steinberg, L. (1981). Transformations in family relations at puberty. *Developmental Psychology, 17,* 833–840.

Steinberg, L. (1983). The varieties and effects of work during adolescence. In M. Lamb, A. Brown, & B. Rogoff (Eds.), *Advances in developmental psychology* (Vol. 3). Hillsdale, NJ: Erlbaum.

Steinberg, L. (1987). The impact of puberty on family relations: Effects of pubertal status and pubertal timing. *Developmental Psychology, 23,* 833–840.

Steinberg, L. (1988). Reciprocal relation between parent-child distance and pubertal maturation. *Developmental Psychology, 24,* 122–128.

Steinberg, L. (1991). Developmental considerations in youth advocacy. In J. C. Westman (Ed.), *Who speaks for the children? The handbook of individual and class child advocacy* (pp. 23–27). Sarasota: Professional Resource Exchange.

Steinberg, L., & Dornbusch, S. M. (1991). Negative correlates of part-time employment during adolescence: Replication and elaboration. *Developmental Psychology, 27*(2), 304–313.

Steinberg, L., & Hill, J. (1978). Patterns of family interaction as a function of age, the onset of puberty, and formal thinking. *Developmental Psychology, 14,* 683–684.

Steinberg, L., Mounts, N. S., Lamborn, S. D., & Dornsbusch, S. M. (1991). Authoritative parenting and adolescent adjustment across varied ecological niches. *Journal of Research on Adolescence, 1*(1), 19–36.

Steinhauer, P. D. (2001). Clinical and service applications of the theory of resiliency with particular reference to adolescents. *International Journal of Adolescent Medicine and Health, 13*(1), 53–73.

Stephenson, A. L., Henry, C. S., & Robinson, L. C. (1996). Family characteristics and adolescent substance use. *Adolescence, 31*(121), 59–77.

Stewart, S. M., Bond, M. H., McBride-Chang, C., Fielding, R., Deeds, O., & Westrick, J. (1998). Parent and adolescent contributors to teenage misconduct in Western and Asian high school students in Hong Kong. *International Journal of Behavioral Development, 22*(4), 847–869.

Stice, E., & Barrera, J. (1995). A longitudinal examination of the reciprocal relations between perceived parenting and adolescents' substance use and externalizing behaviors. *Developmental Psychology, 31*(2), 322–334.

Stiffman, A. R., Church, H., & Earls, F. (1992). Predictive modeling of change in depressive disorder and counts of depressive symptoms in urban youth. *Journal of Research on Adolescence, 2*(4), 295–316.

Stinson, M. S., Whitmire, K., & Kluwin, T. N. (1996). Self-perceptions of social relationships in hearing-impaired adolescents. *Journal of Educational Psychology, 88*(1), 132–143.

Stirtzinger, R., Campbell, L., Green, A., DeSouza, C., & Dawe, I. (2001). Multimodal school-based intervention for at-risk, aggressive, latency-age youth. *Canadian Journal of School Psychology, 17*(1), 27–46.

Stocker, C., & Dunn, J. (1991). Sibling relationships in adolescence. In R. M. Lerner, A. C. Petersen, & J. Brooks-Gunn (Eds.), *Encyclopedia of adolescence* (Vol. 2, pp. 1046–1048). New York: Garland.

Straker, G., Mendelsohn, M., Moosa, F., & Tudin, P. (1996). Violent political contexts and the emotional concerns of township youth. *Child Development, 67,* 46–54.

Straus, M. A., & Yodanis, C. L. (1996). Corporal punishment in adolescence and physical assaults on spouses in later life: What accounts for the link? *Journal of Marriage and Family, 58,* 825–841.

Strouse, J. S., Buerkel-Rothfuss, & Long, E. C. J. (1995). Gender and family as moderators of the relationship between music video exposure and adolescent sexual permissiveness. *Adolescence, 30*(119), 505–521.

Subkoviak, M. J., Enright, R. D., Wu, C.-R., Gassin, E. A., Freedman, S., Olson, L. M., & Sarinopoulos, I. (1995). Measuring interpersonal forgiveness in late adolescence and middle adulthood. *Journal of Adolescence, 18,* 641–655.

Suitor, J. J., & Reavis, R. (1995). Football, fast cars, and cheerleading: Adolescent gender norms, 1978–1989. *Adolescence, 30*(118), 265–272.

Sullivan, M. L. (1993). Culture and class as determinants of out-of-wedlock childbearing and poverty during late adolescence. *Journal of Research on Adolescence, 3*(3), 295–316.

Summers, P., Forehand, R., Armistead, L., & Tannenbaum, L. (1998). Parental divorce during early adolescence in Caucasian families: The role of family process variables in predicting the long-term consequences for early adult psychological adjustment. *Journal of Consulting and Clinical Psychology, 66*(2), 327–336.

Surbey, M. K. (1987). Part II. Ethological perspectives on specific psychiatric disorders: Anorexia nervosa, amenorrhea, and adaptation. *Ethology and Sociobiology, 8,* 47S–61S.

Surbey, M. K. (1990). Family composition, stress, and the timing of human menarche. In T. E. Zeigler & F. B Zigler (Eds.) *Socioendocrinology of primate reproduction.* New York: Wiley-Liss.

Susman, E. J. (1997). Modeling developmental complexity in adolescence: Hormones and behavior in context. *Journal of Research on Adolescence, 7*(3), 283–306.

Sussman, T., & Duffy, M. (1996). Are we forgetting about gay male adolescents in AIDS-related research and prevention? *Youth & Society, 27*(3), 379–393.

Swanson, D. P., Spencer, M. B., & Petersen, A. (1998). Identity formation in adolescence. In K. Borman & B. Schneider (Eds.), *The adolescent years: Social influences and educational challenges: Ninety-seventh yearbook of the National Society for* the Study of Education, Part I (pp. 18–41). Chicago: National Society for the Study of Education.

Swenson, C. C., & Kennedy, W. A. (1995). Perceived control and treatment outcome with chronic adolescent offenders. *Adolescence, 30*(119), 565–578.

Switzer, G. E., Simmons, R. G., Dew, M. A., & Regalski, J. M. (1995). The effect of a school- based helper program on adolescent self-image, attitudes, and behavior. *Journal of Early Adolescence, 15*(4), 429–455.

T

Takahashi, K., & Majima, N. (1994). Transition from home to college dormitory: The role of preestablished affective relationships in adjustment to a new life. *Journal of Research on Adolescence, 4*(3), 367–384.

Takanishi, R., & Hamburg, D. A. (1996). Great transitions: Preparing American youth for the 21st century—the role of research. *Journal of Research on Adolescence, 6*, 379–396.

Talbani, A., & Hasanali, P. (2000). Adolescent females between tradition and modernity: Gender role socialization in South Asian immigrant culture. *Journal of Adolescence, 23*(5): 615–627.

Tanner, J. M. (1962). *Growth at adolescence*. Springfield, IL: Thomas.

Tanner, J. M. (1970). Physical growth. In P. H. Mussen (Ed.), *Carmichael's manual of child psychology* (Vol. 1, pp. 77–155). New York: Wiley.

Tanner, J. M. (1973). Growing up. *Scientific American, 229*, 34–43.

Tanner, J. M. (1991). Menarche, secular trend in age of. In R. M. Lerner, A. C. Petersen, & J. Brooks-Gunn (Eds.), *Encyclopedia of adolescence* (Vol. 1, pp. 637–641). New York: Garland.

Taylor, A. (2002). Keeping up with the 🍁 kids in a wired world. *Transition*, Autumn, 3–6.

Taylor, C. S. (1990). *Dangerous society*. East Lansing: Michigan State University Press.

Taylor, C. S. (1993). *Girls, gangs, women, and drugs*. East Lansing: Michigan State University Press.

Taylor, C. S. (1996). *The unintended consequences of incarceration: Youth development, the juvenile corrections systems, and crime.* Paper presented at the Vera Institute Conference, Harriman, NY.

Taylor, D. M. (1997). The quest for col- 🍁 lective identity: the plight of disadvantaged ethnic minorities, *Canadian Psychology, 38*(3), 174–190.

Taylor, D. M. (2002). The quest for iden- 🍁 tity: From minority groups to generation Xers. Westport, Connecticut: Praeger.

Taylor, L. E. (1995). Joining the old boys' 🍁 club. *Canada and the World Backgrounder. 60*(4), 12–14.

Taylor, R. D. (1996). Adolescents' perceptions of kinship support and family management practices: Association with adolescent adjustment in African American families. *Developmental Psychology, 32*(4), 687–695.

Taylor, R. D., & Roberts, D. (1995). Kinship support and maternal and adolescent well-being in economically disadvantaged African-American families. *Child Development, 66*, 1585–1597.

Taylor, R., Casten, R., Flickinger, S., Roberts, D., & Fulmore, C. D. (1994). Explaining the school performance of African-American adolescents. *Journal of Research on Adolescence, 4*, 21–44.

Taylor, R. J. (1995). Wasted lives and 🍁 wounded people. *Canada and the World Backgrounder, 61*(1), 8–11.

Taylor-Gibbs, J. (1991). Black adolescents at risk: Approaches to prevention. In R. M. Lerner, A. C. Petersen, & J. Brooks-Gunn (Eds.), *Encyclopedia of adolescence* (Vol. 1, pp. 73–84). New York: Garland.

Terrell, N. E. (1997). Street life: Aggravated and sexual assaults among homeless and runaway adolescents. *Youth & Society, 28*(3), 267–290.

The Boys and Girls Club of British 🍁 Columbia (Winter, 2003). Asset building: Evaluating the process . . . Measuring the outcomes. *Asset Building Newsletter, 5*, 11–21. Retrieved from: www.lions-quest.ca/pdf%20files/NetworkerJan03.pdf.

The Double Cohort (2003). Fact Sheet. 🍁 Published by the Ontario Undergraduate Student Alliance & College Student Alliance. Retrieved from: www.thedoublecohort.ca/dcfs.html.

The Health of Canada's Children: A 🍁 CICH Profile 3rd Edition (2001). *Factsheet: Youth*. Canadian Institute of Child Health. Retrieved from: www.cich.ca/youth.htm.

Theissen, V., & Nickerson, C. (1999). 🍁 *Canadian gender trends in education and work*. (T-00-4E.) Applied Research Branch, Strategic Policy. Ottawa: Human Resources Development Canada.

Thelen, E., & Smith, L. B. (1998). Dynamic systems theories. In W. Damon (Series Ed.) & R. M. Lerner (Vol. Ed.), *Handbook of child psychology: Vol. 1. Theoretical models of human development* (5th ed., pp. 563–633). New York: Wiley.

Thomas, A., & Chess, S. (1977). *Temperament and development*. New York: Brunner/Mazel.

Thomas, G., Farrell, M. P., & Barnes, G. M. (1996). The effects of single-mother families and nonresident fathers on delinquency and substance abuse in black and white adolescents. *Journal of Marriage and the Family, 58*, 884–894.

Thompson, A. M., & Chad, K. E. 🍁 (2000). The relationship of pubertal status to body image, social physique anxiety, preoccupation with weight and nutritional status in young females. *Canadian Journal of Public Health. 91*(3), 207–211.

Thompson, K. L., Bundy, K. A., & Broncheau, C. (1995). Social skills training for young adolescents: Symbolic and behavioral components. *Adolescence, 30*(119), 723–734.

Thompson, M. R. (1997). Understanding the essence of the relationship between Big and Little Brothers and Sisters: A phenomenological study. *Journal of Child and Youth Care, 11*(3), 53–62.

Thornberry, T. P., Smith, C. A., & Howard, G. J. (1997). Risk factors for teenage fatherhood. *Journal of Marriage and the Family, 59*, 505–522.

Thorndike, E. L. (1904). The newest psychology. *Educational Review, 28*, 217–227.

Timko, C., Stovel, K. W., Baumgartner, M., & Moos, R. H. (1995). Acute and chronic stressors, social resources, and functioning among adolescents with juvenile rheumatic disease. *Journal of Research on Adolescence, 5*(3), 361–385.

Tisak, M. S., & Tisak, J. (1996). My sibling's but not my friend's keeper: Reasoning about responses to aggressive acts. *Journal of Early Adolescence, 16*(3), 324–339.

To, T., Cadarette, S. M., & Liu, Y. (2001). Biological, social, and environmental correlates of preschool development. *Child: Health, Care, and Development, 27*(2), 187–200.

Tobach, E. (1971). Some evolutionary aspects of human gender. *Journal of Orthopsychiatry, 41,* 710–715.

Tobach, E. (1972). The meaning of cryptanthroparion. In L. Ehrman, G. Omenn, & E. Caspari (Eds.), *Genetics, environment, and behavior* (pp. 219–239). New York: Academic Press.

Tobach, E. (1981). Evolutionary aspects of the activity of the organism and its development. In R. M. Lerner & N. A. Busch-Rossnagel (Eds.), *Individuals as producers of their development: A life-span perspective* (pp. 37–68). New York: Academic Press.

Tobach, E., & Schneirla, T. C. (1968). The biopsychology of social behavior of animals. In R. E. Cooke & S. Levin (Eds.), *Biologic basis of pediatric practice* (pp. 68–82). New York: McGraw-Hill.

Todt, E., Drewes, R., & Heils, S. (1994). The development of interests during adolescence: Social context, individual differences, and individual significance. In R. K. Silbereisen & E. Todt (Eds.), *Adolescence in context: The interplay of family, school, peers, and work in adjustment* (pp. 82–95). New York: Springer.

Tomkins, Qu A. (2002). Growth status and menarche in urban and rural China. *Annals of Human Biology, 2002, 29*(3), 348–352.

Tonkin, R. S. (1997). Evaluation of a summer camp for adolescents with eating disorders. *Journal of Adolescent Health, 20*(6), 412–413.

Tonry, M. (1999). Why are U.S. incarceration rates so high? *Crime and Delinquency, 45*(4), 419–437.

Torres, R., Fernandez, F., & Maceira, D. (1995). Self-esteem and value of health as correlates of adolescent health behavior. *Adolescence, 30*(118), 403–412.

Travers, R., & Schneider, M. (1996). Barriers to accessibility for lesbian and gay youth needing addictions services. *Youth & Society, 27*(3), 356–378.

Treboux, D., & Busch-Rossnagel, N. A. (1995). Age differences in parent and peer influences on female sexual behavior. *Journal of Research on Adolescence, 5*(4), 469–487.

Tremblay, R. E, Boulerice, B., Haren, P. W., McDuff, P., Perusse, D., Pihl, R. O., & Zoccolillo, M. (1995). Do children in Canada become more aggressive as they approach adolescence? In *Growing up in Canada: National Longitudinal Survey of Children and Youth*. Ottawa: Statistics Canada.

Tremblay, T., & Gagne, F. (2001). Beliefs of students talented in academics, music, and dance concerning the heritability of human abilities in these fields. *Roeper Review, 23*(3), 173–177.

Trickett, E. J., Barone, C., & Buchanan, R. M. (1996). Elaborating developmental contextualism in adolescent research and intervention: Paradigm contributions from community psychology. *Journal of Research on Adolescence, 6*(3), 245–269.

Tsuzaki, S., Matsuo, N., Ogata, T., & Osano, M. (1989). Lack of linkage between height and weight and age at menarche during the secular shift in growth of Japanese children. *Annals of Human Biology, 16*(5), 429–436.

Tubman, J. G., Windle, M., & Windle, R. C. (1996). The onset and cross-temporal patterning of sexual intercourse in middle adolescence: Prospective relations with behavioral and emotional problems. *Child Development, 67,* 327–343.

Turiel, E. (1969). Developmental processes in the child's moral thinking. In P. H. Mussen, J. Langer, & M. Covington (Eds.), *Trends and issues in developmental psychology* (pp. 92–133). New York: Holt.

Turner, H. A., & Finkelhor, D. (1996). Corporal punishment as a stressor among youth. *Journal of Marriage and Family, 58,* 155–166.

Turner, P. K., Runtz, M. G., & Galambos, N. L. (1999). Sexual abuse, pubertal timing, and subjective age in adolescent girls: a research note. *Journal of Reproductive & Infant Psychology, 17*(2), 111–119.

Turner, R. A., Irwin, C. E., & Millstein, S. G. (1991). Family structure, family processes, and experimenting with substances during adolescence. *Journal of Research on Adolescence, 1*(1), 93–106.

Turner, S., & Scherman, A. (1996). Big Brothers: Impact on Little Brothers' self-concepts and behaviors. *Adolescence, 31*(124), 875–882.

U

Ulijaszek, S. J., Evans, E., & Miller, D. S. (1991). Age at menarche of European, Afro-Caribbean, and Indo-Pakistani schoolgirls living in London. *Annals of Human Biology, 18*(2), 167–175.

Underwood, M. K., Kupersmidt, J. B., & Coie, J. D. (1996). Childhood peer sociometric status and aggression as predictors of adolescent childbearing. *Journal of Research on Adolescence, 6*(2), 201–223.

Ungar, M. (2001). The social construction of resilience among "problem" youth in out-of-home placement: A study of health-enhancing deviance. *Child and Youth Care Forum, 30*(3), 137–154.

United States Department of Commerce. (1993). *Poverty in the United States: 1993* (Current Population Reports, Series P-60, No. 178). Washington, DC: U.S. Government Printing Office.

United States Department of Health and Human Services. (1996). *Trends in the well-being of America's children and youth: 1996*. Washington, DC: Author.

United States General Accounting Office. (1993). *School-linked human services: A comprehensive strategy for aiding students at risk of school failure* (GAO/HRD-94-21). Washington, DC.

University of Alberta Health Centre (2001). Health Information Page. Women, Weight, and Body Image. Retrieved from: www.ualberta.ca/HEALTHINFO/bodyim.htm#women.

Upchurch, D. M. (1993). Early schooling and childbearing experiences: Implications for postsecondary school attendance. *Journal of Research on Adolescence, 3*(4), 423–443.

Urberg, K. A., Degirmencioglu, S. M., & Pilgrim, C. (1997). Close friend and group influence on adolescent cigarette smoking and alcohol use. *Developmental Psychology, 33*(5), 834–844.

Urberg, K. A., Degirmencioglu, S. M., & Tolson, J. M. (1998). Adolescent friendship selection and termination: The role of similiarity. *Journal of Social & Personal Relationships, 15*(5), 703–710.

Urberg, K. A., Degirmencioglu, S. M., Tolson, J. M., & Halliday-Scher, K. (1995). The structure of adolescent peer networks. *Developmental Psychology, 31*(4), 540–547.

Urberg, K. A., Degirmencioglu, S. M., Tolson, J. M., & Halliday-Scher, K. (2000). Adolescent social crowds: Measurement and relationship to friends. *Journal of Adolescent Research, 15*(4), 427–445.

Urdan, T., Midgley, C., & Wood, S. (1995). Special issues in reforming middle level schools. *Journal of Early Adolescence, 15*(1), 9–37.

Usdan, M. (1994, January). The relationship between school boards and general purpose government. *Phi Delta Kappan*, pp. 374–377.

Useem, E. L. (1991). Student selection into course sequences in mathematics: The impact of parental involvement and school policies. *Journal of Research on Adolescence, 1*(3), 231–250.

V

Valaitis, R. (2002). "They don't trust us; we're just kids." Views about community from predominantly female inner city youth. *Health Care for Women International, 23*(3), 248–266.

Vallerand, R. J., Fortier, M. S., & Guay, F. (1997). Self-determination and persistence in a real-life setting: Toward a motivational model of high school dropout. *Journal of Personality and Social Psychology, 72*(5), 1161–1176.

Van de Ven, P. (1995). Talking with juvenile offenders about gay males and lesbians: Implications for combating homophobia. *Adolescence, 30*(117), 19–42.

Van der Velde, M. E. G., Feij, J. A., & van Emmerik, H. V. (1998). Change in work values and norms among Dutch young adults: Aging or societal trends? *International Journal of Behavioral Development, 22*(1), 55–76.

Van Schoiack Edstrom, L., Frey, K. S., & Beland, K. (2002). Changing adolescents' attitudes about relational and physical aggression: An early evaluation of a school-based intervention. *School Psychology Review, 31*(2), 201–216.

Vanier Institute of the Family (2000). ♣ *Profiling Canada's Families II.* Ottawa: Vanier Institute of the Family.

Vartanian, L. R., & Powlishta, K. K. (1996). A longitudinal examination of the social-cognitive foundations of adolescent egocentrism. *Journal of Early Adolescence, 16*(2), 157–178.

Vernberg, E. M., Ewell, K. K., Berry, S. H., & Abwender, D. A. (1994). Sophistication of adolescents' interpersonal negotiation strategies and friendship formation after relocation: A naturally occurring experiment. *Journal of Research on Adolescence, 4*(1), 5–19.

Vicary, J. R., Klingaman, L. R., & Harkness, W. L. (1995). Risk factors associated with date rape and sexual assault of adolescent girls. *Journal of Adolescence, 18*, 289–306.

Villarruel, F. A., & Lerner, R. M. (Eds.). (1994). *Promoting community-based programs for socialization and learning.* San Francisco: Jossey-Bass.

Vitaro, F., Arseneault, L., & Tremblay, ♣ R. E. (1997). Dispositional predictors of problem gambling in male adolescents. *American Journal of Psychiatry, 154*(12), 1769–1770.

Vitaro, F., Brendgen, M., & Tremblay, ♣ R. E. (2000). Influence of deviant friends on delinquency: Searching for moderator variables. *Journal of Abnormal Child Psychology, 28*(4), 313–325.

Vitaro, F., Ferland, F., Jacques, C., & ♣ Ladouceur, R. (1998). Gambling, substance use, and impulsivity during adolescence. *Psychology of Addictive Behaviors, 12*(3), 185–194.

Vitaro, F., Ladouceur, R., & Bujold, A. ♣ (1996). Predictive and concurrent correlates of gambling in early adolescent boys. *Journal of Early Adolescence, 16*(2), 211–228.

Vitaro, F., Larocque, D., Janosz, M., & ♣ Tremblay, R. E. (2001). Negative social experiences and dropping out of school. *Educational Psychology, 21*(4), 401–415.

Vitaro, F., Tremblay, R. E., Kerr, M., ♣ Pagani, L., & Bukowski, W. M. (1997). Disruptiveness, friends' characteristics, and delinquency in early adolescence: A test of two competing models of development. *Child Development, 68*(4), 676–689.

Vondracek, F. W. (1994). Vocational identity development in adolescence. In R. K. Silbereisen & E. Todt (Eds.), *Adolescence in context: The interplay of family, school, peers, and work in adjustment* (pp. 284–303). New York: Springer.

Vondracek, F. W. (1999, May). *Applications of systemic models in the study of vocational development.* Paper presented at the Fourth National

Conference of the Society for Vocational Psychology, a section of the Counseling Psychology Division of the American Psychological Association, on Examining the interaction of person in environment: Role of context factors in vocational development, Milwaukee, WI.

Vondracek, F. W., Lerner, R. M., & Schulenberg, J. E. (1986). *Career development: A life-span developmental approach.* Hillsdale, NJ: Erlbaum.

Vondracek, F. W., Schulenberg, J., Skorikov, V., Gillespie, L. K., & Wahlheim, C. (1995). The relationship of identity status to career indecision during adolescence. *Journal of Adolescence, 18*, 17–29.

Vondracek, F.W., & Skorikov, V.B. (1997). Leisure, school, and work activity preferences and their role in vocational identity development. *Career Development Quarterly, 45*(4), 322–340.

Vondracek, F.W., Schulenberg, J., Skorikov, V., Gillespie, L. K., & et al. (1995). The relationship of identity status to career indecision during adolescence. *Journal of Adolescence, 18*(1), 17–29.

Vuchinich, S., Angelelli, J., & Gatherum, A. (1996). Context and development in family problem solving with preadolescent children. *Child Development, 67*, 1276–1288.

Vuchinich, S., Hetherington, E. M., Vuchinich, R. A., & Clingempeel, W. G. (1991). Parent-child interaction and gender differences in early adolescents' adaptation to stepfamilies. *Developmental Psychology, 27*, 618–626.

W

Wadsworth, B. J. (1971). *Piaget's theory of cognitive development.* New York: McKay.

Wagenaar, A. C., & Perry, C. L. (1994). Community strategies for the reduction of youth drinking: Theory and application. *Journal of Research on Adolescence, 4*(2), 319–347.

Wagner, B. M., Cohen, P., & Brook, J. S. (1996). Parent/adolescent relationships: Moderators of the effects of stressful life events. *Journal of Adolescent Research, 11*(3), 347–374.

Wagner, J. A. (1987). Formal operations and ego identity in adolescence.

Adolescence, 22(85), 23–35.

Wainryb, C. (1995). Reasoning about social conflicts in different cultures: Druze and Jewish children in Israel. *Child Development, 66*, 390–401.

Wainryb, C., Shaw, L. A., & Maianu, C. (1998). Tolerance and intolerance: Children's and adolescents' judgements of dissenting beliefs, speech, persons, and conduct. *Child Development, 69*(6), 1541–1555.

Waldner-Haugrud, L. K., & Magruder, B. (1996). Homosexual identity expression among lesbian and gay adolescents: An analysis of perceived structural associations. *Youth & Society, 27*(3), 313–333.

Walker, L. J. (1984). Sex differences in the development of moral reasoning: A critical review. *Child Development, 55*, 677–691.

Walker, L. J., & Taylor, J. H. (1991). Family interactions and the development of moral reasoning. *Child Development, 62*, 264–283.

Walker, L., & Richards, B. (1976). The effects of a narrative model on children's moral judgments. *Canadian Journal of Behavioral Science, 8*, 169–177.

Walker, L. J. & Henning, K. H. (1999). Parenting Style and the Development of Moral Reasoning. *Journal of Moral Education, 28*(3), 359–374.

Walker, L. J. (1991). Moral reasoning in a Communist Chinese society. *Journal of Moral Education, 1991, 20*(2), 139–156.

Walker, T. R., & Ehrenberg, M. R. (1998). An exploratory study of young persons' attachment styles and perceived reasons for parental divorce. *Journal of Adolescent Research, 13*(3), 320–342.

Walsh, M. M., Pepler, D. J., & Levene, K. S. (2002). A model intervention for girls with disruptive behaviour problems: The Earlscourt Girls Connection. *Canadian Journal of Counselling, 36*(4), 297–311.

Warton, P. M., & Goodnow, J. J. (1991). The nature of responsibility: Children's understanding of "your job." *Child Development, 62*, 156–165.

Wassef, A., Collins, M. L., Ingham, D., & Mason, G. (1995a). In search of effective programs to address students' emotional distress and behavioral problems. II: Critique of school- and community-based programs. *Adolescence, 30*(120), 757–777.

Wassef, A., Ingham, D., Collins, M. L., & Mason, G. (1995b). In search of effective programs to address students' emotional distress and behavioral problems. I: Defining the problem. *Adolescence, 30*(119), 523–538.

Wassef, A., Mason, G., Collins, M. L., O'Boyle, M., & Ingham, D. (1996). In search of effective programs to address students' emotional distress and behavioral problems. III: Student assessment of school-based support groups. *Adolescence, 31*(121), 1–16.

Waterman, A. S. (1982). Identity development from adolescence to adulthood: An extension of theory and a review of research. *Developmental Psychology, 18*, 341–358.

Watkins, M. (1997). Out of commission: When Ottawa decided to ignore the recommendations of the Royal Commission on Aboriginal Peoples. *This Magazine, 31*(il), 11–12.

Wechsler, D. (2003). *Wechsler Intelligence Scale for Children Manual* (4th ed). San Antonio TX: The Psychological Corporation.

Wehlage, G., Rutter, R., Smith, G., Lesko, N., & Fernandez, R. (1989). *Reducing the risk: Schools as communities of support.* New York: Falmer.

Weinbender, M. L. M., & Rossignol, A. M. (1996). Lifestyle and risk of premature sexual activity in a high school population of Seventh-Day Adventists: Valuegenesis 1989. *Adolescence, 31*(122), 265–281.

Weinberg, R. A., & Erickson, M. F. (1996). Minnesota's Children, Youth, and Family Consortium: A university-community collaboration. *Journal of Research on Adolescence, 6*(1), 37–53.

Weir, E. (2001). Drug-facilitated date rape. *Canadian Medical Association Journal, 165*(1), 80.

Weiss, H. B., & Greene, J. C. (1992). An empowerment partnership for family support and education programs and evaluations. *Family Science Review, 5*, 131–148.

Weiss, L. H., & Schwarz, J. C. (1996). The relationship between parenting types and older adolescents' personality, academic achievement, adjustment, and substance use. *Child Development, 67*, 2101–2114.

Weller, A., Florian, V., & Mikulincer, M. (1995). Adolescents' reports of a parental division of power in a multicultural society. *Journal of Research on Adolescence, 5*(4), 413–429.

Wentzel, K. R. (1991). Relations between social competence and academic achievement in early adolescence. *Child Development, 62*, 1066–1078.

Wentzel, K. R. (1993). Motivation and achievement in early adolescence: The role of multiple classroom goals. *Journal of Early Adolescence, 13*(1), 4–20.

Wentzel, K. R. (1996). Social and academic motivation in middle school: Concurrent and long-term relations to academic effort. *Journal of Early Adolescence, 16*(4), 390–406.

Wentzel, K. R. (1997). Student motivation in middle school: The role of perceived pedagogical caring. *Journal of Educational Psychology, 89*(3), 411–419.

Wentzel, K. R. (1998). Social relationships and motivation in middle school: The role of parents, teachers, and peers. *Journal of Educational Psychology, 90*(2), 202–209.

Wentzel, K. R., & Asher, S. R. (1995). The academic lives of neglected, rejected, popular, and controversial children. *Child Development, 66*, 754–763.

Wentzel, K. R., & Caldwell, K. (1997). Friendships, peer acceptance, and group membership: Relations to academic achievement in middle school. *Child Development, 68*(6), 1198–1209.

Wentzel, K. R., & Erdley, C. A. (1993). Strategies for making friends: Relations to social behavior and peer acceptance in early adolescence. *Developmental Psychology, 29*(5), 819–826.

Wentzel, K. R., & Feldman, S. S. (1996). Relations of cohesion and power in family dyads to social and emotional adjustment during early adolescence. Journal of Research on Adolescence, 6(2), 225–244.

Wentzel, K. R., Feldman, S. S., & Weinberger, D. A. (1991). Parental child rearing and academic achievement in boys: The mediational role of social-emotional adjustment. *Journal of Early Adolescence, 11*(3), 321–339.

Wentzel, K. R., Weinberger, D. A., Ford, M. E., & Feldman, S. S. (1990). Academic achievement in preadolescence: The role of multiple classroom goals. *Journal of Early Adolescence, 13*(1), 4–20.

Werner, E. E., & Smith, R. S. (1992). *Overcoming the odds: High risk children from birth to adulthood.* Ithaca, NY: Cornell University Press.

Werner, E., & Smith, R. (1982). *Vulnerable but invincible.* New York: McGraw-Hill.

Whalen, S. P., & Wynn, J. R. (1995). Enhancing primary services for youth through an infrastructure of social services. *Journal of Adolescent Research, 10*(1), 88–110.

Wheeler, H. A, Adams, G. R., & Keating, L. (2001). Binge eating as a means for evading identity issues: The association between an avoidance identity style and bulimic behavior. *Identity: An International Journal of Theory and Research, 1*(2), 161–178.

Whitbeck, L. B. (1987). Modeling efficacy: The effect of perceived parental efficacy on the self-efficacy of early adolescents. *Journal of Early Adolescence, 7*(2), 165–177.

Whitbeck, L. B., Simons, R. L., & Kao, M. (1994). The effects of divorced mothers' dating behaviors and sexual attitudes on the sexual attitudes and behaviors of their adolescent children. *Journal of Marriage and the Family, 56*, 615–621.

Whitbeck, L. B., Simons, R. L., Conger, R. D., & Lorenz, F. O. (1989). Value socialization and peer group affiliation among early adolescents. *Journal of Early Adolescence, 9*(4), 436–453.

Whitbourne, S. K., & Tesch, S. A. (1985). A comparison of identity and intimacy statuses in college students and alumni. *Developmental Psychology, 21*(6), 1039–1044.

White, S. H. (1968). The learning-maturation controversy: Hall to Hull. *Merrill-Palmer Quarterly, 14*, 58–65.

White, S. H. (1970). The learning theory tradition and child psychology. In P. H. Mussen (Ed.), *Carmichael's manual of child psychology* (3rd ed., pp. 657–701). New York: Wiley.

Whiting, B. B., & Whiting, J. W. M. (1991). Preindustrial world, adolescence in. In R. M. Lerner, A. C. Petersen, & J. Brooks-Gunn (Eds.), *Encyclopedia of adolescence* (Vol. 2, pp. 814–849). New York: Garland.

Wickrama, K. A. S., Conger, R. D., & Lorenz, F. O., Elder, G. H., Jr. (1998). Parental education and adolescent self-reported physical health. *Journal of Marriage and the Family, 60*, 967–978.

Wigfield, A., & Eccles, J. S. (1994). Children's competence beliefs, achieve-ment values, and general self-esteem: Change across elementary and middle school. *Journal of Early Adolescence, 14*(2), 107–138.

Wigfield, A., Eccles, J. S., MacIver, D., Reumann, D. A., & Midgley, C. (1991). Transitions during early adolescence: Changes in children's domain-specific self-perceptions and general self-esteem across the transition to junior high. *Developmental Psychology, 27*, 552–565.

Wilkinson, L. (2002). Factors influenc-ing the academic success of refugee youth in Canada. *Journal of Youth Studies, 5*(2), 173–193.

Williams, C. (2001). Family disruptions and childhood happiness. *Canadian Social Trends.* Catalogue No. 11-008. Ottawa: Statistics Canada.

Willms, D. (1999). *Inequalities in liter-acy skills among youth in Canada and the United States.* Statistics Canada. Catalogue Number 89–552-MIE, No. 6. Ottawa: Ministry of Industry.

Wilson, R.J., & Martinussen, R.L. (1999). Factors affecting the assess-ment of student achievement. *Alberta Journal of Educational Research, 45*(3), 267–277.

Windle, M. (1994). A study of friendship characteristics and problem behaviors among middle adolescents. *Child Development, 65*, 1764–1777.

Windle, M., Miller-Tutzauer, C., & Domenico, D. (1992). Alcohol use, suicidal behavior, and risky activities among adolescents. *Journal of Research on Adolescence, 2*(4), 317–330.

Windle, M., Miller-Tutzauer, C., Barnes, G. M., & Welte, J. (1991). Adolescent perceptions of help-seeking resources for substance abuse. *Child Development, 62*, 179–189.

Wintre, M. & Gallander, Y. M. (2000). First-year students' adjustment to uni-versity life as a function of relation-ships with parents. *Journal of Adolescent Research, 15*, 9–37.

Witt, S. D. (1997). Parental influence on children's socialization to gender roles. *Adolescence, 32*(126), 253–259.

Wong, C. T., Day, J. D., Maxwell, S. E., & Meara, N. M. (1995). A multitrait-multimethod study of academic and social intelligence in college students. *Journal of Educational Psychology, 87*(1), 117–133.

Wong, S. K. (1998). Peer relations and Chinese-Canadian delinquency. *Journal of Youth and Adolescence, 27*(5), 641–659.

Wong, S. K. (1999). Acculturation, peer relations, and delinquent behavior of Chinese-Canadian youth. *Adolescence, 34*(133), 108–119.

Wood, P. B., & Clay, W. C. (1996). Perceived structural barriers and aca-demic performance among American Indian high school students. *Youth & Society, 28*(1), 40–61.

Worell, J. (1981). Life-span sex roles: Development, continuity, and change. In R. M. Lerner & N. A. Busch-Rossnagel (Eds.), *Individuals as pro-ducers of their development: A life-span perspective* (pp. 313–347). New York: Academic Press.

World Health Organization. (1993). *The health of young people: A challenge and a promise.* Geneva: Author.

World Wide Legal Information Association (1996). *Canadian con-stitutional law.* Retrieved from: http://wwlia.org/ca-const.htm.

Wright, D. W., Peterson, L., & Barnes, H. L. (1990). The relation of parental employment and contextual variables with sexual permissiveness and gen-der role attitudes of rural early ado-lescents. *Journal of Early Adolescence, 10*(3), 382–393.

Wu, Z. (1999). Premarital cohabitation and the timing of first marriage. *Canadian Review of Sociology and Anthropology, 36*(1), 109–127.

Wu, Z., & Balakrishnan, T. R. (1995). Dissolution of premarital cohabitation in Canada. *Demography 32*, 521–532.

Y

Yates, M., & Youniss, J. (1996). Community service and political-moral identity in adolescents. *Journal of Research on Adolescence, 6*(3), 271–284.

Yau, J., & Smetana, J. G. (1996). Adolescent-parent conflict among Chinese adolescents in Hong Kong. *Child Development, 67*, 1262–1275.

Yax, L. K. (1999). *Resident population estimates of the United States by age group and sex: April 1, 1990 to October 1, 1999.* Washington, DC: U. S. Census Bureau, Population

Estimates Program, Population Division.

Yildirim, A. (1997). Gender role influences on Turkish adolescents' self-identity. *Adolescence, 32*(125), 216–231.

Young, M. H., Miller, B. C., Norton, M. C., & Hill, E. J. (1995). The effect of parental supportive behaviors on life satisfaction of adolescent offspring. *Journal of Marriage and Family, 57,* 813–822.

Youniss, J., & Dean, A. (1974). Judgment and imagery aspects of operations: A Piagetian study with Korean and Costa Rican children. *Child Development, 45,* 1020–1031.

Youniss, J., Yates, M., & Su, Y. (1997). Social integration: Community service and marijuana use in high school seniors. *Journal of Adolescent Research, 12*(2), 245–262.

YouthNet International (2003). *Programs that Work*. Retrieved from: http://www.iyfnet.org/

Youthquest (2002). Youthquest! Low-cost, high impact: Programs for Lesbian, Gay, Bisexual and transgender youth. *Youthquest! 2002 Strategic services plan*. Retrieved from: www.youthquest.bc.ca/servplan2002/needsassessment.htm#_ftnref2.

Z

Zabin, L. S., Astone, N. M., & Emerson, M. R. (1993). Do adolescents want babies? The relationship between attitudes and behavior. *Journal of Research on Adolescence, 3,* 67–86.

Zane, J. (2001). Muslim youth in Canadian schools: Education and the politics of religious identity. *Anthropology and Education Quarterly, 32*(4), 399.

Zani, B., DiPalma, A., & Vullo, C. (1995). Psychosocial aspects of chronic illness in adolescents with thalassaemia major. *Journal of Adolescence, 18,* 387–402.

Zarbatany, L., Ghesquiere, K., & Mohr, K. (1992). A context perspective on early adolescents' friendship expectations. *Journal of Early Adolescence, 12*(1), 111–126.

Zaslow, M. J. (1988). Sex differences in children's response to parental divorce: I. Research methodology and postdivorce family forms. *American Journal of Orthopsychiatry, 58*(3), 355–378.

Zaslow, M. J. (1989). Sex differences in children's response to parental divorce: II. Samples, variables, ages, and sources. *American Journal of Orthopsychiatry, 59*(1), 118–141.

Zaslow, M., Tout, K., Smith, S., & Moore, K. (1998). Implications of the 1996 welfare legislation for children: A research perspective. *SRCD Social Policy Report, 12* (3).

Zeldin, S. (1995). Community-university collaborations for youth development: From theory to practice. *Journal of Adolescent Research, 10*(4), 449–469.

Zeldin, S., & Price, L. A. (1995). Creating supportive communities for adolescent development: Challenges to scholars: An introduction. *Journal of Adolescent Research, 10*(1), 6–14.

Zhang, J., & Jin, S. (1996). Determinants of suicide ideation: A comparison of Chinese and American college students. *Adolescence, 31*(122), 451–467.

Zimet, G. D., Sobo, E. J., Zimmerman, T., Jackson, J., Mortimer, J., Yanda, C. P., & Lazebnik, R. (1995). Sexual behavior, drug use, and AIDS knowledge among Midwestern runaways. *Youth & Society, 26*(4), 450–462.

Zimiles, H., & Lee, V. (1991). Adolescent family structure and educational progress. *Developmental Psychology, 27*(2), 314–320.

Zimmerman, M. A., Salem, D. A., & Maton, K. I. (1995). Family structure and psychosocial correlates among urban African-American adolescent males. *Child Development, 66,* 1598–1613.

Zimmerman, R. S., Sprecher, S., Langer, L. M., & Holloway, C. D. (1995). Adolescents' perceived ability to say "no" to unwanted sex. *Journal of Adolescent Research, 10*(3), 383–399.

Zoccolillo, M., Vitaro, F., & Tremblay, R. E. (1999). Problem drug and alcohol use in a community sample of adolescents. *Journal of the American Academy of Child and Adolescent Psychiatry, 38*(7), 900–907.

CREDITS

Photographs

CO photos PhotoDisk/Teens.

Chapter 1 Page 4 Young-Wolff, PhotoEdit; page 5 Jonathan Nourok, PhotoEdit; page 8 Bruce D. Ravelli; page 10 Nancy Galambos; page 11 Michael Newman, PhotoEdit; page 13 Bob Daemmrich, The Image Works; page 17 Copyright © 2002, Dick Hemingway; page 20 Monika Graff, The Image Works.

Chapter 2 Page 28 Copyright © Elena Rooraid/PhotoEdit; page 29 Alexander Scott/Masterfile; page 35 Celia Fisher; page 34 Anne Westhues; page 36 Mary Kate Denny, PhotoEdit; page 37 © Chemical Design Ltd./SPL/Science Source/Photo Researchers Inc.; page 43 Topham, The Image Works; page 51 Paul B. Baltes.

Chapter 3 Page 59 Spencer Grant, Stock Boston; page 65 Michele Surbey; page 66 Young-Wolff, PhotoEdit; page 68 Elizabeth Susman; page 70 Copyright © Gary Conner/PhotoEdit; page 71 Paul Conklin, PhotoEdit; page 72 David Magnusson.

Chapter 4 Page 84 D. Young-Wolff, PhotoEdit; page 90 Peter Menzel, Stock Boston; page 91 John J. Mitchell; page 92 Dick Blume, The Image Works; page 94 David R. Frazier, Photo Researchers, Inc.; page 95 Rich Weinberg; page 99 Felicia Martinez, PhotoEdit.

Chapter 5 Page 105 Mary Kate Denny, PhotoEdit; page 109 Bob Daemmrich, Stock Boston; page 114 Nancy Eisenberg; page 116 Tony Freeman, PhotoEdit; page 117 William Damon; page 120 Mary Kate Denny, PhotoEdit; page 123 Peter Benson.

Chapter 6 Page 130 David Young-Wolff, PhotoEdit; page 135 Bob Daemmrich, Stock Boston; page 136 Gerry Adams; page 139 Sally Archer; page 140 David Young-Wolff, PhotoEdit; page 142 James Marcia; page 145 Richard Hutchings, PhotoEdit; page 147 Donald M. Taylor; page 148 Dauphin Friendship Centre Aboriginal Festival.

Chapter 7 Page 157 (top) Spencer Grant/PhotoEdit; page 157 (bottom) Michael Schwartz, The Image Works; page 161 Bob Daemmrich, The Image Works; page 163 Jeylan T. Mortimer; page 164 Stock Boston; page 167 Bill Aron, PhotoEdit.

Chapter 8 Page 180 Donald J. Hernandez; page 181 (left) © Mary Evans Picture Library/Photo Researchers, Inc.; page 181 (right) Bob Daemmrich, The Image Works; page 184 Rafael Macia, Photo Researchers, Inc.; page 185 Bill Lai, The Image Works; page 188 Marion F. Ehrenberg; page 190 Photo Researchers, Inc.; page 195 David Young-Wolff, PhotoEdit.

Chapter 9 Page 206 Mike Doyle, Unicorn Stock Photos; page 207 Robert Brenner, PhotoEdit; page 209 Michael Newman, PhotoEdit; page 210 Mike Mazzaschi, Stock Boston; page 211 Spencer Grant, Stock Boston; page 217 Brett Laursen.

Chapter 10 Page 225 Michael Newman, PhotoEdit; page 228 David Young-Wolff, PhotoEdit; page 229 Ritch Savin-Williams; page 230 Kevin Alderson; page 233 Spencer Grant, PhotoEdit; page 234 Eleanor Maticka-Tyndale; page 240 Michael Newman, PhotoEdit; page 244 Patricia East.

Chapter 11 Page 253 Mark C. Burnett, Stock Boston; page 255 George J. Sefa Dei; page 256 Tony Freeman, PhotoEdit; page 257 Elizabeth Crews Photography; page 262 CP Photo/Paul Chiasson; page 264 Will Hart, PhotoEdit; page 266 K. Solveig/Masterfile.

Chapter 12 Page 274 David Young-Wolff, PhotoEdit; page 275 © David Muscroft/SuperStock; page 276 © David Young-Wolff/PhotoEdit; page 277 Gregory T. Fouts; page 278 Will Hart, PhotoEdit; page 279 Tony Freeman, PhotoEdit; page 284 Mark Richards, PhotoEdit.

Chapter 13 Page 292 Lisa Crockett; page 293 Andrew Stawicki/Toronto Star; page 295 © Jérome Sessini/InVisu/ Corbis/Magmaphoto.com; page 298 © Dick Hemingway; page 300 James Garbarino; page 301 Dr. P. Marazzi/Science Photo Library, Photo Researchers, Inc.; page 303 Mary Lewis, Unicorn Stock Photos; page 304 David R. (Dan) Offord; page 305 Nancy Richmond, The Image Works; page 306 Jacksonville Journal Courier, The Image Works.

Chapter 14 Page 314 Jodie Roth; page 316 Rene Johnston/Toronto Star; page 317 Mary Kate Denny, PhotoEdit; page 324 Nancy Higgitt; page 325 Myrleen Ferguson Cate, PhotoEdit; page 330 Bill Aron/PhotoEdit; page 331 Jean Rhodes.

Chapter 15 Page 338 David Young-Wolff, PhotoEdit; page 339 Eric R. Berndt, Unicorn Stock Photos; page 340 Julian Tanner; page 342 Bob Daemmrich, Stock Boston; page 345 Michael Newman, PhotoEdit; page 349 Stephen Hamilton.

Appendix Page 355 (left) David Parker/Science Photo Laboratory, Photo Researchers, Inc.; page 355 (top right) Elena Rooraid, PhotoEdit; page 355 (bottom right) Ray Stott, The Image Works; page 356 Bill Aron, PhotoEdit; page 358 © Richard T. Nowitz/CORBIS; page 360 Michael Newman, PhotoEdit; page 362 (left) © Hulton-Deutsch/CORBIS; page 362 (top right) © Vince Streano/CORBIS; page 362 (bottom right) Andrew Lichtenstein, The Image Works; page 363 Lorrie K. Sippola; page 367 John Nesselroade; page 368 Rick Madonik/Toronto Star.

Figures and Tables

Chapter 2 Table 2-1 From CONCEPTS AND THEORIES OF HUMAN DEVELOPMENT 2nd edition by Richard M. Lerner, 1996, Random House. Reprinted by permission of the author.

Chapter 3 Figures 3.1, 3.2, 3.3, & 3.4 Figures redrawn from GROWTH AT ADOLESCENCE 2nd edition by J. M. Tanner. Copyright © 1962. Reprinted by permission of Blackwell Scientific Publications; Figure 3.5 Illustration courtesy of Nelson H. Prentiss. Graph by Ilil Arbel from "Growing Up" by J. M. Tanner in *Scientific American*, September 1973, v. 229. Copyright © 1973 by Scientific American, Inc.; Table 3-1 "Ethnic Differences in Growth and Development" by Jean Hiernaux, *Eugenics Quarterly*, 1968, 15, pp. 12–21. Reprinted by permission of Kenneth C. Land, Duke University, Editor of *Social Biology*; Figure 3.7 From "Pubertal Processes in Girls' Psychological Adaptations" in BIOLOGI-CAL-PSYCHOSOCIAL INTERACTIONS IN EARLY ADOLESCENCE: A Life-Span Perspective ed. by R. Lerner and T. T. Foch, Erlbaum, 1987. Reprinted by permission of Lawrence Erlbaum Associates, Inc.; Figures 3.8 & 3.9 From "Differential Maturation Among Girls and Its Relation to Social Adjustment: A Longitudinal Perspective" by Magnusson, et al., in LIFE-SPAN DEVEL-OPMENT AND BEHAVIOR ed. by P. B. Baltes, D. L. Fetherman, and R. M. Lerner, Erlbaum, 1986. Reprinted by permission of Lawrence Erlbaum Associates, Inc.; IFP Box 3.1 "Don't Talk Back!" by R. M. Lerner and C. K. Olson, *Parents,* February 1995.

Copyright © 1995 by Gruner & Jahr USA Publishing. Reprinted from PARENTS magazine by permission.

Chapter 4 Applications Box 4.1 Reprinted by permission of International Youth Foundation, YouthNet International; Table 4-1 From CONCEPTS AND THEORIES OF HUMAN DEVELOPMENT 2nd edition by Richard M. Lerner, 1986, Random House. Reprinted by permission of the author; IFP Box 4.1 "The Imaginary Audience" by R. M. Lerner and C. K. Olson, *Parents*, February 1994. Copyright © 1994 by Gruner & Jahr USA Publishing. Reprinted from PARENTS magazine by permission.

Chapter 5 Table 5-1 Reprinted by permission of Thomas Lickona; Table 5-2 From "Beyond the 'Village' Rhetoric: Creating Healthy Communities for Children and Adolscents" by Benson, Leffert, Scales & Blyth, *Applied Developmental Science*, 2(3), 1998. Reprinted by permission of Lawrence Erlbaum Associates, Inc.; Figures 5.1, 5.2, & 5.3 From "Developmental Assets: Measurement and Prediction of Risk Behaviors Among Adolescents" by N. Leffert, P. Benson, P. Scales, A. Sharma, D. Drake, & D. Blyth, *Applied Developmental Science*, 2, 1998. Reprinted by permission of Lawrence Erlbaum Associates, Inc.; Figures 5.4, 5.5, & 5.6 From "The Contribution of Developmental Assets to the Prediction of Thriving Among Adolescents" by Scales, et al. from *Applied DevelopmentalScience*, 4(1), 2000. Reprinted by permission of Lawrence Erlbaum Associates, Inc.; Figure 5.7 From "Applying Developmental Science in the Twenty-First Century: International Scholarship for Our Times" by R. M. Lerner, C. B. Fisher, R. A. Weinberg, *International Journal of Behavioral Development*, vol. 24 (2000), pp. 24–29. Reprinted by permission of Taylor & Francis Ltd.

Chapter 6 Table 6-1 From CONCEPTS AND THEORIES OF HUMAN DEVELOPMENT 2nd edition by Richard M. Lerner, 1986, Random House. Reprinted by permission of the author; Applications Boxes 6.1 and 6.2 Reprinted by permission of International Youth Foundation, YouthNet International.

Chapter 7 Table 7.1 From "Sex-Role Stereotypes: A Current Appraisal" by I. K. Broverman, S. R. Vogel, D. M. Broverman, F. E. Clarkson, & P. S. Rosenkrantz in *Journal of Social Issues*, v. 28, 1972. Copyright © 1972. Reprinted by permission of Blackwell Publishers; Applications Box 7.1 Reprinted by permission of International Youth Foundation, YouthNet International.

Chapter 8 Table 8-1 From "A Developmental Contextual Perspective on Parenting" by Lerner, et al. in HANDBOOK OF PARENTING: Biology and Ecology of Parenting, Vol. 2, ed. by J. H. Bornstein, R. M. Lerner, D. R. Castellino, P. A. Terry, F. A. Villarruel, & M. H. McKinney, Erlbaum, 1995. Reprinted by permission of Lawrence Erlbaum Associates, Inc.; Tables 8.2, 8.3, 8.4, & 8.5 From AMERICA'S CHILDREN by Donald Hernandez. Copyright © 1993 by Russell Sage Foundation, New York, NY. Reprinted by permission; IFP Box 8.1 "Teens and Tweens" by R. M. Lerner & L. C. Hoopfer, *Family Circle*, October 1993. Copyright © 1993 by Gruner & Jahr USA Publishing. Reprinted from FAMILY CIRCLE magazine by permission.

Chapter 9 Applications Box 9.1 Reprinted by permission of International Youth Foundation, YouthNet International.

Chapter 10 IFP Box 10.1 "Teen Idols" by R. M. Lerner & C. K. Olson, *Parents*, September 1995. Copyright © 1995 by Gruner & Jahr USA Publishing. Reprinted from PARENTS magazine by permission; Figure 10.1 Reproduced with the permission of The Alan Guttmacher Institute from the Alan Guttmacher Institute, SEX AND AMERICA'S TEENAGERS, New York; The Alan Guttmacher Institute, 1994; Applications Box 10.2 Reprinted by permission of International Youth Foundation, YouthNet International.

Chapter 11 Figure 11.1 From GREAT TRANSITIONS: Preparing Adolescents for a New Century. Copyright © 1995 by Carnegie Corporation of New York. Reprinted with permission; Applications Box 11.1 Reprinted by permission of International Youth Foundation, YouthNet International.

Chapter 12 Table 12-1 From "Trajectory and Forms of Institutional Participation" by Eckert in PATHWAYS THROUGH ADOLESCENTS: Individual Development in Relation to Social Contexts ed. by L. J. Crockett and A. C. Crouter, Erlbaum, 1995. Reprinted by permission of Lawrence Erlbaum Associates, Inc.; Application Box 12.1 Reprinted by permission of International Youth Foundation, YouthNet International.

Chapter 13 Table 13-1 Children's Defense Fund, *The State* of *Amenca's Children Yearbook 2001*. Washington, D. C.: Children's Defense Fund, 2000. Used with permission of the Children's Defense Fund; Table 13-2 "Indicators of Child Well-Being" from KIDS COUNT DATA BOOK 2000:

State Profiles of Child Well-Being by the Annie R. Casey Foundation. Copyright © 2000. Reprinted by permission. http://www.kidscount.org; Table 13-3 From "Theories of Human Development: Contemporary Perspectives" by Richard M. Lerner in HANDBOOK OF CHILD PSYCHOLOGY ed. by W. Damon. Volume 1 *Theoretical Models* of *Human Development* ed. by R. M. Lerner. Copyright © 1998. Reprinted by permission of John Wiley & Sons, Inc.; Applications Box 13.1 Reprinted by permission of International Youth Foundation, YouthNet International; Applications Box 13.2 Reprinted by permission of International Youth Foundation, YouthNet International; IFP Box 13.1 Adapted from "Keeping Tabs... Without Being a Nag" by R. M. Lerner & C. K. Olson, *Parents*, September 1996. Copyright © 1996 by Gruner & Jahr USA Publishing. Reprinted from PARENTS magazine by permission.

Chapter 14 Table 14-1 Table from A *Three-Part Definition of Positive Youth Development*, by S. F. Hamilton, unpublished manuscript, 1999. Reprinted by permission of Stephen F. Hamilton, Cornell University; Applications Box 14.1 Adapted from Jacobs, F. (1998). The Five-Tiered Approach to Evaluation: Context and Implementation. In H. Weiss and F. Jacobs (Eds.) (1998). Evaluating Family Programs. Hawthorne, NY: Aldine de Gruyter. Source: Jacobs, F. H. and Kapuscik, J. L. (2000). Making It Count: Evaluating Family Preservation Services. Medford, MA: Tufts University, Eliot-Pearson Department of Child Development. Reprinted by permission of F. H. Jacobs; Applications Box 14.2 From GREAT TRANSITIONS: Preparing Adolescents for a New Century. Copyright © 1995 by Carnegie Corporation of New York. Reprinted with permission.

Chapter 15 Applications Box 15.1 Reprinted by permission of International Youth Foundation, YouthNet International.

Appendix Figure A.l From LIFE SPAN DEVELOPMENTAL PSYCHOLOGY: Introduction to Research Methods by Baltes, Reese, and Nesselroade, Brooks/Cole, 1977. Reprinted by permission of John R. Nesselroade; Applications Box A. 1 "Ethical Standards for Research with Children" by Society for Research in Child Development. Reprinted by permission.

NAME INDEX

SUBJECT INDEX